Essays in International Economics

PRINCETON SERIES OF COLLECTED ESSAYS

This series was initiated in response to requests from students and teachers who want the best essays of leading scholars available in a convenient format. Each book in this series serves scholarship by gathering in one place previously published articles representing the valuable contribution of a noted authority to his field. The format allows for the addition of a preface or introduction and an index to enhance the collection's usefulness. Photoreproduction of the essays keeps costs to a minimum and thus makes possible publication in a relatively inexpensive form.

Essays in International Economics

PETER B. KENEN

PRINCETON UNIVERSITY PRESS
PRINCETON, NEW JERSEY

Copyright © 1980 by Princeton University Press
Published by Princeton University Press, Princeton, New Jersey
In the United Kingdom: Princeton University Press,
Guildford, Surrey

Printed in the United States of America by Princeton
University Press, Princeton, New Jersey

For Joanne, Marc, Stephanie, and Judith

Contents

Preface

The papers collected in this volume are drawn from those I wrote in my first twenty years of work as an economist. The earliest paper, "On the Geometry of Welfare Economics," was written in 1956, when I was a graduate student, and published in 1957. The most recent paper, "New Views of Exchange Rates and Old Views of Policy," was written in 1977 and published in 1978. Coincidentally, those two papers also define the range of my work during the two decades represented in this book. The first paper is theoretical, dealing with the gains from trade and optimal protection. The second deals with empirical work bearing on the theory of macroeconomic policy under alternative exchange-rate regimes.

I have found it fairly easy to organize the book. The papers fall neatly into three groups. The first part of the book, *Trade, Tariffs, and Welfare*, contains six papers on pure trade theory. Three of them focus on positive problems, the other three on normative problems. The second part, *International Monetary Theory and Policy*, contains eight papers on international liquidity, monetary integration, and exchange-rate theory. Two of them present empirical work. The last part of the book, *Monetary Reform and the Dollar*, contains nine articles arranged chronologically. They comment on two decades of debate about the international monetary system, the role of the dollar, and the policies of the United States.

I find it somewhat harder to explain why I have chosen these and omitted other papers. Flattery has played a role—the frequency with which others have mentioned or assigned my papers. (Naturally, laudatory citations get more weight than critical citations.) Memory has also played a role—the recollections of discovery and of finding the right phrase, along with the less pleasant recollections of false starts and dead ends. These papers were the hard ones. (Values of outputs should not be measured by values of inputs unless we can claim to be in long-run equilibrium, but we do it all the time.) My criteria, moreover, were different for the papers in the first parts of the book than for those in the last part. The papers on trade and monetary theory are those that broke new ground of one sort or another, or gave new ways to look at old ideas. The papers in the third part, on the political economy of the monetary system, are chosen to reflect the evolution of my thinking on the subject and the evolution of the subject itself.

The first paper in this book, "Nature, Capital, and Trade," is one that broke new ground. It is concerned with the foundations for the supply side of the Heckscher-Ohlin model. The paper was inspired by work going on around me at Columbia University—the work on human capital by Gary Becker and the work on labor skills and international trade by Donald Keesing. The second paper builds upon the first, using a more general two-country model to draw additional conclusions about the interplay between international trade and investment. Both papers use elaborate apparatus, but the idea that they illustrate is very simple. An economy can be described as having a natural endowment comprising inert stocks of land and labor. They are inert until they are improved by applying capital. Thereafter, they supply factor-service flows that are the inputs to production—the point of entry into the standard Heckscher-Ohlin model. Investment in the natural endowment is subject to diminishing returns, so that the allocation of the capital stock between land and labor is easily determined once one knows the prices of their factor-service flows. Furthermore, free trade in commodities can equalize the factor-service prices, as in the standard model, without also equalizing the returns to capital. Accordingly, free trade can coexist with international capital movements. At the end of the first article, I offer an application. When one takes account of human capital (investment in labor) as well as tangible capital (investment in land), one can reverse the Leontief paradox: U.S. exports use more capital per worker, including human capital, than U.S. import-competing production. If I were rewriting these papers now, I would be less concerned with fitting the superstructure to the new foundation and more concerned with emphasizing the basic notion. That notion was original, more so than any other represented in this book, and that is why I put these papers first.

The next two papers deal with the demand side of the conventional Heckscher-Ohlin model. In "Distribution, Demand, and Equilibrium in International Trade," I show how one must take account of the demand side before saying anything about factor scarcities. Product prices determine factor prices, which determine in turn the distribution of income. The income distribution, however, helps to determine the composition of demand, and one must know the composition of demand, as well as the output mix, to be able to construct an offer curve and thus to determine the trade pattern at each set of product prices. In brief, this paper shows how to describe geometrically all of the relationships that lie behind the simple offer curve. The next paper, "On the Geometry of Welfare Economics," was written earlier but is the sequel logically. As movements along an ordinary offer curve involve redistributions of domestic income, they cannot have clear-cut welfare implications. An increase in the foreign demand for a country's exports, improving its terms of trade, will move it outward on its offer curve, but this outcome by itself does not imply an increase of economic welfare; some citizens will gain and others will lose. To make unambiguous statements about welfare, one must show that the gainers can compensate the losers, and this article supplies the requisite geometry. Borrowing techniques from James Meade and Robert Baldwin, it shows how to derive the situation utility-possibility curve employed by Paul Samuelson to sort out issues in welfare economics and how one can construct an offer curve incorporating compensation. Thus, both of these papers find their way into this book because they give new ways to look at familiar propositions.

The last two papers in this part are likewise concerned with trade and welfare. One shows that the welfare effects of tariff changes depend on the levels of the tariffs involved and draws some implications for customs-union theory. The other shows how emigration affects the welfare of those left behind in the source country. This was, I believe, the first paper to sort out the issues clearly and to deal with them in the context of the Heckscher-Ohlin model. It shows that the effects on economic welfare derive from the effects on the global output mix and that their distribution between host and source countries depends on the pattern of commodity trade.

The second part of the book, on international monetary theory and policy, contains two papers on international liquidity, two on monetary integration, and four on aspects of exchange-rate theory.

Economists seem hesitant to accept the obvious unless it can be built into a formal model. That is why I wrote the first paper in this part, "International Liquidity and the Balance of Payments of a Reserve-Currency Country." My point was one that Robert Triffin had already made, but he had appealed to history and I tried to invoke pure theory. As Triffin saw it—and I agreed—the monetary system of the late 1950s was due to face a difficult dilemma. If the United States continued to run a balance-of-payments deficit, supplying the world with dollar reserves, holders of dollars would come to doubt the quality of those reserves. If the United States ended its deficit, it would maintain the quality of the reserves outstanding but would reduce the growth rate of reserves, and some countries might adopt predatory policies to drain reserves away from others. To make this point abstractly, I built a model of the gold-exchange standard in which the demand for dollar reserves was assumed to vary directly with the strength of the U.S. reserve position—the ratio of its gold reserves to dollar liabilities. I showed that the gold-exchange standard would be stable for as long as that ratio was larger than unity but that the ratio would decline as reserves expanded, driving the system into a "crisis zone" where it would become unstable. We were far from the crisis zone when I wrote the paper, and I wound up on an optimistic note.

Furthermore, I made a couple of suggestions that I would reject to-day. I said, for instance, that the system could be kept out of the crisis zone if new reserve currencies were brought into being—a suggestion that holds much less charm today, as we face the problems of a monetary system having several reserve centers. Nevertheless, the framework I supplied was useful to others; Officer and Willett, for example, used it to examine the behavior of the system in the crisis zone. And I went on to use it in my quantitative work on the asset preferences of central banks.[1]

The second paper looks at international liquidity from a different standpoint. It examines the demand for reserves *in toto* rather than the asset composition of demand. The paper was inspired by dissatisfaction with the measure used most often to gauge the adequacy of reserve supplies—the ratio of reserves to imports—and was the first to use what has since been called the disturbance approach to the demand for reserves. That demand, the paper argues, depends on the need for balance-of-payments financing, not on the levels of payments or receipts, and the need for financing can be represented to a first approximation by the variability of the balance of payments (of reserve flows themselves). The theory was primitive. So were the estimates. For that very reason, however, the paper led to large amounts of work by others, including attempts to measure the costs of holding reserves and to model the optimization of reserve stocks. As I look back upon this paper and the work that followed it, I wonder if the effort was not misdirected. A full-grown theory of the demand for reserves necessarily subsumes the whole theory of balance-of-payments adjustment and forces it into a narrow stock-optimizing framework. Fritz Machlup, who criticized my work at the time, has argued that reserves are determined residually and influence national policies asymmetrically. Central banks do not try to get rid of large reserves and do not often try to build up their reserves at the expense of other policy objectives. Reserve positions influence national policies only when they are at risk, because of large balance-of-payments deficits—and this brings us back to ordinary balance-of-payments theory. I tend to agree.

The next two papers in this part are more closely linked than their titles would suggest. In the first, "Toward a Supranational Monetary System," I try to define the institutional requirements for successful monetary integration. Following James Ingram, I stress the need for capital mobility (asset-market integration) to cushion the process of balance-of-payments adjustment, but I also emphasize the impor-

[1] *Reserve Asset Preferences of Central Banks and Stability of the Gold-Exchange Standard,* Princeton Studies in International Finance, Princeton University, Princeton, N.J., 1963.

tance of a unified fiscal system. I argue, in particular, that the stabilizers built into the fiscal system serve to offset cyclical and structural imbalances in interregional payments, allowing regions to finance or correct imbalances at tolerable cost. In the second paper, "The Theory of Optimum Currency Areas: An Eclectic View," I bring these same arguments to bear on the problem of delineating currency areas—those within which it is best to peg exchange rates and between which it is best to let them float.

In that second paper, however, I make one more point. The degree to which domestic output is diversified may be important for the choice between exchange-rate regimes. Countries (regions) with diversified economies may not have much need to alter their exchange rates. External disturbances may average out, *ex ante*, and when there is need to reallocate resources because of external or internal disturbances, diversification reduces the costs by enhancing domestic mobility. (If making this same point today, I would of course restate it in terms of real exchange rates, as Roland Vaubel does in his work on European monetary integration.) This argument has been cited frequently, most recently by Tower and Willett, but I am dissatisfied with my formulation. As a practical matter, the countries that have opted for flexible exchange rates are those that have the largest, most diversified economies. More generally, my paper and most others on the subject are dated by the theory of exchange-rate determination on which they are based. Until recently, we taught that exchange rates are determined in markets dominated by current-account flows and that current-account balances are affected quickly by exchange-rate changes, producing smooth adjustment to external disturbances. That is not what we teach today. But these two papers are precursors of my monograph on monetary integration,[2] and they influenced my recent book with Polly Reynolds Allen,[3] which examines the problems of economic integration and the delineation of currency areas in the context of a multi-country macroeconomic model that takes the new asset-market view of exchange-rate determination.

The four papers on exchange-rate theory were written at different times, using different methodologies, to focus on particular issues. In the first, "Trade, Speculation, and the Forward Exchange Rate," I reformulate the partial-equilibrium theory of forward exchange handed down from Keynes, by way of S. C. Tsiang and others. In Tsiang's important paper, the forward foreign-exchange rate is determined by three groups of actors—speculators, hedgers, and arbi-

[2] *Capital Mobility and Financial Integration: A Survey*, Princeton Studies in International Finance, Princeton University, Princeton, N.J., 1976.

[3] *Asset Markets, Exchange Rates, and Economic Integration*, Cambridge University Press, London and New York, 1980.

trageurs. In my paper, I show that a single, utility-maximizing firm will speculate, hedge, and arbitrage at various times and in various ways, and that its attitude toward risk is critical for the behavior of the forward rate. I demonstrate, for instance, that covered interest parity holds only under very special circumstances—those one would describe today as meaning risk neutrality. Each optimizing firm, however, will maintain its own "marginal" interest parity; it will arbitrage among sources of finance, domestic and foreign, with the aim of minimizing borrowing costs. Martin Feldstein was right to point out that the paper does not treat utility and risk with sufficient rigor. But it was the first to derive conditions for forward-market equilibrium from conditions for portfolio optimization and to work with stocks (wealth holders' positions) rather than with flows.

During the negotiations on reform of the monetary system, in 1972-74, the United States proposed the use of "objective indicators" to guide the process of balance-of-payments adjustment. Countries with large (or rising) reserves would be expected to inflate or to revalue their currencies; countries with small (or falling) reserves would be expected to deflate or devalue. I was sympathetic to the notion but worried about the choice of indicator. When in doubt, I simulate, and my results are summarized in "Floats, Glides, and Indicators." It examines the behavior of exchange rates and reserves when changes in exchange rates are mandated automatically by changes in reserves, levels of reserves, and moving averages of market exchange rates. Each indicator is made to perform under alternative assumptions about the functioning of the foreign-exchange market, the sizes of the bands surrounding the pegged rates, and the sizes of the changes in the pegs. My simulations warn against the use of reserve levels, the indicator favored by the United States, because they cause large oscillations in exchange rates. I have thought of carrying this work further, to examine in the context of a simple model the implications of alternative rules for managing a floating rate.

The last two papers in this part come out of larger studies—the book with Polly Allen, mentioned earlier, and my econometric work on the U.S. balance of payments.[4] One of them is methodological. It compares ways to specify portfolio adjustment and the consequences for the short-run behavior of a macroeconomic model under alternative exchange-rate regimes. The other looks at an old question in the light of recent theory and empirical work. How effective are monetary and fiscal policies under pegged and floating rates? The evidence, it says, supports the familiar view that monetary policy is more

---

[4] *A Model of the U.S. Balance of Payments*, Lexington Books, D. C. Heath, Lexington, Mass., 1978.

effective with a floating rate and is made all the more effective by high capital mobility. The answer with respect to fiscal policy is somewhat more complicated. The paper also looks at "insulation" under floating rates and shows that it cannot take place immediately. Full insulation is, indeed, a long-run property. But simulations based on my balance-of-payments model for the United States show that there is partial insulation in the short run.

In 1964, at a meeting in Bellagio, a group of economists prepared a report on the international monetary system. It identified three issues—adjustment, liquidity, and confidence. The papers in the last part of this book touch on all three issues but emphasize the links between them. The first paper, for example, was written in 1962, soon after the negotiation of the first swap agreements and of the General Arrangements to Borrow, supplementing the resources of the International Monetary Fund. Those devices were designed to strengthen confidence in the wake of the gold-price scare of 1960-61 and turbulence in foreign-exchange markets, but the paper argues that they did more for liquidity than they did for confidence. It goes on to propose ways of consolidating the new *ad hoc* arrangements, with a view to the development of a reserve system based on overdraft financing rather than holdings of national currencies, and makes a case for giving exchange-rate guarantees on dollars held by foreign official institutions. Like most of those that follow, this paper is dated, but the ideas are not. In a recent paper on long-run reform, J. J. Polak has suggested the transformation of IMF quotas into SDR-denominated overdraft facilities, and exchange-rate guarantees are implicit in proposals for creating a "substitution account" under the aegis of the IMF.

The second paper deals quite explicitly with the links between adjustment and financing (liquidity), and it raises a question that has never been resolved. How soon and how fast should adjustment take place, and are there ways of regulating access to financing in order to optimize the process? The paper puts the problem in general terms. It comes up today in three guises—debates about the scope of IMF "surveillance" and the ways to make it most effective, debates about "conditionality" of access to IMF resources, and debates about the impact of Eurocurrency borrowing on the quality of the adjustment process.

The third paper was written in 1969, two years before the closing of the gold window and the first devaluation of the dollar. It hints at the need to realign exchange rates but indicates no urgency about the problem. In fact, it rules out unilateral action of the sort taken two years later, arguing that the United States should continue to play a passive nth country role in the exchange-rate system. Hence, the paper calls for multilateral agreement on rules for periodic changes in exchange rates within the framework of the Bretton Woods system. The paper marks the end of my long flirtation with a multiple reserve-currency system and the start of my interest in another theme—the need to consolidate *all* reserve assets under the auspices of the IMF. The last page of the article offers in a single sentence a plan for a comprehensive substitution account.

The same theme is developed in the fourth paper, "Convertibility and Consolidation," written in 1972, just after the formation of the Committee of Twenty to plan for the reform of the monetary system. The main purpose of the paper, however, was quite different—to clarify semantic issues in the debate about the future of the system. Those were the days when U.S. and European spokesmen agreed on the need for a "symmetrical" system but could not agree on anything of substance. Symmetry meant different things to different governments. For U.S. spokesmen, it implied more vigorous adjustment on the part of surplus countries. For European spokesmen, it implied a reduction in the special role of the dollar—the imposition of "mandatory asset settlement" (convertibility), so that the United States could not finance its deficit by creating additional dollar reserves.

This paper and the two that follow it comprise a running commentary on the work of the Committee of Twenty. The one I have just summarized was written just after the Committee was created. The next was written a year later, in 1973, just after the IMF meetings in Nairobi (but before the Arab oil "embargo" and the increase in the oil price). It warned against an unworkable agreement—the Rhinopotamus that might be put together by the negotiators. The last was written in 1974, when the Committee was winding up its work without hope of agreement. Its title, "Reforming the Monetary System—You Can't Get There from Here," describes its content accurately. With the benefit of perfect hindsight, I show why it was clear from the very start that there would be no agreement on reform of the system!

There was, of course, agreement of a different sort two years later, at the Jamaica meeting of the Interim Committee, and it is the subject of the next paper, "International Monetary Relations After Jamaica," written in 1976, soon after the agreement was put in place.

The last two papers in this book are somewhat more ambitious. One deals with the problems of controlling liquidity under a floating-rate regime. It was written for the conference in memory of J. Marcus Fleming and owes more to his work than it acknowledges. The other is my only venture into the international monetary problems of the less-developed countries. It deals with the case for debt relief—the costs to the creditors and gains to the debtors.

The papers in this book are reprinted without editing. (I have altered a paragraph in one paper and corrected typographical errors in another.) Therefore, you will still find an error in one diagram, to which I drew attention in a last-minute footnote, and some warts in other papers. Several footnotes, moreover, refer to papers in this book but cite the original places of publication. If I were editing these papers systematically, I would make many changes and add many references. It is not the purpose of this series, however, to bring work up to date, but rather to make it more accessible. I have only two regrets. I cannot make mention of colleagues' work with which I should have been familiar when I did my own, and I cannot take account of thoughtful comments from those who found problems in these papers and took the time to correspond with me about them.

On a separate page, I thank those who have given me permission to reprint these papers. Here, I add my thanks to my collaborators—to Elinor Yudin Sachse, with whom I wrote "The Demand for International Reserves," and to Polly Reynolds Allen, with whom I wrote "Portfolio Adjustment in Open Economies."

Acknowledgments

The author wishes to thank the publishers of the following papers for permission to reprint them here.

"Nature, Capital, and Trade" is reprinted from *The Journal of Political Economy*, Vol. 73 (No. 5, 1965), pp. 437-460. Copyright © 1965 by the University of Chicago.

"Toward a More General Theory of Capital and Trade" is reprinted from P. B. Kenen and R. Lawrence, eds., *The Open Economy: Essays on International Trade and Finance*, New York, Columbia University Press, 1968, pp. 100-123.

"Distribution, Demand, and Equilibrium in International Trade: A Diagrammatic Analysis" was originally published in *Kyklos*, Vol. 12 (No. 4, 1959), pp. 629-638. The version used here was reprinted first in R. E. Caves and H. G. Johnson, eds., *Readings in International Economics*, Homewood, Ill., Richard D. Irwin, Inc., 1968, pp. 90-98.

"On the Geometry of Welfare Economics: A Suggested Diagrammatic Treatment of Some Basic Propositions" is reprinted from *The Quarterly Journal of Economics*, Vol. 71 (No. 3, 1957), pp. 426-447. Copyright © 1957 by the President and Fellows of Harvard College. Reprinted by permission of John Wiley & Sons, Inc.

"A Note on Tariff Changes and World Welfare" is reprinted from *The Quarterly Journal of Economics*, Vol. 88 (No. 4, 1974), pp. 692-697. Copyright © 1974 by the President and Fellows of Harvard College. Reprinted by permission of John Wiley & Sons, Inc.

"Migration, the Terms of Trade, and Economic Welfare in the Source Country" is reprinted from J. N. Bhagwati et al., *Trade, Balance of Payments and Growth: Papers in International Economics in Honor of Charles P. Kindleberger*, Amsterdam, North-Holland Publishing Company, 1971, pp. 238-260.

"International Liquidity and the Balance of Payments of a Reserve-Currency Country" is reprinted from *The Quarterly Journal of Economics*, Vol. 74 (No. 4, 1960), pp. 572-586. Copyright © 1960 by the President and Fellows of Harvard College. Reprinted by permission of John Wiley & Sons, Inc.

With Elinor Yudin [Sachse], "The Demand for International Reserves" is reprinted from *The Review of Economics and Statistics*, Vol. 47 (No. 3, 1965), pp. 242-250. Copyright © 1965 by the President and Fellows of Harvard College. Reprinted by permission of North-Holland Publishing Company, Amsterdam.

"Toward a Supranational Monetary System" is reprinted from

"Techniques to Control International Reserves" is reprinted from R. A. Mundell and J. J. Polak, eds., *The New International Monetary System*, New York, Columbia University Press, 1977, pp. 202-222.

"Debt Relief as Development Assistance" is reprinted from J. N. Bhagwati, ed., *The New International Economic Order: The North-South Debate*, Cambridge, Mass., The MIT Press, 1977, pp. 50-77.

Essays in International Economics

Trade, Tariffs, and Welfare

Nature, Capital, and Trade[1]

PETER B. KENEN

THE factor-endowments analysis of foreign trade, based on the works of Heckscher and Ohlin,[2] has been justly praised as a major intellectual achievement of modern economic thought. In Corden's words, "It is a monolithic, formal structure, rigorous, and with every deductive nook and cranny of it thoroughly explored. If one accepts its restrictive assumptions, a vast number of conclusions can be squeezed out of it."[3] Yet those who praise its tautness and elegance are also quick to warn that its principal predictions are at sharp variance with casual observation and with well-established fact. They distrust the conclusion that free trade without transport costs would equalize factor prices, and they balk at the chief corollary to this famous theorem, that a single tariff could eliminate all trade if factors of production are mobile among countries. They are puzzled by Leontief's celebrated computations[4] showing that the exports of the United States are less

[1] Early versions of this paper were presented in seminars at Columbia, Berkeley, Chicago, and the London School of Economics, and at the 1963 Winter Meetings of the Econometric Society. One such version has been published under the title "Growth Theory, Trade Theory and International Investment," in *Trade and Development* (Geneva: Librarie Droz, 1965). A comprehensive version of the algebraic model will be published with the title "Toward a More General Theory of Capital" (hereinafter cited as "Theory of Capital").

I am indebted to several readers for criticism and suggestions, especially to G. C. Archibald, G. S. Becker, H. G. Johnson, Z. Sebestyen, W. P. Travis, and E. B. Yudin. The first drafts of this paper were prepared in 1962–63, when I held a Ford Foundation Faculty Research Fellowship; I am grateful to the Ford Foundation and to the International Economics Workshop, Columbia University, for generous support of the project.

[2] E. Heckscher, "The Effect of Foreign Trade on the Distribution of Income," reprinted in *Readings in the Theory of International Trade*, ed. H. E. Ellis and L. A. Metzler (Philadelphia, Pa.: Blakiston Co., 1949); and B. Ohlin, *Interregional and International Trade* (Cambridge, Mass.: Harvard University Press, 1933). For compact surveys of recent developments, see J. Bhagwati, "The Pure Theory of International Trade," *Economic Journal*, LXXIV (March, 1964), 17–26; W. M. Corden, *Recent Developments in the Theory of International Trade* (Princeton, N.J.: International Finance Section, 1965), pp. 24–34; and M. Michaely, "Factor Proportions in International Trade," *Kyklos*, XVII (1964), 529–50.

[3] Corden, *op. cit.*, p. 30.

[4] W. W. Leontief, "Factor Proportions and the Structure of American Trade" (hereinafter cited as "Factor Proportions"), *Review of Economics and Statistics*, XXXVIII (November, 1956), 386–407.

capital intensive than its import-competing production, even though the United States is deemed to have more capital per worker than any other major country. Finally, they must grapple with the several major studies challenging a basic supposition of the model, that processes display a strong factor-ordering.[5]

In this paper, I shall show that most of these apparent anomalies descend from the *simpliste* concept of capital used in the factor-endowments analysis. The excess of paradox so many have decried may not be proper cause for condemning trade theory but, rather, for changing the notion of capital to which we have become accustomed. Because trade theory is concerned with long-run phenomena, it must treat capital as a stock of "waiting," not as a collection of tangible assets.[6] It then proceeds, however, as though this disembodied stock were just like any other factor of production. Pure "waiting" is regarded as a substitute for land or labor and is deemed to have a real wage that can be ascertained from the production functions.[7] I shall propose a different view of capital and shall graft it onto the Heckscher-Ohlin

[5] See, for example, K. J. Arrow, H. B. Chenery, B. S. Minhas, and R. M. Solow, "Capital-Labor Substitution and Economic Efficiency," *Review of Economics and Statistics*, XLIII (August, 1961), 225–51; and B. S. Minhas, *An International Comparison of Factor Costs and Factor Use* (Amsterdam: North-Holland Publishing Co., 1963), chap. iv. For trenchant criticism of Minhas' work, see W. W. Leontief, "International Factor Costs and Factor Use," *American Economic Review*, LIV (June, 1964), 335–45.

[6] See R. E. Caves, *Trade and Economic Structure* (Cambridge, Mass.: Harvard University Press, 1960), pp. 94–96.

[7] For an ingenious justification of this approach, see P. A. Samuelson, "Parable and Realism in Capital Theory: The Surrogate Production Function" (hereinafter cited as "Parable and Realism in Capital Theory"). *Review of Economic Studies*, XXIX (June, 1962), 193–206.

model. I shall then explore the several connections between capital formation, foreign trade, and foreign investment, deriving new results that seem to me more plausible than those that obtain in conventional analyses.

I. TRADE AND INVESTMENT IN CONVENTIONAL MODELS

Not too long ago, the factor-price equalization theorem was widely regarded as a mere curiosity. Recent work, however, assigns it a central role in the Heckscher-Ohlin model. In order to predict the structure of foreign trade by comparing national factor endowments, one must employ most of the restrictive assumptions required for factor-price equalization, then impose additional constraints on demand. The two-country, two-product, two-factor model requires three separate sets of assumptions:

1. that factors of production are completely uniform within countries and between them, that all markets are perfectly competitive, and that there is perfect internal mobility;
2. that the production functions are the same in the two countries, that they evince constant returns to scale, and that they can be ranked uniquely by factor-intensity regardless of factor prices;
3. that demand conditions are also alike and that they yield unitary income elasticities for all consumer goods.

The first set of assumptions generates the usual marginal equalities; each factor's real wage will equal its marginal physical product, and each product's price will equal its marginal cost. The second set impounds technology as a separate cause of trade, washes out effects of scale on the supply side, and defines a single-valued functional relationship between each country's product prices and that country's factor prices. The third set of assumptions impounds demand as a separate cause of trade and washes out effects of scale on the demand side.[8] The first and second sets, however, nearly suffice for factor-price equalization; one has only to suppose that there are no trade barriers or transport costs and that the two countries are not so dissimilar as to specialize completely in a single product.

If free trade were to equalize two countries' factor prices, it would also preclude all factor movements. When, for example, net saving occurred in one of the two countries, a change in the terms of trade would maintain equality in national interest rates,[9] thereby forestalling any flow of funds from the country with net saving to the outside world. When, further, one country levied a tariff, no matter how small, and one of the factors had perfect mobility, all trade would cease between the two countries. This important corollary, due to Mundell,[10] can be proved quite easily. If factor prices were equalized by trade, the smallest tariff would drive them apart; it would raise the real wage in the country that imports the labor-intensive product and would raise the interest rate in the country that imports the capital-intensive product.[11] If capital were perfectly mobile between the two countries, it

would start to flow from the first to the second, and the flow of capital would not cease until it had equalized the two countries' interest rates and had also equalized the two countries' wage rates. At this point, however, the two countries' product prices would also be equalized before paying any duty, and the smallest tariff would be prohibitive; there would be no basis for commodity trade. In brief, one cannot study factor movements in the Heckscher-Ohlin model unless one first posits "extraneous" assumptions serving to preclude factor-price equality.[12]

Factor-price equalization does not imply global equality in incomes per capita, as differences in labor-force participation and in supplies of capital per worker could still make for differences in real incomes. But even when conjoined to tariffs and transport costs, these two differences in economic structure do not provide a systematic explanation for the huge variation in incomes per capita that is a most impressive and compelling fact of modern economic life.[13] Again, one is compelled to introduce "extraneous" assumptions into the Heckscher-Ohlin

[8] For a more detailed discussion of the conventional model, see the surveys by Bhagwati (*op. cit.*) and Michaely (*op. cit.*); see also R. W. Jones, "Factor Proportions and the Heckscher-Ohlin Theorem," *Review of Economic Studies*, XXIV (1956–57), 1–10; and Caves, *op. cit.*, chaps. iii–iv, vi–vii.

[9] Here I assume—and shall do so throughout—that an international equality of rental rates on reproducible capital goods implies an equality of national interest rates; for proof and exceptions, see P. A. Samuelson, "Equalization by Trade of the Interest Rate along with the Real Wage," (hereinafter cited as "Equalization by Trade"), *Trade, Growth and the Balance of Payments* (Chicago: Rand-McNally & Co., 1965), pp. 35–52.

[10] R. A. Mundell, "International Trade and Factor Mobility," *American Economic Review*, XLVII (June, 1957), 321–35; see also Caves, *op. cit.*, chap. v.

[11] Here I exclude Metzler's case, in which the foreign offer curve is so inelastic that prices change perversely in the country imposing the tariff; see L. A. Metzler, "Tariffs, the Terms of Trade, and the Distribution of National Income," *Journal of Political Economy*, LVII (February, 1949), 1–29. Note, however, that the Mundell corollary would hold in this case too.

[12] This can, of course, be done without also precluding commodity trade based on differences in factor endowments; see J. E. Meade, *Trade and Welfare* (London: Oxford University Press, 1955), in which the analysis of factor movements is based on the sequential introduction of transport costs and "corner solutions" involving complete specialization.

[13] For a dissenting view, see W. P. Travis, *The Theory of Trade and Protection* (Cambridge, Mass.: Harvard University Press, 1964), chap. vii. There, it is argued that, directly or indirectly, tariffs do account for much of the observed international difference in incomes per capita.

model in order to account for demonstrable fact. When, in addition, tariffs and transport costs prevent an alignment of wage rates and interest rates, differences in national capital supplies should generate differences in interest rates that would draw capital from rich lands to poor, thereby reducing disparities in incomes. This, at least, is what one would infer from the Heckscher-Ohlin model, after abstracting from differences in risk. Yet recent flows of capital have been quite different, shunning the low-income countries except to bring out minerals or directly to exploit their tropical climates.

I shall not pause to dwell on other findings that seem to contradict the Heckscher-Ohlin model—Leontief's results concerning U.S. trade and the recent work on the theory of production that appears to rule out strong factor-ordering. These results have to be qualified, but even when properly modified, each of them challenges the simple presumption that trade is directly related to factor endowments.[14] In each case, again, a satisfactory confrontation between theory and fact can only be achieved by importing additional, special assumptions into the factor-endowments analysis.

On close inspection, however, most of the anomalies and contradictions that generate dissatisfaction with the Heckscher-Ohlin model appear to derive from the peculiar concept of capital used in that model and, more importantly, in many recent works on economic growth. It is the supposition that disembodied

"waiting" can enter the production function as a separate input which equalizes interest rates in the Heckscher-Ohlin model, thereby precluding foreign investment when free trade prevails. This same supposition of homogeneity is also employed by Leontief and by the studies of the production function that challenge the assumption of strong factor-ordering. Admittedly, the study of foreign trade requires an abstract treatment of capital; trade theory must assume that the stock of capital can be reallocated among industries and among countries. But one should not suppose that disembodied "waiting" enters directly into the production function. Production is accomplished by using the services furnished by the several incarnations of a country's "waiting," the services of many different capital assets. When, in addition, one tries to forecast trade patterns at a particular moment of time, the varied incarnations of a nation's capital acquire great significance; one must examine the several ways that "waiting" is embodied and the contribution of each embodiment to the many processes defining the output mix.

To meet these requirements of trade theory, I shall employ a concept of capital different from those used in the past. It is derived from two separate strands of thought, each of them concerned with a single facet of the problem. In his work on resource use and U.S. foreign trade, Vanek presupposes a complementarity between capital and land.[15] He also finds that U.S. trade may conserve scarce land rather than scarce capital (see Table 1). The apparent capital intensity of U.S. import-competing production may, in fact, reflect its very

---

[14] Leontief's results must be doubly qualified because they are based on a very special model and because the best data are never perfect proxies for the abstractions of economic theory. On these points see, e.g., S. Valivanis, "Factor Proportions and the Structure of American Trade: Comment," *Review of Economics and Statistics*, XL, suppl. (February, 1958), 111-13; and Caves, *op. cit.*, pp. 275-80.

[15] J. Vanek, *The Natural Resource Content of U.S. Foreign Trade, 1870-1955* (Cambridge, Mass.: M.I.T. Press, 1963), chap. vii.

heavy land use (high resource-product content) and a lavish use of capital to improve scarce U.S. land.

Schultz, Becker, and others have drawn our attention to a similar relationship between capital and labor.[16] Enormous sums are spent each year to train the U.S. labor force, and these investments have outpaced investments in tangible wealth (see Table 2). Measured investment in human beings was valued at some $880 billion in 1957 and was two-thirds as large as tangible wealth.

Combining these two separate findings, I shall build a simple model that treats "capital" and "nature" as the aboriginal agents of production. I shall suppose that every country has fixed stocks of land and labor, its natural endowment, but shall also suppose that these stocks are wholly inert—that they must be improved by acts of investment

TABLE 1

CAPITAL, LABOR, AND RESOURCE-PRODUCT (LAND) USE PER MILLION DOLLARS U.S. EXPORTS AND U.S. IMPORT-COMPETING PRODUCTION, 1947

Inputs	Exports	Imports
Capital ($ thousands) 1947 prices....................	2,085	2,244
Labor (man-years)...........	179	164
Resource product ($ thousands) 1947 prices........	340	630

Source: Capital and labor data from Leontief, "Factor Proportions," *op. cit.*, Table 1, Part A; resource-product data from Vanek, *op. cit.*, p. 132.

before they can contribute to current production. I shall also assume that a single, malleable capital good or service is used to improve the natural endowment and that it can be employed with

[16] T. W. Schultz, "Reflections on Investment in Man," *Journal of Political Economy*, LXX, suppl. (October, 1962), 1–8; and G. S. Becker, *Human Capital* (New York: National Bureau of Economic Research), 1965.

equal ease to build roads, drain swamps, or train apprentices. In actual fact, of course, acts of investment would differentiate the natural endowment (and would require very different inputs rather than a single capital good). But I shall treat these changes in factor quality as though they were changes in factor

TABLE 2

ESTIMATES OF VARIOUS STOCKS OF CAPITAL IN THE UNITED STATES, 1957

Form of Capital	$ Billions 1956 Prices	Growth Rate 1939–57 (Per Cent)
Reproducible tangible wealth...............	1,270	2.01
Educational capital in labor force.............	535	4.09
On-the-job training, male workers.............	347	5.36

Source: Schultz, *op. cit.*, p. 6.

quantity, pretending that investment in the natural endowment generates a single undifferentiated factor-service flow from land and a second flow from labor and that these two flows are the only inputs into production.

Like most other models used to study foreign trade, mine will employ a number of assumptions that rudely distort economic reality. I shall invoke the three sets of assumptions used in the conventional Heckscher-Ohlin model (but I shall not require global uniformity in factor quality, and I shall read the second set, pertaining to production, as though it referred to the factor-service flows stemming from labor and land). I shall also pretend that all investment is financed by credits from a central fund whose assets will measure the capital stock and that all accounts are kept in real terms, using the price of the capital good as the *numéraire*. These assumptions are designed to suppress the many intractable problems encountered in capital theory—those that relate to the heterogeneity of capital goods and their varied ages.[17] To this same end, I shall study capital formation, displacement, and trade in a stationary state, where the stock of capital is absolutely fixed and perfectly allocated. To deal with saving and investment, I shall postulate once-over growth in the total loan fund (an act of net saving rather than a flow) and shall then examine the implications of the corresponding permanent increase in stationary-state replacement investment.[18]

II. ALLOCATION AND DISPLACEMENT IN A CLOSED ECONOMY

Consider, then, two countries (I and II) with fixed supplies of land and labor. Each country's land is uniform, as is its labor force, but they need not be the same from one country to the other. Each country's stocks of land and labor will be inert until they are improved by a series of investments. Such an investment will evoke a finite factor-service flow, with z_1 units of land service brought forth from a single acre and z_2 units of labor service brought forth from a single worker. Let these flows be steady while they last, but let the investments depreciate by "sudden death" and let them have the same life expectancy, v years. To be quite precise, define a factor-service supply function:

$$z_i = f_i(k_i), \qquad i = 1, 2, \qquad (1)$$

where k_i is the point-input investment in a single acre ($i = 1$) or a single worker ($i = 2$) and where z_i is the yearly factor-service flow evoked by that investment. Let the factor-service supply function look like OPS in Figure 1, with constant elasticity, $0 < \eta < 1$, and let the elasticities be equal for all i.[19]

Let there be a separate loan fund in each of the two countries. The real value of its claims will measure the country's capital stock; the interest income on its credits will measure the annual income to capital. The fund will finance workers so that they may purchase training. It will likewise finance landlords seeking to increase the rental value of their holdings. Its interest rate, r, will be set exactly to equate the demand for credit by workers and landlords with the fixed supply of credit flowing through the fund.[20] The workers and landlords will pay off their debts with some of the gross proceeds of their factor-service sales. And if they have no preference for present over future income, each year's debt-service payment (principal and interest) will be the same fraction, g, of the total loan, k_i.[21] The yearly real income of a worker or landlord is defined by:

$$y_i = w_i z_i - g k_i, \qquad i = 1, 2, \qquad (2)$$

[17] See, e.g., Samuelson, "Parable and Realism in Capital Theory," *loc. cit.*, and J. Robinson, "Accumulation and the Production Function," *Economic Journal*, LXIX (September, 1959), 422–42. These problems are actually compounded in my model, because it takes account of investment in man as well as investment in tangible assets.

[18] For a more detailed treatment of the relationship between the total loan fund (the capital stock) and the yearly flow of replacement investment, see my "Theory of Capital."

[19] Strictly, let $f_i(0) = 0$, and let $0 < (k_i/z_i)f_i' = \eta < 1$, so that $f_i'' = (\eta - 1)(f_i'/k_i) < 0$. The isoelasticity condition (within and between countries) simplifies several of the formulas that follow; for the case in which $\eta_1 \neq \eta_2$, see my "Theory of Capital."

[20] In a stationary state, the supply of credit will exactly equal the current flow of debt repayments; the total loan fund will not grow as by reinvesting its annual interest income.

[21] Barring a preference for present over future income, a worker or landlord will arrange his debt-service payments so as to equalize his annual income across its v-year life-span. But his gross receipts will also be equal for v successive years because z_i is a steady flow, and he will repay his debts in equal annual installments, u_i. (See J. E. Meade, *A Neo-Classical Theory of Economic Growth* [London: George Allen & Unwin, 1961], pp. 134–44.) In this

where w_i is the real wage of the ith factor service (its money wage divided by the price of the capital good), so that $w_i z_i$ measures his gross annual receipts from

case, however, the present value of the u_i, discounted at the interest rate r, must exactly equal k_i:

$$k_i = u_i \sum_{t=1}^{v} (1+r)^{-t} = u_i \frac{(1+r)^v - 1}{r(1+r)^v}.$$

Hence, the fraction g, henceforth described as the gross amortization rate, is defined by

$$g = \frac{u_i}{k_i} = \frac{r(1+r)^v}{(1+r)^v - 1}.$$

Note for future reference that

$$e_{gr} = \frac{dg}{dr} \frac{r}{g} = 1 - \frac{vr}{(1+r)[(1+r)^v - 1]},$$

so that $0 < e_{gr} < 1$.

factor-service sales and gk_i measures his debt-service payment.

As z_i is a steady flow lasting for v years, the worker or landlord will maximize his lifetime earnings if he maximizes y_i. He must borrow and invest until his marginal receipts are driven down to g, his marginal debt-service payment to the central fund. To optimize investment, then,

$$w_i f_i' = g. \tag{3}$$

If $\tan \theta = (g/w_i)$ in Figure 1, this condition holds at P on the function OPS, and $0k_i$ is optimal investment. The corresponding service flow is $0z_i$, which also serves to measure the investor's gross receipts in units of the ith factor service.

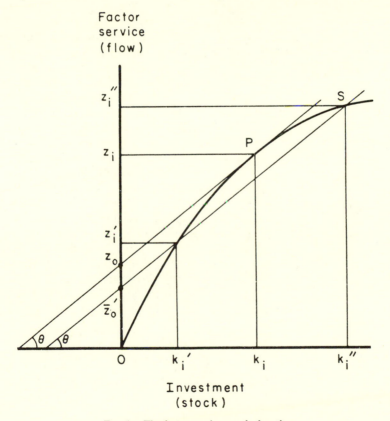

Fig. 1.—The factor-service supply function

Furthermore, $z_0 z_i$ measures the debt-service payment (gk_i/w_i), and $0z_0$ measures real income (y_i/w_i), both of them computed in ith factor-service units.[22]

Suppose, next, that the nation's natural endowment totals N_1 acres and N_2 workers and that past investments in that endowment have been spaced out evenly. Under these assumptions, $(N_1/v)k_1$ of investments in land and $(N_2/v)k_2$ of investments in labor will "die off" every year, and new investment must offset this attrition if it is to call forth stable factor-service flows. In a stationary state, then,

$$Z_i = F_i(K_i) = N_i f_i(k_i), \qquad i = 1, 2, \quad (4)$$

where

$$K_i = \frac{N_i k_i}{v}, \qquad (5)$$

so that $F_i' = v f_i' = \eta(Z_i/K_i)$, and equations (2) and (3) give way to

$$Y_i = N_i y_i = w_i Z_i - v g K_i, \qquad (6)$$

$$w_i F_i' = vg. \qquad (7)$$

Equations (1) and (4) are very similar in their formal properties, conveying the same basic suppositions regarding the role of capital in the economy. But there is a major difference between the two equations. The microeconomic function, equation (1), connects a single act of investment, k_i, with a finite v-year service

flow, z_i. The aggregate relationship, equation (4), connects a yearly flow, K_i, with a perpetual stream of factor service, Z_i. The definition of K_i given by equation (5) pertains to a stationary state; hence equation (4) pertains to that same special state.[23]

Finally, one can represent the yearly interest income on the capital stock by

$$Y_r = K(vg - 1), \qquad (8)$$

where K is the gross total of replacement investment in the entire natural endowment, $K_1 + K_2$, and likewise measures the annual output of the malleable capital good.[24] Consequently,

$$\begin{aligned} Y &= (Y_1 + Y_2) + Y_r \\ &= (w_1 Z_1 + w_2 Z_2) - K, \end{aligned} \qquad (9)$$

which is to measure the national income as gross national product at factor cost, $w_1 Z_1 + w_2 Z_2$, *less* depreciation, K, but to allow for the depreciation of "human capital" as well as tangible capital.

If gross annual investment, K, is optimally allocated in the stationary state, satisfying (7), gross national product will be at a maximum,[25] and the two service flows, Z_1 and Z_2, will obey the relationship traced by $G'G'$ in Figure 2, the gross factor-service frontier. The slope of this frontier, moreover, will be equal (absolutely) to the wage-rate ratio (w_1/w_2), henceforth called w,[26] and its tangent-intercepts will measure gross national product. When, then, $\tan \alpha$ is equal to w, $0Z_1$ of land service and $0Z_2$ of labor service will be forthcoming every

---

[22] One can, indeed, derive eq. (3) directly from Fig. 1. Any level of investment different from $0k_i$ will reduce real income; at $0k_i'$ and $0k_i''$, for example, the investor's income is reduced to $0z_0'$. Note, further, the importance of the restriction $0 < \eta < 1$: Replace f_i' with $\eta(z_i/k_i)$ in eq. (3), then replace g in eq. (2):

$$y_i = w_i z_i (1 - \eta) > 0.$$

Income to the owner of a natural factor will always be positive; it is, in fact, a quasi-rent deriving from declining marginal returns to capital invested in a single worker or a single acre.

[23] The same distinction can be drawn between eqs. (2) and (6).

[24] The capital stock is measured by (K/r) $(vg - 1)$, which yields eq. (8). For the derivation of this definition, see my "Theory of Capital."

[25] See Mathematical Appendix, eqs. (A1)–(A3).

[26] See Mathematical Appendix, eq. (A5).

year, and $0Z_2{}^*$ will measure gross national product in units of labor service.

To pass from gross national product to national income, one must deduct depreciation or, more precisely, the factor-service content of replacement investment. In order to do so, use Euler's theorem to write out the constant-cost production function for the capital good:

$$K = w_1 Z_{1k} + w_2 Z_{2k}, \qquad (10)$$

where Z_{ik} is the input of the ith factor service and w_i is its real wage (marginal product) in the capital-goods sector. Then write:

$$Y = w_1(Z_1 - Z_{1k}) + w_2(Z_2 - Z_{2k})$$
$$= w_1 Z_{1n} + w_2 Z_{2n}, \qquad (11)$$

where Z_{in} is the net supply of the ith factor service available to the consumer-goods sector (or for net additions to the capital stock).

This same subtraction is performed in Figure 2. First, one must select the proper K-isoquant, the one that will

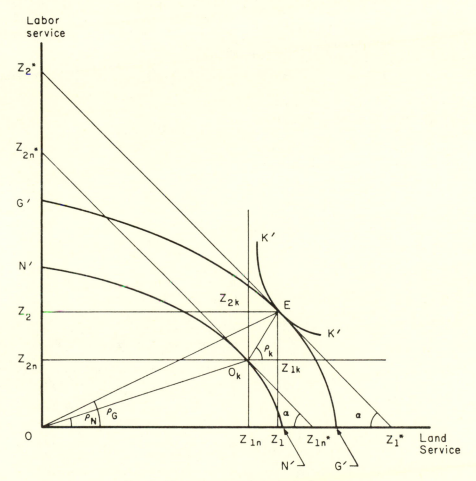

FIG. 2.—The gross and net factor-service frontiers

supply a sufficient quantity of capital goods to sustain $G'G'$ in fixed position. Let this be the isoquant $K'K'$ with origin 0_k. Next, one must place this particular K-isoquant tangent to $G'G'$ at E, thereby subtracting 0_kZ_{1k} of land service from the gross supply, $0Z_1$, and subtracting 0_kZ_{2k} of labor service from the gross supply, $0Z_2$. Repeating this procedure for each wage-rate ratio (each point on $G'G'$), one can trace out $N'N'$, the net factor-service frontier, defining Z_{2n} for each Z_{1n}. As $N'N'$ and $G'G'$ have equal slopes at 0_k and E,[27] the slope of this frontier will be equal (absolutely) to the wage-rate ratio, and its tangent intercepts will measure maximum national income.[28] When $\tan \alpha$ gives w, $0Z_{1n}$ of land service and $0Z_{2n}$ of labor service will be forthcoming for the production of final output, and $0Z_{2n}^*$ will measure maximum national income in units of labor service.

Figure 2 identifies three factor-service ratios that play a strategic role in subsequent analysis:

$R = Z_2/Z_1$, the gross factor ratio for the whole economy, measured by $0Z_2/0Z_1$ or by $\tan \rho_G$ in Figure 2;

$R_n = Z_{2n}/Z_{1n}$, the net factor ratio for the whole economy, measured by $0Z_{2n}/0Z_{1n}$ or by $\tan \rho_N$ in Figure 2;

[27] The slope of $G'G'$ is dZ_2/dZ_1, the slope of $K'K'$ is dZ_{2k}/dZ_{1k}, and each of them is equal to $-w$ at E. Hence, the slope of $N'N'$ is

$$\frac{dZ_{2n}}{dZ_{1n}} = \frac{dZ_2 - dZ_{2k}}{dZ_1 - dZ_{1k}}$$

$$= \frac{dZ_2/dZ_1 - (dZ_{2k}/dZ_{1k})(dZ_{1k}/dZ_1)}{1 - (dZ_{1k}/dZ_1)}$$

$$= -w.$$

[28] As $0Z_1^*$ and $0Z_2^*$ measure maximum gross national product, while $Z_1^*Z_{1n}^*$ and $Z_2^*Z_{2n}^*$ measure gross investment at least factor-service cost, the differences between them, $0Z_{1n}^*$ and $0Z_{2n}^*$, must measure maximum national income.

$R_k = Z_{2k}/Z_{1k}$, the factor ratio of the capital-goods industry, measured by $0_kZ_{2k}/0_kZ_{1k}$ or by $\tan \rho_k$ in Figure 2.

These three ratios are related:[29]

$$R_n - R = (R - R_k)\frac{Z_{1k}}{Z_{1n}}, \qquad (12)$$

so that the three ratios can be ordered uniquely when any pair of them is known. When, for instance, $R_k > R$, then $R > R_n$. This simple ordering will be important in tracing the effects of capital formation, the pattern of foreign trade, and the direction of net foreign lending, the three tasks that lie ahead. With w held constant, it can be shown that[30]

$$\frac{dR}{dK}\frac{K}{R} = 0, \quad \text{and} \quad \frac{dR_k}{dK}\frac{K}{R_k} = 0. \quad (13)$$

Therefore,[31]

$$\frac{dR_n}{dK}\frac{K}{R_n} = \frac{R - R_k}{R}\left[\left(\frac{Z_{1k}}{Z_{1n}}\right)\left(\frac{Z_2}{Z_{2n}}\right)\right]$$
$$\times (1 - \eta). \qquad (14)$$

Net capital formation, measured by the corresponding increase in K, will not alter the gross factor ratio if it does not change the wage-rate ratio. Nevertheless, it will always alter the net factor ratio (unless $R_k = R$) and will thereby generate a change in the output mix. Figure 3 will help to show the reasons for this outcome. There, the straight line $0EE'$ traces points of equal slope on successive gross frontiers (not shown in

[29] This relationship obtains from the definitions of Z_{in} and of the factor ratios; as $Z_{2n} = Z_2 - Z_{2k}$, $R(Z_{1n}) = [R(Z_1) - R_k(Z_{1k})]$.

[30] The first of these results is proved in the Mathematical Appendix; see eq. (A8). It derives from the assumption that all η are equal. The second result derives from the assumption of constant returns to scale in the capital-goods sector.

[31] This result is obtained by differentiating eq. (12); for details, see my "Theory of Capital."

the diagram). When capital formation expands the gross frontier from E to E', gross national product in labor-service units rises from $0Z_2^*$ to $0Z_2^{*'}$. Its growth rate is $(Z_2^*Z_2^{*'}/0Z_2^*)$ or $(EE'/0E)$. If national income grew apace with gross national product, its growth rate would be $(0_k0_k''/00_k)$ equal to $(EE'/0E)$, and it would rise from $0Z_{2n}^*$ to $0Z_{2n}^{*''}$. Points of equal slope on successive net frontiers would lie on $00_k0_k''$, and the net factor ratio would not change. But national income grows more slowly than gross national product[32] and will only rise to some such level as $0Z_{2n}^{*'}$. The point 0_k will be displaced to $0_k'$, reducing the net factor ratio, and the expansion path for the net frontier, $00_k0_k'$, of course, will not be linear. If $R = R_k$, 0_k and $0_k'$ would both lie on $0EE'$, and R_n would not change with capital formation. It is the combination of two separate circumstances (that $R \neq R_k$ and that investment in the natural endowment is subject to diminishing factor-service returns) that gives the non-linear expansion path predicted by equation (14).

To complete the construction of a

[32] It can, in fact, be shown that

$$\frac{dY}{dK}\frac{1}{Y} - \frac{d(Y+K)}{dK}\frac{1}{Y+K}$$

$$= \frac{Y_r - Y}{Y(Y+K)} < 0.$$

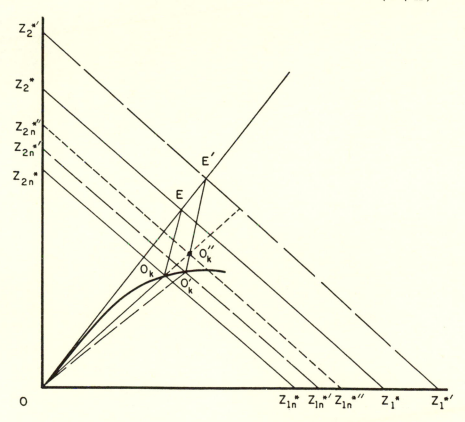

Fig. 3.—Displacement of the net factor-service frontier

single economy, suppose that Z_{1n} and Z_{2n} are fully employed producing two consumer goods, X_1 and X_2, and that the production functions for these commodities are homogeneous of first degree, with strong factor-ordering. Put formally, let

$$X_j = \frac{w_1}{p_j} Z_{1j} + \frac{w_2}{p_j} Z_{2j} = \frac{w_2}{p_j} Z_{1j}$$
$$\times (w + R_j), \qquad j = 1, 2, \tag{15}$$

where p_j is the price of X_j divided by the price of the capital good (so that w_i/p_j is the real wage of the ith factor service in the jth industry), where Z_{1j} and Z_{2j} are the land-service and labor-service inputs to the jth industry, and where R_j is Z_{2j}/Z_{1j}, the factor-service ratio in the jth industry. For strong factor-ordering, let R_2 exceed R_1 at all wage-rate ratios. In this case, and barring complete specialization in one of the two final products, $R_2 > R_n > R_1$ at all wage-rate ratios.[33] Furthermore,

$$Q = \frac{X_2}{X_1} = \frac{p_1}{p_2} \frac{Z_{12}(w + R_2)}{Z_{11}(w + R_1)}$$
$$= p \frac{R_n - R_1}{R_2 - R_n} \frac{w + R_2}{w + R_1}, \tag{16}$$

where Q is the output mix and p is the price ratio (p_1/p_2).[34]

This equation can be used for two important purposes. First, it can supply the vital relationship between the price ratio, p, and the wage-rate ratio, w. Solving for p and holding Q constant,[35]

$$e_{pw} = \frac{dp}{dw} \frac{w}{p} = \frac{w(R_2 - R_1)}{(w + R_1)(w + R_2)}. \tag{17}$$

[33] This is because $Z_{2n} = Z_{21} + Z_{22}$ with full employment, so that $R_n(Z_{1n}) = R_1 Z_{11} + R_2 Z_{12}$, giving $R_2 - R_n = (R_2 - R_1)(Z_{11}/Z_{1n}) \geq 0$.

[34] The ratios Q and p correspond to a point on a transformation curve that translates $N'N'$ into a product space. That curve will display the usual properties; Q and p will be inversely related. For details, see my "Theory of Capital."

As $R_2 > R_1$ at all wage-rate ratios, $0 < e_{pw} < 1$, and the relationship between p and w is monotonic. This relationship will be used below to reaffirm factor-price equalization. Second, equation (16) can reproduce Rybczynski's theorem concerning the relationship between the output mix and the net factor ratio.[36] Fixing the wage-rate ratio (and, therefore, p, R_1 and R_2),

$$\frac{dQ}{dR_n} \frac{R_n}{Q} = \frac{R_n(R_2 - R_1)}{(R_2 - R_n)(R_n - R_1)}. \tag{18}$$

An increase in R_n will raise the ratio Q, "biasing" the output mix in favor of X_2 (intensive in Z_2); a decrease in R_n will reduce the ratio Q, "biasing" the output mix in favor of X_1 (intensive in Z_1).

With these formulas in hand, consider the effects of saving and investment in a closed economy. As in the older classical models, capital formation will work directly to depress the interest rate, r, even though there is no change in the wage-rate ratio. It can be shown that[37]

$$e_{rk} = \frac{dr}{dK} \frac{K}{r} = \frac{\eta - 1}{e_{gr}} < 0, \tag{19}$$

because $0 < e_{gr} < 1$, and $\eta < 1$. But this is not the full effect of capital formation. Combining equations (14) and (18):

$$e_{Qk} = \frac{dQ}{dK} \frac{K}{Q} = (R - R_k)$$
$$\times \frac{(R_2 - R_1)(1 - \eta)}{(R_2 - R_n)(R_n - R_1)} \frac{Z_{1k}}{Z_{1n}} \frac{Z_1}{Z_{1n}}, \tag{20}$$

[35] For the derivation of equation (17), see H. Uzawa, "On a Two-Sector Model of Economic Growth," *Review of Economic Studies*, XXX (June, 1963), 108–9; see also my "Theory of Capital." Eq. (17) can even be applied when Q changes too. Such a situation can be partitioned into a change in the output mix with no change in factor prices, followed by a change in factor prices with no further change in output.

[36] T. N. Rybczynski, "Factor Endowment and Relative Commodity Prices," *Economica*, XXII (November, 1955), 336–41.

[37] See Mathematical Appendix, eq. (A9); for e_{gr}, see n. 21.

which takes its sign from $(R - R_k)$. If, further, e_{Qk} is not zero, net saving will alter the price ratio, p, and will thereby cause a secondary change in the interest rate, r. With unitary income elasticities of demand for both consumer goods, an increase of Q will generate an excess supply of X_2, lowering its price and raising p; a decrease of Q will generate an excess supply of X_1, lowering its price and lowering p. In addition, one can show that, when K is held constant,[38]

$$e_{rp} = \frac{dr}{dp}\frac{p}{r} = \frac{w(R_k - R)}{(w+R)(w+R_k)\,e_{gr}\,e_{pw}}, \quad (21)$$

which takes its sign from $(R_k - R)$. If, then, $R_k > R$, as in Figure 2, e_{Qk} is negative, and net saving will reduce the output ratio, Q, forcing a decline in p. It will also cause a secondary fall in the interest rate, for e_{rp} is positive. If, instead, $R_k < R$, e_{Qk} is positive, and net saving will augment the ratios Q and p. But it will still provoke a secondary fall in r, for e_{rp} is negative. In either case, the secondary change in the interest rate will reinforce the constant-price primary change given by equation (19).

If $R_k = R$, however, net investment will not alter Q or p and cannot cause a secondary change in the interest rate. The system will display a species of balanced growth. With continuous saving and investment, moreover, the system will always approach balanced growth. When R_k does not equal R initially, the change in factor-service prices caused by net investment will operate to bring them into alignment. When $R_k > R$, the wage-rate ratio falls with capital formation, raising the gross factor ratio and reducing R_k. When $R_k < R$, the wage-rate ratio rises, reducing the gross factor ratio and raising R_k. As saving and in-

vestment proceed, these changes cumulate until R_k equals R and balanced growth ensues.[39]

III. FOREIGN TRADE AND FOREIGN INVESTMENT

To study foreign trade and foreign investment, I shall add two more assumptions to the basic list at the start of this paper:

a. that each country manufactures both of the consumer goods, X_1 and X_2, and that these goods are traded without any transport costs, but there is no trade in the capital good;[40]

b. that the two countries' natural endowments yield a strict ordering of gross factor ratios: let $_IR \le {}_{II}R$ whenever factor prices are the same in both countries.[41]

Under these assumptions and those in the basic list, my model reproduces the best known propositions of the Heckscher-Ohlin model but with a number of modifications.

Under assumption a, free trade will equalize the two countries' product prices. And under the assumptions regarding production, equation (16), which links p and w, will exist and be identical in the two countries. Hence, free trade will equalize the two countries' wage-

---

[38] See Mathematical Appendix, eqs. (A10)–(A13).

[39] But further net investment will still depress the interest rate; e_{rk} is always negative. This is one of several major differences between the variety of balanced growth obtaining in my model and that which obtains in conventional two-factor models. For the other differences, see my "Theory of Capital."

[40] The exclusion of trade in the capital good does not, as might at first be thought, limit generality. As free trade in consumer goods will suffice to equalize the two countries' factor prices, w_1 and w_2, it will also equalize the price of the capital good. Trade in the capital good is not required and would only complicate the forecast of trade flows.

[41] The difference in gross factor ratios may be ascribed to a difference in quantities of crude land and labor or to a difference in their qualities (in susceptibility to improvement by investment). For a more extensive treatment, see my "Theory of Capital."

rate ratios and will thereby equalize the real factor-service prices, w_1 and w_2.[42]

Under assumption b and the assumptions regarding demand, a knowledge of the output ratios, $_IQ$ and $_{II}Q$, permits one to forecast the pattern of trade. If, for instance, $_{II}Q > {}_IQ$ at common product prices, Country I will export X_1 and Country II will export X_2. It is, indeed, sufficient to know the net factor ratios. When the p's and w's are equal in both countries,

$$_{II}Q - {}_IQ = ({}_{II}R_n - {}_IR_n)$$

$$\times \frac{p(R_2 - R_1)}{(R_2 - {}_{II}R_n)(R_2 - {}_IR_n)} \frac{w + R_2}{w + R_1}, \quad (22)$$

so that $({}_{II}Q - {}_IQ)$ takes its sign from $({}_{II}R_n - {}_IR_n)$.

Thus far, then, my model gives familiar results. It generates equality in real factor-service prices whenever it fulfills the conventional assumptions for factor-price equalization. It generates a pattern of commodity trade reflecting the physical factor endowments (net factor ratios) of the trading countries. But my model also offers several new propositions concerning international trade and investment:

1. Although the net factor ratios do not take direct account of capital supplies, a difference in capital scarcity, measured by relative interest rates, can affect the ordering of net factor ratios and the composition of commodity trade.

2. Free trade will not equalize two countries' interest rates and cannot thereby compensate for a difference in capital scarcity; a change in tastes, technology or capital supplies will consequently generate foreign lending or investment, not merely cause a change in the terms of trade.

3. Mundell's corollary no longer holds; a tariff may still lead to foreign investment but will not thereby wipe out trade; furthermore, its impact will depend on its incidence.

Each of these three propositions descends from my treatment of capital formation—the basic supposition that a nation's capital is wholly and pervasively embodied in its natural endowment and does not appear separately in the production functions.[43]

The several factor ratios used in my model are not the same as the capital-to-labor ratios featured in conventional

---

[42] Rewriting eq. (16),

$$p = \frac{X_2/Z_{12}}{X_1/Z_{11}} \frac{w + R_1}{w + R_2}.$$

But R_j and X_j/Z_{1j} depend on w alone, not on the scale of output, and the relationship will be identical in both countries. Furthermore, $0 < e_{pw} < 1$, implying that the inverse of this relationship is single valued. In consequence, each country's wage-rate ratio will depend uniquely and identically on that country's price ratio.

[43] They do not derive from my assumption that there is no trade in the capital good or, more generally, from the combination of two traded products (X_1 and X_2) with three factors of production (Z_1, Z_2, and K). Capital is not a factor of production in the ordinary sense; it does not have a real wage obtained from the production functions. Hence, the addition of one more commodity (or trade in the capital good) would not serve to equalize national interest rates. My results, below, should be compared with Samuelson's ("Equalization by Trade," $op.$ $cit.$, p. 52). He has shown that a model with one primary factor (labor) and reproducible capital goods that enter directly into production will, in fact, generate equality in interest rates and take on Ricardian properties. When interest rates are equalized by trade, the two countries' production functions may be regarded as "the simple linear ones of the Ricardian, labor-theory-of-value, constant-cost case." My model, by contrast, posits two primary factors (land and labor) and assumes that the reproducible capital good is not used directly in production. In consequence, interest rates must be equalized by international lending—by transfers between the two countries' loan funds. When they are equalized, moreover, my model becomes a straightforward Heckscher-Ohlin construct, not a Ricardian construct, involving an exchange of consumer goods based on the difference in land-service and labor-service endowments.

two-factor models and in important empirical studies explaining the structure of foreign trade.[44] The net factor ratios, $_IR_n$ and $_{II}R_n$, do not describe capital supplies; the final-product factor ratios, R_1 and R_2, do not describe capital requirements and cannot be used to rank the two industries according to capital intensity. Yet one can still measure capital scarcity in a meaningful way by looking at interest rates and can show that a difference in capital scarcity may affect trade structure by way of its impact on the net factor ratios. Use equation (12) to order the net factor ratios when the p's and w's are equal in both countries:[45]

A difference in capital scarcity will also cause a difference in factor incomes. Free trade will equalize the factor-service prices, w_i, but will not equalize the real incomes, y_i. These will differ between countries, even with free trade, if natural endowments of land and labor differ in quality or if they embody different quantities of capital. One can, in fact, establish that $_{II}y_i < _Iy_i$ whenever $_{II}r > _Ir$, abstracting from differences in factor quality.[46] When, then, the interest rate is higher in Country II, reflecting greater capital scarcity, real yearly income to a single acre or a single worker will tend to be lower in Country II. In brief, my

$$_{II}R_n - _IR_n = \frac{(_{II}R - _IR) + (R_k - _IR)[(_{II}g - _Ig)/_{II}g][(w + _{II}R)/(w + R_k)](_IK/_IY)}{(_{II}Z_{1n}/_{II}Z_1)(_IZ_{1n}/_IZ_1)[(_IY + _IK)/_IY]}. (23)$$

When interest rates are equal in the two countries, the gross amortization rates, $_Ig$ and $_{II}g$, will also be equal. The sign of $_{II}R_n - _IR_n$ will come to depend on the sign of $_{II}R - _IR$. The latter sign, in turn, will depend on the difference in natural endowments (in the supplies of crude land and crude labor and in their quality). When interest rates are not the same in the two countries, implying a difference in capital scarcity, the rest of the numerator comes into play. If, for instance, $_{II}r > _Ir$ so that $_{II}g > _Ig$, the difference in interest rates will augment or diminish the difference in net factor ratios, depending on the sign of $R_k - _IR$. If, indeed, the difference in interest rates is sufficiently large, and $R_k < _IR$, that difference can reverse the iso-interest ordering of net factor ratios and, therefore, the flow of trade; Country I will export X_2, and Country II will export X_1.

model offers an extensive, realistic account of the very large international differences in per capita incomes that are so prominent in the real world. These may be ascribed to geographic differences in labor-force participation and in supplies of tangible capital—the elements appearing in conventional models—but may also be ascribed to geographic differences in labor productivity due, in turn, to differences in stocks of "human capital" and in the quality of natural endowments.

I come now to the most important new proposition concerning international trade and investment: Free trade will

---

[44] See, e.g., Arrow, *et al.*, *op. cit.*; Leontief, "Factor Proportions;" Minhas, *op. cit.*; and Travis, *op. cit.*

[45] For the derivation of eq. (23), see my "Theory of Capital."

[46] The constant-elasticity factor-service supply function, eq. (1), can be written in the form:

$$z_i = \gamma_i k_i^\eta, \qquad 0 < \gamma_i, \qquad 0 < \eta < 1.$$

Exploiting the restatement of y_i in n. 22 and the equilibrium condition in eq. (3),

$$\frac{_{II}y_i}{_Iy_i} = \left[\left(\frac{_{II}\gamma_i}{_I\gamma_i}\right)\left(\frac{_Ig}{_{II}g}\right)^\eta\right]^{1/(1-\eta)}.$$

Differences in factor incomes can then be directly attributed to quality differences $(_{II}\gamma_i/_I\gamma_i)$ and to differences in capital scarcity $(_Ig/_{II}g)$.

not equalize national interest rates in the model set out here; it cannot substitute for foreign investment serving to optimize global production. I shall prove this proposition by a simple illustration that does not require any new formulas, then explore its implications very much more thoroughly.

Suppose that $_I r = _{II} r$ to start, and that $_I R = _{II} R$ at each set of factor prices. Under these conditions, there will be no trade between the two countries; they will have identical net factor ratios when they confront the same set of prices. Suppose, next, that $_I R = R_k = _{II} R$ at the prevailing wage-rate ratio, and disturb the situation by an act of net saving in Country I. There will be no change in Country I's prices, for $e_{Qk} = 0$ in both countries, and capital formation cannot bring on trade. Yet $_I r$ will fall when saving occurs, for $e_{rk} < 0$ in both countries, and Country I must lend to Country II in order to restore interest-rate equality and thereby to maximize worldwide income. Free trade does not substitute for factor movements—for transfers between loan funds—nor do factor movements generate trade.[47]

Similar results obtain when the two countries are trading initially. To analyze this situation, define

$$\delta = \frac{_I r}{_{II} r}. \qquad (24)$$

Then set $_I p = _{II} p$, as would be true with costless free trade, and use equation (21) to compute the change in relative interest rates caused by a disturbance, τ, affecting the price ratios $_I p$ and $_{II} p$:

$$\frac{d\delta}{d\tau} = \delta \left(\frac{d_I r}{d\tau} \frac{1}{_I r} - \frac{d_{II} r}{d\tau} \frac{1}{_{II} r} \right)$$

$$= \delta \left[{}_I e_{rp} \left(\frac{d_I p}{d\tau} \frac{1}{_I p} \right) \right. \qquad (25)$$

$$\left. - {}_{II} e_{rp} \left(\frac{d_{II} p}{d\tau} \frac{1}{_{II} p} \right) \right].$$

This equation simplifies substantially in each of the four cases considered below—when there is an autonomous change in demand or technology, when there is saving in Country I without any transfer between the two loan funds, when there is saving in Country I when transfers occur, and when an *ad valorem* tariff is imposed. In each of these four cases, let $_I r = _{II} r$ initially, and let $_{II} R > _I R$ when wage rates are equal, so that Country I will export X_1 and p $(= _I p = _{II} p)$ will be its terms of trade.

A change in demand or technology.—First, let τ be a change in demand or technology that does not disrupt the free-trade regime and does not induce any net investment.[48] In this case, equation (25) can be written in the form:

$$\frac{d\delta}{d\tau} = \frac{\delta w (_{II} R - _I R)}{(w + _I R)(w + _{II} R) e_{gr} e_{pw}}$$
$$\times \left(\frac{dp}{d\tau} \frac{1}{p} \right), \qquad (26)$$

because e_{gr} and the change in prices will be identical in both countries. As $_{II} R > _I R$, by assumption, a disturbance that raises p, improving the terms of trade for Country I, also raises $_I r$ relative to $_{II} r$.

---

[47] This last statement is not quite accurate. Net lending will always require an offsetting flow of goods; so will the interest payment following the loan. When Country I lends to Country II, the latter uses the loan proceeds to buy additional consumer goods (X_1 and X_2) from Country I, releasing its own factor services to its capital-goods industry and thereby expanding its net frontier. As there is no net saving in Country II, even at a higher level of net geographic product, Country II will not repay its debt; Country I will obtain a perpetual interest income from Country II and will use that income stream to buy both consumer goods from Country II. But neither of these trade flows is based upon comparative advantage; each flow involves a one-way movement of both consumer goods.

[48] The change in demand or technology must be deemed to occur in both countries simultaneously; otherwise, they will no longer have the same demand or production functions.

Country II must lend to Country I to equalize interest rates and maximize the income of the world as a whole.

Capital formation without capital transfers.—Because e_{rk} is always negative, an act of net investment in Country I will lower $_Ir$ on impact and will thereby lower $_Ie_{gr}$.[49] Before any change in w or p, equation (26) can be written in the form:

$$\frac{d\delta}{d\tau} = \frac{\delta w \Delta_k}{(w+R_k)(w+_{II}R)_{II}e_{gr}e_{pw}}$$
$$\times \left(\frac{dp}{d\tau}\frac{1}{p}\right), \quad (27)$$

where

$$\Delta_k = (_{II}R - _IR) + (R_k - _IR)$$
$$\times \left[\frac{_{II}e_{gr}(w+_{II}R)}{_Ie_{gr}(w+_IR)} - 1\right]. \quad (28)$$

The sign of $d\delta/d\tau$ depends on the sign of Δ_k and the sign of $dp/d\tau$. But the latter depends on the constant-price "bias" of Country I's growth and, therefore, on $_Ie_{Qk}$, given by equation (20). In consequence, the sign of $d\delta/d\tau$ depends upon the sign of $R_k - _IR$.

If $R_k \geq _IR$, then Δ_k is positive. In addition, $_Ie_{Qk} \leq 0$, so that net investment reduces $_IQ$ or leaves it unchanged. Country I experiences "export-biased" or "product-neutral" growth, its terms of trade decline, and $dp/d\tau$ is always negative.[50] When $R_k \geq _IR$, in short, the price change produced by saving in Country I

widens the difference between the two interest rates; $_Ir$ falls further relative to $_{II}r$, and factor-price equalization actually serves to strengthen the case for net lending by the growing country.[51]

If $R_k < _IR$, the outcome is doubly uncertain. One cannot attach a sign to Δ_k or to $dp/d\tau$. Capital formation raises $_IQ$, and Country I undergoes "import-biased" growth, yet this may not improve its terms of trade. But two conclusions hold despite this uncertainty: (1) Although $d\delta/d\tau$ may be positive when $R_k < _IR$, it may not fully offset the primary decline in Country I's interest rate. (2) When, further, $_IR$ is very large relative to R_k, Δ_k turns negative and $dp/d\tau$ turns positive; hence $d\delta/d\tau$ turns negative again, enlarging the difference between the two interest rates.

Capital formation when capital is mobile.—When the two loan funds are free to engage in foreign lending, saving and investment may alter the net factor ratios in both countries and may therefore alter both countries' output ratios. The signs of the changes in p and θ must be studied differently, using two new definitions:

$$_TK = _IK + _{II}K$$
$$_TQ = \frac{_IX_2 + _{II}X_2}{_IX_1 + _{II}X_1} = \frac{_IQ + \beta_{II}Q}{1 + \beta}, \quad (29)$$

where

$$\beta = \frac{_{II}X_1}{_IX_1} = \frac{_{II}K}{_IK}\frac{p + _IQ}{p + _{II}Q}. \quad [52]$$

Consider, first, how Country I would allocate an increase in its total loan fund so as to maintain equality in interest

---

[49] Using the formula in n. 21,

$$\frac{d e_{gr}}{a r} = \frac{(vg-1)(1-e_{gr})}{r/(1+r)} > 0,$$

because $0 < r_{gr} < 1$ and $vg > 1$ (see eq. [8], above). Hence, $_Ie_{gr}$ falls with the fall in $_Ir$.

[50] For proof that "product-neutral" growth worsens the terms of trade when income elasticities of demand are unity, see W. M. Corden, "Economic Expansion and International Trade: A Geometrical Approach," *Oxford Economic Papers*, VIII (June, 1956), 223–28.

[51] For similar results in a "classical" model, see D. M. Bensusan-Butt, "A Model of Trade and Accumulation," *American Economic Review*, XLIV (September, 1954), 511–29.

[52] This last formulation relies on a proof that $_{II}Y/_IY = _{II}K/_IK$, when interest rates are equal. This is because $Y/K = (vg/\eta) - 1$.

rates before any change in wage rates or prices. With interest rates the same to start and w held constant, $d_I r/d_T K$ must equal $d_{II} r/d_T K$, so that:

$$\frac{d_I K}{d_T K}\frac{_T K}{_I K}=\frac{d_{II} K}{d_T K}\frac{_T K}{_{II} K}. \quad (30)$$

Both countries will partake of any increase in $_T K$, and an increase arising entirely in Country I will call forth net lending from Country I to Country II.

Consider, next, the change in the global output ratio, $_T Q$. With unitary income elasticities of final demand and the same demand conditions in both countries, the pattern of consumption cannot change unless there is a change in relative prices. If, then, $_T Q$ is raised by capital formation, the price ratio, p, must also rise, so as to align the output ratio and the pattern of consumption. When, further, w is held constant:

$$\frac{d_T Q}{d_T K}\frac{_T K}{_T Q}$$

$$=V\left[_I e_{Qk}\frac{_I Q}{p+_I Q}\left(\frac{d_I K}{d_T K}\frac{_T K}{_I K}\right)\right. \quad (31)$$

$$\left.+_{II} e_{Qk}\frac{\beta_{II} Q}{p+_{II} Q}\left(\frac{d_{II} K}{d_T K}\frac{_T K}{_{II} K}\right)\right],$$

where

$$V=\frac{p(1+\beta)+_I Q+\beta_{II} Q}{(1+\beta)(_I Q+\beta_{II} Q)}>0.$$

One can show that this expression takes its sign from:

$$\Delta_T=\frac{R_k-_I R}{w+_I R}{_I K}+\frac{R_k-_{II} R}{w+_{II} R}{_{II} K}, \quad (32)$$

so that $_T Q$ and p will rise when Δ_T is positive, while $_T Q$ and p will fall when Δ_T is negative. At this point, moreover, equation (26) applies, as interest rates were equal before the change in prices. When $_{II} R>_I R\geq R_k$, then, capital formation, augmenting $_T Q$ and p, will call

forth a secondary transfer of funds from Country II to Country I, offsetting a part of the primary outflow from the country that has saved. When $R_k\geq{_{II} R}>_I R$, capital formation, decreasing $_T Q$ and p, will call forth a secondary transfer of funds from Country I to Country II, reinforcing the primary outflow from the country that has saved. If, finally, $_{II} R>R_k>_I R$, output and prices can move either way, or might even be unchanged.

This final case, moreover, is the one that will prevail after a sufficient time. When Δ_T is not zero initially, saving will alter p and w and will drive Δ_T toward zero. If Δ_T is positive, w will rise, raising R_k and reducing the gross factor ratios; if it is negative, w will fall, reducing R_k and raising the gross factor ratios. When Δ_T has vanished, balanced growth ensues. Subsequent saving will still be reallocated so as to equalize the two countries' interest rates, but there will be no further cause for secondary transfers.

Impact of a tariff.—Let the disturbance, τ, be an *ad valorem* tariff, π. As Country I will export X_1 under free trade,

$$\frac{d_{II} p}{d\tau}-\frac{d_I p}{d\tau}\approx\pi p, \quad (33)$$

where p is the free-trade price ratio. Next, let

$$\frac{d_I p}{d\tau}\frac{1}{_I p}=-\pi\sigma,$$

$$\text{so that }\frac{d_{II} p}{d\tau}\frac{1}{_{II} p}\approx(1-\sigma)\pi, \quad (34)$$

where $0\leq\sigma\leq 1$ if neither country's offer curve is inelastic over the relevant range.[53]

[53] If Country I's offer curve were perfectly elastic, its domestic prices would not change when confronted by a tariff, and σ would be zero. If Coun-

Using these new arguments and equation (25),

$$\frac{d\delta}{d\tau} \approx \frac{w\delta\pi\,(_{II}R - {}_{I}R)\Delta_\pi}{(w + {}_{I}R)(w + {}_{II}R)\,e_{gr}\,e_{pw}}, \quad (35)$$

where

$$\Delta_\pi = \frac{w + {}_{I}R}{w + R_k}\frac{_{II}R - R_k}{_{II}R - {}_{I}R} - \sigma, \quad (36)$$

so that Δ_π is negative when $R_k > {}_{II}R > {}_{I}R$, and it is positive when $_{II}R > {}_{I}R > R_k$. If, then, $R_k > {}_{II}R$, the imposition of a tariff by either country will cause Country I to lend to Country II. If, instead, $_{I}R > R_k$, the imposition of a tariff will cause Country II to lend to Country I. If $_{II}R \geq R_k \geq {}_{I}R$, however, the impact of the tariff depends on its incidence. The first argument of equation (36) can be as low as zero and as high as unity and lies in the same range as the coefficient σ. This result, moreover, is most likely to prevail if the system has been growing steadily. If, indeed, it has attained a state of balanced growth before a tariff is imposed, $\Delta_T = 0$ in equation (32), and $_{II}R > R_k > {}_{I}R$.[54] In brief, one cannot forecast the direction of net lending merely by inspecting the pattern of trade. Nor can one suppose, as in the conventional two-factor model, that the introduction of a single tariff will eliminate all trade.

IV. AN APPLICATION

One could not begin to test the model I have outlined here. It employs far too many artificial constructs. Yet it also offers a more plausible account of important processes than the conventional model from which it is built and gives us new insights into several ancient problems.

First, it suggests an important connection between the terms of trade and capital movements. An improvement in the terms of trade due to a change in demand or technology leads to foreign borrowing; a similar improvement brought about by trade restrictions may lead to foreign lending. Second, the model furnishes a framework for studying the consequence of capital formation and may thereby aid us in the study of development. It argues, for example, that "social-overhead" capital may be the strict complement to "directly productive" capital, for much of the former is, in fact, investment in the labor force and is the progenitor of vital factor services. It likewise illuminates a puzzling fact about the less-developed countries—the low return to investment in countries where capital seems very scarce. This apparent paradox may merely reflect a mal-allocation of capital and a corresponding distortion in rates of return. Recall that the return to capital is the product of two terms: (1) its marginal physical product in generating service flows and (2) the real wage rate earned by those service flows. A disproportionate increase in one service flow will drive down the real wage of that factor service and the corresponding rate of return. A small increase in a nation's stock of tangible capital assets can drastically reduce the rate of return unless the stock of capital invested in man is growing commensurately.

In brief, my model warns us to take the broadest view when studying capital, growth, and trade. To illustrate the gains from taking such a view, I turn

---

try II's offer curve were perfectly elastic, σ would be unity. If either country's offer curve were inelastic, perverse results might occur (see Metzler, *loc. cit.*).

[54] In this case, eq. (36) takes a very simple form:

$$\Delta_\pi = \frac{_{I}K}{_{I}K + {}_{II}K} - \sigma.$$

once again to Leontief.[55] In his famous article on U.S. foreign trade,[56] he offers us new data on the U.S. skill mix in export and import-competing production

[55] One could also illustrate my basic point with reference to the recent work by Arrow *et al.* (*op. cit.*). Two of their findings bear directly on the conventional Heckscher-Ohlin model: (1) that industries have different elasticities of substitution between labor and tangible capital; (2) that "factor-neutral" coefficients of efficiency differ among countries and are always highest in the United States. The first result forbids an invariant ordering of processes according to factor intensity; the capital-to-labor rankings will vary with factor prices. The second result implies a systematic international difference in technology, preventing full factor-price equalization. But these results are based on computations using tangible capital; they make no allowance for investment in man. In consequence, the computed elasticities of substitution do not really state the terms on which a single industry or national economy can trade off capital for labor. Furthermore, the factor-neutral differences in efficiency may reflect differences in factor quality or the role of capital invested in skills. If U.S. workers embody more capital than Japanese workers, one would expect the factor-neutral arguments to be higher in the United States—and would look to the labor-intensive industries for the largest differences. This is precisely what one finds. There is "some slight indication, in comparing Japan and the United States, that the American advantage in efficiency tends to be least in capital-intensive industries" (*ibid.*, p. 247).

[56] Leontief, "Factor Proportions," *op. cit.*, p. 399.

(Table 3). Leontief suggests that these statistics bear out his own supposition concerning U.S. foreign trade—that U.S. labor is more efficient that foreign labor, so that the United States is indeed a labor-abundant country exporting labor-intensive products. Yet skills may reflect investment in man, and when we take this tack, perspectives change radically.

As a limiting case, suppose that skill differences are wholly due to the quantity of capital invested in the labor force and that the wage differences ascribed to skill represent the gross return on that

TABLE 3

PERCENTAGE DISTRIBUTION OF TOTAL LABOR INPUT PER MILLION DOLLARS OF U.S. EXPORT PRODUCTION AND U.S. IMPORT-COMPETING PRODUCTION, 1947

Skill Group	Exports	Imports
I. Professional, technical, etc.	13.75	12.24
II. Clerical, sales, etc.	22.07	17.00
III. Craftsmen and foremen	15.15	11.79
IV. Operatives	30.05	28.38
V. Laborers	18.98	30.59

Source: Leontief, "Factor Proportions," *op. cit.*, Table 2.

TABLE 4

ANNUAL WAGE INCOME AND INVESTMENT IN SKILL, ALL SECTORS, 1959

(Dollars)

SKILL GROUP	MEAN WAGE INCOME*	EXCESS OVER LABORERS	INVESTMENT IN SKILL†	
			At 12.7% Return	At 9.0% Return
I. Professional, etc.	9,414	6,011	47,336	66,790
II. Clerical, etc.	5,935	2,532	19,937	28,131
III. Craftsmen, etc.	5,982	2,579	20,311	28,658
IV. Operatives	4,913	1,510	11,894	16,782
V. Laborers‡	3,403	....	....	....

* Weighted average of mean wage and salary incomes for principal occupations; total income used in lieu of wage income for farmers and self-employed managers.

† Computed by dividing the wage differences in the second column by the rates of return given in the column stubs; rates of return have not been corrected for finite asset life.

‡ Farmers and farm proprietors treated as laborers, regardless of Census classification or treatment in Leontief's study of skills.

Source: Mean wage income based on Census data for principal occupations; rates of return from J. Mincer, "On-the-Job Training: Costs, Returns, and Some Implications," *Journal of Political Economy*, LXX (suppl.) (October, 1962), 66.

capital.[57] Using these two suppositions, one can compute the quantity of capital required to convert a man-year of crude labor into a man-year of skill (Table 4).[58] Next, one can use the percentages furnished by Leontief to compute the capital embodied in a typical man-year of labor used in U.S. exports and in U.S. import-competing production (Table 5). As U.S. export production is more skill intensive than U.S. import-competing production, it is also more intensive in human capital.

Finally, I have grafted my very crude

estimates onto Leontief's impeccable statistics (Table 6).[59] Using the 12.7 per cent rate of return (the more conservative), one does not quite dispatch the Leontief paradox, but the 9.0 per cent rate of return does indeed reverse the factor intensities (and does so decisively when combined with the consumer-price deflator for human capital).[60] The paradox succumbs at last.

[59] In order to do so, I have had to convert my estimates of human capital into 1947 dollars and have done so in two ways. For the issues involved in the choice of deflator, see Kenen and Yudin, *op. cit.*

[60] These computations can be assailed with all of the objections leveled at Leontief. In particular, the use of input-output analysis assumes that every product is processed from start to finish in the

[57] The corresponding rate of return is, of course, an average yield, different from *r* in the model above. The procedure set out here has also been suggested by Bhagwati (*op. cit.*, p. 23), and a complementary attack on the problem is described by D. B. Keesing (see his "Labor Skills and International Trade," *Review of Economics and Statistics*, XLVII [August, 1965].)

[58] These estimates understate investment in the labor force; they neglect the capital required to produce an unskilled worker. For a detailed account of these computations and alternative estimates using, first, median in lieu of mean wage income and, second, Leontief's data on non-agricultural labor and capital, see P. B. Kenen and E. B. Yudin, *Skills, Human Capital and U.S. Foreign Trade* (New York: International Economics Workshop, Columbia University, 1965 [mimeographed]). I am grateful to Miss Yudin for undertaking the laborious computations summarized here.

TABLE 5

HUMAN CAPITAL PER MILLION DOLLARS OF U.S. EXPORT PRODUCTION AND U.S. IMPORT-COMPETING PRODUCTION, 1947

(1959 Dollars per Man-Year)

RATE OF RETURN (PER CENT)	$ THOUSANDS	
	Exports	Imports
12.7................	17.56	14.95
9.0................	24.78	21.10

Source: Based on skill distributions and investments in skill given in preceding tables.

TABLE 6

TANGIBLE AND TOTAL CAPITAL REQUIREMENTS PER MILLION DOLLARS OF U.S. EXPORT PRODUCTION AND U.S. IMPORT-COMPETING PRODUCTION, 1947

(Thousands of 1947 Dollars per Man Year)

ITEM	HUMAN CAPITAL DEFLATED BY			
	Hourly Earnings		Consumer Prices	
	Exports	Imports	Exports	Imports
Tangible capital (Leontief)......	11.62	13.66	11.62	13.66
Tangible and human capital:				
At 12.7% rate of return......	21.38	21.97	25.08	25.12
At 9.0% rate of return.......	25.39	25.38	30.61	29.83

Source: Tangible capital from Leontief, "Factor Proportions," *op. cit.*, Table 1, Part A; human capital from the preceding table, converted to 1947 dollars using, first, the BLS index of average hourly earnings in manufacturing and, second, the consumer price index.

Much more work can be done with my basic suppositions. In tandem with Becker's distinction between "specific" and "general" training,[61] they may help us to explain trade structure in detail and the evolution of comparative advantage. They can also be employed to study economic growth and interregional factor

United States. It is also weakened by the inclusion of trade in raw materials—trade that reflects natural-resource endowments rather than labor and reproducible capital. To skirt these two problems, I have computed the *direct* labor and capital requirements per million dollars of *manufactured* exports and import-competing products. Using the 9 per cent rate of return and the CPI deflator, I obtain

migration. But they must be refined and thoroughly articulated before they can be used to fullest advantage.

the following capital requirements (in thousands of 1947 dollars per man year):

	Exports	Imports
Tangible capital (as in Leontief)....	6.86	8.66
Tangible and human capital........	24.22	24.24

These computations do not quite banish the paradox but show the same general pattern as the figures given in the text. For details, including wage and skill data, see Kenen and Yudin, *op. cit.*

[61] Becker, *op. cit.*, pp. 11–29.

MATHEMATICAL APPENDIX

ALLOCATION AND DISPLACEMENT IN A CLOSED ECONOMY

To maximize gross national product with fixed factor-service prices, w_i, and a fixed investment flow, K, differentiate the Lagrangian argument:

$$G = (w_1 Z_1 + w_2 Z_2) - \lambda (K_1 + K_2 - K). \tag{A1}$$

The first-order conditions for maximum G are:

$$\frac{\partial G}{\partial K_i} = w_i F_i' - \lambda = 0, \qquad i = 1, 2,$$

$$\frac{\partial G}{\partial \lambda} = K_1 + K_2 - K = 0. \tag{A2}$$

These conditions are satisfied by equation (7) of the text, when $\lambda = vg$.[62] Next, differentiate equations (A2) to form:

$$\begin{bmatrix} w_1 F_1'' & 0 & 1 \\ 0 & w_2 F_2'' & 1 \\ 1 & 1 & 0 \end{bmatrix} \begin{bmatrix} dK_1 \\ dK_2 \\ -vdg \end{bmatrix} = \begin{bmatrix} -F_1' dw_1 \\ -F_2' dw_2 \\ dK \end{bmatrix}. \tag{A3}$$

Applying Cramer's rule,

$$\frac{dK_i}{dw_i} = \frac{F_i}{|H|}, \qquad \text{and} \qquad \frac{dK_j}{dw_i} = -\frac{F_i}{|H|} \tag{A4a}$$

$$\frac{dK_i}{dK} = -\frac{w_j F_j''}{|H|} \qquad\qquad \begin{array}{l} i = 1, 2 \\ j = 1, 2 \\ i \neq j \end{array} \tag{A4b}$$

$$\frac{dg}{dw_i} = -\frac{F_i' \, w_j F_j''}{v \ |H|}, \qquad \text{and} \qquad \frac{dg}{dK} = -\frac{1}{v} \frac{w_1 F_1'' w_2 F_2''}{|H|} \tag{A4c}$$

where $|H| = -(w_1 F_1'' + w_2 F_2'')$.

[62] The second-order conditions for maximum G are satisfied by the restriction $F_i'' < 0$. Eqs. (A2) also serve to maximize national income.

Using (A4a) and equation (7) of the text,

$$\frac{dZ_2/dw_i}{dZ_1/dw_i} = \frac{F_2'(dK_2/dw_i)}{F_1'(dK_1/dw_i)} = -\frac{F_2'}{F_1'} = -w, \qquad (A5)$$

proving that the slope of $G'G'$ in Figure 2 is equal (in absolute value) to the wage-rate ratio.
Using (7) once again,

$$w = \frac{Z_2}{Z_1}\frac{K_1}{K_2} = R\frac{K_1}{K_2}, \qquad (A6)$$

so that

$$\frac{K_1}{K} = \frac{w}{w+R}, \qquad \frac{K_2}{K} = \frac{R}{w+R}, \qquad (A7a)$$

$$|H| = -w_2F_2''\frac{w+R}{w}. \qquad (A7b)$$

Therefore, (A4b) gives

$$\frac{dK_1}{dK}\frac{K}{K_1} = \frac{dK_2}{dK}\frac{K}{K_2} = 1, \qquad (A8a)$$

$$\frac{dR}{dK}\frac{K}{R} = \left(\frac{dZ_2}{dK_2}\frac{K_2}{Z_2}\right)\left(\frac{dK_2}{dK}\frac{K}{K_2}\right) - \left(\frac{dZ_1}{dK_1}\frac{K_1}{Z_1}\right)\left(\frac{dK_1}{dK}\frac{K}{K_1}\right) = 0, \qquad (A8b)$$

proving that an increase in replacement investment (resulting from an increase in the capital stock) will not alter R if it does not alter w.
Using (A4c) and (A7b),

$$\frac{dr}{dK}\frac{K}{r} = \left(\frac{dg}{dK}\frac{K}{g}\right)\left(\frac{dr}{dg}\frac{g}{r}\right) = \frac{wK}{vg}\left(\frac{w_1F_1''}{w+R}\right)\left(\frac{dr}{dg}\frac{g}{r}\right) = (\eta-1)\left(\frac{dr}{dg}\frac{g}{r}\right), \qquad (A9)$$

which gives equation (19) of the text. Furthermore,

$$\frac{dr}{dp}\frac{p}{r} = \left(\frac{dg}{dw}\frac{w}{g}\right)\left(\frac{dw}{dp}\frac{p}{w}\right)\left(\frac{dr}{dg}\frac{g}{r}\right) = \left[\left(\frac{dg}{dw_1}\frac{w_1}{g}\right)\left(\frac{dw_1}{dw}\frac{w}{w_1}\right) + \left(\frac{dg}{dw_2}\frac{w_2}{g}\right)\left(\frac{dw_2}{dw}\frac{w}{w_2}\right)\right]$$

$$\times\left(\frac{dw}{dp}\frac{p}{w}\right)\left(\frac{dr}{dg}\frac{g}{r}\right) = -\left[\frac{w_2F_2''}{|H|}\left(\frac{dw_1}{dw}\frac{w}{w_1}\right) + \frac{w_1F_1''}{|H|}\left(\frac{dw_2}{dw}\frac{w}{w_2}\right)\right]\left(\frac{dw}{dp}\frac{p}{w}\right)\left(\frac{dr}{dg}\frac{g}{r}\right). \qquad (A10)$$

But from the definition of w,

$$\frac{dw_1}{dw}\frac{w}{w_1} = 1 + \frac{dw_2}{dw}\frac{w}{w_2}. \qquad (A11)$$

And from equation (10) of the text,[63]

$$\frac{dw_2}{dw}\frac{w}{w_2} = -\frac{w}{w+R_k}. \qquad (A12)$$

[63] Holding K constant:

$$\frac{dw_2}{dw} = -\left[Z_{1k}\left(\frac{dw_1}{dw}\frac{w}{w_1}\right) + w\left(\frac{dZ_{1k}}{dw}\right) + \left(\frac{dZ_{2k}}{dw}\right)\right]\frac{w_2}{Z_{2k}}.$$

When, then, K is constant,

$$\frac{dr}{dp}\frac{p}{r} = \left(\frac{w}{w+R} - \frac{w}{w+R_k}\right)\left(\frac{dw}{dp}\frac{p}{w}\right)\left(\frac{dr}{dg}\frac{g}{r}\right), \tag{A13}$$

which gives equation (21) of the text.

But along any isoquant, $K'K'$, $\left(\dfrac{dZ_{2k}}{dw}\right) = -w\left(\dfrac{dZ_{1k}}{dw}\right)$, so that

$$\frac{dw_2}{dw}\frac{w}{w_2} = -w\frac{Z_{1k}}{Z_{2k}}\left(\frac{dw_1}{dw}\frac{w}{w_1}\right) = -\frac{w}{R_\eta}\left[1 + \left(\frac{dw_2}{dw}\frac{w}{w_2}\right)\right],$$

which gives (A12) directly.

PETER B. KENEN

Toward a More General Theory
of Capital and Trade

MOST THEORIES OF PRODUCTION, GROWTH, AND TRADE treat capital as though it were an ordinary input. The stock of capital appears directly in the production function, just like land or labor, and has a separate marginal product. Processes are classified by capital intensity, and countries are classified by capital scarcity.[1] Elsewhere, I have offered a

---

[1] For examples in growth theory, see R. M. Solow, "A Contribution to the Theory of Economic Growth," *Quarterly Journal of Economics*, LXX (1956), J. E. Meade, *A Neo-Classical Theory of Economic Growth* (London: George Allen & Unwin, 1961); and H. Uzawa, "On a Two-Sector Model of Economic Growth," *Review of Economic Studies*, XXIX (1961–62), and XXX (1963). For examples in trade theory, see E. Heckscher, "The Effects of Foreign Trade on the Distribution of Income," in *Readings in the Theory of International Trade*, H. E. Ellis and L. A. Metzler (eds.) (Philadelphia: Blakiston, 1949); B. Ohlin, *Interregional and International Trade* (Cambridge: Harvard University Press, 1933); J. E. Meade, *Trade and Welfare* (London: Oxford University Press, 1955); and W. P. Travis, *The Theory of Trade and Protection* (Cambridge: Harvard University Press, 1964). For important empirical applications, see K. J. Arrow, H. B. Chenery, B. S. Minhas, and R. M. Solow, "Capital-Labor Substitution and Economic Efficiency," *Review of Economics and Statistics*, XLIII (1961); W. W. Leontief "Factor Proportions and the Structure of American Trade: Further Theoretical and Empirical Analysis," *Review of Economics and Statistics*, XXXVIII (1956); and B. S. Minhas, *An International Comparison of Factor Costs and Factor Use* (Amsterdam: North-Holland Publishing Co., 1963).

different approach.[2] Capital can be regarded as the progenitor of other inputs, having an indirect marginal product. Combined with land and labor, the "natural endowment," it furnishes the service flows used in production. This essay will illustrate the merits of my new approach. It will reexamine several propositions in the pure theory of foreign trade, reworking the familiar Heckscher-Ohlin model in order to secure more plausible results than trade and growth theories have been able to supply using the conventional concept of capital.

The theory of capital developed here has several antecedents. Its fundamental supposition, that capital and nature are complementary, is basic to the Austrian theory of capital and has sometimes crept into writings on foreign trade.[3] My own views, however, derive from the more recent works of Vanek,[4] Schultz,[5] and Becker.[6] Vanek postulates a complementarity between capital and land, then argues that U.S. trade may conserve scarce land rather than scarce capital, answering Leontief's celebrated paradox.[7] Schultz and Becker postulate a complementarity between capital and labor. They suggest that outlays on schooling and training are forms of investment, and that the capital invested in man contributes importantly to total output. Combining these suggestions in a formal model, I shall treat each input stream, the service flows from land and labor, as though they were produced by acts of investment, assigning a pervasive role to capital formation.

THE ALLOCATION OF INVESTMENT

Let each country have a fixed stock of labor, N_1 men, and a fixed stock of land, N_2 acres. Suppose, however, that these stocks must be improved before they can contribute to current production. More formally, let

[2] P. B. Kenen, "Nature, Capital and Trade," *Journal of Political Economy*, LXXIII (1965).

[3] See C. Iverson, *International Capital Movements* (London: Oxford University Press, 1935); and R. Nurkse, "Causes and Effects of Capital Movements," in *Equilibrium and Growth in the World Economy: Economic Essays by Ragnar Nurkse*, G. Haberler and R. M. Stern (eds.) (Cambridge: Harvard University Press, 1961).

[4] J. Vanek, *The Natural Resource Content of United States Foreign Trade* (Cambridge: MIT Press, 1963).

[5] T. W. Schultz, "Reflections on Investment in Man," *Journal of Political Economy*, LXX Supplement (1956).

[6] G. S. Becker, "Investment in Human Capital: A Theoretical Analysis," *Journal of Political Economy*, LXX Supplement (1956).

[7] Leontief, "Factor Proportions."

there be a single, malleable capital good that can be used with equal ease to make all improvements in the "natural endowment," and let it be combined with that endowment to generate a single, undifferentiated service flow from labor and a second flow from land. Further:

1. Let all markets be purely competitive, all inputs be fully employed, and all decision units have perfect foresight.
2. Let all accounts be kept in real terms, with the price of the capital good as *numeraire*.
3. Let all investments have the same lifespan (v years), and let them depreciate by sudden death.
4. Let all production functions be homogeneous of first degree in the factor services, be twice differentiable with diminishing marginal products, and have an invariant ranking by factor intensity.
5. Let demand conditions be independent of the income distribution, with unitary income elasticities of demand for all final products.

The first of these assumptions is common to most models built at a comparable level of abstraction. The second gives a simple way to value all assets and incomes. The third permits us to avoid several intractable problems in capital theory, pertaining to the heterogeneity of capital goods and their varied ages.[8] The fourth and fifth assumptions allow us to ignore the influence of scale on both sides of the market; they are especially helpful in tracing the growth path of a closed economy and in the study of foreign trade.

Now let each investment in the "natural endowment" be financed by a loan from a central fund (whose total claims will measure the capital stock); let each worker and landlord borrow from that fund in order to improve himself or his holdings, then earn income by selling the factor-service flows that come from the improvement. Furthermore, let each investor maximize the present value of his income stream (let there be no preference for present over future earnings). Under these additional assumptions, a loan from the central fund will be repaid in equal annual instalments spanning the v-year life of the factor-service flow produced by the investment for which the loan was made.[9] A worker will borrow in order to train himself and will have repaid his debt when he leaves the

---

[8] See J. Robinson, "Accumulation and the Production Function," *Economic Journal*, LXIX (1959); and P. A. Samuelson, "Parable and Realism in Capital Theory: The Surrogate Production Function," *Review of Economic Studies*, XXIX (1962).

[9] Meade, *Neo-Classical Theory*, pp. 134–44.

labor force; a landlord will borrow in order to improve his land and will have repaid his debt when his land reverts to its natural state.

To study the behavior of a single investor, define:

z_i The annual supply of the ith factor service (input) flowing from a unit of the ith natural factor ($i = 1$ for labor, $i = 2$ for land).

k_i The number of units of the homogeneous capital good needed to evoke the flow z_i.

w_i The real annual wage earned by a unit of the ith factor service (its money wage divided by the price of the capital good).

y_i The real annual income earned by the owner of a unit of the ith natural factor (his money wage divided by the price of the capital good).

r The interest rate.

g The gross amortization rate linking the yearly debt-service payment (interest and principal) to the face value of the corresponding loan.

Now relate k_i, an act of investment, to z_i, the steady v-year service flow to which it gives rise. Write:

$$z_i = f_i(k_i), \quad i = 1, 2 \tag{1}$$

such that $f_i(0) = 0$, $f_i' = \eta_i(z_i/k_i) > 0$, and $f_i'' = (\eta_i - 1)(f_i'/k_i) < 0$, where the η_i are constant (and, by implication, fall between zero and unity). The first of these restrictions on the factor-service supply functions asserts that the "natural endowment" is wholly inert until it is improved by an act of investment; it does not furnish services useful in production. The second and third restrictions convey another important assumption—that investment in the "natural endowment" is subject to diminishing factor-service returns.

As all investments are financed by loans from the central fund, k_i represents the real value of the debt incurred by an investor, while gk_i represents his annual debt-service payment. In consequence, his income is:

$$y_i = w_i z_i - gk_i, \quad i = 1, 2 \tag{2}$$

Furthermore, the present value of the stream gk_i must equal k_i, so that:

$$k_i = gk_i \sum_{t=1}^{v} (1 + r)^{-t} = gk_i \frac{(1 + r)^v - 1}{r(1 + r)^v} \tag{3}$$

As z_i is a steady flow lasting v years, a worker or landlord will maximize the present value of his income stream by maximizing y_i. To reproduce his behavior, differentiate (2) with respect to k_i and set the derivative equal to zero:[10]

$$w_i f_i' = g, \quad i = 1, 2 \tag{4}$$

A worker or landlord will borrow and invest up to the point at which the marginal revenue from factor-service sales equals the marginal debt-service cost of investing in himself or his holdings.[11]

Now let us pretend that optimal (income-maximizing) quantities of capital have been invested in each of the nation's N_1 workers and each of its N_2 acres, and that past investments have been spaced out evenly. On these suppositions, N_i/v of "old" investments will die off each year, and:

$$\left. \begin{aligned} Z_i &= N_i z_i \\ K_i &= \frac{N_i}{v} k_i \\ Y_i &= N_i y_i = w_i Z_i - v g K_i \\ K &= \sum_i K_i \end{aligned} \right\} \quad i = 1, 2 \tag{5}$$

Here, Z_i is the aggregate annual supply of the ith factor service; K_i is the aggregate annual investment required to sustain Z_i; Y_i is the real annual income earned by all the owners of the ith natural factor; and K is the aggregate annual investment required to sustain the two factor-service flows (and measures the annual output of the capital good).[12]

The level of investment, K, also represents the real value of new lending in this stationary state, while gK represents the aggregate annual

---

[10] The sufficient second-order condition for maximum y_i is $w_i f_i'' < 0$, and is satisfied by the third restriction imposed on (1).

[11] Note, further, that (3) and (4) give:

$$y_i = w_i z_i (1 - \eta_i)$$

The income derived from factor-service sales is a steady, v-year stream of positive quasi-rents, bearing a close resemblance to land rent in the Ricardian model. Its sign derives from the assumption of diminishing factor-service returns to investment in the "natural endowment." The analogy is completed below, when it is shown that net capital formation reduces the interest rate and raises y_i, just as population growth reduces the real wage and raises land rent in the Ricardian model.

[12] Note the vital difference between z_i and Z_i. The former is a v-year flow; the latter is perpetual. Similarly, k_i is a single act of investment, while K_i is the annual flow needed to perpetuate a stationary state.

debt-service payment required to amortize a single year's lending. The balance outstanding on all past loans measures the capital stock, and is given by:[13]

$$C = \frac{K}{r}(vg - 1) \tag{6}$$

Interest income is defined in relation to this stock:

$$rC = K(vg - 1) \tag{6a}$$

Hence, one can go on to measure national income:

$$Y = Y_1 + Y_2 + rC = w_1 Z_1 + w_2 Z_2 - K = w_2 Z_1(w + R) - K \tag{7}$$

where $w = w_1/w_2$, henceforth described as the wage-rate ratio, and $R = Z_2/Z_1$, henceforth described as the gross factor ratio. This equation measures national income as gross national product at factor cost *less* depreciation, K, on the stock of capital (including both human and tangible capital). Alternatively, write:

$$Z_i = Z_{ik} + Z_{in}, \quad i = 1, 2 \tag{8}$$

where Z_{ik} is the amount of the ith factor service required to produce the capital good, while Z_{in} is the amount left for the production of final output. Furthermore, write:

$$K = \beta_k(R_k, 1)Z_{1k} \tag{9}$$

where $R_k = Z_{2k}/Z_{1k}$. As w_i is the real wage rate of the ith factor service in the capital-goods industry:

$$w_1 = \beta_k(R_k, 1) - \beta_k' \cdot R_k$$

$$w_2 = \beta_k' \tag{10}$$

[13] If all debt-service payments are made at the start of the year, the unpaid balance on a loan t years after issue is defined by:

$$C_t = K(1 + r)^t - gK[(1 + r)^{t-1} + \cdots + (1 + r) + 1]$$
$$= K(g/r)[1 - (1 + r)^{t-v}], \quad t < v$$

In effect, each amortization payment earns interest from the time it is made through the start of year t. The balance outstanding on all past loans is then defined by:

$$C = \sum_{t=0}^{v} C_t = K(g/r) \sum_{t=0}^{v} [1 - (1 + r)^{t-v}]$$

so that:

$$K = w_1 Z_{1k} + w_2 Z_{2k} \tag{8a}$$

Therefore:

$$Y = w_1 Z_{1n} + w_2 Z_{2n} = w_2 Z_{1n}(w + R_n) \tag{7a}$$

where $R_n = Z_{2n}/Z_{1n}$, henceforth described as the net factor ratio.[14]

In order to complete the two-factor model, let there be two final products, X_1 and X_2, with $R_1 < R_2$ at all w. Here, of course, $R_1 = Z_{21}/Z_{11}$ and $R_2 = Z_{22}/Z_{12}$, where Z_{ij} is the input of the ith factor service to the jth final product. For full employment, let:[15]

$$Z_{in} = \sum_j Z_{ij}, \quad i = 1, 2; \; j = 1, 2 \tag{11}$$

and write:

$$\left. \begin{aligned} X_j &= \beta_j(R_j, 1) Z_{1j} \\ \frac{w_1}{p_j} &= \beta_j(R_j, 1) - \beta_j' \cdot R_j \\ \frac{w_2}{p_j} &= \beta_j' \end{aligned} \right\} \; j = 1, 2 \tag{12}$$

where p_j is the price of the jth final product expressed in units of the capital good.

Finally, write:

$$Q = \frac{X_2}{X_1} \tag{13}$$

and:

$$Q^c = \theta(p) \tag{14}$$

where $p = p_1/p_2$, the product-price ratio, and Q^c is the ratio in which X_1 and X_2 are consumed at each and every level of national income.

---

[14] One more variant will be used below. Write:

$$K = w_2 Z_{1k}(w + R_k)$$

and:

$$Y = w_2[Z_1(w + R) - Z_{1k}(w + R_k)] = w_2 Z_{1n}(w + R_n)$$

so that:

$$(R - R_n) = (R_k - R)(Z_{1k}/Z_{1n})$$

One can always rank the three factor ratios by ranking any pair. When $R_k > R$, then $R > R_n$; when $R_k = R$, then $R = R_n$; and when $R_k < R$, then $R < R_n$.

[15] In consequence:

$$(R_2 - R_n) = (R_2 - R_1)(Z_{11}/Z_{1n})$$

We have, in all, 38 equations in 42 unknowns.[16] But in a closed economy:

$$Q = Q^c \tag{15}$$

If, then, N_1, N_2, and K are given, we can solve for all the other terms in the system.

Yet one can write a simpler version of the system, to solve for g, r, p, w, Q^c, Q, k_1, k_2, R, R_n, R_k, R_1, and R_2, given N_1, N_2, and K:

$$g - \frac{r(1 + r)^v}{(1 + r)^v - 1} = 0 \tag{16}$$

$$g - \frac{w \cdot \beta_k{}' \cdot \eta_1 \cdot f_1(k_1)}{k_1} = 0 \tag{17}$$

$$p - \frac{\beta_2{}'}{\beta_1{}'} = 0 \tag{18}$$

$$Q^c - Q = 0 \tag{19}$$

$$Q^c - \theta(p) = 0 \tag{20}$$

$$\frac{w \cdot \eta_1 \cdot f_1(k_1)}{k_1} - \frac{\eta_2 \cdot f_2(k_2)}{k_2} = 0 \tag{21}$$

$$R \cdot N_1 f_1(k_1) - N_2 f_2(k_2) = 0 \tag{22}$$

$$N_1 k_1 + N_2 k_2 - vK = 0 \tag{23}$$

$$\beta_2(R_2, 1)(R_n - R_1) - Q \cdot \beta_1(R_1, 1)(R_2 - R_n) = 0 \tag{24}$$

$$(R - R_n)N_1 f_1(k_1) - \frac{(R_k - R_n)K}{\beta_k(R_k, 1)} = 0 \tag{25}$$

$$\beta_k{}'(R_k + w) - \beta_k(R_k, 1) = 0 \tag{26}$$

$$\beta_1{}'(R_1 + w) - \beta_1(R_1, 1) = 0 \tag{27}$$

$$\beta_2{}'(R_2 + w) - \beta_2(R_2, 1) = 0 \tag{28}$$

This simpler system and variants on it will serve as the basis for subsequent analysis.

[16] These 38 equations are the two equations (1), the two equations (2), equation (3), the two equations (4), the seven equations (5), equations (6) and (7), the two equations (8), equation (9), the two equations (10), the two equations (11), the six equations (12), equation (13), equation (14), and the definitions of R, R_n, R_1, R_2, R_k, w, and p. The 42 unknowns are N_1, N_2, z_1, z_2, k_1, k_2, w_1, w_2, y_1, y_2, r, g, Z_1, Z_2, K_1, K_2, K, Y_1, Y_2, Y, C, Z_{1n}, Z_{2n}, Z_{1k}, Z_{2k}, Z_{11}, Z_{12}, Z_{21}, Z_{22}, X_1, X_2, p_1, p_2, R, R_n, R_1, R_2, R_k, Q, Q^c, w, and p.

DISPLACEMENT AND ADJUSTMENT
IN A CLOSED ECONOMY

Once the stock of capital is optimally allocated, satisfying these equations, changes in N_1, N_2, and K will cause systematic changes in the economy.[17] To study displacement and adjustment in this system, write out the total derivatives of equations (16) through (28):

$$g^* - \left[1 - \frac{vr}{(1+r)[(1+r)^v - 1]}\right]r^* = 0 \qquad (29)$$

$$g^* - \left[w^* + \frac{\beta_k''}{\beta_k'} R_k \cdot R_k^* - (1 - \eta_1)k_1^*\right] = 0 \qquad (30)$$

$$p^* - \left[\frac{\beta_2''}{\beta_2'} R_2 \cdot R_2^* - \frac{\beta_1''}{\beta_1'} R_1 \cdot R_1^*\right] = 0 \qquad (31)$$

$$Q^{c*} - Q^* = 0 \qquad (32)$$

$$Q^{c*} - \left(\frac{dQ^c}{dp}\right)\left(\frac{p}{Q^c}\right) \cdot \left(\frac{dp}{dw}\right)\left(\frac{w}{p}\right)w^* = 0 \qquad (33)$$

$$(1 - \eta_1)k_1^* - (1 - \eta_2)k_2^* - w^* = 0 \qquad (34)$$

$$\eta_1 k_1^* - \eta_2 k_2^* + R^* - (N_2^* - N_1^*) = 0 \qquad (35)$$

$$\left(\frac{K_1}{K}\right)k_1^* + \left(\frac{K_2}{K}\right)k_2^* - \left[K^* - \left(\frac{K_1}{K}\right)N_1^* - \left(\frac{K_2}{K}\right)N_2^*\right] = 0 \quad (36)$$

$$\frac{R_n(R_2 - R_1)R_n^*}{(R_2 - R_n)(R_n - R_1)} - \left[\frac{R_2(R_n + w)R_2^*}{(R_2 + w)(R_2 - R_n)} + \frac{R_1(R_n + w)R_1^*}{(R_1 + w)(R_n - R_1)}\right]$$
$$- Q^* = 0 \quad (37)$$

$$\left(\frac{R - R_n}{R}\right)\eta_1 k_1^* - \left(\frac{Z_{2n}}{Z_2}\right)R_n^* - \left(\frac{Z_{2k}}{Z_2}\right)\left(\frac{R_n + w}{R_k + w}\right)R_k^* + R^*$$
$$- \left(\frac{R - R_n}{R}\right)(K^* - N_1^*) = 0 \quad (38)$$

---

[17] An increase in N_1 represents an increase in the nation's labor force. An increase in N_2 can, perhaps, be viewed as an increase in its stock of land or, more plausibly, as a proxy for "disembodied" technological progress affecting that stock's quality (its susceptibility to improvement by investment). An increase in K represents net saving; it measures the increase in stationary-state replacement investment corresponding to a permanent change in the stock of capital (the total claims of the central loan fund),

$$\left(\frac{\beta_k{}''}{\beta_k{}'}\right)R_k \cdot R_k{}^* + \left[\frac{w}{(R_k + w)}\right]w^* = 0 \tag{39}$$

$$\left(\frac{\beta_1{}''}{\beta_1{}'}\right)R_1 \cdot R_1{}^* + \left[\frac{w}{(R_1 + w)}\right]w^* = 0 \tag{40}$$

$$\left(\frac{\beta_2{}''}{\beta_2{}'}\right)R_2 \cdot R_2{}^* + \left[\frac{w}{(R_2 + w)}\right]w^* = 0 \tag{41}$$

where asterisks denote relative rates of change ($g^* = dg/g$, $w^* = dw/w$, and so on).

To make this system more compact, use (39) through (41) to replace $R_k{}^*$, $R_1{}^*$, and $R_2{}^*$ wherever they appear, then use (29) through (38) to solve for r^*, g^*, p^*, w^*, Q^*, $k_1{}^*$, $k_2{}^*$, R^*, and $R_n{}^*$. From (29), obtain:

$$r^* = e_{rg} \cdot g^*, \quad e_{rg} = \left[1 - \frac{vr}{(1 + r)[(1 + r)^v - 1]}\right]^{-1} > 0 \tag{29a}$$

because $vr < [(1 + r)^v - 1]$. Rewrite (30), as:

$$g^* = \left(\frac{R_k}{R_k + w}\right)w^* - (1 - \eta_1)k_1{}^* \tag{30a}$$

Then rewrite (31), as:

$$p^* = e_{pw} \cdot w^*, \quad e_{pw} = \frac{w(R_2 - R_1)}{(R_1 + w)(R_2 + w)} > 0 \tag{31a}$$

because $R_1 < R_2$ at all factor prices.[18] From (32) and (33), obtain:

$$Q^* = e_{cp} \cdot e_{pw} \cdot w^*, \quad e_{cp} = \left(\frac{dQ^c}{dp}\right) \cdot \left(\frac{p}{Q^c}\right) > 0 \tag{33a}$$

[18] Note, in passing, that (18) and (31a) can be invoked to reaffirm factor-price equalization in a two-country, two-product model. As $\beta_1{}'$ and $\beta_2{}'$, the arguments of (18), are functions of w, one can write (18) in the general form:

$$p = h(w), \quad w = h^{-1}(p)$$

As (31a) asserts that the first of these functions is single-valued and monotonic, the second is likewise single-valued and monotonic. If, then, two countries have identical production functions for X_1 and X_2, if trade between them fosters an equality in product prices, and if neither country is completely specialized in X_1, or X_2 (so that $\beta_1{}'$ and $\beta_2{}'$ exist in both countries), the two countries will display the same wage-rate ratios, w, and the same factor-service prices, w_1 and w_2.

with well-behaved demand functions. From (34) and (36), derive:

$$k_1{}^* = \frac{[R(\eta_2/\eta_1) + w][K^* - (K_1/K)N_1{}^* - (K_2/K)N_2{}^*] + [R\phi/(1 - \eta_1)]w^*}{w + R\phi} \qquad (34a)$$

$$k_2{}^* = \frac{\phi[R + w(\eta_1/\eta_2)][K^* - (K_1/K)N_1{}^* - (K_2/K)N_2{}^*] - [w/(1 - \eta_2)]w^*}{w + R\phi} \qquad (36a)$$

where $\phi = (1 - \eta_1)\eta_2/(1 - \eta_2)\eta_1$.[19] From (35), obtain:

$$R^* = \eta_2 k_2{}^* - \eta_1 k_1{}^* + (N_2{}^* - N_1{}^*) \qquad (35a)$$

Rewrite (37), as:

$$Q^* = e_{QR_n} \cdot R_n{}^* - e_{Qw} \cdot w^*, \quad e_{QR_n} = \frac{R_n(R_2 - R_1)}{(R_2 - R_n)(R_n - R_1)} > 0,$$

and

$$e_{Qw} = -\frac{w(R_n + w)}{(R_2 - R_n)(R_n - R_1)}\left[\frac{\beta_2{}'(R_n - R_1)}{\beta_2{}''(R_2 + w)^2} + \frac{\beta_1{}'(R_2 - R_n)}{\beta_1{}''(R_1 + w)^2}\right] > 0 \qquad (37a)$$

because $R_1 < R_2$ at all w,[20] while $\beta_1{}'' < 0$ and $\beta_2{}'' < 0$ when all production functions display diminishing marginal products. Finally, from (38), write:

$$R_n{}^* = \left(\frac{Z_2}{Z_{2n}}\right)\left[R^* + \left(\frac{R - R_n}{R}\right)(\eta_1 k_1{}^* - K^* + N_1{}^*)\right.$$

$$\left. + \left(\frac{Z_{1k}}{Z_{2n}}\right)\left(\frac{R_n + w}{R_k + w}\right)\left(\frac{w}{R_k + w}\right)\left(\frac{\beta_k{}'}{\beta_k{}''}\right)w^* \right] \qquad (38a)$$

Now use (34a), (35a), (36a), and (38a) to write out the changes in k_1, k_2, R, and R_n that could happen with a constant wage-rate ratio (those that would come about in consequence of $N_1{}^*$, $N_2{}^*$, and K^*, were $w^* = 0$):

$$k_1^{**} \equiv \frac{R(\eta_2/\eta_1) + w}{w + R\phi}\left[K^* - \left(\frac{K_1}{K}\right)N_1{}^* - \left(\frac{K_2}{K}\right)N_2{}^*\right]$$

$$= \left[\frac{R(\eta_2/\eta_1) + w}{w + R\phi}\right]\left[K^* - \frac{w \cdot N_1{}^* + R(\eta_2/\eta_1) \cdot N_2{}^*}{w + R(\eta_2/\eta_1)}\right] \qquad (42)$$

[19] These formulations derive from (21) and (23), which yield:

$$(K_1/K) = 1 - (K_2/K) = w/[w + R(\eta_2/\eta_1)]$$

[20] When $R_1 < R_2$ and neither X_i is zero, $R_1 < R_n < R_2$ (see note 15).

$$k_2^{**} \equiv \phi\left(\frac{\eta_1}{\eta_2}\right)k_1^{**} \tag{43}$$

$$R^{**} \equiv (\phi - 1)\eta_1 k_1^{**} + (N_2^* - N_1^*) \tag{44}$$

$$R_n^{**} \equiv \left(\frac{Z_2}{Z_{2n}}\right)\left\{(N_2^* - N_1^*) - \left(\frac{R - R_n}{R}\right)(K^* - N_1^*)\right.$$
$$\left. + \left[(\phi - 1) + \left(\frac{R - R_n}{R}\right)\right]\eta_1 k_1^{**}\right\} \tag{45}$$

Reinserting these new terms into the equations that were used to define them:

$$k_1^* = k_1^{**} + \frac{R\phi \cdot w^*}{(w + R\phi)(1 - \eta_1)} \tag{46}$$

$$k_2^* = \phi\left(\frac{\eta_1}{\eta_2}\right)k_1^{**} - \frac{w \cdot w^*}{(w + R\phi)(1 - \eta_2)} \tag{47}$$

$$R^* = R^{**} - e_{Rw} \cdot w^*, \quad e_{Rw} = \left(\frac{\eta_2}{1 - \eta_2}\right)\left(\frac{w + R}{w + R\phi}\right) > 0 \tag{48}$$

$$R_n^* = R_n^{**} - e_{R_n w} \cdot w^*, \quad e_{R_n w} = \left(\frac{w + R_n}{R_n}\right)\left(\frac{Z_1}{Z_{1n}}\right)$$
$$\times \left[\left(\frac{\eta_2}{1 - \eta_2}\right)\left(\frac{R}{w + R\phi}\right) - \left(\frac{Z_{1k}}{Z_1}\right)\left(\frac{\beta_k'}{\beta_k''}\right)\frac{w}{(w + R_k)^2}\right] > 0 \tag{49}$$

The sign of $e_{R_n w}$ derives from the fact that $\beta_k'' < 0$.

To complete this version of the basic model, use (33a), (37a), and (49) to write:

$$w^* = \frac{e_{QR_n} \cdot R_n^{**}}{e_{cp} \cdot e_{pw} + e_{QR_n} \cdot e_{R_n w} + e_{Qw}} \tag{50}$$

so that the change in w depends on the change in the net factor ratio induced by K^*, N_1^*, and N_2^*. Then use (29a), (30a), and (46) to write:

$$r^* = e_{rg}\left[\frac{w(R_k - R\phi)w^*}{(R_k + w)(R\phi + w)} - (1 - \eta_1)k_1^{**}\right] \tag{51}$$

so that the change in r depends on the signs of $(R_k - R\phi)$, w^*, and k_1^{**}.

When w^* is zero, we shall speak of product-market balanced growth.

When r^* is zero, we shall speak of capital-market balanced growth. And, when $w^* = r^* = 0$, we shall speak of full-scale balanced growth.

How can the last result occur? Clearly, it requires that R_n^{**} be zero. But it also requires that k_1^{**} be zero. Otherwise, r^* would not vanish when w^* had vanished. When k_1^{**} is zero, however, equation (42) becomes:

$$K^* - N_1^* = \frac{R(\eta_2/\eta_1)}{w + R(\eta_2/\eta_1)}(N_2^* - N_1^*) \tag{52}$$

And (45) becomes:

$$R_n^{**} = \left(\frac{Z_2}{Z_{2n}}\right)\left[\frac{w + R_n(\eta_2/\eta_1)}{w + R(\eta_2/\eta_1)}\right](N_2^* - N_1^*) \tag{53}$$

Hence R_n^{**} is not zero when k_1^{**} is zero unless $N_1^* = N_2^*$ and, from (52), $K^* = N_1^* = N_2^*$. This is the only instance of full-scale balanced growth. All other sets of changes in the "natural endowment" and capital stock will alter the wage-rate ratio, the interest rate, or both.

One could, of course, devise a series of cases in which r^* would vanish, and another set of cases in which w^* would vanish. Furthermore, wage-rate change will affect R_n^{**} and can force the economy toward product-market balanced growth. But this result is far from certain; changes in K, N_1, and N_2 may, instead, induce continuous changes in w and r.

To study such a case of continuous change, set $\eta_1 = \eta_2 = \eta$, so that:[21]

$$k_1^{**} = (K^* - N_1^*) - \left(\frac{R}{R + w}\right)(N_2^* - N_1^*) \tag{54}$$

$$R_n^{**} = \left(\frac{Z_2}{Z_{2n}}\right)\left(\frac{Z_{1k}}{Z_{1n}}\right)\left[\left(\frac{Y}{K}\right)\left(\frac{w + R_k}{w + R}\right)(N_2^* - N_1^*) \right.$$
$$\left. + \left(\frac{R - R_k}{R}\right)(1 - \eta)k_1^{**}\right] \tag{55}$$

$$r^* = -e_{rg}\left[\frac{w(R - R_k)w^*}{(w + R_k)(w + R)} + (1 - \eta)k_1^{**}\right] \tag{56}$$

When, then, $k_1^{**} > 0$, the signs of the changes in w and r come to depend on $(N_2^* - N_1^*)$ and on $(R - R_k)$. When, for instance, $N_2^* \geqslant N_1^*$ and $R > R_k$, the net factor ratio will rise, raising the wage-rate ratio, and the increase in the latter will depress the interest rate. When, instead,

[21] This is the "linear version" of the general model (so named because the gross factor ratio is not affected by capital formation); it is the one that was used in my earlier paper, cited in note 2.

Table 1

Table 1

Changes in the Rate of Interest (with $\eta_1 = \eta_2 = \eta$ and $k_1^{**} > 0$)

Rankings	R_n^{**} and w^*	Wage-Induced r^*	Total r^*
With $N_2^* > N_1^*$, and			
$R > R_k$	+	−	−
$R = R_k$	+	0	−
$R < R_k$	?	?	?
With $N_2^* = N_1^*$, and			
$R > R_k$	+	−	−
$R = R_k$	0	0	−
$R < R_k$	−	−	−
With $N_2^* < N_1^*$, and			
$R > R_k$	?	?	?
$R = R_k$	−	0	−
$R < R_k$	−	−	−

$N_2^* < N_1^*$ and $R < R_k$, the net factor ratio will decline, reducing the wage-rate ratio, but, as before, the interest rate will fall. In each instance, moreover, two forces are at work on the rate of interest; k_1^{**} induces a "primary" change, and w^* induces a "secondary" change. The full range of results (for $k_1^{**} > 0$) is set out in Table 1. Notice that r^* is always negative, save when $N_2^* > N_1^*$ while $R < R_k$, and when $N_2^* < N_1^*$ while $R > R_k$.

Now let $K^* = N_1^*$ and let $N_2^* = 0$, so that:

$$R_n^{**} = \left(\frac{Z_2}{Z_{2n}}\right)\left(\frac{Z_{1k}}{Z_{1n}}\right)\left(\frac{w + R_k}{w + R}\right) T \cdot K^* \tag{57}$$

where:

$$T = \left(\frac{R - R_k}{R_k + w}\right)(1 - \eta) - \left(\frac{Y}{K}\right) \tag{58}$$

and where:

$$dT = -(1 - \eta)\left(\frac{R}{R + w}\right)\left[\frac{R - R_k}{R_k + w} - \frac{Y}{K}\right]K^* - \frac{w^*}{R_k + w}\left\{\eta R_k\left(\frac{R + w}{R_k + w}\right)\right.$$

$$\left. -\left(\frac{w}{R_k + w}\right)\left(\frac{R + w}{R_k + w}\right)\left(\frac{\beta_k{}'}{\beta_k{}''}\right)(1 - \eta) + w\left(\frac{R - R_k}{R + w}\right)\left[\frac{R - R_k}{R_k + w} - \frac{Y}{K}\right]\right\} \tag{59}$$

Here, we must compare $[(R - R_k)/(R_k + w)]$, $[(R - R_k)/(R_k + w)](1 - \eta)$, and (Y/K), and this is done in Table 2. When, for instance,

$$[(R - R_k)/(R_k + w)](1 - \eta) > (Y/K),$$

Table 2

Changes in R_n^{**} (with $\eta_1 = \eta_2 = \eta$, $K^* = N_1{}^*$, and $N_2{}^* = 0$)

		Change in R_n^{**}		
Ranking	$T, R_n^{**},$ and w^*	K effect	w effect	Total
$\dfrac{R - R_k}{R_k + w}(1 - \eta) > \dfrac{Y}{K}$	+	−	−	−
$\dfrac{R - R_k}{R_k + w}(1 - \eta) = \dfrac{Y}{K}$	0	−	0	−
$\dfrac{R - R_k}{R_k + w} > \dfrac{Y}{K} > \dfrac{R - R_k}{R_k + w}(1 - \eta)$	−	−	+	?
$\dfrac{R - R_k}{R_k + w} = \dfrac{Y}{K}$	−	0	+	+
$\dfrac{Y}{K} > \dfrac{R - R_k}{w + R_k} > 0$	−	+	?	?
$\dfrac{R - R_k}{R_k + w} < 0$	−	+	+	+

R_n^{**} and w^* are positive, as is $[(R - R_k)/(R_k + w)] = (Y/K)$. In consequence, all arguments of (59) are unambiguously negative, and R_n^{**} declines. But, when R_n^{**} and w^* have fallen to zero, the first argument of (59) is still negative, so that R_n^{**} has also to turn negative. Product-market balanced growth is not a stable state.

To end this exploration of the closed economy, consider one more simple case in which R_n^{**} will always go to zero. Let $K^* > N_1{}^* = N_2{}^*$ (which includes the simpler case of capital formation without any change in the "natural endowment"). In this instance:

$$R_n^{**} = \left(\frac{Z_2}{Z_{2n}}\right)\left(\frac{Z_{1k}}{Z_{1n}}\right)\left(\frac{R - R_k}{R}\right)(1 - \eta)(K^* - N_1{}^*) \qquad (60)$$

This case is covered by the middle section of Table 1; for all orderings of R and R_k, the interest rate declines. In this case, moreover, R_n^{**} will go to zero from any starting point, for $(\partial R/\partial w)(w/R) < 0$ [see equation (48)] and $(\partial R_k/\partial w)(w/R_k) > 0$ [see equation (39)]. Factor-market balanced growth will occur eventually and, once it is attained, will be self-perpetuating. When it has been reached, however, r^* will take the sign of $(K^* - N_1{}^*)$, declining with an increase in capital per worker.

TRADE AND INVESTMENT IN A
TWO-COUNTRY MODEL

To study foreign trade and foreign investment, let there be two countries, I and II, and adopt five more assumptions:

1. That both final products, X_1 and X_2, are traded without transport cost, but there is no trade in the capital good.
2. That both countries have identical production functions, and each country produces both final products.
3. That demand conditions are the same in both countries (with unitary income elasticities).
4. That all factor-service supply functions have the same elasticities $(_I\eta_i = {}_{II}\eta_i = \eta)$ and all investments have the same factor-service lives $(_Iv = {}_{II}v = v)$.
5. That the two countries' natural endowments yield a strict ordering of gross factor ratios: $_IR < {}_{II}R$ whenever $_Iw = {}_{II}w$ and $_Ir = {}_{II}r$.[22]

Under the first of these assumptions, free trade will equalize the two countries' product prices. Under the second, equation (18), linking p and w, exists and is the same in the two countries. Hence, free trade will equalize the two countries' factor prices.[23]

But, with factor-price equalization and identical demand conditions, the two-country model can be set out with common p and w, with common R_k, R_1, R_2, and Q^c (all of which depend on p or w), and in terms of $_Ig$, $_{II}g$, $_Ir$, $_{II}r$, $_IQ$, $_{II}Q$, $_Ik$, $_{II}k$, $_Ik_2$, $_{II}k_2$, $_IR$, $_{II}R$, $_IR_n$, and $_{II}R_n$, given $_IK$ and $_{II}K$, $_IN$ and $_{II}N_1$, and $_IN_2$ and $_{II}N_2$. To solve this whole system, we need twenty equations: the (common) equations (18), (20), (26), (27), and (28); the two sets of equations (16), (17), (21), (32), (24), and (25); and one new equation linking the common Q^c with global production:

$$Q^c = \left(\frac{_IX_2 + {}_{II}X_2}{_IX_1 + {}_{II}X_1}\right) = \frac{\beta_2(R_2, 1)}{\beta_1(R_1, 1)}\left[\frac{(_IR_n - R_1) + (_{II}R_n - R_1)U}{(R_2 - {}_IR_n) + (R_2 - {}_{II}R_n)U}\right] \quad (61)$$

where

$$U = \left(\frac{w + {}_IR_n}{w + {}_{II}R_n}\right)\left(\frac{_{II}Y}{_IY}\right) = \left(\frac{w + {}_IR_n}{w + {}_{II}R_n}\right)\left(\frac{v \cdot {}_{II}g - \eta}{v \cdot {}_Ig - \eta}\right)\left(\frac{_{II}K}{_IK}\right)$$

[22] The role of this iso-interest restriction is clarified in note 25.

[23] See note 18; see also P. A. Samuelson, "The Prices of Factors and Goods in General Equilibrium," *Review of Economic Studies*, XXI (1953–54).

With identical demand conditions, moreover, the output ratios $_IQ$ and $_{II}Q$ determine the pattern of trade. If $_{II}Q > {}_IQ$ at the common product prices fixed by free trade, country I will export X_1 and country II will export X_2. It is, in fact, sufficient to know the net factor ratios if one wants to forecast the structure of trade. When prices are equal in the two countries:

$$_{II}Q - {}_IQ = \frac{\beta_2(R_2, 1)}{\beta_1(R_1, 1)} \left[\frac{(R_2 - R_1)(_{II}R_n - {}_IR_n)}{(R_2 - {}_{II}R_n)(R_2 - {}_IR_n)} \right] \tag{62}$$

so that $_{II}Q > {}_IQ$ whenever $_{II}R_n > {}_IR_n$.

Thus far, then, this model gives familiar results. It generates equality in factor-service prices whenever the conventional assumptions are fulfilled, and, with the conventional restrictions on final demand, it generates a pattern of merchandise trade reflecting the physical factor endowments (net factor ratios) of the trading countries. But the model also offers several new results concerning international trade and investment.[24]

The net factor ratios $_IR_n$ and $_{II}R_n$ are not directly descriptive of capital supplies; they are not the same as the capital-to-labor ratios featured in conventional two-country models. Nor are the factor ratios R_1 and R_2 directly descriptive of capital requirements; they cannot be used to order the production functions according to capital intensity. Hence, statements about the capital intensities of export and import-competing production have no true counterparts in the model studied here. Yet, one can still measure capital scarcity by comparing interest rates. Furthermore, a difference in national interest rates will affect the ordering of net factor ratios, thereby affecting the pattern of trade. On the fourth assumption introduced above, one can rank the two countries' net factor ratios when those two countries face the same prices:

$$_{II}R_n - {}_IR_n = {}_{II}\left(\frac{Y + K}{Y}\right)\left(\frac{w + {}_{II}R_n}{w + {}_{II}R}\right)\left[(_{II}R - {}_IR)\left(\frac{w + {}_IR_n}{w + {}_IR}\right) \right.$$

$$\left. - (_IR_n - {}_IR)\left(\frac{_{II}g - {}_Ig}{_{II}g}\right)\left(\frac{w + {}_{II}R}{w + {}_IR}\right) \right] \tag{63}$$

When interest rates are equal in the two countries, the gross amortization rates will be equal too, and the second argument of (63) will vanish

[24] Some of these results, concerning the effects of changes in demand on international movements of capital and the similar effects of import tariffs, were set out in my earlier paper (cited in note 2) and will not be repeated here.

completely. The ordering of net factor ratios will depend on the ordering of gross factor ratios, and the latter will reflect an underlying difference in "natural endowments."[25] When interest rates are different in the two countries, reflecting a difference in capital scarcity, the second argument of (63) will come into play. If, for instance, $_{II}r > _{I}r$ (so that $_{II}g > _{I}g$), while $R_k > _{I}R$ (so that $_{I}R_n < _{I}R$), the difference in interest rates will augment the iso-interest difference in net factor ratios, making for more trade. If, instead, $R_k > _{I}R$, the same difference in interest rates will narrow the difference in net factor ratios, making for less trade (and may even overturn the iso-interest difference, reversing the pattern of merchandise trade).[26]

A difference in capital scarcity will also cause a difference in net factor incomes. Free trade will align the factor-service prices, w_i, but will not always equalize the net factor incomes, y_i. These incomes will differ

---

[25] The constant-elasticity factor-service supply function can be written in the form:

$$Z_i = N_i(\gamma_i \cdot k_i^{\eta_i})$$

where γ_i is a constant reflecting factor quality. But (4) can be written as:

$$g = w_i \cdot \eta_i \cdot \gamma_i \cdot k_i^{\eta_i - 1}$$

so that:

$$\log Z_i = \log N_i + \frac{1}{1 - \eta_i} \log \gamma_i + \frac{\eta_i}{1 - \eta_i} [\log w_i + \log \eta_i - \log g]$$

And:

$$\log R = \log \left(\frac{N_2}{N_1}\right) + \frac{1}{1 - \eta_2} \log \left(\frac{\gamma_2}{\gamma_1}\right) - \frac{\eta_2}{1 - \eta_2} \log \left(\frac{w\eta_1}{\eta_2}\right)$$

$$+ \frac{\eta_2 - \eta_1}{(1 - \eta_1)(1 - \eta_2)} [\log (w_1\eta_1) + \log \gamma_1 - \log g]$$

With $_{I}w = _{II}w$ and $_{I}\eta_i = _{II}\eta_i = \eta_i$, then:

$$\log \left(\frac{_{II}R}{_{I}R}\right) = \left[\log \left(\frac{N_2}{N_1}\right)_{II} - \log \left(\frac{N_2}{N_1}\right)_{I}\right]$$

$$+ \frac{1}{1 - \eta_2} \left[\log \left(\frac{\gamma_2}{\gamma_1}\right)_{II} - \log \left(\frac{\gamma_2}{\gamma_1}\right)_{I}\right]$$

$$+ \frac{\eta_2 - \eta_1}{(1 - \eta_1)(1 - \eta_2)} \left[\log \left(\frac{_{I}g}{_{II}g}\right) + \log \left(\frac{_{II}\gamma_1}{_{I}\gamma_1}\right)\right]$$

The first argument of this equation measures the difference in relative quantities (in acres per worker). The second measures the difference in relative quantity. The third combines two terms relating to absolute quality and to relative capital scarcity, but this term vanishes when, as in the text, $\eta_2 = \eta_1$.

[26] This inference assumes that $_{II}R > _{I}R$. When $\eta_I \neq \eta_2$, however, the ordering of gross factor ratios can itself be altered by a difference in interest rates (see note 25).

between countries if those countries' "natural endowments" differ in quality or if they embody different investments.[27] In consequence, the model set forth here furnishes a comprehensive explanation of international differences in real incomes. These may be ascribed to national differences in supplies of tangible capital and labor-force participation (the elements that enter conventional models), but can also be ascribed to national differences in stocks of "human capital" and in the quality of "natural endowments."[28]

I come now to the most important new proposition furnished by this model of capital formation. In the conventional Heckscher-Ohlin construct, free trade will equalize national interest rates, and capital movements are wholly redundant.[29] An act of net saving in country I, for example, will not cause it to invest in country II, for interest rates will be aligned by changes in the terms of trade resulting from country I's domestic investment. In the model studied here, free trade will not equalize two countries' interest rates; it is not a substitute for capital

---

[27] By way of proof, use the arguments of notes 11 and 25 to write:

$$\log \left(_{II}y_i/_{I}y_i\right) = \log \left[\left(_{II}g/_{I}g\right)\left(_{II}k_i/_{I}k_i\right)\right]$$

$$= \frac{\log \left(_{II}\gamma_i/_{I}\gamma_i\right) - \eta_i \log \left(_{II}g/_{I}g\right)}{1 - \eta_i}$$

Differences in factor incomes can then be attributed to differences in quality $\left(_{II}\gamma_i/_{I}\gamma_i\right)$ and, inversely, to differences in capital scarcity $\left(_{II}g/_{I}g\right)$.

[28] Denoting the (conventional) supplies of labor and capital by L' and K', the corresponding real wages by w_1' and w_2', and the total population by N, gross national product per capita can be written in the form:

$$G/N = (L'/N)[w_1' + w_2'(K'/L')]$$

Because free trade will equalize the w_i' between countries, differences in national outputs per capita must be due to differences in tangible capital per worker (K'/L') and in labor-force participation (L'/N). In the model studied here:

$$G/N = (N_1/N)z_1(w_1 + w_2 \cdot R)$$

Once again, free trade will equalize the w_i between countries, but differences in national outputs per capita can now be due to differences in (N_1/N), labor-force participation, in z_1, the labor-service flow from a single worker, and in R, land-service flow per unit of labor-service flow. Differences in z_1 and R, moreover, can reflect differences in capital scarcity and in the quality of "natural endowments."

[29] See P. A. Samuelson, "Equalization by Trade of the Interest Rate along with the Real Wage," in *Trade, Growth and the Balance of Payments* R. E. Caves, H. G. Johnson and P. B. Kenen (eds.) (Chicago: Rand-McNally, 1965).

movements serving to optimize world production.[30]   I shall prove this proposition by a simple illustration that does not require any new formulae, and will then examine it somewhat more thoroughly.

Suppose that $_I r = {}_{II} r$ initially, and that $_I R = {}_{II} R = R_k$ at a common set of prices in the two countries. Under these conditions, $_I R_n = {}_{II} R_n$, and there will be no trade. Now, disturb this situation by an act of net saving in country I, and let that saving be invested inside country I itself. There will be no change in $_I R_n$, for $_I R_n^{**} = 0$ when $_I R = R_k$ [see equation (55)]. Hence capital formation will not cause a change in prices and will not bring on trade. Yet $_I r$ will decline with this capital formation, falling by $e_{rg}(1 - \eta)_I K^*$ [see equation (56)], and some of country I's net saving must be moved to country II in order to restore interest-rate equality. Notice, moreover, that this transfer of capital will not lead to trade, for $_{II} R_n^{**} = 0$ when, as here, $_{II} R = R_k$. In brief, free trade cannot substitute for capital movements, and movements of capital need not bring on trade.[31]

This proof was contrived to forestall foreign trade, but similar results obtain when the two countries are trading initially. To study such a case,

---

[30] This result, it should be stressed, does not depend on my assumption that there is no trade in the capital good or, more generally, on my combination of two traded products with three factors of production, Z_1, Z_2, and K. Capital is not a factor of production in the ordinary sense. Hence, the addition of one more commodity (or trade in the capital good) would not serve to equalize national interest rates. My results, below, should be compared with Samuelson's ("Equalization by Trade"). He shows that a model with one primary factor (labor) and reproducible capital goods that enter directly into production will, in fact, equalize national interest rates and take on Ricardian properties. When free trade has equalized the two countries' interest rates, their production functions can be regarded as "the simple linear ones of the Ricardian labor-theory-of-value, constant-cost case." My model, by contrast, posits two primary factors, land and labor, and assumes that the reproducible capital good is not used directly in production. In consequence, interest rates must be equalized by international lending (by transfers between the two countries' loan funds). Once they have been equalized (and if there are no differences in factor quality), my model becomes a straightforward Heckscher-Ohlin construct, not a Ricardian construct, with trade based on differences in land and labor endowments.

[31] The last statement is not quite accurate. A capital movement always requires an offsetting flow of goods; so does the interest payment to which it gives rise. When country I lends to country II, the latter will use the loan proceeds to buy some of every final product in country I, releasing its own factor services to produce additional capital goods and expand its output. With no saving in country II, even at the higher level of net geographic product, that country will not repay its debts. Instead, country I will obtain a perpetual interest-income stream from country II and will use that income stream to buy some of country II's final output. But neither of these trade flows is based on the principle of comparative advantage; each one involves a one-way flow of both final products.

define:

$$s \equiv \frac{_{II}r}{_{I}r} \tag{64}$$

and let $s = 1$ to start. Then use (54) and (56) to write:

$$
\left.
\begin{aligned}
s^* &= (_{II}r^* - {}_{I}r^*) \equiv s_w{}^* + s^{**} \\[2mm]
s_w{}^* &\equiv -e_{rg}\left[\frac{w(_{II}R - {}_{I}R)}{(_{I}R + w)(_{II}R + w)}\right]w^* \\[2mm]
s^{**} &\equiv -e_{rg}(1 - \eta)(_{II}k_1^{**} - {}_{I}k^{**})
\end{aligned}
\right\} \tag{65}
$$

Since $s_w{}^* \neq 0$ when $_{I}R \neq {}_{II}R$ and $w^* \neq 0$, any change in factor-service prices can create a difference in national interest rates. Hence, factor-price equality ($_{I}w = {}_{II}w$ and $_{I}w^* = {}_{II}w^*$) does not guarantee interest-rate equality.

But what happens to w^* when the k_1^{**} are different from zero; what are the effects of capital formation and changes in the nations' "natural endowments"? To answer this question, one must differentiate equation (61) and solve it for w^*. First, write:

$$
\begin{aligned}
e_{cp} \cdot e_{pw} \cdot w^* &= (R_2 - R_1)(1 + U)V[_{I}R_n \cdot {}_{I}R_n{}^* + {}_{II}R_n \cdot U \cdot {}_{II}R_n{}^*] \\[2mm]
&+ \left\{\frac{w}{(w + R_1)^2}\left(\frac{\beta_1{}'}{\beta_1{}''}\right)\left[\frac{(w + {}_{I}R_n) + (w + {}_{II}R_n)U}{(_{I}R_n - R_1) + (_{II}R_n - R_1)U}\right]\right. \\[2mm]
&\quad \left. \times \frac{w}{(w + R_2)^2}\left(\frac{\beta_2{}'}{\beta_2{}''}\right)\left[\frac{(w + {}_{I}R_n) + (w + {}_{II}R_n)U}{(R_2 - {}_{I}R_n) + (R_2 - {}_{II}R_n)U}\right]\right\}w^* \\[2mm]
&+ UV(R_2 - R_1)(_{II}R_n - {}_{I}R_n)U^* \tag{66}
\end{aligned}
$$

where

$$V \equiv \frac{1}{[(_{I}R_n - R_1) + (_{II}R_n - R_1)U][(R_2 - {}_{I}R_n) + (R_2 - {}_{II}R_n)U]} > 0$$

and where:

$$
\begin{aligned}
U^* &= \left(\frac{_{I}R_n \cdot {}_{I}R_n{}^*}{w + {}_{I}R_n} - \frac{_{II}R_n \cdot {}_{II}R_n{}^*}{w + {}_{II}R_n}\right) + \frac{w(_{II}R_n - {}_{I}R_n)w^*}{(w + {}_{I}R_n)(w + {}_{II}R_n)} \\[2mm]
&+ \left(\frac{vg}{vg - \eta}\right)\left(\frac{s^{**} + s_w{}^*}{e_{rg}}\right) + (_{II}K^* - {}_{I}K^*) \tag{67}
\end{aligned}
$$

When $s = 1$, however, equation (63) gives:

$$\frac{w(_{II}R_n - {}_IR_n)w^*}{(w + {}_IR_n)(w + {}_{II}R_n)} = \left(\frac{Y + K}{Y}\right)\frac{w(_IR - {}_{II}R)w^*}{(w + {}_IR)(w + {}_{II}R)}$$

$$= -\left(\frac{vg}{vg - \eta}\right)\left(\frac{s_w{}^*}{e_{rg}}\right) \tag{68}$$

so that:

$$U^* = \left(\frac{_IR_n \cdot {}_IR_n{}^*}{w + {}_IR_n} - \frac{_{II}R_n \cdot {}_{II}R_n{}^*}{w + {}_{II}R_n}\right) - \left(\frac{vg}{vg - \eta}\right)$$

$$\times (1 - \eta)(_{II}k_1^{**} - {}_Ik_1^{**}) + (_{II}K^* - {}_IK^*) \tag{67a}$$

Returning, now, to (66), use (67a) and (49) to replace U^*, ${}_IR_n{}^*$, and ${}_{II}R_n{}^*$, then solve for w^*:

$$w^* = \frac{V(R_2 - R_1)}{e_{cp} \cdot e_{pw} + e_{v_1w} + e_{v_2w}}\left\{W\left[\frac{_IR_n \cdot {}_IR_n^{**}}{w + {}_IR_n} + \frac{_{II}R_n \cdot U \cdot {}_{II}R_n^{**}}{w + {}_{II}R_n}\right]\right.$$

$$+ U(_{II}R_n - {}_IR_n)\left[(_{II}K^* - {}_IK^*)\right.$$

$$\left.\left. - \left(\frac{vg}{vg - \eta}\right)(1 - \eta)(_{II}k_1^{**} - {}_Ik_1^{**})\right]\right\} \tag{69}$$

where:

$$W \equiv (w + {}_IR_n) + (w + {}_{II}R_n)U > 0$$

$$e_{v_1w} \equiv VW(R_2 - R_1)\left[\frac{_IR_n}{w + {}_IR_n}\,(_Ie_{R_nw}) + \frac{_{II}R_n \cdot U}{w + {}_{II}R_n}\,(_{II}e_{R_nw})\right] > 0 \left.\begin{array}{c}\\\\\\\\\\\\\\\end{array}\right\} \tag{70}$$

$$e_{v_2w} \equiv -VW\left\{\frac{w}{(w + R_1)^2}\left(\frac{\beta_1{}'}{\beta_1{}''}\right)[(R_2 - {}_IR_n) + (R_2 - {}_{II}R_n)U]\right.$$

$$+ \frac{w}{(w + R_2)^2}\left(\frac{\beta_2{}'}{\beta_2{}''}\right)[(_IR_n - R_1) + (_{II}R_n - R_1)U]\right\} > 0$$

Consider, now, the leading cases. First, let ${}_IK^* = {}_IN_1{}^* = {}_IN_2{}^*$, and ${}_{II}K^* = {}_{II}N_1{}^* = {}_{II}N_2{}^*$, giving full-scale balanced growth in each country. Here, of course, ${}_Ik_1^{**} = {}_{II}k_1^{**} = 0$, and, in consequence, ${}_IR_n^{**} = {}_{II}R_n^{**} = 0$, so that s^{**} vanishes completely. Furthermore, (69) gives:

$$w^* = \frac{V(R_2 - R_1)U(_{II}R_n - {}_IR_n)(_{II}K^* - {}_IK^*)}{e_{cp} \cdot e_{pw} + e_{v_1w} + e_{v_2w}} \tag{71}$$

If, then, $_{II}K^* > {}_IK^*$ while $_{II}R > {}_IR$, w will rise, and (65) tells us that $_{II}r$ will fall relative to $_Ir$. Capital must flow to country I, the slower-growing country, in order to equalize the two countries' interest rates.[32] Put differently, full-scale balanced growth does not preclude capital movements unless it proceeds at the very same rate in the two countries.

Next, let $_IK^* > {}_IN_1^*$, let $_{II}K^* > {}_{II}N_1^*$, and let $_IN_1^* = {}_IN_2^* = {}_{II}N_1^* = {}_{II}N_2^*$ (an instance of net capital formation per worker but uniform growth in "natural endowments"). Here, $_Ik_1^{**} > 0$, $_{II}k_1^{**} > 0$, and $_{II}k_1^{**} - {}_Ik_1^{**} = {}_{II}K^* - {}_IK^*$ [see equation (54)], while $_IR_n^{**}$ takes its sign from $_IR - R_k$ and $_{II}R_n^{**}$ takes its sign from $_{II}R - R_k$ [see equation (60)]. Here, too:

$$w^* = \frac{V(R_2 - R_1)}{e_{cp} \cdot e_{pw} + e_{v_1 w} + e_{v_2 w}} \left\{ W\left[\frac{{}_IR_n \cdot {}_IR_n^{**}}{w + {}_IR_n} + \frac{{}_{II}R_n \cdot U \cdot {}_{II}R_n^{**}}{w + {}_{II}R_n} \right] \right.$$

$$\left. + U({}_{II}R_n - {}_IR_n)\left[\frac{\eta(vg - 1)}{vg - \eta} \right]({}_{II}K^* - {}_IK^*) \right\} \quad (72)$$

When, then, $_{II}K^* \gg {}_IK^*$ (so that $s^{**} < 0$), while $_{II}R > {}_IR \gg R_k$, w will rise, s_w^* will be negative, and capital must flow from country II to country I. Conversely, when $_{II}K^* < {}_IK^*$, while $R_k \gg {}_{II}R > {}_IR$, w will fall, s_w^* will be positive, and capital must flow from country I to country II. Notice, however, that, when $_{II}K^* > {}_IK^*$ while $R_I \gg {}_{II}R$, or when $_{II}K^* < {}_IK^*$ while $_IR \gg R_k$, the sign of the capital flow is thoroughly ambiguous. In the first of these two cases, s^{**} is negative; there will be a "primary" growth-induced flow from country II to country I. In the same case, however, $_IR_n^{**} < 0$ and $_{II}R_n^{**} < 0$, so that the signs of w^* and s_w^* are uncertain. In the second of these cases, s^{**} is positive; there will be a "primary" growth-induced flow from country I to country II. But $_IR_n^{**} \gg 0$ and $_{II}R_n^* > 0$, so that the signs of w^* and s_w^* are again uncertain.

Consider, now, the simplest case, one in which $_IK^* = {}_{II}K^*$ and there is no change in "natural endowments." Here, s^{**} is zero, as with full-scale balanced growth; there is no "primary" capital flow. When $_{II}R > {}_IR \gg R_k$, however, $_IR_n^{**} \gg 0$ and $_{II}R_n^{**} > 0$, so that w will rise, s_w^* will be negative, and capital must flow from country II to country I. When, instead, $R_k \gg {}_{II}R > {}_IR$, w will fall, s_w^* will be positive, and capital

---

[32] If, of course, $_IR > {}_{II}R$, w will fall, but s_w^* will still be negative and capital will still flow to the slower-growing country. If, finally, $_IR = {}_{II}R$, there will be no capital transfer despite the difference in growth rates.

must flow from country I to country II. When, finally $_{II}R > R_k > {}_IR$, the signs of w^* and s_w^* are uncertain; capital can flow in either direction, or may not flow at all.

This final case deserves a bit more attention, for one can show that wage-rate change must lead the system to this zone, and that, eventually, capital will cease to move. When $_IK^* = {}_{II}K^* = K^*$ and there is no change in "natural endowments," the sign of the change in the wage-rate ratio is given by:

$$\frac{_IR_n \cdot {}_IR_n^{**}}{w + {}_IR_n} + \frac{_{II}R_n \cdot U \cdot {}_{II}R_n^{**}}{w + {}_{II}R_n}$$

$$= U(1 - \eta)\left(\frac{w + {}_{II}R_n}{w + R_k}\right)\left(\frac{K}{Y}\right)\frac{Y + K}{Y} \, M \cdot K^* \quad (73)$$

where:

$$M = \left(\frac{_IR - R_k}{w + {}_IR}\right)\left(\frac{_IK}{{}_{II}K}\right) + \left(\frac{_{II}R - R_k}{w + {}_{II}R}\right) \quad (74)$$

But $_IR$ and $_{II}R$ decline when w^* is positive [see equation (48)], while R_k rises in the same circumstance [see equation (39)]. When, then, M is positive and w rises, M itself must fall; when M is negative and w falls, M itself must rise. With capital formation proceeding at the same rates in the two countries, the system will converge on product-market balanced growth and, once there, will stay there.

Distribution, Demand, and Equilibrium in International Trade: A Diagrammatic Analysis*

By PETER B. KENEN†

SOME TWENTY YEARS AGO, Professors Leontief and Lerner brought the community indifference map into common use in international trade theory.[1] Since then, however, economists have repeatedly observed that the community indifference map is an unsatisfactory tool of analysis because it is unstable. Whenever international prices change, each country's product-mix will change and its income distribution will be altered. In consequence, community indifference curves will change shape and position.[2]

Yet most treatises and texts on international trade still employ the community indifference map to depict equilibrium in the two-country, two-commodity case.[3] Though faulty, it has proved too convenient to be quickly discarded. It is nevertheless possible to adduce most of the important propositions in international trade theory without employing community indifference curves. In another article, I have reproduced the major welfare propositions of trade theory using a device which fixes the (ordinal) utility of all but one of the persons within a country and assigns the gains from trade or from optimal protection to the remaining

---

* *Kyklos,* Vol. XII (fasc. 4, 1959), pp. 629–38.

† Columbia University.

[1] Wassily W. Leontief, "The Use of Indifference Curves in the Analysis of Foreign Trade," *Quarterly Journal of Economics,* May, 1933, reprinted in *Readings in the Theory of International Trade* (Philadelphia, 1949); Abba P. Lerner, "The Diagrammatic Representation of Demand Conditions in International Trade," *Economica,* August, 1934, reprinted in his *Essays in Economic Analysis* (New York, 1953).

[2] See, e.g., Tibor De Scitovszky, "A Reconsideration of the Theory of Tariffs," *Review of Economic Studies,* Summer, 1942, reprinted in *Readings, loc. cit.;* and Paul A. Samuelson, "Social Indifference Curves," *Quarterly Journal of Economics,* February, 1956.

[3] See, e.g., James E. Meade, *A Geometry of International Trade* (London, 1952); Donald B. Marsh, *World Trade and Investment* (New York, 1951); and Charles P. Kindleberger, *International Economics* (Homewood, 1958).

person.[4] Here, I set out a second diagrammatic method which takes explicit account of variations in the distribution of income and traces their impact upon the pattern of international trade.

I

We shall deal with two commodities, cloth and steel, and two factors of production, labor and capital. We assume throughout that pure competition prevails in all markets, that the supplies of labor and capital are fixed and fully employed, and that production functions are linear and homogeneous. We assume at the outset that all workers have equal incomes and identical indifference maps and that all capitalists have equal incomes and identical indifference maps.

We begin our argument with the production transformation curve *BLA* in the northwest quadrant of Figure 1. That schedule describes the combinations of cloth and steel that can be produced and the ratio of steel to cloth prices at which each combination will be forthcoming. If, for example, the ratio of steel to cloth prices equals the slope of the line *CLD* and, therefore, the slope of *BLA* at *L*, *LM* ($= OH$) units of steel and *LH* ($= OM$) units of cloth will be produced. The national income measured in units of steel will be *OC*:

$$\text{National income} = \text{Steel output} \times \text{Price of steel}$$
$$+ \text{Cloth output} \times \text{Price of cloth}$$
$$= OH \times \text{Price of steel} + HL \times \text{Price of cloth}.$$

Hence:

$$\frac{\text{National income}}{\text{Price of steel}} = OH + HL \times \frac{\text{Price of cloth}}{\text{Price of steel}}.$$
$$= OH + HC = OC.$$

We next consider the rectangle *OEFG* in the southwest quadrant of Figure 1. That construction is the Stolper-Samuelson box.[5] It describes the supplies of capital (*OG* or *EF*) and of labor (*OE* or *FG*) available for the production of steel and cloth and the ways in which they may be combined. If *OW* units of capital and *WJ* ($= GK$) units of labor are used to produce steel, *WG* ($- JK$) units of capital and *KF* units of labor are available to produce cloth. The steel output corresponding to this combination of inputs is that associated with the steel isoquant a_s, defined relative to the axes *OE* and *OG*, passing through *J*. The cloth output corresponding to this combination of inputs is that associated with the cloth isoquant a_c, defined relative to the axes *FG* and *FE*, passing through

[4] "On the Geometry of Welfare Economics," *Quarterly Journal of Economics,* August, 1957.

[5] Wolfgang Stolper and Paul A. Samuelson, "Protection and Real Wages," *Review of Economic Studies,* November, 1941, reprinted in *Readings, loc. cit.*

J. As these isoquants are tangent at J, the combination of inputs just described is "efficient"; steel output cannot be increased (decreased) without decreasing (increasing) cloth output.

The point J, therefore, is the counterpart of some point on the production transformation curve BLA. To locate its counterpart we first observe that steel production at F corresponds to steel production at B (OB units), for at F all of the labor and capital available are employed in the steel industry making steel output a maximum and cloth output zero. We next observe that a movement along FIO from F toward O reduces steel output in proportion to the distance travelled from F, for our production functions evince constant returns to scale. If, then, the distance OF denotes a steel output of OB units, the distance OI denotes a steel output of OH, for OFB and OIH are similar triangles. Now the isoquant a_s passes through I and J. At J, therefore, steel output is OH units. At J, furthermore, cloth output is at a maximum given steel output. Hence production at J implies a cloth output of HL units, the largest compatible with a steel output of OH, and corresponds to production at L on BLA.

Now let us recall that production at J implies a unique ratio of wage rates to rates of return on capital; the ratio of wage rates to the return on capital must equal the slope of a_c at J. If, then, we construct at F the line FN having a slope equal to that of a_c at J, we may measure the wage bill (the total of labor income) in units of capital. It is GN. Concomitantly, the national income measured in units of capital is ON, leaving OG as the share of capitalists in the national income. This proposition can be quickly proved:

$$\text{National income} = \text{Labor force} \times \text{Wage rate}$$
$$+ \text{ Capital stock} \times \text{Return on capital}$$
$$= FG \times \text{Wage rate} + OG \times \text{Return on capital.}$$

Hence:

$$\frac{\text{National income}}{\text{Return on capital}} = FG \times \frac{\text{Wage rate}}{\text{Return on capital}} + OG$$
$$= GN + OG = ON.$$

Suppose, now, that the international rate of exchange of steel for cloth (the system of international prices) *were* given by the slope of CLD. Then OH of steel and OM of cloth *would be* produced in the country we are examining and the national income of that country measured in units of steel would be OC. The ratio of wage rates to the return on capital would equal the slope of FN, the wage bill in units of capital would be GN, the income of capitalists OG, and the national income ON.

Let us mark off on the abscissa of our diagram a distance OC' equal to OC, drop perpendiculars from C' and from N through P, and draw the diagonal OP. As OGQ and ONP are similar triangles, $OG/ON =$

GQ/NP. $GQ (= OR)$ is therefore the income of capitalists measured in units of steel and RC' is the income of labor. We now construct the indifference map of the capitalists relative to the axes OC' and OS and the capitalists' budget restraint RS. The latter is, of course, a line of identical slope to that of CLD. The capitalists' equilibrium position is the point T, where an indifference curve Ω_c is tangent to RS. The capitalists will consume VT $(= OU)$ units of cloth and UT $(= OV)$ units of steel.

Extending the lines QR and UT until they meet in O', we draw the workers' indifference map relative to the axes $O'R'$ and $O'S'$ and their budget restraint $R'S'$. The workers' equilibrium position is at T, where the indifference curve Ω_L is tangent to $R'S'$. The workers will consume $V'T'$ $(= O'U')$ units of cloth and $U'T'$ $(= O'V')$ units of steel.

Clearly, the aggregate consumption of cloth is $OU + O'U'$ or OY $(= ZX)$. In that case, however, aggregate consumption of steel, $OV + O'V'$, must equal XY $(= OZ)$. This may be easily demonstrated:

Labor income   = Workers' steel consumption × Price of steel
                      + Workers' cloth consumption × Price of cloth
                      = $O'V'$ × Price of steel + $O'U'$ × Price of cloth.

And:

Capitalists' income = Capitalists' steel consumption × Price of steel
                      + Capitalists' cloth consumption × Price of cloth
                    = OV × Price of steel + OU × Price of cloth.

But:

National income   = Labor income + Capitalists' income
                      = $(O'V' + OV)$ × Price of steel
                      + $(O'U' + OU)$ × Price of cloth.

Hence:

$$\frac{\text{National income}}{\text{Price of steel}} = (O'V' + OV) + XZ \times \frac{\text{Price of cloth}}{\text{Price of steel}}$$
$$CO = (O'V' + OV) + CZ$$
$$CO - CZ = O'V' + OV) = ZO.$$

Our country, then, produces at L and trades at X; it imports MY units of cloth and exports HZ units of steel.

II

Our diagram may be used to illustrate a number of important propositions in the theory of international trade.

First, it indicates that factor proportions do not measure factor scarcity. The capital-to-labor ratio, OG/OE, may be smaller than in other countries, yet cloth—the imported commodity—uses capital less intensively than steel; $JK/KF < OW/WJ$. The "scarce factor" explana-

FIGURE 1

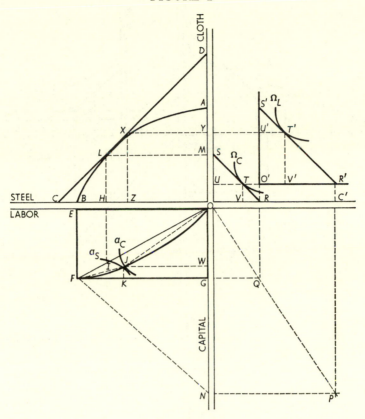

FIGURE 2

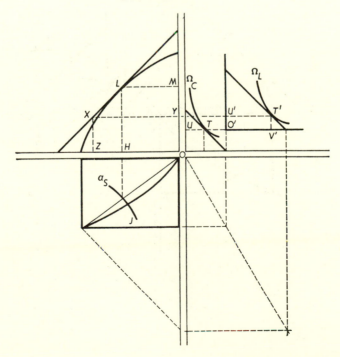

FIGURE 3

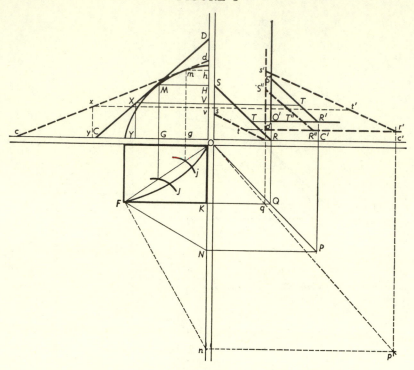

FIGURE 4

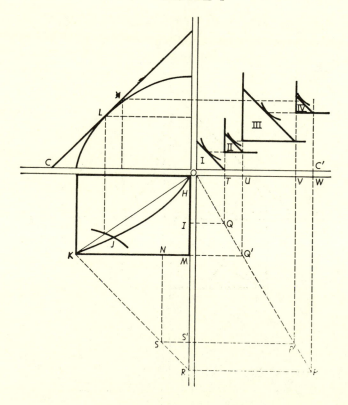

tion of specialization, then, must either be abandoned or so much modified as to render it tautological. Scarcity can only be interpreted in the light of demand conditions.[6]

Our second objective is closely akin to the first. It is to stress the role of demand and distribution in ordering the pattern of international specialization. Suppose that the systems of indifference curves in Figure 1 were transposed; suppose that workers strongly preferred steel to cloth and capitalists strongly preferred cloth to steel. Under these circumstances our solution would be that described in Figure 2. That diagram differs from Figure 1 only with respect to the character of the indifference maps. The transposition of the indifference systems, however, has reversed the pattern of specialization. As workers evince a strong preference for steel over cloth, $O'V'$ is longer, and $O'U'$ shorter, than in Figure 1. And as capitalists evince a strong preference for cloth over steel, OV is shorter, and OU longer, than in Figure 1. But workers in our example have larger incomes than capitalists, so the increase of $O'V'$ exceeds the decrease of OV, and the decrease of $O'U'$ swamps the increase of OU. OY $(= OU + O'U')$ is consequently smaller than in Figure 1 and less than OM, while OZ $(= OV + O'V')$ is larger than in Figure 1 and greater than OH. Our country now imports ZH of steel and exports MY of cloth.

Our final exercise involves a change in the terms of trade. It is generally supposed that an improvement in the terms of trade (an increase of export prices relative to import prices) augments economic welfare. It is of course possible to prove that such an improvement *makes possible* an increase of welfare, for the losers can be compensated. Our diagram, however, allows us to illustrate circumstances in which improved terms of trade seriously injure one group in the community. In Figure 3 we have assumed trade to take place at X and production at M; HV units of cloth are exported and GY units of steel are imported. To production at M there corresponds the point J on $FJjO$ and the ratio KN/FK of wage rates to returns on capital. The income of capitalists expressed in units of steel is OR, and their equilibrium position is at T. The incomes of workers expressed in steel is RC' $(= R'O')$, and their equilibrium position is at T'.

We now suppose that the price of steel decreases, causing the international ratio of exchange to shift from CD to cd. Cloth output increases and steel output decreases, bringing production from M to m and from J to j. At j, the factor price ratio favors labor, causing labor's share of the national income to rise from KN/ON to Kn/On. Marking off a distance

6 This point has recently been made by R. W. Jones ("Factor Proportions and the Heckscher-Ohlin Theorem," *Review of Economic Studies*, 1956/57, pp. 1–10), and by Kelvin Lancaster ("Protection and Real Wages: A Restatement," *Economic Journal*, June 1957, pp. 200–210). The implications of this analysis for the Leontief scarce-factor paradox are thoroughly explored in those articles.

$c'O$ equal to cO on the abscissa of our diagram and dropping perpendiculars from c' and n we produce the point p and the diagonal Op in place of OP. Note that the angle pOn is smaller than the angle PON. This can be established using our national income identities:

$$On \times \text{Return on capital} = Oc' \times \text{Price of steel}.$$

Hence:

$$Oc'/On \; (= np/On) = \frac{\text{Return on capital}}{\text{Price of steel}}.$$

But the ratio return on capital/price of steel is the marginal product of capital in steel production which has declined with the change in production from J to j. The ratio np/On, therefore, must be smaller than the ratio NP/ON, and the angle pOn must be smaller than the angle PON.

As a result of the change in international prices, production and factor returns, the income of capitalists expressed in steel is reduced from OR to Or. At the same time, the budget line has diminished in slope to reflect the change in commodity prices. The equilibrium position for capitalists is consequently removed from T to some such point as t, a distinctly inferior position.

But the income of labor expressed in steel has risen from RC' to rc', and the axes for labor's indifference map—$O'R'$ and $O'S'$—have been replaced by $o'r'$ and $o's'$. Labor's equilibrium position is therefore changed from T' to t'. Aggregate demand for cloth decreases from $OV \; (= YX)$ to $Ov \; (= yx)$, increasing exports of cloth to vh and imports of steel to gy.

Labor has clearly gained by the change in the terms of trade. This may be confirmed by transferring the initial budget line, $R'S'$ to the new axes $o'r'$ and $o's'$. The initial equilibrium position of labor, T'', on that budget line, $R''S''$, obviously falls on a lower indifference curve than the new equilibrium position, t', on the budget line $r's'$.

III

At the beginning of this discussion we assumed "that all workers have equal incomes and identical indifference maps and that all capitalists have equal incomes and identical indifference maps." We can now relax that assumption. Let us suppose that OI capitalists in Figure 4 have one set of indifference maps and IM have a different set, and that KN of the labor force have one set of indifference maps and NM another. Beginning with production at L and J and with a ratio of factor returns equal to MR/KM, we may divide the national income measured in units of capital into four parts: OI, IM, MS' and $S'R$. That MS' and $S'R$ stand in the same relation to MR as do KN and NM to KM can easily be established, for KSN and SRS' are similar triangles. We may then proceed as in Figure 1. Dropping perpendiculars from OR to the diagonal OP we locate the points Q, Q', and P', mark off the incomes of each group of persons on the axis OC', and construct the indifference maps pertaining to each group. The first group of capitalists, OI, receives an income equal to OT units of steel and operates on the indifference map I. The second group of capitalists, IM, receives an income equal to TU units of steel and operates on the indifference map II. The first group of workers, KN, receives an income equal to UV units of steel and operates on the indifference map III. And the second group of workers receives an income equal to VW units of steel and operates on the indifference map IV. The position of each indifference map depends, of course, upon the equilibrium position of the preceding group. Adding up the cloth consumption of our four groups, we secure the trading point X.

The procedure just described might be extended to treat differences in income among persons. If, for instance, the stock of capital OI were divided among three persons, one of them owning OH units, the others sharing HI equally, we could treat OH and HI as separate groups. We should, in fact, have to do so. Though the indifference maps of the three persons are identical (they all belong to the group OI), the person owning OH units might purchase steel and cloth in different proportions than the persons sharing HI units. The three persons owning OI units of capital could be treated as a single group for purposes of demand analysis only if their individual indifference maps evinced unit elasticity of demand for cloth and steel.

Finally, the diagram used in this discussion can also be employed to construct an offer curve. Were we to alter slightly the international ratio of exchange, CLD, in Figure 1 we would generate a new production point, L, and a new trading point, X. Repeating this process, we would eventually secure a schedule showing the amounts of cloth and steel that would be traded at various sets of prices. This schedule *is* an offer curve.

ON THE GEOMETRY OF WELFARE ECONOMICS*

A Suggested Diagrammatic Treatment
of Some Basic Propositions

By Peter B. Kenen

I

This essay comprises four sections. In the first, we point out that the familiar Bowley-Edgeworth box diagram which suffices to describe an exchange equilibrium cannot be used to describe an equilibrium involving production. In the second, we construct a modified box diagram that allows a complete and explicit treatment of the welfare implications of changes in production. In the third, we relate our modified box diagram to some recent work in welfare economics. And in the fourth, we apply our modified box diagram to the analysis of certain propositions in the theory of international trade.

By means of the traditional Bowley-Edgeworth diagram we are able to identify the family of efficient income distributions — distributions of two commodities, fixed in total supply, between two persons or groups of persons. The line $O_I O_{II}$ in Figure I is the locus of these efficient distributions, the contract curve. Choosing a point on the production transformation curve $Y_0 X_0$, we have dropped perpendiculars to both axes of the diagram, measuring off the fixed amounts $O_I X$ of commodity X and $O_I Y$ of commodity Y. In the rectangle $O_I X O_{II} Y$ we have drawn two sets of indifference curves: those of Person (or Group) One, relative to the origin O_I, and those

* I am grateful to Professors Gottfried Haberler, Wassily Leontief and Robert Baldwin and to Messrs. Egon Neuberger and Herbert Levine who have read early drafts of the present paper and provided invaluable criticism. I would also thank Professor Robert Dorfman who assisted with the proofs presented in the mathematical appendix. Naturally, none of those mentioned bears any responsibility for my conclusions or for the errors which may remain. This paper was written during my residence at Harvard University in 1955–56, made possible by a generous grant from the Earhart Foundation.

of Person (or Group) Two, relative to the origin O_{II}. The contract curve $O_I O_{II}$ is the locus of points of tangency between the indifference curves of Person One and of Person Two.

A movement from one to another of the points on the contract curve must make one person better off at the expense of the other. A movement from A to C will transfer Person One from the indifference

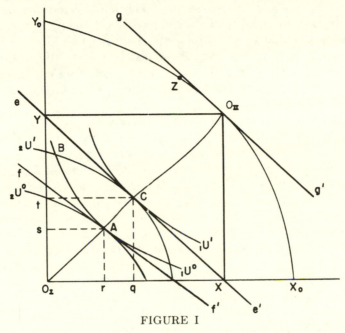

FIGURE I

curve $_1U^0$ to the higher curve $_1U^1$ and will force Person Two from $_2U^0$ to the lower curve $_2U^1$. To move from A to C we would transfer from Person Two to Person One rq of commodity X and st of commodity Y. At A, Person One requires $O_I r$ of X and $O_I s$ of Y, leaving rX of X and sY of Y to Person Two; at C, Person One requires $O_I q$ of X and $O_I t$ of Y, leaving qX of X and tY of Y to Person Two.

Concomitantly, a movement from some point like B, off the contract curve, to a point on the contract curve could make one person better off without harming the other, or might make both persons better off. At B, Person One is on the indifference curve $_1U^0$ and Person Two on the indifference curve $_2U^1$. Moving from B to A, we could make Person Two better off without harming Person One. Moving from B to C, we could make Person One better off without harming Person Two. Or moving from B to a point between A and C, we could make both better off.

These remarks imply still a third characteristic of the contract curve $O_I O_{II}$. If we wish to increase the utility of one of our two persons but are initially on the contract curve, we should move to another point on the contract curve. This way, we will provide the desired increase in one person's utility at a minimum of (psychic) cost to the second person.

Note, finally, that the familiar condition of purely competitive equilibrium, the equality of the commodity price ratio, p_x/p_y, to the consumers' marginal rates of substitution, assigns to each point on the contract curve a unique set of relative prices. If an observed equilibrium is to occur at C, p_x/p_y must equal the slope of the line ee'; if the observed equilibrium is to occur at A, p_x/p_y must equal the slope of the line ff'.

Much of modern welfare economics has drawn on these and other properties of the box diagram.[1] But the construction cannot be applied to many of the most interesting problems in welfare economics because it takes no account of the conditions required for an equilibrium in production. If those conditions are to be fulfilled, the great majority of the points on a Bowley-Edgeworth contract curve can never be realized. By way of illustration, assume that we are in full equilibrium at point C but want to move to point A. The instant we leave point C, the shape of the box $O_I X O_{II} Y$ will begin to change, so that A will disappear.[2] The cause of this change in the shape of the box diagram is the necessary condition for equilibrium in production that the commodity price ratio equal the marginal rate of transformation, the slope of the production transformation curve $Y_0 X_0$. Full equilibrium at C requires that the lines ee' and gg' must have the same slopes; p_x/p_y must at once equal the slopes of $_1 U^1$ and $_2 U^1$ at C and the slope of $Y_0 X_0$ at O_{II}. In order to move from C to A, we must reduce the price ratio p_x/p_y until it is equal to the slope of ff'. But as ff' is less steep than gg', the corner of the box, O_{II}, would have to move northwest along $Y_0 X_0$, say to Z, until the slope of $Y_0 X_0$ were equal to ff'. The dimensions of the box must change.[3]

The lines ee' and ff' might, of course, have the same slopes, a box

1. Cf., e.g., Tibor de Scitovsky, "A Note on Welfare Propositions in Economics," *Review of Economic Studies*, IX(1) (Nov. 1941), and Kenneth E. Boulding, "Welfare Economics" in *A Survey of Contemporary Economics*, Vol. II, ed. B. Haley (Richard D. Irwin Inc., 1952).

2. A similar point is made by Paul A. Samuelson in his article on "The Evaluation of Real National Income," *Oxford Economic Papers*, N.S., II (Jan. 1950), 16.

3. This argument abstracts from the effect of the changed distribution of income upon the supplies of factors of production. Throughout this essay we assume that the factors of production are fixed in total supply.

of dimensions $O_I X$ and $O_{II} Y$ being, then, consistent with several exchange equilibria on the contract curve $O_I O_{II}$. But such special cases do not vitiate the force of our general observation. When the analyses of production and consumption are joined, the traditional box diagram is deprived of significance, since the slightest movement

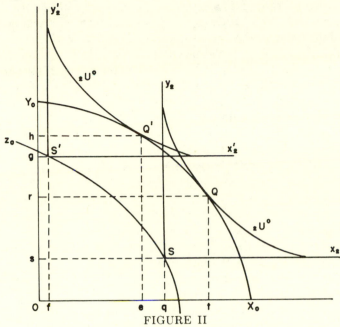

FIGURE II

along the contract curve generally causes the box to change shape and the contract curve to dissolve.

II

In place of the Bowley-Edgeworth box diagram we shall now derive a diagram combining equilibrium in production with equilibrium in exchange. To this end, we shall assume that: (1) the economy is purely competitive; (2) the supplies of the factors of production are fixed; (3) all commodities are produced under conditions of constant or increasing cost so that the production transformation curve will itself evince increasing (opportunity) costs; and (4) each person's (ordinal) utility index is unaffected by the amounts of goods consumed by the other person.

Consider, now, the production transformation curve $Y_0 X_0$ of Figure II, of negative slope throughout and, pursuant to our third assumption, concave to the origin O. We begin by fixing Person Two on one of his indifference curves, $_2U^0$, which is drawn relative to the axes Sy_2 and Sx_2 and which we have superimposed on Y_0X_0 with its axes parallel to OX_0 and OY_0, and tangent to Y_0X_0 at Q. This construction equates the marginal rate of transformation to Person Two's marginal rate of substitution. If, therefore, these are equal to the commodity price ratio, p_x/p_y, Ot of X and Or of Y will be produced and Person Two will consume qt of X and sr of Y. sS ($= Oq$) of X and qS ($= Os$) of Y will be left to Person One.

If, now, we displace $_2U^0$ to another point on Y_0X_0, keeping it tangent to Y_0X_0 and its axes parallel to OX_0 and OY_0, we will generate a new point which, like S, indicates the amounts of X and Y remaining for Person One to consume. When, for example, $_2U^0$ is tangent to Y_0X_0 at Q', Oe of X and Oh of Y will be produced and Person Two will consume fe of X and gh of Y. Person One will be left with gS' ($= Of$) of X and fS' ($= Og$) of Y.

We can, in short, generate a curve, z_0, which we will call Person One's *availability locus*. This curve will be of negative slope throughout, concave to the axis OX_0 and, *at each point such as* S *and* S', *of slope equal to that of* Y_0X_0 *at the corresponding points* Q *and* Q'.[4] This last property of the *availability locus* is a happy one. It means that the curve z_0 describes both the amounts of X and Y which are left to Person One and the price ratio at which they will be available. The price ratio is, of course, the slope of z_0.

We shall soon see that this property of the *availability locus* permits Person One to equate his marginal rate of substitution — the slope of one of his indifference curves defined relative to OX_0 and OY_0 — to the price ratio p_x/p_y, by ascending his preference map until one of his indifference curves is tangent to z_0. But first let us note that as Sx_2 and Sy_2 are displaced along Y_0X_0, the point S will eventually cross OY_0 or, in the other direction, OX_0. In either circumstance, Person Two's demand for some commodity, Y or X, will exceed the amount being produced. In a closed economy, therefore, the *availability locus* can be meaningfully defined only in the quadrant bounded by OX_0 and OY_0. But later on, when we admit of the possibility of trade with an outside world, we will have cause to consider the segments of z_0 lying south of OX_0 and west of OY_0.

4. A simple geometric proof of the equality of slopes for a curve perfectly analogous to z_0 is given by J. E. Meade (*A Geometry of International Trade*, Allen and Unwin, 1953, pp. 13–14). Professor Meade generates his trade indifference curves by passing a transformation curve along an indifference curve in the same way we have passed an indifference curve along a transformation curve. An algebraic proof of this theorem is given in the mathematical appendix to this paper.

Finally, observe that we may define a family of *availability loci*. By placing Person Two on a lower indifference curve and following the procedure just described, we can generate a new *availability locus*. Because Person Two's indifference curves do not cross, successive *availability loci* will not cross; the new one will lie uniformly to the northeast of z_0. In the limiting case where Person Two is allowed no X and no Y, the *availability locus* will coincide with the production transformation curve $Y_0 X_0$.

Let us then draw a family of *availability loci* in a new diagram, Figure III, numbering them to reflect the direction of change in

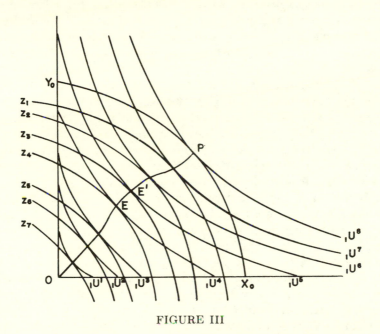

FIGURE III

Person Two's welfare; curves of higher number correspond to increases in Person Two's utility. Further, let us define, relative to the origin O, a system of indifference curves for Person One, $_1U^1$ through $_1U^8$. We have already observed that Person One will maximize his real income by moving to that point at which the particular *availability locus* confronting him is tangent to one of his indifference curves. If, for example, Person Two's utility has been so fixed as to confront Person One with z_4, he will move to the point E where $_1U^4$ is tangent to z_4; if, instead, he faces z_3, he will move to E' where $_1U^5$ is tangent to z_3. Points such as E and E' are fully efficient in the Paretian sense; each marginal rate of substitution will equal the marginal rate of transformation and the price ratio p_x/p_y.[5] But there will be formed a set of these Pareto optima, each member of the set corresponding to a different level of Person Two's utility. The line OP which traces out this set we shall call the modified or Paretian contract curve, Figure III itself being the modified box diagram which we proposed to provide.

The reader may quickly satisfy himself that OP shares with the Edgeworth contract curve the properties which we have ascribed to the latter. A movement along the curve must increase the welfare of one person at the expense of the second. A movement from a point off the curve to a point on the curve could increase the utility of one person without harming the second, or could increase the utility of both. And a movement along the curve is the most economical way to increase one person's utility because it minimizes the other person's loss.

There is one difficulty involved in this construction. Whereas, from the Edgeworth box diagram, we may read off the consumption of both persons, the modified box diagram of Figure III tells us the consumption of only one. To determine how much of the commodities X and Y Person Two receives in a particular situation we have first to find out how much of X and Y are being produced. We must measure the slope of the indifference curves at the chosen position of equilibrium and locate that point on the production transformation curve Y_0X_0 of Figure III which has the same slope. From that point we must drop perpendiculars to the axes of the diagram to measure off the total outputs of X and Y. Subtracting from the totals the consumption of Person One, we then emerge with the amounts available to Person Two. But as partial compensation for this cumbersome feature, the modified box diagram has the advantage over the Edgeworth construction that it may be readily extended to an n-person economy. Fixing n-minus-one of the consumers on indifference curves, we can successively subtract from the production transformation curve the amounts that they would consume at each set of relative prices, just as we subtracted Person Two's consumption from Y_0X_0 in Figure II. In this way, we can derive an *availability locus* for the *nth* person that takes account of the aggregate demand of all the other consumers.[6]

5. As we have assumed that the factors of production are fixed in supply, we neglect here the set of equilibrium conditions that must hold in the factor markets. But certain of these are implied in the usual construction of the production transformation curve. (*Vide*, e.g., Wolfgang Stolper and Paul A. Samuelson, "Protection and Real Wages," *Review of Economic Studies*, IX (Nov. 1941), 66.)

6. But, like the community indifference curves of the sort Scitovsky constructs, the members of a family of n-person *availability loci* can cross each other.

But there is a more fundamental difference between the Edgeworth and Paretian box diagrams. Each point on OP involves a simultaneous and consistent equilibrium in production and exchange; at each point on the Paretian contract curve, all of the marginal rates of substitution are equal, not only to the price ratio p_x/p_y, but also to the marginal rate of transformation. The Paretian contract curve takes into account the changes in production that are neglected by — and destructive of — the Edgeworth construction. We can move along it without causing it to dissolve.

III

Among the most powerful and ingenious of the welfare economist's tools is the situation utility-possibility curve devised by Professor Samuelson.[7] The situation utility-possibility curve is "a frontier curve or envelope giving, for each amount of one person's utility, the maximum possible amount of the other person's utility."[8]

The derivation of the situation utility-possibility curve is straightforward. Returning to Figure I, we select some point on the production transformation curve Y_0X_0, say O_{II}, form the box $O_I XO_{II} Y$, and derive the Edgeworth contract curve $O_I O_{II}$. Now to each point on that contract curve there corresponds a pair of values $_1U^i$ and $_2U^i$, of the utility indices of Persons One and Two. To the contract curve itself, therefore, must correspond some curve in the utility space of Figure IV, say abc. Samuelson has christened this curve the *point* utility-possibility curve because it describes the set of potential income distributions that may be generated by a box of fixed size, by the point O_{II} of Figure I.

The precise slope and position of the point utility-possibility curve depend, of course, upon the manner in which we choose to measure the utility of each consumer. And the calibration of an ordinal utility index is, by definition, arbitrary. But the slope of the point utility-possibility curve must always be negative, simply because a movement along the Edgeworth contract curve entails an increase

There are an infinite number of ways in which the utilities of the first n-minus-one persons can be altered to generate a second *availability locus*. (Cf. Tibor de Scitovsky, "A Reconsideration of the Theory of Tariffs," *Review of Economic Studies*, IX (Summer, 1942), and Paul A. Samuelson, "Social Indifference Curves," this *Journal* LXX (Feb. 1956). 4–8.)

7. Samuelson, "Evaluation of Real National Income," *loc. cit.;* also his *Foundations of Economic Analysis*, pp. 244–48, and J. de V. Graaf, "On Optimum Tariff Structures," *Review of Economic Studies*, XVII (1949–50), 47–50, on which I have drawn heavily.

8. Samuelson, "Evaluation of Real National Income," *op. cit.*, p. 6.

in the utility of one consumer at the expense of the second consumer.[9]

To every point on Y_0X_0 in Figure I, there corresponds a similar point utility-possibility curve as, to each, there corresponds a box that produces an Edgeworth contract curve. Let us, then, choose some point on the horizontal axis of Figure IV and move due north through the family of point utility-possibility curves *abc*, *def*, etc., that are generated by the transformation curve Y_0X_0. We must eventually come to a stop; we shall reach that point utility-possibility curve which lies at the greatest perpendicular distance from our start-

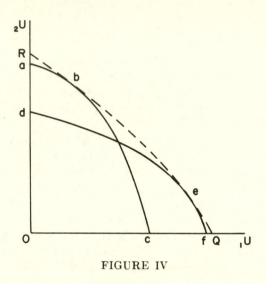

FIGURE IV

ing point. At this frontier we will be touching the *situation* utility-possibility curve that is generated by Y_0X_0 of Figure I, and by repeating this procedure at each point along the abscissa of Figure IV we could trace out the entire situation utility-possibility curve *RQ* of Figure IV. But we can reach the same result more directly: the *situation* utility-possibility curve is simply the envelope formed by the family of *point* utility-possibility curves.

Each point on the situation utility-possibility curve at once involves a particular collection of the commodities X and Y and a particular distribution of these commodities between Persons One and Two. The point b, for example, is attained by producing O_IX of commodity X and O_IY of commodity Y (Figure I) and distributing them uniquely between the two consumers. We have seen, however,

9. An algebraic demonstration of this same point is given by Graaf, *op. cit.*, p. 59.

that of the multitude of possible distributions of a given collection of goods, only a small subset are consistent with full equilibrium; at only a few of the points on $O_I O_{II}$ is the price ratio equal to the slope of gg'. If, then, the situation utility-possibility curve is to describe a set of feasible income distributions, the point b on RQ must belong to that subset.

Fortunately, the consumers' marginal rates of substitution, equal to each other at every point on abc, are equal at b to that marginal rate of transformation which is required to call forth $O_I X$ of commodity X and $O_I Y$ of commodity Y. The price ratio at b will equal the slope of gg' so that the point b will belong to the required subset and the situation utility-possibility curve *will* describe a set of feasible equilibria. In the mathematical appendix to this paper we offer a rigorous proof of this proposition. But those readers who are familiar with Paretian general equilibrium theory should find our assertion intuitively acceptable.[1] The situation utility-possibility curve describes the maximum of utility which can be attained by one person when the utility of the other is fixed. Given the value of all but one consumer's utility, however, a purely competitive system will maximize the utility of the remaining consumer. Whence purely competitive behavior, involving precisely those equalities between the marginal rates of substitution and of transformation which are required if RQ is to be a locus of feasible equilibria, yields exactly that result described by the situation utility-possibility curve.

The argument of the preceding paragraphs suggests a close connection between the situation utility-possibility curve and the Paretian contract curve of Figure III. For the contract curve is also a locus of constrained maxima. It is derived by fixing Person Two on one of his indifference curves, confronting Person One with the set of consumption possibilities which are then available to him and allowing him to maximize his utility. The situation utility-possibility curve and the Paretian contract curve, then, are but two ways of describing the same set of Paretian optima, the situation utility-possibility curve being the translation into a utility-space of the contract curve OP of Figure III, just as the point utility-possibility curve was the translation into that same utility-space of the Edgeworth contract curve $O_I O_{II}$ of Figure I.[2]

1. For an admirable description of Pareto's argument and results, cf. Nancy Ruggles, "The Welfare Basis of the Marginal Cost Pricing Principle,"*Review of Economic Studies*, XVII (1949–50), 33–34, and Samuelson, *Foundations, op. cit.*, pp. 212–14.
2. Note, however, that though the situation utility-possibility curve can be derived directly from the Paretian contract curve, the procedure cannot be

This point-to-point correspondence between the situation utility-possibility curve and the Paretian contract curve endows the latter with considerable significance. By examining the Paretian contract curve we may determine the impact upon potential economic welfare of changes in the commodity collection available to the community. This is because a uniform outward (northeast) shift of the situation utility-possibility curve permits an increase in the community's potential economic welfare; it allows an increase in one consumer's utility without injury to the second consumer, satisfying the familiar compensation criterion.[3] More important, such a shift permits improvement in an index of social welfare.[4] But because we can determine the effect of a change in the transformation curve upon the Paretian contract curve, and because we can derive the situation utility-possibility curve from the Paretian contract curve, we can apply the contract curve to the solution of problems in welfare economics. We can determine the impact of changes in factor supplies, in productivity or in other circumstances, upon the situation utility-possibility curve.

By way of illustration, consider the two panels of Figure V. In both we have drawn an *availability locus*, zz', and the Paretian contract curve, OP, which marks the tangencies of the family of curves zz' with Person One's indifference curves. To each panel we have added a second *availability locus*, ww', which we assume to be generated by the same indifference curve as was zz' but by an altered transformation curve. The curves zz' and ww', then, allow Person Two the same order of satisfaction. In both panels, zz' and ww' have been drawn so as to intersect, and the line OK has been added to map the set of points of intersection. That region over which ww' is to the northeast of zz' we have called Region I and that region over which zz' is to the northeast of ww' we have called Region II. The locus of intersections, OK, forms the boundary between Regions I and II.

Figure Va has been constructed to illustrate the *sole sufficient condition* for an unambiguous increase in potential welfare. The Paretian contract curve belonging to the initial situation, OP, has been drawn so as to fall entirely in Region I. The reader can easily see that when zz' is replaced with ww' (when the production trans-

reversed. The Paretian contract curve supplies more information than the situation utility-possibility curve.

3. *Vide*, e.g., Scitovsky, "A Note on Welfare Propositions in Economics," *loc. cit.*; also his "A Reconsideration of the Theory of Tariffs," *op. cit.*, pp. 91–92.

4. Provided, of course, the individual's utility indices are made to count in the social welfare function. (Cf. Samuelson, *Foundations, op. cit.*, pp. 243 *et seq.* and F. M. Fisher, "Income Distribution, Value Judgments and Welfare," this *Journal*, LXX (Aug. 1956), 381.)

formation curve shifts), Person One can immediately climb to a higher indifference curve than he had attained facing zz'. Where zz' and OP intersect, one of Person One's indifference curves must be tangent to zz'. But because that indifference curve is convex to the origin, it must intersect ww' to the southeast and northwest of its point of tangency with zz' and within Region I. There must then be some higher indifference curve tangent to ww' within Region I, say at A, so that with Person Two's utility fixed, Person One will gain by the

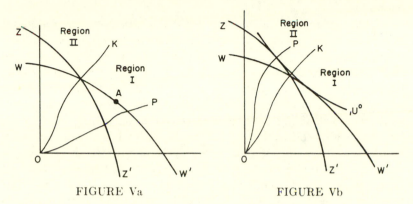

FIGURE Va   FIGURE Vb

change from zz' to ww'. Moreover, as OP has been drawn *entirely* within Region I, a similar increase in Person One's utility could occur for each value of Person Two's utility index. Hence the situation utility-possibility curve that corresponds to the family of *availability loci* ww' will lie entirely outside that generated by the family zz' and the change in the production transformation curve that replaced zz' with ww' will have provided an increase in potential economic welfare. (The situation utility-possibility curve corresponding to the initial transformation curve and the family zz' is, of course, the translation into a utility-space of the initial contract curve, OP, while that corresponding to the altered transformation curve and the family ww' is the translation of the set of points A.)

But the arrangement pictured in Figure Va is not a *necessary* condition for an increase in welfare. Consider Figure Vb. In this diagram the Paretian contract curve has been drawn through Region II. But the indifference curve $_1U^0$, tangent to zz' where the latter intersects OP, is not sharply curved and dips below ww'.* Under these circumstances and provided that they are repeated for all equivalent pairs of *availability loci* zz' and ww', the situation utility-possibility

* Erratum: it is not so drawn in Figure Vb. This error in the drawing was discovered too late to be corrected.

curve that pertains to the family ww' will once more lie entirely outside that pertaining to the family zz'.

Joining our analyses of Figures Va and Vb, we may say that an unambiguous increase in potential economic welfare *will* occur if the Paretian contract curve of the initial situation, OP, lies entirely within Region I, that region of the modified box diagram over which the initial *availability loci* are to the southwest of the altered *availability loci*, but that an increase *might* occur were OP in the opposite region.

This theorem is much more general than that formulated by Samuelson. He confines himself to the proposition that "If the production-possibility function of one situation lies uniformly outside that of a second situation, then the utility-possibility function of the one will also be outside that of the other."[5] This statement is correct; when the production transformation curve is shifted uniformly outward, the *availability locus* generated by a particular indifference curve will also shift out and the curves zz' and ww' will not cross. Samuelson's formulation, then, relates to a special case of the arrangement illustrated in Figure Va; we have only to imagine that Region I is coextensive with the quadrant enclosed by Ox and Oy. But Samuelson could have gone farther. Even when there occurs a "twist" in the production transformation curve so that the initial and altered *availability loci* intersect, there may still result an unambiguous increase in potential economic welfare. To be sure, Samuelson is aware of this possibility. "An outward shift in the utility-possibility function may have occurred," he writes, "as the result of a *twist* of the production-possibility curve. This is because people's tastes for different goods may be such that the points on the new production schedule that lie inward may be points that would never be observed in any optimal competitive market."[6] But lacking an apparatus which relates the situation utility-possibility curve to a commodity space — the Paretian contract curve — he could not derive the precise and sufficient condition we have formulated. That our theorem manifestly requires a detailed knowledge of each consumer's preference function and the community's production transformation curve is admittedly a profound impediment to its application. But to know precisely how much information we need and lack is a small step forward from total ignorance.

5. Samuelson, "Evaluation of Real National Income," *op. cit.*, p. 17.
6. *Ibid.*

IV

Throughout our discussion, we have emphasized the connection between the distribution of income and the price system, pointing out that each position on the situation utility-possibility curve corresponds to a particular set of relative prices. Unless, therefore, a government has the power to discriminate among the various members of the community and to confront them with different sets of prices — or to fix production and consumption by fiat, it cannot alter the distribution of income without accepting and facilitating changes in the price system and in the composition of production. In particular, the government must accommodate its tax structure to that set of prices which corresponds to the desired income distribution; it must revise all taxes on internal and foreign trade whenever it alters the income distribution. This point is too often ignored in analyses of international trade.[7] Discussions of trade and tariffs rarely take account of the influence of the internal distribution of income upon foreign trade and tariff policy, however they may stress the obverse relationship, the impact of trade upon the domestic distribution of income.[8]

One advantage of our technique is that it lays bare this neglected link between trade policy and the distribution of income. By way of illustration, let us consider successively the case for free international trade and the case for optimal protection, delving beneath the situation utility-possibility curves that are generated by these policies and examining the appropriate Paretian contract curves.

We first explore the case for free trade, employing Figure VI. There we have drawn an *availability locus*, z_1, derived from one of Person Two's indifference curves, $_2U^1$ (not shown). In the absence of international trade and with Person Two confined to $_2U^1$, the economy would come to rest at Q, where z_1 is tangent to Person One's indifference curve $_1U^1$. But suppose that trade is begun with the outside world and that our two-person, two-commodity economy is confronted with a fixed system of international prices which differs from the system that prevailed within the economy before trade. Suppose, for example, that its inhabitants are able to exchange FD of domestically-produced X for FB of foreign-produced Y, the slope of the line DB or terms of trade being different from the slope of z_1 at Q.

7. But cf. Graaf, *op. cit.*, pp. 56–57.
8. *Vide*, e.g., Stolper and Samuelson, *loc. cit.*, and Lloyd Metzler, "Tariffs, the Terms of Trade and the Distribution of National Income," *Journal of Political Economy*, Feb. and Aug. 1949. These authors are concerned to show that the imposition of a tariff can change the absolute and relative returns to particular factors of production.

It would now be possible for Person One to reach the indifference curve $_1U^2$, higher than $_1U^1$, although Person Two were to remain on the same indifference curve, $_2U^1$, which generated z_1. In this example, Person Two will wish to consume FR more of Y than is being produced at home. But this does not disrupt our argument. For Person One is trading X for Y and receiving FB of Y for FD of X; he can easily supply Person Two with FR of Y, the difference between the latter's requirements and the total domestic output, and still gain from his trade with the outside world.

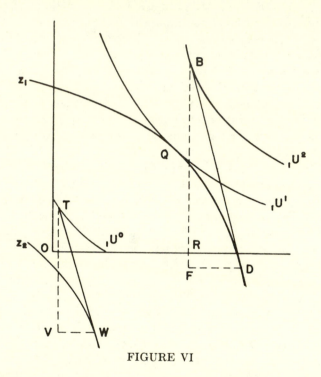

FIGURE VI

Trade, of course, does not take place this way. And it may adversely affect one of our two consumers. If, for example, Person Two were to earn his income producing commodity X, he would absorb some of the gains from trade. As both the price and domestic output of X are increased by the opening of trade, Person Two would move to an *availability locus* to the southwest of z_1, perhaps so far to the southwest that Person One could not trade his way back to the indifference curve $_1U^1$ from which he started. Similarly, Person Two might be a worker and Person One a capitalist and commodity X could require more labor per unit of capital than commodity Y, so that Person One might be disadvantaged by the opening of trade.[9]

On the other hand, we have shown that free trade *can* make one person better off without injuring the other. Were we to repeat the construction of Figure VI for each of the family of *availability loci*, we could generate a locus of Pareto optima to which there would correspond a situation utility-possibility curve. That curve would lie uniformly outside of its pre-trade counterpart, implying that free trade is preferable to autarky.

The situation utility-possibility curve that is generated by free trade has two peculiarities, each worthy of brief note.

First, the price ratio implied at each point on the free trade situation utility-possibility curve is the same as that at every other point. Unlike the situation utility-possibility curve generated in a closed economy, it is not the locus of points of tangency between indifference curves and *availability loci*. It instead traces two sets of points of tangency, between a price line of fixed slope and indifference curves, and between that price line and *availability loci*. But if our country confronted, not a fixed set of international prices, but a foreign offer curve of less than infinite elasticity, the price ratio would have to change with the distribution of income. We shall revert to this construction when we consider the optimum tariff argument and Figure VII.

Second, the free trade situation utility-possibility curve includes points like T in Figure VI which have the peculiar property that they permit Person Two to be better off than he could *ever* be in the absence of trade. The *availability locus* z_2 to which T pertains lies southwest of the origin of the diagram, O, so that in the absence of trade Person Two could never reach it. But he could reach T once trade is opened if, in the pre-trade equilibrium, Person One had been located at some point on the indifference curve $_1U^0$ and the gains from trade were assigned to Person Two rather than to Person One. An observable equilibrium might also occur at T if, with the opening of trade, the domestic distribution of income were allowed to change in favor of Person Two.

Finally, let us note that the amount, the gain, the very existence of trade, will all depend upon the *intra*national distribution of income. Suppose, for example, that two countries were to enjoy precisely the same factor endowments and that there were two persons (or groups of persons) within each country, Person One of Country A having the same preference field as Person One of Country B and Person Two of Country A having the same preference field as Person Two of Country B. A reading of such standard works as Professor Ohlin's

9. Stolper and Samuelson, *op. cit.*, pp. 66–68.

Interregional and International Trade[1] or Professor Leontief's "The Use of Indifference Curves in the Analysis of Foreign Trade"[2] might cause us to conclude that no trade would take place between Country A and Country B. If, however, domestic economic policies or institutional arrangements in the two countries cause them to be differently located on their (identical) Paretian contract curves, relative prices in the two countries would differ and they could trade. It is indeed possible that two quite similar countries could jointly gain more from trade and that there could occur a larger volume of trade between them than would arise from the juxtaposition of two countries of vastly different factor endowments or of consumers of very different tastes. Neither differences in factor endowments nor differences in tastes — nor the two together — are truly necessary or sufficient to cause trade.[3]

More generally, the amount that any one country will trade, and its gains from trade will depend partly upon the initial domestic distribution of income.

Let us now turn to the optimum tariff argument. It has long been known[4] that a country can always improve its position by imposing upon its external trade some tariff or set of tariffs, provided that it confronts a less than infinitely elastic foreign offer curve and provided that other countries do not retaliate. Recently, however, the optimum tariff argument has been extended. Whereas Scitovsky[5] had assumed production to be fixed, treated only the case of an inelastic foreign offer curve and applied as his welfare criterion the compensation principle, more recent expositors of the argument have allowed for changes in production, permitting them to consider both inelastic and elastic foreign offer curves, and have applied as their measure of gain the situation utility-possibility curve.[6] This extension of the case for protection has, however, deprived the earlier analysis of simplicity

1. Harvard University Press, 1933.
2. This *Journal*, XLVII (May 1933).
3. Ohlin asserts the contrary (*op. cit.*, p. 49), but may comprehend by "the influence of demand" the distribution of income within each trading country. Similarly, Leontief's community indifference curves are necessarily a function of the distribution of income; a change in the distribution of income will change their shape and cause the tangency of an indifference curve and international price ratio to occur at some different point, altering the amount of trade, the system of prices and the gains from trade.
4. References to the works important to the development of the argument are given by Graaf, *op. cit.*, p. 47.
5. Scitovsky, "A Reconsideration of the Theory of Tariffs," *op. cit.*, *passim*.
6. Graaf, *loc. cit.*, and Robert Baldwin, "The New Welfare Economics and the Gains in International Trade," this *Journal*, LXVI (Feb. 1952). I have drawn heavily upon this article in the presentation that follows.

and clarity.   Moreover, and with but one exception,[7] the newer
formulations have not explored the connection between the domestic
distribution of income and the optimum rate of duty; they have generally treated the optimum tariff as somehow independent of income
distribution.   For these reasons and as still another exercise in the
application of the modified box diagram and Paretian contract curve,
we shall devote the remaining paragraphs of this paper to a diagrammatic exposition of the optimum tariff argument.

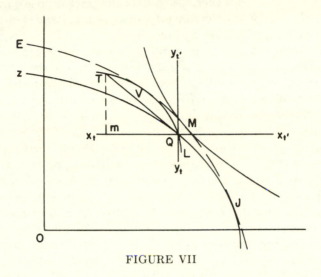

FIGURE VII

We shall suppose that our two-person, two-commodity economy
is confronted by a less than infinitely elastic foreign offer curve, the
curve TL drawn in Figure VII relative to the axes $x_t x_t'$ and $y_t y_t'$.
When the price ratio p_x/p_y is less than the value of the slope of TL
at the point Q, foreigners will wish to export commodity Y and to
import commodity X; the northwest quadrant, bounded by Qx_t and
$Qy_{t'}$, will interest us.   When, on the other hand, the price ratio is
greater than the value of the slope of TL at Q, foreigners will wish to
export commodity X and to import commodity Y; the southeast
quadrant, bounded by $Qx_{t'}$ and Qy_t, will interest us.

To find that free trade equilibrium which corresponds to the
availability locus z and to the less than perfectly elastic offer curve
TL we have now to pass TL along z, keeping $x_t x_t'$ parallel to the
abscissa of the diagram and Q on the curve z.   At each point such as
Q we must construct the tangent to z and extend it until it intersects

7. Graaf, *op. cit.*, pp. 56–57.

TL, as at T. Of the series of points T that are so generated, that one will be the point of free trade equilibrium at which T is also a point of tangency between the price ratio TQ and one of Person One's indifference curves (not shown). Person One will then be prepared to trade Qm of X for mT of Y. The point T of Figure VII is precisely analogous to the point B of Figure VI.

To each of the family of *availability loci* z, of course, there will correspond a free trade equilibrium. In contrast to the situation pictured in Figure VI, however, the equilibrium price ratio is quite likely to be different for each *availability locus;* the system of prices will change with the distribution of income.

Now suppose that some tariff is imposed upon trade between Person One and the outside world. We can readily show that there is some tariff which will allow Person One to reach a point like M, and a higher indifference curve, $_1U^1$, than he could attain by unrestricted trade. As when we sought the free trade point T, let us again pass the offer curve TL along z. But this time, let us form of the set of curves TL that are produced, an envelope curve E. Baldwin has shown that E, the optimum tariff locus, possesses one happy property. Its slope at any point V will be the same as the slope of z where z is intersected by the offer curve tangent to E at V.[8] If, then, some indifference curve $_1U^1$ is tangent to E, as at M, Person One's marginal rate of substitution, being equal to the slope of E, will equal the domestic marginal rate of transformation; M is a fully efficient and feasible position of equilibrium. By imposing a tariff that will produce equilibrium at M, then, we can make Person One better off than with free trade, without injuring Person Two.

The procedure just outlined could be repeated for each of the curves z, producing an optimum tariff locus E and an optimum tariff position M for each domestic distribution of income, and forming a situation utility-possibility curve that would lie entirely outside the free trade curve. Hence the optimal tariff yields an increase in potential welfare.

But the optimum tariff rate, like the free trade price ratios that are produced by the offer curve TL, is likely to vary with the distribution of income. There will be as many optimal tariffs as there are potential free trade equilibria, or, more precisely, a unique optimal ad valorem tariff rate for each point on the situation utility-possibility curve that is generated by the set of points M.

8. Robert Baldwin, "Equilibrium in International Trade; a Diagrammatic Analysis," this *Journal*, LXII (Nov. 1948), 754. An alternative proof can be obtained by slightly altering Note I of the attached mathematical appendix.

We have finally to note that to one of the possible free trade positions there may correspond no optimum tariff. At J, on z, the tariff locus JE will just touch the *availability locus;* the slope of z is there equal to the slope of TL at Q. If, through J, there passed the no-trade Paretian contract curve, making J a position of equilibrium in the absence of trade, no tariff could improve upon Person One's position. But by the same token, there would be no trade in the absence of a tariff.

The foregoing analysis of the case for free trade and the case for the optimum tariff have been offered as an illustration of the use to which the *availability loci*, modified box diagram and Paretian contract curve can be profitably applied. Until now, there have been few geometric devices available to the economist for the description and examination of problems involving both production and consumption — for the diagrammatic exposition of simple systems of general equilibrium. The present paper is intended to help fill this empty corner in the economist's toolbox.

MATHEMATICAL APPENDIX

Note I. *To prove that the slope of the curve z_0 of Figure II is equal at* S *to the slope of the curve* $Y_0 X_0$ *at* Q.

Let the transformation curve be $f(x,y) = 0$ and the chosen indifference curve for Person Two be $u(x_2,y_2) = c$, where (x,y) denotes the total output of the two goods and (x_2,y_2) denotes Person Two's share. Then Person One's share is $(x_1,y_1) = (x - x_2, y - y_2)$. Note that if x be regarded as an independent variable, then all the other variables are functions of it alone by virtue of these equations and the condition that the indifference curve be tangent to the transformation curve at Q, namely:

$$\frac{u_1(x_2,y_2)}{u_2(x_2,y_2)} = \frac{f_1(x,y)}{f_2(x,y)} .$$

Thus as x changes, the rate of change of y is, from the transformation function and this equation:

$$\frac{dy}{dx} = -\frac{f_1}{f_2} = -\frac{u_1}{u_2}.$$

If the utility of Person Two is not changed, total differentiation of $u(x_2,y_2) = c$ gives:

$$\frac{dy_2}{dx_2} = \frac{\dfrac{dy_2}{dx}}{\dfrac{dx_2}{dx}} = -\frac{u_1}{u_2} = \frac{dy}{dx} .$$

Finally, using this result,

$$\frac{dy_1}{dx_1} = \frac{\dfrac{dy_1}{dx}}{\dfrac{dx_1}{dx}} = \frac{\dfrac{dy}{dx} - \dfrac{dy_2}{dx}}{1 - \dfrac{dx_2}{dx}} = \frac{\dfrac{dy}{dx} - \dfrac{dy}{dx}\dfrac{dx_2}{dx}}{1 - \dfrac{dx_2}{dx}} = \frac{dy}{dx} ,$$

so that the z_0 curve at the point x_1, y_1 has the same slope as the transformation curve at the point x, y. In this proof we have made the economically plausible assumption that $\dfrac{dx_2}{dx} < 1$.

Note II. *To prove that at each point on the situation utility-possibility curve, all the consumers' marginal rates of substitution are equal to the marginal rate of transformation so that the situation utility-possibility curve is the locus of fully efficient and feasible equilibria.*

Let the two utility functions be $_1U(x_1, y_1)$ and $_2U(x_2, y_2)$ and the transformation function be $f(x_1 + x_2, y_1 + y_2) = 0$. If we fix Person One's utility at, say, $_1U^0$, and maximize the utility of Person Two, we obtain a point on the situation utility-possibility curve. Indeed the situation utility-possibility curve is the locus of all such points and is generated by varying $_1U^0$.

Formally speaking, the problem is to maximize $_2U(x_2, y_2)$ subject to the two constraints

$$_1U(x_1, y_1) = {}_1U^0 ,$$
$$f(x_1 + x_2, y_1 + y_2) = 0 .$$

If a set of quantities x_1, x_2, y_1, y_2 is to furnish a solution to this problem, it is necessary that all four partial derivatives of the appropriate Lagrangean function vanish, this function being
$$L(x_1, x_2, y_1, y_2) = {}_2U(x_2, y_2) + \lambda \left[{}_1U(x_1, y_1) - {}_1U^0 \right] + \mu f(x_1 + x_2, y_1 + y_2).$$
These four conditions are:

$$\frac{\partial L}{\partial x_1} = \lambda_1 U_1 + \mu f_1 = 0 ,$$

$$\frac{\partial L}{\partial y_1} = \lambda_1 U_2 + \mu f_2 = 0 ,$$

$$\frac{\partial L}{\partial x_2} = {}_2U_1 + \mu f_1 = 0 ,$$

$$\frac{\partial L}{\partial y_2} = {}_2U_2 + \mu f_2 = 0 .$$

From the first two of these

$$\frac{_1U_1}{_1U_2} = \frac{f_1}{f_2},$$

and from the second two

$$\frac{_2U_1}{_2U_2} = \frac{f_1}{f_2},$$

whence

$$\frac{_1U_1}{_1U_2} = \frac{_2U_1}{_2U_2}.$$

This shows that at any point on the situation utility-possibility curve Person One's marginal rate of substitution is equal to Person Two's marginal rate of substitution.

Furthermore, if we let $x = x_1 + x_2$ and $y = y_1 + y_2$, then at any point on the transformation function

$$\frac{dy}{dx} = -\frac{f_1}{f_2}.$$

Thus

$$\frac{_1U_1}{_1U_2} = \frac{_2U_1}{_2U_2} = -\frac{dy}{dx},$$

which asserts that the two marginal rates of substitution equal the marginal rate of transformation. Hence all the points on the situation utility-possibility curve satisfy the conditions for Pareto optima.

PETER B. KENEN

COLUMBIA UNIVERSITY

A NOTE ON
TARIFF CHANGES AND WORLD WELFARE *

PETER B. KENEN

This note seeks to simplify and unify earlier results obtained by Vanek [1] and Baldwin,[2] describing the effects on world welfare of unilateral tariff reductions and of a customs union. It deals with two products, x and y, and with n countries, and uses as a proxy for world welfare the sum of the n countries' x and y outputs valued at world prices. More directly and importantly, it measures the change in world welfare by the change in y output *given* x output — by the change in the placement of the world's transformation curve.[3]

Formally, world output is given by

$$(1) \qquad y = \Sigma \ f_j(x_j)$$

$$(2) \qquad x = \Sigma \ x_j,$$

where $j = 1, \ldots, n$, and the functions $f_j(x_j)$ are the transformation curves for the individual countries. In each country, moreover, the usual assumptions of trade theory (pure competition and increasing opportunity costs) give

$$(3) \qquad p(1 + t_j) = -f_j',$$

where p is the world price of y in terms of x, and t_j represents the domestic price effect of a tariff levied by the jth country. When $t_j > 0$, the country may be deemed to have a tariff on y (and to export x); when $t_j < 0$, it may be deemed to have a tariff on x (and to export y).[4]

To start, let us reproduce the most familiar proposition — that free trade is required to maximize world welfare. As welfare will be maximized when y is maximized for each and every x, differentiate (1) constrained by (2) and set the derivatives equal to zero. Then

---

* The author is indebted to Polly Allen, Anne Krueger, James Henderson, and Neil Wallace for comments on earlier drafts.

1. Jaroslav Vanek, "Unilateral Trade Liberalization and Global World Income," this *Journal*, LXXVIII (Feb. 1964), 139–47.

2. Robert E. Baldwin, "Customs Unions, Preferential Systems and World Welfare," in M. Connolly and A. Swoboda, eds., *International Trade and Money* (London: George Allen & Unwin, 1973).

3. An outward shift in this curve is sufficient to produce an outward shift in the world's situation-utility-possibility curve — see, e.g., Peter B. Kenen, "On the Geometry of Welfare Economics," this *Journal*, LXXI (Aug. 1957), 426–47. But it is not necessary to cause such a shift. Increased efficiency in exchange (e.g., the consumption effects of tariffs reduction not studied here) could do so too.

4. When $t_j < 0$, however, it does not measure the ad valorem tariff. If $t_j'(>0)$ is the tariff rate on x, $(1+t_j') = 1/(1+t_j)$, and $t_j = -t_j'/(1+t_j') < 0$. Notice that $t_j > 0$ can also represent the external price effect of an export subsidy on x, and that $t_j < 0$ can represent the effect of an export subsidy on y.

(4) $f_j' = -\lambda,\ j = 1,\ \ldots,\ n,$

where λ is the Lagrangean multiplier attached to the constraint. The n countries must have the same marginal rates of substitution, and (3) tells us that this cannot happen if any $t_j \neq 0$.

Consider next the impact of changes in tariff rates. Differentiate totally (1), (2), and (3), forming

$$
(5)\quad
\begin{vmatrix}
1 & 0 & p(1+t_1) & \ldots & & p(1+t_n) \\
0 & 0 & 1 & 1 \ldots & & 1 \\
0 & (1+t_1) & f_1'' & 0 \ldots & & 0 \\
. & . & 0 & & & . \\
. & . & . & & & . \\
. & . & . & & 0 & . \\
. & (1+t_n) & 0 & \ldots 0 & & f_n''
\end{vmatrix}
\begin{vmatrix}
dy \\ dp \\ dx_1 \\ . \\ . \\ . \\ dx_n
\end{vmatrix}
=
\begin{vmatrix}
0 \\ dx \\ -p\,dt_1 \\ . \\ . \\ . \\ -p\,dt_n
\end{vmatrix},
$$

and use Cramer's Rule to solve for the change in y output (and world welfare) caused by a change in the ith country's tariff:

(6) $(dy/dt_i) = - (p^2/f_i'')\,[\sum_j (t_j - t_i)(1+t_j)/f_j'']/$
          $[\sum_j (1+t_j)/f_j''].$

As all the f_j'' are negative (including f_i''), the sign of (6) depends uniquely on the weighted sum of the tariff differences $(t^j - t_i)$.[5]

This brings us directly to Vanek's chief result — that the impact on world welfare of a unilateral tariff change depends on the initial (relative) height of the tariff to be altered and on the size of the change itself. Suppose that the ith country has the highest tariff on product y, so that $t_i > 0$ and $(t_j - t_i) < 0$ for all $j \neq i$. In this instance, $(dy/dt_i) < 0$, and a small reduction in the ith country's tariff has to increase world welfare.[6] If, however, some t_j is larger than t_i, or dt_i is large enough to reverse the sign of some $(t_j - t_i)$, the impact of a cut in the ith country's tariff could well be perverse.[7] When, in

---

5. This formulation is similar to those obtained by James E. Meade in *Trade and Welfare* (Oxford: Oxford University Press, 1955), although it is derived quite differently.

6. The same thing would be true if the ith country had the highest tariff on product x. Here, $t_i < 0$ and $(t_j - t_i) > 0$ for all $j \neq i$, so that $(dy/dt_i) > 0$, but tariff reduction means an increase in t_i. It should, of course, be emphasized that tariff reductions that increase world welfare may decrease the welfare of the country making them. As usual, there is a systematic difference between cosmopolitan and national interests (but one that can be bridged by lump sum transfers).

7. Notice, further, that a tariff change leads also to a change in all other countries' prices, since
$(dp/dt_j) = -(p/f_j'')/[\sum_j (1+t_j)/f_j''] < 0.$

With x-output fixed for the world as a whole, an increase in a single tariff on y (or reduction in a single tariff on x), reducing x-output in the country changing its tariff, must increase x-output in all other countries and, therefore, must

fact, t_i is low relative to other tariffs, there is a strong presumptive case against any cut; the largest "wrong-signed" differences $(t_j - t_i)$ would have the largest weights $(1+t_j)$ in (6), above.

Two interesting corollaries follow directly:

COROLLARY 1. *When* n$=2$, *unilateral free trade does not maximize world welfare. Let the first of two countries export* x *and the second export* y, *so that*

(7)
$$(dy/dt_2) = - (dy/dt_1)\,[(1+t_1)/(1+t_2)]$$
$$= - [p^2/f_1''f_2'')\,(1+t_1)\,(t_1-t_2)]/$$
$$[(1+t_1)/f_1'' + (1+t_2)/f_2''].$$

If neither country has a tariff, neither should impose one; as always, global free trade maximizes world welfare. If both countries have tariffs and one will not budge, the other can contribute to world welfare by cutting its own — even moving to free trade — but would do better to replace its import tariff with an export subsidy equal in size to the first country's tariff. It would thereby nullify the first country's tariff, installing an efficient substitute for world-wide free trade.

COROLLARY 2. *When* n>2, *there is a unique welfare-maximizing tariff rate for each country, given all the other rates. As world welfare is largest when* $(dy/dt_i) = 0$ *for all* i,

(8)
$$\sum_j (t_j - t_i)\,(1+t_j)/f_j'' = 0,$$

or

(8a)
$$t_i{}^* = [\sum_j t_j(1+t_j)/f_j'']/[\sum_j (1+t_j)f_j''],$$

for j$\neq$i, *where* $t_i{}^*$ *is the tariff rate that maximizes world welfare, given all the other rates. When some* t_j *are positive and others negative,* $t_i{}^*$ *can conceivably be zero; unilateral free trade by the* i[th] *country might maximize world welfare. But when* $t_j \geqslant 0$ *for all* j$\neq$i, *this cannot be so; the* i[th] *country must impose an import tariff (if it imports* y*) or an export subsidy (if it exports* y*), and its tariff or subsidy must lie between the extreme* t_j's.

We turn now to the impact of a customs union, merging the first two countries of an *n*-country world and mounting a common

---

lower the world price of y. This effect, however, could cause some countries to stop exporting y and start exporting x, and one or more $t_j < 0$ would then turn positive, altering the sign of (6) as a whole. We exclude this possibility here and hereafter.

tariff, t_c, bounded by the members' tariffs before they were unified.[8] Prior to any change in t_3 through t_n,

(9) $dy = (dy/dt_1) dt_1 + (dy/dt_2) dt_2 = (dy/dt_1)(t_c - t_1)$
        $+ (dy/dt_2)(t_c - t_2).$

Combining (6) and (9), we obtain

(10) $$dy = - [p^2/f_1''f_2''] \frac{T_u + T_e}{[\sum_j (1+t_j)/f_j'']}$$

for $j = 1, \ldots, n$, where

$$T_u = (1+t_c)(t_1 - t_2)^2;$$
$$T_e = \sum_k \{ [f_2''(t_1 - t_k)(t_1 - t_c) + f_1''(t_k - t_2)(t_c - t_2)](1+t_k)/f_r'' \}$$

for $k = 3, \ldots, n$.

Clearly, T_u has to be nonnegative for all t_1 and t_2, reflecting the simplest and inevitable consequence of a customs union. When two countries merge their tariffs, they align their marginal rates of transformation, removing one departure from global efficiency.

The sign of T_e, however, depends on the ordering of national tariffs and on the pattern of trade after the union is formed. It reflects the impact of unification on the global level of protection, and is the more likely to be positive when the common tariff is low. Consider sequentially the several possibilities:

A. Let both members' tariffs be extreme (e.g., $t_1 > t_k > t_2$, for all t_k). Then $T_e > 0$ whenever, as assumed above, t_c is bounded by t_1 and t_2.[9]

B. Let one member's tariff be extreme (e.g., $t_1 > t_2 > t_k$, for one or more t_k, and no $t_k > t_1$). Then T_e is not certain to be positive unless $[(t_1 - t_c)/(t_c - t_2)] > [f_1''(t_2 - t_k)/f_2''(t_1 - t_k)]$ for all t_k, and this is the more likely to happen when t_c is set to maximize the change in the rate that was extreme (i.e., close to t_2 when t_1 was extreme).

C. Let neither member's tariff be extreme (e.g., $t_3 \ldots t_r > t_1 > t_{r+1} \ldots t_{r+m} > t_2 > t_{r+m+1} \ldots t_n$). Then there is no simple sufficient condition that renders $T_e > 0$. For any fixed t_c, however, it is the more likely to be positive as m approaches n.

In case A, the customs union serves always to reduce one of the

---

8. If t_1 and t_2 have opposite signs initially, t_c will be determined by an interaction of the trade pattern and the agreement establishing the customs union. Suppose that $t_1 > 0 > t_2$ initially and that the agreement fixes the common import tax on y at $t_{1c} > 0$ and the common tax on x at $t_{2c} < 0$. If the new union as a whole imports y, t_{1c} will be the only import tax affecting intra-union prices; if it imports x, t_{2c} will be the only import tax.

9. Some terms in T_e, however, must change sign in the process of unification. If, for instance, $t_c = t_1$, all $(t_k - t_2)$ will switch sign as t_c supplants t_2. Hence $T_e > 0$ does not guarantee gains from a union.

extreme national tariffs, raising y output and world welfare. In case B, the union is more likely to raise world welfare when t_c approaches the smaller of the members' tariffs. And in case C, the union is more likely to raise world welfare, the closer t_c to the smaller of the members' tariffs, the fewer the outside rates that bracket them, and the smaller the gap between the members' tariffs and the highest rates levied by outsiders.

Our findings thus far are consistent with Baldwin's, albeit more general. (Because he dealt only with three countries, he could not study C above.) Yet when we examine the options available to the k countries outside the union, our findings begin to differ substantially.

In a three-country world, the problem is quite simple. Whatever the ordering of national tariffs before the union is formed, the outsider's tariff will be at one extreme once the union is in being. This is trivially true, for t_c and t_3 are the only tariffs. Hence, one can apply Corollary 1 above. The third country can always enlarge world welfare by cutting its own tariff (even to zero), and it can maximize world welfare, given $t_c \neq 0$, by subsidizing exports rather than by taxing imports. But when $n > 3$, the problem is more complicated.

When t_1 and t_2 are the largest tariffs in the whole array, the substitution of t_c is bound logically to leave some other rate at one end of the array, inviting one outsider to reduce its tariff, thereby to enlarge y output and world welfare. That country should not necessarily move to free trade; equation (8a) applies, so that the new tariff, t_k^*, has to be a weighted average of the other countries' rates (with t_c replacing t_1 and t_2). (If, of course, all countries act altruistically or in the anticipation of compensating transfer payments, adjusting their tariffs to maximize y output, the first shift to a new t_k^* will leave some other rate exposed at the edge of the array; and the country with that tariff would be the one to make the next adjustment. Taking t_c to be fixed, the outside world as a whole could leapfrog its way to the most efficient stance — a uniform subsidy on exports to the union.)

In every other case, however, creation of a customs union need not call for cuts in other countries' tariffs. In case B, construction of t_c may not expose some new t_k at the end of the array; the formation of a union may call for an increase in some of the t_k's. In case C, moreover, no new rate, t_k, can be exposed at the edge of the array.

Notice, however, one curiosity. If the outside world was wholly altruistic before the customs union came into being, all t_k would have been set between t_1 and t_2, pursuant to (8a), and case A would prevail. In this happy instance, $T_e > 0$, and a customs union will increase welfare. And when t_c has been constructed, one or more t_k is made to be extreme, furnishing a simple, unambiguous basis for further reductions in the outsiders' tariffs.

PRINCETON UNIVERSITY

MIGRATION, THE TERMS OF TRADE, AND ECONOMIC WELFARE IN THE SOURCE COUNTRY*

Peter B.KENEN

Those of us whose happier professional duties include the frequent reading of Charles P.Kindleberger's work unite in admiring his intellectual mobility. He has toiled in more fields than many others could cultivate, harvesting rich crops in every one of them. But one constant in a long career is Kindleberger's interest in mobility itself — in the theory and implications of factor movements. His doctoral dissertation dealt with short-term capital[1]. His most recent writings have been concerned with financial integration, direct investment, and other current issues on capital account[2]. Along the way, moreover, he has looked at people, applying the Lewis model to Western Europe's growth and thinking through the implications of emigration from the Mediterranean basin[3].

This brief paper honors him by imitation, the sincerest flattery. It seeks to identify the welfare implications of net emigration, viewed from the standpoint of the source region or country and in the context of the Heckscher-Ohlin model. It proceeds from a single set of assumptions, sufficient to obtain all of its conclusions but has in tow a long mathematical appendix deriving a number of those same conclusions under less restrictive sets of assump-

* I am grateful to Jaroslav Vanek and Ronald Jones for spotting errors in earlier drafts and to several colleagues and students for suggesting improvements and qualifications. Remaining errors and excessive claims to originality are, of course, my own personal achievements.

[1] *International Short-Term Capital Movements* (New York: Columbia University Press, 1937).

[2] *Europe and the Dollar* (Cambridge: The M.I.T. Press, 1966) Chaps. 1, 2, and 5.

[3] *Europe's Postwar Growth: The Role of Labor Supply* (Cambridge: Harvard University Press, 1967) and "Emigration and Economic Growth", Banca Nazionale del Lavoro *Quarterly Review*, No. 74 (September 1965).

tions. In addition to the several standard suppositions of the Heckscher-Ohlin model, listed in due course, it supposes that workers migrate in response to wage differences (or, more precisely, the present value of expected differences), that each migrant takes with him an average-sized family and that no migrant owns any productive property or claims to the income from any such property. These extra suppositions guarantee that migrants gain by moving (if their expectations are fulfilled) and that the welfare gain or loss for persons remaining in the source country depends, in the first instance, on the change in labor's average product (or the present value of future average product). Movements of average-sized families do not change the ratio of labor force to population, so that labor's average product and per capita income, the first approximation to economic welfare, have always to move in the same direction.

11.1. The One-Product Closed Economy

The most common treatment of the problem studied here is a simple aggregate production-function version usually inflicted on unsuspecting students. It derives from the theory of optimum population expounded by Meade[4] and is basic to much recent work on international capital movements, not just migration[5].

Starting with a single product, perfect competition, and constant returns to scale, one commonly invokes the law of variable proportions to ascertain three consequences of net emigration. If the source country is located initially where its marginal product of labor is positive, declining, and smaller than the average product, net emigration has these effects:

1. Total product falls.
2. The marginal product of labor rises and that of capital declines, redistributing income in favor of labor.
3. The average product of labor rises, raising per capita income.

---

[4] James E.Meade, *Trade and Welfare* (London: Oxford University Press, 1955) pp. 84-85. Note, however, the several important qualifications which Meade himself attaches on subsequent pages.

[5] See e.g., G.D.A.MacDougall, "The Benefits and Costs of Private Investment from Abroad: A Theoretical Approach", in: *Readings in International Economics*, eds. R.E. Caves and H.G.Johnson (Homewood, Ill.: Richard D.Irwin, 1968) pp. 172-194.

The second of these three effects does not inhibit definitive inference, because the third effect suggests that, with lump-sum transfers, all remaining residents could be made to gain. If, then, the analysis is sound, public policy should encourage emigration or, at the very least, should not discourage it[6].

But this analysis should not please a sophomore, let alone an author of public policy. Consider a one-product economy with constant returns to scale, described by fig. 11.1[7]. Its initial labor force is OL_0; its capital stock is OK_0; its total output is given by the isoquant P_t; and its wage-rental ratio is given by the slope of P_t at Q_t (by $\tan \beta$). Its national income (in units of capital) is OV_t, of which OK_0 goes to the capitalists and $K_0 V_t$ goes to the workers. Now let emigration cut back the labor force to OL_1 and consider the condition of those who stay behind. Prior to emigration, those parties earned OV_0 of income, corresponding to P_0 of output. Emigration, however, reduces available output to P_1, smaller than P_0, reducing, not raising, the welfare of those who stay behind[8]. The conventional analysis falls into error because it compares noncomparable numbers. It compares the average product of the initial labor force (including the emigrants-to-be) with the average product of the final labor force.

Even as amended, however, the model described by fig. 11.1 leaves many questions without answers. One would like to know, for instance, whether the loss of the migrants' tax payments differs from the total cost of the public services that would have been consumed by the migrants and their families. One would also like to know whether the transfer of human capital attending emigration should be treated as a loss to the source country[9]. Most importantly, one would like to know whether this simple analysis can survive

---

[6] If, of course, the marginal product is declining but equal to average product, there can be no change in the latter or in the welfare of remaining residents. Initial population is, on this view, optimal. If, finally, the marginal product is declining but larger than the average product, emigration will reduce average product and the welfare of remaining residents. Initial population is sub-optimal.

[7] This exposition was suggested by Ronald Jones (who referred me to a similar construction by Harry Johnson). I cannot thank Johnson directly, as his intellectual output far exceeds my bibliographical input.

[8] The new output P_1 will be produced at E, with OL_1 of labor and OK_0 of capital, and there will be a redistribution of income in favor of labor, as the wage-rental ratio at E is larger than $\tan \beta$. This refinement, however, does not undermine the basic analysis or conclusion.

[9] For footnote, see next page.

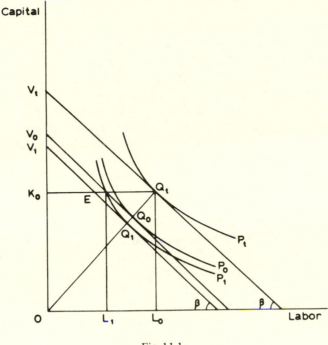

Fig. 11.1.

the introduction of additional commodities and of foreign trade[10]. What follows is an effort to answer this last question (ignoring all the rest).

[9] This is a vexed issue on which much has been written; see, e.g., C.P.Kindleberger, "Emigration and Economic Growth", H.B.Grubel and A.D.Scott, "The International Flow of Human Capital" (*American Economic Review*, Vol. 65 (May 1966) pp. 268-275, and the survey by E.S. Djimopoulos, "Temporary Labor Migration: Effects on the Country of Emigration", International Economics Workshop, Columbia University, 1969 (mimeographed). Clearly, one must avoid double counting. The present value of the human capital embodied in a migrant is part of the present value of his marginal product and has already been subtracted from source-country output. But one has still to ask if some part of that same loss could have been avoided with perfect advance knowledge of the migrant's plans. If employers or government agencies furnish an irretrievable portion of the human capital embodied in a migrant and could have withheld some of that capital for a different use (without impairing the migrant's ability to migrate), one would have to treat that portion of the capital as an *avoidable* loss, if not an additional loss.

[10] MacDougall ("The Benefits and Costs of Private Investment...", pp. 186-188) discusses this issue, but his model does not allow him to study it thoroughly.

11.2. The Two-Product Closed Economy

Consider a single country obeying all the rules of a factor-proportions (Heckscher-Ohlin) model, but, in the first instance, having no foreign trade. It produces two commodities (apples and blankets) under perfect competition and constant returns to scale. It has two factors of production (labor and capital) that are fully employed by its two industries but are used in different proportions by those two industries; let apple production be more capital intensive than blanket production at all sets of factor prices. All persons within the economy have the same tastes, with unitary income elasticities of demand for the two commodities. Each person, moreover, consumes both commodities at all sets of product prices (so that the closed economy must produce both of them)[11].

The relevant circumstances of this economy are described by fig. 11.2. Its initial labor force is B_0L_0; its capital stock is B_0K. The point P_0 lies on the efficiency locus (not drawn here), where the blanket isoquant I_b drawn with reference to B_0, is tangent to the apple isoquant I_a drawn with reference to A_0. The slopes of the two isoquants at P_0 give the initial wage-rental ratio; it is measured by $\tan\beta$. Next, construct A_0G_0 with slope equal to $\tan\beta$. The distance B_0G_0 measures the national income in units of capital, with capital itself earning B_0K and labor earning KG_0. Income per worker is given by B_0G_0/KA_0.

If, now, emigration reduces the labor force to B_0L_1, there will be several major changes in the economy. Note, first, what would happen if there were no change in equilibrium factor and product prices. With constant returns to scale, the new production point P_1 must lie on B_0P_0 and on a line parallel to A_0P_0 drawn from the new factor-box corner A_1; there can be no change in the industries' factor proportions if there is, as yet, no change in factor prices. At P_1, however, blanket output has fallen absolutely [by $(B_0P_0-B_0P_1)/$

---

[11] Note that perfect competition, constant returns to scale, strong factor ordering and incomplete specialization suffice to generate a single-valued functional relationship between marginal products (factor prices) and relative product prices; see, e.g., P.A. Samuelson, *Collected Scientific Papers* (Cambridge: The M.I.T. Press, 1966), Vol. 2, pp. 888-908. This fact is used many times below. The other assumptions concerning demand conditions are used to forecast changes in consumption when we confront income changes and also to construct the representative indifference curve shown in fig. 11.3. If workers and capitalists have the same tastes, with unitary income elasticities, changes in factor prices can have no effect upon the position of a representative (or collective) indifference curve.

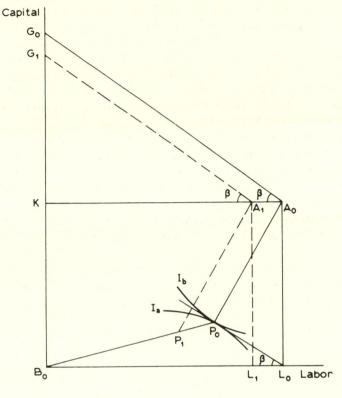

Fig. 11.2.

B_0P_0], while apple output has risen absolutely [by $(A_1P_1-A_0P_0)/A_0P_0$] [12].
National income has fallen to B_0G_1, but income per worker has risen to
B_0G_1/KA_1 [13].

Thus far, it would seem, net emigration benefits the remaining population
by raising income per worker. There are, however, two objections to this
conclusion. First, it falls into the same trap as the conventional one-product

---

[12] This is a familiar proposition, adapted from T.M.Rybczynski, "Factor Endowment and Relative Commodity Prices", *Readings in International Economics*, pp. 78-89.

[13] In proof, write $B_0G_0/KA_0 = B_0K/KA_0 + \tan\beta$, and $B_0G_1/KA_1 = B_0K/KA_1 + \tan\beta$, so that $B_0G_1/KA_1 - B_0G_0/KA_0 = (B_0K/KA_0)(A_1A_0/KA_1) > 0$.

analysis — comparing noncomparable populations. Second, at unchanged prices, there would be disequilibrium in the product markets.

If, as assumed, emigrants possess no capital, they had no claim to any part of the income $B_0 K$ prior to emigration; their total income was $G_0 G_1$, a pro rata share of total labor income. Hence, the constant-price income per worker of a remaining resident was $B_0 G_1 / K A_1$ prior to emigration and is not changed by emigration.

If, further, blanket output falls and apple output rises, while the total and average incomes of remaining residents are not changed by emigration, the outflow of workers must generate an excess supply of apples (an excess demand for blankets). Emigration reduces the total demand for both commodities, and there can be no offsetting increase of purchases by those who stay behind. The price of blankets must rise relative to that of apples, and national income must be redistributed in favor of labor (the factor used intensively in the production of blankets). When, finally, this occurs, potential welfare must decline. The gainers (workers) cannot compensate the losers (capitalists).

This last proposition can be proved quite simply. Examine fig. 11.3, the commodity-space counterpart of fig. 11.2. Here, the closed economy's initial transformation curve is $\bar{A}_0 E_0 \bar{B}_0$, and its initial equilibrium is at E_0 (with product prices given by $\tan \pi$). Its national income is OY_0 measured in apples; it produces and consumes OB_0 of blankets and OA_0 of apples. With net emigration, the transformation curve shrinks and twists becoming $\bar{A}_1 E_1 \bar{B}_1$. At constant product prices, national income would be OY_1, measured in apples (lower by the $Y_0 Y_1$ generated and received by the now-absent migrants); production would move to OB_1 of blankets and OA_1 of apples; and consumption would move to OB_2 of blankets and OA_2 of apples. There would be $B_1 B_2$ excess demand for blankets and $A_1 A_2$ excess supply of apples. The price of blankets must rise relative to that of apples until the points E_1 and F_1 merge on the new transformation curve. Consider, however, one further property of the income level OY_1. This was the initial income of the nonmigrant workers and capitalists, taken together, so that they were consuming OB_2 of blankets and OA_1 of apples prior to emigration. They were able to attain point F_1 on the "representative" indifference curve U_1. When, then, emigration and the consequent disequilibrium in the product markets drives them to a new consumption point, between F_1 and E_1, it forces them onto a lower indifference curve, reducing the welfare of the remaining population. The higher price of blankets at this new point means, of course, an increase in the wage-rental ratio, so that workers gain and capitalists

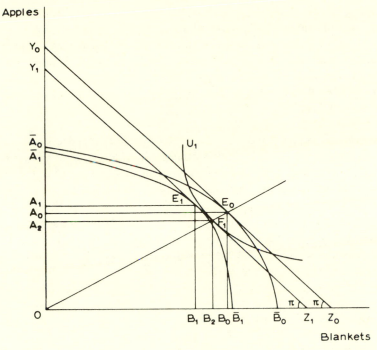

Fig. 11.3.

lose, but the former are unable to compensate the latter by, say, lump-sum transfers; total real income has declined[14]

One can make this last point differently, thereby to stress the vital role of the assumption, soon to be relaxed, that the economy is closed to foreign trade. If the remaining residents of the economy could export A_1A_2 of apples and import B_1B_2 of blankets at relative prices equal to $\tan\pi$, they could produce at E_1 and consume at F_1 (on the indifference curve U_1). Emigration would not alter their welfare. It is the absence of this opportunity that causes the welfare loss[15].

Summarizing for the closed two-product economy, net emigration has these three effects:

[14] See note 11.
[15] Note that immigration has symmetrical effects. Here, the *initial* population enjoys a welfare gain, as immigration generates an excess supply of blankets, reducing their relative price and allowing the initial population to "import" apples from the now larger economy of which they are part. The initial population captures gains from trade.

1. A reduction of total output, measured at constant prices, but no change in the constant-price income per worker of the remaining population.

2. A rise in the price of the labor-intensive product that raises the marginal product of labor and lowers the marginal product of capital, aiding the remaining workers and injuring the capitalists.

3. An overall welfare loss for the remaining population, as the workers cannot compensate the capitalists.

These results affirm the principal conclusions of our amended one-product model. Doing so, incidentally, they contradict the very notion of an optimum population. Whatever the initial population (the capital-labor ratio), emigration will always increase the marginal product of labor but, by the very price effect which guarantees that increase, will always serve to lower overall potential welfare. Workers should oppose public policies restricting emigration (whether or not they plan themselves to emigrate), but the government of a closed economy, concerned about the welfare of all its citizens, should always encourage immigration, not emigration[16].

11.3. The Two-Product Open Economy

We turn now to trading economies and deal, ad seriatum, with three situations: (1) An economy confronting fixed terms of trade (the traditional small-country case). (2) An economy confronting a fixed but imperfectly elastic foreign offer curve. (3) A two-country system in which emigration from the first is immigration to the second, and the global change in the output mix is the chief determinant of the change in welfare.

The first of these three cases is nearly trivial. If product prices are fixed by foreign trade, there can be no price effect, no redistribution of national in-

[16] Notice, moreover, that this same argument favors *continuous* immigration. Prior immigrants have only to be viewed as part of the now-initial population, eligible for compensation when further arrivals generate a new excess supply of the labor-intensive commodity and reduce the marginal product of labor. Notice, further, that the argument developed above extends automatically to another set of facts. If the average migrant owns as much capital as the average nonmigrant, leaves its physical embodiment behind, but keeps title to the income, there will still be no change in constant-price income per worker (as the ratio of capital to labor income will not change with net migration), but the price effects described above will still occur (as the ratio of capital goods to labor will still change). These different facts, however, require external commodity trade to effect transfers of property income.

come, and no need for compensation. The excess demand for blankets caused by emigration can be satisfied by larger blanket imports or smaller blanket exports, depending upon the initial trade pattern, and the remaining population is not affected by emigration[17].

The second of these cases is not much more difficult. As before, emigration will generate an excess demand for blankets and excess supply of apples. In this instance, however, prices will change, income will be redistributed in favor of labor, and welfare changes will ensue. If the source country exports blankets (and its remaining residents would also export blankets if prices were unchanged after emigration), the excess demand for blankets as a result of emigration serves to reduce export supply, moving the system along the foreign offer curve and raising the relative price of blankets. This increase in price, however, amounts to an improvement in the terms of trade. Lump-sum transfers, therefore, can increase the welfare of remaining residents[18]. If, contrarily, the source country imports blankets, the excess demand for blankets caused by emigration amounts to an increase in import demand, moving the system along the foreign offer curve in the opposite direction. The resulting increase in the price of blankets amounts to a deterioration in the terms of trade, reducing the welfare of the remaining population[19].

To illustrate these propositions, fig. 11.4a is adapted from fig. 11.2. Here, initial output is at E_0 on the initial transformation curve (not shown) and on the budget line $Z_0 Y_0$, while initial consumption is at F_0, on that same budget line. Export supply is $Q_0 E_0$ of blankets. After emigration, output is at E_1, on the new transformation curve $\bar{A}_1 E_1 \bar{B}_1$, and the budget line $Z_1 Y_1$, while

---

[17] This simplest case could easily be illustrated using fig. 11.3. If, initially, consumption took place at a point on $Y_0 Z_0$ southeast of E_0 (at F_0, not now shown), the economy would be exporting apples in exchange for blankets. Emigration would still shift production to E_1 and consumption to F_1 (but F_1 would lie to the southeast of its present position, on a ray not now shown between the origin, O, and the initial consumption point F_0). There would be a change in the volume of trade, but the remaining residents would stay at their initial consumption point F_1 and on their initial indifference curve, U_1.

Notice, however, that this simplest case begs one important question: What is there to generate the wage differential motivating emigration? We shall not confront this issue until we reach case 3, when it will take on enormous importance. Notice, further, that continuing emigration will eventually terminate blanket production, causing factor-price effects. Commodity prices will still be fixed by trade, but the marginal product of labor will have to rise with any further emigration. This will redistribute income in favor of labor (and may also serve to halt the outflow of labor by closing the initial wage differential).

[18] For footnote, see page 101.

[19] For footnote, see page 101.

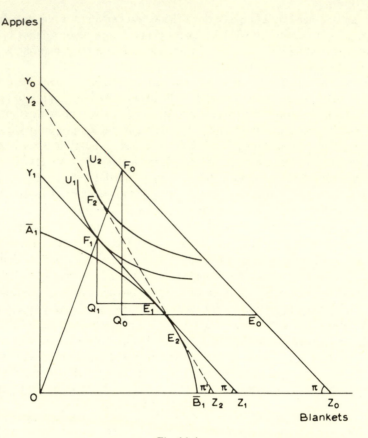

Fig. 11.4a.

consumption is at F_1, at the intersection of $Z_1 Y_1$ and the ray OF_0. Export supply is $Q_1 E_1$ (smaller than $Q_0 E_0$ because F_1 must be southwest of F_0, while E_1 must be northwest of E_0). The budget line $Z_1 Y_1$, however, was that of the remaining population prior to emigration, so that the indifference curve U_1 denotes the initial welfare level of that population. When, then, the reduction of export supply raises the relative price of blankets (from $\tan \pi$ to, say, $\tan \pi'$), the remaining population can achieve the higher welfare level denoted by U_2[20].

[20] For footnote, see next page.

[18] If the remaining residents would import blankets after emigration, emigration could have different welfare implications. An improvement in the terms of trade of the whole economy could be a deterioration in the terms of trade of the remaining population, diminishing its welfare. This possibility is illustrated in the diagram below (a modification of fig. 11.4a in the text). Here, initial exports are $Q_0 E_0$ of blankets, but the

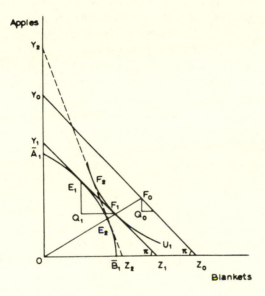

Fig. 11.4b.

constant-price exports of the remaining population would be $Q_1 E_1$ of apples. Emigration will increase the relative price of blankets, as in all other cases studied thus far, but an insufficient increase will leave remaining residents on a representative indifference curve lower than U_1. The new budget line must be steeper than $Z_2 Y_2$ to guarantee an increase in welfare.

[19] Notice the absence of a qualification analogous to that required by the "export" case (and treated in detail in note 18). This is because a country importing blankets prior to emigration has also to do so after emigration. If E_0 were northwest of F_0 in fig. 11.4a, then E_1 would have to be northwest of F_1; E_1 would have to be northwest of E_0 to increase apple output, while F_1 must be on OF_0, southwest of F_0.

[20] The price ratio $\tan \pi'$ will bring equilibrium if one could place the origin of the foreign offer curve at E_2 and have that curve intersect U_2 and $Z_2 Y_2$ at their own intersection, F_2.

To sum up, emigration will increase the economic welfare of the remaining population (by allowing the gainers to compensate the losers) if the source country exports the labor-intensive product (and if the remaining population would do so too in the absence of price changes).

The third case to be considered is the most difficult. Suppose, however, that there is free trade with zero transport costs, so that product prices are the same in both countries under study. Suppose, further, that those countries produce apples and blankets under the same economic conditions, have identical tastes (with unitary income elasticities), but differ in a single, critical way: Let the production functions of one country display a product-neutral, factor-neutral superiority in economic efficiency, thereby to raise its real wage rate and attract the other's labor[21]. This will be the host country; the other will be the source country.

Under these additional assumptions, a migration from source to host country will not affect the incomes of those who remain in the source country, or of the initial host-country residents, until it affects relative prices. It does, however, increase the incomes of the migrants, so that it enlarges total demand for both commodities. This same migration, however, also enlarges constant-price world blanket output and reduces constant-price world apple output, creating an excess supply of blankets and an excess demand for apples, in the world as a whole. It reduces source-country blanket output and enlarges host-country blanket output, but the greater efficiency of the host country makes for a net increase in world blanket output. Similarly, it enlarges source-country apple output and reduces host-country apple output, but the greater efficiency of the host country makes for a net decrease in world apple output. The world price of blankets must decline relative to that of apples, redistributing income in favor of capital within each country[22].

Welfare implications follow directly — and are the opposite of those that were obtained in the closed economy or case (2), earlier. If the source country exports blankets (and its remaining residents would do so too in the ab-

---

[21] If there were no such efficiency difference, the similarity between the two countries would guarantee factor-price equalization under free trade (so long as neither country specialized completely). The introduction of a product-neutral, factor-neutral difference does not prevent the equalization of *relative* factor prices and, therefore, industry factor requirements, but does prevent the equalization of absolute marginal products and, therefore, absolute factor returns. It thereby motivates labor migration (and would cause capital to move along with labor if we were not, arbitrarily, keeping it at home).

[22] Note that this result, if sufficiently extreme, could disappoint the expectations of the migrants themselves and reduce their welfare.

sence of price changes), emigration reduces the welfare of its remaining residents; lump-sum transfers cannot compensate the losers (workers). If, instead, the source country imports blankets, emigration increases the welfare of its remaining residents; lump-sum transfers can be used to compensate the losers.

These results, however, depend uniquely on the choice of reasons for the wage difference needed to explain migration. If efficiency differences had certain biases (product or factor), the argument would change. And if there were no difference of this sort, but a tariff, transport costs, complete specialization, or factor reversals were the cause of higher wages in one country, one might have to use a different approach[23]. There is, in brief, no simple, general method for measuring the consequence of labor migration.

Mathematical Appendix

This appendix furnishes more rigorous proofs of several propositions offered in the text (devoting particular attention to the necessity or sufficiency of the assumptions used in their derivation).

The Basic Model

Consider two commodities ($i = 1,2$) and two countries ($j = 1,2$). Each production function is homogeneous of first degree in labor and capital and is the same in both countries, save for a factor-neutral efficiency term:

$$x_{ij} = a_{ij}[f_i(k_{ij})]\left(\frac{L_{ij}}{L_j}\right), \qquad f_i'(k_{ij}) > 0, f_i''(k_{ij}) < 0 \qquad (11.1)$$

where x_{ij} is ith product output in the jth country (per member of that country's labor force), a_{ij} represents factor-neutral efficiency, k_{ij} is the capital-labor ratio, L_{ij} is labor input, and L_j is the jth country's total labor force. Let $x_{ij} > 0$ at all times.

---

[23] If, for instance, factor reversals were the cause of the wage difference, the welfare changes would be different. Suppose that blankets are labor intensive in the source country and capital intensive in the host country. Migration will reduce blanket output in both countries and will increase apple output, raising the relative price of blankets. This price effect will favor source-country labor and host-country capital, and will increase the welfare of the remaining source-country population if that country (and its remaining population) is the one which exports blankets. In this and other instances, however, migration is apt to be self-limiting; it can, for example, eliminate the factor reversal or complete product specialization that are its initial causes.

With full employment and perfect competition:

$$\sum_i L_{ij} = L_j \tag{11.2}$$

$$\sum_i L_{ij} k_{ij} = L_j k_j \tag{11.3}$$

$$y_{ij}^k = a_{ij}[f_i'(k_{ij})] \tag{11.4}$$

$$y_{ij}^w = a_{ij}[f_i(k_{ij}) - f_i'(k_{ij})k_{ij}] \tag{11.5}$$

where k_j is the jth country's overall capital-labor ratio, while y_{ij}^k and y_{ij}^w are the real wages (incomes) accruing to units of capital and labor, each measured in units of the ith product.

The product-price and factor-price ratios are

$$p_j = \frac{y_{2j}^k}{y_{1j}^k} \tag{11.6}$$

$$v_j = \frac{y_{ij}^w}{y_{ij}^k} \tag{11.7}$$

The demand functions for the first product are

$$c_{1j}^k = g_j^k(y_{1j}^k, p_j) \tag{11.8}$$

$$c_{1j}^w = g_j^w(y_{1j}^w, p_j) \tag{11.9}$$

$$c_{1j} = c_{1j}^w + c_{1j}^k k_j. \tag{11.10}$$

At this juncture, there are 15 endogenous variables for each country (the pairs x_{ij}, k_{ij}, L_{ij}, y_{ij}^k, and y_{ij}^w, plus p_j, v_j, c_{1j}^k, c_{1j}^w, and c_{1j}) and 14 equations (the pairs (11.1), (11.4), (11.5) and (11.7), plus (11.2), (11.3), (11.8), (11.9) and (11.10)). Consider, then three ways to close the system[24].

---

[24] A fourth, closing the economy itself, is to write $x_{1j} = c_{1j}$. This instance, however, is adequately covered in the text and does not, in any case, lend itself to the strategy adopted here.

A. In a single country facing fixed terms of trade

$$p_j = \bar{p} \ . \tag{11.11a}$$

B. In a single country facing a fixed foreign offer curve:

$$(x_{1j} - c_{1j})L_j = s_j(p_j), \qquad (x_{1j} - c_{1j})s_j'(p_j) < 0 \ . \tag{11.11b}$$

C. In a two-country system with no barriers to trade

$$\sum_j (x_{ij} - c_{ij})L_j = 0 \tag{11.11c}$$

$$p_j = p \ . \tag{11.12}$$

In cases (A) and (B), there are 15 equations, equal in number to the endogenous variables. In case (C), there are 31 equations, equal in number to the 30 national variables plus the additional (common) variable p. In each case, there are four exogenous variables for each country (a_{ij}, k_j, and L_j).

Transformation of the Model
All versions of this model can be written more compactly. Using eqs. (11.1), (11.2) and (11.3),

$$x_{1j} = a_{1j} \, [f_1(k_{1j})] \left[\frac{k_{2j} - k_j}{k_{2j} - k_{1j}} \right] \tag{11.13}$$

where $x_{1j} > 0$ implies $k_{2j} > k_j > k_{1j}$ whenever $k_{2j} > k_{1j}$, as is assumed hereafter[25]. Using eqs. (11.1), (11.4) and (11.5), and invoking Euler's theorem:

$$f_i'(k_{ij})(v_j + k_{ij}) = f_i(k_{ij}) \ . \tag{11.14}$$

---

[25] Similarly,

$$x_{2j} = a_{2j} [f_2(k_{2j})] \left[\frac{k_j - k_{1j}}{k_{2j} - k_{1j}} \right].$$

Or, using eqs. (11.14) and (11.15),

$$x_{2j} = p \left[\left(\frac{v_j + k_{2j}}{v_j + k_{1j}} \right) \left(\frac{k_j - k_{1j}}{k_{2j} - k_j} \right) \right] x_{1j} \ .$$

Then, from eqs. (11.4) through (11.10):

$$p = \left(\frac{a_{2j}}{a_{1j}}\right)\left[\frac{f_2'(k_{2j})}{f_1'(k_{1j})}\right]$$ (11.15)

$$c_{1j} = g_j^w(y_{1j}^w,p) + g_j^k(y_{1j}^k,p)k_j$$ (11.16)

$$y_{ij}^k = a_{ij}[f_i'(k_{ij})]$$ (11.17)

$$y_{ij}^w = y_{ij}^k v_j .$$ (11.18)

Now there are nine endogenous variables for each country (the pairs k_{ij}, y_{ij}^k and y_{ij}^w, plus x_{1j} c_{1j} and v_j) and nine equations (the pairs (11.14), (11.17) and (11.18), plus (11.13), (11.15) and (11.16)), plus the common price ratio p and the three versions of (11.11).

Now differentiate eqs. (11.13) through (11.18), using dotted terms to denote percentage rates of change. From eqs. (11.13) and (11.14):

$$\dot{x}_{1j} = \dot{a}_{1j} + Q_j \dot{v}_j - \left(\frac{k_j}{k_{2j}-k_j}\right)\dot{k}_j$$ (11.19)

where

$$Q_j = \left(\frac{1}{k_{2j}-k_{1j}}\right)\left[\sigma_{1j}k_{1j}\left(\frac{v_j+k_{2j}}{v_j+k_{1j}}\right) + \sigma_{2j}k_{2j}\left(\frac{k_j-k_{1j}}{k_{2j}-k_j}\right)\right],$$

while

$$\sigma_{ij} = \left(\frac{\delta k_{ij}}{\delta v_j}\right)\left(\frac{v_j}{k_{ij}}\right) > 0 ,$$

so that[26] $Q_j > 0$. From eqs. (11.14) and (11.15):

$$\dot{p} = (\dot{a}_{2j}-\dot{a}_{1j}) + e_j^{pv}\dot{v}_j$$ (11.20)

where

$$e_j^{pv} = \frac{v_j(k_{2j}-k_{1j})}{(v_j+k_{1j})(v_j+k_{2j})} > 0 .$$

---

[26] For footnote, see next page.

From eq. (11.16):

$$c_{1j} = E_j^y \dot{a}_{1j} - \left[z_j e_j^{ky} - \left(\frac{k_{1j}}{v_j + k_{1j}} \right) E_j^y \right] \dot{v}_j - E_j^p \dot{p} + z_j \dot{k}_j \qquad (11.21)$$

where $0 < z_j = k_j(c_{1j}^k/c_{1j}) < 1$; where $e_j^{ky} = (\delta c_{1j}^k/\delta y_{1j}^k)(y_{1j}^k/c_{1j}^k) > 0$ and $e_j^{wy} = (\delta c_{1j}^w/\delta y_{1j}^w)(y_{1j}^w/c_{1j}^w) > 0$, so that $E_j^y = [e_j^{wy} + z_j(e_j^{ky} - e_j^{wy})] > 0$; and where $e_j^{kp} = -(\delta c_{1j}^k/\delta p)(p/c_{1j}^k) > 0$ and $e_j^{wp} = -(\delta c_{1j}^w/\delta p)(p/c_{1j}^w) > 0$, so that $E_j^p = [e_j^{wp} + z_j(e_j^{kp} - e_j^{wp})] > 0$. Then, from eqs. (11.17) and (11.18):

$$\dot{y}_{ij}^k = \dot{\alpha}_j^k - \left(\frac{v_j}{v_j + k_{ij}} \right) \left(\frac{1}{e_j^{pv}} \right) \dot{p} \qquad (11.22)$$

$$\dot{y}_{ij}^w = \dot{\alpha}_j^w + \left(\frac{k_{ij}}{v_j + k_{ij}} \right) \left(\frac{1}{e_j^{pv}} \right) \dot{p} \qquad (11.23)$$

where

$$\dot{\alpha}_j^k = \frac{(v_j + k_{2j})\dot{a}_{2j} - (v_j + k_{1j})\dot{a}_{1j}}{(k_{2j} - k_{1j})} ,$$

[26] From note 2, moreover,

$$\dot{x}_{2j} = \dot{a}_{2j} + \left[\left(\frac{v_j + k_{1j}}{v_j + k_{2j}} \right) \left(\frac{k_{2j} - k_j}{k_j - k_{1j}} \right) \right] Q_j \dot{v}_j + \left(\frac{k_j}{k_j - k_{1j}} \right) \dot{k}_j .$$

In consequence,

$$(\dot{x}_{2j} - \dot{x}_{1j}) = (\dot{a}_{2j} - \dot{a}_{1j}) + (T_j k_j)\dot{k}_j - \left[(v_j + k_j)\left(\frac{k_{2j} - k_j}{v_j + k_{2j}} \right)(T_j Q_j) \right] \dot{v}_j$$

where $T_j = (k_{2j} - k_{1j})/[(k_{2j} - k_j)(k_j - k_{1j})] > 0$. Using eq. (11.20), then

$$(\dot{x}_{2j} - \dot{x}_{1j}) = \left[1 + (v_j + k_j)\left(\frac{k_{2j} - k_j}{v_j + k_{2j}} \right)(T_j Q_j)\left(\frac{1}{e_j^{pv}} \right) \right](\dot{a}_{2j} - \dot{a}_{1j})$$

$$+ (T_j k_j)\dot{k}_j - \left[(v_j + k_j)\left(\frac{k_{2j} - k_j}{v_j + k_{2j}} \right)(T_j Q_j)\left(\frac{1}{e_j^{pv}} \right) \right]\dot{p} .$$

An increase of the capital-labor ratio (or of a_{2j} relative to a_{1j}) will shift the transformation curve, raising x_{2j} relative to x_{1j} at each set of product prices ($\dot{p}=0$). An increase of p will move an economy along its transformation curve, raising x_{1j} relative to x_{2j}. These familiar results underlie the diagrams used in the text.

while

$$\dot{\alpha}_j^w = \dot{\alpha}_j^k - \left(\frac{\dot{a}_{2j} - \dot{a}_{1j}}{e_j^{p\upsilon}}\right) .$$

Finally, from eqs. (11.11a) and (11.11b):

$$\dot{p} = 0 \qquad\qquad (11.24)$$

$$(x_{1j}\dot{x}_{1j} - c_{1j}\dot{c}_{1j}) + (x_{1j} - c_{1j})\dot{L}_j = -e^s(x_{1j} - c_{1j})\dot{p} \qquad (11.25)$$

where $e^s = -s_j'(p)[p/(x_{1j} - c_{1j})] > 0$. And from eq. (11.11c):

$$\sum_j [(x_{1j}\dot{x}_{1j} - c_{1j}\dot{c}_{1j}) + (x_{1j} - c_{1j})\dot{L}_j] L_j = 0 . \qquad (11.26)$$

Factor-Supply Changes and Economic Welfare

Next, postulate a welfare (utility) function for an individual worker or capitalist and the corresponding budget constraint:

$$U_j^t = U_{j.}^t(c_{1j}^t, c_{2j}^t), \qquad t = w, k \qquad (11.27)$$

$$(pc_{1j}^t + c_{2j}^t) - y_{2j}^t = 0 . \qquad (11.28)$$

Maximizing eq. (11.27) subject to (11.28), we have

$$\left(\frac{\delta U_j^t}{\delta c_{1j}^t}\right) = \lambda p \qquad\qquad (11.29)$$

$$\left(\frac{\delta U_j^t}{\delta c_{2j}^t}\right) = \lambda \qquad\qquad (11.30)$$

where λ is a Lagrangian multiplier.

Differentiating eqs. (11.27) through (11.30) totally and setting $dU_j^t = 0$, we can solve for the change in y_{2j}^t needed to keep U_j^t constant:

$$\dot{y}_{2j}^{*t} = m_j^t \dot{p} \qquad\qquad (11.31)$$

where $m_j^t = (c_{1j}^t/y_{1j}^t) \leqslant 1$. Consider, then, two situations:

1. If there are no lump-sum transfers between workers and capitalists, the sign of the realized welfare change is given by:

$$\dot{G}_j^t = \dot{y}_{2j}^t - \overset{*}{\dot{y}}_{2j}^t \ . \tag{11.32}$$

Or, using eqs. (11.22) and (11.23), we have

$$\dot{G}_j^k = \dot{\alpha}_j^k - \left[\left(\frac{v_j + k_{1j}}{k_{2j} - k_{1j}}\right) + m_j^k\right]\dot{p} \tag{11.33}$$

$$\dot{G}_j^w = \dot{\alpha}_j^w + \left[\left(\frac{k_{2j}}{v_j}\right)\left(\frac{v_j + k_{1j}}{k_{2j} - k_{1j}}\right) - m_j^w\right]\dot{p} \ . \tag{11.34}$$

Changes in factor supplies ($\dot{L}_j$ and $\dot{k}_j$) have no welfare impact unless they alter product prices. But when, as their consequence, $\dot{p} > 0$, then $\dot{G}_j^k < 0$ and $\dot{G}_j^w > 0$; this is because

$$\left(\frac{k_{2j}}{v_j}\right)\left(\frac{v_j + k_{1j}}{k_{2j} - k_{1j}}\right) > 1 > m_j^w \ .$$

2. If there are lump-sum transfers, the sign of the realized welfare change is given by:

$$\dot{G}_j = \dot{y}_{2j} - \overset{*}{\dot{y}}_{2j} \tag{11.35}$$

where

$$\overset{*}{\dot{y}}_{2j} = \left(\frac{y_{1j}^w}{y_{1j}}\right)\overset{*}{\dot{y}}_{2j}^w + k_j\left(\frac{y_{1j}^k}{y_{1j}}\right)\overset{*}{\dot{y}}_{2j}^k = \left(\frac{c_{1j}^w + k_j c_{1j}^k}{y_{1j}}\right)\dot{p} = \left(\frac{c_{1j}}{y_{1j}}\right)\dot{p} \tag{11.36}$$

and

$$\dot{y}_{2j} = \left(\frac{y_{1j}^w}{y_{1j}}\right)\dot{y}_{2j}^w + k_j\left(\frac{y_{1j}^k}{y_{1j}}\right)\dot{y}_{2j}^k = \dot{\alpha}_j^k - \left(\frac{y_{1j}^w}{y_{1j}}\right)\left(\frac{\dot{a}_{2j} - \dot{a}_{1j}}{e_j^{pv}}\right)$$

$$+ \left[\frac{v_j(k_{2j} - k_{1j})}{e_j^{pv}(v_j + k_{2j})(v_j + k_j)}\right]\dot{p} \ . \tag{11.37}$$

The last term in eq. (11.37), however, reduces to $(x_{1j}/y_{1j})\dot{p}$, so that eq. (11.35) becomes:

$$\dot{G}_j = \dot{\alpha}_j^k - \left(\frac{y_{1j}^w}{y_{1j}}\right)\left(\frac{\dot{a}_{2j} - \dot{a}_{1j}}{e_j^{pv}}\right) + \left(\frac{x_{1j} - c_{1j}}{y_{1j}}\right)\dot{p} \ . \tag{11.38}$$

Once again, changes in factor supplies leave welfare unaffected unless they alter product prices. Here, however, their price effect is thoroughly familiar: if factor-supply changes improve the terms of trade, they increase welfare; if they worsen the terms of trade, they decrease welfare[27].

We have, therefore, to ascertain the signs of $\dot{p}$ in each version of the model (setting $\dot{a}_{ij} = 0$ to concentrate on changes in factor supplies).

Taking, first, the simplest case, eq. (11.24) now asserts that an economy with fixed terms of trade cannot experience any welfare change consequent upon a change in factor supplies. As $\dot{p} = 0$, by hypothesis, $\dot{G}_j^k = \dot{G}_j^w = \dot{G}_j = 0$.

Taking, next, the other single-country case, we use eqs. (11.19) through (11.21) and (11.25) to write,

$$\dot{p} = \left(\frac{e_j^{pv}}{D_j}\right)\left\{\left[x_{1j}\left(\frac{k_j}{k_{2j}-k_j}\right) + c_{1j}z_j\right]\dot{k}_j - (x_{1j}-c_{1j})\dot{L}_j\right\} \qquad (11.39)$$

where

$$D_j = e_j^{pv}\left[(x_{1j}-c_{1j})e^s+c_{1j}E_j^p\right] + x_{1j}Q_j + c_{1j}\left[z_je_j^{ky}\left(\frac{k_{1j}}{v_j+k_{1j}}\right)E_j^y\right].$$

The sign of D_j depends entirely on that of its final term (as all other terms are positive). Hereafter, therefore, let all income elasticities be constant, and let workers and capitalists have the same tastes. Under these circumstances, $E_j^y = e_j^{ky}$ and $z_j = k_j/(v_j+k_j)$, the capitalists' share in national income, while the final term of D_j reduces to

$$c_{1j}\left[e_j^{ky}\left(\frac{k_j-k_{1j}}{k_{2j}-k_{1j}}\right)e_j^{pv}\right] > 0.$$

With balanced growth in factor supplies ($\dot{L}_j \neq 0, \dot{k}_j = 0$), the sign of $\dot{p}$ depends entirely upon the trade pattern. If $x_{1j} > c_{1j}$, $\dot{L}_j > 0$ implies $\dot{p} < 0$ (giving $\dot{G}_j^k > 0$ and $\dot{G}_j^w < 0$). If $x_{1j} < c_{1j}$, $\dot{L}_j > 0$ implies $\dot{p} > 0$ (giving $\dot{G}_j^k < 0$ and $\dot{G}_j^w > 0$). In either case, of course, $\dot{L}_j > 0$ (overall growth in factor supplies) worsens the terms of trade; $\dot{G}_j < 0$.

With unbalanced growth, the outcome can differ. Consider, in particular, the results of immigration (so that $\dot{k}_j = -\dot{L}_j < 0$). Rewriting eq. (11.39), we have

---

[27] If $x_{1j} > c_{1j}$, then $\dot{p} > 0$ is an improvement in the terms of trade and gives $\dot{G}_j > 0$. If $x_{1j} < c_{1j}$, then $\dot{p} < 0$ is an improvement in the terms of trade and gives $\dot{G}_j > 0$.

$$\dot{p} - \left(\frac{e_j^{pv}}{D_j}\right)\left[x_{1j}\left(\frac{k_{2j}}{k_{2j}-k_j}\right)-c_{1j}(1-z_j)\right]\dot{L}_j$$

$$= -\left(\frac{e_j^{pv}}{D_j}\right)y_{1j}^w\left[\left(\frac{k_{2j}}{k_{2j}-k_{1j}}\right)\left(\frac{v_j+k_{1j}}{v_j}\right)-m_j^k\right]\dot{L}_j . \tag{11.40}$$

As $m_j^k < 1$, this expression takes its sign from $\dot{L}_j$. When, then, $\dot{L}_j > 0, \dot{p} < 0$; $\dot{G}_j^k > 0$, $\dot{G}_j^w < 0$, and the sign of $\dot{G}_j$ depends on the trade pattern. If $x_{1j} > c_{1j}$ initially and (at constant prices) after immigration, $\dot{G}_j < 0$; if, instead, $x_{1j} < c_{1j}$, $\dot{G}_j > 0$.

The two-country situation is more complex; generalized treatment is not too useful. Consider, however, the case of net migration (so that $L_1\dot{L}_1 = -L_2\dot{L}_2$), and use eqs. (11.19) through (11.21) and (11.26) to write

$$\dot{p} = \left(\frac{1}{D}\right)\left\{\left[x_{12}\left(\frac{k_{22}}{k_{22}-k_2}\right)-x_{11}\left(\frac{k_{21}}{k_{21}-k_1}\right)\right]\right.$$

$$\left. -\left[c_{12}\left(\frac{v_2}{v_2+k_2}\right)-c_{11}\left(\frac{v_1}{v_1+k_1}\right)\right]\right\}\dot{L}_1 \tag{11.41}$$

where

$$D = \left[x_{11}\left(\frac{Q_1}{e_1^{pv}}\right)+x_{12}\left(\frac{Q_2}{e_2^{pv}}\right)\left(\frac{L_2}{L_1}\right)\right]+\left[c_{11}e_1^{kp}+c_{12}e_2^{kp}\left(\frac{L_2}{L_1}\right)\right]$$

$$+\left[c_{11}\left(\frac{k_1-k_{11}}{k_{21}-k_{11}}\right)e_1^{ky}+c_{12}\left(\frac{k_2-k_{12}}{k_{22}-k_{12}}\right)e_2^{ky}\left(\frac{L_2}{L_1}\right)\right]$$

Although $D > 0$, the sign of eq. (11.41) remains in doubt. Additional restrictions are needed. Assume, therefore, that $a_{11} = (1+\gamma)a_{12}$, which assumption (joined to others made earlier) gives $v_j = v_0$, $k_{ij} = k_{i0}$, and $y_{i1}^w = (1+\gamma)y_{i2}^w$, so that $\dot{L}_1$ takes its sign from γ. Further, assume that all tastes are the same and that $e_j^{ky} = 1$. Under this additional assumption,

$$c_{1j} = y_{1j}^k(v_0+k_j)[g(p)] \tag{11.42}$$

where $g(p) = m_j^k = m_j^w \leqslant 1$. Rewriting eq. (11.41), we have

$$\dot{p} = -\left(\frac{1}{D}\right)y_{12}^w\left[\left(\frac{v_0+k_{10}}{v_0}\right)\left(\frac{k_{20}}{k_{20}-k_{10}}\right)-g(p)\right](\gamma\dot{L}_1) . \tag{11.43}$$

As $g(p) < 1$ and $\gamma \dot{L}_1 > 0$, then $\dot{p} < 0$ under all circumstances. Hence, $\dot{G}_j^k > 0$, $\dot{G}_j^w < 0$, and $\dot{G}_1$ takes its sign from the trade pattern. If, at initial prices, $x_{11} > c_{11}$ for the relevant population, $\dot{G}_1 < 0$; if $x_{11} < c_{11}$ for that population, $\dot{G}_1 > 0$.

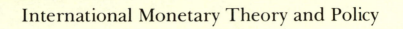

International Monetary Theory and Policy

INTERNATIONAL LIQUIDITY AND THE BALANCE OF PAYMENTS OF A RESERVE-CURRENCY COUNTRY*

By Peter B. Kenen

I

Several experts have recently warned that the world's monetary reserves must increase if the growth of international trade and the spread of convertibility are to continue. Some fear that a shortage of liquidity must throttle world trade.[1] Others, more cautious, suggest that such a shortage may force governments facing payments crises to adopt remedies that may inhibit the further growth of trade.[2]

Under present circumstances, a demand for extra liquidity may be satisfied by an increase of the world's monetary gold stock; new gold production will enlarge world reserves. But a number of experts think this source inadequate.[3] They argue that the reserve-currency countries, Britain and the United States, must also supply additional cash to the rest of the world — that these two countries must run payments deficits on current-*cum*-capital account. I propose to explore some of the implications of this proposition — to investigate certain of the dynamic properties of the new gold-exchange standard.

Throughout, I shall assume that there is only one reserve-currency country (America) and one reserve currency (the dollar). Hence, governments and banks that are repositories of international liquidity can hold only gold or dollars. In addition, I shall assume that their choice as between gold and dollars is governed by the interest reward that dollar balances offer and by the foreigners' estimate of the risk that the dollar price of gold may rise. This risk, in turn, will be assumed to vary inversely with the American reserve ratio — the ratio of American gold to short-term liabilities (foreign-

* I am indebted to Professors J. W. Angell and H. G. Johnson and to Mr. Richard Cooper for comments on an earlier draft of this paper.
1. Roy Harrod, "Imbalance in International Payments," *International Monetary Fund Staff Papers*, 1953.
2. International Monetary Fund, *International Liquidity and Reserves*, 1958, and Robert Triffin, "The Return to Convertibility," Banca Nazionale del Lavoro, *Quarterly Review*, March 1959.
3. Triffin, *op. cit.*

owned dollar balances).[4] For the present, I shall also assume that
the foreign institutions that hold dollars may also hold gold. This
is a drastic simplification, but will render the presentation more
manageable. I modify it in an appendix to this paper.

The assumptions just listed produce three equations:

$$R = D + G_f, \tag{1}$$
$$G = G_a + G_f, \tag{2}$$
$$D/R = \theta(i, G_a/D), \tag{3}$$

where R is the total of reserves (other than those of America); D is
the stock of foreign-owned dollar balances; G is the world's gold stock;
G_a is America's gold stock, inclusive of the gold that is used to back
America's own money supply; G_f is the rest of the world's gold stock;
and i is the rate of return that dollar balances offer. I assume that
G and i are exogenously determined.

Equations 1 and 2 are definitional. Equation 3 is behavioral
and is assumed to have the following properties:

(a) $\partial (D/R)/\partial(G_a/D) > 0$ and $\partial^2(D/R)/\partial(G_a/D)^2 < 0$;
(b) $\partial(D/R)/\partial i > 0$.

These conditions say that foreigners will want to hold a larger fraction
of their reserves as dollar balances the larger the American reserve
ratio (given interest rates) and the larger the return their balances
yield (given the American reserve ratio). We neglect the possibility
that foreigners may look at America's "free" gold instead of her gross
gold stock when appraising the American reserve ratio.

II

To begin our analysis, we connect the change in world reserves,
dR, to America's balance of payments on current-*cum*-capital account,
B, defined as an increase in America's net stock of liquid assets.
Neglecting domestic American gold production:

$$B = dG_a - dD. \tag{4}$$

If, now, we designate the *desired* change in world reserves as
dR^*, we may write the American payments position that must be
maintained to secure dR^* as:[5]

$$B^* = -(dR^* - dG). \tag{4a}$$

---

4. One reader has suggested that changes in the absolute American gold
stock is the proximate determinant of foreign confidence in the dollar. This is a
plausible alternative, but not as plausible, I think, as my hypothesis. The
supposition made here, moreover, is akin to that which underlies most of our
thinking about banking systems.

5. From equations 1 and 2, $B = (dG - dG_f) - (dR - dG_f)$, which gives
$B = -(dR - dG)$. Substituting B^* and dR^* for B and dR, we obtain equation 4a.

Equation 4a merely reaffirms my earlier assertion: If new gold production cannot satisfy the world's demand for reserves (if $dR^* > dG$), the reserve-currency country must run a payments deficit. It does not say that America will lose gold when she runs a payments deficit, nor that America's reserve ratio will fall. Although in deficit, America may gain gold if foreigners wish to add more dollars to their reserves than they gain by way of America's deficit.[6] America's reserve ratio may even rise when she runs a payments deficit.[7]

But foreigners may decline to hold all of the dollars they may gain by way of America's payments deficit. They will then drain away part of America's gold stock; and if the American reserve ratio is initially smaller than unity, they will thereby erode America's reserve ratio.[8] An American payments deficit, then, could undermine confidence in the dollar and might consequently wreck the gold-exchange standard. A decline in America's reserve ratio due to an American deficit could cause other countries to switch from dollars to gold, further eroding America's reserve position. The system could disintegrate. It is the main task of this paper to identify the circumstances under which this will happen.

To begin, we extract from equations 1 and 2 a definition of the American reserve ratio, G_a/D, in terms of D/R and G/R:

$$G_a/D = 1 - [(1 - G/R)/(D/R)]. \tag{5}$$

Equation 5 argues that each combination of D/R with G/R is consistent with but one American reserve ratio, and that an increase of D/R will increase the American reserve ratio when G/R is smaller than unity and will decrease the reserve ratio when G/R is larger than unity. But G/R is itself linked to America's ratio.[9] If G_a/D itself exceeds unity, G/R will also exceed unity and America's reserve ratio will be a decreasing function of D/R. If, by contrast, G_a/D is smaller than unity, G/R will be smaller than unity and America's

6. The change in America's gold stock, dG_a, may be written as $dG - dG_f$ or as $dD + B$. Even if B is negative, dG_a may be positive.

7. The change in America's reserve ratio, $d(G_a/D)$, may be written as $(G_a/D)\,(dG_a/G_a - dD/D)$ or as $(1/D)[dD(1 - G_a/D) + B]$. This may be positive even when B is negative.

8. Even if they decide to hold the dollars they gain, moreover, their demand for dollars may not suffice to stabilize America's reserve ratio. This is because the condition for stability in the reserve ratio (footnote 7, above) is more stringent than the condition for stability in the gold stock itself (footnote 6, above).

9. This is because $G/R = (G_a + G_f)/(D + G_f)$, which may be rewritten as $G/R = (G_a/D + G_f/D)/(1 + G_f/D)$.

reserve ratio will be an increasing function of D/R. These possibilities are illustrated by Figure I, where $(G/R)_1 < (G/R)_2 < 1$, and $(G/R)_3 > (G/R)_4 > 1$.

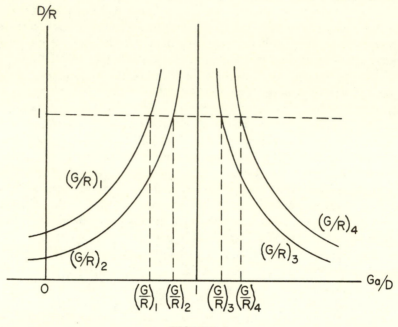

FIGURE I

Using equations 3 and 5, we may trace the path taken by America's reserve ratio when America runs a payments deficit and may investigate the stability of our system. We set $i = i_0$ and superimpose a representation of equation 3 upon the family of equations 5 to form Figure II. With i fixed, equation 3 gives D/R for each American reserve ratio, and equation 5 gives the reserve ratio that is consistent with each pair of values for D/R and G/R. Hence the points P_0, P_1, etc., in Figure II give those combinations of D/R and the American reserve ratio that are mutually consistent. Defining that G/R which produces the point of tangency P_0 as $(G/R)_{\min}$, we may classify the possibilities as follows: For G/R greater than unity there will be just one such consistent combination of D/R and G_a/D for each G/R. For G/R less than unity, there may be more; there will be two for all $(G/R)_{\min} < G/R < 1$, one for $G/R = (G/R)_{\min}$, and none for $G/R < (G/R)_{\min}$.

Clearly, the parameter G/R is decisive to a particular solution of our system. Let us, then, digress to explore the connection between G/R and America's payments position. If $0 < dG < dR$, America runs a payments deficit (B is negative). But:

$$d(G/R) = (G/R)(dG/G - dR/R) = (dR/R)(dG/dR - G/R)$$

$$(6).$$

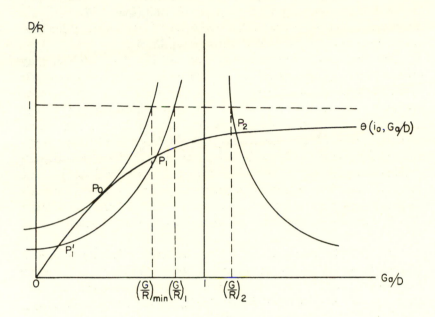

FIGURE II

If, therefore, dR is positive (world reserves are increasing), an American payments deficit must reduce G/R whenever new gold production is smaller relative to the increment in world reserves than the world's total gold stock relative to total reserves. If, then, G/R is initially larger than unity, an increase in world reserves larger than new gold production *must* reduce G/R. If, by contrast, G/R is initially smaller than unity, an increase in world reserves larger than new gold production *may* reduce G/R, but need not do so.

We may now return to Figure II. Suppose, to start, that G/R is greater than unity. The system will begin at some point like P_2. If America runs a deficit, raising world reserves by more than new gold production, G/R must fall, carrying the system's equilibrium along $\theta(i_0, G_a/D)$, toward P_1. The reserve ratio and D/R will both fall. This trend will continue until G/R falls to equality with dG/dR, so that $dG/dR - G/R = 0$. Once at that level (say at $(G/R)_1$ and P_1 in Figure II), G/R will be stationary, provided only that reserves and the gold stock continue to increase in the same ratio. The system will have attained a sustainable position.[1] I say "sustainable" and not "stable" because we have not yet examined the dynamic properties of the system, only a set of plausible solutions. We have not determined that the system *will* move from P_2 to P_1 as G/R declines, only that it must if it is to attain a new equilibrium.

We may now distinguish two possibilities. First, dG/dR may exceed $(G/R)_{\min}$, as does $(G/R)_1$ in Figure II. In this instance, our system will have a sustainable solution, for G/R itself will come to rest at a value exceeding $(G/R)_{\min}$. Second, dG/dR may be smaller than $(G/R)_{\min}$. In this case, the system will not have a sustainable solution. Which result will actually obtain depends, of course, upon the initial position $(G/R)_2$, upon the shape and position of $\theta(i_0, G_a/D)$, and upon the rates of change of reserves and of the gold stock. The outcome, therefore, is dependent partly upon the size of America's continuing payments deficit.[2] The larger that deficit, the smaller dG/dR, and the greater the risk that dG/dR will be smaller than $(G/R)_{\min}$.

In principle, America can control the path taken by G/R and can act to insure that a sustainable solution is attained. America can reduce its deficit to raise dG/dR or, for a given dG/dR, can raise its short-term interest rates, lifting $\theta(i, G_a/D)$ and reducing $(G/R)_{\min}$. The first policy, however, would defeat the objective set at the outset of this discussion. It would reduce the rate of accumulation of reserves, dR, relative to the desired rate, dR^*. The second may be inconsistent with America's domestic economic objectives. It could slow America's growth and encumber antirecession policy. America might be unable to expand her money supply to stimulate bank lending for domestic recovery.[3]

1. If, of course, we seek a constant rate of increase in reserves, $(dR/R)^*$, not a constant absolute increase, dR^*, and if $(dR/R)^*$ is larger than dG/G, the system will not come to rest; $d(G/R)$ will always be negative. The only continuing rate (dR/R) that would stabilize G/R would be $(dR/R) = (dG/G)$. This would set B^* at $-dG(R/G - 1)$.

2. As $B = -(dR - dG)$, $dG/dR = dG/(dG - B)$. When America is in deficit, however, B is negative. The larger the deficit, then, the smaller dG/dR.

3. In addition, an increase of interest rates could reduce America's long-term lending abroad, reducing the payments deficit and, again, slowing the accumulation of reserves by other countries.

Up to now, we have supposed that the initial G/R is greater than unity. Let us now suppose that G/R and G_a/D are initially smaller than unity. The system might then begin at a position like P_1 in Figure II. In these circumstances, an American deficit large enough to set dG/dR smaller than $(G/R)_1$ would cause G/R to fall, pushing the equilibrium point to the left on $\theta(i_0, G_a/D)$. The American reserve ratio and D/R would decline. Again, however, the decline of G/R would proceed at a diminishing (absolute) rate, slowing the displacement of P_1, and a sustainable position would be generated provided dG/dR were greater than $(G/R)_{\min}$. If, by contrast, the American deficit were small enough to set dG/dR larger than $(G/R)_1$, G/R would rise. In this case, a sustainable solution would necessarily exist.[4]

The system might begin at a point like P_1' in Figure II. But I shall postpone the analysis of this situation until we have explored the dynamic properties of our system.

Let us summarize to this point:

1. If we wish to increase reserves faster than the rate at which the monetary gold stock is increasing, the reserve-currency country (America) must run a payments deficit.

2. If, initially, $G/R > 1$, America's deficit must reduce the equilibrium values of the American reserve ratio, G_a/D, and D/R, for G/R will be larger than dG/dR.

3. If, initially, $G/R < 1$, America's deficit may increase or decrease the equilibrium values of the reserve ratio and D/R as dG/dR exceeds or falls short of the initial G/R.

4. For all initial values of G/R greater than $(G/R)_{\min}$, a continuing deficit of constant size must reduce or increase G/R until $G/R = dG/dR$. Thereafter, G/R, D/R, and America's reserve ratio will come to rest, provided reserves and the world's gold stock continue to increase in the same ratio.[5]

5. $G/R = dG/dR$ will be a solution to our system, giving sustainable values for D/R and the American reserve ratio, provided

4. If dG is positive and America is running a deficit, dG/dR must be positive but smaller than unity. By assumption, however, dG/dR is greater than the initial G/R. Hence the ratio G/R must rise but must stop rising before it reaches unity. There must also be a sustainable solution for dG/dR greater than unity, but this implies that America is running a payments surplus and lies beyond the immediate purview of our discussion.

5. Note, however, that this proposition has been established only for initial values of G_a/D and D/R greater than those pertaining to $(G/R)_{\min}$. We have not yet investigated points like P_1', in Figure II.

dG/dR exceeds or is equal to $(G/R)_{\min}$. If this condition is not satisfied, we cannot produce mutually consistent values for D/R and the reserve ratio at $G/R = dG/dR$.

6. To satisfy condition (5), America's monetary authorities may either reduce America's deficit, raising dG/dR relative to $(G/R)_{\min}$, or may raise interest rates to lower $(G/R)_{\min}$ relative to dG/dR.

III

Thus far, we have been concerned to trace the values of America's reserve ratio and D/R that are given by an initial value for G/R and the displacement of that ratio by an American payments deficit. We shall now examine the dynamics of our model to ask whether America's ratio and D/R will actually converge upon their equilibrium values when America runs a deficit. To this end, we shall assume a simple lag in the adjustment of D/R to G_a/D, rewriting equation 3 as:

$$(D/R)_t = \theta[i_o, (G_a/D)_{t-1}]. \tag{3a}$$

Consider, now, the several cases that may arise.

Let us start at P_1 in Figure III and suppose that G/R is suddenly

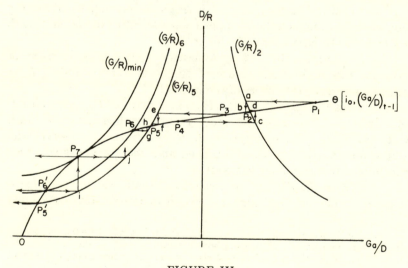

FIGURE III

reduced from that level which generated P_1 to a new level $(G/R)_2$. The system would travel the route $P_1, a, b, \ldots P_2$. It would converge upon a new equilibrium. If, by contrast, the system were initially at P_4, giving values for the reserve ratio and D/R smaller than those pertaining to P_2, the system would travel the route $P_4, c, d, \ldots \ldots P_2$. Again, it would oscillate into the new equilibrium. No matter what its initial position, then, a system displaying the properties of our model will converge upon the appropriate equilibrium when G/R is greater than unity.

Suppose, next, that G/R were established at $(G/R)_5$ in Figure III. If the initial values of D/R and America's reserve ratio were given by P_3, the system would travel along $P_3, e, f, \ldots \ldots P_5$. It would converge upon its new solution. If it were initially at P_6, it would travel the path $P_6, g, h, \ldots \ldots P_5$. It would again approach its equilibrium. For G/R smaller than unity, then, the system must approach its equilibrium without oscillating provided it begins from points to the right of P_7. Suppose, however, that the system were to start at P_5' or P_6', positions to the left of P_7. If G/R were to increase, the system would again converge upon its new equilibrium. If, for example, we were at P_6' and G/R were to rise from $(G/R)_6$ to $(G/R)_5$ the system would travel along $P_6', i, j, \ldots \ldots P_5$. Note that it would not seek P_5' but would instead attain its upper equilibrium P_5. If, however, G/R were to decline, the system would disintegrate. If, for example, we were at P_5' and G/R fell from $(G/R)_5$ to $(G/R)_6$, the American reserve ratio would decline precipitously, seeking an intersection with the hyperbola given by $(G/R)_6$. If that hyperbola were steeply sloped in the neighborhood of P_5', the system could achieve this intersection at a positive G_a/D. But the new American reserve ratio would be smaller than that prevailing at P_5'. D/R would consequently fall again, lowering G_a/D once more. Our model is unstable in this region. If, therefore, the system were to start from a point to the left of P_7 it would converge upon its (upper) equilibrium with an increase of G/R, but would disintegrate with a decline in G/R.

Consider, finally, the dynamics of P_7, given by $(G/R)_7 = (G/R)_{min}$. If G/R were to increase, the system would approach a new equilibrium. But if G/R were to fall, the system would disintegrate. P_7, then, partakes of the properties of points to its right with respect to an increase of G/R and of points to its left with respect to a decrease.[6]

---

6. Formally speaking P_7 is unstable in both directions. But the chain of changes that would be caused by an increase of G/R is bounded by another equilibrium, while that which would be started by a decline of G/R is not analogously confined.

The dynamic properties of our model may be summarized as follows:

1. If an American deficit raises G/R, the system will achieve its new equilibrium no matter what the initial position.

2. If an American deficit reduces G/R, the system will approach a new equilibrium if it begins from a point to the right of P_7, but will disintegrate if it begins at or to the left of P_7.

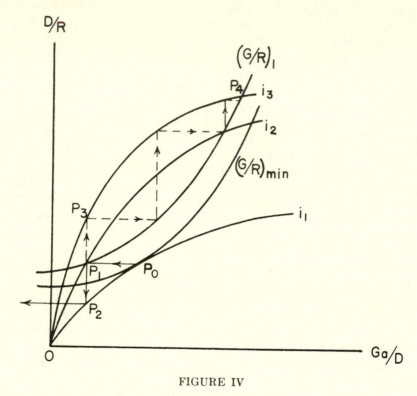

FIGURE IV

3. The system will oscillate into its new equilibrium if the new G/R is greater than unity; it will converge upon that equilibrium asymptotically if the new G/R is smaller than unity.

If, of course, the system threatens to disintegrate because G/R is falling and it is initially at or to the left of P_7, America's monetary authorities may raise interest rates. Indeed, they must, for it is too late to cut America's deficit. If, for example, the system were initially at P_0 in Figure IV and G/R were to fall to $(G/R)_1$, the system would begin to fall apart, traveling along $P_0, P_1, P_2 \ldots \ldots$ America would have to raise interest rates immediately from i_1 to i_2 to arrest this collapse at P_1. P_1, however, remains unstable with respect to a further decline in G/R. America, then, would do better to set its short-term interest rates at i_3, because the system would then travel to a new and stable equilibrium along $P_0, P_1, P_3 \ldots \ldots P_4$.[7]

IV

To the limited extent that the model developed here resembles our present-day gold-exchange standard, it has important implications for policy formation.

On the one hand, it reminds us that an American payments deficit is prerequisite to an increase of world reserves larger than new gold production. At the same time, it suggests that the United States should not yet be alarmed if her payments deficit reduces her reserve ratio, G_a/D, because the present ratio is still above unity. Under present circumstances we should expect America's reserve ratio to fall when the United States runs a deficit, but need not fear that such a decline will spark a collapse of the gold-exchange standard.

On the other hand, our model warns that a continuing United States deficit of constant absolute size could carry the gold-exchange standard into its region of peril. If the deficit is large enough to drive dG/dR below $(G/R)_{min}$, we will face delicate policy problems. If, of course, we could estimate $(G/R)_{min}$, we might be able to stem the United States deficit before the system reached $(G/R)_{min}$. This would raise dG/dR relative to $(G/R)_{min}$, but would demand a nice calculation of foreigners' preferences.

In brief, this analysis suggests that the more rapid the increase of world reserves, the sooner must that increase be curtailed. The larger America's deficit, the earlier will we approach $(G/R)_{min}$ and the region of instability. This suggests that we should begin to seek substitutes for an increase of gold or dollar balances to raise world liquidity.[8]

The recent increase of International Monetary Fund resources may be a partial substitute for an increase of national reserves and an American deficit. But other countries may include America's

7. P_4 is a stable equilibrium with respect to a further decline in G/R because $(G/R)_1$ is larger than the $(G/R)_{min}$ which corresponds to the new function $\theta[i_3, G_a/D)_{t-1}]$.

8. This is the burden of Triffin's recent proposal for an overhaul of international financial arrangements ("Tomorrow's Convertibility," Banca Nazionale del Lavoro, *Quarterly Review*, June 1959).

obligations to the International Monetary Fund in her liabilities when appraising America's reserve ratio. What is worse, some of the Fund's dollars will find their way back into national balances as they are used by the Fund. An increase of IMF resources must eventually diminish America's reserve ratio and might cause foreigners to cut D/R.

An increase in the price of gold could also diminish the need for an American payments deficit. But it would also shake foreigners' confidence in the dollar. A higher price for gold would raise G/R and America's reserve ratio, but could also raise $(G/R)_{min}$ by shifting $\theta(i, G_a/D)$ downwards. It could wreck the gold-exchange standard.

Barring a radical reform of international finance, the development of additional reserve currencies would seem to remain as the most promising avenue to increased liquidity. But this alternative raises a host of new problems which I cannot adequately analyze with the simple devices used here.

APPENDIX

PRIVATE BALANCES AND THE STABILITY OF THE SYSTEM

My model differs from reality in several important respects. There are actually several reserve currencies, a complication that could build new sources of instability into the gold-exchange standard at the same time that it could give America an additional degree of freedom. In present circumstances, foreigners' decisions to hold or disgorge dollars must be affected by interest rates in London and by the anticipated dollar price of sterling, as well as by interest rates in New York and the dollar price of gold. Second, the foreigners' demand function for dollars, equation 3, vastly oversimplifies the problem it portrays.

We shall not explore the first of these complications here, but will examine the second. Our equation 3 assumes that the demand for dollar balances is entirely independent of the distribution of reserves among countries. In point of fact, some countries, especially the other reserve-currency countries, hold few dollars and much gold. If, then, these nations run a payments surplus, the world demand for dollars must decline, given total reserves (or must rise more slowly than otherwise if total reserves are rising). At the same time, some institutions within each country may be barred by law or convention from holding gold. This possibility ties the demand for dollars to the distribution of reserves *within* each foreign country.

Let us consider this last problem in more detail, as it has a bearing upon the stability of our system. Suppose that the dollar balances foreigners hold are divided between the central bank (designated below by the subscript c) that can hold gold, and commercial banks (designated below by the subscript p) which cannot. We then have:

$$D = D_c + D_p, \tag{A-1}$$
$$R_c = D_c + G_f. \tag{A-2}$$

Our demand functions are:

$$D_c/R_a = \alpha(i, G_a/D, \ldots \ldots), \tag{A-3}$$
$$D_p = \beta(i, G_a/D, \ldots \ldots). \tag{A-4}$$

Note that equations A-3 and A-4 are fundamentally dissimilar. We cannot write A-4 to specify D_p/R_p because that ratio is, by definition, unity.[1]

We then have:

$$
\begin{aligned}
D/R &= (D_c/R_c)\,(R_c/R) + D_p/R \\
&= (D_c/R_c)\,(1 - D_p/R) + D_p/R. \tag{A-5}
\end{aligned}
$$

And we can write:

$$\frac{\partial(D/R)}{\partial(G_a/D)} = \alpha_G'\,(1 - D_p/R) + \beta_G'\,(1 - D_c/R_c)(1/R), \tag{A-6}$$

where α_G' is the partial derivative of D_c/R_c with respect to G_a/D and β_G' is the partial derivative of D_p with respect to G_a/D. If these two partials are positive and if D_p/R and D_c/R_c are each less than unity, the argument of equation A-6 will be positive. This may be regarded as the normal case.

In addition:

$$\frac{\partial^2(D/R)}{\partial(G_a/D)^2} = \alpha_G''\,(1 - D_p/R) + \beta_G''\,(1 - D_c/R_c)\,(1/R)$$
$$- (2/R)\alpha_G'\,\beta_G'. \tag{A-7}$$

1. One is tempted to write A-3 as $\alpha\,(i, G_a/D, R_c, \ldots\ldots)$ to suggest that governments may wish to hold more (or fewer) dollars relative to total reserves at higher levels of R_c. But I do not know what sign to give the partial of D_c/R_c with respect to R_c. It could be positive or negative throughout or might change signs as R_c varies. Similarly, one might write A-4 as a function of R_c, but here too the sign of the partial is in doubt. If an increase of reserves caused the government to relax exchange controls limiting D_p, D_p would rise with R_c. But if an increase of reserves caused bankers to grow bullish on the price of home currency in terms of dollars, D_p might fall with a rise in R_c. At the same time, the influence of G_a/D upon D_p may be small if the banks are barred from holding gold. It would have a significant influence only if it simultaneously reflected expectations as to the future price of home currency and the dollar.

The argument of equation A-7 will be negative if A-6 is positive and if the second-order partial derivatives α_G'' and β_G'' are negative, as assumed earlier.

In short, our new D/R will rise at a decreasing rate when G_a/D increases. It will look much like the demand function $\theta(i, G_a/D)$, used earlier and portrayed in Figure II, except that we shall have a new demand schedule for each *combination* of R and i, not merely for the separate values of i. This means that D/R will change whenever G/R is changed by a change in R. But much depends upon this difference between our new model and the one discussed earlier. For:

$$\frac{\partial (D/R)}{\partial R} = -(1/R)\,(D_p/R)\,(1 - D_c/R_c). \qquad \text{(A-8)}$$

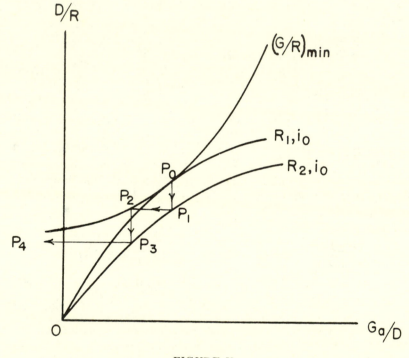

FIGURE V

Equation A-8 argues that D/R will decline as R increases, for D_c/R_c is normally smaller than unity. In consequence, an increase of R will cause the demand schedule to sag, raising $(G/R)_{\min}$. Our new system is more likely to encounter $(G/R)_{\min}$ before G/R is stabilized. What is worse, the system grows dangerously unstable in the neighborhood of $(G/R)_{\min}$. Even if America sets its deficit to stabilize G/R at $(G/R)_{\min}$, the gold-exchange standard may disintegrate. This is because *any* increase of reserves at $(G/R)_{\min}$ will cutback D/R. If, for example, the system starts at $(G/R)_{\min}$ in Figure V an increase of reserves just sufficient to maintain G/R at $(G/R)_{\min}$ will depress the demand for dollars from R_1 to R_2. Unless American interest rates rise promptly to restore D/R, the system will travel into chaos along $P_0, P_1, P_2, P_3, \ldots \ldots$

The existence of private dollar balances insensitive to changes in R can imperil the gold-exchange standard.[2]

2. If, of course, $D_p = \beta(i, G_a/D, R \ldots \ldots)$, an hypothesis similar to that proposed in note 1, this collapse need not occur. For then, the argument of equation A-8 would be transformed into

$$(1/R)\,(1 - D_c/R_c)\left[\frac{\partial D_p}{\partial R} - D_p/R\right].$$

This statement will be positive if $\partial D_p/\partial R$ exceeds D_p/R. But I can see no a priori reason to suppose that this partial derivative is positive, let alone larger than D_p/R.

COLUMBIA UNIVERSITY

The Demand for International Reserves*

PETER B. KENEN and ELINOR B. YUDIN

If economists could measure the need for reserves, they might be able to agree on the right way to reform the international monetary system. Most of the economists who propose drastic reform do so because they anticipate a shortage of reserves; some even believe that the shortage is upon us. Those who advocate more gradual change believe that reserves are adequate now and for the next several years; some even believe that reserves are excessive.

Unfortunately, there is no way to measure the adequacy of reserves—not even to make historical comparisons. Scitovsky's comments illustrate several of the problems involved in appraising the global stock of reserves:

If the world supply of reserves were adequate, the drawing down of some countries' reserves to unduly low levels would be matched by some other countries' excessive accumulation of reserves, and the desire to eliminate balance-of-payments deficits in the former would be matched by the desire to eliminate the surpluses in the latter.[1]

On this definition, global reserves would not be adequate unless countries behaved symmetrically toward payments surpluses and payments deficits. Hence, Scitovsky's criterion assumes that every government or central bank has a precise demand for reserves; if it acts to restrict aggregate expenditure when its reserves fall below a certain level, it will also act to stimulate expenditure when reserves exceed that same level. Behavior, however, may not be this simple. A government willing to tolerate losses of reserves without taking restrictive action may still prefer to accumulate more reserves than to expand demand and court inflation. Even if each country had a unique demand for reserves, moreover, a fixed global total of reserves could be more or less "adequate" depending on its distribution. Finally, Scitovsky's criterion, like most others, involves important normative judgments, implicitly endorsing global price stability as a policy objective and assuming that a symmetrical response to deficits and

* The authors are Professor of Economics and research assistant in the International Economics Workshop, Columbia University. They are indebted to fellow members of the Workshop and to the Seminar in International Economics, Harvard University, for criticism and suggestions. Professor Jon Cunnyngham provided valuable guidance in the design of computations. Research on the project was financed by a Ford Foundation grant to the International Economics Workshop, Columbia University.
[1] Tibor Scitovsky in [8], 208.

surpluses will accomplish payments adjustments with appropriate speed.[2]

It is even difficult to measure the stock of reserves, as the several reserve assets and reserve credits now in use are not perfect substitutes for one another; equal amounts of gold, currency, and credit may make unequal contributions to a nation's external liquidity. Liquidity is a state of mind. Most of the economists concerned with these problems take account of central-bank gold and foreign currency, IMF gold tranches, and automatic drawing rights under bilateral credit arrangements. Others count all assets susceptible of mobilization at moments of crisis—all IMF drawing rights, the long-term foreign assets of official institutions, and "potential" bilateral credits. Some prefer to deal with gross assets and gross drawing rights, others make allowance for "liquid" liabilities.

Yet quantitative methods may answer important factual questions pertaining to liquidity. We may ask, for example, if national holdings of reserves, defined consistently if not perfectly, exhibit any marked regularity or rational pattern. If they do, we may be able to describe the national demand for reserves of a "typical" country, then to appraise the distribution of global reserves.

The Measurement of Payments Disturbances

Measurement always requires a yardstick. A dollar total of reserves, gross or net, is meaningless. But the yardstick generally used to measure liquidity—the ratio of reserves to imports—does not tell us very much. This familiar ratio merely shows how long a country could finance its imports if it were suddenly deprived of all its foreign-exchange earnings. A better yardstick would direct our attention to the more likely contingency. It would compare the level of reserves to the variations in payments and receipts that countries actually expect to experience.

Governments have many reasons for holding reserve assets, including the requirements of domestic monetary legislation or long-standing custom. But the paramount reason for holding reserves is the commitment to maintain stable exchange rates in the face of payments disturbances. Trade and private service flows, government transactions and capital movements are subject to several disturbances—secular, cyclical, seasonal, and random. Under a system of flexible exchange rates, the net current impact of all these disturbances would be manifest as changes in the exchange rates. If ex-

---

[2] Several recent studies stress these important normative issues—the links between the question of adequacy and the problem of adjustment. See Caves [1]; Machlup et al., [4], 53-54; and the Report of the Group of Ten [5], 4-5.

change rates were perfectly rigid, by contrast, the net current impact of these disturbances would be manifest as changes in official reserves and official liabilities—the counterparts of central-bank intervention supporting the exchange rates. Under the arrangements that actually prevail, small changes in exchange rates occur automatically, absorbing some disturbances.[3] Changes in policy, moreover, especially in exchange controls, have suppressed or offset significant disturbances. However, most of the countries surveyed in this study have been compelled to intervene in the foreign-exchange market and the larger disturbances afflicting trade and payments are usually reflected in their reserves.

The adequacy of official reserves and credit facilities must be appraised in relation to expected future disturbances, not in relation to those of the past. But the size and duration of future disturbances may perhaps be gauged by examining past disturbances, manifest as changes in official reserves. In Triffin's words:

The order of magnitude of deficits calling for reserve financing might first be gauged quantitatively on the basis of past experience. This first approximation should then be revised, upward or downward, in the light of other pertinent evidence about the probable course of external and internal developments.[4]

Recorded changes in reserves do not measure past disturbances with any great accuracy—even with respect to countries that have abjured exchange control and have not altered their exchange rates. Changes in domestic policy, especially in monetary policy, can offset substantial disturbances, and the endogenous responses of the private sector have also been important in many instances. Finally, reserves may sometimes change autonomously, as central banks may intervene in the foreign-exchange market when there has been no apparent disturbance, selling gold and foreign currency when the exchange rate is above its "lower support point," and buying when the rate is below its "upper support point." They also engage in forward foreign-exchange operations and intergovernmental credit transactions that distort statistics on reserves and thereby distort any measure of disturbances derived from those statistics. Yet changes in reserves remain the best available measure of disturbances. In their very nature, moreover, they are certain to reflect the disturbances sufficient in size or duration to compel official intervention—disturbances requiring the use or acquisition of official reserves.

[3] In one important case studied here (Canada), the exchange rate was allowed to fluctuate extensively. More important, the rate was deliberately altered. In two other cases (Germany and the Netherlands), there were smaller but significant changes in exchange rates, interrupting the continuity of the data.

[4] Robert Triffin [7], 35.

Inspection of the major countries' published reserve statistics suggested that the monthly changes in each nation's reserves can be described stochastically—that the changes may even be normally distributed.[5] If this were so, a country's balance of payments could be described as a simple random walk. But the monthly changes in reserves also displayed a significant serial correlation; successive observations were not independent. If, then, a country's balance of payments is to be described stochastically, one must use a Markov process rather than a random walk. We consequently sought to describe each country's balance of payments by a simple autoregressive scheme:

$$\Delta R_t = \rho \Delta R_{t-1} + \varepsilon_t, \quad 0 < \rho < 1 \qquad (1)$$

where ε_t has $N(\bar{\varepsilon}, \sigma_\varepsilon^2)$. In other words, the monthly "surplus" or "deficit" in the balance of payments, as measured by the change in gross reserves, ΔR_t, was treated as reflecting a current disturbance, ε_t, drawn from a normal population with mean $\bar{\varepsilon}$ and variance σ_ε^2, and the "carry-forward" of all past disturbances embodied in $\rho \Delta R_{t-1}$. The past disturbances will be subject to cumulative decay when $0 < \rho < 1$.[6]

---

[5] The reserve statistics used in this study span the five-year period 1958-1962. They include official holdings of gold and convertible foreign exchange, the net IMF position (whether positive or negative), and, prior to 1959, the net EPU position of member countries. All data were drawn from *International Financial Statistics*. It might have been better to include credits available through EPU, rather than credits drawn or granted, and to have included the IMF gold tranche which cannot turn negative, rather than the net IMF position which does turn negative when countries draw on their credit tranches. But these substitutions would not have altered many of the month-to-month changes. The monthly changes in reserves were computed directly from the gross reserve figures, but adjusted to exclude the discontinuities introduced by the termination of EPU (January 1959). One might also have adjusted the published statistics for drawings on bilateral credit facilities, for the creation of and drawings on IMF "standby" credits, for changes in "liquid" liabilities, or for "special" intergovernment capital transactions such as debt prepayments. These adjustments would have had significant effects on the British statistics and, at the end of the period under study, on the statistics of several continental European countries.

[6] The supposition that ε_t is normally distributed obtains support from theory, not just casual observation. If the balance of payments can be viewed as a sum of separate transactions, each of them subject to a stochastic disturbance, the change in reserves will itself display a disturbance equal to the sum of the component disturbances. Although the components of the sum may not be normally distributed, the Central Limit Theorem suggests that the sum will have a normal distribution. The supposition that $0 < \rho < 1$ also obtains support from theory. Some of the constituent disturbances are likely to vanish soon after they appear. Others are likely to endure for several months or years unless they are offset by endogenous responses or by public policy. These offsets, however, will only take hold with the passage of time, eroding the disturbance gradually. A disturbance ε_0, therefore, may be deemed to have a net effect $\rho^k \varepsilon_0$, k months later. These points are discussed at much greater length in a paper by the junior author, Elinor B. Yudin, *The Demand for Reserves* (International Economics Workshop, Columbia University, 1964, mimeo.). That paper also contains a detailed description of the computations presented below.

This compound hypothesis, if valid, would be quite convenient, allowing the complete description of a country's payments experience in terms of three parameters: $\bar{\varepsilon}$, the mean of the net disturbance; σ_ε^2, its variance; and ρ, its carry-forward or duration.[7] To test this hypothesis, we have computed simple least-squares estimates of:

$$\Delta R_t + \bar{e} + p\Delta R_{t-1}, \qquad (\text{1a})$$

where $\bar{e}$ approximates $\bar{\varepsilon}$, p is an estimate of ρ, and σ_e (the standard error of estimate) is an estimate of σ.[8] We then ran separate statistical tests on the several parts of our composite hypothesis—that $0 < \rho < 1$, that ε_t is normally distributed, and that a simple Markov scheme suffices to describe the monthly balance of payments.

Estimates of $\bar{e}$, p, and σ_e for 14 countries are arrayed in table 1.[9] Eight countries' data displayed significant positive values for p; one more series (Germany) displayed a positive value just short of statistical significance.[10] Five other national series gave negative values for p, but only one of these (Finland) was significantly different from zero. In the majority of cases, then, our results were consistent with the supposition that $0 < \rho < 1$. An even larger majority of countries conformed to the next supposition; ten sets of residuals e_t satisfied a Chi-square test for normal fit at the 0.05 level of significance.

[7] The values of the parameters, $\bar{\varepsilon}$, σ_ε^2, and ρ, obtained below, will, of course, reflect the choice of time interval (the use of monthly data). But the relative national values of each parameter should not be much affected by this arbitrary choice. Although quarterly estimates of the three parameters would probably differ from the monthly estimates studied here, they are apt to differ in similar degree from one country to the next. It is the relationship among national values, moreover, that matters for the cross-sectional analysis in the next section.

[8] If the residuals e_t are normally distributed, implying that the ε_t are normally distributed, a simple least-squares estimate of $\bar{e}$ and p will approach the desirable large sample properties of asymptotic consistency and efficiency.

[9] Additional estimates were made for the changes in reserves reported by 13 other countries (Brazil, Chile, Colombia, El Salvador, Greece, India, Iran, Iraq, Lebanon, Mexico, Pakistan, Peru, and the Philippines) usually classified as "less-developed" countries. Nine of these countries' reserves gave values for p that were not significantly different from zero; two (Greece and Pakistan) gave significant positive values, two more (Iran and Iraq) gave significant negative values. The latter pair also showed significant (negative) second-order autocorrelation. Four countries' residuals (Brazil, El Salvador, Iraq, and Lebanon) failed the Chi-square test for normality at the 0.05 level, but only one (Lebanon) failed the Bartlett test for homoscedasticity. One would expect—and one finds—that the changes in reserves for these countries are more nearly random than those for the countries in table 1. Most of the underdeveloped countries still use strict exchange controls and have small reserves. Any enduring payments disturbance is usually met by changes in direct controls, so that the monthly changes in reserves should be regarded as the consequence of imperfect synchronization in exchange control, rather than the measure of the payments disturbances.

[10] When the most recent past quarterly change in reserves was substituted for ΔR_{t-1}, the German data gave a significant positive p.

TABLE 1.—AUTOREGRESSIVE EQUATIONS: MONTHLY CHANGES IN
RESERVES, 1958-1962

| Country | Parameters (and standard errors) | | Standard Error of Estimate (σ_e) (millions of dollars) | e_t Normally Distributed[b] |
	$\bar{e}$ (millions of dollars)	p		
Austria	5.40 (2.66)[a]	0.4664 (0.1198)[a]	18.9958	yes
Belgium	7.65 (4.47)	0.4216 (0.1165)[a]	32.4678	yes
Canada	2.99 (8.64)	0.4914 (0.1149)[a]	66.3340	no
Denmark	2.70 (2.14)	−0.2176 (0.1306)	16.4670	yes
Finland	1.32 (1.12)	−0.3785 (0.1280)[a]	8.3367	yes
Germany	10.12 (33.14)	0.2022 (0.1284)	256.4864	no
Italy	22.32 (9.05)	0.4661 (0.1139)[a]	61.5243	yes
Japan	9.16 (5.02)	0.6457 (0.1001)[a]	33.2173	yes
Netherlands	20.17 (6.87)[a]	−0.0853 (0.1294)	49.3806	no
New Zealand	0.22 (1.97)	0.4331 (0.1177)[a]	15.2923	yes
Norway	1.91 (1.34)	−0.1796 (0.1303)	10.2767	yes
Sweden	3.36 (2.21)	0.3307 (0.1237)[a]	16.4466	yes
Switzerland	17.08 (8.78)	−0.0631 (0.1494)	66.6481	yes
United Kingdom	14.69 (16.77)	0.3302 (0.1244)[a]	127.4753	no[c]

[a] Significantly different from zero at the 0.05 level.
[b] Distributions listed as "yes" are those that satisfied the Chi-square test for normality at the 0.05 level of signifance.
[c] Would satisfy the Chi-square test for normality at the 0.01 level of significance.

There is no satisfactory test for the sufficiency of the simple Markov scheme, but two imperfect tests give consistent results. The first test was performed by inserting an additional term into equation (1a):

$$\Delta R_t = \bar{e} + p_1 \Delta R_{t-1} + p_2 \Delta R_{t-2}. \qquad (1b)$$

Not one computed p_2 was significantly different from zero, suggesting that the simple scheme set forth by equation (1) provides a sufficient stochastic description of the payments disturbances.[11] The second test applied the Durbin-Watson ratio to the residuals, e_t, generated from equation (1a). There was no evidence of autocorrelation, positive or negative.[12]

[11] This test is imperfect because ΔR_{t-1} and ΔR_{t-2} will be intercorrelated when $p_1 > 0$.
[12] This test is also imperfect, as the Durbin-Watson test should not be applied to data generated from an autoregressive transform. See J. Durbin and G. S. Watson [2], 410.

Our hypothesis, however, involves one additional supposition—that σ_ε^2 is constant through time. To test this assumption of homoscedasticity, we split each country's residuals, e_t, into two equal groups at the mid-point of the monthly series (June 1960), made separate estimates of σ_ε^2 for the two subperiods, and applied the Bartlett test. Our results, arrayed in table 2, were less satisfactory than expected. Six of the 14 sets of residuals showed a change in variance during the five-year period 1958-1962.

TABLE 2.—TESTS FOR STABILITY OF THE STANDARD ERRORS (σ_e)

Country	Bartlett Test (χ^2)	Linear Trend Coefficients and Standard Errors	
		λ	σ_λ
Austria	7.908[b]	14.3987[a]	4.4660
Belgium	0.017	1.5601	13.0310
Canada	30.603[b]	305.0469[a]	86.5924
Denmark	0.290	1.9199	3.0062
Finland	2.228	− 0.9648	0.7330
Germany	0.835	−370.1011	1141.2093
Italy	4.275[a]	87.3123	53.7158
Japan	6.231[a]	27.6118[a]	13.1164
Netherlands	1.405	− 82.6399	58.6199
New Zealand	0.008	− 1.1795	1.9708
Norway	2.116	1.4701	1.1071
Sweden	5.070[a]	− 2.2450	4.7838
Switzerland	5.544[a]	172.4060[a]	69.6477
United Kingdom	0.971	161.9592	186.5336

[a] Significantly different from zero at the 0.05 and 0.01 levels.
[b] Significantly different from zero at the 0.05 level, but not at the 0.01 level.

Viewed from a different standpoint, however, these same results inspire more pleasure than chagrin, supporting the contention that reserves must grow through time. The Brookings group endorses this important hypothesis:

While the range of potential swings in the balance of payments will probably continue to be a moderate percentage of the total volume of international transactions, these swings have widened greatly in recent years, and the trend of recent developments suggests that they are likely to widen further in the future.[13]

We have obtained additional support for the Brookings view by running a set of simple trend estimates, displayed in table 2. Treating every e_t^2 as a point-estimate of σ_e^2, we have made regression estimates of linear trend:

$$(2) \qquad e_t^2 = e_0^2 + \lambda T. \qquad (2)$$

[13] See W. Salant et al. [6], 136; also the Report of the Group of Ten [5], 8. Triffin [7], ch. 3 made the same point much earlier, but did not explicitly relate his argument for growth in reserves to the evolution of payments disturbances.

Four of the λ's were statistically significant, and nine of the 14λ's were positive, suggesting gradual growth in the amplitude of payments disturbances.

Our composite hypothesis ($0 < \rho < 1, \varepsilon_t$ normal, and σ_ε^2 constant) is rarely satisfied by any one country's data. Belgium and New Zealand are the only ones whose data pass all tests at the 0.05 level of significance. The Italian, Japanese, Swedish, and British statistics could do so too, but only if the tests for normality and homoscedasticity were substantially relaxed (by accepting the hypotheses of normality and homoscedasticity unless they are contradicted at the 0.01 level of significance rather than the 0.05 level). A majority of national estimates, however, passed each of our tests taken one at a time—even the test for homoscedasticity. Hence, we were content to use our computed parameters, $\bar{e}, p$, and σ_ε^2, as yardsticks with which to appraise the need for reserves—as the input to a series of cross-sectional relationships seeking to measure the demand for reserves.

The Demand for Reserves

If countries hold reserves to cope with disturbances—to maintain stable exchange rates—the demand for reserves should depend on expectations as to the size and duration of those disturbances. Each country's demand for reserves should therefore depend on the central bank's expectations concerning the anticipated mean disturbance, $\bar{\varepsilon}$, the variance of disturbances, σ_ε^2, and the "carry-forward," ρ.[14] Yet any attempt to measure the "typical" demand for reserves by a cross-sectional analysis of information on national payments disturbances must make two heroic assumptions:

First, we are obliged to assume that each central bank or government holds the reserves it desires. This assumption can never be fulfilled with precision, if only because the stock of reserves circulates continuously.[15] Nor can it be fulfilled for all countries together unless the total of reserves is sufficiently large.[16]

[14] Alternatively, the demand for reserves might be deemed to depend on the distribution of a single number, jointly generated by these three parameters—on the distribution of anticipated *cumulative* surpluses and deficits. One could derive such a distribution from the three parameters studied in the text, but this would be extremely laborious and should not be necessary. The three parameters, $\bar{\varepsilon}, \sigma_\varepsilon^2$ and ρ, specify that distribution completely and sufficiently. One might also try to link the level of reserves to the *total* variance, rather than the variance around $\bar{\varepsilon}$. This procedure would avoid the necessity for separate consideration of $\bar{\varepsilon}$ and ρ in the equations that follow. But it would also misrepresent the stochastic character of the balance of payments adduced in the previous section.

[15] One might, perhaps, surmount this first objection by seeking to explain *average* national reserves over a period of years. But experiments along these lines gave similar results to those reported in the text (the experiments on single-year reserves).

[16] This second *caveat* does not much impair the validity of our approach because we

Second, we are obliged to assume that the distribution of future disturbances, as forecast by the central banks, resembles the distribution of past disturbances. The values of $\bar{e}$, p and σ_e must be regarded as satisfactory proxies for $\bar{\varepsilon}$, ρ, and σ_ε, and these, in turn, must be thought to resemble the parameters that the authorities contemplate when they appraise the sufficiency of their reserves. This assumption cannot be exactly fulfilled because recorded changes in reserves will always reflect the influence of policies initiated to control the nation's balance of payments and regulate its stock of reserves. A country that deems itself short of reserves may act directly to reduce payments disturbances—or will willingly accommodate a "structural" surplus—thereby compressing σ_e, reducing p, and enlarging $\bar{e}$. We shall assume that the values of σ_e and p shown in table 1 are not materially affected by national policies—that they are satisfactory proxies for σ_e and ρ, the "true" parameters. We shall also assume that these "true" parameters do not greatly differ from those that central banks project for the future. But we do not have similar confidence in our estimates of $\bar{e}$, as any deliberate attempt to adjust reserve holdings is certain to affect the mean monthly change and, therefore, our values for $\bar{e}$. A country that anticipates a "structural" deficit ($\bar{\varepsilon} < 0$) and lacks sufficient reserves to finance such a deficit is obliged to defend its position. In consequence, its $\bar{e}$ may differ substantially from its anticipated mean disturbances, $\bar{\varepsilon}$.[17]

We now suppose that the demand for reserves depends on $\bar{\varepsilon}$, σ_ε, and ρ. As a linear approximation:

$$R_{it} = \beta_0 - \beta_1 \bar{\varepsilon}_1 + \beta_2 \rho_i + \beta_3 \sigma_{ei}, \tag{3}$$

where R_{it} measures the ith country's gross reserves at the start of the tth month. To compute a cross-sectional least-squares estimate of this relationship, we employed the parameters arrayed in table 1, but made a systematic adjustment in those statistics. When p was not significant (or significant but negative), it was arbitrarily fixed at zero. The corresponding estimate of $\bar{e}$ was replaced by the mean change in reserves,

---

do not study all the major countries simultaneously. We have deliberately excluded the United States—the main supplier of reserves over the past few years. We have also excluded France because its reserve data were not sufficiently continuous.

[17] In the period under study, of course, the several national values of $\bar{e}$ jointly reflected the massive United States deficits of 1958-1962. These deficits may be viewed as "structural" disturbances afflicting other countries—as an overwhelming increase in the "supply" of reserves, posing an intractable identification problem. We think it equally correct, however, to view them as reflecting European policies deliberately designed to acquire reserves, and, therefore, overlaying or distorting the "true" $\bar{\varepsilon}$. One can hardly accuse the European countries of excessive zeal in accomplishing a restoration of payments equilibrium. On the contrary, the major European countries were quite content to acquire reserves by way of the United States deficit.

and the corresponding estimate of σ_e was replaced by the simple standard deviation of the monthly change in reserves.[18] Our first least-squares estimates sought to "explain" the distribution of gross reserves at December 31, 1957 ("initial" reserves). Our second estimate sought to "explain" gross reserves at December 31, 1962 ("terminal" reserves):[19]

$$R_{57} = \quad 68.11 + \quad 5.77\,\bar{e} + \quad 77.17\,p$$
$$\quad (177.81) \quad (15.96) \quad (378.12)$$
$$+ \quad 19.34\,\sigma_e\,, \bar{R}^2 = .95, \tag{3a}$$
$$(2.16)*$$

$$R_{62} = -\,159.80 + 95.89\,\bar{e} + 1136.62\,p$$
$$\quad (206.91) \quad (18.57)* \quad (440.00)*$$
$$+ \quad 16.69\,\sigma_e\,, \bar{R}^2 = .96 \tag{3b}$$
$$(2.51)*$$

These equations offer strong support for our hypothesis that the demand for reserves depends on the size and duration of disturbances. They attribute great explanatory power to σ_ε (represented by the "adjusted" values of σ_e). They also apply the anticipated sign to β_2, the coefficient attached to p, and β_2 is significant with respect to "terminal" reserves. In both equations, however, β_1 takes the "wrong" (positive) sign, and the influence of $\bar{\varepsilon}$ attains striking significance in the second equation. These results support our *caveat* concerning the computed mean of the disturbances, $\bar{e}$. The $\bar{e}$ may reflect intended reserve accumulation, not the projected mean disturbance determining demand. We therefore delete this variable from subsequent equations.[20]

When $\bar{e}$ is deleted from our first two equations, we obtain these results:

$$R_{57} = \quad 89.80 + \quad 70.23\,p + 19.95\,\sigma_e$$
$$\quad (160.61) \quad (362.40) \quad (1.26)*$$
$$\bar{R}^2 = .95, \tag{3a'}$$

$$R_{62} = \quad 200.96 + 1021.19\,p + 26.98\,\sigma_e$$
$$\quad (355.51) \quad (802.14) \quad (2.78)*$$
$$\bar{R}^2 = .88. \tag{3b'}$$

The equations still "explain" the distribution of reserves quite well,

---

[18] Computations using the "unadjusted" values of $\bar{e}$, p, and σ_e suggested that this adjustment did not have much effect on our final results. As expected, it did increase the standard error of β_2 (pertaining to p), but not by enough to alter our conclusions. Estimates were also made using σ^2, "adjusted" and "unadjusted," and the results of these computations were slightly different from those described below. In general, the coefficient of multiple correlation ($\bar{R}^2$) was lower, and the influence of p was sometimes less pronounced.

[19] The standard errors of the regression coefficients appear in parentheses beneath the coefficients. Asterisks denote statistical significance at the 0.05 level.

[20] Note, in passing, that $\bar{e}$ and σ_e are highly intercorrelated.

but β_2 (pertaining to ρ) is no longer significant in the "terminal" equation. Furthermore, the coefficient of multiple correlation, $\bar{R}^2$, declines abruptly with respect to "terminal" reserves, falling below the $\bar{R}^2$ for "initial" reserves. As the "terminal" $\bar{R}^2$ was consistently lower than the "initial" $\bar{R}^2$ in other experiments, we may perhaps infer that the very large increase in reserves generated by the United States payments deficit was not well distributed among other countries.

One would expect the demand for reserves to reflect additional circumstances and considerations, not just expectations concerning disturbances. We have sought to take account of two such considerations—the opportunity cost of holding reserves and the level of "liquid" liabilities that governments regard as claims on their reserves—but have not been successful.

We did not try to devise a direct measure of opportunity cost. Instead, we supposed that reserve accumulation is usually accomplished at the expense of capital formation—public or private, domestic or foreign—and that the "social marginal product" of capital varies inversely with per capita income. On this supposition, per capita income should correlate directly with total reserves. A country with a high per capita income should hold more reserves than a country with a low per capita income.[21]

We had equal difficulty measuring "liquid" liabilities, as the published figures are notoriously poor. There are no statistics for Switzerland, a major banking center, and the British data are organized quite differently from other countries' figures. In the end, we added the gross liabilities of central banks and governments to the net liabilities of "deposit money banks," both as reported in *International Financial Statistics*.[22] Once again, we employed a linear approximation:

$$R_{it} = \beta_0 + \beta_2\rho_i + \beta_3\sigma_e + \beta_4(Y/P)_i + \beta_5 L_{it}, \qquad (4)$$

where $(Y/P)_i$ represents per capita income in the ith country and L_{it} represents that country's liabilities. The addition of per capita income and of liabilities did not much improve the overall fit:

---

[21] The statistics for per capita income were obtained from income data in *International Financial Statistics*. They pertain to 1960.

[22] For the United Kingdom, we used the "old" series on sterling balances, excluding British indebtedness to the IMF. For the Canadian banks, we used foreign currency deposits *less* banks' claims on their foreign branches. When "explaining" initial reserves, we used liabilities at December 31, 1957; when "explaining" terminal reserves, we used liabilities at December 31, 1962. We ran several computations using other constructs (central bank liabilities taken alone, then official and bank liabilities without allowance for bank assets), but we did not find significant departures from the pattern described in the text.

$$R_{57} = -371.78 + 305.95\,p + 20.63\,\sigma_e$$
$$(275.32) \quad (336.44) \quad (1.19)*$$
$$+ 0.39\,(Y/P) \quad - \quad 0.02L_{57},$$
$$(0.21) \quad\quad (0.01)$$
$$\bar{R}^2 = .96, \tag{4a}$$

$$R_{62} = \quad 715.40 + 977.98\,p + 28.06\,\sigma_e$$
$$(681.78) \quad (836.39) \quad (2.96)*$$
$$- 0.51\,(Y/P) - \quad 0.03\,L_{62},$$
$$(0.52) \quad\quad (0.02)$$
$$\bar{R}^2 = .88. \tag{4b}$$

Indeed, liabilities took on the "wrong" (negative) sign in both equations, while per capita income took on the "wrong" (negative) sign in the 1962 equation.

In a final experiment, we replaced liabilities with the domestic money supply, M_{it}, to allow for the impact of domestic legislation on the demand for reserves and for the contention that "excessive" domestic liquidity represents a potential claim on reserves.[23] This permutation was not informative. Our results were much as with liabilities:

$$R_{57} = -320.31 + 351.11\,p + 20.92\,\sigma_e$$
$$(290.16) \quad (383.28) \quad (1.55)*$$
$$+ 0.35\,(Y/P) - 0.02M_{57},$$
$$(0.22) \quad\quad (0.02)$$
$$\bar{R}^2 = .96, \tag{4c}$$

$$R_{62} = \quad 757.13 + 576.12\,p + 25.44\,\sigma_e$$
$$(720.22) \quad (980.99) \quad (4.25)*$$
$$+ 0.47\,(Y/P) + 0.02M_{62},$$
$$(0.57) \quad\quad (0.04)$$
$$\bar{R}^2 = .87. \tag{4d}$$

Although central banks insist that "liquid" liabilities and the domestic money supply are relevant to any appraisal of their reserves, we could not establish any connection between either item and actual reserves. The prospective volatility of the balance of payments, measured by σ_e, accounted for the bulk of the total variation in the several central banks' holdings of reserves.

The strong partial correlation between R_{it} and σ_e, however, could conceivably reflect the influence of country size. Large countries, one

[23] See Holtrop [3]. We did not employ liabilities and the money stock in the same equation as they are closely correlated.

might argue, hold large reserves and likewise experience large disturbances, as measured by the changes in their reserves. To exclude this possibility, we recomputed each of our cross-sectional equations with the addition of national income as a proxy for size. As national income did not display explanatory power and did not alter our other results, we doubt that those results are spurious or accidental.

The Distribution of Reserves

Our cross-sectional equations cannot be used to detect an absolute "excess" or "deficiency" of gross reserves. But they can be used cautiously to appraise the distribution of reserves—to estimate the gross reserves each nation would hold if it conformed to "average" behavior and the relative "excess" or "shortfall" in national holdings compared to "average" behavior. Table 3 presents two sets of calculations based

TABLE 3.—EXCESS (+) AND SHORTFALL (−) OF GROSS RESERVES
COMPUTED FROM "BEST" EQUATIONS

Country	1957			1962			
	Actual Reserves	Computed Reserves	Excess (+) or Short-fall (−)	Actual Reserves	Computed Reserves	Excess (+) or Short-fall (−)	$\bar{e}$
Austria	523.00	491.33	31.67	1081.00	1041.72	39.28	5.3991
Belgium	1148.00	770.89	377.11	1753.00	1406.53	346.47	7.8446
Canada	1926.00	1432.61	493.39	2547.00	2270.03	276.97	2.9886
Denmark	172.00	445.99	−273.99	261.00	982.56	−721.56	1.4833
Finland	180.00	279.37	− 99.37	317.00	765.13	−448.13	1.3186
Germany	5197.00	5277.10	− 80.10	6964.00	7286.80	−322.80	29.4500
Italy	1354.00	1336.97	17.03	3644.00	2145.22	1498.78	22.3195
Japan	524.00	774.07	−250.07	2022.00	1410.68	611.32	9.1578
Netherlands	1009.00	1090.82	− 81.82	1946.00	1824.01	121.99	15.6167
New Zealand	152.00	417.76	−265.76	171.00	945.71	−774.71	.2228
Norway	197.00	319.53	−122.53	304.00	817.54	−513.54	1.7833
Sweden	501.00	440.62	60.38	801.00	975.55	−174.55	3.3577
Switzerland	1898.00	1429.63	468.37	2872.00	2266.14	605.86	16.2333
United Kingdom	2374.00	2648.29	−274.29	3311.00	3856.40	−545.40	14.6865

on the "best" regression equations we were able to develop. The first three columns of that table list actual and computed reserves for 1957, along with the relative "excess" (+) or "shortfall" (−), the discrepancy between computed and actual holdings. The next three columns list the corresponding figures for 1962, and the final column lists the computed mean disturbance ($\bar{e}$ adjusted for nil or negative p). Computed reserves are derived from the simple regression relationship between R_{it} and σ_e (the only consistently significant relationship we have identified):

$$R_{57} = 113.74 + 19.88\,\sigma_e\,, \quad \bar{R}^2 = .96, \tag{5a}$$
$$\quad\;\; (98.47) \quad (1.15)*$$

$$R_{62} = 548.99 + 25.95\,\sigma_e\,, \quad \bar{R}^2 = .87. \tag{5b}$$
$$\quad\;\; (233.07) \quad (2.73)*$$

We do not attach great significance to these computations, but have been impressed by certain regularities:

First, we detect a considerable change in the distribution of reserves between 1957 and 1962. The correlation between the successive relative national positions (between columns 3 and 6 of table 3) is a mere 0.49.

Second, we find support for our contention that "new" reserves were not well distributed over this period. Countries displaying large relative deficiencies in 1957 should, perhaps, have made the largest gains in reserves by 1962. In this case, their data would have displayed the largest mean changes, i.e., the largest values for $\bar{e}$. Had this been so, in turn, there should have been a negative correlation between the third and seventh columns of table 3. In actual fact, there was no such correlation.[24]

Finally, our computations conform to *a priori* expectations in several strategic respects: They reveal a persistent and substantial relative deficiency in British reserves, sharp gains across the period in the relative positions of Japan and Italy, a deterioration in the relative position of Canada resulting from its payments crisis in 1962, and, surprisingly, a very slight relative deficiency for Germany.[25]

---

[24] As one would expect, the sixth and seventh columns of table 3 were positively correlated, but not very strongly.

[25] It should be noted in this connection that the level and variation in German reserves caused that country to appear as the extreme observation in the cross-sectional analysis, but that the exclusion of Germany from the entire analysis did not change the pattern or significance of our overall findings. Furthermore, alternative estimates of relative "excesses" and "shortfalls" based on equations including per capita income, liabilities, and p (similar to equations 4a and 4b in the text) did not give very different results in respect of distribution. The relative "excess" of Canadian reserves increased on this computation, while the position and pattern of change for several small countries, especially Austria, Belgium, and Sweden, was rather different.

REFERENCES

[1] R. E. Caves, "International Liquidity: Toward a Home Repair Manual," *Review of Economics and Statistics*, XLVI (May 1964).

[2] J. Durbin and G. S. Watson, "Testing for Serial Correlation in Least Squares Regression. I," *Biometrica* (1950).

[3] M. W. Holtrop, "Method of Monetary Analysis Used by De Neder-landsche Bank," International Monetary Fund *Staff Papers* (Feb. 1957).

[4] F. Machlup et al., *International Monetary Arrangements: The Problem of Choice* (Princeton, 1964).

[5] *Ministerial Statement of the Group of Ten and Annex Prepared by Deputies* (Aug. 1964).

[6] W. Salant et al., *The United States Balance of Payments in 1968* (Washington: The Brookings Institution, 1963).

[7] R. Triffin, *Gold and the Dollar Crisis* (New Haven, 1961).

[8] United States Congress, Subcommittee on International Exchange and Payments of the Joint Economic Committee, *Hearings: International Payments Imbalances and Need for Strengthening International Financial Arrangements* (Washington, 1961).

TOWARD A SUPRANATIONAL MONETARY SYSTEM

Peter B. Kenen

After a decade of debate, academic and official, the leading governments are finally agreed on the need to create international reserves in a more orderly way. This agreement, to be sure, is still incomplete. The several official proposals for reform of the monetary system differ importantly, and the differences will not be easy to resolve. Yet the very decision to negotiate on rival plans is itself a major achievement. Less than five years ago, the principal American spokesman could argue that the reserve-creating capabilities of the present system "are clearly as promising as any of the more familiar proposals,"[1] and three years ago, the Group of Ten still believed that "there is no immediate need to reach a decision as to the introduction of a new type of reserve asset."[2]

Even now, however, the official dialogue on reform is too narrowly focused on technical questions — on the "backing" for the new reserve asset and its relationship to gold, on the size of the

[1]Robert V. Roosa, "Assuring the Free World's Liquidity," Federal Reserve Bank of Philadelphia, *Business Review, Supplement,* September 1962, p. 12.

[2]*Ministerial Statement of the Group of Ten: Annex Prepared by Deputies,* reprinted in the *Federal Reserve Bulletin,* August 1964, p. 988. The Group of Ten includes Belgium, Canada, France, Germany, Italy, Japan, the Netherlands, Sweden, the United Kingdom and the United States.

new fiduciary issue and its distribution. There has not been sufficient systematic discussion of basic aims or of the connection between new reserve creation and the evolution of the world economy. Too often, of course, a debate on first principles results in a rotund declaration devoid of operational content. But international reserves are, at most, time-buying aids to the execution of national policies, and decisions affecting the creation of reserves cannot be made wisely and harmoniously unless there is agreement regarding the proper deployment of national policies affecting international financial stability.

No such agreement prevails today, and none is in prospect.[3] Indeed, the disagreement on methods of reserve creation testifies to deep disarray on principles. The sharp cleavage between "anglo-saxon" and "continental" views arises because of a difference in policy aims and, in particular, because many Europeans hold that the United States and United Kingdom are dangerously tolerant of inflation.[4] Accordingly, the continental countries are determined to limit reserve creation very strictly, even among the industrial countries. They also oppose reserve creation by the International Monetary Fund, because they distrust the financial policies of the less-developed countries, who have a voice in IMF decisions. A second disagreement, concerning the interconvertibility of reserve assets and their relationship to gold, likewise reflects an imperfect faith in other countries' policies. The French demand that new reserves be closely linked to gold derives in part from a belief that every country should be empowered to veto an expansion of world reserves, by exchanging the new reserve asset for gold, so as to limit other countries' deficits.

My chief point is that the case for a reform of the monetary system and the mountain of monetary plans confronting us.

[3]A detailed study of the "adjustment process" has been undertaken by the OECD. But the study of adjustment policies has been segregated from the planning of reform, as though the two problems were separate.

[4]The continental fear of inflation, may, in turn, reflect experience far more than dogma. One can, in fact, interpret much of the recent transatlantic dialogue on the U.S. payments problem in simple historical terms. The canons of central banking call upon deficit countries to deflate, accepting unemployment, and on surplus countries to inflate, accepting higher prices. The memories of those who make policy, however, cause them to rebel against this prescription. Twentieth-century American history has taught the United States to fear unemployment as the gravest economic evil, while twentieth-century European history has taught the continental countries to fear inflation above all.

should be appraised in the light of first principles.[5] Because the international monetary system must serve the international economy, its designers must pay painstaking attention to the strengths and weaknesses of that economy—and to the international political environment within which the monetary system has to function. Before writing a new constitution for the international monetary system, we must first identify the potential threats to international financial stability—to ask how payments problems can and may arise. Next, we must ask if those threats can be forestalled, whether by deliberate changes in national policies or by automatic adaptations in the market place. Finally, we must ask how the disturbances that actually emerge, as deficits or surpluses, can and should be met, and what role reserves should play in the insuing process of adjustment. In other words, we have to ask how the creation of international money is most apt to affect the speed and the quality of policy responses in the constituent national economies.

In order to answer these questions, we shall have to wander in a very arid wilderness. To identify the most important attributes of a supranational monetary system, we shall have to pick our way through the modern theory of the balance of payments, a desert no less dry or forbidding than Sinai itself.[6]

Modern balance-of-payments theory identifies several separate disturbances afflicting a nation's external transactions. It argues, moreover, that each such disturbance has to be met by a unique constellation of policies if the nation is to honor its domestic commitments to full employment, stable prices, and steady

[5]For compact summaries of the major plans, see R. G. Hawkins and S. E. Rolfe, "A Critical Survey of Plans for International Monetary Reform," C. J. Devine Institute of Finance, New York University, *Bulletin*, November 1965, and F. Machlup, *Plans for Reform of the Monetary System*, Princeton, N.J.: International Finance Section, 1964; also, *Report of the Study Group on the Creation of Reserve Assets*, Rome: Banca d'Italia, 1965.

[6]The exposition that follows will draw heavily on the writings of J. E. Meade, *The Balance of Payments*, London: Oxford University Press, 1961, and H. G. Johnson (especially his "Toward a General Theory of the Balance of Payments," in *International Trade and Economic Growth*, London: George Allen & Unwin, 1958). It will also borrow from recent work on the theory of optimum currency areas (see especially, R. A. Mundell, "A Theory of Optimum Currency Areas," *American Economic Review*, Vol. 51, No. 4, September 1961, pp. 657–664, and R. I. McKinnon, "Comment," *American Economic Review*, Vol, 53, No. 4, September 1963, pp. 717–725, and on Richard Cooper's study of Atlantic economic policy, soon to be published by the Council on Foreign Relations.

growth. To illustrate this principle, I shall ask you to contemplate a simple two-country world in which there are no international movements of labor or capital, and in which money wage rates cannot be reduced except by raising unemployment to intolerable heights.

These suppositions can be stated formally, using the familiar identities of national-income accounting:

$$Y = E + X - M$$
$$B = X - M$$

where Y is national income, E is national expenditure (including its import content), X and M are exports and imports, respectively, and B is the balance of trade in goods and services.[7] To start, let

$$Y = Y*$$
$$B = B* = 0$$

where $Y*$ is the full-employment or "target" level of national income and $B*$ is the "target" balance of foreign trade. Next, write out changes in E, X and M as:

$$dE = dE^a + (1 - s) \, dY$$
$$dX = dX^a$$
$$dM = dM^a + m(dY)$$

where s is the "marginal propensity to save," m is the "marginal propensity to import," and the arguments dE^a, dX^a and dM^a are income-autonomous disturbances affecting domestic expenditure, exports, and imports. Combining these three statements with the definitions of Y and $B,$ one obtains the conventional Keynesian multipliers for an open economy:[8]

[7]If there are no international movements of capital, balanced foreign trade implies balanced foreign payments.

[8]These formulae ignore "foreign repercussions" because they treat changes in each country's exports as if they were fully autonomous rather than dependent on changes in the other country's income. But the formulae with foreign repercussions, though much more complicated, convey the same messages as those in the text. The more important defect of these formulae, to which I shall return in a subsequent note, pertains to their application at full employment. If labor is fully employed, an increase in money income will be fully dissipated in rising prices, not manifest in rising real output and income, dY. Price and real-income changes will, of course, have similar effects on the trade balance (albeit by different routes), but may call for somewhat different policy responses.

$$dY = \frac{dE^a + dX^e - dM^a}{m + s}$$

$$\frac{dE^a + dB^a}{m + s}$$

$$dB = \frac{-m(dE^a) + s(dB^a)}{m + s}$$

If $Y = Y^*$ and $B = B^*$ to start, any autonomous change in domestic spending, dE^a, or in foreign trade, dB^a, will bring about an unwanted change in Y or B, and any such departure from the target values will require a change in national policies.

Notice, however, that the two disturbances lead to dissimilar changes in the trade balance. An autonomous decline in domestic spending ($dE^a < 0$), occasioned perhaps by a change in monetary policy, government spending, or tax rates, will depress national income ($dY < 0$) and will cause a surplus in the trade balance ($dB > 0$). An autonomous decrease of exports or increase of imports ($dB^a < 0$), occasioned by a change in tastes or costs of production, will also depress national income, but will cause a deficit in the trade balance ($dB < 0$). The two types of disturbance will consequently call for somewhat different changes in national policies.

A country confronting a decline in domestic expenditure can always prevent an unwanted fall in its national output and income by deliberately inducing a shift in the trade balance — by devaluing its currency to stimulate exports and reduce imports or by erecting new trade barriers. Indeed, a shift in the trade balance, dB^a, equal in absolute size to the shortfall of domestic spending, dE^a, would precisely suffice to stabilize national income. Following these policies, however, the country would drive its trade balance further into surplus, and the other country's balance further into deficit, for dE^a and dB^a take opposite signs in the trade-balance equation.[9] The efficient response to a decline in expenditure is, then, directly to combat that decline by cutting interest rates or tax rates, or raising government expenditure, for these actions would prevent or reverse the change in national income and in the trade balance.

[9] The course of action described here, often described as a "beggar-my-neighbor" policy, was frequently pursued and roundly condemned during the inter-war period.

A country confronting an autonomous decrease of exports or increase of imports can prevent a fall in national income by inducing an expansion of domestic expenditure — by adjusting its interest rates or fiscal policies to foster a countervailing dE^a. Doing so, however, the country would compound its external problem by driving the trade balance further into deficit. In this case, the most efficient policy response is to offset the trade-balance disturbance directly by changing the exchange rate or altering trade controls. If successful in correcting the trade balance, these policies would also stabilize national income and employment, for the initial dB^a would be cancelled from both multipliers.[10]

These simple principles of economic policy are not new or controversial, and are applied, with occasional lapses, by most major countries. But if they are relevant to national conduct, they should also influence the design and appraisal of monetary plans. If, for example, trade-balance disturbances are frequent or severe, and countries abjure the use of trade controls, the monetary system should surely countenance changes in exchange rates. Yet devaluations and revaluations are not regarded as normal policy measures. On the contrary, they are treated as remedies of last resort, not to be used unless all other policies fail.[11] What is worse, an emerging official consensus strongly favors the rapid correction of deficits and corresponding limitations on reserve creation, so that deficit countries will be compelled to take early action. This prescription would make sense if deficits were always due to excess demand, but when deficits are due to trade-balance dis-

[10]A change in the exchange rate would be equally efficient in two other cases: (1) As suggested in an earlier note, an autonomous increase in domestic expenditure will increase wages and prices when the economy is fully employed to start, and once they are raised, prices are not cut back easily. In consequence, a temporary rise in domestic expenditure may leave in its wake an enduring deterioration in the trade balance, requiring a change in the exchange rate. (2) An autonomous outflow of capital, hitherto excluded by the assumption that there are no international factor movements, requires an improvement in the trade balance to prevent an imbalance in over-all payments, and this can be accomplished by devaluation. In this second case, however, devaluation is an efficient response but is not sufficient; it must be accompanied by a reduction of domestic expenditure to stabilize income as the trade balance improves. Alternatively, the monetary authorities may choose to stem the capital outflow by raising interest rates, but must then relax their fiscal policies to offset the effects of higher interest rates on domestic spending and national income; on this point, see R. A. Mundell, "The Appropriate Use of Monetary and Fiscal Policy for Internal and External Stability," International Monetary Fund, *Staff Papers*, Vol. 9, No. 1, March 1962 pp. 70 ff.

[11]See, for example, *Ministerial Statement*, paragraph (7), pp. 978–979.

turbances, and exchange rates are fixed, the deficit countries may have to reduce their internal wages and prices relative to those abroad, thereby generating a countervailing increase of exports and decrease of imports. Such a reduction in wages and prices calls for a restriction of domestic demand. The prompt elimination of a payments deficit caused by a trade-balance disturbance may therefore require the creation of more unemployment than prudence or conscience can allow. The process of adjustment to a trade-balance change has instead to be spread out, and an ample financing of the intervening deficit will be required, even by the manufacture of new reserves. In brief, the international monetary system has to deal differently with different disturbances — to foster efficient national policies.

To amplify and qualify this proposition, I should like to draw an extended analogy between international payments adjustment and interregional payments adjustment. The separate regions of a single country will, at times, run deficits in their external trade and cannot resort to devaluation or to trade controls. In these ways, they resemble the members of an "integrated" international economy committed to the maintenance of fixed exchange rates and freely flowing trade. Countries, however, are different from regions in important respects, so that a supranational monetary system has to differ in design and operation from a national monetary system.

To pursue this analogy, I shall use the same simple model as before, treating dY, dB, dB^a, and dE^a as changes in national or regional income, trade, and expenditure. I shall also extend the model to take fleeting account of the labor and capital movements that may result from various disturbances.

If payments experience were dominated by expenditure changes, dE^a's rather than dB^a's, there would be a unique relationship between the internal and external problems of countries or regions. Assuming, once again, that those countries or regions begin with full employment and balanced trade, those that experience inflation will display trade-balance deficits, while those that experience deflation will experience trade-balance surpluses. In such a world, moreover, labor and capital mobility cannot substantially mitigate the internal and external problems caused by the disturbances. If expenditure were increased in one country or region, the corresponding shortage of labor could be fully satisfied by an inflow of labor, but other countries or regions would then experience labor shortages (a decrease of supply with unchanged demand). Labor mobility, much like trade itself, serves merely to diffuse an expenditure disturbance. An inflow of capital, by contrast, would be quite helpful from the external standpoint, but would exacerbate the internal problem. An autonomous increase of spending in one country or region, driving up interest rates, would attract outside funds and finance all or part of the trade-balance deficit. The inflow, however, would also sustain bank liquidity in the deficit country or region, short-circuiting the automatic monetary processes that would otherwise serve to curb the increase of expenditure.[12]

The combinations inflation-*cum*-deficit and deflation-*cum*-surplus are common occurences in international monetary annals. They are, indeed, so familiar that central bankers are apt to recommend restrictive policies whenever a country lapses into deficit. But one would not expect to encounter these combinations as frequently in interregional payments experience. The regions of a single country are subject to a common national monetary policy and, in substantial degree, to a common fiscal policy, leaving little scope for disparate changes in regional expenditure.

There are twelve Federal Reserve Banks in the United States, but their separate powers are sharply circumscribed by law and practice. They cannot run the monetary printing press at will to generate independent trends in expenditure. The several states have somewhat more fiscal autonomy; they can tax and spend on their own initiative. Yet this autonomy is also circumscribed, partly by legal and market constraints on the states' ability to borrow, partly by the internal mobility of American capital and labor which threatens to punish any community whose tax rate or spending on public services moves far out of line. Furthermore, Federal taxes and spending, being much larger, tend to swamp state-by-state differences,[13] while the Federal tax system tends also

[12]The capital movement would likewise work to raise interest rates in the outside world, but this would be salutary, not harmful, because it would compress effective demand, thereby offsetting the increase in demand for the outside world's goods occasioned by the increase of import demand in the deficit country or region.

[13]The geographic distribution of Federal expenditures is, of course, subject to change, but these variations are best regarded as autonomous changes in the governmental demand for regional exports, so as to separate the macroeconomic and microeconomic aspects of fiscal policy. For a more detailed discussion of these and related issues, see G. H. Borts and J. L. Stein, *Economic Growth in a Free Market*, New York: Columbia University Press, 1964; and J. T. Romans, *Capital Exports and Growth among U.S. Regions*, Middletown, Conn.: Wesleyan University Press, 1965.

to average out regional differences in effective tax rates by allowing the deduction of state and local taxes from income subject to Federal tax.

A supranational monetary system would also have to align expenditure trends in its constituent national economies in order to combat the combinations of inflation-*cum*-deficit and deflation-*cum*-surplus. It would have to accomplish a coordination of monetary and fiscal policies to simulate the centralization of policies characteristic of a national economy. But if it were constructed for this task alone, a supranational system might damage some of its members, and in the absence of a supranational political system empowered to prevent or punish defection, it might not last for long. If its operations prevented member countries from achieving important domestic objectives, it would evoke insistent demands for secession or, at the very least, for the application of trade controls amounting to *de facto* secession. To see why an unswerving alignment of policies could get in the way of national goals, we have again to study trade-balance disturbances.[14]

If payments experience were dominated by trade-balance disturbances, dB^a's rather than dE^a's, there would be a different and more difficult relationship between the internal and external problems confronting national and regional economies. When a country or region suffers an autonomous decline in the demand

[14]Differences in rates of economic growth and in its character could also engender serious tensions. If population, investment, and technology advance at different rates in constituent countries or regions, output targets, Y^*, will also change at different rates. In this case, an alignment of actual expenditure trends may lead to cumulative gaps between potential and actual performance, and the economies with the highest growth rates may come to experience overt unemployment. If, further, economic growth leads to a systematic change in the composition of production costs, or demand patterns, calling for adjustments in the terms of trade, payments problems will arise despite the alignment of trends in expenditure This class of problems is more apt to arise between countries than regions, because knowledge, capital, and labor move less freely between countries than within them. A substantial mobility of knowledge and capital serves, *ex ante*, to even out regional growth rates: a substantial mobility of labor serves, *ex post*, to reduce the differences in unemployment rates resulting from the residual differences in growth rates. In general, resource mobility is an efficient response to any disturbance that would, in its absence, require a change in the terms of trade. For a more rigorous treatment of these growth problems, with a formal statement of the conditions for external and internal balance, see my "*Déséquilibres des Paiements et Etalon Monétaire International*," Banque Nationale de Belgique, *Bulletin d'Information et de Documentation*, January 1965.

for its exports, it will display deflation-*cum*-deficit; when it enjoys an autonomous increase, it will display inflation-*cum*-surplus. These changes in demand, moreover, happen quite frequently in export and import markets alike; they are the inevitable counterparts of product substitution, the advent of new competitors, and changes in relative costs of production due to different rates of change in money wages and in man-hour output. They have struck at whole countries and at regions inside countries. Consider, as examples, Britain's experience in the 1920s, when a deep depression was combined with a payments deficit, and the similar but less severe American experience in the late 1950s.[15] Consider, too, the current plight of Appalachia due to the substitution of oil for coal as an industrial and household fuel, and the stagnation of New England in the late 1940s and early 1950s due to the growth of Southern textile production.[16]

An adjustment of monetary and fiscal policies cannot fully answer a trade-balance disturbance. A decrease of spending by the deficit country and an increase by the surplus country will, of course, restore external balance, but will also aggravate each country's domestic problem. An increase of spending by the deficit country and a decrease by the surplus country will restore internal balance all around, but will work to aggravate the payments problem. When, therefore, trade flows are disturbed, the countries or regions affected either have to reallocate resources, between or within them, or foster a change in the pattern of world demand favoring the products of the deficit country.

Here, then, factor mobility can help. When consumers in one of two countries switch from home to foreign goods, that country will experience deflation-*cum*-deficit, and the other will experience inflation-*cum*-surplus. If labor moves freely between them, however, responding to differences in market conditions, both countries may be able to regain full employment without any change in

[15] It is commonly agreed that Britain's depression was due to the sluggish evolution of her export industries before the First World War and was then compounded by the decision, in 1925, to reestablish convertibility at the pre-war exchange rate. The American balance-of-payments problem first emerged in 1958 with a sharp deterioration in the U.S. trade balance, and was associated with a stagnation of exports and a sharp increase of manufactured imports. At one point in 1959, the United States even displayed a merchandise-trade deficit. The prolongation of the U.S. payments problem, however, must be ascribed to different causes, notably the increase in capital exports during and after 1960.

[16] One might also associate the prolonged expansion of the West Coast economy with a trade-balance disturbance—the growth of demand for its defense-related exports.

national policies; the deficit country will have a labor surplus, the surplus country will have a labor shortage, and an exodus of labor from the deficit country can resolve each country's problem.[17] This same transfer of labor, moreover, will work to relieve the imbalance in their external trade; the shrinkage of employment, output, and income in the deficit country will reduce its demand for imports, and a corresponding expansion in the surplus country will augment its imports. It is, indeed, conceivable that the migration required to eliminate each country's employment problem will exactly suffice to erase the imbalance in foreign trade.[18]

Extending this same argument, several authors have maintained that a perfect mobility of labor between countries or regions is the necessary and sufficient condition for participation in a monetary union—for maintaining a fixed exchange rate between their currencies.[19] But though it may suffice in certain circumstances, mobility may not be required for a fixed-rate regime to function efficiently. When labor does not move between countries or regions, a trade-balance disturbance will call for a change in the terms of trade; prices must fall in the deficit country or rise in the surplus country so as to induce a countervailing shift in the pattern of world demand—an increase in spending on the products of the country with the deflation-*cum*-deficit. But the size of the requisite change in prices and the terms of trade depends upon consumer and producer responses to changes in relative prices. If a country or region is wholly dependent on a single export, actually and potentially, and the demand for its export declines, it must accept a deterioration in its terms of trade and real wage rates sufficient to restore fully the global demand for that single export. If, instead, it can export a variety of products, its terms of trade and real wage rates do not have to fall so far. Producer substitution inside the country will be joined to consumer substitution, inside and outside, restoring full employment and the trade balance at a smaller sacrifice, transitional and permanent.

A diversification of output and internal labor mobility, geo-

[17]But if there is a difference in the two countries' labor requirements per unit of output, migration may not fully solve both countries' problems.

[18]A corresponding mobility of capital, however, could exacerbate the two countries' problems. The decline of economic activity in the deficit country, reducing its interest rates, could increase its foreign lending and enlarge its payments deficit.

[19]See, for example, Mundell. "A Theory of Optimum Currency Areas," *American Economic Review*, September 1961, pp. 657 ff.

graphic and occupational, may consequently serve as effective substitutes for the international or interregional labor mobility that has been so much emphasized by recent writers. This same diversification of output may serve a related purpose. If output and exports are thoroughly diversified and the disturbances affecting foreign trade are independent of one another, a country or region may count on the law of large numbers to keep its foreign trade in balance and also to protect its domestic economy from external perturbations. This possibility is sometimes acknowledged, but has not attracted sufficient attention. It is, I submit, precisely because of this internal diversification that major industrial countries do not often display the painful combinations of deflation-*cum*-deficit and inflation-*cum*-surplus: the many disturbances affecting their foreign trade tend to average out rather than accumulate.[20] For the same reason, smaller less-developed countries and regions of a single country, being less diversified, display these combinations frequently and painfully. It is, finally, for this reason that economists who favor fixed exchange rates are often willing to exempt the less-developed countries. Because the economies of the latter are not well diversified, there is insufficient averaging of trade-balance disturbances, and when those disturbances appear, large changes in the terms of trade are sometimes needed to reestablish external and internal balance. The less-developed countries must be allowed to alter their exchange rates.

Although regions may experience deflation-*cum*-deficit more often than countries, they may be more fortunate in other respects. As labor moves more freely between regions than countries, regions need not always accept major changes in their terms of trade and real wage rates when they encounter trade-balance disturbances. Workers may begin to leave a depressed region when wage rates start to fall, reducing the region's labor surplus and limiting the decline, requisite and actual, in the terms of trade. In addition, regions derive several advantages from participation in a national economy. When, for example, an American community suffers deflation-*cum*-deficit, its Federal tax payments diminish at once, slowing the decline in its purchasing power and compressing the cash outflow on its balance of payments. There is also an inflow of Federal money—of unemployment benefits.

[20]When, indeed, these combinations do occur, they are apt to come from the capital account (where large disturbances can bunch up quite readily), or to result from general changes in wage rates or productivity; they may also represent the cumulative growth effects mentioned in a previous note.

Furthermore, regions can borrow (or sell off securities) in the national capital market more easily than countries can borrow abroad.[21] Finally, regions afflicted by deflation-*cum*-deficit can often obtain discretionary aid from the central government; special programs of financial and technical assistance to depressed areas have been enacted by a number of countries, including the United States.

Lacking comparable powers and instruments to compensate its member countries, a supranational monetary system perhaps has to function somewhat differently from a national monetary system.[22] As we have not yet developed efficient machinery for making international transfer payments and cannot count on private capital transactions to finance obdurate payments problems, a supranational monetary system must be able to bestow large amounts of credit on countries afflicted by trade-balance disturbances (or variations in capital flows). It must be empowered to pay a high bribe price for the maintenance of stable exchange rates and for compliance with its rules—to dissuade deficit countries from restricting international trade and investment, and to encourage the gradual changes in domestic costs and prices required to offset autonomous shifts in exports, imports, and capital flows.[23]

By implication, the managers of such a system must seek to discriminate between disturbances. They must require a prompt

[21]This point has been emphasized by J. C. Ingram; see especially his contribution to *Factors Affecting the United States Balance of Payments*, Washington D. C.: Government Printing Office, 1962.

[22]One can, of course, cite instances in which countries have obtained similar external aid. The Marshall Plan effected massive transfers to countries with difficult payments problems; more recently, the IMF has granted special drawing rights to less-developed countries dependent on exports of primary products. But these international arrangements operate sporadically and are primitive compared to the machinery for regional transfers that has been built into advanced national economies.

[23]From time to time, moreover, the system must be willing to finance a deficit country that is not making any change in domestic costs or prices but is, instead, attempting institutional reforms. It is sometimes said that adaptations of this sort are not legitimate substitutes for conventional cost-price adjustments, precisely because they should be made even in the absence of a payments deficit. But this argument forgets that once they have been made, there will be no need for cost-price adjustments (and if these are made too, they will have to be reversed). It also ignores a pervasive fact of economic and political life—that some things which should be done will not be attempted until the onset of a crisis. Sometimes, indeed, a crisis is required merely to identify the need for adaptation, let alone to galvanize those who must make the changes, be they in government or in the private sector.

response to deficits resulting from excess domestic demand and, correspondingly, should not grant much credit to the deficit country; but they must allow a slow response to deficits resulting from external disturbances and should grant ample credit to the deficit country. Failing to make this distinction, they will either be too tolerant of deficits due to excess demand or too intolerant of deficits due to trade-balance shifts and changes in capital flows. If too tolerant of the former, they will permit individual countries to export their policy errors; if too intolerant of the latter, they will impose undue hardship on countries already suffering the painful domestic consequences of shifts in world demand or production. In either case, they are bound to provoke international dissension, and in a world that does not yet possess supranational political institutions with coercive powers over national policy, they will witness a renewed disintegration of the international economy, rather than the further integration that is — or ought to be — the ultimate aim of international financial arrangements.[24]

It is the further implication of my analysis that any supranational monetary system designed to function automatically — to be proof against the fallibility of man — is also apt to fail. A system of fully flexible exchange rates, favored by many economists, would make speedy changes in the terms of trade, correcting trade-balance disturbances whenever they arose. It would also protect the world at large from errors in national policy, inflationary or deflationary, but would do so by "bottling up" the errors in the countries committing them, and punishing those countries' citizens. A country restricting domestic demand would experience an appreciation of its own currency, and this would compound the consequences of its mistake by creating additional slack in its economy.[25] Flexible exchange rates, then, are not fully efficient at coping with disturbances in national expenditure.

[24]It is regrettably easy to document this gloomy forecast. One has only to list the succession of measures taken by the United States during the past few years — the tying of foreign aid, the increase of "Buy-American" preferences governing Federal procurement, the taxation of capital outflows, and most recently, the resort to quantitative restrictions on foreign investment, called "guidelines" for the sake of form, but no less damaging to an integrated international economy.

[25]There is a further problem with flexible exchange rates: When international capital movements are sensitive to differences in national interest rates, an increase in one country's interest rate, attracting foreign capital, will cause that country's currency to appreciate and will thereby shift global spending onto other countries' goods, causing those countries to experience inflation. Full flexibility, then, may actually sensitize — not immunize — the world economy to errors in national monetary policies.

A full-fledged gold standard would also function automatically,[26] but might not be sufficiently generous in dealing with trade-balance shifts. Under a gold standard, a deficit country would be compelled to cut back its money stock as it lost reserves; it would be obliged to reinforce the deflationary pressures that emanate directly from external disturbances. With the passage of time, wages and prices would begin to fall in the deficit country (and would also rise in the surplus country), accomplishing the change in relative prices needed to neutralize external disturbances. But this would be a costly way to combat imbalances — and one that most governments sought to avoid long before they acknowledged an explicit commitment to maintain full employment.[27]

This is, perhaps, the point at which to recapitulate and offer some suggestions regarding the design of a supranational monetary system. Such a system, it is clear, cannot apply the same standards and sanctions to all the countries of the world. The major industrial nations may be ready to refrain from restricting their trade; they may also be able to maintain stable exchange rates — though this is far from certain and may not be desirable. The less-developed economies, by contrast, lack the resilience and flexibility that diversified production confers; they are exposed to external disturbances. They also lack a large armory of policy instruments and the internal political cohesion required to master external disturbances by adjusting domestic wages and prices. They must be encouraged to change their exchange rates to resolve their payments problems.[28]

Furthermore, the major industrial countries have still to foster a sufficient international mobility of capital, knowledge, and labor among themselves. International transfers of capital and technical knowledge can generate more uniform rates of growth in output and demand. International transfers of labor can cut down the costs of trade-balance adjustment. It is, incidentally, the chief function of private direct investment to redistribute capital and knowledge among the industrial countries, because transfers of

[26]I have in mind a textbook gold standard, under which the national money supply would be governed by the central bank's holdings of gold, not De Gaulle's gold standard, under which central banks would hold their reserves in gold but would retain autonomy in monetary policy.

[27]See, for example, R. Nurkse, *International Currency Experience*, Geneva: League of Nations, 1944, Chap. 4; and A. I. Bloomfield, *The International Gold Standard, 1880–1914*, New York: Federal Reserve Bank of New York, 1959.

[28]They should, indeed, be urged to alter their exchange rates in lieu of using trade controls to foster development by further import substitution.

this sort occur much more freely among the far-flung branches of a single firm than between competing firms. And it is for this reason, if no other, that restrictions on private direct investment may damage the world economy. These restrictions may be quite effective in correcting payments deficits, but are correspondingly destructive of a vital equilibrating mechanism, which would be beneficial to the whole international economy over the longer run.

A supranational monetary system encompassing these same industrial countries should, in turn, display three separate attributes:

1. It should provide for a continuous confrontation and reconciliation of national objectives. All countries cannot run trade-balances surpluses at once; nor can they all achieve over-all surpluses unless international reserves are made to grow at the corresponding rate. No country, moreover, can enlarge its foreign lending unless some other country is willing to borrow more (and also enlarge domestic expenditure relative to output). Going one step further, it is important to formulate and ratify the domestic aims of each constituent national economy. The international community cannot censure any country for failing to restore external balance without weighing the domestic opportunity cost of faster or larger external adjustment. More generally, one cannot define an "optimum policy mix" for a single country or group of countries without first articulating a consistent constellation of national and international objectives; the very concept of optimality implies a correspondence between instruments and aims.

2. The system should provide for a close coordination of national policies pertaining to domestic demand. This is the necessary substitute for a supranational financial policy to standardize trends in national expenditure and thereby to forestall the emergence of inflation-*cum*-surplus or deflation-*cum*-deficit anywhere within the system. A partial coordination of national policies has already been achieved among the industrial countries; frank and wide-ranging discussions in Working Party Three of the OECD have begun to exert a significant influence on national policies, especially monetary policies. But a closer coordination is needed, and it should be extended to fiscal policies.

3. The system should be capable of financing obdurate deficits, whether by the transfer of existing reserves from one country to another or by the creation of new reserves. It should, of course, be able to insist that countries making use of its credit facilities give evidence of progress toward external balance. It should even be able to withhold assistance from countries that misbehave — those that permit domestic inflation or resort to trade controls. But if it is forbidden to finance long-lasting deficits, it cannot expect deficit countries to obey its injunctions against the use of trade restrictions and to accomplish painful changes in domestic costs and prices.

These three activities, and notably the last two, also have to be linked in a special way. The connections among them, moreover, are often misunderstood.

Much of what is written on the monetary system proposes that national policies be "disciplined" by limiting reserve creation — that rationing reserves will force an alignment of trends in expenditure. This prescription assumes that most imbalances arise from divergent expenditure trends, and implies that the remaining imbalances can be handled by modest adjustments in the policy mix (such as countervailing changes in monetary and fiscal policies) arranged by consultation and negotiation.

If my own analysis is correct, the conventional prescription mismates instruments and aims, and may be destructive of the monetary system. It would be more logical — and very much easier — to seek the required alignment of national policies through multilateral consultation, then to gear reserve creation for the financing of residual deficits. It is, in fact, necessary to proceed this way if, at this juncture, the monetary system is obliged to operate by purchasing compliance, rather than by punishing aberrant policies. If it were forbidden to finance the most difficult adjustments, it could not provide meaningful incentives. Put differently, any attempt to regulate the quality of payments policies by negotiation would not succeed if, by reining-in on credit creation, the system had already required a rapid suppression of every imbalance.[29]

[29]There is the further difficulty that a deflationary departure from accepted standards of national policy cannot be punished by restricting reserve creation; in this instance, limitations on access to credit would damage the innocent (who would be in deficit) rather than the guilty (who would be in surplus).

Some will surely object that adherence to any such monetary system calls for a considerable sacrifice of national sovereignty. But the sacrifice of sovereignty took place long ago. It occurred when the major industrial countries opted for stable exchange rates and pledged themselves to work for freer international trade and investment. To honor these commitments, nations must behave much as if they were the regions of a single country, and the international monetary system should be designed to reward them when they act that way.

THE THEORY OF OPTIMUM CURRENCY AREAS: AN ECLECTIC VIEW

Peter B. Kenen

Introduction

When should exchange rates be fixed and when should they fluctuate? What criteria define the optimum currency area, within which the exchange rates should be pegged immutably, but whose rates should fluctuate, or at least be varied, vis-à-vis the outside world? We owe the first explicit formulation of this question to our conference chairman, Robert Mundell, and I shall preface my reply by summarizing his.[1]

In his very terse treatment of the subject, Mundell does not pause to give us many definitions, but two of them emerge inside his argument—a definition of optimality and a definition of an economic region. Optimality relates to the state of the labor market. If the prevailing exchange-rate regime, fixed or flexible, can maintain external balance without causing unemployment (or, on the other side, demand-induced wage inflation), that regime is optimal. If the currency regime within a given area causes unemployment somewhere in that area (or compels some other portion of that same area to accept inflation as the antidote to unemployment), it is not optimal. In Mundell's own words:

> In a currency area comprising different countries with national currencies the pace of employment in deficit countries is set by the willingness of surplus countries to inflate. But in a currency area comprising many regions and a single currency, the pace of inflation is set by the willingness of central authorities to allow unemployment in deficit regions.
>
> ... But a currency area of either type cannot prevent both unemployment and inflation among its members. The fault lies not with the type of currency area, but with the domain of the currency area. The optimum currency area is not the world.[2]

1. Robert A. Mundell, "A Theory of Optimum Currency Areas," *American Economic Review*, 60, no. 4 (September 1961): 657–65.
2. *ibid.*, p. 659. Mundell's definition of optimality is quite similar to Meade's; see James E. Meade, *The Balance of Payments* (London: Oxford University Press, 1951), pp. 104–7 and 114–24.

One could readily adopt many other points of view. Thus, McKinnon has employed a different definition of optimality

> . . . To describe a single currency area within which monetary-fiscal policy and flexible external exchange rates can be used to give the best resolution of three (sometimes conflicting) objectives: (1) the maintenance of full employment; (2) the maintenance of balanced international payments; (3) the maintenance of a stable internal average price level. Objective (3) assumes that any capitalist economy requires a stable-valued liquid currency to insure efficient resource allocation. . . . The inclusion of objective (3) makes the problem as much a part of monetary theory as of international trade theory. The idea of optimality, then, is complex and difficult to quantify precisely. . . .[3]

I shall have something more to say about McKinnon's third objective, especially his reasons for calling it to our attention. But most of my analysis will make use of the simpler labor-market criterion.

Mundell's other definition, likewise implicit rather than explicit, relates to the delineation of an economic region. It is, again, quite simple and leads his analysis to powerful results. But those same results may not be too helpful from the standpoint of policy and will cause the two of us to part company at an early stage. Mundell's notion of a region is functional not literal. You will not find his regions on an ordinary map but must instead use an input-output table. As I understand the substance of his argument, a region is defined as a homogeneous collection of producers that use the same technology, face the same demand curve, and suffer or prosper together as circumstances change. Thus:

> . . . Suppose that the world consists of two countries, Canada and the United States, each of which has separate currencies. Also assume that the continent is divided into two regions which do not correspond to national boundaries —the East, which produces goods like cars, and the West, which produces goods like lumber products.[4]

Here, Mundell has used the geographer's language, but solely for expositional convenience. It is, in fact, the difference in the product mix that distinguishes East from West.

Combining his labor-market view of optimality and his rather special

3. Ronald I. McKinnon, "Optimum Currency Areas," *American Economic Review*, 53, no. 4 (September 1963): 717. In McKinnon's model, flexible exchange rates can generate a conflict between (1) and (3) because depreciation will augment the demand for "tradable" output, draw labor away from "non-tradable" output, and cause a general increase in wages and prices.
4. Mundell, "Theory of Optimum Currency Areas," p. 659.

definition of a region, Mundell proceeds to furnish an elegant answer to the question of currency areas. He asks us to suppose that consumers shift their spending from cars to lumber products—from eastern goods to western goods. The East, of course, develops a current-account deficit in its balance of payments and an excess supply of labor. The West develops a current-account surplus and an excess demand for labor.

If workers cannot move from East to West, some way must be found to augment the demand for cars (eastern goods) and diminish the demand for lumber products (western goods). The East has to accept worse terms of trade—a decrease in the price of cars relative to lumber products sufficient to reallocate aggregate demand and thereby to eliminate the disequilibria in both regions' labor markets. And if money wage rates are sticky in both regions, eastern currency must be made cheaper in terms of western currency, whether by depreciation (a free-market change) or devaluation (a calculated alteration in a pegged exchange rate). East and West should not be joined in a monetary union, nor be made to peg their currencies once and for all; they do not comprise an optimum currency area.

What happens, however, if workers can move freely between East and West? The westward migration of unemployed eastern workers will serve to ameliorate the labor-market problems of both regions and, at the same time, will help to solve their payments problem. As workers move from East to West, their purchases of cars will be transformed from home demand into extra eastern exports; their purchases of lumber products will be transformed from western exports into extra home demand. In brief, Mundell contends that interregional factor mobility can substitute for changes in regional exchange rates, and that the entire zone through which labor can move freely delineates the right domain for a monetary union or for fixed exchange rates; with labor mobility, East and West do comprise an optimum currency area.

Peripheral Objections

Aspects of this argument call for further work. What should be done, for instance, when there is a major difference in the labor intensities of eastern and western production? Migration might then leave a residual imbalance in one region's labor market—an enduring excess supply in the East or excess demand in the West. And are we really sure that factor movements can restore a perfect balance in the regions' trade even when it does resolve both of their employment problems? Rather special patterns of consumer demand and methods of production may be needed in each region if a simple labor movement and the corresponding change in the locus of demand are to end an imbalance in two regions' labor markets and also to equilibrate the trade flow between them. Notice, finally, that the increase of demand for lumber products could stimulate additional investment in the West, leading to an increase in its income and imports large enough to open up a current-account deficit in its balance of payments.[5]

But the main lines of the argument are not at issue. Nor can one accuse Mundell of failing to perceive the ultimate, unhappy implication of his argument. When regions are defined by their activities, not geographically or politically, perfect interregional labor mobility requires perfect occupational mobility. And this can only come about when labor is homogeneous (or the several regions belonging to a single currency area display very similar skill requirements). In consequence, Mundell's approach leads to the sad certainty that the optimum currency area has always to be small. It must, indeed, be coextensive with the single-product region. In Mundell's own words:

> ...If, then, the goals of internal stability are to be rigidly pursued, it follows that the greater is the number of separate currency areas in the world, the more successfully will these goals be attained...But this seems to imply that regions ought to be defined so narrowly as to count every minor pocket of unemployment arising from labor immobility as a separate region, each of which should apparently have a separate currency![6]

Mundell and I agree that "such an arrangement hardly appeals to common sense," and we likewise agree on some of the reasons.[7] If every community, however small, could issue its own currency, money would no longer serve to lead us out of barter; and if each region's central bank could run its own printing press with complete autonomy, we would soon have to face the difficult problem that McKinnon posed.

5. See Marina v. N. Whitman, *International and Interregional Payments Adjustment: A Synthetic View. Princeton Studies in International Finance*, No. 19 (Princeton: Princeton Univ. Press, 1967). Mrs. Whitman suggests that this variety of current-account deficit may even be needed to maintain overall balance in interregional payments, for some of the additional investment in the West may be financed by capital imports from the East.

6. Mundell, "Theory of Optimum Currency Areas," p. 662.

7. One of them, in fact, anticipates McKinnon's view, and can best be summarized by quoting Mundell again: "The thesis of those who favor flexible exchange rates is that the community in question is not willing to accept variations in its real income through adjustments in its money wage rate or price level, but that it is willing to accept virtually the same changes...through variations in the rate of exchange.... Now as the currency area grows smaller and the proportion of imports in total consumption grows, this assumption becomes increasingly unlikely." (*Ibid.*, p. 663.)

Investors would be deprived of a "stable-valued liquid currency" to hold as a store of value or use as a standard of value when allocating capital among single-product regions.[8]

It has, of course, been argued that changes in exchange rates, actual or possible, do not much deter international investment and, *in extenso*, might not be barriers to a satisfactory allocation of capital among single-product regions.[9] This argument, however, draws heavily on the very special experience of Canada; it assumes that exchange rates will not wobble much; and, most importantly, it forecasts that forward markets will come into being so that traders and investors can translate uncertainty into calculable costs. Given a multitude of microregions, each with its own currency, the foreign exchange markets might be quite thin; few banks and brokers would be able or willing to deal in the host of currencies that would then abound and might not be capable of taking on net positions, long and short, large enough to guarantee stabilizing speculation. To make matters worse, single-product regions may suffer significant disturbances in their foreign trade and payments, so that exchange rates may fluctuate quite widely. More on this point soon.

I come now to another collection of arguments that Mundell and McKinnon have not explored sufficiently. Economic sovereignty has several dimensions, two of them particularly relevant to the problem of managing aggregate demand and maintaining full employment. Fiscal and monetary policies must go hand in hand, and if there is to be an "optimum policy mix," they should have the same domains.[10] There

8. If there were a single region larger than the rest, or more prudent in managing its money, that region's currency might well come into use as an interregional standard of value. In such a case, however, many debts and claims internal to smaller regions would come to be denominated in that "key currency," driving other currencies out of common use. One wonders if the courts of the other microregions would be willing to enforce contracts of this type. Doing so, after all, they would help to undermine their own regions' currencies, much as the Supreme Court of the United States would have undermined the legal status of the dollar if it had upheld the gold-clause contracts in the 1930's.

9. See, e.g., Egon Sohmen, *Flexible Exchange Rates* (Chicago: University of Chicago Press, 1961), p. 19.

10. This term, another of our chairman's contributions to our jargon, is usually employed to denote the combination of monetary and budgetary policies needed to maintain external and internal balance. If, of course, exchange rates are left free to fluctuate, furnishing external balance, the two internal instruments need not be aligned precisely. Yet an "optimum policy mix" is not unimportant to domestic demand management, taken by itself. Too much reliance on one of the two instruments, monetary or budgetary, can have severe and deplorable consequences for particular sectors of the domestic economy. When, as this is written, interest rates are driven high to make good deficiencies in fiscal policy, construction is hit hard, as is investment in public facilities that have to be financed by bond issues subject to approval by the electorate.

should be a treasury, empowered to tax and spend, opposite each central bank, whether to cooperate with monetary policy or merely to quarrel with it. From other viewpoints, too, the domain of fiscal policy ought to coincide with the currency area or, at least, be no larger than the monetary zone. Otherwise, the treasury will face a host of problems.[11]

How would taxes be collected if a single fiscal system were to span a number of currency areas, each of them entitled to alter its exchange rate? How would a treasury maintain the desired distribution of total tax collections? Suppose that the treasury levied an income tax to be paid in each resident's regional currency and that the West was printing money faster than the East, causing a more rapid rise in prices and incomes. Unless the West's currency were to depreciate *pari passu* with the faster rise in money incomes, the West would come to pay a larger fraction of the tax (and if the tax were graduated, might also have to furnish a larger share of the goods and services absorbed by the government, as its tax payments would rise faster than its prices). The same problem would arise even more dramatically if the treasury relied on property taxation. Property values and property assessments might not keep pace with money incomes, and even if the difference in rates of inflation were exactly matched by the change in the exchange rate, there could be a significant redistribution of the tax burden.[12]

In which currency, moreover, would the central government pay for goods and services? Which one would it use to pay its civil servants?[13] And what may be the thorniest practical problem, in which currency should the central government issue its own debt instruments? None of these difficulties would be insurmountable, but ulcer rates in govern-

11. At one point, Meade appears to take a different point of view, arguing for flexible exchange rates within a common market (see James E. Meade, "The Balance-of-Payments Problems of a European Free-Trade Area," *Economic Journal*, 67, no. 3 (September 1957): 379–96. But Meade is not talking of an economic union with a common fiscal system.

12. Analogous problems would arise in respect to transfer payments—and are not hypothetical. Many close observers of the European scene argue that exchange rates can no longer change within the European Economic Community, for any change would undermine the precarious agreement that will govern contributions to the fund financing EEC farm price supports.

13. Notice, in this connection, that a major difference between the currency composition of government receipts and the currency composition of government spending would force the treasury into the exchange market where, willfully or otherwise, it might well become the single speculator capable of altering regional exchange rates. In this case, "the speculative argument against flexible exchange rates would assume weighty dimensions" (Mundell, "Theory of Optimum Currency Areas," p. 663).

ment are already far too high, and ought not to be increased unnecessarily.

In our day, too, government activities may well be subject to important economies of scale. This is surely true in matters of defense and may be true of civil functions. If, then, an optimum currency area should be no smaller than the rather large domain of a least-cost government, it may have to span a great number of single-product regions. If, further, a fiscal system does encompass many such regions, it may actually contribute to internal balance, offsetting the advantage claimed for fragmentation. It is a chief function of fiscal policy, using both sides of the budget, to offset or compensate for regional differences, whether in earned income or in unemployment rates. The large-scale transfer payments built into fiscal systems are interregional, not just interpersonal, and the rules which regulate many of those transfer payments relate to the labor market, just like the criterion Mundell has employed to mark off the optimum currency area. When one looks at fiscal policy in macroeconomic terms, one comes to the unhappy view espoused by Mundell; budgetary policies cannot help but cause inflation in already-prosperous parts of an economy if they are designed to stimulate demand and thereby to eliminate local unemployment. Yet this is not the only way to look at fiscal policy. Given the big numbers, total taxation, and total expenditure, the budget can still combat localized recessions. When a region or community suffers a decline in its external sales, a trade-balance deficit, and internal unemployment,

> ...its federal tax payments diminish at once, slowing the decline in its purchasing power and compressing the cash outflow on its balance of payments. There is also an inflow of federal money—of unemployment benefits. Furthermore, a region can borrow (or sell off securities) in the national capital market more easily than countries can borrow abroad. Finally, regions can...obtain discretionary aid from the central government; special programs of financial and technical assistance to depressed areas have been enacted by a number of countries, including the United States.[14]

On balance, then, a region may come out ahead by foregoing the right to issue its own currency and alter its exchange rate, in order to participate in a major fiscal system.

To sum up, an efficient fiscal system must be made to span many single-product regions and should be coextensive with (or no larger

14. Peter B. Kenen, "Toward a Supranational Monetary System," mimeographed (International Economics Workshop: Columbia University, 1966), pp. 13–14.

than) a single, if non-optimal, currency area. The logic of Mundell's approach, however impeccable, should not cause us to convene another San Francisco conference, there to carve the world up, rather than unite it, so that single-product regions can have their own currencies and can let them fluctuate.

And here, perhaps, Mundell and I are not far apart. The purpose of his argument, he tells us at the end, is not to recommend that there be more currencies, but merely to determine when one ought to recommend that existing currencies be fixed or flexible. He asks us to agree that "the validity of the argument for flexible exchange rates...hinges on the closeness with which nations correspond to regions. The argument works best if each nation (and currency) has internal factor mobility and external factor immobility."[15] On first reading this last passage, incidentally, I was certain that "regions" had been redefined. Here, it would appear that a region is delineated by factor mobility, not by its principal activity and, therefore, the degree to which its industries suffer the same changes in product demand. Yet when one reads these sentences a little bit differently, the seeming inconsistency vanishes at once. For "regions" let me substitute "optimum currency areas," then paraphrase the argument.[16] Exchange rates should be fixed between single-product regions when labor moves freely between them, for then there is no need to change the terms of trade when a region encounters an external disturbance; and when there is mobility across all the regions making up a nation, that whole nation is an optimum currency area. When, further, workers can move freely between any pair of countries, those two countries jointly form an optimum currency area and can peg their currencies, one to the other. When, contrarily, there is no mobility between the single-product regions of a single nation, it may be very difficult to maintain full employment and price stability throughout its territory; the nation must rely on rather sophisticated internal policies to reallocate demand rather than augment or curb it. When, finally, labor does not move between a pair of countries, their currencies should fluctuate, one against the other, so as to accomplish changes in their terms of trade. Regions, to repeat, are still to be defined by their activities; optimum currency areas are to be defined by the interregional mobility of labor.

15. Mundell, "Theory of Optimum Currency Areas," p. 664.
16. I dwell on this small point in order to be spared another dozen papers by students who believe that they have discovered a fatal flaw in Mundell's analysis and that the whole argument must therefore be wrong.

A Competing Principle

But now it is my task to show that Mundell's approach is not wholly adequate—that marking off zones of perfect labor mobility may not be the best way to delineate optimum currency areas, for perfect mobility rarely prevails. Other criteria will have to be employed when, at the millennium, central bankers come to us and ask if an exchange rate should be fixed or flexible. In my view, diversity in a nation's product mix, the number of single-product regions contained in a single country, may be more relevant than labor mobility. I hope, indeed, to make three points:

> 1) That a well-diversified national economy will not have to undergo changes in its terms of trade as often as a single-product national economy.
> 2) That when, in fact, it does confront a drop in the demand for its principal exports, unemployment will not rise as sharply as it would in a less-diversified national economy.
> 3) That the links between external and domestic demand, especially the link between exports and investment, will be weaker in diversified national economies, so that variations in domestic employment "imported" from abroad will not be greatly aggravated by corresponding variations in capital formation.

The first of these three points can be made most easily. A country that engages in a number of activities is also apt to export a wide range of products. Each individual export may be subject to disturbances, whether due to changes in external demand or in technology. But if those disturbances are independent, consequent on variations in the composition of expenditure or output, rather than massive macroeconomic swings affecting the entire export array, the law of large numbers will come into play. At any point in time, a country can expect to suffer significant reversals in export performance, but also to enjoy significant successes. Its aggregate exports, then, are sure to be more stable than those of an economy less thoroughly diversified. From the standpoint of external balance, taken by itself, economic diversification, reflected in export diversification, serves, ex ante, to forestall the need for frequent changes in the terms of trade and, therefore, for frequent changes in national exchange rates.[17]

17. Anyone familiar with random processes knows, of course, that they may not average out quickly or perfectly. That is why the gambler has to have a bankroll and why central banks have to have reserves. If, in fact, one views the balance of payments as a simple sum of stochastic processes, the deficit or surplus, measured by the change in central bank reserves, should obey the central limit

One has at once to qualify this simple proposition. A diversification of output and exports cannot guarantee domestic stability, even when external shocks tend to average out. There must be sufficient occupational mobility to reabsorb the labor and capital idled by adverse disturbances. Here, two possibilities arise. If, on the one hand, external disturbances are truly independent because each export product is quite different from the rest, export earnings will be stable but factor mobility may be very low. Products that differ when classified by final use may differ in their modes of manufacture, so that the factors of production used in making one of them may not be adaptable to making any other. If, on the other hand, the several separate exports of a single country are, in fact, close substitutes when classified by final use, disturbances afflicting external demand will not be fully independent—the law of large numbers will not apply—but there may be more mobility between export industries. Products that are similar in final use are apt to have similar factor requirements, and workers who are idled by an export disturbance may be more readily absorbed in other activities.

My second point is closely related to the first but deals with the consequence of export fluctuations after they appear. A diversification of output will mitigate the damage done by external shocks, not merely diminish the likelihood of major shocks. To make this point, I shall contrast four distinct economies, asking what they have to do to maintain external balances when they are afflicted by exogenous disturbances. These four economies are perfectly competitive and make use of a single variable input, standardized labor, but they differ in two ways.[18] Output is diversified in the first and second countries; each of them produces an export good and an import-competing good. The third and fourth economies, by contrast, are not diversified; they specialize completely in export production. Furthermore, the first and third are small economies, with no influence at all on world prices,[19] while the second

theorem, exhibiting a normal or nearly normal distribution, and a central bank's reserves ought to be an increasing function of the variance or standard deviation of that normal distribution. Surprisingly enough, these things are true; see Peter B. Kenen and Elinor B. Yudin, "The Demand for International Reserves," *Review of Economics and Statistics*, 97, no. 3 (August 1965): 242–50. For a further look at the balance of payments as a somewhat fancier stochastic process, see my *Computer Simulation of the United States Balance of Payments*, mimeographed (International Economics Workshop: Columbia University, 1965).

18. For a more formal representation of these economies, and proofs of the theorems that follow, examine the Appendix.

19. Hence, the first and third resemble the model economies considered in McKinnon's note on optimum currency areas, except that they do not produce "non-tradable" commodities and cannot shift labor (or domestic demand) to and from their local sectors when domestic prices change.

and fourth are large economies, facing a determinate demand for their exports.

Consider, first, a simple exogenous disturbance, an increase in wage rates more rapid than in import prices. Here, all four economies must make the same exchange-rate change to stabilize employment; the requisite devaluation or depreciation must equal the difference between the rates of change of wages and of import prices. Yet the four economies behave rather differently when their central banks opt for fixed exchange rates. In each case, employment is certain to decline, but the changes in employment will not be identical. In the small-country case, the two-product economy will suffer a smaller decline in employment if its export industry has the larger elasticity of demand for labor with respect to real wage rates.[20] In the large-country case, this same condition has to hold, but does not suffice; there is, indeed, a strong presumption that the two-product national economy will suffer the larger change in employment.[21] Facing this type of exogenous disturbance, then, diversified economies may be at a handicap.[22]

Consider, next, a different class of exogenous disturbances, more like the one that figures in Mundell's analysis. Seen by the small countries, this type of shock will appear as an exogenous change in the terms of trade; seen by the large countries, it will appear as an exogenous change in export demand at given terms of trade. Here, there are perceptible differences in the size of the exchange-rate change needed for internal balance, not just in the size of the change in employment occurring when the central banks opt for fixed exchange rates. Whether small or large, the two-product economy is bound to experience the smaller change in its exchange rate.[23] Furthermore, product diversification always serves to shield the labor force from this class of shock. The two-product economy suffers the smaller change in employment under fixed exchange rates, and the larger the fraction of the labor force engaged in import-competing production, the smaller the change in employment occasioned by a change in the terms of trade or demand for exports.[24]

20. See equation (4.5) of the Appendix.
21. See equation (4.6) of the Appendix.
22. Notice, moreover, that this strange result derives from the mere fact of diversification, not from mobility inside an economy. Both parts of the labor force, in export- and import-competing production, are affected the same way by changes in the money wage relative to import prices.
23. See equations (4.7) and (4.8) of the Appendix.
24. See equations (4.9) and (4.10) of the Appendix, and notice once again that the extra stability afforded a diversified economy derives from the mere fact that it has more industries, not from any labor flow inside the country. The two disturbances considered here do not affect employment in the import-competing

I come now to my third point concerning diversification. Here, I shall combine the first of those three points, concerning the advantages conferred ex ante by export diversity, with my earlier remark, concerning the connection between export demand and the stability of capital formation.

Suppose that an economy is operating at full steam, with no idle capacity in any of its sectors. An increase of demand for that country's exports will introduce damaging inflationary pressures. And those pressures will be amplified in two separate ways—by the familiar Keynesian multiplier and by an increase in capital formation as exporters undertake to satisfy their customers. Exports and investment will increase together, giving a double thrust to aggregate demand. From the standpoint of external balance, this may not be bad. Imports will rise faster and are more apt to offset the initial rise in exports, narrowing the gap in the current-account balance. But from the standpoint of internal balance, the increase of investment induced by the rise in exports will put a larger strain on domestic policy.[25]

Clearly, a country will be least exposed to this compound instability if its exports are thoroughly diversified and the disturbances afflicting

---

industry. For labor mobility to play a part in stabilizing overall employment, there must be a change in the exchange rate or a decrease of the money wage relative to import prices; these would stimulate production in the import-competing industry and transfer idle workers from the export industry.

25. In the paper cited earlier, Mrs. Whitman has supplied an elegant analysis of these phenomena and, what may be most important, of the complications introduced when some of the investment is financed by foreigners. Here, some simple algebra can illustrate my point. Using the familiar Keynesian relationships:

$$dY = dC + dI + dX - dM,$$
$$dC = (1 - s)\, dY,$$
$$dM = m \cdot dY,$$
$$dB = dX - dM.$$

Introduce a simple link between exports and investment:

$$dI = r \cdot dX.$$

Then:

$$dY = (1 + r)\, dX/(s + m) \qquad \text{and} \qquad dB = (s - rm)\, dX/(s + m).$$

The change in income is an increasing function of the link between exports and investment, while the change in the trade balance is a decreasing function of that same connection, r. Note, in passing, that a diversified economy may have a rather small marginal propensity to import (see Whitman, *International and Interregional Payments*, p. 8), so that dY and dB may be increasing functions of diversification; external disturbances will not spill back out. This may be the chief counterargument to my own contention that diversified economies are the least vulnerable to external shocks and have the least need for flexible rates to maintain internal balance.

those exports are, in consequence, fairly well randomized. The corresponding fluctuations in domestic investment may not average out as well, since an increase of demand for any single export may increase investment in that export industry, while an equal decrease of demand for some other export may not cause a corresponding decrease in investment. Here, much will depend on the capital-intensities of the nation's industries and on investors' judgments regarding the duration of the export disturbance. Yet the asymmetries, if they exist, cannot be large enough to vitiate my basic point. Diversity in exports, protecting the economy from external shocks, will surely help to stabilize capital formation, easing the burden that has to be borne by internal policies.

Again, a major caveat: My argument does not apply when changes in export demand arise from business-cycle swings. When those occur, the whole range of exports will be hit, and export diversification cannot forestall "imported" instability.

This point has been made before and has, indeed, been offered as the principal criterion for choosing a particular exchange-rate regime. Fixed rates, it is said, are much to be preferred if one's own authorities, especially the central bank, are less adept or more prone to err than those of other countries. With fixed rates, the outside world can be made to bear some part of the consequences of one's own mistakes.[26] If, conversely, foreigners are less adept at economic management, flexible exchange rates are much to be preferred, to insulate a stable domestic economy from another country's errors.

These are potent arguments and may even be decisive. They did, in fact, dominate the Canadian debate a few years ago. But surely they do not belong to the theory of optimum currency areas. Optimality has always to be judged from a global point of view,[27] and these defensive arguments are far from cosmopolitan. Countries which adopt fixed

26. This point is the counterpart of another by Mundell: That fiscal policy is more potent under flexible exchange rates "because leakages through foreign trade are closed by changes in the exchange rate," and that the potency of monetary policy is increased even more because of its effects on capital movements; an increase of interest rates, attracting foreign capital, forces an appreciation of the home currency and a concomitant deflationary change in the current-account balance. See Robert Mundell, "Flexible Exchange Rates and Employment Policy," *Canadian Journal of Economics and Political Science*, 27, no. 4 (November 1961): 516; also Sohmen, *Flexible Exchange Rates*, p. 84.

27. If not in other areas of economic thought, certainly in matters pertaining to exchange rates. How many times have we to remind our students—and ourselves as well—that an exchange rate is common to two countries, not the exclusive national property of one or the other? How many times have we heard and ridiculed the remarkable recommendation that "all currencies should fluctuate except the U.S. dollar"?

exchange rates to diffuse their own mistakes inflict those same mistakes on their trading partners; countries which adopt flexible exchange rates compound the consequences of their neighbors' errors.

Conclusion

Where, then, do I wind up? Fixed rates, I believe are most appropriate —or least inappropriate—to well-diversified national economies. *Ex ante*, diversification serves to average out external shocks and, incidentally, to stabilize domestic capital formation. *Ex post*, it serves to minimize the damage done when averaging is incomplete. It is also a prerequisite to the internal factor mobility that Mundell has emphasized, because a continuum of national activities will maximize the number of employment opportunities for each specialized variety of labor.

One more desideratum emerges from my argument. Countries with fixed rates have also to be armed with potent and sophisticated internal policies. Remember that diversified national economies may be particularly vulnerable to the "monetary" shocks represented by a change in money wages relative to import prices. Hence, they must maintain rather close control over money-wage rates, or at least be able to align the rate of change of the money wage with rates of change prevailing abroad. Furthermore, fixed-rate countries must be armed with a wide array of budgetary policies to deal with the stubborn "pockets of unemployment" that are certain to arise from export fluctuations combined with an imperfect mobility of labor.

In brief, I come quite close to endorsing the status quo. The principal developed countries should perhaps adhere to the Bretton Woods regime, rarely resorting to changes in exchange rates.[28] The less-developed countries, being less diversified and less well-equipped with policy instruments, should make more frequent changes or perhaps resort to full flexibility.

Appendix

To sort out the effects of diversification, consider the economies described in the text.

The Small Two-Product Economy

As labor is the only variable input, the two outputs, X_1 and X_2, can be

---

[28] If so, however, they must have large reserves. For a longer argument along these same lines, see my "Toward a Supranational Monetary System," cited above.

written as functions of employment, N_1 and N_2, and those functions will display diminishing returns:

$$X_1 = g_1(N_1), \qquad g_1' > 0, g_1'' < 0 \qquad (1.1)$$
$$X_2 = g_2(N_2), \qquad g_2' > 0, g_2'' < 0 \qquad (1.2)$$

Next, define total employment, N, and real income, Y, using the price of the export product as numeraire:

$$N = N_1 + N_2 \qquad (1.3)$$

$$Y = X_1 + \frac{1}{p} \cdot X_2 \qquad (1.4)$$

$$p = P_1/P_2 \qquad (1.5)$$

Furthermore, labor will be paid a money wage, W, equal to the value of its marginal product, so that:

$$W = P_1 \cdot g_1' \qquad (1.6)$$
$$W = P_2 \cdot g_2' \qquad (1.7)$$

Now define the domestic consumption of X_1 and X_2 on the supposition that there is no net saving, so that expenditure will always equal income:

$$X_1^c = C(Y, p) \qquad (1.8)$$
$$X_2^c = (Y - X_1^c)p \qquad (1.9)$$

Note that (1.8) and (1.9) imply a continuous equality between exports and imports.[29] Finally, define the foreign-currency prices of the two products, P_1^f and P_2^f, and write the exchange rate, R, in units of foreign currency per unit of home currency. Then:

$$RP_1 = P_1^f \qquad (1.10)$$
$$RP_2 = P_2^f \qquad (1.11)$$

If W, R, P_1^f and P_2^f are treated as exogenous, the eleven equations given above uniquely determine X_1, X_2, N_1, N_2, Y, p, P_1, P_2, X_1^c, and X_2^c.

The Large Two-Product Economy

Use (1.1) through (1.9) and (1.11) above, but replace (1.10) with a demand function for exports, X_1^e:

$$X_1^e = X_1 - X_1^c = E(RP_1/P_2^f, t) \qquad (1.10')$$

where t is an exogenous disturbance.

29. Exports will be $(X_1 - X_1^c)$ and imports will be valued at $(X_2^c - X_2)/p$. Invoking (1.9) and (1.4), above, imports can be written as $(Y - X_1^c - X_2/p)$, which is $(X_1 - X_1^c)$.

The Small One-Product Economy

,Use (1.1), (1.5), (1.6), and (1.8) through (1.11), but replace (1.3) and (1.4) with:

$$N = N_1 \qquad (1.3')$$
$$Y = X_1 \qquad (1.4')$$

This economy has nine equations and an equal number of endogenous variables; equations (1.2) and (1.7) have dropped out, but so too have X_2 and N_2.

The Large One-Product Economy

Use (1.1), (1.3'), (1.4'), (1.5), (1.6), (1.8), (1.9), (1.10'), and (1.11). This economy, like the one before has nine equations and nine endogenous variables.

To simplify subsequent analysis, rewrite the essential part of each economic model. For the small two-product case:

$$N = N_1 + N_2 \qquad (2.1)$$

$$Y = g_1(N_1) + \frac{1}{p} \cdot g_2(N_2) \qquad (2.2)$$

$$p = P_1^f / P_2^f \qquad (2.3)$$

$$RW = P_1^f \cdot g_1' \qquad (2.4)$$

$$RW = P_2^f \cdot g_2'. \qquad (2.5)$$

For the large two-product case, use (2.1), (2.2), and (2.5), above, but replace (2.3) and (2.4) with

$$p = P_1 / P_2^f \qquad (2.3')$$

$$W = P_1 \cdot g_1' \qquad (2.4')$$

and combine (1.8) and (1.10') into

$$g_1(N_1) = C(Y, p) + E(p, t). \qquad (2.6)$$

For the small one-product case, use (2.3) and (2.4) above, but replace (2.1) and (2.2) with

$$N = N_1 \qquad (2.1')$$

$$Y = g_1(N_1), \qquad (2.2')$$

and for the large one-product case, use (2.1'), (2.2'), (2.3'), (2.4'), and (2.6).

Differentiate (2.1) through (2.5) to furnish four equations for the small two-product country:

$$dN_1 + dN_2 - dN = 0 \qquad (3.1)$$

$$g_1' \, dN_1 + g_1' \, dN_2 - dY - (X_2/p)\overset{*}{p} = 0 \qquad (3.2)$$

$$\frac{1}{e_1 \cdot N_1} dN_1 - \overset{*}{p} = (\overset{*}{P_2^f} - \overset{*}{W} - \overset{*}{R}) \qquad (3.3)$$

$$\frac{1}{e_1 \cdot N_1} dN_1 - \frac{1}{e_2 \cdot N_2} dN_2 - \overset{*}{p} = 0 \qquad (3.4)$$

where $\overset{*}{p}$, $\overset{*}{P_2^f}$, $\overset{*}{W}$, and $\overset{*}{R}$ are the percentage rates of change in p, P_2^f, W, and R, and where $e_1 = -(g_1'/g_1'')/N_1$ and $e_2 = -(g_2'/g_2'')/N_2$, the elasticities of N_1 and N_2 with respect to real wage rates. Here, the percentage change in relative prices, $\overset{*}{p}$, is exogenous; the four equations (3.1) through (3.4) suffice merely to solve for dN_1, dN_2, dN, and dY.

Differentiate (2.1), (2.2), (2.3'), (2.4'), (2.5), and (2.6) to obtain five equations for the large two-product country: equations (3.1) through (3.4) and

$$g_1' \, dN_1 - c_1 \cdot dY + (n^c \cdot X_1^c + n^e \cdot X_1^e)\overset{*}{p} = dX_1^{ea} \qquad (3.5)$$

where $c_1 = (\partial C/\partial Y)$, the marginal propensity to spend on X_1; where $n^c = -(\partial C/\partial p)(p/X_1^c)$, the price elasticity of home demand for X_1; where $n^e = -(\partial E/\partial p)(p/X_1^e)$, the price elasticity of foreign demand for X_1, and where dX_1^{ea} is the autonomous change in export demand, $(\partial E/\partial t)\, dt$. Here, the percentage change in relative prices, $\overset{*}{p}$, is endogenous; the five equations (3.1) through (3.5) suffice to solve for dN_1, dN_2, dN, dY, and $\overset{*}{p}$.

Differentiate (2.1'), (2.2'), (2.3), and (2.4) to obtain two equations for the small one-product country:

$$g_1' \, dN - dY = 0 \qquad (3.6)$$

$$\frac{1}{e_1 \cdot N} dN - \overset{*}{p} = (P_2^f - \overset{*}{W} - \overset{*}{R}). \qquad (3.7)$$

Here, again, $\overset{*}{p}$ is exogenous; equations (3.6) and (3.7) suffice merely to solve for dN and dY.

Finally, differentiate (2.1'), (2.2'), (2.3'), (2.4'), and (2.6) to obtain three equations for the large one-product country: Equations (3.6), (3.7), and (3.5), but with total N replacing N_2 in (3.5). These three equations suffice to solve for dN, dY, and $\overset{*}{p}$.

Now write out the changes in employment, dN, attaching a super-script to each result so as to identify the case from which it comes. In the small one-product country:

$$dN^{1s} = Ne_1(\overset{*}{P_2^f} - \overset{*}{W} - \overset{*}{R} + \overset{*}{p}).\tag{4.1}$$

In the small two-product country

$$dN_1 = N_1 \cdot e_1(\overset{*}{P_2^f} - \overset{*}{W} - \overset{*}{R} + \overset{*}{p}),$$

$$dN_2 = N_2 \cdot e_2(\overset{*}{P_2^f} - \overset{*}{W} - \overset{*}{R}),$$

$$dN^{2s} = [Ne_1 + N_2(e_2 - e_1)](\overset{*}{P_2^f} - \overset{*}{W} - \overset{*}{R}) + (N_1 \cdot e_1)\overset{*}{p}.\tag{4.2}$$

In the large one-product country

$$dN^{1l} = \frac{1}{D_1}\,[n^\alpha(\overset{*}{P_2^f} - \overset{*}{W} - \overset{*}{R}) + dX_1^{ea}]\tag{4.3}$$

where $n^\alpha = (n^c \cdot X_1^c + n^e \cdot X_1^e)$ and $D_1 = g_1'(1 - c_1) + n^\alpha/Ne_1$ (with $D_1 > 0$ because $c_1 < 1$ when X_2 is not an inferior good). Finally, in the large two-product country

$$dN_1 = \frac{1}{D_2}\,\{[(n^\alpha + c_1 \cdot X_2/p) + c_1(N_2 \cdot e_2)g_1'](\overset{*}{P_2^f} - \overset{*}{W} - \overset{*}{R}) + dX_1^{ea}\},$$

$$dN_2 = (N_2 \cdot e_2)(\overset{*}{P_2^f} - \overset{*}{W} - \overset{*}{R}),$$

$$dN^{2l} = \frac{1}{D_2}\,\left\{\left[\frac{Ne_1 + N_2(e_2 - e_1)}{N_1 \cdot e_1}\,(n^\alpha + c_1 \cdot X_2/p) + (N_2 \cdot e_2)g_1'\right]\right.$$

$$\left. \times (\overset{*}{P_2^f} - \overset{*}{W} - \overset{*}{R}) + dX_1^{ea}\right\}\tag{4.4}$$

where $D_2 = D_1 + [n^\alpha(N_2/N) + c_1 \cdot X_2/p]/(N_1 \cdot e_1)$. The new arguments figuring in D_2 represent the two effects of product diversification. The term $n^\alpha(N_2/N)$ is the direct effect of splitting the labor force into N_1 and N_2. The term $c_1 \cdot X_2/p$ is an indirect terms-of-trade effect, measuring the change in home spending on X_1 resulting from a change in relative prices that alters the X_1 value of X_2 output and, to that extent, alters the national income. It takes this form because the X_1 value of national income, Y, is used as an argument in the demand function for X_1, equation (1.8), above.

Now let $\overset{*}{p} = 0$ in (4.1) and (4.2), let $dX_1^{ea} = 0$ in (4.3) and (4.4), and let $\overset{*}{R} = 0$ for fixed exchange rates. Pairing off the countries according to size:

$$dN^{1s} - dN^{2s} = N_2(e_1 - e_2)(\overset{*}{P_2^f} - \overset{*}{W}) \tag{4.5}$$

$$dN^{1l} - dN^{2l} = \frac{1}{D_2}\left\{N_2(e_1 - e_2)(n^\alpha + c_1 \cdot X_2/p)/(N_1 \cdot e_1)\right.$$

$$\left. - g_1'\left[N_2 \cdot e_2 + (1 - c_1)Ne_1\left(\frac{D_2 - D_1}{D_1}\right)\right]\right\}$$

$$\times (\overset{*}{P_2^f} - \overset{*}{W}) \tag{4.6}$$

In the small-country case, the condition $e_1 > e_2$ is sufficient to diminish variations in employment arising from disparities between $\overset{*}{P_2^f}$ and $\overset{*}{W}$. In the large-country case, $e_1 > e_2$ is needed but does not suffice; the other argument of (4.6) is unambiguously positive. When $\overset{*}{P_2^f} \neq \overset{*}{W}$, then, the diversified economy may suffer larger changes in employment.[30]

Next, let $\overset{*}{P_2^f} = \overset{*}{W}$ to study the external shocks $\overset{*}{p}$ and dX_1^{ea}. Whereas, before, all four economies had to make the very same changes in exchange rates for internal balance ($dN = 0$), here, each economy must make a different change. Using (4.1) through (4.4), compute the requisite changes in exchange rates and the pairwise differences. As:

$$\overset{*}{R}^{1s} = \overset{*}{p},$$

$$\overset{*}{R}^{2s} = (1 - \overset{*}{V})p,$$

$$\overset{*}{R}^{1l} = \frac{dX_1^{ea}}{n^\alpha},$$

$$\overset{*}{R}^{2l} = \frac{(1 - V)\, dX_1^{ea}}{n^\alpha + c_1 \cdot X_2/p + N_2 \cdot e_2(1 - V)g_1'},$$

where $V = (N_1 \cdot e_1)/[(N_1 \cdot e_1) + (N_2 \cdot e_2)]$, then:

$$\overset{*}{R}^{1s} - \overset{*}{R}^{2s} = (1 - V)\overset{*}{p} \tag{4.7}$$

$$\overset{*}{R}^{1l} - \overset{*}{R}^{2l} = \frac{Vn^\alpha + c_1 \cdot X_2/p + N_2 \cdot e_2(1 - V)g_1'}{n^\alpha[n^\alpha + c_1 \cdot X_2/p + N_2 \cdot e_2(1 - V)g_1']}\, dX_1^{ea}. \tag{4.8}$$

The one-product economy is bound to experience the larger change in its exchange rate.

30. Mere size, however, is advantageous. In the one-product case, for example: $dN^{1s} - dN^{1l} = \frac{1}{D_1} Ne_1(1 - c_1)g_1'(\overset{*}{P_2^f} - \overset{*}{W})$. The small country will experience the larger change in aggregate employment.

If, now, $\overset{*}{R} = 0$, $\overset{*}{p}$ and dX_1^{ea} lead to different changes in aggregate employment:

$$dN^{1s} - dN^{2s} = (N_2 \cdot e_2)\overset{*}{p} \tag{4.9}$$

$$dN^{1l} - dN^{2l} = \left(\frac{D_2 - D_1}{D_1 \cdot D_2}\right) dX_1^{ea}$$

$$= \left[\frac{n^\alpha(N_2/N) + c_1 \cdot X_2/p}{(N_1 \cdot e_1)D_1 \cdot D_2}\right] dX^{ea} \tag{4.10}$$

In each case, the diversified national economy suffers the smaller change in employment.

TRADE, SPECULATION, AND THE FORWARD EXCHANGE RATE

Peter B. Kenen

If Great Britain had been paradise for the last two hundred years, economic analysis might still be quite primitive. Our subject advances most rapidly when theorists are challenged by policy problems, and it owes its greatest debt to Britain's afflictions. The history of trade theory illustrates this proposition. So does the theory of forward exchange.

The interest-parity doctrine, constructed by Keynes and christened by Einzig,[1] replied to the dilemma that Britain confronted in the early 1920's – domestic stagnation combined with a payments deficit. Keynes showed that changes in forward exchange rates have the same effect on capital flows as changes in the difference between national interest rates. He urged intervention to support forward sterling in lieu of raising Bank rate higher, thereby to strengthen Britain's reserves without doing damage to the British economy. When Britain faced the same dilemma in the late 1950's, another generation of economists revived Keynes's suggestion,[2] inspiring additional advances in analysis.

The modern theory of forward exchange, as set out by Spraos, Tsiang, and Sohmen,[3] builds upon Keynes's contribution – his treatment of the

---

[1] J. M. Keynes, *A Tract on Monetary Reform* (London: Macmillan and Co., 1923), pp. 122-32; and P. Einzig, *A Dynamic Theory of Forward Exchange* (London: Macmillan and Co., 1961), p. 146.

[2] See, *e.g.*, A. E. DeJasay, "Forward Exchange: The Case for Intervention", *Lloyds Bank Review*, L (October, 1958), 35-45; and J. Spraos, "Speculation, Arbitrage and Sterling", *Economic Journal*, LXIX, No. 1 (March, 1959), 1-21.

[3] J. Spraos, *loc. cit.*; *idem*, "The Theory of Forward Exchange and Recent Practice", *The Manchester School of Economics and Social Studies*, XXI, No. 2 (May, 1953), 87-117; S. C. Tsiang, "The Theory of Forward Exchange and Effects of Government Intervention on the Forward Exchange Market", *International Monetary Fund Staff Papers*, VII, No. 1 (April, 1959), 75-106; and E. Sohmen, *Flexible Exchange Rates: Theory and Controversy* (Chicago: University of Chicago Press, 1961), chap. iv.

forward exchange rate as an ordinary price that must move to equate
supply and demand. But the treatment of transactions in forward exchange is much more complete. As the *modus operandi* of Bank rate was
usually expounded in respect of bill-market arbitrage – movements of
funds between two countries' money markets – Keynes stressed the forward exchange operations arising from this type of capital transfer.[4]
Recent writers on forward exchange have studied the many constituents
of forward supply and demand, examining separately transactions arising
from trade, from the several types of international investment, and from
pure speculation on changes in the spot rates. In so doing, they have
made important changes in Keynes's chief conclusion. Because the supply
and demand for forward exchange reflect commercial "covering" and
speculation, as well as interest arbitrage, the equilibrium price for forward
exchange can be quite different from interest parity, even when there is
just one relevant interest rate in each of the countries concerned.

But this functional classification of forward transactions may also
obscure the essential similarity of all such transactions. Purchases and
sales of forward exchange are undertaken for one reason, no matter what
their form or the principal business activity of buyer and seller. They are
used to alter the currency composition of each party's balance sheet – to
align his net position in each currency, whether "long" or "short", with
his expectations concerning the exchange rates. A merchant, investor, or
banker who holds foreign-currency assets or who incurs foreign-currency
debts may make profits or take losses in his own currency if the spot
exchange rate is subject to change during the life of his assets or debts.
To diminish his exposure to exchange risk, he must reduce his net position
in foreign exchange, as by incurring foreign-currency debt to offset net

---

[4]   Even now, interest parity is usually expressed in terms of the Treasury bill rates:
If r_a is the quarterly interest rate on three-month Treasury bills in New York, r_b is
the corresponding rate in London, R is the spot price of sterling expressed in dollars,
and $R_f = R(1 - \alpha_f)$ is the three-month forward price of sterling, an American
investor averse to exchange risk will have no profit incentive to transfer funds between
New York and London when:

$$(1 + r_a) = (1 + r_b) \cdot (R_f/R) = (1 + r_b)(1 - \alpha_f).$$

When this condition holds, however:

$$(r_b - r_a)/(1 + r_b) = \alpha_f,$$

describing the bill-rate interest parity for forward sterling.

assets or by acquiring foreign-currency assets to offset net debt.[5] Transactions in forward foreign exchange create these extra debts and claims without imposing interest costs or a loss of interest income. A sale of forward foreign exchange creates a new debt in foreign currency and a new claim in the seller's own currency. A purchase of forward foreign exchange creates a new claim in foreign currency and a new debt in the seller's own currency.

To illustrate the basic similarity of purpose in all forward exchange transactions, I examine the spot and forward operations of an export-import firm. I show that it engages in "covering" (or "hedging"), arbitrage, and speculation in the normal course of business, and I develop the several connections among these activities – connections that cannot appear when the activities are studied separately or assigned to different parties.[6] I also stress the relationship between the firm's balance sheet (a set of stocks) and its transactions in foreign exchange (a set of flows).[7]

I   The trader-speculator

The first version of the model studied here supposes that all foreign trade is invoiced in the exporter's currency and is conducted on a cash basis. Exporters are paid in full on the execution of sales contracts (and employ their cash receipts to purchase or produce the goods they must deliver under the contracts). Importers must borrow to make their cash payments, and can do so readily at foreign or domestic banks. The banks

---

[5]   It is, of course, conventional to define exposure to exchange risk as a long or short position in foreign currency, and I follow this convention here. But a firm whose net worth is always expressed in its home currency also courts exchange risk, for its home currency depreciates whenever any other currency appreciates. No one with financial assets or financial debts can escape exchange risk, properly defined.

[6]   See, *e.g.*, J. E. Stein, *The Nature and Efficiency of the Foreign Exchange Market* ("Essays in International Finance", No. 40 [Princeton, N. J.: International Finance Section, Princeton University, 1962]), pp. 15 ff. Stein regards the banks as the "professional risk bearers" (speculators) who take over exchange risks from merchants and investors.

[7]   In this respect and several others, my treatment of the problem resembles the Fleming-Mundell model (J. M. Fleming and R. A. Mundell, "Official Intervention on the Forward Exchange Market: A Simplified Analysis", *International Monetary Fund Staff Papers*, XI, No. 1 [March, 1964]).

lend freely to all comers, but at rising interest rates; the average rate paid by any one borrower to any one bank is an increasing function of his current borrowing from that particular bank.[8] Finally, I assume that the spot exchange rate is fixed (albeit not immutably), that all bank loans and forward exchange transactions have the same maturity (ninety days), and, at the start, that the volume of trade is given.

To put these assumptions more formally, define:

R, R_e, R_f The spot price of pounds prevailing today (the current spot price), the spot price traders expect to encounter ninety days from now (the expected or deferred spot price), and the ninety-day forward price of pounds prevailing today, all expressed in dollars per pound;

M_a, M_b American and British imports paid for today (current trade), both expressed in dollars;

$_bP, {}_aP$ Spot purchases of British currency (pounds) and American currency (dollars) resulting from current trade (current spot purchases);

$_bP_e, {}_aP_e$ Spot purchases of British and American currency ninety days from now resulting from current trade (deferred spot purchases);

$_bP_f, {}_aP_f$ Ninety-day forward purchases of British and American currency resulting from current trade (current forward purchases);

C_{aa}, C_{ab} New dollar loans to American and British traders furnished by American banks (current American bank loans);

C_{ba}, C_{bb} New sterling loans to American and British traders furnished by British banks (current British bank loans);

r_{aa}, r_{ab} The average rates of interest on C_{aa} and C_{ab}; and

r_{ba}, r_{bb} The average rates of interest on C_{ba} and C_{bb}.

If, then, all imports are financed by bank credit:

$$M_i = C_{ai} + C_{bi} R, \qquad i = a, b. \tag{1}$$

If average interest rates rise with the level of new borrowing, and banks

---

[8] To be more realistic, one should probably assume that the average interest rate is an increasing function of the borrower's total indebtedness, not his new borrowing from a particular bank. But this would greatly complicate the algebra that follows.

do not discriminate by nationality:[9]

$$r_{ai} = \beta_a(C_{ai}), \quad \text{with} \quad r'_{ai} \equiv (d\beta_a/dC_{ai}) > 0, \quad \text{and}$$

$$r_{bi} = \beta_b(C_{bi}R), \quad \text{with} \quad r'_{bi} \equiv (d\beta_b/dC_{bi})/R > 0. \tag{2}$$

Next, define the current dollar value of the change in each importer's balance sheet (his expected net worth) resulting from current trade and from new transactions in forward exchange:[10]

$$V_a = {}_bP_f R_e - {}_bP_f R_f - [C_{aa}(1 + r_{aa}) + C_{ba}(1 + r_{ba})R_e]$$

$$V_b = \{{}_aP_f/R_e - {}_aP_f/R_f - [C_{ab}(1 + r_{ab})/R_e + C_{bb}(1 + r_{bb})]\}R. \tag{3}$$

A forward purchase of foreign exchange appears twice in each equation – as the expected home-currency equivalent of a foreign-currency asset $({}_bP_f R_e$ and ${}_aP_f/R_e)$ and as an obligation to deliver home currency $({}_bP_f R_f$ and ${}_aP_f/R_f)$. Debts to foreign banks also appear at their expected home-currency value $[C_{ba}(1+r_{ba}) R_e$ and $C_{ab}(1+r_{ab})/R_e]$. Hence, each balance-sheet change contains two terms weighted by the expected spot rates, R_e and $(1/R_e)$, and these can be collected to define two new terms measuring each trader's exposure to exchange risk:

$$E_a = [C_{ba}(1 + r_{ba}) - {}_bP_f]R$$

$$E_b = - [C_{ab}(1 + r_{ab}) - {}_aP_f]. \tag{4}$$

E_a measures the current dollar value of the American's net sterling debt (his "short" position in foreign currency); E_b measures the current dollar value of the British trader's net dollar claim (his "long" position in foreign currency). E_a and E_b are defined asymmetrically so that they will take the same sign when both traders expect the same change in the spot rate.[11]

---

[9]　Note that r_{bi} is defined as a function of $C_{bi}R$, the dollar equivalent of C_{bi}, to facilitate direct comparison between r'_{ai} and r'_{bi}. Note, further, that total dollar interest costs are $C_{ai}r_{ai}$, and that marginal interest costs are $(r_{ai} + C_{ai}r'_{ai})$. If marginal interest costs rise with total borrowing:

$$\frac{d(r_{ai} + C_{ai}r'_{ai})}{dC_{ai}} = 2r'_{ai} + C_{ai}r''_{ai} > 0,$$

whence $\varepsilon_{ai} \equiv r''_{ai}(C_{ai}/r'_{ai}) > -2$. Similarly, $\varepsilon_{bi} \equiv r''_{bi}(C_{bi}R/r'_{bi}) > -2$. The case for these restrictions appears in the appendix.

[10]　We do not require the corresponding change in each exporter's balance sheet, since the exporter is paid promptly in domestic currency.

[11]　See p. 149, below.

As each trader must pay for his imports in foreign currency, he will exchange the proceeds of home-currency bank borrowing for spot foreign currency. In consequence:

$$_bP = C_{aa}/R, \quad \text{and} \quad _aP = C_{bb}R. \tag{5}$$

He must also buy spot foreign exchange to pay off his net foreign-currency debt, but only when that debt matures. Therefore:

$$_bP_e = C_{ba}(1 + r_{ba}) - {}_bP_f = E_a/R$$
$$_aP_e = C_{ab}(1 + r_{ab}) - {}_aP_f = - E_b. \tag{6}$$

Finally, solve equations (4) for forward purchases:

$$_bP_f = C_{ba}(1 + r_{ba}) - E_a/R$$
$$_aP_f = C_{ab}(1 + r_{ab}) + E_b. \tag{7}$$

If, next, one rewrites R_e as $R(1-\alpha_e)$ and R_f as $R(1-\alpha_f)$, where α_e is the expected percentage discount on spot sterling and α_f is the actual percentage discount on forward sterling, equations (3) give way to:

$$V_a = E_a(\alpha_e - \alpha_f) - [C_{aa}(1 + r_{aa}) + C_{ba}R(1 + r_{ba})(1 - \alpha_f)]$$
$$V_b = E_b[(\alpha_e - \alpha_f)/(1 - \alpha_f)(1 - \alpha_e)]$$
$$- [C_{ab}(1 + r_{ab})/(1 - \alpha_f) + C_{bb}R(1 + r_{bb})]. \tag{8}$$

These equations reproduce Tsiang's important contribution:[12] Although each trader may engage in "spot-market speculation", achieving his desired net position, E_i, by borrowing from foreign banks, his operations can be viewed as comprising "forward-market speculation", combined with covered debt arbitrage that minimizes interest cost. When $(\alpha_e - \alpha_f)$ is positive, a trader can seek speculative profits by selling pounds forward, then buying them spot when he must deliver them. By combining C_{ai} and C_{bi} correctly, moreover, a trader can finance his imports at least interest cost and no net exposure to exchange risk. Note, too, that positive values of $(\alpha_e - \alpha_f)$ invite the American trader to incur net sterling debt $(E_a > 0)$ so as to increase expected net worth, and invite the British trader to incur

---

[12] Tsiang, *op. cit.*, p. 92; also Spraos, "Speculation, Arbitrage and Sterling", pp. 5-6.

net dollar claims $(E_b > 0)$; similarly, negative values invite the American trader to incur net sterling claims $(E_a < 0)$, and invite the British trader to incur net dollar debt $(E_b < 0)$. In general, any difference between the expected spot discount, α_e, and the actual forward discount, α_f, supplies an incentive for traders to speculate – to take on net positions in foreign currency.

II The foreign exchange market and interest parity

If the traders represented by these equations can be regarded as "typical", their purchases of spot and forward exchange can be used as proxies for the corresponding aggregates. Hence, current trade and speculation will generate excess supplies of spot and forward dollars when:

$$S \equiv {}_bP R - {}_aP = C_{aa} - C_{bb} R = [M_a - M_b] + [C_{ab} - C_{ba} R] > 0$$

$$S_e \equiv {}_bP_e R - {}_aP_e = E_a + E_b > 0$$

$$S_f \equiv {}_bP_f R_f - {}_aP_f = [C_{ba}(1 + r_{ba}) R (1 - \alpha_f) - C_{ab}(1 + r_{ab})]$$
$$- [E_a(1 - \alpha_f) + E_b] > 0. \qquad (9)$$

When S is positive, of course, current trade and speculation will work to increase British reserves. When S_e is positive, they will work to increase British reserves ninety days hence, provided the exchange rate has not changed in the interim. When S_f is positive, the forward rate must change or must be stabilized by official intervention.[13]

If the forward market is in equilibrium $(S_f = 0)$, the last of these three definitions can be rearranged as follows:

$$\frac{(C_{ab} - C_{ba} R)(1 + r_{ab}) + [E_a(1 - \alpha_f) + E_b]}{C_{ba}(1 + r_{ba}) R} = \left[\frac{r_{ba} - r_{ab}}{1 + r_{ba}} \right] - \alpha_f. \qquad (10)$$

But the first argument on the lefthand side of equation (10) also figures

---

13 Note, however, that S has no argument denoting the deferred effects of past trade and speculation, while S_e has no argument denoting the then-current effects of future trade and speculation. S_f, by contrast, describes the entire excess supply of forward dollars. Note, too, that S_e is defined at the current spot rate, not the expected spot rate; if an R_e different from R prevails ninety days hence, the definition of S_e will no longer hold.

in the definition of excess spot demand (S), so that equation (10) can be rewritten:

$$\frac{[S + (M_b - M_a)](1 + r_{ab}) + [E_a(1 - \alpha_f) + E_b]}{C_{ba}(1 + r_{ba})R} = \left[\frac{r_{ba} - r_{ab}}{1 + r_{ba}}\right] - \alpha_f. \quad (10a)$$

This equation reproduces another major finding of the recent contributors: Classic interest parity is a very special case. The forward discount on the pound would be at loan-rate parity when the righthand side of equation (10a) vanished completely, when $\alpha_f = (r_{ba} - r_{ab})/(1 + r_{ba})$. In order for this to happen, however, the lefthand side of the equation would have to vanish, too. Loan-rate parity would always emerge if S were zero, trade were balanced, and there were no speculation.[14] But these conditions will rarely prevail, as exchange-rate speculation is not an aberration linked solely to anticipations of devaluation. Whenever α_e differs from α_f, even when α_e is equal to zero, traders have profit incentives to speculate, and will take on net positions; the E_i are not likely to be zero.

III Maximization and marginal parity

If traders were to maximize expected net worth and were indifferent to risk, they would take on enormous foreign-currency positions whenever α_e was different from α_f. If, instead, the traders were averse to exchange risk, weighing it carefully when reaching for profit, they would not take on net positions in foreign exchange unless prospective gains outweighed prospective risk. To put this second supposition more formally, define the typical trader's utility function as:

$$U_i = \psi_i(V_i, |E_i|), \qquad i = a, b. \quad (11)$$

---

14 It would also be maintained in another special case. Spot-market equilibrium requires that $S + S'_e = 0$, where S'_e is the value of S_e generated by past speculation, and can be represented by $E'_a + E'_b$. With spot-market equilibrium and balanced trade, the sign of equation (10a) depends on:

$$[E_a(1 - \alpha_f) + E_b] - [E'_a + E'_b](1 + r_{ab}),$$

reflecting the evolution of speculation, and loan-rate parity will be obtained when $E_a = E'_a(1 + r_{ba})$ and $E_b = E'_b(1 + r_{ab})$. In proof, assume loan-rate parity and substitute for α_f in the argument above.

setting $(\partial U_i/\partial V_i) > 0$ and $(\partial U_i/\partial E_i) < 0$. An increase in prospective net worth raises utility; an increase in exposure to exchange risk reduces utility. Then define $\alpha_a^* \equiv (\alpha_e - \alpha_f)$ and $\alpha_b^* \equiv \alpha_a^*/(1 - \alpha_f)(1 - \alpha_e)$, the prospective profit rates on the net positions E_a and E_b, so as to rewrite equations (8) more compactly:

$$V_i = E_i \alpha_i^* - \frac{[C_{ai}(1 + r_{ai}) + C_{bi} R(1 + r_{bi})(1 - \alpha_f)]}{1 - z_i \alpha_f}, \qquad (8a)$$

where $z_a = 0$ and $z_b = 1$.

The use of the absolute value, $|E_i|$, in equation (11) is meant to imply that traders are equally averse to "long" and "short" positions of identical size – to net debts and net claims in foreign currency. The sign of E_i cannot be inferred from the utility function or its derivatives, but it can be obtained from the sign of the expected profit rate, α_i^*, as $E_i \alpha_i^*$ must augment V_i rather than reduce it. The construction of the utility function also implies that the size of the expected profit rate does not affect the trader's attitude toward risk, save by affecting prospective net worth, V_i. Finally, the utility function is written as though the trader's total foreign-currency position, the series of net debts or net claims acquired in the preceding eighty-nine days, does not affect his current decisions. This supposition is not realistic. But there is little to be gained by writing U_i as a function of past debts and claims as well as current debts and claims, for the former are not altered by the trader's new decisions. It is sufficient to remember that these predetermined debts and claims are quite apt to influence current behavior – that they will alter the in-difference curves linking V_i and E_i. If, for example, an American trader has assumed net sterling claims during the most recent eighty-nine days, but has now come to anticipate a positive profit rate on net sterling debt, he is likely to take on larger net debts than he would have incurred if he did not already hold net sterling claims, thereby to offset his net sterling claims.[15]

A trader may be deemed to maximize utility while obeying the trade constraint given by equation (1). To simulate his operations, construct the Lagrangian function:

$$L_i = \psi_i(V_i, |E_i|) + \lambda_i(C_{ai} + C_{bi} R - M_i). \qquad (12)$$

---

[15] For a more elaborate treatment of this problem (with a similar conclusion), see Tsiang, *op. cit.*, pp. 88-90.

Then differentiate this function with respect to E_i, C_{ai}, C_{bi} and λ_i, and set the first partial derivatives equal to zero:[16]

$$\frac{\partial L}{\partial E} = \frac{\partial U}{\partial E} + \frac{\partial U}{\partial V}\left(\frac{dV}{dE}\right) = 0$$

$$\frac{\partial L}{\partial C_a} = \frac{\partial U}{\partial V}\left(\frac{dV}{dC_a}\right) + \lambda = 0$$

$$\frac{\partial L}{\partial C_b} = \frac{\partial U}{\partial V}\left(\frac{dV}{dC_b}\right) + \lambda R = 0$$

$$\frac{\partial L}{\partial \lambda} = C_a + C_b R - M = 0. \tag{13}$$

From the first of these conditions:

$$-\left(\frac{\partial U}{\partial E}\right)\Big/\left(\frac{\partial U}{\partial V}\right) = \left(\frac{dV}{dE}\right) = \alpha_i^*, \tag{14}$$

which asserts that the marginal rate of substitution between net worth, V_i, and exposure to exchange risk, E_i, must equal the marginal profit rate foreseen by the trader. Figure 1 illustrates this condition for the American trader. The curves $_1U$ and $_2U$ are his indifference curves relating E_a and V_a, and $_0V_a$ denotes net worth when E_a is zero. If $\tan\theta$ represents the profit rate α_a^*, the trader will locate at T_1, taking on $_1E_a$ dollars worth of sterling debt and raising net worth to $_1V_a$.[17] By rotating the ray defining angle θ, one can construct an "offer curve" like $_0V_aT_1T_2$, depicting the trader's demand for sterling debt as a function of the expected rate of profit.[18]

From the second and third of the marginal conditions (and the additional assumption that traders borrow in both centers, so that C_{ai} and

---

[16] I omit the subscript i when it is not needed to avoid ambiguity.

[17] As the indifference curves are defined in respect of the absolute value of E_a, Figure 1 can be employed to describe the trader's acquisitions of sterling claims when α_a^* is negative. It can also be employed to describe the British trader's acquisitions of dollar claims ($E_b > 0$) and dollar debt ($E_b < 0$).

[18] Note, in passing, that this curve could perhaps bend backward and that this effect, if sufficiently strong, could cause $_bP_t$ to behave peculiarly. I return to this problem below.

C_{bi} are both positive):

$$\left(\frac{dV}{dC_a}\right)R = \left(\frac{dV}{dC_b}\right). \tag{15}$$

But:

$$\frac{dV}{dC_a} = -\left[\frac{1 + r_{ai} + C_{ai}r'_{ai}}{1 - z_i\alpha_f}\right],$$

$$\frac{dV}{dC_b} = -R\left[\frac{1 + r_{bi} + C_{bi}Rr'_{bi}}{1 - z_i\alpha_f}\right](1 - \alpha_f). \tag{16}$$

Whence:

$$\alpha_f = \frac{(r_{bi} + C_{bi}Rr'_{bi}) - (r_{ai} + C_{ai}r'_{ai})}{(1 + r_{bi} + C_{bi}Rr'_{bi})}. \tag{17}$$

Each trader will arrange his total borrowing so that the discount on forward sterling stands at its marginal loan-rate parity. Unlike the average parity examined earlier, this marginal parity will always prevail (unless the difference in bank lending rates is so large that traders borrow all they need from one country's banks). Marginal loan-rate parity is internal to the cost calculations of the individual trader, and can be maintained by adjustments in the locus of commercial borrowing. Average loan-rate parity, by contrast, depends on a particular constellation of market aggregates.

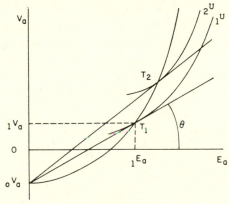

Figure 1

IV Stability, displacement, and adjustment

To study the trader's responses when α_e, α_f and M_i change, take the total derivatives of equations (13), writing:

$$
\begin{bmatrix}
\dfrac{\partial^2 L}{\partial E^2} & \dfrac{\partial^2 L}{\partial C_a \partial E} & \dfrac{\partial^2 L}{\partial C_b \partial E} & 0 \\[2ex]
\dfrac{\partial^2 L}{\partial C_a \partial E} & \dfrac{\partial^2 L}{\partial C_a^2} & \dfrac{\partial^2 L}{\partial C_a \partial C_b} & 1 \\[2ex]
\dfrac{\partial^2 L}{\partial C_b \partial E} & \dfrac{\partial^2 L}{\partial C_a \partial C_b} & \dfrac{\partial^2 L}{\partial C_b^2} & R \\[2ex]
0 & 1 & R & 0
\end{bmatrix}
\begin{bmatrix}
dE_i \\[2ex] dC_{ai} \\[2ex] dC_{bi} \\[2ex] d\lambda_i
\end{bmatrix}
=
\begin{bmatrix}
-\left(\dfrac{\partial U}{\partial V}\right)d\alpha_i^* \\[2ex]
\left(\dfrac{z_i \lambda_i}{1 - z_i \alpha_f}\right)d\alpha_f \\[2ex]
-\lambda_i R\left[\dfrac{1}{1-\alpha_f} - \dfrac{z_i}{1 - z_i \alpha_f}\right]d\alpha_f \\[2ex]
dM_i
\end{bmatrix}
$$

$$\tag{18}$$

Applying Cramer's rule:

$$
\frac{dE_i}{d\alpha_i^*} = -\left(\frac{\partial U}{\partial V}\right)\frac{|H_1|}{|H|} = -\left(\frac{\partial U}{\partial V}\right)\bigg/\left(\frac{\partial^2 L}{\partial E^2}\right),
$$

$$
\frac{dC_{ai}}{d\alpha_i^*} = -R\left(\frac{dC_{bi}}{d\alpha_i^*}\right) = -R\left(\frac{\partial U}{\partial V}\right)\left[R\left(\frac{\partial^2 L}{\partial C_a \partial E}\right) - \left(\frac{\partial^2 L}{\partial C_b \partial E}\right)\right]\frac{1}{|H|}, \tag{19}
$$

where H is the bordered Hessian on the lefthand side of (18), and H_1 is the principal minor of H obtained by deleting the first row and column.[19] As $(\partial^2 L/\partial E^2)$ must be negative when L_i is a maximum, $(dE_i/d\alpha_i^*)$ is always positive.[20] An increase in the profit rate foreseen by the trader will cause him to enlarge his net position. As $R\,(\partial^2 L/\partial C_a\,\partial E) = (\partial^2 L/\partial C_b\,\partial E)$, moreover, $(dC_{ai}/d\alpha_i^*)$ and $(dC_{bi}/d\alpha_i^*)$ are zero. Changes in the profit rate will not directly alter the locus of borrowing. Furthermore:

$$
\frac{dE_i}{d\alpha_f} = \left(\frac{dE_i}{d\alpha_i^*}\right)\left(\frac{d\alpha_i^*}{d\alpha_f}\right) + \frac{R\lambda_i}{1-\alpha_f}\left[R\left(\frac{\partial^2 L}{\partial C_a \partial E}\right) - \frac{\partial^2 L}{\partial C_b \partial E}\right]\frac{1}{|H|},
$$

$$
\frac{dC_{ai}}{d\alpha_f} = -R\left(\frac{dC_{bi}}{d\alpha_f}\right) = -\left(\frac{\partial^2 L}{\partial E^2}\right)\left[\frac{R^2 \lambda_i}{1-\alpha_f}\right]\frac{1}{|H|} = -\left[\frac{R^2 \lambda_i}{1-\alpha_f}\right]\frac{1}{|H_1|}
$$

$$
= \frac{-\dfrac{dV}{dC_a}}{(1-\alpha_f)\left[\dfrac{d^2 V}{dC_a^2} + \left(\dfrac{d^2 V}{dC_b^2}\right)\bigg/R^2\right]}. \tag{20}
$$

---

[19]   For proof that $|H_1|/|H| = 1/(\partial^2 L/\partial E^2)$, see equation (A.6) of the appendix.

[20]   See equations (A.4) through (A.6) of the appendix. Note that the sign of $(dE_i/d\alpha_i^*)$ rules out a backward-bending "offer curve" ($_0 V_a T_1 T_2$) in Figure 1.

Hence $(dE_i/d\alpha_f)$ simplifies to $(dE_i/d\alpha_i^*)(d\alpha_i^*/d\alpha_f)$, and this must be negative because $(d\alpha_i^*/d\alpha_f)$ is negative. An increase in the discount on forward sterling causes a reduction in net dollar claims (net sterling debt) because it reduces the profitability of speculation against sterling. In addition, $(dC_{ai}/d\alpha_f)$ is negative and $(dC_{bi}/d\alpha_f)$ is positive, for $|H_1|$ must be positive when L_i is a maximum, while λ_i is equal to $-(\partial U/\partial V)(dV/dC_a)$ and is therefore positive.[21] An increase in the discount on forward sterling causes a shift in the locus of borrowing – more borrowing from Britain and less from America. Finally, one can show that:

$$\frac{dE_i}{dM_i} = -\left(\frac{\partial^2 L}{\partial C_a \partial E}\right)\bigg/\left(\frac{\partial^2 L}{\partial E^2}\right) = -\left[\frac{\partial^2 U}{\partial V \partial E} + \frac{\partial^2 U}{\partial V^2}\left(\frac{dV}{dE}\right)\right]\left(\frac{dV}{dC_a}\right)\bigg/\left(\frac{\partial^2 L}{\partial E^2}\right),$$

$$\frac{dC_{ai}}{dM_i} = \left[1 - R\left(\frac{dC_{bi}}{dM_i}\right)\right] = \left(\frac{d^2 V}{dC_b^2}\right)\bigg/\left[R^2\left(\frac{d^2 V}{dC_a^2}\right) + \left(\frac{d^2 V}{dC_b^2}\right)\right]. \quad (21)$$

Hence, (dE_i/dM_i) takes the sign of $[(\partial^2 U/\partial V \partial E)+(\partial^2 U/\partial V^2)(dV/dE)]$, not yet specified. We do not know how an increase in the level of trade affects the volume of speculation. But $0<(dC_{ai}/dM_i)<1$, and $0< R\,(dC_{bi}/dM_i)<1$. We can say that an increase in the level of trade will increase traders' borrowing from both financial centers.

We usually suppose that demand curves slope downward, and most recent writers on forward exchange have made the same assumption. Consider, however, the changes in $_bP_f$ and $_aP_f$, the two traders' purchases of forward foreign exchange, attending a decrease in the corresponding prices, R_f and R_f' (where $R_f' = 1/R_f$). Differentiating equations (7) and allowing, in the process, for changes in trade:

$$-\frac{d_bP_f}{dR_f} = \frac{d_bP_f}{d\alpha_f}\left(\frac{1}{R}\right) = \left\{\left[\left(\frac{dC_{ba}}{d\alpha_f}\right)(1 + r_{ba} + C_{ba}Rr_{ba}')R + \left(\frac{dE_a}{d\alpha_a^*}\right)\right]\right.$$

$$\left. + \left[\left(\frac{dC_{ba}}{dM_a}\right)(1 + r_{ba} + C_{ba}Rr_{ba}')R - \left(\frac{dE_a}{dM_a}\right)\right]\left(\frac{dM_a}{d\alpha_f}\right)\right\}/R^2,$$

$$-\frac{d_aP_f}{dR_f'} = -\frac{d_aP_f}{d\alpha_f}\left(R_f^2/R\right) = \left\{\left[\left(\frac{dC_{bb}}{d\alpha_f}\right)(1 + r_{ab} + C_{ab}r_{ab}') + \left(\frac{dE_b}{d\alpha_b^*}\right)(R/R_f^2)\right]\right.$$

---

[21] For the sign of $|H_1|$ and the final formulation of $(dC_{ai}/d\alpha_f)$, see equation (A.3) of the appendix. As $(dV/dC_a) < 0$, and each of the derivatives in the denominator is also negative, the whole argument will always be negative.

$$-\left[\left(\frac{dC_{ab}}{dM_b}\right)(1 + r_{ab} + C_{ab}\, r'_{ab}) + \left(\frac{dE_b}{dM_b}\right)\right]\left(\frac{dM_b}{d\alpha_f}\right)\left(\frac{1}{R}\right)\right\}/R_f'^2 . \qquad (22)$$

As $(dC_{bi}/d\alpha_f)$ and $(dE_i/d\alpha_i^*)$ are always positive, the first argument of each equation will also be positive. Furthermore, C_{ba} and C_{ab} are increasing functions of imports. Yet one cannot attach a sign to the second argument of each equation without first ascertaining the signs of (dE_i/dM_i) and $(dM_i/d\alpha_f)$.

Some recent writers on forward exchange assume that a decline in the cost of forward cover will stimulate imports – that $(dM_a/d\alpha_f)$ is positive and $(dM_b/d\alpha_f)$ is negative because α_f is the discount on the forward pound – and some of them lean heavily on this assumption to secure other important results.[22] Traders who "cover" commercial risks, it is argued, will use the forward rate to calculate the home-currency price of imports; they will regard a decline in the cost of forward foreign exchange as equivalent to – and more relevant than – a decrease in the cost of spot exchange. My equations (1) through (8) do not display a separate term that corresponds to "covering". But I can obtain the conventional signs for $(dM_a/d\alpha_f)$ and $(dM_b/d\alpha_f)$ by supposing that the level of trade depends on a component of expected net worth, and asking how an increase in the forward discount affects that component. One cannot suppose that the level of trade depends on the whole of V_i, for a change in α_f would then give ambiguous results. Holding M_i fixed:[23]

$$\frac{dV_a}{d\alpha_f} = \left[E_a + \alpha_a^*\left(\frac{dE_a}{d\alpha_a^*}\right)\right]\left(\frac{d\alpha_a^*}{d\alpha_f}\right) + C_{ba}\, R\,(1 + r_{ba}),$$

$$\frac{dV_b}{d\alpha_f} = \left[E_b + \alpha_b^*\left(\frac{dE_b}{d\alpha_b^*}\right)\right]\left(\frac{d\alpha_b^*}{d\alpha_f}\right) - C_{ab}\,(1 + r_{ab})/(1 - \alpha_f)^2 . \qquad (23)$$

---

22   See Sohmen, *op. cit.*, pp. 72-76, 137-38; Tsiang, *op. cit.*, pp. 92-94, 105; and Einzig, *op. cit.*, pp. 53-58.

23   Differentiating V_a with respect to α_f and holding M_a constant:

$$\frac{dV_a}{d\alpha_f} = \left[E_a + \alpha_a^*\left(\frac{dE_a}{d\alpha_a^*}\right)\right]\left(\frac{d\alpha_a^*}{d\alpha_f}\right) - \left[\left(\frac{dC_{aa}}{d\alpha_f}\right)(1 + r_{aa} + C_{aa}r'_{aa})\right.$$

$$\left. + \left(\frac{dC_{ba}}{d\alpha_f}\right)(1 + r_{ba} + C_{ba}\,Rr'_{ba})\,(1 - \alpha_f)R\right] + C_{ba}\, R(1 + r_{ba}) .$$

But $(dC_{aa}/d\alpha_f) = - R(dC_{ba}/d\alpha_f)$, while $(1 + r_{aa} + C_{aa}\, r'_{aa}) = (1 + r_{ba} + C_{ba}r'_{ba})$ $(1 - \alpha_f)$, so that the argument in brackets vanishes completely. A similar procedure gives $(dV_b/d\alpha_f)$.

As $(d\alpha_i^*/d\alpha_f)$ is always negative, $(dV_a/d\alpha_f)$ might also be negative when E_a is positive, while $(dV_b/d\alpha_f)$ might be positive when E_b is negative. If, however, the level of imports is independent of the speculative argument in V_i, depending only on "nonspeculative" net worth, $(V_i - E_i\alpha_i^*)$, an increase in α_f will increase M_a and decrease M_b because it will cut the cost of American borrowing and raise the cost of British borrowing.

Yet the slopes of the demand curves, given by equations (22), will still be in doubt unless $(dE_a/dM_a)\leq0$ and $(dE_b/dM_b)\geq0$. If the demand curves are both to slope downward, one must set $(dE_i/dM_i)=0$ by setting $[(\partial^2 U/\partial V \partial E)+(\partial^2 U/\partial V^2)(dV/dE)]=0$ in equation (21). This is tantamount to saying that trade and speculation are *doubly* independent. To obtain $(dM_a/d\alpha_f)>0$ and $(dM_b/d\alpha_f)<0$, I had to suppose that a change expected in net worth due to speculation would not alter imports. To obtain $(dE_i/dM_i)=0$, I have to suppose that a change in "nonspeculative" net worth will not alter the volume of speculation, E_i.

To prove this second statement, denote the marginal rate of substitution between V_i and E_i by ϕ, and differentiate ϕ with respect to V_i, holding E_i constant:

$$\frac{\partial\phi}{\partial V} = -\left[\frac{\partial^2 U}{\partial V \partial E} + \phi\left(\frac{\partial^2 U}{\partial V^2}\right)\right]\bigg/\left(\frac{\partial U}{\partial V}\right) = -\left[\frac{\partial^2 U}{\partial V \partial E} + \frac{\partial^2 U}{\partial V^2}\left(\frac{dV}{dE}\right)\right]\bigg/\left(\frac{\partial U}{\partial V}\right),$$

$$(24)$$

as $\phi=(dV/dE)$ when V_i is a maximum. When (dE_i/dM_i) is zero, then, $(\partial\phi/\partial V)$ is also zero, and the trader's indifference curves will be vertically

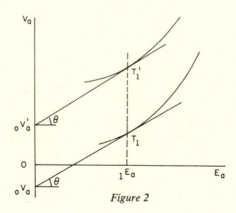

Figure 2

aligned, as in Figure 2. A change in "nonspeculative" net worth, $_0V_a$ in the diagram, due to a change in the level of trade, in interest rates, or in α_f, will not cause a change in the trader's net foreign-currency position, E_i.[24]

Two-way independence between trade and speculation lurks in all the recent models that treat speculation, arbitrage, and commercial "covering" as separate activities. The authors of those models, however, would seem to have chosen this mode of analysis for its expositional convenience, without perceiving its full significance or its role in their results. But two-way independence is an excessively strict supposition, for it rules out several intriguing results, yet does not even guarantee a stable forward market. To be sure of comparative-static stability in the forward market, one must be able to show that a rise in the price of the forward dollar will generate an excess supply of dollars – that (dS_f/dR_f') is positive. This may not be true, even when the two demand curves for forward exchange are negatively sloped. Differentiating equation (9) with respect to the forward price of the dollar, R_f', and using the arguments of equation (22):

$$\frac{dS_f}{dR_f'} = -\left[\left(\frac{d_b P_f}{dR_f}\right)R_f^3 + \left(\frac{d_a P_f}{dR_f'}\right) + {}_bP_f R_f^2\right]$$

$$= R(1-\alpha_f)^2 \left\{\left[\sum_i \left(\frac{dC_{bi}}{d\alpha_f}\right) R(1 + r_{ai} + C_{ai} r_{ai}')\right]\right.$$

$$\left. + \left[\frac{dE_a}{d\alpha_a^*}(1-\alpha_f) + \frac{dE_b}{d\alpha_b^*}(1-\alpha_f)^{-2}\right]\right.$$

$$\left. + (1-\alpha_f)\left[\left(\frac{d^2 V_a}{dC_{aa}^2}\right)\left(\frac{dC_{aa}}{d\alpha_f}\right)\left(\frac{dM_a}{d\alpha_f}\right) - \left(\frac{d^2 V_b}{dC_{bb}^2}\right)\left(\frac{dC_{ab}}{d\alpha_f}\right)\left(\frac{1-\alpha_f}{R^2}\right)\left(\frac{dM_b}{d\alpha_f}\right)\right]\right.$$

$$\left. - \left[\frac{dE_a}{dM_a}(1-\alpha_f)\frac{dM_a}{d\alpha_f} + \frac{dE_b}{dM_b}\left(\frac{dM_b}{d\alpha_f}\right)\right] - [{}_bP_f R]\right\}. \qquad (25)$$

The first three arguments of this equation, representing arbitrage, specu-

---

[24] One can see the full effects of setting $(dE_i/dM_i) = 0$ by looking at the Hessian H. With $(dE_i/dM_i) = 0$, H can be partitioned into two submatrices: the first contains one element, $(\partial^2 L/\partial E^2) < 0$, supplying a sufficient second-order condition for maximum prospective gains from speculation; the second is H_1 with $|H_1| > 0$, supplying a sufficient second-order condition for minimum borrowing cost. Note, further, that one can obtain $(dE_i/dM_i) = 0$ with $(\partial^2 U/\partial V \partial E) \gtreqless 0$. But with $(\partial^2 U/\partial V \partial E) > 0$,

lation, and the role of trade, will all be positive, provided $(dM_a/d\alpha_f)$ is positive and $(dM_b/d\alpha_f)$ is negative (*i.e.*, with one-way independence).[25] The fourth argument has an uncertain sign unless one assumes two-way independence, but the fifth will be negative in every circumstance. Hence, one cannot put a sign to equation (25) merely by assuming two-way independence. One must make a separate assumption concerning market

the sign of $(\partial^2 L/\partial E^2)$ comes into doubt, as:

$$\frac{\partial^2 L}{\partial E^2} = \left(\frac{\partial^2 U}{\partial E^2}\right) + \phi\left(\frac{\partial^2 U}{\partial V \partial E}\right) + \phi\left[\left(\frac{\partial^2 U}{\partial V \partial E}\right) + \phi\left(\frac{\partial^2 U}{\partial V^2}\right)\right] = \left(\frac{\partial^2 U}{\partial E^2}\right) + \phi\left(\frac{\partial^2 U}{\partial V \partial E}\right),$$

when $(dE_i/dM_i) = 0$, and this may not be negative even if $(\partial^2 U/\partial E^2) < 0$. If further $(\partial^2 U/\partial V \partial E) < 0$, one must have $(\partial^2 U/\partial V^2) > 0$, which is implausible, although not impossible. In short, one can best obtain $(dE_i/dM_i) = 0$ by setting $(\partial^2 U/\partial V \partial E) = (\partial^2 U/\partial V^2) = 0$, which gives strict independence between $(\partial U/\partial E)$ and V_i (between the marginal disutility of exposure to exchange risk and prospective net worth, including gains from speculation), not merely between $(\partial U/\partial E)$ and $(V_i - E_i\alpha_i^*)$ or $_0V_a$ in Figure 2.

[25] The new formulation of the trade term in equation (25) derives from equations (20), (21), and (16). For:

$$\left(\frac{dC_{ba}}{dM_a}\right) R = -\left(\frac{d^2V_a}{dC_{aa}^2}\right)\left(\frac{dC_{aa}}{d\alpha_f}\right)(1 - \alpha_f) \Bigg/ \left(\frac{dV_a}{dC_{aa}}\right),$$

where

$$\left(\frac{dV_a}{dC_{aa}}\right) = -(1 + r_{aa} + C_{aa} r'_{aa});$$

$$\left(\frac{dC_{ab}}{dM_b}\right) = -\left(\frac{d^2V_b}{dC_{bb}^2}\right)\left(\frac{1}{R^2}\right)\left(\frac{dC_{ab}}{d\alpha_f}\right)(1 - \alpha_f) \Bigg/ \left(\frac{dV_b}{dC_{ab}}\right),$$

where

$$\left(\frac{dV_b}{dC_{ab}}\right) = -(1 + r_{ab} + C_{ab} r'_{ab}) / (1 - \alpha_f).$$

It should be remembered that (d^2V_a/dC_{aa}^2) and $(dC_{aa}/d\alpha_f)$ are negative; so, too, are the corresponding arguments for Britain. Note that equation (25) can also be written in the familiar elasticities form:

$$\frac{dS_f}{dR'_f} = [_bP_f R_f/R'_f]\left[_b\eta_f + {_a\eta_f}\left(\frac{_aP_f}{_bP_f R_f}\right) - 1\right],$$

where $_b\eta_f$ and $_a\eta_f$ are the elasticities of demand for forward exchange. Haberler was among the first to show that the corresponding spot-market condition is, in fact, a statement that the market is stable. (See G. Haberler, "The Market for Foreign Exchange and Stability of the Balance of Payments", *Kyklos*, III [1949], 193-218).

stability. I assume that the market is stable in the sections that follow. I also assume that the level of trade is independent of the expected gains from speculation so as to obtain the conventional signs for $(dM_a/d\alpha_f)$ and $(dM_b/d\alpha_f)$. But I do not impose two-way independence.

V Speculation, intervention, and the reserves

Suppose that the traders come to anticipate a depreciation of spot sterling – that there is an increase in α_e. From equations (9):

$$\frac{dS}{d\alpha_e} = 0$$

$$\frac{dS_e}{d\alpha_e} = \left[\frac{dE_a}{d\alpha_a^*} + \frac{dE_b}{d\alpha_b^*}(1 - \alpha_e)^{-2}\right] > 0$$

$$\frac{dS_f}{d\alpha_e} = -\left[\frac{dE_a}{d\alpha_a^*}(1 - \alpha_f) + \frac{dE_b}{d\alpha_b^*}(1 - \alpha_e)^{-2}\right] < 0. \tag{26}$$

Taken by itself, speculation against sterling will not cause any current change in Britain's reserves, and will cause an increase after ninety days. But the excess demand for forward dollars $(dS_f < 0)$ produced by speculation will lead to a change in α_f, the discount on forward sterling, unless the authorities intervene to stabilize the forward pound. In the absence of such intervention it is necessary that:

$$\left(\frac{dS_f}{d\alpha_e}\right)d\alpha_e + \left(\frac{dS_f}{d\alpha_f}\right)d\alpha_f = 0, \quad \text{or} \quad -\left(\frac{dS_f}{d\alpha_e}\right)\Big/\left(\frac{dS_f}{d\alpha_f}\right) = \left(\frac{d\alpha_f}{d\alpha_e}\right) > 0. \tag{27}$$

Forward sterling will tend toward a discount $(d\alpha_f > 0)$ when the forward market is assumed to be stable. This change in the forward rate is likely to affect Britain's reserves, though the sign of the change is not at all certain. The current and deferred effects of the increase in α_f take their signs from:

$$\left(\frac{dS}{d\alpha_f}\right) = \left[\left(\frac{dC_{aa}}{dM_a}\right)\left(\frac{dM_a}{d\alpha_f}\right) - R\left(\frac{dC_{bb}}{dM_b}\right)\left(\frac{dM_b}{d\alpha_f}\right)\right] - R\left[\frac{dC_{ba}}{d\alpha_f} + \frac{dC_{bb}}{d\alpha_f}\right] \tag{28}$$

$$\left(\frac{dS_e}{d\alpha_f}\right) = -\left[\frac{dE_a}{d\alpha_a^*} - \frac{dE_b}{d\alpha_b^*}(1 - \alpha_f)^{-2}\right] + \left[\frac{dE_a}{dM_a}\left(\frac{dM_a}{d\alpha_f}\right) + \frac{dE_b}{dM_b}\left(\frac{dM_b}{d\alpha_f}\right)\right]. \tag{29}$$

The first or "trade" term of equation (28) will always be positive, as $(dM_a/d\alpha_f)>0$ and $(dM_b/d\alpha_f)<0$ when the level of trade is independent of speculative gains; but the second or "arbitrage" term will always be negative, as $(dC_{bi}/d\alpha_f)$ is always positive. And if the first effect is larger than the second, speculation against sterling can actually add to Britain's reserves, rather than reducing them. Tsiang has also called attention to this possibility, but in a different context. Objecting to official intervention in the forward market, he argues that it may protect a nation's reserves, but "at the cost of worsening, to some extent, the current balance of trade".[26] The "worsening" at issue, however, is the cancellation of the "trade" effect in equation (28), and if there is a case for official intervention, it rests on the supposition that this "trade" effect is too small to offset the "arbitrage" effect, so that $(dS/d\alpha_f)$ is negative. Put differently, official intervention does not worsen the trade balance; it merely forgoes the (insufficient) trade-balance gain concomitant with speculation.

The deferred effects of speculation are also ambiguous, as one cannot attach a sign to (dE_i/dM_i) in equation (29) without assuming two-way independence. Furthermore, $(dM_a/d\alpha_f)$ and $(dM_b/d\alpha_f)$ have opposite signs, so that the second argument of equation (29) might turn either way, no matter what the sign of (dE_i/dM_i). Finally, solve equations (9) for $(S+S_e)$ to obtain the total change in Britain's reserves, current and deferred:

$$(S + S_e) = (M_a - M_b) + (C_{ba} R r_{ba} - C_{ab} r_{ab}) - (_bP_f R)\alpha_f - S_f. \qquad (30)$$

Differentiating this equation totally and invoking equation (27) to dispose of its last term:

$$\left(\frac{dS_e}{d\alpha_e}\right) + \left[\frac{dS}{d\alpha_f} + \frac{dS_e}{d\alpha_f}\right]\left(\frac{d\alpha_f}{d\alpha_e}\right) = \left(\frac{dE_a}{d\alpha_a^*}\right)\alpha_f + \left\{\left[\frac{dM_a}{d\alpha_f} - \frac{dM_b}{d\alpha_f}\right]\right.$$

$$+ R\left[\frac{dC_{ba}}{d\alpha_f} + \frac{dC_{ba}}{dM_a}\left(\frac{dM_a}{d\alpha_f}\right)\right](r_{ba} + C_{ba} R r'_{ba})$$

$$+ \left[\frac{dC_{bb}}{d\alpha_f} - \frac{dC_{ab}}{dM_b}\left(\frac{dM_b}{d\alpha_f}\right)\right](r_{ab} + C_{ab} r'_{ab})$$

$$\left. - R\left[\left(\frac{d_bP_f}{d\alpha_f}\right)\alpha_f + _bP_f\right]\right\}\left(\frac{d\alpha_f}{d\alpha_e}\right). \qquad (31)$$

All of the arguments of equation (31) are positive, save for the last pair

---

26 *Op. cit.*, p. 105.

of terms in brackets; the sign of $(d_b P_f / d\alpha_f)$ will always be in doubt unless one assumes two-way independence, and the last term will always be negative.[27] Hence, the total effect of speculation on Britain's reserves – current and deferred, direct and indirect – must remain ambiguous; two-way independence and forward market stability do not suffice to clarify the sign of equation (31).

Yet the case for intervention in the forward market is not weakened by these new results, as the proponents of intervention make no claim at all regarding the total effect described by equation (31). They merely suppose that the (beneficial) "trade" effect of speculation is smaller than the (adverse) "arbitrage" effect – that $(dS/d\alpha_f)$ is negative – so that speculation against sterling will reduce Britain's reserves as soon as it appears. They argue, moreover, that the authorities will be able to "unwind" their forward positions without any later loss of reserves. This modest case for intervention draws strong support from equations (26). If the authorities support forward sterling, meeting the excess demand for forward dollars defined by $(dS_f / d\alpha_e)$, there will be no change in the forward rate (no change in α_f). In this case, $(dS / d\alpha_e)$ and $(dS_e / d\alpha_e)$ in equations (26) will describe the full reserve effects, current and deferred, of speculation against sterling. There will be no current change in British reserves, and the increase in reserves occurring ninety days later will suffice to discharge the commitments incurred by the authorities. They will gain $(dS_e / d\alpha_e)$ dollars ninety days after their intervention and will have to pay out $(dS_f / d\alpha_e)$ dollars. But:

$$\left(\frac{dS_e}{d\alpha_e}\right) = -\left(\frac{dS_f}{d\alpha_e}\right) + \alpha_f\left(\frac{dE_a}{d\alpha_e}\right). \tag{32}$$

The authorities' deferred receipts will exceed their obligations, supplying a profit on counterspeculation if the forward pound stood at a discount when intervention first occurred.[28]

---

[27]   The demand for forward sterling, $_b P_t$, is the difference between $C_{ba}(1 + r_{ba})$ and E_a / R, and it would seem that this could be negative. But if E_a / R is positive (the case that raises doubt), E_b will also be positive, and $_a P_t$ will be positive. As $_b P_t R_f = {_a P_t}$, then, $_b P_t$ must be positive.

[28]   The comparison between $(dS_e / d\alpha_e)$ and $(dS_t / d\alpha_e)$ deserves special emphasis, as it is the relevant test of the risk incurred by the authorities. Too many people are prone to make an irrelevant comparison between the *level* of reserves and the authorities' forward commitments.

If speculation continued unabated at the end of the ninety-day period, the authorities

VI Modifications in the model

This entire paper has been constructed on a particular set of assumptions regarding institutional arrangements: Trade was financed in the exporter's currency and was conducted on a cash basis. But similar conclusions can be derived for very different institutional arrangements. I do not examine all permutations, but outline one other case to show how the rest of them can be attacked and that the analysis is very similar to the one presented in the preceding sections.

Suppose that trade is invoiced in the importer's currency and that payments are made when goods are delivered, ninety days after contracts are signed. Let the exporters borrow from foreign and domestic banks to finance their operations while awaiting payment for the goods they have sold. In this case, one can write:

$$(1 - g_i)\,X_i = C_{ai} + C_{bi}\,R\,, \tag{33}$$

where X_i represents export proceeds valued in dollars at the current spot rate, and g_i represents the gap between export proceeds and the dollar total of exporters' costs.[29] Next, write V_i^x, the current dollar value of the change in net worth due to the exporter's current sales and his forward exchange transactions:

$$V_a^x = X_a\,(R_e/R) + {}_bP_f\,R_e - {}_bP_f\,R_f - \left[C_{aa}\,(1 + r_{aa}) + C_{ba}\,(1 + r_{ba})\,R_e\right],$$
$$V_b^x = \{X_b/R_e + {}_aP_f/R_e - {}_aP_f/R_f - \left[C_{ab}\,(1 + r_{ab})/R_e + C_{bb}\,(1 + r_{bb})\right]\}\,R\,. \tag{34}$$

Finally, define the exporter's exposure to exchange risk in the usual way:

$$E_a^x = \left[C_{ba}\,(1 + r_{ba}) - X_a/R - {}_bP_f\right]R\,,$$
$$E_b^x = -\left[C_{ab}\,(1 + r_{ab}) - X_b - {}_aP_f\right]. \tag{35}$$

---

would have to renew their positions to stabilize the forward rate. But their commitments are not apt to cumulate, as Tsiang suggests (*op. cit.*, pp. 105-6), unless the traders enlarge their net positions, E_i, at the close of the period. Tsiang's error consists in neglecting the fact that the traders must discharge their own obligations after ninety days. One is not likely to make this sort of error if one works with net positions, as in this paper, rather than current flows. (For more extensive comments on "cumulation", see J. H. Auten, "Counter-Speculation and the Forward-Exchange Market", *Journal of Political Economy*, LXIX, No. 1 [February, 1961], 50-51.)

[29] Hence $0 < g_i < 1$. The use of this device permits me to write equation (33) as an equality, not an inequality.

Whence:

$$V_i^x = E_i^x \alpha_i^* + \frac{X_i(1 - \alpha_f)}{(1 - z_i \alpha_f)^2} - \left[\frac{C_{ai}(1 + r_{ai}) + C_{bi}R(1 + r_{bi})(1 - \alpha_f)}{1 - z_i \alpha_f}\right], \qquad (36)$$

which is identical to equation (8a) save for the addition of the trade term, $X_i(1 - \alpha_f)/(1 - z_i \alpha_f)^2$, which corresponds explicitly to commercial "covering". The addition of this term, however, makes little difference for the analysis if one regards the level of exports as demand-determined. Using the same utility function as in the importer-borrower case, one can form the Lagrangian function:

$$L_i^x = \psi_i^x(V_i^x, |E_i^x|) + \lambda_i^x \left[C_{ai} + C_{bi}R - (1 - g_i)X_i\right], \qquad (37)$$

and can differentiate L_i^x with respect to E_i^x, C_{ai}, C_{bi}, and λ_i^x. The first-order conditions for maximum L_i^x will be the same as equations (13), except that $(1 - g_i)X_i$ replaces M_i in the final equation, and the only change in equation (18) describing displacement is the substitution of $dX_i(1 - g_i)$ for dM_i. One therefore obtains the same equations (19) and (20) as in the importer-borrower case, while (21) gives way to:

$$\frac{dE_i}{dX_i} = -(1 - g_i)\left[\frac{\partial^2 U}{\partial V \partial E} + \frac{\partial^2 U}{\partial V^2}\left(\frac{dV}{dE}\right)\right]\left(\frac{dV}{dC_a}\right) / \left(\frac{\partial^2 L}{\partial E^2}\right),$$

$$\frac{dC_{ai}}{dX_i} = \left[(1 - g_i) - R\left(\frac{dC_{bi}}{dX_i}\right)\right] = \frac{(1 - g_i)\left(\frac{d^2 V}{dC_b^2}\right)}{R^2\left(\frac{d^2 V}{dC_a^2}\right) + \left(\frac{d^2 V}{dC_b^2}\right)}, \qquad (38)$$

which take the same signs as equations (21).

Finally, define the arguments that correspond to S, S_e, and S_f. As traders must convert foreign-currency borrowing into home currency:

$$S^x = C_{ab} - C_{ba}R. \qquad (39)$$

As before, moreover:

$$S_e^x = E_a^x + E_b^x. \qquad (40)$$

And equations (35) give:

$$S_f^x = \left[C_{ba}(1 + r_{ba})R(1 - \alpha_f) - C_{ab}(1 + r_{ab})\right]$$
$$- \left[E_a^x(1 - \alpha_f) + E_b^x\right] - \left[X_a(1 - \alpha_f) - X_b\right], \qquad (41)$$

adding a trade-balance term to the argument of S_f in equation (9). When one differentiates these three equations with respect to the expected discount on spot sterling, α_e, one obtains the same arguments as in equation (26) and can make the same case for forward-market intervention in the face of speculation. But these three equations respond rather differently to changes in the forward rate. To isolate this difference directly, examine the response of S^x, the excess supply of dollars on the spot market:

$$\frac{dS^x}{d\alpha_f} = \left[\left(\frac{dC_{ab}}{dX_b}\right)\left(\frac{dX_b}{d\alpha_f}\right) - R\left(\frac{dC_{ba}}{dX_a}\right)\left(\frac{dX_a}{d\alpha_f}\right)\right] - R\left[\frac{dC_{ba}}{d\alpha_f} + \frac{dC_{bb}}{d\alpha_f}\right]. \tag{42}$$

The second or "arbitrage" argument of equation (42) is the same as that of equation (28) defining $(dS/d\alpha_f)$. But the first or "trade" argument is rather different. One could, of course, banish the significant difference between the two "trade" terms by a mechanical substitution of $(dM_a/d\alpha_f)$ for $(dX_b/d\alpha_f)$, and $(dM_b/d\alpha_f)$ for $(dX_a/d\alpha_f)$.[30] The signs of $(dM_i/d\alpha_f)$, however, were obtained by making special assumptions in the importer-borrower case, and these assumptions cannot hold in the present case, as changes in the forward rate can no longer alter the importer's balance sheet.

Yet one can still attach the appropriate signs to $(dX_i/d\alpha_f)$. Equations (34) imply that an exporter can be regarded as "covering" all his commercial receipts and speculating, if at all, on the forward market. If this is true, however, he can be expected to use the forward rate when quoting the foreign-currency prices at which he makes his export sales. One can write:

$$X_a = (p_a q_a)(R/R_f), \quad \text{with} \quad q_a = f_a(p_a/R_f),$$
$$X_b = (p_b q_b) R_f, \quad \text{with} \quad q_b = f_b(p_b R_f), \tag{43}$$

where the q_i are the export quantities, the p_i are the (constant) export prices in the exporters' currencies, and the f_i define the demand for each country's exports as a function of the price paid by the importers. These equations yield:

$$\frac{dX_a}{d\alpha_f} = -X_a(\eta_a - 1)/(1 - \alpha_f),$$

$$\frac{dX_b}{d\alpha_f} = X_b(\eta_b - 1)/(1 - \alpha_f), \tag{44}$$

---

[30] There would still be a difference between the two "trade" arguments, since the

where the η_i are the price elasticities of demand for imports defined in the usual way.[31] When, therefore, each country confronts an elastic demand for its exports, $(dX_a/d\alpha_f)$ must be negative and $(dX_b/d\alpha_f)$ positive. The "trade" term of equation (42) is consequently positive, aligning my two models in the most important way.[32]

VII Summary

The model of forward exchange operations with which you have just tangled is quite special and restrictive in several of its features. It assumes a symmetrical aversion to risk – to long and short positions in foreign exchange – and pretends that trader-speculators work with a "point estimate" of the future spot rate. But my model is more general than most of its predecessors, for it does not segregate the several components of the demand for forward exchange. It deals with a single firm involved in foreign trade and shows that such a firm will engage in "covering", "arbitrage", and "speculation" in the normal course of its credit operations.

My model can be made to yield many of the propositions stressed by other recent writers. It shows, for example, that all speculation can be treated as a combination of spot-market arbitrage in assets or debt coupled to open forward positions. It also reproduces the modern formulation of classic interest parity. The forward rate will not stand at "average interest parity" save in special circumstances, but will almost always stand

---

loan weights applied to the trade changes are different. But all the loan weights are positive (see equations [21] and [38]), so that the two "trade" arguments would both be positive.

[31] To be precise: $\eta_a = -f'_a [(p_a/R_t)/q_a]$, and $\eta_b = -f'_b [(p_b R_t) / q_b]$.

[32] Note, further, that a weaker restriction on η_a and η_b suffices to remove any new ambiguity as to $(dS_t^x/d\alpha_f)$: S_t^x differs from S_t by another "trade" term, $-[X_a (1 - \alpha_f) - X_b]$ in equation (41). Differentiating this new term with respect to α_f and using the arguments of equation (44):

$$\left[\left(\frac{dX_b}{d\alpha_f} \right) - \left(\frac{dX_a}{d\alpha_f} \right) \right] (1 - \alpha_f) + X_a \right] = [X_b (\eta_b - 1) + X_a \eta_a (1 - \alpha_f)] / (1 - \alpha_f),$$

and the righthand side of this equation cannot be negative unless the elasticities are very low. If, in fact, $X_a = X_b$ to start, the righthand side cannot be negative unless $(1 - \eta_b) / \eta_a > (1 - \alpha_f)$, and this is impossible unless $\eta_b < 1$.

at "marginal parity", because this marginal condition is internal to the profit calculations of the individual borrower or investor. You have also encountered new results. First, this paper has explored the substantive implications of "two-way independence" between trade and speculation. When, as here, trade and speculation are conducted by one enterprise, the demand curve for forward foreign exchange may be backward sloping, and the forward market may be unstable. But my model also shows that "two-way independence" does not guarantee stability; one needs a more restrictive elasticities condition, much like the familiar Lerner-Robinson condition. And when one assumes market stability, one can dispense with "two-way independence", so as to study the several connections between trade and speculation.

Finally, this analysis supplies a strong presumptive case for official intervention to combat speculation. It shows how speculation will affect reserves, allowing for the cross-effects of trade and speculation, and how intervention will dispel these effects, preventing any change in official reserves. Intervention can prevent any "current" loss of reserves; when speculation has died down, moreover, the authorities can unwind their forward positions without any "deferred" loss of reserves. They can "match" their net positions with those of the speculators. The net profit or loss on counterspeculation depends entirely on the forward premium or discount at which the authorities stabilize the forward rate.

APPENDIX

Consider the bordered Hessian $|H|$ appearing in equation (18) of the text. For maximum L_i, it is necessary and sufficient that $(-1)^{(4-m)}|H_m| < 0$, where H_m is the $(4-m)$th order trailing principal minor of the Hessian obtained by deleting the first m rows and columns.[33] In consequence, $|H_1|$ must be positive, being of third order. Furthermore:

$$|H_1| = 2R\left(\frac{\partial^2 L}{\partial C_a \, \partial C_b}\right) - R^2\left(\frac{\partial^2 L}{\partial C_a^2}\right) - \frac{\partial^2 L}{\partial C_b^2}. \qquad (A.1)$$

---

[33] See, e.g., J. R. Hicks, *Value and Capital* (2nd edition; London: Oxford University Press, 1946), pp. 304-5.

And:

$$\frac{\partial^2 L}{\partial C_a^2} = \frac{\partial^2 U}{\partial V^2}\left(\frac{dV}{dC_a}\right)^2 + \frac{\partial U}{\partial V}\left(\frac{d^2 V}{dC_a^2}\right),$$

$$\frac{\partial^2 L}{\partial C_b^2} = \frac{\partial^2 U}{\partial V^2}\left(\frac{dV}{dC_b}\right)^2 + \frac{\partial U}{\partial V}\left(\frac{d^2 V}{dC_b^2}\right) = \frac{\partial^2 U}{\partial V^2}\left(\frac{dV}{dC_a}\right)^2 R^2 + \frac{\partial U}{\partial V}\left(\frac{d^2 V}{dC_b^2}\right),$$

$$\frac{\partial^2 L}{\partial C_a \partial C_b} = \frac{\partial^2 U}{\partial V^2}\left(\frac{dV}{dC_a}\right)\left(\frac{dV}{dC_b}\right) = \frac{\partial^2 U}{\partial V^2}\left(\frac{dV}{dC_a}\right)^2 R. \qquad (A.2)$$

So that:

$$|H_1| = -\left(\frac{\partial U}{\partial V}\right)\left[R^2\left(\frac{d^2 V}{dC_a^2}\right) + \left(\frac{d^2 V}{dC_b^2}\right)\right], \qquad (A.3)$$

where:

$$(d^2 V/dC_a^2) = -(2r'_{ai} + C_{ai} r''_{ai})/(1 - z_i\alpha_f) = -r'_{ai}(2 + \varepsilon_{ai})/(1 - z_i\alpha_f),$$

and:

$$(d^2 V/dC_b^2) = -[(2r'_{bi} + C_{bi} r''_{bi})(1 - \alpha_f)/(1 - z_i\alpha_f)] R^2$$
$$= -[r'_{bi}(2 + \varepsilon_{bi})(1 - \alpha_f)/(1 - z_i\alpha_f)] R^2.$$

For $|H_1| > 0$, $(d^2 V/dC_a^2)$ and $(d^2 V/dC_b^2)$ must be negative, so that ε_{ai} and ε_{bi} must each exceed -2. In effect, marginal borrowing cost must be an increasing function of current borrowing.

Maximum L_i also requires $|H| < 0$, being of fourth order. But:

$$|H| = \left(\frac{\partial^2 L}{\partial E^2}\right)|H_1| + \left[R\left(\frac{\partial^2 L}{\partial C_a \partial E}\right) - \left(\frac{\partial^2 L}{\partial C_b \partial E}\right)\right]^2, \qquad (A.4)$$

where:

$$\frac{\partial^2 L}{\partial C_a \partial E} = \left[\frac{\partial^2 U}{\partial V \partial E} + \frac{\partial^2 U}{\partial V^2}\left(\frac{dV}{dE}\right)\right]\left(\frac{dV}{dC_a}\right),$$

$$\frac{\partial^2 L}{\partial C_b \partial E} = \left[\frac{\partial^2 U}{\partial V \partial E} + \frac{\partial^2 U}{\partial V^2}\left(\frac{dV}{dE}\right)\right]\left(\frac{dV}{dC_b}\right) = \left(\frac{\partial^2 L}{\partial C_a \partial E}\right)R, \qquad (A.5)$$

so that the second argument of (A.4) vanishes completely, and:

$$|H| = \left(\frac{\partial^2 L}{\partial E^2}\right)|H_1|. \qquad (A.6)$$

Hence $(\partial^2 L/\partial E^2)$ must be negative if L_i is a maximum. This result has already been employed in the construction of Figure 1, as the increasing slope of the trader's indifference curves requires that:

$$\left(\frac{\partial^2 U}{\partial E^2}\right) + \phi\left(\frac{\partial^2 U}{\partial V\,\partial E}\right) + \phi\left[\left(\frac{\partial^2 U}{\partial V\,\partial E}\right) + \phi\left(\frac{\partial^2 U}{\partial V^2}\right)\right] < 0, \qquad \text{(A.7)}$$

where ϕ is the marginal rate of substitution between V_i and E_i. In equilibrium, however, $\phi = (\mathrm{d}V/\mathrm{d}E)$, and the argument of equation (A.7) is the formula for $(\partial^2 L/\partial E^2)$.

FLOATS, GLIDES AND INDICATORS

A comparison of methods for changing exchange rates*

Peter B. KENEN

A model of the spot market for foreign exchange is used to study the behavior of exchange rates, official reserves, and speculators' profits when exchange rates are flexible, pegged, and regulated by gliding-parity rules based on averages of spot rates, levels and changes in reserves, and the basic balance. The behavior of the spot rate and efficacy of various gliding-parity rules is shown to depend on the way that speculators form expectations. Some rules, however, are more efficient in minimizing fluctuations of exchange rates and trade volume, especially rules based on changes in reserves and averages of past market rates. Rules based on levels of reserves prove to be least efficient.

1. Introduction

Official and academic discussions of the international monetary system emphasize the need to change exchange rates promptly and precisely, without disrupting world trade and payments. This paper looks at several ways to achieve that objective. It uses a simple mathematical model to simulate the determination of a spot exchange rate under a large number of exchange-rate regimes. The regimes include free-market flexibility, a pegged rate that can be set free to float temporarily, and systems in which 'objective indicators' are employed to signal the need for changes in parity. The indicators studied in this paper are based on the equilibrium exchange rate, a moving average of actual market rates, the level of official reserves, changes in reserves, and the so-called basic balance.

The mathematical model has been programmed to generate a month-by-month history of the spot exchange rate, merchandise trade, official reserves, and foreign-exchange speculation, following the introduction of a permanent exogenous increase in one country's prices or the volume of its imports. The program

*Work on this project was financed by the National Science Foundation under Grant GS-41498 and by the International Finance Section, Princeton University. The present versions of the model and program reflect suggestions made in seminars at The Johns Hopkins University, the University of Pennsylvania, Princeton University, the U.S. Treasury, and the International Monetary Fund. Nancy Happe and Dennis Warner of Princeton University rendered valuable research assistance.

replicates that history for each exchange-rate regime, allowing us to study the several regimes' performance in a consistent, controlled environment. It also permits experimentation in a number of directions, allowing us to study each regime in many environments. Here, for example, I will look at four modes of foreign-exchange speculation and at two disturbances affecting foreign trade. I will also look at the effects of varying the lags in the response of trade volume to changes in the terms of trade, and at the effects of varying the relevant price elasticities. Finally, I shall alter the size of the band surrounding the parity (the points at which the central bank is obliged to intervene), the permissible frequency of changes in parity, and the sizes of the changes.

I begin by describing the underlying model, turn next to the specification of the exchange-rate regimes, then report on a number of simulations designed to compare the characteristics of those regimes.[1]

2. The model

Consider a single spot market for foreign exchange inhabited by traders, professional speculators, and a central bank. Traders buy home and foreign currency to pay for exports and imports ordered in earlier periods (months). Speculators buy or sell home currency to profit from anticipated changes in the spot exchange rate. The central bank intervenes to peg the exchange rate whenever it reaches an upper or lower limit defined in relation to a predetermined parity.

The traders' demands for home and foreign currency depend on current trade flows. These flows, however, derive from earlier orders for goods, and each order is made to depend on the terms of trade prevailing in the month when it is placed. Formally,

$$XO(I) = AX \cdot TT(I)^{-EX}, \tag{1}$$

$$MO(I) = AM \cdot TT(I)^{EM}, \tag{2}$$

and

$$TT(I) = PH(I)/[PF(I) \cdot RM(I)], \tag{3}$$

where $XO(I)$ is the volume of export orders placed in the Ith month, $MO(I)$ is the volume of import orders, $TT(I)$ is the terms of trade, $PH(I)$ is the level of home prices, $PF(I)$ is the level of foreign prices, and $RM(I)$ is the spot exchange rate (market rate) in units of home currency per unit of foreign currency. The scalars AX and AM are chosen so that the annual volume of trade will be 100.0 when $TT(I)$ is unity, and each simulation is started with $PH(I) = PF(I) =$

---

[1] For a complete description of the model and examples of the output see Kenen (1974a). The notation used below derives from the vocabulary of the FORTRAN program MXRT-III documented there.

$RM(I) = 1.00$, so that $TT(I)$ has always to begin at unity. The price elasticities EX and EM can be varied from one simulation to the next. Here, they are set at 1.0 (the 'low elasticities' case) or at 1.5 (the 'high elasticities' case).

Exogenous disturbances are introduced using a variable, $PR(I)$, that can take two forms. A *permanent* disturbance is created by starting $PR(I)$ at unity and raising it by five percentage points across the first twelve months of each simulation,

$$PR(I) = PR(I-1) + [0.01(5/12)], \qquad I = 1, 2, \ldots, 12, \qquad (4)$$

and $PR(I) = PR(I-1)$, thereafter. A *stochastic* disturbance is created by starting $PR(I)$ at unity and adding a random component in each and every month,

$$PR(I) = 1.00 + V \cdot DN(I), \qquad I = 1, 2, \ldots, N, \qquad (5)$$

where N is the number of months spanned by the simulation. The series $DN(I)$ is distributed normally with zero mean and unit variance, and the scalar V is set at $(0.075/1.645)$, so that the interval ± 0.075 contains 95 percent of the random shocks.

To generate an exogenous change in home prices, permanent or stochastic, we have only to set $PH(I) = PR(I)$. This is the disturbance used most often below. To generate an exogenous change in import volume, we have only to replace the scalar AM in eq. (2) with the variable $AM \cdot PR(I)$.[2]

The current demand for home currency to pay for exports is a weighted sum of export orders, and the current demand for foreign currency to pay for imports is a weighted sum of import orders,

$$XP(I) = \sum_J W_J \cdot [XO(I-J) \cdot PH(I-J)], \qquad (6)$$

$$MP(I) = \sum_J W_J \cdot [MO(I-J) \cdot PF(I-J)]. \qquad (7)$$

Two sets of weights are used here. For 'fast' trade adjustment, $W_1 = W_6 = 0.10$, $W_2 = W_5 = 0.15$, and $W_3 = W_4 = 0.25$; for 'slow' trade adjustment, $W_J = 0.0667$ for $J = 1, 2, 3$, and $J = 10, 11, 12$, and $W_J = 0.10$ for $J = 4, 5, \ldots, 9$.

One other trade series, current export volume, is used to measure the real effects of changes in exchange rates,

$$XV(I) = \sum_J W_J \cdot XO(I-J). \qquad (8)$$

It is compared below with a hypothetical measure of export volume, $XQ(I)$,

---

[2] One could also generate a permanent increase in foreign prices by setting $PF(I) = PR(I)$.

obtained in two steps. First, use eqs. (1)–(3) to define

$$XQ(I) = AX \cdot [PH(I)/PF(I)]^{-EX} \cdot EQ(I)^{EX}, \qquad (9)$$

and

$$MQ(I) = AM \cdot [PH(I)/PF(I)]^{EM} \cdot EQ(I)^{-EM}, \qquad (10)$$

where $EQ(I)$ is the spot rate that would clear the foreign-exchange market in the absence of all lags, speculative flows, and official intervention – the comparative-static equilibrium rate. Next, set

$$XQ(I) \cdot PH(I) - MQ(I) \cdot PF(I) \cdot EQ(I) = 0, \qquad (11)$$

to solve for $EQ(I)$, and calculate $XQ(I)$ using that solution.[3]

The treatment of trade flows in this model has two major implications. First, it pretends that traders are naive. They place orders on the basis of contemporaneous prices, not anticipated prices, and they fail to allow for the possibility that the exchange rate will have changed by the time they must make payments. They do not cover their currency needs by dealing in spot or forward exchange when they place new orders. Second, trade volume is completely insensitive to the current spot rate, so that the model has to rely on foreign-exchange speculation – movements of private funds responsive to expectations – to bridge temporarily the inevitable gaps between the traders' demands and supplies of home and foreign currency.

This second implication needs to be emphasized. In the model set out here and, I venture to suggest, in the real world as well, the markets for foreign exchange could not function without the assistance of speculators. The Walrasian process by which currency dealers transact business could not establish market-clearing prices. The existence of speculation does not guarantee dynamic stability; much will depend on the volume of speculation and on the speed with which the speculators alter their positions. But speculation is not an extraneous activity. It performs a vital social role.[4]

[3] The rate $EQ(I)$ is also used to guide expectations and, in one regime, to signal parity changes. The stochastic simulations described below take two views of $EQ(I)$. One set of simulations makes it reflect the stochastic shocks; the other makes it exclude them (it remains at unity throughout).

[4] The same point has been made by Britton (1970). It evokes a phenomenon detected in recent history – the tendency for the trade balance to describe a 'J curve' after a devaluation. A devaluation does not alter instantly the volume of trade, but inflates the home-currency cost of imports already ordered and invoiced in foreign currency. This effect is powerful in my model. Although the elasticities EX and EM are chosen to satisfy the Marshall–Lerner–Robinson condition, they begin to operate only with a lag, imparting comparative-static stability, but not dynamic stability. [For more on the 'J curve' and doubts about its durability, see Magee (1973).] The point made here is *not* the one made by Friedman (1953), that profitable speculation will stabilize prices. The notion of stability implicit in his argument relates to the amplitude of price fluctuations. Mine relates to the existence of a market-clearing price. The two notions, however, have important intersections; see Williamson (1973). Furthermore, I shall use Friedman's notion of stability to rank exchange-rate regimes – to ask how they interact with various modes of speculation to influence the amplitude of fluctuations in the exchange rate and volume of trade.

It is important, then, to model carefully the behavior of the speculators – how they form their expectations and how they adjust their positions in home and foreign currencies – and to ask what happens to them in each simulation. If they repeatedly suffer large losses, they will be driven out of business, and the market for foreign exchange will cease to function smoothly, if it is able to function at all.

I begin by trying to straddle a paradox – by pretending that the speculators have great faith in the rules governing the monetary system but know those rules only to a first approximation. They do not stage massive raids in the foreign-exchange market when large movements of reserves warn them that the central bank may back away from its commitments. But neither do they know exactly how or when the rules currently in use will mandate a parity change. The first part of this supposition does not jibe with recent history – the chronicle of huge capital movements prompted by strong signals that the rules might be broken. That history, however, can be read as testimony to the speculators' disbelief in the central banks' determination to stand by their own rules, and this disbelief has no proper place in my experiments. I am concerned to study the ways in which certain rules would work, not to simulate the ways in which they might be broken, and it is therefore appropriate for me to assume that the rules of the system have been made to last – and to ascribe the same view to the speculators. I am more troubled by the second part of my composite supposition. If a rule for making parity changes is well-established and well-known, sufficiently so to be credible, speculators are certain to exploit it. They are bound to move funds across the foreign-exchange market as soon as they have any cause to expect a parity change. But I am unable to deal with this problem in the present context. I must apply the rules mechanistically, not 'presumptively' or stochastically so as to deceive the speculators.[5]

My next supposition is not quite so drastic. As my model permits no more than one parity change each month, and the change can be made only before the foreign-exchange market has opened for the month, I shall assume that the speculators enter each month's market with a single point-estimate of the future spot rate – the rate they expect to prevail one month in the future – and shall not let them change that point-estimate during the course of the current month,

---

[5]Some simulations examined below use the various rules to mandate very small parity changes, thereby to minimize the profit opportunities available to those who know the rules (and to minimize the correlation between the changes in the parity and in the market rate). This approach, however, may not be consonant with current thinking in governments and central banks. They appear to contemplate infrequent changes, not a true glide, and infrequent changes might have to be quite large. (Small changes, moreover, could not always break the correlation between the parity and the market rate. They might not be able to mandate a change in the parity until the market rate had reached the edge of its band and was poised to move along with the band. This is one defect of reserve-based rules, compared with rate-based rules, as significant changes in reserves are likely to occur only when the market rate is already at the edge.)

no matter what happens in the market. They will sell foreign currency (buy home currency) during the month if the current spot rate, $RM(I)$, is higher than their estimate of the future spot rate, $AR(I)$. To be precise, the difference between these two rates is made to determine the size of the speculators' *desired* long position in home currency, defined by a sequence of transactions and equations.

Trace the calculations of a speculator facing an exchange rate $RM(I)$ during the current month and forecasting a rate $AR(I)$ for the coming month. By selling one unit of foreign currency, he can obtain $RM(I)$ units of home currency. When, next month, he sells that home currency, he hopes to obtain $[RM(I)/AR(I)]$ units of foreign currency. His prospective profit is $[RM(I)/AR(I)-1]$ per unit of foreign currency sold, and his willingness to make such sales is treated as a linear function of his prospective profit.[6] His desired *short* position in foreign currency is defined by

$$SFA(I) = S[RM(I)-AR(I)]/AR(I), \tag{12}$$

and the corresponding *long* position in home currency is

$$SHA(I) = SFA(I) \cdot RM(I). \tag{13}$$

The speculative coefficient S, linking $SFA(I)$ to prospective profit, is scaled in multiples of export value, so that the volume of speculative flows is related to the volume of commercial business handled by the market. (In most simulations reported below, the speculators' short positions in foreign currency would be twenty times initial monthly export value if the anticipated profit rate were 100 percent.)

Speculators are assumed to reach $SFA(I)$ by a familiar stock-adjustment route. Their current purchases of home currency are defined by

$$CSH(I) = Q[SHA(I)-SH(I-1)], \quad 0 < Q \leq 1, \tag{14}$$

where $CSH(I)$ is the number of units of home currency purchased during the Ith month, $SH(I-1)$ is the actual long position in home currency inherited

---

[6]For a more sophisticated formulation, see Hettich (1974). He has grafted utility maximization onto my model, causing $SFA(I)$ to depend on the variance of expectations, not just on the mean. Note in passing that the argument in the text depends on a hidden assumption. In order to sell a currency short, speculators must be able to borrow unlimited amounts (and to do so at the same constant interest rate regardless of currency). Hettich suggests another formulation. Suppose that there is a forward market inhabited only by speculators (who make all their commitments there) and by arbitrageurs (whose supply of funds is infinitely elastic with respect to the covered interest-rate differential). Suppose, further, that interest rates are the same in both countries, so that the *sign* of the covered differential depends only on the forward premium. If speculators sell foreign currency forward, expecting its spot price to fall in the future, arbitrageurs will buy it forward and sell the same amount of foreign currency spot. The positions defined by eqs. (12)–(15) of the text will represent the spot positions of arbitrageurs, not speculators, but will fulfill the same role in the model.

from the previous month, and Q is the stock-adjustment coefficient. At the beginning of each simulation, $SH(I)$ is set at zero; thereafter,

$$SH(I) = SH(I-1)+CSH(I). \tag{15}$$

The stock-adjustment coefficient Q is set at 0.50 in the simulations examined here.[7]

Two questions remain: How do speculators form their expectations concerning next month's spot rate? And how should we measure the profits they earn during a simulation?

In two modes of speculation simulated here, the anticipated spot rate is formed regressively. Speculators are deemed to believe that there is a 'normal' rate to which the market rate must some day return. Formally,

$$AR(I) = RM(I-1)+C[NR(I)-RM(I-1)], \qquad 0 < C \leqq 1, \tag{16}$$

where $RM(I-1)$ is the actual spot rate one month ago, and $NR(I)$ is the 'normal' rate to which $RM(I)$ is thought to tend. In the first mode of speculation, the 'normal' rate is the current parity, $PA(I)$, adjusted crudely for the likelihood of change,

$$NR(I) = PA(I)+[PA(I)-PA(I-12)]/12. \tag{17}$$

In the second mode, the 'normal' rate is a moving average of the comparative-static equilibrium rate defined by eq. (11) above,

$$NR(I) = \sum_{J} EQ(I-J+L)/3, \qquad J = 1, 2, 3, \tag{18}$$

where L is a lag operator used to define the range of the speculators' foresight (and is set at 3 in most simulations).

Under the mode described by eq. (17), speculators gamble on the supposition that the market rate will tend to a level resembling the current parity.[8] The coefficient C tells us how fast they expect it to do so (and is set at 0.75 hereafter). Under the mode described by eq. (18), speculators gamble on the supposition that the market rate will tend to a level resembling the contemporaneous equilibrium rate defined by the basic trade equations and the price or trade disturbance.[9]

---

[7]Except for those summarized by table 4, below. For simulations using different values of Q and S (and of C, D, and E, defined later), see Kenen (1974b).

[8]A similar formulation is used by Grubel (1965).

[9]This mode resembles the rational-expectations model of speculation, applied in a similar context by Black (1972).

The remaining modes of speculation base expectations on actual experience. The third employs a simple adaptive mechanism,

$$AR(I) = AR(I-1) + D[RM(I-1) - AR(I-1)], \quad 0 < D \leqq 1. \quad (19)$$

Speculators correct their previous forecasts by a fraction of the error made last month. (As large values of that fraction can destabilize the market, D is set at 0.10 hereafter.) The fourth mode is extrapolative,

$$AR(I) = AR(I-1) + E[RM(I-1) - RM(I-2)], \quad 0 < E \leqq 1. \quad (20)$$

Speculators alter their earlier views on the basis of experience, but use a fraction of the recent change in the market rate, not of their own past error. (The fraction E is set at 0.25 throughout this paper.)

It is easy to measure the speculators' profits when their holdings of home currency have gone to zero at the end of a simulation. Their terminal holdings of foreign currency measure the profits they realized during the simulation. Those holdings are

$$SF(I) = -\sum_J [CSH(J)/RM(J)], \quad J = 1, 2, \ldots, I. \quad (21)$$

But when home-currency holdings are not zero at the end, we must ask how much foreign currency the speculators could obtain in exchange for those holdings and have therefore to decide at what exchange rate to convert them.[10] There is, of course, no right rate for this purpose (because the process of conversion would affect the rate), but we shall pretend that speculators can dispose of their holdings at the market rate prevailing when the simulation ends. The speculators' profits, including unrealized profits, are defined by

$$PO(I) = SF(I) + SH(I)/RM(I). \quad (22)$$

As a practical matter, $PO(I)$ rarely differs in sign from other measures one might choose to use.[11]

3. Solving the model

To solve the whole model for the current spot rate, $RM(I)$, we have first to define and solve a market-clearing equation,

$$XP(I) - MP(I) \cdot RMT(I) + CSH(I) = 0, \quad (23)$$

[10]The difficulty resembles one identified by Telser (1959) in his critique of Baumol (1957).
[11]The program calculates two other measures. One divides $SH(I)$ by the final value of $AR(I)$; the other divides it by the final value of $EQ(I)$.

where $RMT(I)$ is a 'tentative' market rate. As this equation is quadratic in $RMT(I)$, rules must be used to choose between its roots.[12] If, of course, one root is negative, the program chooses the other.[13] If both roots are positive, the program takes several steps. When, for example, the larger root is smaller than $RM(I-1)$, the previous market rate, it treats that root as $RMT(I)$. When the two roots bracket $RM(I-1)$, the program computes the excess demand for home currency that would prevail currently if the market rate were constant. If there would be excess demand, it chooses as $RMT(I)$ the smaller root of the quadratic; it acts on the assumption that an excess demand for home currency will reduce the price of foreign currency.

These and other procedures used to solve the model assume that the market for foreign exchange is organized to generate the usual price responses – that the price of foreign currency will rise when that currency is in short supply. They also assume that speculation will perform its basic function – that the process of competitive bidding will end in the discovery of a market-clearing rate. As indicated earlier, this outcome is not certain. Suppose that there is an excess supply of home currency, causing $RMT(I)$ to rise. This will raise the cost of imports, $MP(I) \cdot RMT(I)$ in eq. (19), an effect that will add to the excess supply of home currency, rather than reducing it. Market stability requires that $CSH(I)$ rise more than the increase in the cost of imports, and $CSH(I)$ depends on the parameters S and Q in eqs. (12) and (14). The structure of the model guarantees that speculators will move money in the right direction; their demand for home-currency balances is an increasing function of the current market rate, given the expected rate. But we must choose values for S and Q which make sure that the *size* of the movement of money exceeds the increase in the cost of imports.

When exchange rates are fully flexible or floating temporarily, the solution of the market-clearing equation is the solution of the model itself; the tentative market-clearing rate, $RMT(I)$, is the spot rate, $RM(I)$. When rates are pegged, however, there is more to do. First, we must define the upper and lower limits for spot-market fluctuations (the points at which the central bank is obliged to intervene to stabilize the spot rate). These are given by

$$PU(I) = PA(I)[1+0.01 \cdot BD], \tag{24}$$

and

$$PL(I) = PA(I)[1-0.01 \cdot BD], \tag{25}$$

[12]Substituting and rearranging terms,

$$[S \cdot Q/AR(I)] \cdot RMT(I)^2 - [MP(I)+S \cdot Q] \cdot RMT(I) + [XP(I)-Q \cdot SH(I-1)] = 0,$$

where $AR(I)$, $XP(I)$, $MP(I)$, and $SH(I-1)$ are specified entirely by exogenous or past events and by the parity, $PA(I)$, discussed below.

[13]Because $[S \cdot Q/AR(I)]$ and $[MP(I)+S \cdot Q]$ are non-negative, it is impossible for both roots to be negative. If the roots are not real, the program reduces the stock-adjustment coefficient Q and tries again to solve the quadratic. For details, see Kenen (1974a).

where $PA(I)$ is the current parity, discussed below, and BD is the allowable margin for spot-market fluctuations expressed as a percentage of the current parity. (Unless otherwise indicated, BD is set at 2.5 percent in the simulations studied below.) Next, we must ask if $RMT(I)$ lies between these limits. If it does, the situation is the same as it would be with flexibility; $RM(I)$ is $RMT(I)$, completing the solution. If instead $RMT(I)$ lies outside these limits, one of them must take effect. If $PL(I) > RMT(I)$, the central bank must buy foreign currency to support its price; it must peg $RM(I)$ at $PL(I)$. If $PU(I) < RMT(I)$, the central bank must sell foreign currency to keep down its price; it must peg $RM(I)$ at $PU(I)$.

Finally, to measure the volume of intervention required to peg the spot exchange rate, define and solve,

$$DF(I) = XP(I)/RM(I) - MP(I) + CSH(I)/RM(I). \tag{26}$$

The central bank's reserves at the end of each month are defined accordingly,

$$RE(I) = RE(I-1) + DF(I). \tag{27}$$

In all simulations studied here, $RE(I)$ begins at 20.0 (at 20 percent of the initial annual value of exports).

At the conclusion of each simulation, the program computes a set of summary statistics. Two of these are used extensively below. The first is a measure of variability in export volume relative to equilibrium volume,

$$100\left[\sum_I \{XV(I) - XQ(I)\}^2/N\right]^{\frac{1}{2}},$$

where, as before, N is the number of months spanned by the simulation ($N = 120$ here). The second summary statistic is a measure of the variability in reserves,

$$100\left[\sum_I DF(I)^2/N\right]^{\frac{1}{2}}.$$

4. The exchange-rate regimes

The simulations presented in this paper examine nine exchange-rate regimes and several permutations of certain regimes.

(1) *Flexible rates.* The spot rate is market determined. The central bank abstains from intervention, and $RM(I) = RMT(I)$ in each and every month.[14]

[14]Used in combination with the first (parity-based) mode of speculation, this regime generates an anomaly. The parity on which expectations are based has no operational significance.

(2) *Fixed rates*. The parity is fixed forever (at unity). The central bank intervenes to keep the market rate between $PU(I)$ and $PL(I)$.

(3) *Temporary float*. The market rate is set free to float whenever reserves have fallen to 75 percent of their initial level (and would fall further during the current month) or when they have risen to 125 percent of their initial level (and would rise further during the month). The float is allowed to continue for twelve months, at which time a new parity is declared.[15]

(4) *Parity at equilibrium*. This regime flatters central banks and governments. It assumes that they are able to identify the comparative-static equilibrium rate, $EQ(I)$, and have the courage of their convictions. They change the parity from month to month, aligning it with a moving average of equilibrium rates,

$$PA(I) = MAQ(I), \tag{28}$$

where

$$MAQ(I) = \sum_J EQ(I-J)/3, \qquad J = 1, 2, 3. \tag{29}$$

In some simulations, however, parity changes take place only twice a year, and the parity can lag behind the moving average.

Each of the remaining exchange-rate regimes uses a numerical indicator to mandate changes in parity. In each of them, moreover, the size of the permissible parity change is fixed at an annual rate (at 5 or 10 percent of the initial parity), so that the size of each parity change depends on the frequency with which the changes can occur.[16] When, for example, the annual rate is five percent and monthly changes are allowed, each devaluation or revaluation will be five-twelfths of one percent of the initial parity. When the annual rate is five percent and only semiannual changes are allowed, each devaluation or revaluation will be 2.5 percent of the initial parity. Two of the remaining exchange-rate regimes employ rate-based indicators; two employ reserve-based indicators; one employs the basic balance. They are defined as follows:

(5) *Moving average of equilibrium rates*. This regime uses the moving average $MAQ(I)$, defined above, but does so differently than the fourth regime. The central bank is given these instructions:

Whenever $[PA(I-1)-MAQ(I-1)]$ is larger than 2.0 percent of the initial parity, revalue (reduce the parity) by the permissible amount.

[15]Given by $PA(I) = [RM(I-1)+RM(I-2)]/2$. New trigger points are also set to govern future floats (at 75 and 125 percent of reserves in the month when the float began).

[16]I have also studied forms of these regimes in which the size of each parity change is not predetermined, but depends on the strength of the signal given by the indicator. These 'continuous' forms resemble most closely the ones employed in theoretical work on policy changes, speeds of adjustment, and the stability of macroeconomic models, but they do not perform very differently from the 'discontinuous' forms described in the text. Examples are given in subsequent notes.

Whenever $[PA(I-1)-MAQ(I-1)]$ is smaller than -2.0 percent of the initial parity, devalue (raise the parity) by the permissible amount.

When neither condition obtains (or no change is permitted during the current month because changes can be made only semiannually), the prior parity is retained.[17]

(6) *Moving average of market rates.* This regime employs an indicator recommended by several proponents of gliding parities.[18] Define a sixth-month moving average of spot exchange rates,

$$MAM(I) = \sum_J RM(I-J)/6, \qquad J = 1, 2, \ldots, 6, \tag{30}$$

and use it just as $MAQ(I)$ was used by the fifth regime. (Some simulations examined below use a twelve-month moving average.)

(7) *Reserve level.* This regime embodies an automatic version of the 'presumptive indicator' proposed by the United States in recent international negotiations.[19] It employs the difference between the current level of reserves, $RE(I)$, and the initial level, which it treats as the target or desired level. The central bank follows these instructions:

Whenever $RE(I-1)$ is larger than 115 percent of initial reserves *and* $RE(I-1) \geq RE(I-2)$, revalue by the permissible amount.

Whenever $RE(I-1)$ is smaller than 85 percent of initial reserves *and* $RE(I-1) \leq RE(I-2)$, devalue by the permissible amount.

These instructions are designed to prevent any change in parity after reserves have started to return to their target level. In some simulations, however, they are amended by an additional clause: There can be no revaluation if the basic balance is in deficit and no devaluation if it is in surplus. Here, of course, the

---

[17]The two percent trigger point used in this rule (and the next) is not altogether arbitrary; it is chosen to allow parity changes before the market rate reaches the edge of its band, thereby to emphasize a major difference between the rate-based and reserve-based regimes. The continuous counterpart of this rule (and the next) is

$$PA(I) = PA(I-1)+0.01(K/DQ)[MAQ(I-1)-PA(I-1)],$$

where K is the monthly change used in the 'discontinuous' rule above (e.g., five-twelfths of one percent), and DQ is calibrated to cause parity changes similar to those produced by the discontinuous rule. When, for example, the trigger point is 2.0 percentage points, DQ is set at $\frac{1}{4} \times 0.02$. It is made one-fourth as large as its discontinuous counterpart because, without this modification, the continuous form causes cumulative changes in parity.

[18]See Murphy (1965). For other academic and official antecedents, see Underwood (1973), who traces the origins of several rules studied in this paper; also Halm (1970). For the most recent official incarnations, see International Monetary Fund (1974), especially pp. 51–75.

[19]U.S. Treasury (1973). Similar proposals were made by Modigliani and Kenen (1966) and Triffin [in Hinshaw (1971)]. Underwood (1973) argues that the same notion was central to the Keynes Plan for the postwar system.

basic balance is the trade balance,

$$BB(I) = XP(I) - MP(I) \cdot RM(I). \tag{31}$$

There are no long-term capital flows in the model.[20]

(8) *Reserve change.* This regime embodies a suggestion made by Cooper (1970). It uses the most recent changes in reserves:

> Whenever $DF(I-1)$ *and* $DF(I-2)$ are larger than 0.20 reserve units (one percent of the initial level), revalue by the permissible amount.
> Whenever $DF(I-1)$ *and* $DF(I-2)$ are smaller than -0.20 reserve units, devalue by the permissible amount.

This formulation, however, furnishes no remedy for a small but permanent deficit $[0 > RE(I) \geq -0.20]$ that would cause reserves to drain away slowly. Hence, some simulations amend it to mandate a supplementary devaluation (revaluation) when $DF(I)$ has been negative (positive) for twelve consecutive months and there has been no parity change during that period.[21]

(9) *Basic balance.* This regime seeks to formalize the frequent assertion that parities should be changed only if there are persistent 'basic' imbalances.[22] It makes two quarterly measurements,

$$BQ1(I) = \sum_J BB(I-J)/3,$$

and

$$BQ2(I) = \sum_J BB(I-3-J)/3, \qquad J = 1, 2, 3, \tag{32}$$

then substitutes $BQ1(I)$ for $DF(I-1)$, and $BQ2(I)$ for $DF(I-2)$ in the instructions for the eighth regime.

5. Non-stochastic simulations

Four sets of simulations are examined in this section. The first is designed to

[20]The continuous counterpart is

$$PA(I) = PA(I-1) - 0.01(K/DR)[RE(I-1) - 20.0],$$

causing a devaluation whenever actual reserves are smaller than target reserves. When the trigger point is 15 percent of initial reserves, DR is set at $\frac{1}{4} \times 0.15 \times 20.0$, following the method used for the fifth regime.

[21]The continuous counterpart is

$$PA(I) = PA(I-1) - 0.01(K/DD) \cdot DF(I-1),$$

causing a devaluation whenever there is a deficit. When the trigger point is one percent of initial reserves, DD is set at $\frac{1}{4} \times 0.01 \times 20.0$. The continuous counterpart of the ninth regime uses $BQ1(I)$, defined in the text, in lieu of $DF(I-1)$.

[22]See, e.g., Bergsten (1972) and International Monetary Fund (1974, pp. 52–63), which attributes to the EEC Monetary Committee the opinion that the basic balance might be 'the most satisfactory leading indicator for adjustment action'.

select a small subset of rules for intensive analysis. The second studies the influence of the environment (the size of elasticities, speed of trade adjustment, and form of exogenous disturbance) on the performance of those rules. The third studies the effects of altering the volume of speculation and the speculators' foresight. The fourth studies the effects of altering the size and frequency of changes in parity and of widening the band around parity.

5.1. A comprehensive view

The first set of simulations looks at the effects across ten years of a permanent five percent increase in home prices (completed in the first year), assuming 'low' price elasticities and 'fast' trade adjustment. The volume of speculation is standardized at twenty times export value; the stock-adjustment coefficient is fixed at 0.50; and speculators are allowed to look three months ahead when expectations are regressive to the equilibrium rate. The limits to the band around parity are set at 2.5 percent; the annual change in parity is held to 5.0 percent; and parity changes are permitted monthly. Tables 1.1 through 1.4 deal with the outcomes for four modes of speculation.[23]

Because this first set of results includes 52 separate simulations, it is impossible to dwell on each of them. Instead, I organize my comments to answer two general questions: (1) Does the mode of speculation have a systematic impact on the outcomes of the simulations? (2) Do the simulations for any one regime allow us to render a tentative judgment concerning the efficiency of that regime?

5.1.1. *The modes of speculation.* The manner in which speculators form expectations affects the profitability of speculation, the speed with which the market rate reaches its final equilibrium, the variability of export volume, and the variability of reserves.

Under expectations regressive to parity (table 1.1) all exchange regimes lead to losses. This result is not surprising. The exogenous disturbance calls for a permanent five percent depreciation of the home currency. Expectations regressive to parity, even if adjusted for the likelihood of parity changes, cannot alert the speculators to this necessity. Significantly, the losses are relative large under flexible exchange rates (as expectations are then based on a fixed notional parity) and under a temporary float (as the new parity is not declared until the float has ended); in both instances, expectations lag behind events. Similar results obtain when expectations are adaptive (table 1.3) and extrapolative (table 1.4), as expectations formed in these two ways are likewise backward-looking. Positive profits occur only when expectations are regressive to the equilibrium rate (table 1.2), and even when this mode of speculation gives rise to losses, as it does

[23]Results for the continuous formulations of the gliding-parity rules are summarized in Appendix A.

Table 1.1

Summary statistics for five percent price disturbance, low price elasticities and fast trade adjustment; speculators' expectations regressive to parity.

Exchange regime	Parity changes	Parity		Market rate		Reserves		Variability		Profit
		Max	Final	Max	Final	Min	Final	Export volume	Reserve changes	
Prototypes										
Flexible rate	0	1.000	1.000	1.050	1.050	20.0	20.0	8.04	–	−0.137
Pegged rate	0	1.000	1.000	1.025	1.025	− 1.2	− 1.2*	19.15	18.48	−0.031
Temporary float	1	1.044	1.044	1.070	1.050	11.8	11.8	12.54	17.50	−0.200
Parity at equilibrium	14	1.050	1.050	1.069	1.050	20.0	20.0	3.62	0.00	−0.036
Glides										
Average of equilibrium	8	1.033	1.033	1.059	1.050	19.9	19.9	3.93	0.88	−0.047
Average of market rate	13	1.054	1.054	1.073	1.050	17.1	17.1	9.78	6.86	−0.145
Reserve level	67	1.137	0.996*	1.109	0.995*	14.3	30.8	30.31	25.87	−0.539
Reserve change	3	1.012	1.012	1.038	1.038	8.6	8.6*	11.75	10.58	−0.069
Basic balance	9	1.037	1.037	1.063	1.050	18.2	18.2	7.21	5.71	−0.104
Amended glides										
Average of market rate	10	1.042	1.042	1.064	1.050	15.7	15.7	9.72	7.94	−0.118
Reserve level	14	1.058	1.058	1.084	1.050	14.3	14.3	12.33	9.83	−0.166
Reserve change	6	1.025	1.025	1.051	1.050	14.8	14.8	9.15	7.86	−0.105
Basic balance	16	1.037	1.033*	1.063	1.047*	18.2	18.2	7.48	5.71	−0.099

*Changing in final (tenth) year.

Table 1.2

Summary statistics for five percent price disturbance, low price elasticities and fast trade adjustment; speculators' expectations regressive to equilibrium rate.

Exchange regime	Parity changes	Parity		Market rate		Reserves		Variability		Profit
		Max	Final	Max	Final	Min	Final	Export volume	Reserve changes	
Prototypes										
Flexible rate	0	1.000	1.000	1.058	1.050	20.0	20.0	2.35	–	−0.021
Pegged rate	0	1.000	1.000	1.025	1.025	−5.4	−5.4*	18.28	21.77	−0.004
Temporary float	1	1.045	1.045	1.050	1.050	14.9	14.9	6.59	12.09	0.037
Parity at equilibrium	Parity changes ineffective; results resemble flexible-rate solution									
Glides										
Average of equilibrium	8	1.033	1.033	1.051	1.050	18.9	18.9	0.78	4.56	0.002
Average of market rate	8	1.033	1.033	1.050	1.050	17.9	17.9	1.96	7.53	0.015
Reserve level	19	1.079	1.079	1.052	1.052	16.4	18.2*	4.79	11.38	0.037
Reserve change	3	1.012	1.012	1.038	1.038	7.1	7.1*	8.99	12.28	0.008
Basic balance	8	1.033	1.033	1.050	1.050	14.5	14.5	7.05	12.35	0.037
Amended glides										
Average of market rate	8	1.033	1.033	1.050	1.050	16.0	16.0	4.76	10.79	0.034
Reserve level	Same as simple glide									
Reserve change	6	1.025	1.025	1.050	1.050	15.6	15.6	4.35	9.06	0.018
Basic balance	9	1.037	1.037	1.050	1.050	14.9	14.9	6.52	12.03	0.036

*Changing in final (tenth) year.

Table 1.3

Summary statistics for five percent price disturbance, low price elasticities and fast trade adjustment; speculators' expectations adaptive.

Exchange regime	Parity changes	Parity		Market rate		Reserves		Variability		Profit
		Max	Final	Max	Final	Min	Final	Export volume	Reserve changes	
Prototypes										
Flexible rate	0	1.000	1.000	1.089	1.064*	20.0	20.0	16.10	–	–0.405
Pegged rate	0	1.000	1.000	1.025	1.025	– 4.2	– 4.2*	19.11	21.62	–0.029
Temporary float	1	1.073	1.073	1.074	1.050*	15.0	16.1	12.50	12.27	–0.151
Parity at equilibrium	14	1.050	1.050	1.076	1.059*	18.9	18.9	12.46	4.03	–0.289
Glides										
Average of equilibrium	8	1.033	1.033	1.059	1.053*	17.0	17.0	8.21	7.32	–0.158
Average of market rate	15	1.058	1.054	1.075	1.059*	17.4	17.4	12.00	7.32	–0.216
Reserve level	53	1.108	0.996*	1.081	1.021*	16.5	22.9*	18.42	14.86	–0.290
Reserve change	6	1.025	1.025	1.051	1.050	13.9	13.9	8.28	10.45	–0.085
Basic balance	10	1.042	1.042	1.068	1.057*	18.0	18.0	10.18	5.65	–0.216
Amended glides										
Average of market rate	11	1.046	1.046	1.062	1.049*	14.2	14.2	10.18	11.60	–0.099
Reserve level	16	1.067	1.067	1.077	1.055*	16.5	17.1	12.79	10.46	–0.199
Reserve change	8	1.033	1.033	1.055	1.049*	14.4	14.4	8.47	10.38	–0.089
Basic balance	17	1.042	1.037*	1.068	1.055*	17.6	17.6	9.37	6.76	–0.197

*Changing in final (tenth) year.

Table 1.4

Summary statistics for five percent price disturbance, low price elasticities and fast trade adjustment; speculators' expectations extrapolative.

Exchange regime	Parity changes	Parity		Market rate		Reserves		Variability		Profit
		Max	Final	Max	Final	Min	Final	Export volume	Reserve changes	
Prototypes										
Flexible rate	0	1.000	1.000	1.050	1.050	20.0	20.0	8.04	–	−0.137
Pegged rate	0	1.000	1.000	1.025	1.025	− 1.2	− 1.2*	19.15	18.48	−0.031
Temporary float	1	1.044	1.044	1.050	1.050	14.9	14.9	11.98	9.08	−0.138
Parity at equilibrium	14	1.050	1.050	1.050	1.050	20.0	20.2	7.70	1.44	−0.136
Glides										
Average of equilibrium	Parity changes ineffective; results resemble flexible-rate solution									
Average of market rate	8	1.033	1.033	1.050	1.050	19.7	19.7	8.32	1.91	−0.138
Reserve level	19	1.079	1.079	1.052	1.052	16.7	18.3*	10.80	7.93	−0.150
Reserve change	1	1.004	1.004	1.029	1.029	2.7	2.7*	16.46	15.20	−0.044
Basic balance	Parity changes ineffective; results resemble flexible-rate solution									
Amended glides										
Average of market rate	8	1.033	1.033	1.050	1.050	18.4	18.4	9.34	4.78	−0.139
Reserve level	Same as simple glide									
	6	1.025	1.025	1.050	1.050	14.5	14.5	11.03	7.63	−0.139
Reserve change										
Basic balance	Parity changes ineffective; results resemble flexible-rate solution									

*Changing in final (tenth) year.

with flexible exchange rates, the losses are smaller than they are under other modes.[24]

The mode of speculation tends also to influence the speed with which the spot exchange rate reaches equilibrium. Here, however, the three modes that always cause losses differ importantly among themselves. The first and fourth modes, together with the second, cause the rate to reach its long-term equilibrium during the decade covered by each simulation, unless it is prevented from doing so by an insufficient change in parity – a characteristic of a regime rather than a mode of speculation. With adaptive expectations, by contrast, the market rate is almost always changing after ten years. It is converging on its equilibrium level in most simulations – an assertion supported by prolonging the simulations for an additional decade – but the convergence is very slow.

Turning to the implications of speculation for the variability of export volume, the results appear to be consistent with Friedman's (1953) conjecture that profitability enhances stability. Taking the 13 exchange-rate regimes one at a time, there is a strong positive correlation between the profitability of speculation and the variability of export volume. With a temporary float, for example, we find the following.

Mode	Export variability	Speculators profits
Regressive to parity	12.54 (4)	−0.200 (4)
Regressive to equilibrium	6.59 (1)	+0.037 (1)
Adaptive	12.50 (3)	−0.151 (3)
Extrapolative	11.98 (2)	−0.138 (2)

There are only two exceptions to this outcome (the glides based on changes in reserves and on the amended moving average of market rates), but even in these instances, profitable speculation leads to the least export instability. The positive correlation, however, does not hold across exchange-rate regimes within a given mode of speculation. I return to this problem below.

There is less to be said about the variability of reserves, although one can detect certain regularities. In eight of the nine gliding-parity cases, extrapolative expectations cause the smallest fluctuations. In fact, this mode of speculation serves often to preclude any change in reserves; parity changes are triggered quickly enough to keep the market rate inside its band. At the opposite extreme, expectations regressive to equilibrium tend to cause large movements in reserves under all regimes that do not allow a rapid change in the exchange rate.

[24]The losses shown under flexibility, however, have disturbing implications for the survival of speculators and the viability of the regime. They derive in part from the tendency for the market rate to overshoot the comparative-static equilibrium rate on which expectations are based – a tendency that is common to most of the gliding-parity rules because they restrict the month-to-month movements of the market rate. Notice that the maximum market rate is higher under flexibility than under any other exchange-rate regime in table 1.2.

Finally, a procedural decision: Because the adaptive mode of speculation produces so many simulations that do not settle down a full decade after a disturbance, making it quite difficult to compare exchange-rate regimes, I shall say nothing further about this mode. It may be a realistic representation of speculation but is not especially suitable for present purposes.

5.1.2. The exchange-rate regimes. An efficient exchange-rate regime should satisfy a number of criteria. First, the spot exchange rate should be able to attain its final equilibrium (here, to depreciate by five percent). Second, the rate should not move in a fashion that causes unnecessary fluctuations in trade volume (here, variations in export volume around the comparative-static equilibrium level). Third, there should not be large movements in reserves, as these could raise doubts in the minds of speculators concerning the determination of the central bank to stand by the rules of the regime. Fourth, speculators should be able to make profits or, at the very least, should be spared large losses when they behave in a stabilizing fashion.

I begin by applying these criteria to the first four exchange-rate regimes, then look at the five gliding-parity rules.

Because the simulations studied here require a permanent five percent change in the exchange rate, a pegged rate cannot satisfy the first three criteria. The market rate moves quickly to the edge of the band, but cannot move any further. Thereafter, there is a deficit in the balance of payments, and the central bank runs out of reserves.[25] Export variability is quite large, as trade volume is prevented from achieving the level implied by the comparative-static equilibrium rate. (The index of variability does not measure short-term instability in this particular instance.) When, instead, the central bank is sufficiently well-informed to keep the parity in line with the comparative-static equilibrium rate, these problems disappear. The market rate reaches its long-term equilibrium, and export volume is quite stable. In two simulations, moreover, there are no changes in reserves.[26] In all simulations, however, speculators suffer larger losses than they do when the parity is pegged forever, even in table 1.1, when their expectations are guided more or less correctly by the parity itself.

Flexible exchange rates and temporary floats straddle the extremes described by the other two prototypical regimes. The market rate reaches its long-term equilibrium in every simulation. Export volume is more stable than it is with pegged exchange rates, but less stable than it is when the parity is aligned with the comparative-static equilibrium rate. There are, of course, no changes in reserves with full flexibility, and the changes are smaller with temporary floats than when

[25]The size of the cumulative loss of reserves varies with the mode of speculation because, with expectations regressive to the equilibrium rate, speculators are not willing to support the market rate. They do not believe that it will return to its initial level.

[26]There is a negligible increase in table 1.4, as the parity moves too rapidly, causing the lower limit of the band to collide with the market rate.

the parity is pegged permanently. The central bank cannot run out of reserves. As noted earlier, however, flexible rates are unkind to speculators in the market modelled here. Losses are larger than with pegged rates and, in table 1.1, larger also than they are when the parity is aligned with the comparative-static equilibrium rate.[27]

In the fifth exchange-rate regime, the comparative-static equilibrium rate is used only to nudge the parity, not directly to select it, as it was in the fourth. One might therefore expect to find more variability in export volume and in reserves. But the differences between the two regimes are not very large. The fifth does quite well by all criteria. The parity comes to rest rapidly in all simulations at a level which permits the market rate to reach its equilibrium. The index of export variability is smaller than it is for any other gliding-parity rule (and in table 1.2 smaller even than it is for the fourth regime). In all simulations, moreover, the fifth regime does better than the temporary float, and it is never inferior to full flexibility. It leads to larger reserve losses than the fourth regime, but causes smaller changes than the temporary floats.

Although the fifth regime is less efficient than the fourth, its kinship with the latter gives it great power compared to all other gliding-parity rules. It uses an accurate forecast of the direction in which the exchange rate should move. The others employ historical information, telling us where the rate has been. In consequence, it is the most efficient rule, viewed from the standpoint of stabilization. It does not always yield the largest profits, but neither does it cause the largest losses. Yet some of the other regimes behave fairly well.

When parity changes are based on an average of market rates, the simulations satisfy my first criterion. The change in the parity is a bit too large in table 1.1, allowing the market rate to overshoot its long-term level, but it settles down after small oscillations. The ranking by other criteria, however, varies with the mode of speculation. When, for example, expectations are regressive to equilibrium, the regime is second-best in its effects on the stability of exports and reserves; when they are regressive to parity, it is only third-best.

Finally, compare the two versions of this regime – the version that employs a six-month moving average with the (amended) version that employs a twelve-month average. The former is better when expectations are regressive to equilibrium (save with regard to profitability) and is slightly better with extrapolative expectations. The latter is slightly better when expectations are regressive to parity (save with regard to variations in reserves). The differences, however, are not large.

The seventh regime has attracted much attention because it uses a formula resembling the one proposed by the United States to regulate 'presumptively' the process of balance-of-payments adjustment. The incarnation studied here,

---

[27]In that same instance, the losses with flexibility are smaller than the losses with a temporary float, but speculators reap large profits from the float in table 1.2, because they build up long positions in foreign currency before the float begins.

however, has disastrous properties. In two out of four simulations, the parity is changing during the tenth year. In the other two (and in one of the first two), the market rate is 'stuck' at the end of the decade, causing a deficit or surplus in the balance of payments, changing the stock of reserves, and promising additional parity changes. When expectations are regressive to parity, export volume is less stable than under any other rule, even under pegged exchange rates, and the variability of reserves is larger than it is under other gliding parities. With other modes of speculation the outcomes are better, absolutely and comparatively, but export volume is less stable than it is under flexibility and under the two rate-based glides.[28]

The difficulty with the reserve-level rule is fundamental, not fortuitous. The rule marries a *flow* control to a *stock* target, a union that is always apt to be unstable.[29] The exchange rate can regulate the balance of payments – the rate of change of reserves. It cannot regulate the level of reserves. When, therefore, an increase in home prices causes reserves to fall below their target level, the rule leads to a series of devaluations large enough to drag the market rate beyond its equilibrium, to generate a surplus in the balance of payments, and to drive reserves through their upper limit. At that point, the rule leads to a series of revaluations, shoving the spot rate around again and producing a new deficit. The cycle is repeated. The reserve-level rule cannot stabilize the stock of reserves without destabilizing the exchange rate and volume of trade.

The amended version of the seventh regime, in which the sign of the basic balance can override a signal to revalue or devalue, does a bit better than the simple formulation. In table 1.1, for example, the behavior of the basic balance checks the cumulative change in the parity, bringing the market rate and reserves to rest. The stock of reserves, however, remains far from target, precisely because the parity does not change sufficiently to generate a surplus in the balance of payments and reconstitute reserves. In other words, the amendment serves sometimes to stabilize the foreign-exchange market, but only by interfering with the stated aim of the rule itself.

The eighth regime has no fundamental flaw, even though it uses data on reserves. It matches a flow control to a flow target. The parity and market rate settle down. Earlier comments, however, identify one defect. This regime mandates a devaluation whenever the monthly deficit is larger than 0.20 reserve units. It does not mandate any change when the imbalance is smaller. In each simulation, the regime ceases to signal the need for devaluation as soon as the deficit is cut back to 0.20 reserve units, and the cumulative change in the parity is far too small. The market rate cannot reach its long-term equilibrium, and there is a residual deficit at the end of each simulation. Reserves go on falling, just as they do with pegged rates, and the two indexes of variability are inflated.

[28]Furthermore, the seventh regime loses out to the eighth when the latter is amended to eliminate residual imbalances.
[29]See Phillips (1954).

Fortunately, the amended version of the rule corrects this imperfection completely. It causes supplementary changes in parity (three in table 1.1) that allow the market rate to reach its equilibrium. Reserves are stable at the end of each simulation, and the indexes of variability are reduced.

The ninth regime uses the basic balance by itself and has some strange properties. The market rate settles down at equilibrium and the changes in reserves are not large, but the ranking of this rule is very sensitive to the mode of speculation. In table 1.1, for example, it is second-best among the gliding parities in its effects on export volume (it is better, indeed, than full flexibility) and second-best also in its effects on reserves. In table 1.2, by contrast, it is only fourth-best in its effects on export volume (and far inferior to flexibility) and is the worst of the five gliding parities in its effects on reserves. Notice, finally, that the amended version of this rule is not significantly different from the simple version. The indexes of variability are slightly smaller in table 1.2, but not in table 1.1, and in the latter the amended version causes the parity to go on changing during the tenth year of the simulation.

5.1.3. A subset of regimes. One aim of this first comprehensive survey is to choose a small number of exchange-rate regimes for more intensive study. This is not difficult. (1) The temporary float was seen to combine the features of its antecedents – to cause less variability in exports and reserves than a pegged rate but somewhat more variability than flexibility. Hereafter, then, I omit this regime. (2) The twelve-month moving average of market rates did not behave very differently than the six-month average. Hereafter, then, I omit the twelve-month average. (3) The amended version of the reserve-level rule was much better than the simple version in tables 1.1 and 1.3, and was no worse in other tables. It did not stabilize the stock of reserves at or near the target level, but did check the cyclical movement of the parity characteristic of the simple version, allowing the market rate to settle down. Hereafter, then, I substitute the amended version.[30] (4) The amended version of the reserve-change rule served always to stabilize the stock of reserves by ending residual imbalances. Once again, then, I substitute the amended version. (5) The amended version of the basic-balance rule never behaved much more efficiently than the simple version and destabilized the parity and market rate in table 1.1. Hereafter, then, I omit the amended version.[31]

---

[30]There is a good case for dropping this regime entirely. I retain it for the time being because it has received so much attention, academic and official.

[31]The subset of gliding-parity rules formed this way serve frequently to stabilize exports and reserves more effectively than the continuous forms of the same rules defined in previous notes and described in Appendix A. The principal exceptions occur in respect of the basic-balance rule and when expectations are extrapolative. What is more important for a comparative evaluation of the gliding parities, the two groups of rules are similar in relative effectiveness. The power of any single rule to stabilize export volume depends on the mode of speculation,

5.2. Effects of the environment

Consider the ways in which the several regimes react to changes in the economic environment, using the new subset of exchange-rate regimes and altering three aspects of the environment – the speed with which the volume of merchandise trade responds to changes in home prices and the exchange rate, the sizes of the price elasticities, and the form of the permanent exogenous disturbance. I concentrate on export variability, using the data in table 2,[32] and look first at certain absolute effects.

The stability of export volume is related strongly to the speed with which trade flows adjust to prices, and the correlation is reinforced by high price elasticities. Comparing the 16 pairs of simulations in the first two columns of table 2, we find only four in which export variability is reduced by slowing the speed of adjustment. Comparing the pairs in the third and fourth columns, we find only three in which it is reduced.[33]

The effects of altering the price elasticities are just as strong – and fly in the face of intuition. Textbooks tell us that high price elasticities are good for the stability of the foreign-exchange market. Here, however, high elasticities tend to destabilize export volume. Comparing the first and third columns of table 2, we find only two pairs of simulations in which an increase in the price elasticities reduces the variability of export volume. Comparing the second and fourth columns, we find only two. And when we combine long lags with high elasticities, comparing the first and the fourth columns, we do not find a single exception. The increase of elasticities and lengthening of lags work jointly and powerfully to enlarge the variability of export volume.[34] This last comparison, moreover,

but the rankings of the rules are similar under any single mode. Consider the outcomes when expectations are regressive to the equilibrium rate.

	Ranking by export variability	
Regime	Continuous	Discontinuous
Average of equilibrium rates	1	1
Average of market rates	2	2
Reserve level	5	4[a]
Reserve change	3	3[a]
Basic balance	4	5

[a]Amended versions.

The continuous form of the basic-balance rule does better absolutely and comparatively than the discontinuous form, switching places with the reserve-level rule.

[32]The first column of that table reproduces data from tables 1.1 and 1.2. Data on the outcomes with extrapolative expectations (table 1.4) are omitted from the new table and those that follow, mainly because so many gliding-parity results resemble (or are identical to) those for flexible exchange rates. For data on the variability of reserves, see Appendix B.

[33]The effect on the variability of reserves is even stronger. There are no declines between the first and second columns in Appendix B, and only one decline between the third and fourth.

[34]Notice, in addition, the number of times that high elasticities and slow adjustment combine to prolong the process of adjustment to the exogenous disturbance. In almost every simulation, the market rate is moving at the end of ten years.

Table 2

Variability of export volume with various price and trade disturbances.

| Exchange regime | Five percent price disturbance | | | | Ten percent trade disturbance, high elasticities, slow adjustment |
| | Low price elasticities | | High price elasticities | | |
	Fast adjust	Slow adjust	Fast adjust	Slow adjust	
Speculators' expectations regressive to parity					
Flexible rate	8.04	8.47	7.91	10.62^m	17.67^m
Pegged rate	19.15^r	19.16^r	27.90^r	27.86^r	31.71^r
Parity at equilibrium	3.62	5.71	4.44	8.83^m	13.00^m
Average of equilibrium	3.93	3.78	4.91	5.26^m	13.22
Average of market rate	9.78	17.11^{pmr}	10.26	14.26^m	20.96^m
Amended reserve level	12.33	16.96^r	15.64^r	31.86^{pmr}	35.57^{mr}
Amended reserve change	9.15	11.27^m	9.17	14.10^m	20.95^m
Basic balance	7.21	23.20^{pmr}	16.72^{pmr}	29.79^{pmr}	34.59^{pmr}
Speculators' expectations regressive to equilibrium					
Flexible rate	2.35	5.32	2.28	5.76^m	7.67^m
Pegged rate	18.28^r	17.92^r	27.25^r	26.72^r	29.06^r
Parity at equilibrium	**	4.94	**	**	**
Average of equilibrium	0.78	1.65	1.10	2.00	7.94
Average of market rate	1.96	1.60	3.03	2.88^m	9.11^m
Amended reserve level	4.79^r	7.34^{pmr}	6.04^r	6.27^r	11.36^m
Amended reserve change	4.35	3.82	5.39	5.55	10.23^m
Basic balance	7.05	7.92	7.76	9.63^m	14.02^m

[p] Parity changing in final (tenth) year.
[m] Market rate changing in final (tenth) year.
[r] Reserves changing in final (tenth) year.
** Parity changes ineffective; resembles flexible-rate solution.

helps to explain what is happening. In every simulation, but especially with slow adjustment, current changes in trade volume reflect decisions made in earlier months, on the basis of prices prevailing in those months. The tail is wagging the dog, and high elasticities cause it to wag more vigorously, giving the speculators more work to do.

Look next at the relative effects of changing the speed of adjustment and elasticities, beginning with a series of simple comparisons. Ask how many gliding-parity rules cause less (or no more) variability in export volume than full flexibility. The glide based on the equilibrium rate does so every time – under both modes of speculation and all modes of trade adjustment. The glide based on the market rate does so in three simulations when expectations are regressive to equilibrium; the glide based on changes in reserves does so too, but only with slow trade adjustment. The glide based on the basic balance does so when expectations are regressive to parity and trade adjustment is fast. The glide based on the level of reserves never does so. It continues to display its fundamental flaw, even when amended.[35]

Additional information is obtained by ranking the five gliding-parity regimes. Under expectations regressive to parity, the average of equilibrium rates is the most efficient. The reserve change is second-best in three simulations and third-best in one. At the opposite extreme, the basic balance is second-best once but fourth-best or worst three times, while the reserve level is third-best once but fourth-best or worst three times. Under expectations regressive to equilibrium, the average of equilibrium rates is best in three simulations and second-best in one, while the average of market rates is best once and second-best three times. Here, moreover, the reserve level is always fourth-best, and the basic balance is worst. Finally, compare the glides based on changes in reserves and on the market rate. The former is always one rank ahead of the latter under the first mode of speculation, but the relationship is reversed under the second mode.

The last column of table 2 displays the effects of an exogenous increase in imports, rather than an exogenous increase in home prices. There is, of course, a major difference between these disturbances. The size of the change in the exchange rate required to offset a price disturbance does not depend on the size of the price elasticities. The exchange rate must restore purchasing-power parity. But the size of the change required to offset a trade disturbance is inversely related to the sizes of the price elasticities.[36] Nevertheless, the two types of

---

[35]One can also count the frequency with which each gliding parity is superior to an 'omniscient' central bank (one that sets the parity equal directly to the comparative-static equilibrium rate). Under expectations regressive to parity, the glide based on the equilibrium rate is superior with slow trade adjustment. Under expectations regressive to equilibrium, that glide is superior every time; the one based on the average of market rates is superior three times; and the one based on changes in reserves is superior with slow adjustment.

[36]This is why the final simulation in table 2 uses a ten percent trade disturbance; a five percent disturbance does not often trigger changes in parity because the new equilibrium rate lies within the limits of the band.

disturbance have similar implications for the absolute and relative efficiencies of the exchange-rate regimes. Compare the fourth and fifth columns of table 2. The variability of export volume is always larger with the trade disturbance. Under the first speculative mode, however, the glide based on the equilibrium rate is more efficient than flexibility, just as it was with a price disturbance, and the rankings of the five gliding parities are unchanged.

Table 3

The variability of export volume and speculators' profits with a five percent price disturbance.

Exchange regime	Low elasticities and fast adjustment		High elasticities and slow adjustment	
	Variability of exports	Speculators' profits	Variability of exports	Speculators' profits
Expectations regressive to parity				
Flexible rate	8.04	−0.137	10.62	−0.099
Pegged rate	19.15	−0.031	27.86	−0.029
Parity at equilibrium	3.62	−0.036	8.83	−0.017
Average of equilibrium	3.93	−0.047	5.26	−0.045
Average of market rate	9.78	−0.145	14.26	−0.130
Amended reserve level	12.33	−0.166	31.86	−0.347
Amended reserve change	9.15	−0.105	14.10	−0.117
Basic balance	7.21	−0.104	29.79	−0.547
Expectations regressive to equilibrium				
Flexible rate	2.35	−0.021	5.76	−0.021
Pegged rate	18.28	−0.004	26.72	−0.004
Parity at equilibrium	**	**	**	**
Average of equilibrium	0.78	0.002	2.00	0.003
Average of market rate	1.96	0.015	2.88	0.019
Amended reserve level	4.79	0.037	6.27	0.046
Amended reserve change	4.35	0.018	5.55	0.012
Basic balance	7.05	0.037	9.63	0.062

**Parity changes ineffective; resembles flexible-rate solution.

5.3. Effects of speculation

Table 3 replicates some of the data given in table 2, but adds information on the speculators' profits. It allows us to appraise effects of the economic environment on the profitability of speculation and on the relationship between stability and profitability.

Note first that there is an increase in profitability with slow trade adjustment and high price elasticities. There are only four exceptions to this generalization, and two of them relate to very large changes in the index of variability.[37] But we

---

[37]Under expectations regressive to parity, there are larger losses with the reserve-level and basic-balance rules. The former settles down in the 'low–fast' case, but not in the 'high–slow' case; the latter declines from second-best to worst in relative efficiency. The other exceptions involve the rule using changes in reserves.

can draw no inference from this finding. Although long lags and high elasticities appear to amplify instability, we cannot conclude from the increase in profitability that speculation is indeed stabilizing – that the larger profits (smaller losses) are the rewards for combatting this instability. To do so would be circular logically and would ignore the numerical evidence. The table shows an increase in instability, despite the increase in profitability.

Turning to the correlations across exchange-rate regimes, stability correlates with profitability under the first mode of speculation, and the correlation is quite stable between environments. With low elasticities and fast adjustment, there is a perfect rank correlation across the five gliding parities; the regime that shows the least instability shows the smallest losses. With high elasticities and slow adjustment, the rankings are altered (because the basic-balance rule loses efficiency), but the correlation is still strong. The second mode of speculation however, displays a *perverse* correlation – and this is the one mode of speculation that yields positive profits! The correlation is perfectly perverse with low elasticities and fast adjustment (apart from a tie in profitability), and there is only one reversal with high elasticities and slow adjustment.

These results are important to an appraisal of the several exchange-rate regimes, but may not be entirely fair to the hypothesis that there is an intrinsic positive correlation between stability and profitability. It may be wrong to compare the effects of speculation across sets of circumstances over which the speculators have no control. They do not write the rules for changing parities; they do not select the lags or elasticities. On this view, it would be better to ask if there is a positive correlation between stability and profitability when one varies the behavior of the speculators rather than varying the environment within which they function.

I gave an affirmative answer to this question earlier, citing the positive correlations across modes of speculation in tables 1.1–1.4, and this correlation is repeated in table 3. For any single regime and economic environment, profits are almost always larger (losses smaller) when export volume is more stable. The next table, however, gives cause for caution and shows again how difficult it is to assess the contributions of the gliding parities to the effectiveness of speculation.

The three simulations summarized by table 4 examine the effects of speculation when expectations are regressive to equilibrium – the mode that gave positive profits but perverse correlations across regimes. The three simulations ask what happens when we change the speculators' ability to forecast the equilibrium rate and when we change the volume of speculation.[38] The implications for profitability are those one would expect; the implications for stability are less uniform. When speculators are allowed to look three months ahead, as in the first simulation, their profits are larger (losses smaller) than when they are myopic. There

[38] These simulations come from Kenen (1974b) and differ in certain respects from those shown elsewhere in this paper. Direct numerical comparisons will be misleading.

Table 4

Additional results on export variability and speculators' profits, five percent price disturbance with low price elasticities and fast trade adjustment; expectations regressive to equilibrium rate.[a]

Exchange regime	Speculative coefficient 10 times exports, $L = 3$		Speculative coefficient 10 times exports, $L = 0$		Speculative coefficient 20 times exports, $L = 0$	
	Variability of exports	Speculators' profits	Variability of exports	Speculators' profits	Variability of exports	Speculators' profits
Flexible rate	3.71	−0.023	5.82	−0.042	3.75	−0.041
Pegged rate	18.28	−0.003	18.30	−0.005	18.31	−0.005
Parity at equilibrium	3.65	−0.023	5.00	−0.041	**	**
Average of equilibrium	1.29	0.001	1.65	−0.021	1.90	−0.034
Average of market rate	2.26	0.009	3.11	0.006	3.43	0.017
Amended reserve level	8.44	0.014	8.00	0.013	7.95	0.030
Amended reserve change	5.69	0.009	4.80	0.005	5.29	0.019
Basic balance	6.85	0.016	6.89	0.015	7.32	0.031

[a]Simulations differ from those summarized by the other tables; the stock-adjustment coefficient has been set at unity.
**Parity changes ineffective; resembles flexible-rate solution.

are no exceptions to this generalization. In three of nine instances, however, foresight fails to enhance the stability of export volume. When, next, speculators are made to take larger positions in home and foreign currencies, as in the third simulation, profits get larger, but so do losses. The consequence of any given gamble is a bigger reward or punishment, depending on the quality of the gamble. When, further, the larger positions lead to larger losses, they lead also to more variability in the volume of exports. But when they lead to larger profits, they do not always lead to more stability. There are larger profits in five instances, but more instability in three.

5.4. *Effects of altering the exchange-rate regimes*

The final set of non-stochastic simulations is designed to study the effects of changing the speed of the glide (from five to ten percent), the frequency of parity changes (from monthly to semiannual), and the width of the band surrounding the parity (from 2.5 to 5.0 percent). Table 5.1 summarizes simulations using expectations regressive to parity; table 5.2 summarizes simulations using expectations regressive to equilibrium.[39] I look first at the five gliding parities, one by one, then try to draw general conclusions.

(1) *Glides based on the equilibrium rate.* Here, the several permutations of the glide have no large effects on efficiency. With one small exception (in table 5.1), an increase in the speed of the glide tends to raise slightly the variability of export volume, but it has no consistent effect on the movements of reserves. Reductions in the frequency of parity changes tend also to enlarge the variability of export volume but reduce the movements of reserves because they allow larger parity changes at the beginning of each simulation. An increase in the width of the band has a negligible effect on export volume but has an important effect on reserves. Because the market rate can reach its equilibrium without striking the edge of the band, there are no changes in reserves in any simulation.

(2) *Glides based on the market rate.* When expectations are regressive to equilibrium, this regime is not dramatically sensitive to the changes studied here. An increase in the speed of the glide has only small effects on the variability of exports and on movements of reserves. The shift to semiannual parity changes diminishes modestly both forms of instability. But when expectations are regressive to parity, there are large losses in efficiency and the permutations nteract strongly. When parity changes take place monthly, for example, a faster glide adds slightly to export instability and to movements of reserves. When instead the changes take place twice a year, the faster glide adds hugely to export

[39]As the widening of bands leads frequently to outcomes resembling those shown for flexible rates (in tables 1.1 and 1.2, above), the outcomes are not shown in these tables. Some of them appear in Appendix C. It should be remembered that a reduction in the frequency of parity changes is accompanied by an increase in the size of each change (from one-twelfth to one-half of the permissible annual rate).

Table 5.1

Summary statistics for five percent price disturbance with low price elasticities and fast trade adjustment, various rates and frequencies of glide; speculators' expectations regressive to parity.

| | | Five percent glide | | | | | | Ten percent glide | | | | |
| | | Variability | | Final values | | | | Variability | | Final values | | |
Frequency	Parity changes	Export volume	Reserve changes	Parity	Market rate	Reserves	Parity changes	Export volume	Reserve changes	Parity	Market rate	Reserves
Moving average of equilibrium rate												
Monthly	8	3.93	0.88	1.033	1.050	19.9	4	3.64	0.29	1.033	1.050	20.0
Semiannual	2	5.07	0.00	1.050	1.050	20.0	1	5.17	0.00	1.050	1.050	20.0
Moving average of market rate												
Monthly	13	9.78	6.86	1.054	1.050	17.1	7	10.11	7.09	1.058*	1.050	17.4
Semiannual	11	21.08	13.14	1.025*	1.001*	15.4*	15	45.05	46.42	0.950*	0.965*	24.7*
Amended reserve level												
Monthly	14	12.33	9.83	1.058	1.050	14.3	11	18.68	13.34	1.092	1.064	21.7*
Semiannual	3	11.17	11.01	1.075*	1.082*	14.6	4	25.18	21.72	1.000	1.025*	25.4*
Amended reserve change												
Monthly	6	9.15	7.86	1.025	1.050	14.8	3	7.96	7.08	1.025	1.050	17.4
Semiannual	1	7.53	8.09	1.025	1.050	18.0	1	8.87	10.99	1.050	1.050	17.5
Basic balance												
Monthly	9	7.21	5.71	1.037	1.050	18.2	64	30.78	14.06	1.067*	1.067*	12.8*
Semiannual	1	6.18	4.85	1.025	1.050	19.0	10	23.98	21.15	1.000*	1.001*	10.7

*Changing in final (tenth) year.

Table 5.2

Summary statistics for five percent price disturbance with low price elasticities and fast trade adjustment, various rates and frequencies of glide; speculators' expectations regressive to equilibrium.

		Five percent glide						Ten percent glide				
		Variability		Final values				Variability		Final values		
Frequency	Parity changes	Export volume	Reserve changes	Parity	Market rate	Reserves	Parity changes	Export volume	Reserve changes	Parity	Market rate	Reserves
Moving average of equilibrium rate												
Monthly	8	0.78	4.56	1.033	1.050	18.9	4	0.82	4.81	1.033	1.050	19.0
Semiannual	2	1.03	4.45	1.050	1.050	19.2	1	1.25	4.15	1.050	1.050	19.4
Moving average of market rate												
Monthly	8	1.96	7.53	1.033	1.050	17.9	4	1.60	7.37	1.033	1.050	18.1
Semiannual	2	0.76	5.74	1.050	1.050	18.9	1	0.79	5.73	1.050	1.050	18.9
Amended reserve level												
Monthly	19	4.79	11.38	1.079	1.052	18.2*	10	6.10	13.25	1.083	1.056	22.0*
Semiannual	7	10.16	20.67	1.025	1.050	23.0	8	15.41	47.27	1.000*	1.025*	19.1*
Amended reserve change												
Monthly	6	4.35	9.06	1.025	1.050	15.6	3	2.28	6.79	1.025	1.050	17.6
Semiannual	1	0.96	4.52	1.025	1.050	19.1	1	1.25	4.15	1.050	1.050	19.4
Basic balance												
Monthly	8	7.05	12.35	1.033	1.050	14.5	8	7.05	12.35	1.067	1.050	14.5
Semiannual	2	7.05	12.35	1.050	1.050	14.5	2	16.31	28.53	1.100	1.072	32.7*

*Changing in final (tenth) year.

instability and to fluctuations in reserves. The effects of widening the band depend directly on the speed of the glide. When it is limited to five percent, a wider band amplifies enormously the instability of export volume, but precludes any change in reserves. When it is limited to ten percent, the wider band has similar effects on export volume, but no consistent impact on reserves.[40] Finally, note that two of these simulations have not settled down after a decade; the only ones to do so consistently are those that combine monthly parity changes with a narrow band.

(3) *Glides based on the level of reserves.* Here, there are large changes in outcomes under both modes of speculation. A faster glide, for instance, destabilizes export volume and augments the movements of reserves. A reduction in the frequency of parity changes has the same effect on reserves but does not have a uniform effect on trade volume. With a doubling of the band, the market rate behaves as though it were flexible, and there are no changes in reserves to mandate parity changes. Finally, the system comes to rest in only two of the simulations shown in the tables.

(4) *Glides based on changes in reserves.* Here, again, we find certain interactions, but none of them is strong. When, for example, parity changes take place monthly, faster glides stabilize export volume and reserves. When changes take place twice a year, however, faster glides *destabilize* export volume (and when expectations are regressive to parity, lead also to larger fluctuations in reserves). The effect of limiting frequency is less uniform, taken by itself. It stabilizes export volume in three pairs of simulations but is destabilizing in the fourth, and leads to larger movements of reserves under expectations regressive to parity. A doubling of the band diminishes export variability in some experiments and, as usual, conserves reserves.

(5) *Glides based on the basic balance.* These experiments behave much like those based on the market rate. There are large changes in export performance and in the variability of reserves, and some permutations interact strongly. When, for instance, expectations are regressive to equilibrium, three of the four simulations are identical (apart from the size of the parity change), but the combination of a fast glide with semiannual parity changes causes a large loss of efficiency. And when expectations are regressive to parity, there are cumulative differences among the simulations. A shift to semiannual parity changes tends to reduce export variability, but a faster glide magnifies it. Here, moreover, the implications of a wider band are larger when the glide is slow than when it is fast; the change in export variability is more pronounced.

To summarize this series of experiments, let us try to answer briefly two broad questions: Which regimes work as well with 'jumping' parities (represented by semiannual changes) as they do with a true glide? And which ones work as well

---

[40]See Appendix C.

with rapid changes (represented by the ten percent glide) as they do with slow changes?

Glides based on the equilibrium rate are quite robust; the results are much the same – and very satisfactory – under every permutation. Glides based on changes in reserves, although inferior absolutely, are not much more sensitive to frequency or speed, but glides based on the market rate and on the basic balance are less satisfactory from the standpoint of stability when parity changes are infrequent or the glide is fast, especially when speculators' expectations are connected to the parity itself. Finally, glides based on the level of reserves are not very sensitive to frequency or speed, but always display the cyclical parity changes that destabilize the market rate and the volume of trade.

6. Stochastic simulations

The several sets of simulations studied heretofore have asked how well the five gliding-parity rules can identify a permanent disturbance and bring about the necessary change in the exchange rate. The simulations studied in this section ask a somewhat different question: Which gliding-parity rules can sort out false signals, and which ones succumb to them, causing unnecessary changes in parity?

To investigate this question, I have run several groups of simulations, each of them containing 20 ten-year runs in which the home price index, $PH(I)$, is bombarded by monthly disturbances defined by eq. (5), the stochastic variant of the disturbance series.[41] Each run uses the same set of parameters (low elasticities, fast adjustment, and speculation standardized at twenty times export value); each of them employs a narrow band around parity and a five percent monthly glide. But each run uses a different set of random numbers, $DN(I)$, to generate $PH(I)$. The first group of simulations, summarized by table 6.1, examines the behavior of a flexible exchange rate, a pegged rate, and the five gliding parities when expectations are regressive to parity. The second group, summarized by table 6.2, examines their behavior when expectations are regressive to a stochastic counterpart of the comparative-static equilibrium rate.[42]

[41]The large disturbances used by eq. (5) do not realistically describe movements of price indexes. From this point of view, it would be better to experiment with stochastic fluctuations in import volume. But the price disturbances have convenient properties, including the one mentioned in the next note.

[42]A third group is summarized by Appendix D. It examines the behavior of the gliding-parity rules when expectations are regressive to a non-stochastic equilibrium rate. The difference between the two equilibrium rates crudely approximates the difference between ignorance and knowledge of the nature of the price disturbances. The stochastic rate measures the change in the spot rate, $RM(I)$, required to offset exactly the current stochastic value of the price index; its use in the formation of expectations is tantamount to assuming that speculators mistake each random movement in $PH(I)$ for a permanent change and infer that the exchange rate will have to adjust accordingly. The non-stochastic rate is constant (at unity); its use in the formation of expectations is tantamount to assuming that speculators recognize each random movement to be

Table 6.1

Recapitulation of stochastic simulations; speculators' expectations regressive to parity.[a]

Statistics	Flexible rate	Pegged rate	Equilibrium rate[b]	Market rate	Glide based on		
					Reserve level[c]	Reserve change[c]	Basic balance
Parity changes							
Largest number in one run	–	–	60	9	0	1	39
Mean number in one run	–	–	47	1	0	0	19
Number of runs with none	–	–	0	12	20	15	0
Largest high–low spread	–	–	0.050	0.021	–	0.004	0.063
Mean high–low spread	–	–	0.036	0.004	–	0.001	0.032
Market rate							
Highest maximum rate	1.028	1.025	1.055	1.042	**	1.029	1.067
Lowest minimum rate	0.971	0.975	0.947	0.959	**	0.971	0.950
Largest high–low spread	0.051	0.050	0.096	0.065	**	0.050	0.112
Mean high–low spread	0.035	0.034	0.073	0.037	**	0.035	0.067
Changes in reserves							
Largest variability	–	1.91	4.17	4.12	**	1.83	8.25
Mean variability	–	0.32	0.70	0.50	**	0.31	2.32
Changes in export volume							
Largest variability	22.49	22.46	25.22	22.57	**	22.59	25.72
Mean variability	15.50	15.48	17.35	15.75	**	15.52	18.27

[a]Summary of 20 ten-year simulations using five percent monthly glides.
[b]Using stochastic equilibrium rate.
[c]Amended.
**Identical to pegged-rate case.

Before drawing conclusions from the statistics in these tables, a word on an analytical ambiguity in the question posed above. What do we mean by an 'unnecessary' change in parity? To see how elusive this notion can be, suppose that there were a large stochastic change in the level of home prices, too large to be offset by a movement in the market rate without a change in parity to shift the band. Because the price change would be temporary, there would be no cause for a permanent change in the exchange rate. But if there were no change in the exchange rate, or if it were contained by the band, there would be a large change in export volume after a few months. Export orders would respond to the imperfect synchronization of the home price index and the spot exchange rate. Actual export volume would differ from equilibrium volume, and an exchange-rate regime that refused to signal parity changes would display considerable export variability.[43]

The ambiguity shows up most clearly in table 6.2, where speculators are made to believe that the market rate must follow every movement in home prices, so that random variations in $PH(I)$ cause large fluctuations in the market rate under flexible exchange rates. Although the pegged-rate regime limits these fluctuations, it leads to much more variability in export volume; so do the gliding-parity rules that cause the fewest parity changes. In this instance, moreover, it is hard to find regimes that sort out noise completely; all regimes signal parity changes from time to time, and the statistics on export volume are quite similar across regimes, whether we look at largest values or at averages.

Two regimes, however, have special characteristics. The glide based on the equilibrium rate signals the largest number of parity changes (and signals them in every run), and it tends to cause cumulative parity changes; the spread between the highest and lowest parities obtained in a single run is larger on average than for other regimes. Furthermore, the changes are ill-timed from the standpoint of stability. There is more variability in export volume than with pegged exchange rates, and reserves are more volatile. The glide based on the level of reserves is not much better. Although it does not cause as many parity changes

temporary and infer that the exchange rate will have to return to its long-term stationary level. Similarly, the use of a stochastic rate in the gliding-parity rule based on the equilibrium rate implies that the central bank cannot sort out noise. The use of a non-stochastic rate implies that it can, and declines to make any parity change in response to variations in $PH(I)$. (The results in Appendix D are identical to those for pegged rates in table 6.1.) It is especially important to note that these two equilibrium rates have the same implications for the measurement of $FXQ(I)$, used in the index of export variability, provided we apply concepts consistently. To define $FXQ(I)$ stochastically, one must use the stochastic level of home prices and the stochastic equilibrium rate. The latter will offset the former exactly, and $FXQ(I)$ will be constant at its initial level. To define $FXQ(I)$ non-stochastically, one must use the non-stochastic level of prices and the non-stochastic equilibrium rate. Each of these is constant (at unity) and $FXQ(I)$ is also constant at its initial level. Hence, differences between the indexes of export variability in tables 6.1 and 6.2, on the one hand, and Appendix D, on the other, are due entirely to differences in actual export volume, not to differences in comparative-static levels.

[43]If, of course, traders were not myopic, but based their export and import orders on the *expected* terms of trade, this ambiguity would disappear.

Table 6.2

Recapitulation of stochastic simulations; speculators' expectations regressive to a stochastic equilibrium rate.[a]

Statistics	Flexible rate	Pegged rate	Glide based on				
			Equilibrium rate[b]	Market rate	Reserve level[c]	Reserve change[c]	Basic balance
Parity changes							
Largest number in one run	–	–	60	8	21	27	8
Mean number in one run	–	–	47	3	10	12	1
Number of runs with none	–	–	0	3	2	0	11
Largest high–low spread	–	–	0.050	0.021	0.063	0.025	0.021
Mean high–low spread	–	–	0.036	0.008	0.025	0.015	0.004
Market rate							
Highest maximum rate	1.094	1.025	1.042	1.046	1.055	1.038	1.038
Lowest minimum rate	0.910	0.975	0.954	0.959	0.947	0.959	0.963
Largest high–low spread	0.169	0.050	0.075	0.071	0.088	0.066	0.071
Mean high–low spread	0.134	0.050	0.065	0.056	0.069	0.059	0.054
Changes in reserves							
Largest variability	–	95.81	111.54	97.65	100.66	96.79	96.55
Mean variability	–	58.47	69.20	59.05	62.38	59.78	58.77
Changes in export volume							
Largest variability	6.39	16.31	17.02	15.63	17.35	14.27	16.08
Mean variability	5.19	10.90	11.02	11.05	12.14	10.41	11.00

[a]Summary of 20 ten-year simulations using five percent monthly glides.
[b]Using stochastic equilibrium rate.
[c]Amended.

(and does not cause them in all runs), the changes are cumulative once again. They spread the high and low parities and cause much instability. The glides based on the equilibrium rate cause cumulative parity changes because they employ a stochastic form of that rate.[44] The glides based on the level of reserves cause cumulative changes because a single change can never reverse the direction in which the stock is moving.

Each of the other gliding-parity rules mandates a number of parity changes in table 6.2 and, apart from the one that uses the basic balance, does so in a majority of the stochastic runs. But these rules do not cause cumulative changes. The spread between high and low parities is small, and the average range of changes in the market rate is similar to what it would be under pegged exchange rates.

The outcomes in table 6.1 are quite different from those in table 6.2. Because speculation tends to stabilize the market rate, it causes smaller spreads under flexibility and less variation in reserves under pegged exchange rates.[45] The stabilization of reserves, moreover, means that the reserve-based glides cannot give strong signals. Those that are based on the level of reserves do not cause a single parity change in table 6.1, while those that are based on the flow cause only one revaluation or devaluation in each of five stochastic runs.

Consider, however, the other regimes. Glides based on the stochastic equilibrium rate signal large numbers of parity changes, destabilizing export volume and producing movements of reserves larger than those that occur with pegged rates. Glides based on the market rate mandate parity changes in twelve of twenty runs, but the spreads between the high and low parities are fairly small. (The outcomes for this regime are similar in the two tables.) But glides based on the basic balance behave very badly in table 6.1, compared to their performance in table 6.2 and to other gliding-parity regimes.

To sum up, the equilibrium-rate rule is inferior to pegged exchange rates if the central bank is unable to identify pure noise; when, as in these tables, the glides are based on a stochastic equilibrium rate, parity changes occur in every run, export variability is very large, and there are big movements in reserves. The reserve-level rule is robust when the stochastic variations in prices are sufficiently diffuse to prevent cumulative changes in reserves, as in table 6.1, but once there is enough change in the stock of reserves to trigger a single parity change, the rule begins to misbehave.[46] The basic-balance rule is not satis-

[44]Contrast these results with those obtained in Appendix D, using the non-stochastic equilibrium rate.

[45]There is, of course, more variability in export volume, since the stabilization of the market rate causes it to differ from the index of home prices, changing the terms of trade and altering export orders.

[46]This characteristic of the reserve-level rule showed up strikingly in an additional set of simulations. The stochastic price index was redefined as a random walk,

$$PR(I) = PR(I-1) + V \cdot DN(I).$$

In comparisons like those made by table 6.1, table 6.2, and Appendix D, the reserve-level rule caused the largest or second-largest spread in the parity, and when expectations were regressive to parity, caused the largest variability in export volume.

factory in any instance. There are numerous changes in parity, and they tend to be destabilizing. Exports and reserves are very volatile in both tables. The remaining rules, by contrast, sort out noise more consistently. There are several parity changes in table 6.2, but they do not cumulate, and there are very few parity changes in table 6.1.

7. Conclusions

It is difficult to summarize a survey of so many simulations, but we can extract several regularities. Looking back across the non-stochastic simulations, the glide based on the equilibrium rate seems to be the best from every point of view – better even than full flexibility. At the opposite extreme, the glide based on the level of reserves is the worst from many standpoints.

Yet the best gliding-parity rule might not work well in practice. It does not employ an 'objective' indicator – one that can be measured precisely and promptly. It relies instead on a first approximation to an accurate official assessment of long-term trends in trade and payments (which is why it performs inefficiently in some stochastic runs).[47] Let us therefore set this rule aside, and conclude with a brief comparison of the three 'objective' indicators that are neither best nor worst – the six-month moving average of spot exchange rates, the amended reserve change, and the basic balance.

There are, of course, a number of practical objections to each of these three indicators.[48] Market rates, for example, are easy to measure; they cannot be falsified or concealed. There might be much debate, however, concerning the choice of numeraire in a real world with many currencies. And it could be difficult to prevent manipulation by official intervention in the foreign-exchange market. A central bank determined to postpone a devaluation might buy its home currency while the spot rate remained within its band, forestalling a change in the average of market rates and silencing the indicator. The use of changes in reserves would not lead to this result; a central bank that supported the spot rate would lose reserves more rapidly, evoking an earlier signal to devalue. But changes in reserves are not easy to measure when, as now, governments are free to hold many assets, and they can be hidden temporarily by swapping currency balances with the commercial banks – at home or in the Eurocurrency market. The

---

[47] The comparative-static equilibrium rate is identical to the home price index $PH(I)$ in all but one of the simulations studied here (the one in which the system was disturbed by an autonomous change in import volume). Hence, the gliding-parity rule based on the equilibrium rate could be viewed as a proxy for a rule based on movements in national prices. [Rules of this type are discussed in International Monetary Fund (1974).] Remember, however, that it does not serve this additional purpose anent disturbances afflicting trade and that it by-passes all of the serious problems one would encounter when trying to choose appropriate indexes of national prices. There are no non-traded goods in this model.

[48] For more on these issues, see Cooper (1970) and International Monetary Fund (1974). Cooper favors reserve changes, rather than averages of market rates, on the basis of these practical considerations (especially the fact that many large transactions, official and private, are negotiated outside the spot market and could not affect an average of market rates).

problem' of measurement, however, is truly formidable when we come to the basic balance. Even the countries that report it do not define it identically (because they use different definitions of long- and short-term capital movements). Furthermore, the data needed to compute it, on any definition that might be negotiated, are not available promptly, let alone monthly.

But let us limit this final comparison to the characteristics studied in this paper, using the summary of non-stochastic simulations supplied by table 7. There, I rank the three 'objective' indicators against each other and against a

Table 7

Rankings by stability of export volume, selected non-stochastic simulations.

| | | Glide based on | | |
Simulation	Flexible rate	Market rate	Reserve change	Basic balance
Expectations regressive to parity				
Low elasticities and fast trade adjustment				
Five percent monthly glide	2	4	3	1
Five percent semiannual glide	3	4	2	1
Ten percent monthly glide	2	3	1	4
Ten percent semiannual glide	1	4	2	3
High elasticities and slow trade adjustment				
Five percent monthly glide	1	3	2	4
Expectations regressive to equilibrium				
Low elasticities and fast trade adjustment				
Five percent monthly glide	2	1	3	4
Five percent semiannual glide	3	1	2	4
Ten percent monthly glide	3	1	2	4
Ten percent semiannual glide	3	1	2	4
High elasticities and slow trade adjustment				
Five percent monthly glide	3	1	2	4

fully flexible exchange rate according to their power to stabilize export volume. Three facts emerge from the comparison: (1) Some gliding parities are more efficient than full flexibility, especially when expectations are regressive to equilibrium – the only profitable mode of speculation. (2) The glide based on the basic balance does very badly under one mode of speculation, and when the glide is fast, under the other mode as well. (3) The choice between a glide based on the market rate and one based on changes in reserves must depend on whether we seek to obtain the most efficient performance under the most favorable circumstances (mode of speculation, speed of trade adjustment, and way in which the glide takes place) or whether we seek to guard against the worst performance under the least favorable circumstances. The moving average of market rates is more efficient when expectations are regressive to equilibrium (better in this circumstance than flexibility), but falls to third or fourth place when expectations are regressive to parity. The change in reserves is never in last place and does better than the glide based on the market rate when, with expectations regressive to parity, parity changes take place infrequently.

There are many essential dimensions to the choice among exchange-rate regimes. The tests run here, however, narrow the choice and, in my opinion, give good marks to an indicator based on changes in reserves.

References

Baumol, W.J., 1957, Speculation, profitability, and stability, Review of Economics and Statistics 39, 263–271.

Bergsten, C.F., 1972, Reforming the dollar (Council on Foreign Relations, New York).

Black, S.W., 1972, The use of rational expectations in models of speculation, Review of Economics and Statistics 54, 161–165.

Britton, A.J.C., 1970, The dynamic stability of the foreign-exchange market, Economic Journal 80, 91–96.

Cooper, R.N., 1970, Sliding parities, A proposal for presumptive rules, in: G.N. Halm, ed., Approaches to greater flexibility of exchange rates (Princeton University Press, Princeton) 251–259.

Friedman, M., 1953, The case for flexible exchange rates, in: M. Friedman, Essays in positive economics (University of Chicago Press, Chicago) 157–203.

Grubel, H.G., 1965, Profits from forward exchange speculation, Quarterly Journal of Economics 79, 248–262.

Halm, G.N., 1970, Toward limited flexibility of exchange rates, in: G.N. Halm, ed., Approaches to greater flexibility of exchange rates (Princeton University Press, Princeton) 3–26.

Hettich, J.C., 1974, Speculation and stability in the foreign exchange market, unpublished senior thesis (Princeton University, Princeton).

Hinshaw, R., 1971, The economics of international adjustment (Johns Hopkins University Press, Baltimore).

International Monetary Fund, 1974, International monetary reform, Documents of the Committee of Twenty (International Monetary Fund, Washington).

Kenen, P.B., 1974a, Alternative rules for changing exchange rates (International Finance Section, Princeton University, Princeton).

Kenen, P.B., 1974b, A comparison of exchange-rate regimes, Selectivity, profitability, and speculation, Paper prepared for the Conference on International Monetary Economics (University of Paris–Dauphine).

Magee, S.P., 1973, Currency contracts, pass-through, and devaluation, Brookings Papers in Economic Activity 1, 303–323.

Modigliani, F. and P.B. Kenen, 1966, A suggestion for solving the international liquidity problem, Banca Nazionale del Lavoro Quarterly Review 76, 3–17.

Murphy, J.C., 1965, Moderated exchange rate variability, National Banking Review 3, 151–161.

Phillips, A.W., 1954, Stabilisation policy in a closed economy, Economic Journal 64, 290–323.

Telser, L.G., 1959, A theory of speculation relating profitability and stability, Review of Economics and Statistics 41, 295–302.

Underwood, T.G., 1973, Analysis of proposals for using objective indicators as a guide to exchange rate changes, International Monetary Fund Staff Papers 20, 100–117.

United States Treasury, 1973, The U.S. proposal for using reserves as an indicator of the need for balance-of-payments adjustment, in: Economic Report of the President (Government Printing Office, Washington).

Williamson, J., 1973, Another case of profitable destabilising speculation, Journal of International Economics 3, 77–84.

Appendix A
Results with continuous formulations of gliding-parity rules.
(Summary statistics for five percent disturbance, low price elasticities and fast trade adjustment.)

Exchange regime	Parity changes	Parity		Market rate		Reserves		Variability		
		Max	Final	Max	Final	Min	Final	Export volume	Reserve changes	Profit
Speculators' expectations regressive to parity										
Average of equilibrium	78	1.049	1.049	1.060	1.050	19.2	19.2	6.18	2.58	−0.089
Average of market rate	105	1.057	1.051*	1.065	1.048*	16.9	16.9	9.47	6.17	−0.138
Reserve level	100	1.126	1.121*	1.098	1.093*	14.6	23.5*	21.37	17.28	−0.118
Reserve change	53	1.021	1.021	1.047	1.047	13.6	13.6*	9.34	7.78	−0.096
Basic balance	30	1.022	1.022	1.047	1.047	16.5	16.5*	6.77	4.55	−0.080
Speculators' expectations regressive to equilibrium										
Average of equilibrium	78	1.049	1.049	1.050	1.050	17.6	17.6	2.46	7.64	0.016
Average of market rate	87	1.049	1.049	1.050	1.050	17.3	17.3	3.04	8.17	0.017
Reserve level	110	1.095	1.088*	1.067	1.061*	16.2	21.8*	7.99	12.59	0.027
Reserve change	65	1.021	1.021	1.046	1.046	13.3	13.3*	4.83	8.47	0.014
Basic balance	57	1.022	1.022	1.047	1.047	13.0	13.0*	6.27	11.13	0.027
Speculators' expectations adaptive										
Average of equilibrium	78	1.049	1.049	1.068	1.057*	17.8	17.8	9.80	5.57	−0.194
Average of market rate	102	1.055	1.048*	1.065	1.053*	15.8	15.8	9.76	8.43	−0.133
Reserve level	99	1.103	1.097*	1.076	1.070*	15.0	22.3*	14.81	14.29	−0.119
Reserve change	42	1.027	1.027	1.052	1.049*	13.8	13.8	8.43	9.54	−0.084
Basic balance	25	1.023	1.023	1.049	1.049	14.2	14.2*	7.30	8.94	−0.105
Speculators' expectations extrapolative										
	Parity changes ineffective; results resemble flexible-rate solution									
Average of equilibrium	90	1.040	1.049	1.050	1.050	19.7	19.7	8.27	1.28	−0.138
Average of market rate	102	1.086	1.086*	1.059	1.059*	17.0	18.1*	10.36	6.71	−0.198
Reserve level	83	1.021	1.021*	1.046	1.046*	13.8	13.8*	10.63	6.23	−0.120
Reserve change										
Basic balance	Parity changes ineffective; results resemble flexible-rate solution									

*Changing in final (tenth) year.

Appendix B

Results with various price and trade disturbances.
(Variability of reserves.)

Exchange regime	Five percent price disturbance				Ten percent trade disturbance, high elasticities, slow adjustment
	Low price elasticities		High price elasticities		
	Fast adjust	Slow adjust	Fast adjust	Slow adjust	
Speculators' expectations regressive to parity					
Flexible rate	–	–	–	–	–
Pegged rate	18.48ʳ	19.07ʳ	37.50ʳ	37.97ʳ	37.09ʳ
Parity at equilibrium	**	3.16	0.00	2.94ᵐ	2.75ᵐ
Average of equilibrium	0.88	5.43	3.21	8.34ᵐ	7.99
Average of market rate	6.86	11.35ᵖᵐʳ	11.62	16.51ᵐ	16.21ᵐ
Amended reserve level	9.83	14.53ʳ	16.33ʳ	40.09ᵖᵐʳ	39.43ᵐʳ
Amended reserve change	7.86	11.72ᵐ	10.95	16.66ᵐ	16.46ᵐ
Basic balance	5.71	21.00ᵖᵐʳ	9.53ᵖᵐʳ	31.68ᵖᵐʳ	32.45ᵖᵐʳ
Speculators' expectations regressive to equilibrium rate					
Flexible rate	–	–	–	–	–
Pegged rate	21.77ʳ	22.25ʳ	39.10ʳ	38.72ʳ	37.72ʳ
Parity at equilibrium	**	1.02	**	**	**
Average of equilibrium	4.56	6.59	3.78	6.03	6.03
Average of market rate	7.53	9.38	7.80	8.89ᵐ	8.49ᵐ
Amended reserve level	11.38ʳ	13.82ᵖᵐʳ	11.77ʳ	12.71ʳ	11.86ᵐ
Amended reserve change	9.06	10.20	10.35	11.47	10.92ᵐ
Basic balance	12.35	13.91	13.37	13.84ᵐ	13.35ᵐ

ᵖParity changing in final (tenth) year.
ᵐMarket rate changing in final (tenth) year.
ʳReserves changing in final (tenth) year.
**Parity changes ineffective; resembles flexible-rate solution.

Appendix C
Summary of simulations with five percent bands.

| | Export volume | | | | Reserve changes | | | |
| | Five percent glide | | Ten percent glide | | Five percent glide | | Ten percent glide | |
Exchange regime	Monthly	Semiannual	Monthly	Semiannual	Monthly	Semiannual	Monthly	Semiannual
Speculators' expectations regressive to parity								
Average of equilibrium	4.03	(a)	3.66	(a)	0.00	(a)	0.00	(a)
Average of market rate	24.41*	29.95*	46.36*	51.29*	0.00*	0.00*	15.48*	30.34*
Amended reserve level	(b)	(b)	(b)	(b)	(b)	(b)	(b)	(b)
Amended reserve change	(b)	(b)	(b)	(b)	(b)	(b)	(b)	(b)
Basic balance	15.44*	10.12	34.58*	26.45*	0.00*	0.00	0.00*	0.00*
Speculators' expectations regressive to equilibrium								
Average of equilibrium	(b)	(b)	(b)	(b)	(b)	(b)	(b)	(b)
Average of market rate	(b)	(b)	(b)	(b)	(b)	(b)	(b)	(b)
Amended reserve level	(b)	(b)	(b)	(b)	(b)	(b)	(b)	(b)
Amended reserve change	1.66	1.66	1.66	1.66	3.39	3.39	3.39	3.39
Basic balance	(b)	(b)	(b)	(b)	(b)	(b)	(b)	(b)

[a] Results identical to those for corresponding simulation with 2.5 percent band.
[b] Results identical to flexible-rate case (in table 1.1 or 1.2).
* Reserves, market rate, or parity changing in tenth year.

Appendix D

Stochastic simulations when speculators' expectations are regressive to non-stochastic equilibrium rate.[a]

Statistics	Equilibrium rate[b]	Market rate	Reserve level[c]	Reserve change[c]	Basic balance
Parity changes					
Largest number in one run	0	2	0	1	22
Mean number in one run	0	1	0	0	10
Number of runs with none	20	12	20	15	0
Largest high–low spread	–	0.008	–	0.004	0.033
Mean high–low spread	–	0.002	–	0.001	0.022
Market rate					
Highest maximum value	**	1.025	**	1.025	1.028
Lowest minimum value	**	0.971	**	0.974	0.971
Largest high–low spread	**	0.048	**	0.050	0.051
Mean high–low spread	**	0.035	**	0.034	0.035
Changes in reserves					
Largest variability	**	2.10	**	1.66	6.33
Mean variability	**	0.27	**	0.31	0.92
Changes in export volume					
Largest variability	**	22.46	**	22.46	22.39
Mean variability	**	15.49	**	15.48	15.50

[a]Summary of 20 ten-year simulations using five percent monthly glides.
[b]Using non-stochastic equilibrium rate.
[c]Amended.
**Identical to pegged-exchange-rate case in table 6.1. All outcomes for flexible and pegged rates are identical to those in table 6.1 (because the non-stochastic equilibrium rate is unity and, therefore, identical to the notional or fixed parity used by those regimes).

Portfolio Adjustment in Open Economies:
A Comparison of Alternative Specifications

Polly Reynolds Allen and Peter B. Kenen

Contents: Introduction. — I. The Basic Model. — II. The Market-Clearing Equations. — III. The Closed Economy. — IV. The Open Economy with Flexible Exchange Rates and No Capital Mobility. — V. The Open Economy with Flexible Exchange Rates and Perfect Capital Mobility. — VI. The Open Economy with Pegged Exchange Rates and No Capital Mobility. — VII. The Open Economy with Pegged Exchange Rates and Perfect Capital Mobility. — VIII. Summary and Conclusions.

Introduction

This paper compares two ways to describe the adjustment of money and bond holdings in simple models of open economies. Our concern with this problem arises from our search for a convenient way to specify the process of adjustment in a large multi-country model we are building to study financial integration and from our desire to compare the results obtained in several recent papers dealing with the theory of economic policy under fixed and flexible exchange rates, with and without capital mobility[1]. These papers have a common aim — to marry Mundell's well-known conclusions regarding fiscal and monetary

Remark: This paper derives from the authors' current work on the theory of international financial integration. It has benefitted from discussions with our colleagues, Alan Blinder, William Branson, Martin Hellwig, Dwight Jaffee, and Lars Nyberg, from presentations by Rudi Dornbusch and Pentti Kouri in the Research Seminar on International Economics at Princeton University and from comments at seminars at the University of Chicago and Rutgers University. We are grateful to the International Finance Section and to the Ford Foundation's Research Program on International Economic Order for support of this research.

[1] See, e.g., William H. Branson, "Stocks and Flows International Monetary Analysis", in: *International Aspects of Stabilization Policies*, Ed. by A. Ando, R. Herring, and R. Marston, Federal Reserve Bank of Boston, Conference Series No. 12, Boston, 1974. — Rüdiger Dornbusch, "A Portfolio Balance Model of the Open Economy", *Journal of Monetary Economics*, Vol. 1. Amsterdam, 1975, pp. 3 sqq. — For surveys of earlier work on the problem see: Johan Myhrman, "Balance of Payments Adjustment and Portfolio Theory: A Survey", in: *Recent Issues in International Monetary Economics*, Ed. by E. Claassen and P. Salin, Amsterdam, 1975; Zoran Hodjera, "International Short-Term Capital Movements: A Survey of Theory and Empirical Analysis", IMF, *Staff Papers*, Vol. 20, Washington, D.C., 1973, pp. 683 sqq.; Marina von Neumann Whitman, *Policies for Internal and External Balance*, International Finance Section, Special Papers in International Economics, No. 9, Princeton, N.J., 1970.

policies[1] with the "new view" of capital movements as by-products of portfolio adjustments. Comparisons are not easy, as the contributors to this common aim have adopted different views of the way in which portfolios are altered.

Our immediate objective is methodological — to show how and why the process of adjustment affects results obtained regarding the effectiveness of economic policies. Our findings, however, have broader implications for the interpretation of continuous-time models and of the distinction between short and long runs in a variety of macroeconomic models[2]. Our method is to study two specifications imbedded in a single model of a small open economy. In one version of that model, holders of financial assets alter their portfolios instantaneously. Shifts between money and bonds take place before there can be any change in the size of wealth holders' total portfolios (before there can be any saving or dissaving). We call this the stock version[3]. In the other version of the model, asset holders alter their portfolios gradually. The rates at which they do so depend on the sizes of discrepancies between desired and actual holdings of individual assets. We call this the flow version[4].

I. The Basic Model

The model we employ to study these specifications resembles one developed in Kenen's paper[5]. It is a Keynesian description of a small open

---

[1] The relevant papers are reprinted in Robert A. Mundell, *International Economics*, New York, London, 1968.

[2] Some of these issues are discussed by: Josef May, "Period Analysis and Continuous Analysis in Patinkin's Macroeconomic Model", *Journal of Economic Theory*, Vol. 2, New York and London, 1970, pp. 1 sqq.; Duncan K. Foley, "On Two Specifications of Asset Equilibrium in Macroeconomic Models", *The Journal of Political Economy*, Vol. 83, Chicago, Ill., 1975, pp. 303 sqq.; M. F. Hellwig, "The Demand for Money and Bonds in Continuous Time Models", *Journal of Economic Theory*, forthcoming.

[3] This model and its uses are described in P. R. Allen, *A Suggested Formulation for Open Economy Portfolio Models*, International Finance Section Research Memorandum, Princeton, N. J., 1975, mimeo. — Similar models have been used by Alan S. Blinder and Robert M. Solow, "Does Fiscal Policy Matter?", *Journal of Public Economics*, Vol. 2, Amsterdam, 1973, pp. 319 sqq.; Duncan K. Foley and Miguel Sidrauski, *Monetary and Fiscal Policy in a Growing Economy*, Macmillan Series in Economics, New York, London, 1971.

[4] For a more complete presentation, see P. B. Kenen, *A Portfolio Model of Payments Adjustment with Four Financial Assets*, International Finance Section Working Paper G-75-01, Princeton, N. J., 1975, mimeo.

[5] The more elaborate version studied there has fractional-reserve commercial banking, a simple form of capital formation, and an additional bond denominated in foreign currency. Furthermore, the bonds are consols with variable prices, introducing capital gains and losses as an additional cause for differences between desired and actual wealth. But the specification of policy changes is less satisfactory.

economy in which the prices of all goods are fixed (at unity), so that the domestic arguments can be measured in units of home output. The principal arguments are:

B	the stock of government bonds (bills) measured at face value;
B^h, B^f, B^c	government bonds held by households, foreigners, and the central bank, respectively;
L	the stock of money;
W^h, W^c	the wealth (net worth) of households, and the central bank, respectively;
S^h	saving by households;
Y	national income (output) at factor cost;
Y^d	the disposable (after-tax) income of households;
G	government expenditure on home goods;
T^h, T^f	net transfers to (+) government from households and foreigners, respectively;
X	the volume of exports;
M	the volume of imports in units of foreign output;
R	the stock of external reserves in units of foreign output;
π	the price of foreign currency (exchange rate);
r	the interest rate on government bonds.

Variables with asterisks are desired stocks; thus, $*W^h$ is the stock of wealth desired by households. Variables with hats are desired flows; thus, $\hat{S}^h$ is saving desired by households. Variables with dots are actual flows; thus, $\dot{R}$ is the rate of change of reserves. Differentials like δR denote instantaneous changes, including changes in certain policies and in demand conditions. Differentials like dR denote long-run comparative-static changes — movements from one full-scale equilibrium to another. Finally, equations numbered "a" apply only in the stock version of the model, while those numbered "b" apply only in the flow version.

Households are deemed to lodge their wealth in money and bonds, and they are the only holders of money. Their balance sheet is:

$$W^h = L + B^h \tag{1.1}$$

As neither asset can vary in price, saving is the sole cause of changes in wealth:

$$\dot{W}^h = S^h \tag{1.2}$$

3*

Desired wealth depends on the interest rate and disposable income:

$$*W^h = W (r, Y^d), W_r > 0, W_y > 0, \qquad (1.3)$$

where

$$Y^d = Y + r B^h - T^h. \qquad (1.4)$$

Desired saving, the planned change in wealth, depends on the difference between desired and actual wealth, even in the stock version of the model:

$$\hat{S}^h = \lambda^s (*W^h - W^h), 0 < \lambda^s < (1/W_y), \qquad (1.5)$$

so that the marginal propensity to save, $\lambda^s W_y$, is smaller than unity.

There are at least three ways to write the households' demand for money — as a function of disposable income, Y^d, factor income, Y, or total household income $(Y + r B^h)$. We have chosen factor income[1]:

$$*L = L (r, Y), L_r < 0, L_y > 0. \qquad (1.6)$$

This equation, however, does not play the same role in the stock and flow versions. In the stock version, demands for stocks of money and bonds define the desired allocation of *actual* wealth:

$$W^h = *L + *B^h. \qquad (1.7a)$$

By implication, equation (1.6) describes the market demand for money, and equation (1.7a) describes the market demand for bonds. In the flow version, by contrast, demands for stocks of money and bonds define the intended allocation of *desired* wealth:

$$*W^h = *L + *B^h. \qquad (1.7b)$$

The market demands for money and bonds are flow demands. They describe the intended allocation of current saving between money and bonds. The flow demand for money is:

$$\hat{L} = \lambda^h (*L - L), 0 < \lambda^h < \infty, \qquad (1.8b)$$

---

[1] Selected results involving the use of disposable income are given in subsequent notes. There are important differences in the short-run effects of budget deficits and in the short- and long-run effects of balanced-budget changes in government expenditure. Notice that equation (1.6) contains an element of money illusion. The demand for money is invariant with respect to changes in the home-currency price of imports. This is why the model will not replicate results obtained by Dornbusch, *op. cit.*, and others concerning the real-balance effects of changes in exchange rates.

and the flow demand for bonds is:

$$\hat{B}^h = \hat{S}^h - \hat{L}.$$ (1.9b)

Equations (1.6) through (1.9b) highlight the difference between the stock and flow specifications. In the flow version, desired saving constrains the desired rates of asset accumulation. Thus, an increase of income, while increasing the flow demand for money, also increases desired saving, and if its effect on saving exceeds its effect on the flow demand for money, as assumed later in this paper, it will increase the flow demand for bonds. In the stock version, the level of actual wealth constrains desired asset composition. Here, too, an increase of income will increase desired saving and the demand for money, but because its effect on the latter is instantaneous, there has to be an equal decrease in the stock demand for bonds; the income derivative of $*B^h$ is equal to $-L_y$ [1]. The stock version is built upon the implicit supposition that households partition decisions to save from decisions regarding the allocation of actual wealth.

Although money is held only by households, bonds may be held by households, foreigners, and the central bank. Therefore:

$$B = B^h + B^f + B^c.$$ (1.10)

The stock of money is issued by the central bank. Its balance sheet is:

$$W^c + L = B^c + \pi R.$$ (1.11)

The income of the central bank is $r\,B^c$, and all of it goes to the government. By implication, the central bank does not save, and its wealth can be

[1] For more on this feature of stock models, see May, *op. cit.*; Foley, *op. cit.*; Hellwig, *op. cit.* Hellwig's comments are especially germane. The assertion that $L_y > 0$, he reminds us, is obtained from the theory of the transactions demand for cash, a theory that postulates nontrivial transactions costs. But the notion of instantaneous adjustment used in the stock model is not readily reconciled with the existence of transactions costs. "Therefore," Hellwig says, "there is no presumption in this type of model that the demand for money is increasing in income, if indeed it is possible to justify the existence of the demand for money at all." The flow model used here may be deemed to take implicit cognizance of transactions costs. Furthermore, it may be more readily regarded as a continuous approximation to a discrete (difference-equation) model in which there would be an inventory-theoretic demand for cash balances. The stock version, by contrast, treats money as a riskless portfolio asset. This, in turn, suggests that the demand for money might be more appropriately specified in that version as a function of wealth rather than income. We retain the income specification for purposes of comparability between the two versions.

written as the integral of capital gains resulting from changes in the exchange rate:

$$W^c = \int_0^T R \, \dot{\pi} \, dt, \qquad\qquad (1.12)$$

where R and $\dot{\pi}$ are regarded as functions of time.

The central bank alters B^c by open-market operations in the bond market. These are designed to influence the stock of money. We can therefore suppose that the central bank has a target, $*B^c$, and conducts its open-market operations to achieve that target. But if the bank purchased or sold bonds in ways that were not consonant with the manner in which other bond holders adjusted their portfolios, it could have a disruptive or explosive impact on income and the interest rate. It has therefore to behave in the same manner as all other holders. In the stock version, of course, it can achieve instantaneous changes in $*B^c$ because other holders behave this way. Therefore:

$$\delta \, *B^c = d \, *B^c = dB^c. \qquad\qquad (1.13a)$$

But in the flow version, where other holders adjust their portfolios gradually, the central bank has also to operate gradually when working to achieve a change in its target. It must regulate its open-market purchases and sales according to a flow target, $\hat{B}^c$, such that

$$\dot{B}^c = \hat{B}^c, \qquad\qquad (1.13b)$$

and

$$d \, *B^c = dB^c = \int_0^{T'} \hat{B}^c \, dt, \ T' < T. \qquad\qquad (1.14b)$$

It must conduct its open-market operations, $\dot{B}^c$, at a rate, $\hat{B}^c$, and for an interval, 0 to T', chosen jointly to guarantee that the cumulative change in its bond holdings equals the desired change.

The central bank alters R by open-market operations (intervention) in the foreign-exchange market, but R is not exogenous. When the exchange rate is pegged, the volume of intervention depends on the evolution of the balance of payments:

$$\pi \dot{R} = (X - \pi M) + (T^f - r \, B^f) + \dot{B}^f. \qquad\qquad (1.15)$$

When the exchange rate is perfectly flexible, there is no intervention.

The government has no net worth, but its total payments and receipts define the rate at which the stock of bonds is changing:

$$\dot{B} = (G + rB) - (T^f + T^h + rB^c).$$ (1.16)

Government spending is policy-determined:

$$G = \hat{G}.$$ (1.17)

The transfers T^f and T^h are governed by special assumptions. First, we assume that the government adjusts transfers from foreigners to offset exactly the interest paid to foreigners, so that

$$T^f = r\, B^f.$$ (1.18)

Second, we assume that the government adjusts transfers from households (taxes) to achieve a policy-determined budget surplus or deficit, $\hat{B}$,[1] so that

$$\dot{B} = \hat{B},$$ (1.19)

and from equations (1.10), (1.16), and (1.18),

$$T^h = \hat{G} - \hat{B} + r\, B^h.$$ (1.16')

As in the case of open-market operations, moreover, we may suppose that the government regulates $\hat{B}$ in a fashion consonant with a stock target, *B, such that

$$d*B = dB = \int_0^{T''} \hat{B}\, dt, \ T'' < T.$$ (1.20)

It runs a deficit or surplus $\dot{B}$, at a rate, $\hat{B}$, and for an interval, 0 to T'', chosen jointly to guarantee that the total change in the stock of bonds equals the desired change[2].

[1] This assumption is similar to the one used by Foley and Sidrauski, *op. cit.*

[2] One is tempted to draw the same distinction here that was used in connection with open-market operations — to suppose that there can be an instantaneous increase of debt, δB, in the stock version, just as there was an instantaneous change of central-bank bond holdings, $\delta*B^c$. It must be remembered, however, that an issue of government bonds involves an increase in the stock of a particular asset and, simultaneously, an increase in household wealth. The latter does not take place instantaneously. It is accomplished by altering T^h, the rate at which households make transfers to the government, and T^h is a flow. These two

Our assumptions concerning T^h and T^f allow us to rewrite disposable income and the balance of payments:

$$Y^d = Y - \hat{G} + \hat{B}, \tag{1.4'}$$

$$\pi \dot{R} = X - \pi M + \dot{B}^f. \tag{1.15'}$$

The foreign demand for exports will be written as

$$\hat{X} = X\left(\frac{1}{\pi}\right), X_{\frac{1}{\pi}} < 0. \tag{1.21}$$

The domestic demand for imports will be written as

$$\hat{M} = M(\pi, Y), M_\pi < 0, M_y > 0. \tag{1.22}$$

II. The Market-Clearing Equations

In stock and flow versions alike, all markets are assumed to clear at all times. And because we are dealing with a small country, the demand for imports is always satisfied. We have therefore to deal with only four markets — those for domestic output, government bonds, money, and foreign exchange. The market-clearing equations for output will be the same in both versions of the model. The equations for bonds, money, and foreign exchange will be different.

The excess demand for goods is written in terms of flows:

$$(Y^d - \hat{S}^h) + \hat{G} + (\hat{X} - \pi \hat{M}) - Y = 0. \tag{2.1}$$

It can be rewritten as

$$-\hat{S}^h + \hat{B} + (\hat{X} - \pi \hat{M}) = -\lambda^s [W(r, Y - \hat{G} + \hat{B})$$

$$- W^h] + \hat{B} + [X\left(\frac{1}{\pi}\right) - \pi M(\pi, Y)] = 0. \tag{2.1'}$$

---

effects of a change in the stock of bonds cannot be represented by supposing that new bonds drop like manna from heaven or, in more recent accounts, like leaflets from a helicopter. (This is perhaps the place to note that we have neglected one possibility emphasized by some who make frequent use of helicopters — that households view future tax liabilities as negative wealth. If this were true, changes in the stock of bonds would have no net wealth effects; their gross effects would be offset by the permanent increase of taxes required to pay interest on the bonds.)

In the stock version of the model, the markets for bonds and money are cleared when there are no excess stock demands or supplies. Hence, the market-clearing equation for bonds is[1]:

$$B - {^*}B^h - {^*}B^f - {^*}B^c = 0 ,\qquad(2.2\,a)$$

and the market-clearing equation for money is:

$$^*L - L = 0 .\qquad(2.3\,a)$$

These can be rewritten as

$$B - [W^h - L\,(r,\,Y)] - {^*}B^f - {^*}B^c = 0 ,\qquad(2.2\,a')$$

$$L\,(r,\,Y) - L = 0 .\qquad(2.3\,a')$$

There is an implicit stock demand for foreign exchange (which can be deemed to represent the outside world's stock demand for its own currency), but it is not independent of equations (2.2a') and (2.3a'). It has to be satisfied when they are satisfied.

In the flow version of the model, the markets for bonds and money are cleared when there are no excess flow demands or supplies. In the bond market, then,

$$\hat{B} - \hat{B}^h - \hat{B}^f - \hat{B}^c = 0 ,\qquad(2.2\,b)$$

and in the money market,

$$\hat{L} - \dot{L} = 0 .\qquad(2.3\,b)$$

These can be rewritten as

$$\hat{B} - [\hat{S}^h - \hat{L}] - \hat{B}^f - \hat{B}^c = \hat{B} - \lambda^s\,[W\,(r,\,Y - \hat{G} + \hat{B})$$

$$- W^h] + \lambda^h\,[L\,(r,\,Y) - L] - \hat{B}^f - \hat{B}^c = 0 ,\qquad(2.2\,b')$$

$$\lambda^h\,[L\,(r,\,Y) - L] - \dot{L} = 0 .\qquad(2.3\,b')$$

---

[1] Bond equations are written as excess supplies rather than excess demands, because we are working with the interest rate rather than the price of bonds.

There is an implicit flow demand for foreign exchange. It can be obtained by replacing actual with desired flows in the definition of the balance of payments, equation (1.15′) above, but can also be obtained from equations (2.1′), (2.2b′), and (2.3b′). It has to be satisfied when they are satisfied.

To solve these market-clearing equations, we have first to describe conditions in the market for government bonds and in the market for foreign exchange.

The foreign demand for domestic bonds defines the degree of capital mobility. When there is no mobility,

$$*B^f = \hat{B}^f = 0 , \qquad (2.4)$$

and the interest rate adjusts to clear the bond market. When, instead, there is perfect mobility, the foreign demand is perfectly elastic at a fixed interest rate:

$$r = \bar{r} , \qquad (2.5)$$

and foreign holdings of government bonds adjust to clear the market, so that

$$*B^f = B^f, \quad \text{and} \quad \hat{B}^f = \dot{B}^f . \qquad (2.4′)$$

When the exchange rate is fully flexible,

$$R = \dot{R} = 0 , \qquad (2.6)$$

and the exchange rate adjusts to clear the money market. When, instead, the exchange rate is pegged,

$$\pi = \bar{\pi} = 1 , \qquad (2.7)$$

and reserves adjust to clear the market.

Furthermore, equations (2.6) and (2.7) permit us to rewrite equations (1.12) and (1.11). Because $\pi = 1$ whenever $R \neq 0$,

$$W^c = 0 , \qquad (1.12′)$$

$$L = B^c + R = *B^c + R . \qquad (1.11′)$$

Therefore,

$$\dot{L} = \dot{B}^c + \dot{R} = \hat{B}^c + \dot{R} . \qquad (1.11″)$$

Solution of the Stock Model

Using all of these assertions, we can describe the goods, bond, and money markets of the stock version by

$$- \lambda^s \left[W(r, Y - \hat{G} + \hat{B}) - W^h \right] + \hat{B}$$

$$+ \left[X \left(\frac{1}{\pi} \right) - \pi M (\pi, Y) \right] = 0, \qquad (2.1')$$

$$B - W^h + L (r, Y) - B^f - {}^*B^c = 0, \qquad (2.2\,a')$$

$$L (r, Y) - ({}^*B^c + R) = 0. \qquad (2.3\,a'')$$

This system contains three market-clearing variables (Y, r *or* B^f, and π *or* R) and the endogenous stock W^h.[1] The latter, however, changes only gradually and is deemed to be fixed in the short run. Thus, the total derivatives of the market-clearing equations can be written as[2]:

$$
\begin{bmatrix}
- E_y & - \lambda^s W_r & 0 & -1 & 0 \\
L_y & L_r & -1 & 0 & 0 \\
L_y & L_r & 0 & 0 & -1
\end{bmatrix}
\begin{bmatrix}
\delta Y \\
\delta r \\
\delta B^f \\
- e_\pi \, \delta \pi \\
\delta R
\end{bmatrix}
$$

$$
\begin{bmatrix}
- (1 - \lambda^s W_y) & - \lambda^s W_y & 0 & -1 \\
0 & 0 & 1 & 0 \\
0 & 0 & 1 & 0
\end{bmatrix}
\begin{bmatrix}
\delta \hat{B} \\
\delta \hat{G} \\
\delta\, {}^*B^c \\
\delta X^a
\end{bmatrix}
+
\begin{bmatrix}
- \lambda^s & 0 \\
1 & -1 \\
0 & 0
\end{bmatrix}
\begin{bmatrix}
\delta W^h \\
\delta B
\end{bmatrix}
, \qquad (2.8a)
$$

---

[1] One can rewrite the market-clearing equations (2.1') through (2.3a'') as reduced-form functions of W^h, the stock of bonds, the exogenous policy variables, and a taste parameter, X^a:

$$Y = Y (W^h; B, \hat{B}, \hat{G}, {}^*B^c, X^a), \quad \text{and}$$
$$r = r (W^h; \ldots), \text{ or } B^f = B^f (W^h; \ldots), \quad \text{and}$$
$$\pi = \pi (W^h; \ldots), \text{ or } R = R (W^h; \ldots).$$

[2] The exchange rate is set at unity after differentiation. The signs of the elements in the vector on the left-hand side of (2.8a) reflect an implicit pairing of prices, flows, or stocks with individual markets. We assume that the market for goods is cleared by changes in output (income), that the market for bonds is cleared by changes in the price of bonds (the

where

$$E_y = \lambda^s W_y + M_y \, ,$$

$$e_\pi = (X/\pi) \left[- (1/\pi) (X_1/X) - (\pi M/X) \, \pi \, (M_\pi/M) - (\pi M/X) \right] ,$$

so that E_y is the sum of the marginal propensities to save and import, while e_π is the elasticity of the trade balance with respect to the exchange rate (the Marshall-Lerner-Robinson condition), and is assumed to be positive throughout[1].

The elements in the first vector on the right-hand side of (2.8a) denote three simple policies and an exogenous shift in demand. The terms $\delta \hat{B}$ and $\delta \hat{G}$ are fiscal policies (an increase in the government deficit accomplished by reducing taxes and a balanced-budget increase in government expenditure). The term $\delta^* B^c$ is a monetary policy (an instantaneous open-market purchase of government bonds). The shift in demand, δX^a, is a permanent increase in the foreign demand for domestic output. The elements in the second vector denote changes in stocks that occur over time. The term δW^h is a change in household wealth. The term δB is a change in the stock of government bonds (resulting from $\hat{B}$).

The change in wealth over time is described by equation (1.2) above. But this equation can be rewritten. As the market for goods is always cleared by changes in home output, $\hat{S}^h$ cannot differ from S^h, so that

$$\dot{W}^h = \hat{S}^h = \hat{B} + \lfloor X \left(\frac{1}{\pi} \right) - \pi M \, (\pi, Y) \rfloor \, . \tag{1.2'}$$

This is a dynamic equation in W^h, and the necessary and sufficient conditions for the local stability of the stock version is that $(d\dot{W}^h/dW^h) < 0$. When this condition is satisfied, saving will tend to zero and, in the long run, wealth will cease to change. At that point, then,

$$\hat{S}^h = [X \left(\frac{1}{\pi} \right) - \pi M \, (\pi, Y)] = 0 \, . \tag{2.9a}$$

___

reciprocal of the interest rate) or by changes in the stock of bonds held by foreigners, and that the market for money is cleared by changes in the price of money (the reciprocal of the exchange rate) or by changes in the stock of reserves held by the central bank.

[1] The definitions of terms like E_y are collected for convenience in a glossary at the end of the text.

This condition is used below to ascertain the long-run changes in W^h and the corresponding changes in Y, r or B^f, and π or R.[1]

Solution of the Flow Version

The behavior of wealth over time is similar in the flow version, but the structure of that version requires that we study separately the evolution of its components. It will convenient, then, to rewrite the market-clearing equations in terms of B^f and R. Using equations (1.10) and (1.11′), rewrite equation (1.1):

$$W^h = B - B^f + R, \tag{1.1′}$$

and replace W^h wherever it appears:

$$- \lambda^s [W (r, Y - \hat{G} + \hat{B}) - (B - B^f + R)] + \hat{B}$$

$$+ [X \left(\frac{1}{\pi} \right) - \pi M (\pi, Y)] = 0, \tag{2.1″}$$

$$\hat{B} - \lambda^s [W (r, Y - \hat{G} + \hat{B}) - (B - B^f + R)] +$$

$$\lambda^h [L (r, Y) - (B^c + R)] - \dot{B}^f - \hat{B}^c = 0, \tag{2.2b″}$$

$$\lambda^h [L (r, Y) - (B^c + R)] - \dot{R} - \hat{B}^c = 0. \tag{2.3b″}$$

This system contains three market-clearing variables (Y, r or $\dot{B}^f$, and π or $\dot{R}$) and the endogenous stocks B^f and R.[2] These stocks change slowly,

[1] Whenever the government is running a budget deficit or surplus, there is a second dynamic equation:

$$\dot{B} = \hat{B}.$$

Beyond the interval $0 < t < T''$, however, $\hat{B}$ is assumed to be zero, and dB is stationary at d^*B. The same suppositions govern the flow version, along with analogous suppositions concerning open-market operations. In the flow version,

$$\dot{B}^c = \hat{B}^c.$$

Beyond the internal $0 < t < T'$, however, $\hat{B}^c$ is assumed to be zero, and dB^c is stationary at d^*B^c. All of these suppositions are employed to write the long-run equations for the flow version (equations (2.9b) and (2.10b)) below.

[2] Once again, one can write the market-clearing equations as reduced-form functions of stocks, policy variables, and the taste parameter:

$$Y = Y (B^f, R; B, B^c, \hat{B}, \hat{G}, \hat{B}^c, X^a), \text{ and}$$
$$r = r (B^f, R; \ldots), \text{ or } \dot{B}^f = \dot{B}^f (B^f, R; \ldots), \text{ and}$$
$$\pi = \pi (B^f, R; \ldots) \text{ or } \dot{R} = \dot{R} (B^f, R; \ldots).$$

however, and each is deemed to be fixed in the short run. Thus, the total derivatives of the market-clearing equations are[1]:

$$
\begin{bmatrix}
-E_y & -\lambda^s W_r & 0 & -1 & 0 \\
-(\lambda^s W_y - \lambda^h L_y) & -(\lambda^s W_r - \lambda^h L_r) & -1 & 0 & 0 \\
\lambda^h L_y & \lambda^h L_r & 0 & 0 & -1
\end{bmatrix}
\begin{bmatrix}
\delta Y \\
\delta r \\
\delta B^f \\
-e_\pi \, \delta\pi \\
\delta R
\end{bmatrix}
$$

$$
=
\begin{bmatrix}
-(1 - \lambda^s W_y) & -\lambda^s W_y & 0 & -1 \\
-(1 - \lambda^s W_y) & -\lambda^s W_y & 1 & 0 \\
0 & 0 & 1 & 0
\end{bmatrix}
\begin{bmatrix}
\delta\hat{B} \\
\delta\hat{G} \\
\delta\hat{B}^c \\
\delta X^a
\end{bmatrix}
$$

$$
+
\begin{bmatrix}
-\lambda^s & 0 \\
-\lambda^s & \lambda^h \\
0 & \lambda^h
\end{bmatrix}
\begin{bmatrix}
(\delta B - \delta B^f + \delta R) \\
(\delta B^c + \delta R)
\end{bmatrix}.
\qquad (2.8\,b)
$$

The elements in the first vector on the right-hand side refer to the same policies and shift in demand as those in the system (2.8a), but the monetary policy, $\delta\hat{B}^c$, takes the form appropriate to the flow version. The elements in the second vector denote changes in stocks that occur over time.

Changes in the stock B^f occur with capital mobility, reflecting the market-clearing flows $\dot{B}^f$. These flows are defined by equation (2.2b''). Changes in the stock R occur with pegged exchange rates, reflecting the market-clearing flows $\dot{R}$. These flows are defined by equation (2.3b''). Thus, equations (2.2b'') and (2.3b'') serve not only as market-clearing equations, but also as dynamic equations in B^f and R. These can be used to establish the local stability of the flow version — to show that

---

[1] Here, again, the signs of the elements in the vector on the left-hand side reflect an implicit pairing of prices or flows with individual markets. The pairing is analogous to the one employed in connection with (2.8a).

$\dot{B}^f$ and $\dot{R}$ tend to zero[1]. In the long run, then, B^f and R will cease to change (along with wealth itself), so that

$$- \lambda^s \left[W\left(r, Y - \hat{G}\right) - \left(*B - B^f + R\right) \right] + \lambda^h \left[L\left(r, Y\right) \right.$$

$$- \left(*B^c + R\right) \left. \right] = 0 , \tag{2.9b}$$

$$\lambda^h \left[L\left(r, Y\right) - \left(*B^c + R\right) \right] = 0 . \tag{2.10b}$$

These conditions are used below to ascertain the long-run changes in B^f and R and in the remaining market-clearing variables.

III. The Closed Economy

When there is no trade in goods or bonds, all terms and coefficients pertaining to π, R, $\hat{X}$, $\hat{M}$, and B^f drop out of (2.8a) and (2.8b). Furthermore, equation (1.1') asserts that $\delta W^h = \delta B$. Because there is no foreign trade, there can be no saving unless the government runs a budget deficit, and the cumulative increase of wealth has therefore to equal the cumulative deficit. In both versions of the model, moreover, the second (or third) market-clearing equation becomes redundant. The demands for goods, money, and bonds are not independent when there is no way to satisfy an excess demand for goods by running a trade deficit, an excess demand for money by importing reserves, or an excess demand for securities by importing bonds.

Under these circumstances, then, the stock version of the model takes the simple form:

$$\begin{bmatrix} - \lambda^s W_y & - \lambda^s W_r \\ L_y & L_r \end{bmatrix} \begin{bmatrix} \delta Y \\ \delta r \end{bmatrix} = \begin{bmatrix} - (1 - \lambda^s W_y) & - \lambda^s W_y & 0 \\ 0 & 0 & 1 \end{bmatrix} \begin{bmatrix} \delta \hat{B} \\ \delta \hat{G} \\ \delta *B^c \end{bmatrix}$$

$$+ \begin{bmatrix} - \lambda^s \\ 0 \end{bmatrix} [\delta B] . \tag{3.1a}$$

---

[1] With capital mobility and flexible exchange rates, the necessary and sufficient condition for local stability is that $(d\dot{B}^f / dB^f) < 0$; with no capital mobility and pegged exchange rates, it is that $(d\dot{R}/dR) < 0$. With capital mobility and pegged rates, the condition is more complicated; we state and study it below. With no capital mobility and flexible rates (and in the closed economy), $\dot{B}^f = \dot{R} = 0$, and there are no dynamic equations.

The determinant is $\lambda^s H$, where $H = (L_y W_r - L_r W_y) > 0$[1]. The short-run effects on income and the interest rate are shown in the first part of Table 1. An open-market purchase of government bonds increases income and reduces the interest rate. A larger government deficit increases income and raises the interest rate. A balanced-budget increase in government spending has effects similar to those of a larger deficit. The effects of $\delta \hat{G}$ differ from those of $\delta \hat{B}$ by the factor $[\lambda^s W_y/(1 - \lambda^s W_y)]$, and they will not be shown separately in subsequent tables[2].

Because there are no endogenous changes in stocks, there is no need for a dynamic analysis of this system. The long-run effects of monetary and fiscal policies can be obtained directly from (3.1a), after substituting the operator "d" for "δ" to denote long-run changes. Thus, the effects of $d*B^c$ and $d\hat{G}$ are no different than those of $\delta *B^c$ and $\delta \hat{G}$. This is because $\delta *B^c$ *is* a permanent change in a stock, while $\delta \hat{G}$ *is* a permanent change in a flow. The effects of $d*B$, by contrast, differ in size but not in sign from those of $\delta \hat{B}$. This is because $d*B$ is the permanent change in the stock of debt obtained by letting $\hat{B}$ go to zero (at time T'') and looking back upon its integral[3].

---

[1] Notice that the trace is negative (because $L_r < 0$) and the determinant is positive. These are the necessary and sufficient conditions for a stable market-clearing system when, as here, the system contains two equations. When there are three equations, as in open systems studied below, the determinant must be negative. In those instances, however, the trace-determinant condition is necessary but not sufficient for stability. The notion of stability at issue here is related to the pairing of markets and market-clearing variables described in footnote 2, p. 256. It says that an excess demand or supply in one or more markets will produce the short-run changes in prices, flows, and stocks obtained by solving the system itself — changes like those shown in Tables 1 through 4. It is distinct from the notion of stability discussed above in connection with changes in wealth, reserves, or foreign holdings of government bonds. The trace-determinant conditions are satisfied by every short-run system studied hereafter.

[2] When the demand for money depends on disposable income, not factor income, the policy changes $\delta \hat{G}$ and $\delta \hat{B}$ have different short-run effects:

$$\delta Y = - (1/\lambda^s H) [(1 - \lambda^s W_y) L_r + \lambda^s W_r L_y] \delta \hat{B} + [1] \delta \hat{G},$$
$$\delta r = [L_y/\lambda^s H] \delta \hat{B}.$$

The sign of $(\delta Y/\delta \hat{B})$ is ambiguous, not positive. This is because $(\delta r/\delta \hat{B})$ is larger than it is in Table 1, and a larger increase in the interest rate augments the saving rate (reduces consumption). The balanced-budget multiplier is unity, and $\delta \hat{G}$ has no effect on the interest rate (because it has no effect on disposable income).

[3] The short-run effect of $\delta \hat{B}$ has two parts. Because it is accomplished by reducing taxes, it adds to disposable income and consumption. Because it increases desired wealth (by $W_y \delta \hat{B}$), it depresses consumption. These are the opposite-signed effects contained in the coefficient $(1 - \lambda^s W_y)$. The long-run effect of $d*B$, by contrast, has only one (wealth) component.

The flow version of the model takes this simple form:

$$
\begin{bmatrix} -\lambda^s W_y & -\lambda^s W_r \\ \lambda^h L_y & \lambda^h L_r \end{bmatrix}
\begin{bmatrix} \delta Y \\ \delta r \end{bmatrix}
=
\begin{bmatrix} -(1-\lambda^s W_y) & -\lambda^s W_y & 0 \\ 0 & 0 & 1 \end{bmatrix}
\begin{bmatrix} \delta \hat{B} \\ \delta \hat{G} \\ \delta \hat{B}^c \end{bmatrix}
$$

$$
+
\begin{bmatrix} -\lambda^s & 0 \\ 0 & \lambda^h \end{bmatrix}
\begin{bmatrix} \delta B \\ \delta B^c \end{bmatrix} .
\qquad (3.1\,b)
$$

The determinant is $\lambda^s\lambda^h H$, and the short-run effects on income and the interest rate are those shown in the second part of Table 1. The effects of the fiscal policies $\delta\hat{B}$ and $\delta\hat{G}$ are the same as those obtained for the stock version. The effects of the monetary policy $\delta\hat{B}^c$ may be different in size but not in sign. This result reflects the difference in the way monetary policy must be conducted. In the stock version of the model, it will be recalled, an open-market purchase involves an instantaneous change in the stock of bonds held by the central bank. In the flow version, it involves a gradual change. The effects of the two policies would be the same if $\delta\hat{B}^c$ were conducted at the rate $\lambda^h\delta * B^c$ (if it were scaled to the rate at which households alter their holdings of money).

As there are no endogenous changes in stocks in the flow version, there is again no need for dynamic analysis. The long-run effects of monetary and fiscal policies can be obtained directly from (3.1 b), using long-run rather than instantaneous changes in $*B^c$, etc. They have, of course, to be the same as those in the stock version.

The short-run behavior of the two versions can be compared using a standard IS-LM analysis. The IS curve, denoting equilibrium in the goods market, and the LM curve, denoting equilibrium in the money market, have the same positions and slopes in both versions; see Figures 1a and 1b. An increase of $\hat{B}$ or $\hat{G}$ shifts the IS curve rightward; an increase of $*B^c$ (in the stock version) or $\hat{B}^c$ (in the flow version) shifts the LM curve rightward. The BB curve, denoting equilibrium in the bond market, differs between the two versions (even though, in each version, its slope is not independent of the slopes of the IS and LM curves). In the stock version, the slope of the BB curve, taken from the second row of (2.8a) is $-L_y/L_r$. This is also the slope of the LM curve; the two curves are identical. In the flow version, the slope of the BB curve, taken from the second row of (2.8b), is $-(\lambda^s W_y - \lambda^h L_y)/(\lambda^s W_r - \lambda^h L_r)$,

Figure 1 — *The Closed Economy*

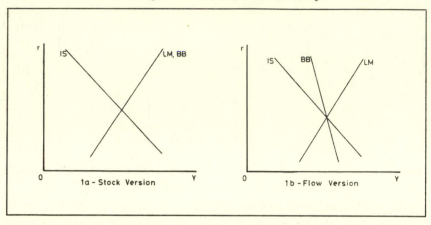

1a - Stock Version
1b - Flow Version

which is a linear combination of the slopes of the IS and LM curves[1]. An exogenous shift in the IS or LM curve is matched by an equivalent shift in the BB curve.

IV. The Open Economy with Flexible Exchange Rates and No Capital Mobility

In the absence of capital mobility, a flexible exchange rate serves always to maintain balanced trade in goods:

$$\hat{X} - \pi\hat{M} = 0 . \tag{4.1}$$

In this circumstance, moreover, equation (1.2′) asserts that $\hat{S}^h$ must equal $\hat{B}$, just as it did in the closed economy. There can be no saving unless there is a government budget deficit.

In the stock version of the model, equation (4.1) is an independent equation, but it does not overdetermine the system. With no capital movements or changes in reserves, the second (or third) row of (2.8a) is again redundant, and equation (4.1) becomes the third market-clearing equation. Differentiating that equation and substituting the result for the third row of (2.8a),

---

[1] The sign of the slope of the BB curve has no importance at this stage. Later, however, we shall assume that $\lambda^s W_y > \lambda^h L_y$, so that the slope will be negative (as drawn in Figure 1b).

Table I — *Flexible Exchange Rates with No Capital Mobility*[a]

Disturbance	Effect on		
	Y	r	π
Short-run in stock version:			
$\delta {}^{*}B^c$	$[W_r/H]$	$-[W_y/H]$	$[W_r/H]\,[M_y/e_\pi]$
$\delta \hat{B}$	$-(1 - \lambda^s W_y)\,[L_r/\lambda^s H]$	$(1 - \lambda^s W_y)\,[L_y/\lambda^s H]$	$-(1 - \lambda^s W_y)\,[L_r/\lambda^s H]\,[M_y/e_\pi]$
$\delta \hat{G}$	$-W_y\,[L_r/H]$	$W_y\,[L_y/H]$	$-W_y\,[L_r/H]\,[M_y/e_\pi]$
δX^a	0	0	$-[1/e_\pi]$
Short-run in flow version:			
$\delta \hat{B}^c$	$[W_r/\lambda^h H]$	$-[W_y/\lambda^h H]$	$[W_r/\lambda^h H]\,[M_y/e_\pi]$
$\delta \hat{B}$	b	b	b
$\delta \hat{G}$	b	b	b
δX^a	0	0	b
Long-run in each version:			
$d {}^{*}B^c$	b	b	b
$d {}^{*}B$	$-[L_r/H]$	$[L_y/H]$	$-[L_r/H]\,[M_y/e_\pi]$
$d \hat{G}$	b	b	b
$d X^a$	0	0	b

[a] The policy-induced changes in income and the interest rate apply also in the closed economy. — [b] Same as short-run effect in stock version.

4*

$$\begin{bmatrix} -E_y & -\lambda^s W_r & -1 \\ L_y & L_r & 0 \\ -M_y & 0 & -1 \end{bmatrix} \begin{bmatrix} \delta Y \\ \delta r \\ -e_\pi \delta\pi \end{bmatrix} =$$

$$\begin{bmatrix} -(1-\lambda^s W_y) & -\lambda^s W_y & 0 & -1 \\ 0 & 0 & 1 & 0 \\ 0 & 0 & 0 & -1 \end{bmatrix} \begin{bmatrix} \delta\hat{B} \\ \delta\hat{G} \\ \delta*B^c \\ \delta X^a \end{bmatrix} + \begin{bmatrix} -\lambda^s \\ 0 \\ 0 \end{bmatrix} [\delta B] . \quad (4.2\,a)$$

The determinant is $\lambda^s H$, just as it was in the closed economy. The effects on income, the interest rate and the exchange rate are shown in Table I. The effects of monetary and fiscal policies on income and the interest rate are the same as in the closed economy. Their effects on the exchange rate reflect their effects on income. As an increase of income induces an increase of imports, and as the policies $\delta*B^c$, $\delta\hat{B}$, and $\delta\hat{G}$ work to increase income, each such policy causes a depreciation. Note, finally, that an autonomous increase of exports, δX^a, leads to an appreciation, but it has no effect on income or the interest rate; the flexible exchange rate insulates the domestic economy from external disturbances.

In the flow version of the model, the rates at which households alter their holdings of money and bonds are not independent of the rate at which they alter their wealth, and no equation is redundant. In different terms, equation (4.1) can be derived from equations (2.1″) through (2.3b″), rather than being independent. In consequence, the system (2.8b) can be used to write the relevant relationships:

$$\begin{bmatrix} -E_y & -\lambda^s W_r & -1 \\ -(\lambda^s W_y - \lambda^h L_y) & -(\lambda^s W_r - \lambda^h L_r) & 0 \\ \lambda^h L_y & \lambda^h L_r & 0 \end{bmatrix} \begin{bmatrix} \delta Y \\ \delta r \\ -e_\pi \delta\pi \end{bmatrix} =$$

$$\begin{bmatrix} \cdot\cdot & \cdot\cdot & \cdot\cdot & \cdot\cdot \\ \cdot\cdot & \cdot\cdot & \cdot\cdot & \cdot\cdot \\ \cdot\cdot & \cdot\cdot & \cdot\cdot & \cdot\cdot \end{bmatrix} \begin{bmatrix} \delta\hat{B} \\ \delta\hat{G} \\ \delta\hat{B}^c \\ \delta X^a \end{bmatrix} + \begin{bmatrix} \cdot\cdot & \cdot\cdot \\ \cdot\cdot & \cdot\cdot \\ \cdot\cdot & \cdot\cdot \end{bmatrix} \begin{bmatrix} \delta B \\ \delta B^c \end{bmatrix} , \quad (4.2\,b)$$

the matrices on the right-hand side being identical to those in (2.8b). The short-run effects of $\delta\hat{B}^c$, etc., are shown in the second part of Table 1. Again, the determinant and policy effects on income and the interest rate are identical to those shown for the closed economy. The behavior of the exchange rate is the same as it was in the stock version.

The IS-LM diagrams, Figures 1a and 1b, can be used to illustrate the resemblance of this first open-economy case to the closed economy. One has only to reinterpret the IS curve. In both versions of the model, the exchange rate adjusts to keep the trade balance at zero. The IS curve can therefore be interpreted as the locus of Y and r combinations which guarantee equilibrium in the goods market, *given* the exchange rate required to balance the trade account. Interpreted this way, the IS curve does not shift with changes in π, while the LM and BB curves are never affected by those changes.

V. The Open Economy with Flexible Exchange Rates and Perfect Capital Mobility

When there is trade in goods and bonds, a flexible exchange rate does not always hold the trade balance at zero, and domestic saving need not equal the government deficit. In consequence, the system (2.8a) furnishes a satisfactory basis for the analysis of the stock version. Here, it takes the form:

$$\begin{bmatrix} -E_y & 0 & -1 \\ L_y & -1 & 0 \\ L_y & 0 & 0 \end{bmatrix} \begin{bmatrix} \delta Y \\ \delta B^f \\ -e_\pi \, \delta\pi \end{bmatrix} = \begin{bmatrix} \cdot\cdot & \cdot\cdot & \cdot\cdot & \cdot\cdot \\ \cdot\cdot & \cdot\cdot & \cdot\cdot & \cdot\cdot \\ \cdot\cdot & \cdot\cdot & \cdot\cdot & \cdot\cdot \end{bmatrix} \begin{bmatrix} \delta\hat{B} \\ \delta\hat{G} \\ \delta *B^c \\ \delta X^a \end{bmatrix}$$

$$+ \begin{bmatrix} \cdot\cdot & \cdot\cdot \\ \cdot\cdot & \cdot\cdot \\ \cdot\cdot & \cdot\cdot \end{bmatrix} \begin{bmatrix} \delta W^h \\ \delta B \end{bmatrix} , \qquad (5.1a)$$

the matrices on the right-hand side being identical to those in (2.8a). The determinant is $-L_y$. The short-run effects on income and the exchange rate are shown in Table 2, along with the effects on the stock of bonds held by foreigners, B^f, and on the flow of bonds, $\dot{B}^f$. The existence of the flow $\dot{B}^f$ is not inconsistent with the assumption of instantaneous

Table 2 — *Flexible Exchange Rates with Perfect Capital Mobility*

Disturbance	Effect on			
	Y	B^f	$\dot{B}^f$	π
Short-run in stock version:				
$\delta *B^c$	$[1/L_y]$	0	$- [\lambda^s W_y/L_y]$	$(1/e_\pi)\,[E_y/L_y]$
$\delta \hat{B}$	0	0	$(1 - \lambda^s W_y)$	$- (1/e_\pi)\,(1 - \lambda^s W_y)$
δX^a	0	0	0	$- (1/e_\pi)$
Short-run in flow version:				
$\delta \hat{B}^c$	$[1/\lambda^h L_y]$	0	$- [\lambda^s W_y/\lambda^h L_y]$	$(1/e_\pi)\,[E_y/\lambda^h L_y]$
$\delta \hat{B}$	0	0	a	a
δX^a	0	0	0	a
Long-run in each version:				
$d*B^c$	a	$- [W_y/L_y]$	0	$(1/e_\pi)\,[M_y/L_y]$
$d*B$	0	1	0	0
dX^a	0	0	0	a

a Same as short-run effect in stock version.

portfolio adjustment. It derives from the manner in which saving takes place. To see that this is true, take the time derivative of equation (2.2a'), the market-clearing equation for bonds in the stock version:

$$\dot{B}^f = \hat{B} - \dot{W}^h + {}^*\dot{L} - \dot{B}^c . \tag{5.2a}$$

But $\dot{B}^c$ is zero in the stock version, while equations (1.11') and (2.3a') say that ${}^*\dot{L} = \dot{L} = 0$ under flexible exchange rates. Combining these assertions with the dynamic equation (1.2')[1]:

$$\dot{B}^f = - (\hat{X} - \pi \hat{M}) . \tag{5.2a'}$$

Differentiating this equation totally and replacing the terms δY and $\delta \pi$ with the short-term policy effects shown in Table 2, we obtain the values for $\delta \dot{B}^f$ listed there.

---

[1] Equation (5.2a') could be derived directly from the balance-of-payments equation (1.15), but this would assume the conclusion we are trying to reach — that the flow $\dot{B}^f$ exists even in the stock version.

The short-run effects of the policies $\delta\hat{B}$ and $\delta*B^c$ are different than they were in the absence of mobility. Deficit spending has no effect on income. It leads only to a capital inflow ($\delta\dot{B}^f > 0$). This is why the exchange rate appreciates, rather than depreciates. An open-market purchase of government securities causes an increase of income, as before, and a capital outflow ($\delta\dot{B}^f < 0$). In consequence, there is a larger depreciation than there was when capital was not mobile. Note, finally, that the introduction of trade in bonds does not change the short-run impact of an exogenous increase in exports. The flexible exchange rate serves again to insulate the domestic economy from a shift in the foreign demand for domestic output.

Turning to stability and long-run behavior, differentiate equation (1.2') with respect to all arguments in (5.1a) and replace the terms δY and $\delta\pi$ with the total derivatives obtainable from (5.1a)[1]:

$$d\dot{W}^h = \lambda^s\,(W_y/L_y)\,d*B^c - \lambda^s\,dW^h\,. \qquad (5.3a)$$

As $(d\dot{W}^h/dW^h) = -\lambda^s$, the system (5.1a) is stable. By implication, saving goes to zero in the long run, and equation (5.3a) can be used to define the long-run change in wealth:

$$dW^h = (W_y/L_y)\,d*B^c\,. \qquad (5.3a')$$

An increase of government debt, $\delta*B$, does not add to household wealth, as all of it is sold to foreigners. Finally, replacing δW^h with the solution for dW^h, we solve (5.1a) for the long-run changes in income, the stock debt held by foreigners, and the exchange rate. These are shown in the final part of Table 2.

The flow version of the model takes the form:

$$
\begin{bmatrix} -E_y & 0 & -1 \\ -(\lambda^s W_y - \lambda^h L_y) & -1 & 0 \\ \lambda^h L_y & 0 & -1 \end{bmatrix}
\begin{bmatrix} \delta Y \\ \delta\dot{B}^f \\ -e_\pi\,\delta\pi \end{bmatrix} =
$$

$$
\begin{bmatrix} \cdot\cdot & \cdot\cdot & \cdot\cdot & \cdot\cdot \\ \cdot\cdot & \cdot\cdot & \cdot\cdot & \cdot\cdot \\ \cdot\cdot & \cdot\cdot & \cdot\cdot & \cdot\cdot \end{bmatrix}
\begin{bmatrix} \delta\hat{B} \\ \delta\hat{G} \\ \delta\hat{B}^c \\ \delta X^a \end{bmatrix}
+
\begin{bmatrix} \cdot\cdot & \cdot\cdot \\ \cdot\cdot & \cdot\cdot \\ \cdot\cdot & \cdot\cdot \end{bmatrix}
\begin{bmatrix} (\delta B - \delta B^f) \\ \delta B^c \end{bmatrix}\,, \qquad (5.1b)
$$

---

[1] As $\hat{B}$ is zero in the long run, it is irrelevant to stability and long-run analysis, and it is deleted from equation (5.3a).

the matrices on the right-hand side being identical to those in (2.8b). The determinant is $-\lambda^h L_y$, and the short-run solutions are shown in the second part of Table 2. There is only one difference between these results and those for the stock version. As in both cases studied above, the effects of an open-market operation, $\delta\hat{B}^c$, differ by the factor $(1/\lambda^h)$ from those in the stock version.

To study stability and long-run behavior in the flow version, use (5.1b) to write the derivative of $\dot{B}^f$ with respect to all arguments:

$$dB^f = -\lambda^s (W_y/L_y) \, d^*B^c + \lambda^s \, d^*B - \lambda^s \, dB^f . \qquad (5.4b)$$

As $(d\dot{B}^f/dB^f) = -\lambda^s$, the system (5.1b) is stable. The flow $\dot{B}^f$ goes to zero in the long run, and equation (5.4b) can be used to define the long-run change in B^f shown in the final part of Table 2. Finally, replacing δB^f in (5.1b), we can solve for the long-run changes in income and the exchange rate.

Again, an IS-LM diagram can be used to illustrate the relationship between stock and flow versions. The IS curve in Figure 2 is the same in both versions but steeper than it was in the closed economy; its slope is $-(\lambda^s W_y + M_y)/\lambda^s W_r$, and M_y is zero in the closed economy. Changes in the exchange rate shift the IS curve because they affect the trade balance. A depreciation moves it rightward, an appreciation, leftward. These shifts guarantee that the IS curve will pass through the intersection of the LM

Figure 2 — *The Open Economy with Flexible Exchange Rates and Capital Mobility: Effects of an Open Market Purchase*

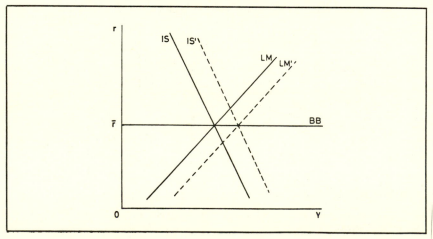

and BB curves. The LM curve is the same as in Figure 1, but the perfect elasticity of foreign demand for bonds at the world interest rate, $\bar{r}$, produces a horizontal BB curve in both versions. Consider, then, the workings of monetary policy. An open-market purchase ($\delta *B^c$ in the stock version and $\delta \hat{B}^c$ in the flow version) shifts the LM curve to the right, as shown in Figure 2. The depreciation of the exchange rate induced by the central bank's additional demand for bonds shifts the IS curve to the right. Monetary policy operates on income by fostering a surplus in the trade balance. A government deficit, by contrast, has no effect on any curve in either version of the model. The supply of new bonds, $\delta \hat{B}$, causes the exchange rate to appreciate and the trade balance to deteriorate by an amount just sufficient to offset the effect of the deficit (tax reduction) on the households' demand for home goods.

VI. The Open Economy with Pegged Exchange Rates and No Capital Mobility

In this case, (2.8a) simplifies to:

$$
\begin{bmatrix} -E_y & -\lambda^s W_r & 0 \\ L_y & L_r & 0 \\ L_y & L_r & -1 \end{bmatrix} \begin{bmatrix} \delta Y \\ \delta r \\ \delta R \end{bmatrix} = \begin{bmatrix} \cdots & \cdots & \cdots & \cdots \\ \cdots & \cdots & \cdots & \cdots \\ \cdots & \cdots & \cdots & \cdots \end{bmatrix} \begin{bmatrix} \delta \hat{B} \\ \delta \hat{G} \\ \delta *B^c \\ \delta X^a \end{bmatrix}
$$

$$
+ \begin{bmatrix} \cdots & \cdots \\ \cdots & \cdots \\ \cdots & \cdots \end{bmatrix} \begin{bmatrix} \delta W^h \\ \delta B \end{bmatrix} , \qquad (6.1a)
$$

the matrices on the right-hand side being identical to those in (2.8a). The determinant is $-H_a$, where $H_a = (\lambda^s H - M_y L_r) > 0$. The short-run solutions are shown in the first part of Table 3.

The signs of the principal policy effects are the same as those obtained with flexible exchange rates. A deficit, $\delta \hat{B}$, increases income and raises the interest rate. An open-market purchase, $\delta *B^c$, increases income and reduces the interest rate. Both policies, moreover, lead to outflows of reserves ($\delta \dot{R} < 0$) at rates which reflect the increase of imports induced by the increase of income. To derive these flow effects, we take the time derivative of equation (1.1'):

$$
\dot{R} = \dot{W}^h - \dot{\hat{B}} + \dot{B}^f . \qquad (6.2a)
$$

Table 3 — *Pegged Exchange Rates with No Capital Mobility*

Disturbance	Effect on			
	Y	r	R	$\dot{R}$
Short-run in stock version:				
$\delta * B^c$	$\lambda^s [W_r/H_a]$	$- [E_y/H_a]$	0	$- \lambda^s [M_y W_r/H_a]$
$\delta \hat{B}$	$- (1 - \lambda^s W_y) [L_r/H_a]$	$(1 - \lambda^s W_y) [L_y/H_a]$	0	$(1 - \lambda^s W_y) [M_y L_r/H_a]$
δX^a	$- [L_r/H_a]$	$[L_y/H_a]$	0	$\lambda^s [H/H_a]$
Short-run in flow version:				
$\delta \hat{B}^c$	$\lambda^s [W_r/H_b]$	$- [E_y/H_b]$	0	$- \lambda^s [M_y W_r/H_b]$
$\delta \hat{B}$	$- \lambda^h (1 - \lambda^s W_y) [L_r/H_b]$	$(1 - \lambda^s W_y) [U_y/H_b]$	0	$\lambda^h (1 - \lambda^s W_y) [M_y L_r/H_b]$
δX^a	$[(\lambda^s W_r - \lambda^h L_r)/H_b]$	$- [(\lambda^s W_y - \lambda^h L_y)/H^b]$	0	$\lambda^{s)\hbar} [H/H_b]$
Long-run in each version:				
$d * B^c$	0	$- [1/(W_r - L_r)]$	$- [W_r/(W_r - L_r)]$	0
$d * B$	0	$[1/(W_r - L_r)]$	$[L_r/(W_r - L_r)]$	0
$d X^a$	$[1/M_y]$	$- [(W_y - L_y)/M_y (W_r - L_r)]$	$[H/M_y (W_r - L_r)]$	0

Setting $\dot{B}^f$ at zero (because there is no trade in bonds) and using the dynamic equation $(1.2')$,

$$\dot{R} = (\hat{X} - \pi\hat{M}) \, . \qquad\qquad (6.2\,a')$$

Differentiating this equation totally and replacing the term δY with the short-run policy effects shown in Table 3, we obtain the values for δR listed there.

The only major differences between the outcomes in Table 3 and the ones obtained with flexible exchange rates pertain to the effects on income and the interest rate of an autonomous increase in exports. There is, of course, an inflow of reserves in lieu of an appreciation, and because there is no change in the exchange rate, there are positive effects on income and the interest rate. The economy is no longer insulated from external disturbances.

To derive the long-run results shown in Table 3, we have again to differentiate the dynamic equation $(1.2')$ with respect to all arguments in $(6.1\,a)$, then to replace the term δY with the total derivative obtained from $(6.1\,a)$:

$$dW^h = - \lambda^s [M_y W_r/H_a] \, d^*B^c + \lambda^s [M_y W_r/H_a] \, d^*B +$$

$$\lambda^s [H/H_a] \, dX^a - \lambda^s [M_y (W_r - L_r)/H_a] \, dW^h \, . \qquad (6.3\,a)$$

As $(d\dot{W}^h/dW^h) = - \lambda^s [M_y (W_r - L_r)/H_a]$, the system $(6.1\,a)$ is stable, and equation $(6.3\,a)$ can be solved for the long-run change in wealth:

$$dW^h = - [W_r/(W_r - L_r)] \, d^*B^c + [W_r/(W_r - L_r)] \, d^*B$$

$$+ [H/M_y (W_r - L_r)] \, dX^a \, . \qquad (6.3\,a')$$

An open-market operation reduces wealth because it reduces the interest rate and causes dissaving; an issue of debt raises wealth because it raises the interest rate; and an increase of foreign demand raises wealth by way of its permanent impact on income. Replacing δW^h in $(6.1\,a)$, we solve for the long-run changes in income, the interest rate, and the stock of reserves. These are shown in the final part of Table 3.

In the flow version of the model:

$$
\begin{bmatrix}
- E_y & - \lambda^s W_r & 0 \\
- (\lambda^s W_y - \lambda^h L_y) & - (\lambda^s W_r - \lambda^h L_r) & 0 \\
\lambda^h L_y & \lambda^h L_r & -1
\end{bmatrix}
\begin{bmatrix}
\delta Y \\
\delta r \\
\delta \dot{R}
\end{bmatrix}
=
$$

$$
\begin{bmatrix}
\cdot\cdot & \cdot\cdot & \cdot\cdot & \cdot\cdot \\
\cdot\cdot & \cdot\cdot & \cdot\cdot & \cdot\cdot \\
\cdot\cdot & \cdot\cdot & \cdot\cdot & \cdot\cdot
\end{bmatrix}
\begin{bmatrix}
\delta\hat{B} \\
\delta\hat{G} \\
\delta\hat{B}^c \\
\delta X^a
\end{bmatrix}
+
\begin{bmatrix}
\cdot\cdot & \cdot\cdot \\
\cdot\cdot & \cdot\cdot \\
\cdot\cdot & \cdot\cdot
\end{bmatrix}
\begin{bmatrix}
(\delta B + \delta R) \\
(\delta B^c + \delta R)
\end{bmatrix}
, \qquad (6.1\,b)
$$

the matrices on the right-hand side being identical to those in (2.8 b). The determinant is $- H_b$, where $H_b = [\lambda^s \lambda^h H + M_y (\lambda^s W_r - \lambda^h L_r)] = [\lambda^s W_r U_y - \lambda^h L_r E_y]$, where $U_y = (M_y + \lambda^h L_y)$, so that $H_b > 0$. The short-run results are shown in the second part of Table 3.

Here we find for the first time significant differences between the short-run responses of the stock and flow versions. An open-market purchase, for example, has the same-signed effects on income, the interest rate, and the flow of reserves, but all effects are smaller in the flow version, even when we standardize the open-market purchase by setting $\delta\hat{B}^c$ equal to $\lambda^h \delta * B^c$. The ratio of stock- to flow-version effects is $(H_b/\lambda^h H_a)$, and $H_b - \lambda^h H_a = \lambda^s M_y W_r > 0$. The reason for these differences resides in the impact of reserve flows on asset markets. An open-market purchase causes an outflow of reserves, reducing the money supply, but outflow has non-negligible implications only in the flow version of the model, where asset markets deal in flows rather than in stocks. There, the induced reduction in the money supply serves immediately to arrest the decline in the interest rate and the increase of income. For this same reason, budget deficits and shifts in the demand for exports also function differently in two versions. These differences are best described diagrammatically, using the IS and LM curves of Figures 3 and 4.

The IS curve in these figures is the same as in Figure 2 above; it allows for leakages through the trade balance. The LM and BB curves are the same as in Figure 1 above, and the BB curve has been deleted; it always moves to the intersection of the IS and LM curves. In the stock version, of course, the LM curve is the locus of points at which the stock demand for money equals the stock supply, and it is not immediately affected by flows of reserves. In the flow version, the LM curve is the

Figure 3 — *The Open Economy with Pegged Exchange Rates and No Capital Mobility: Effects of a Budget Deficit*

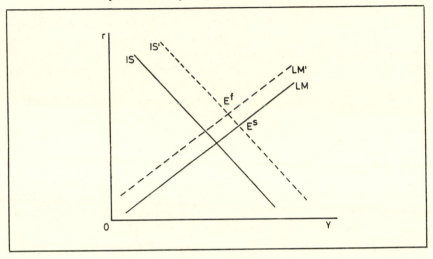

Figure 4 — *The Open Economy with Pegged Exchange Rates and No Capital Mobility: Effects of an Increase in Exports*

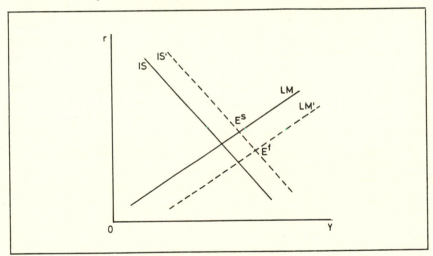

locus of points at which the flow demand for money equals the flow supply, and a flow of reserves will shift it immediately. A balance-of-payments surplus will shift it rightward, a deficit, leftward. Thus, in Figure 3, a budget deficit shifts the IS curve to the right, and the new short-run equilibrium will be at E^s in the stock version and at E^f in the flow version. The short-run increase of the interest rate is larger in the flow version, and the increase of income is smaller. This is because the outflow of reserves shifts the LM curve to the left. In Figure 4, an autonomous increase of exports shifts the IS curve to the right, but in the flow version, also shifts the LM curve in that same direction. There is a larger short-run change in income, and the sign of the change in the interest rate is ambiguous.

This last instance is the only one in which there can be any difference between the two versions in the *sign* of a short-run response. In the stock version of the model, the increase of income resulting from an increase of export demand raises the demand for money, and any increase in the demand for money has as its counterpart an equivalent reduction in the demand for bonds; the income derivative of the stock demand for bonds is $- L_y$. The result is the unambiguous increase of the interest rate shown in Table 3 and Figure 4. In the flow version of the model, the increase of income serves again to raise the demand for money, but can either raise or lower the demand for bonds; the income derivative of that demand is $(\lambda^s W_y - \lambda^h L_y)$. One is tempted to assume that this term is negative. There would then be a perfect symmetry of signs in the stock and flow versions. But this would say that bonds are an income-inferior asset. It is, we believe, more realistic to suppose that saving induced by an increase of income is divided between bonds and money. We shall, indeed, make two assumptions reflecting this belief: (1) that an increase of income leads to an increase in the flow demand for bonds — that $\lambda^s W_y > \lambda^h L_y$, and (2) that the speed with which households adjust their cash balances equals or exceeds the speed with which they adjust their total wealth — that $\lambda^h \geq \lambda^{s\,1}$. The first assumption says that $(\delta r/\delta X^a)$ will be negative in the flow version, as shown in Figure 4. The two assumptions taken together say that $W_y > L_y$, so that a permanent increase of exports will cause a long-run reduction in the interest rate in both versions of the model.

To study long-run behavior in the flow version, we use (6.1b) to write the derivative of $\dot{R}$ with respect to all arguments:

$$d\dot{R} = - \lambda^s \lambda^h (M_y W_r/H_b)\, d*B^c + \lambda^s \lambda^h (M_y L_r/H_b)\, d*B$$

$$+ \lambda^s \lambda^h (H/H_b)\, dX^a - \lambda^s \lambda^h [M_y (W_r - L_r)/H_b]\, dR . \qquad (6.4b)$$

---

[1] This second supposition is consistent with the limitations placed on λ^s and λ^h when they were introduced. The former must be smaller than $(1/W_y)$; the latter has no upper bound.

As $(d\dot{R}/dR) = -\lambda^s\lambda^h [M_y (W_r - L_r)/H_b]$, the system (6.1b) is stable. The flow $\dot{R}$ goes to zero in the long run, and equation (6.4b) can be used to derive the long-run change in R shown in the final part of Table 3. Finally, replacing δR in (6.1b), we can solve for the long-run changes in income and the exchange rate.

VII. The Open Economy with Pegged Exchange Rates and Perfect Capital Mobility

In this fifth and final instance, the stock version takes the form:

$$
\begin{bmatrix}
-E_y & 0 & 0 \\
L_y & -1 & 0 \\
L_y & 0 & -1
\end{bmatrix}
\begin{bmatrix}
\delta Y \\
\delta B^f \\
\delta R
\end{bmatrix}
=
\begin{bmatrix}
\cdot\cdot & \cdot\cdot & \cdot\cdot & \cdot\cdot \\
\cdot\cdot & \cdot\cdot & \cdot\cdot & \cdot\cdot \\
\cdot\cdot & \cdot\cdot & \cdot\cdot & \cdot\cdot
\end{bmatrix}
\begin{bmatrix}
\delta\hat{B} \\
\delta\hat{G} \\
\delta*B^c \\
\delta X^a
\end{bmatrix}
$$

$$
+
\begin{bmatrix}
\cdot\cdot & \cdot\cdot \\
\cdot\cdot & \cdot\cdot \\
\cdot\cdot & \cdot\cdot
\end{bmatrix}
\begin{bmatrix}
\delta W^h \\
\delta B
\end{bmatrix}
, \qquad (7.1a)
$$

the matrices on the right-hand side being identical to those in (2.8a). The determinant is $-E_y$ (the sum of the marginal propensities to save and import). The short-run solutions are shown in the first part of Table 4.

There is one major difference between these results and those shown in Table 3 above, when there was no trade in bonds. The stock of reserves, R, responds instantaneously to the disturbances $\delta*B^c$, $\delta\hat{B}$, and δX^a, because the economy can adjust its cash holdings by buying or selling bonds on the world market. It does not have to do so by changing its trade balance, a process that takes time even in the stock version. Confirming this explanation, the coefficients of R and B^f are identical in each instance. Notice, further, that an open-market operation has no effect on income, even in the short run. Bonds sold by the central bank are bought by foreigners, and there is no change in the stock of money. The instantaneous change in reserves offsets the open-market operation. (This result and one obtained in Table 2 above replicate Mundell's well-known conclusions about the effects of capital mobility. Under fixed exchange rates, the introduction of capital mobility undermines the effectiveness of monetary

Table 4 — *Pegged Exchange Rates with Perfect Capital Mobility*

Disturbance	Effect on				
	Y	B^f	$\dot{B}^f$	R	$\dot{R}$
Short-run in stock version:					
$\delta {*}B^c$	0	-1	0	$\cdot{-}1$	0
$\hat{\delta B}$	$(1-\lambda^s W_y) \cdot [1/E_y]$	$(1-\lambda^s W_y) \cdot [L_y/E_y]$	$[1/E_y^2][\lambda^s L_y \lambda^s W_y \cdot (1+M_y)+M_y(1-\lambda^s W_y) E_y] - [\lambda^s W_y/E_y^2][\lambda^s (W_y-L_y) + M_y]$	$(1-\lambda^s W_y) \cdot [L_y/E_y]$	$[\lambda^s L_y/E_y](1+M_y)[\lambda^s W_y/E_y]$ $[1/E_y^2][\lambda^s L_y \lambda^s W_y]$
δX^a	$[1/E_y]$	$[L_y/E_y]$	0	$[L_y/E_y]$	0
Short-run in flow version:					
$\delta \hat{B}^c$	0	0	-1	0	$\lambda^h (1-\lambda^s W_y) [L_y/E_y]$
$\hat{\delta B}$	a	0	$(1-\lambda^s W_y) [\overset{\downarrow}{U_y/E_y}]$	0	$\lambda^h [L_y/E_y]$
δX^a	a	0	$-[(\lambda^s W_y - \lambda^h L_y)/E_y]$	0	0
Long-run in each version:					
$d{*}B^c$	0	-1	0	-1	0
$d{*}B$	0	1	0	0	0
dX^a	$[1/M_y]$	$-[(W_y-L_y)/M_y]$	0	$[L_y/M_y]$	0

a Same as short-run effect in stock version.

policy. Under flexible exchange rates, it undermines the effectiveness of fiscal policy.)

The flow changes shown in this first part of the table are obtained by taking the time derivatives of equations (2.3a'') and (1.1'), the market-clearing equation for money and the definition of total wealth. From equations (2.3a''), (1.1'), and the dynamic equation[1],

$$\dot{R} = L_y \, (\delta Y/\delta W^h) \, \dot{W}^h$$

$$= (\lambda^s \, L_y/E_y) \, \lambda^s \, [W(r, \, Y - \hat{G} + \hat{B}) - W^h] \,, \qquad (7.2a)$$

$$\dot{B}^f = \dot{R} - (\hat{X} - \pi\hat{M}) \,. \qquad (7.3a)$$

Differentiating with respect to all short-term arguments,

$$\delta\dot{R} = (\lambda^s \, L_y/E_y) \, [\lambda^s \, W_y \, (\delta Y + \delta\hat{B})] \,, \qquad (7.2a')$$

$$\delta\dot{B}^f = \delta\dot{R} + M_y \, \delta Y - \delta X^a \,. \qquad (7.3a')$$

Replacing δY with the policy effects shown in Table 4, we obtain the flow changes $\delta\dot{R}$ and $\delta\dot{B}^f$ listed there.

To study stability and long-run behavior in the stock version, we have again to differentiate the dynamic equation with respect to all arguments in (7.1a), then to replace the term δY with its total derivative:

$$d\dot{W}^h = \lambda^s \, (W_y/E_y) \, dX^a - \lambda^s \, (M_y/E_y) \, dW^h \,. \qquad (7.4a)$$

As $(d\dot{W}^h/dW^h) = - \lambda^s \, (M_y/E_y)$, the system (7.1a) is stable, and we can employ equation (7.4a) to solve for the long-run change in wealth:

$$dW^h = (W_y/M_y) \, dX^a \,. \qquad (7.4a')$$

Replacing δW^h in (7.1a), we can solve for the long-run changes shown in the final part of Table 4.

---

[1] The term $\dot{B}^c$ drops out of these equations because it is zero in the stock version The term $\delta\hat{G}$ is omitted from subsequent equations, as we have deleted it from the analysis.

In the flow version of the model:

$$
\begin{bmatrix}
-E_y & 0 & 0 \\
-(\lambda^s W_y - \lambda^h L_y) & -1 & 0 \\
\lambda^h L_y & 0 & -1
\end{bmatrix}
\begin{bmatrix}
\delta Y \\
\delta \dot{B}^f \\
\delta \dot{R}
\end{bmatrix} =
$$

$$
\begin{bmatrix}
\cdot\cdot & \cdot\cdot & \cdot\cdot & \cdot\cdot \\
\cdot\cdot & \cdot\cdot & \cdot\cdot & \cdot\cdot \\
\cdot\cdot & \cdot\cdot & \cdot\cdot & \cdot\cdot
\end{bmatrix}
\begin{bmatrix}
\delta\hat{B} \\
\delta\hat{G} \\
\delta\hat{B}^c \\
\delta X^a
\end{bmatrix}
+
\begin{bmatrix}
\cdot\cdot & \cdot\cdot \\
\cdot\cdot & \cdot\cdot \\
\cdot\cdot & \cdot\cdot
\end{bmatrix}
\begin{bmatrix}
(\delta B - \delta B^f + \delta R) \\
(\delta B^c + \delta R)
\end{bmatrix}, \quad (7.1\,\text{b})
$$

the matrices on the right-hand side being identical to those in (2.8 b). The determinant is $-E_y$, just as in the stock version, and the short-run solutions are shown in the second part of Table 4.

There are, of course, no short-run changes in R or B^f, as these stocks are held constant when solving for δY, $\delta\dot{B}^f$, and $\delta\dot{R}$. Notice, however, that the flow changes $(\delta\dot{B}^f/\delta\hat{B}^c)$ and $(\delta\dot{R}/\delta\hat{B}^c)$ are identical to the stock changes $(\delta B^f/\delta*B^c)$ and $(\delta R/\delta*B^c)$ in the stock version, while the flow changes induced by $\delta\hat{B}$ resemble the stock changes in the first part of the table.

There is, again, a single difference in sign between the two versions of the model. The stock change $(\delta B^f/\delta X^a)$ is unambiguously positive; the flow change $(\delta\dot{B}^f/\delta X^a)$ is negative on the assumptions adopted above. This outcome is the counterpart of the difference in sign that occurred in respect of the interest rate when there was no trade in bonds, and it has the same interpretation. When, as here, capital is perfectly mobile, stock and flow changes in foreign holdings of domestic bonds take the place of changes in the domestic interest rate. They respond negatively to an excess domestic demand for bonds, just like the interest rate. Lastly, notice that the changes in income are the same in each version. As different rates of change in reserves can have no effect on the interest rate, they cannot affect the size of the change in income.

Finally, consider the long-run properties of the flow version. We use (7.1 b) to write the derivatives of $d\dot{R}$ and $d\dot{B}^f$ with respect to all arguments and combine our results in a new subsystem:

$$
\begin{bmatrix}
-\lambda^h \left[\lambda^s (W_y - L_y) + M_y\right] & -\lambda^s \lambda^h L_y \\
-\left[\lambda^s \lambda^h (W_y - L_y) + (\lambda^h - \lambda^s) M_y\right] & -\lambda^s U_y
\end{bmatrix}
\begin{bmatrix}
dR \\
dB^f
\end{bmatrix}
=
$$

$$
\begin{bmatrix}
\lambda^h E_y & -\lambda^s \lambda^h L_y & -\lambda^h L_y \\
\lambda^h E_y & -\lambda^s U_y & +(\lambda^s W_y - \lambda^h L_y)
\end{bmatrix}
\begin{bmatrix}
d*B^c \\
d*B \\
dX^a
\end{bmatrix}.
\qquad (7.4\,\text{b})
$$

This system satisfies the conditions for long-run stability. The trace is negative; the determinant is $\lambda^s \lambda^h E_y M_y$ and is therefore positive. Solving the system for dR and dB^f, we obtain the long-run effects shown in the final part of Table 4, and replacing δR and δB^f in (7.1a) with the solutions for dR and dB^f, we obtain the corresponding changes in income.

The IS, LM, and BB curves for pegged exchange rates and perfect capital mobility are identical to those shown in Figure 2 for flexible rates and perfect mobility. In this instance, however, it is the LM curve that shifts to the intersection of the IS and BB curves, whereas, with flexible rates, it was the IS curve that shifted to the intersection of the LM and BB curves. Changes in reserves take the place of changes in exchange rates. Furthermore, the differences between the stock and flow versions of the model pertain mainly to the timing of reserve and bond flows, and an IS-LM analysis does not serve to highlight them. It is more illuminating to examine the changes in money and bond holdings over time. Thus, Figure 5 sketches the paths taken by household holdings of wealth, money, and bonds following an autonomous increase in the demand for exports.

In each version of the model, changes in money holdings, L, must equal the changes in reserves, R, given in Table 4, while changes in bond holdings, B^h, must equal the negative of the changes in foreign holdings, B^f. Furthermore, B^h must equal the difference between W^h and L, a fact reflected in the construction of Figure 5. In each version, moreover, an increase of export demand raises income by $1/E_y$, augmenting saving by $\lambda^s W_y/E_y$. This higher rate of saving adds gradually to wealth until wealth reaches its new equilibrium level, and wealth follows the same path in both versions. In the long run, moreover, the composition of wealth will be the same in the stock and flow versions[1]. The one difference be-

---

[1] The assumption that $W_y > L_y$ is reflected in Figure 5 by the larger final value for B^h (the smaller increase in L than in W^h).

Figure 5 — *The Open Economy with Pegged Exchange Rates and Perfect Capital Mobility: Paths of Wealth and Portfolio Adjustment: Effects of an Increase in Exports*

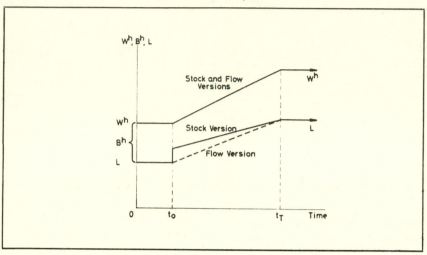

tween the two resides in the timing of the changes in money and bond holdings. Any increase of income raises the stock demand for money. In the stock version of the model, households satisfy this increased demand immediately; they shift discontinuously from bonds to money, as shown by the solid line in Figure 5. In the flow version, by contrast, the composition of portfolios changes gradually; money and bond holdings rise together, as shown by the broken line in the figure. In the stock version, there is an instantaneous stock shift, followed by gradual changes in money and bond holdings, reflecting the gradual growth of wealth. In the flow version, there is no discontinuity; the shift in portfolios required by the increased demand for money takes place over time, together with the changes in money and bond holdings that reflect the growth of wealth.

VIII. Summary and Conclusions

The basic difference between the two versions of the model is the manner in which households enter asset markets — with immediate stock demands for assets, as in the stock version, or with flow demands constituting a gradual adjustment to long-run stock demands for assets, as in the flow version. The immediate stock demands of the stock version indicate the preferred allocation of *existing* wealth; the long-run stock

Table 5 — *Differences between the Stock and Flow Versions in Their Short-Run Responses to Disturbances*

Closed economy	none
Flexible exchange rate, no capital mobility	none
Flexible exchange rate, perfect capital mobility	none
Fixed exchange rate, no capital mobility	Any disturbance that creates a trade deficit and a reserve outflow produces in the flow version an interest rate higher and an output lower than in the stock version. The reverse is true for a disturbance that creates a trade surplus and reserve inflow.
Fixed exchange rate, perfect capital mobility	Any disturbance that affects the stock demand for money, directly or through induced changes in Y and r, induces an *immediate* exchange of bonds and money with foreigners in the stock version, but induces only a *gradual* exchange of bonds and money with foreigners in the flow version. In both versions, induced saving implies gradual accumulation of both assets.

demands of the flow version indicate the preferred allocation of *desired* wealth. In the steady state, when actual wealth equals desired wealth, the immediate and long-run stock demands for assets are identical. Thus, the steady-state outcomes of any disturbance are the same in both versions of the model.

The differences between the two versions in their responses to disturbances lie in the initial changes of the market-clearing variables and in the subsequent paths of adjustment to the common steady state. These differences vary with assumptions about the exchange-rate regime and with the degree of capital mobility. They are summarized in Table 5. One conclusion drawn from this model is that the central bank must adjust its rate of open-market operations to the nature of asset demands. The similarities and differences summarized in Table 5 are based on the assumption that the central bank has an immediate stock demand for bonds in the stock version and a long-run stock demand for bonds in the flow version, and implements the latter at the same rate as households implement their long-run demand for money (i.e., that $\delta B^c = \lambda^h \delta \hat{B}^c$).

The presence or absence of differences between the short-run responses of the two versions depends upon which assets, if any, are exchanged internationally and upon the terms on which they are exchanged.

(1) If there is international trade in more than one asset (the case of a fixed exchange rate and perfect capital mobility), the stock version produces an instantaneous rearrangement of portfolios in response to a disturbance, with a gradual accumulation in holdings of all assets when the disturbance induces saving. The flow version produces a gradual rearrangement of portfolios in response to the change in the preferred allocation of desired wealth caused by the disturbance, along with the growth of the portfolio due to induced saving; there is no immediate rearrangement of portfolios. When only *one* asset is traded internationally, by contrast, that asset can be exchanged only for a flow of goods; thus, even in the stock version of the model, any actual adjustment of portfolios is accomplished gradually as a result of saving. These conclusions about differences in the timing of portfolio adjustments apply generally to models that differ in the specification of market demands for assets.

(2) The two versions have the same short-run outcomes when there is a perfectly elastic foreign supply of bonds and no international exchange of money (flexible exchange rate); they differ in their responses when there is a perfectly elastic supply of money (fixed exchange rate) and no international exchange of bonds. These results stem from the assumption, made here for purposes of comparability, that the immediate stock demand for money in the stock version takes the same form as the long-run stock demand for money in the flow version. When, therefore, the money supply is exogenously determined, as in the case of a flexible exchange rate, the conditions under which there is no excess stock demand for money in the stock version are the same as those under which there is no excess flow demand for money in the flow version[1]. If the stock demands for money in the two versions did not take the same form, the short-run responses would not be identical in the case of a flexible exchange rate and perfect capital mobility or in the cases where no asset was traded internationally (a closed economy or a flexible exchange rate and no capital mobility).

---

[1] If the model had been specified differently, with the immediate stock demand for bonds in the stock version taking the same form as the long-run stock demand for bonds in the flow version, the responses to a disturbance would have been identical in the case of a fixed rate and no capital mobility and would have differed in the case of a flexible rate and perfect capital mobility.

Glossary

$E_y = \lambda^s W_y + M_y$

$e_\pi = (X/\pi) [- (1/\pi) (X_{\left(\frac{1}{\pi}\right)}/X) - (\pi M/X) \pi (M_\pi/M) - (\pi M/X)]$

$H = W_r L_y - L_r W_y$

$H_a = \lambda^s H - M_y L_r$

$H_b = \lambda^s \lambda^h H + M_y (\lambda^s W_r - \lambda^h L_r) = \lambda^h H_a + \lambda^s M_y W_r$

$U_y = M_y + \lambda^h L_y$

* * *

New Views of Exchange Rates and Old Views of Policy

By Peter B. Kenen*

In what sense can it be said that a floating exchange rate confers national autonomy? Can it insulate an economy against disturbances coming from abroad? Can it enhance the effectiveness of domestic monetary and fiscal policies? How does the degree of capital mobility influence our answers to these questions? Experience with limited exchange rate flexibility since 1973 would appear to say that floating rates cannot confer complete autonomy. Furthermore, developments in the theory of exchange rate determination, inspired in part by that experience, have given us new ways of approaching these newly controversial issues.

I propose to deal with these questions in two ways. First, I will present results extracted from a formal algebraic model on which I have been working in collaboration with Polly Allen and which forms the basis for our forthcoming book. Second, I will summarize results obtained from an expanded version of an econometric model first presented in my 1974 article and soon to appear in my forthcoming book.

I

The familiar questions with which I began have to be answered anew because the models used in current work on international theory include phenomena that did not figure in older models. In particular, the current models employ a portfolio or asset-market approach and allows for wealth effects of exchange rate changes in the determination of the balance of payments and the exchange rate. This approach subsumes the more narrowly conceived monetary approach to the balance of payments.

The model from which I draw my findings is summarized in Table 1 and has fea-

*Princeton University.

tures found in many other models (see, especially William Branson; Lance Girton and Dale Henderson; Rudiger Dornbusch, 1977; Russell Boyer). The model describes a small open economy facing fixed prices for the goods and bonds it *buys* abroad, but not for those it *sells* abroad. Capital movements take place exclusively by way of transactions in foreign bonds denominated in foreign currency. The economy is always in equilibrium; all markets are perfectly competitive and clear continuously; and expectations are perfectly stationary. (For models in which expectations figure prominently in the determination of a floating exchange rate, see Dornbusch, 1976; Pentti Kouri.)

The economy produces only one good Q_1, and output is an increasing function of the home currency price of the good p_1. Thus the country's gross domestic product Y is price *times* quantity, as at (1) in Table 1.

Household wealth W^h is held as money L^h, domestic bonds denominated in home currency B^h, and foreign bonds denominated in foreign currency F^h. (Both bonds are bills, so that capital gains and losses arise only because the home currency value of a foreign bond depends on the exchange rate π.) Wealth is written as the sum of the histories of saving S, and of capital gains and losses on foreign bonds, this being the principal dynamic relationship in the model.

Saving is made to depend on foreign and home interest rates, $\bar{r}_0$ and r_1, on disposable income, Y^d, and on wealth. Disposable income is gross domestic product *plus* interest income earned on bond holdings *less* lump sum taxes T^h, paid by households. Consumption C is disposable income *less* saving, and the demands for the two goods, C_0 and C_1, depend on consumption and on the home currency

TABLE 1—THE ALGEBRAIC MODEL

(1) The Supply Side

$$Y = p_1 Q_1, Q_1 = f(p_1), f_1 \geq 0^a$$

(2) Wealth, Saving, and Demands for Goods

$$W^h = L^h + B^h + \pi F^h$$

$$= \int S \, dt + \int F\left(\frac{\delta \pi}{\delta t}\right) dt$$

$$S = S(\bar{r}_0, r_1, Y^d, W^h), S_0 > 0, S_1 > 0,$$
$$0 < S_Y < 1, S_W < 0$$

$$Y^d = Y + \bar{r}_0(\pi F^h) + r_1(B^h) - T^h = C + S$$

$$C = \pi \bar{p}_0^f C_0 + p_1 C_1, C_1$$
$$= C_1(\pi \bar{p}_0^f, p_1, C), C_{10} > 0,$$
$$C_{11} < 0, C_{1C} > 0^b$$

$$C_1^f = C_1^f(\bar{p}_0^f, \frac{p_1}{\pi}, \overline{C}^f), C_{10}^f > 0,$$
$$C_{11}^f < 0, C_{1C}^f > 0$$

(3) Demands for Assets

$$L^h = L(\bar{r}_0, r_1, Y, W^h), L_0 < 0,$$
$$L_1 < 0, L_Y > 0, L_W > 0$$

$$B^h = B(\bar{r}_0, r_1, Y, W^h), B_0 < 0,$$
$$B_1 > 0, B_Y < 0, B_W > 0$$

$$\pi F^h = F(\bar{r}_0, r_1, Y, W^h), F_0 > 0,$$
$$F_1 < 0, F_Y < 0, F_W > 0^c$$

(4) The Central Bank, Money, and Exchange Rate Policy

$$L = \bar{B}^c + \pi R, R = 0 \text{ or } \pi = \bar{\pi}$$

(5) The Government, Fiscal Policy, and Supply of Domestic Bonds

$$D = \bar{G}_1 + r_1(B - \bar{B}^c) + T^f - T^h$$

$$B = \int D \, dt$$

$$T^f = \bar{r}_0(\pi F^h)$$

(6) The Market-Clearing Equations

$$p_1 C_1 + p_1 C_1^f + \bar{G}_1 - p_1 Q_1$$
$$= p_1 C_1^f - \pi \bar{p}_0^f C_0 + \bar{D} - S = 0$$

$$B^h + \bar{B}^c - B = 0$$

$$L^h - L = 0$$

---

a If output depends on labor input and diminishing returns prevail, the simplest Keynesian case can be obtained by assuming that labor supply is perfectly elastic at a fixed money wage (in which case $f_1 > 0$) and the simplest classical case can be obtained by assuming that labor supply is perfectly inelastic and the money wage rate perfectly flexible (in which case $f_1 = 0$).

b The demand functions for goods are assumed to be homogeneous of degree zero in prices and nominal consumption, and to have unitary elasticities with respect to nominal consumption.
c As demands for assets are constrained by actual wealth, it can be shown that $L_W + B_W + F_W = 1$, $L_Y + B_Y + F_Y = 0$, and $L_i + B_i + F_i = 0$, for $i = 0, 1$.

---

prices of the two goods, $\pi \bar{p}_0^f$ and p_1. The foreign demand for the domestic good C_1^f, is defined analogously, using the relevant foreign currency arguments.

The households' demands for money, domestic bonds, and foreign bonds are constrained by wealth and are written in nominal terms as functions of interest rates, income, and wealth, as at (3) in Table 1.

Domestic money is issued by the central bank. Thus, the stock of money L is defined at (4) as the sum of the central bank's holdings of domestic bonds $\bar{B}^c$, and of foreign currency reserves R. The central bank adjusts its holdings of domestic bonds by open-market operations. It adjusts its holdings of reserves to execute exchange rate policy. Under a floating rate, it abstains completely from intervention in the foreign

exchange market and has no need for reserves. It is thus convenient (but not necessary) to suppose that the stock of reserves is zero. Under a pegged rate, the central bank intervenes to guarantee that the rate remains at the desired level $\bar{\pi}$, and its holdings of reserves vary accordingly.

The government buys domestic goods; its demand $\bar{G}_1$ is policy determined in nominal terms. The government's budget constraint is given at (5) in Table 1, where D is its nominal budget deficit, B is the stock of government debt (the supply of domestic bonds) and is determined by the history of budget deficits, and T^f are transfers to foreigners.

If the budget deficit were endogenous as in most macroeconomic models, there could be no clear-cut distinction between goods-market disturbances and asset-market disturbances; any disturbance or policy change impinging on any term in the budget equation would affect the deficit and the supply of bonds. For this and other reasons, it is useful to suppose that the budget deficit is policy determined. The government selects a deficit of predetermined size and duration, achieving its aim by adjusting lump sum taxes T^h continuously. By implication, long-run changes in the stock of debt B are likewise policy determined, being the steady-state counterparts of temporary deficits. Finally, I assume that the government adjusts transfers to foreigners continuously to offset exactly the interest income that households earn from foreigners. This assumption causes the current account balance to equal the trade balance and simplifies the working definition of disposable income.

Under my version of the small country assumption, the supply of foreign goods is perfectly elastic at the foreign currency price $\bar{p}_0^f$, and the supply of foreign bonds is perfectly elastic at the foreign interest rate $\bar{r}_0$. We have thus to write down and solve simultaneously only three market-clearing equations—for the domestic good, the domestic bond, and domestic money, as at (6) in Table 1.

II

Using these three equations, the model can be solved for the market-clearing values of p_1, r_1, and π (or R), given the exogenous and policy variables and two state variables—the stock of domestic debt and the integral of household saving. (Wealth itself is not a state variable because it is affected instantaneously by a change in the exchange rate.) And because the model is stable dynamically, it can also be solved for the steady-state values of those same variables—those that obtain when saving goes to zero.

Before returning to the questions raised at the start of this paper, let me draw attention to three points:

1) The exchange rate is the price of one national money in terms of another. Accordingly, monetarists are fond of saying that the rate is determined in and by the money market, given the effects of disturbances and policies on all other markets. This view is misleading. In my model, as in others, the exchange rate is the price that *clears* the money market, but it is determined jointly with income and the interest rate by the responses of all markets together. A change in the exchange rate affects the home currency prices of foreign goods and of foreign bonds and has therefore to influence the goods and bond markets. In my model, moreover, it affects household wealth and by this route affects saving and absorption.

2) Price elasticities appear pervasively in the solutions. This fact likewise contradicts the simplistic view that the exchange rate is determined in and by the money market. The real or barter side of the economy is *not* irrelevant to the determination of a floating exchange rate. It is relevant, in fact, even to the effects of disturbances arising *in* the money market. (The sizes of the changes in π and Y resulting from an open-market operation depend on goods-market elasticities.)

3) The signs of many outcomes depend on an assumption that the absorption-increasing effects of a change in wealth are not "crowded out" by the absorption-decreasing effects of the concomitant change in the interest rate. To be precise, I assume that saving (absorption) is relatively sensitive to changes in wealth, while the demand for money is relatively sensitive to changes in the interest rate, so that $S_W L_1 > L_W S_1$. This is vital, for example, to my finding that an increase in the stock of debt, the long-run counterpart of a budget deficit, raises the steady-state level of income. (It plays the same role at that point as an analogous assumption made by Alan Blinder and Robert Solow.) It is likewise important to my finding that an increase in the foreign interest rate has a positive effect on income. In that instance, however, I add the supposition that the effects of changes

in $\bar{r}_0$ and r_1 on the demand for money are proportional to their effects on saving. Finally, it plays a strategic role in deciding the influence of capital mobility on the effectiveness of fiscal and monetary policies.

III

What does this model have to say about the ability of a floating exchange rate to insulate the national economy from an external disturbance? Consider first the signs of the effects of an increase in the foreign price. There is an immediate and permanent appreciation of the domestic currency and a temporary increase in income. Thus, insulation is not instantaneous but occurs with the passage of time, as saving and capital flows lead to changes in stocks of wealth and holdings of foreign bonds that cause income to return to its initial level. To put the point generally, in the very short run, a floating exchange rate has the task of clearing the money market. Gradually that task is taken over by changes in wealth, income, and the interest rate. Then the floating exchange rate takes on a different task; it clears the goods market, given the level of spending implied by the steady-state level of income, by acting on the trade balance.

It can thus be said that insulation is achieved, but only in the long run. This is true for a large class of goods-market disturbances, including some that have *domestic* origins. It is achieved against an increase in foreign expenditure, $\bar{C}^f$, but also against a shift of domestic or foreign demand between domestic and foreign goods.

Insulation is not achieved, however, against a foreign asset-market disturbance, not even in the long run. An increase in the foreign interest rate causes the domestic currency to depreciate permanently and increases income. (This result is counterintuitive, as an increase in $\bar{r}_0$ raises saving and is to this extent *de*flationary. However it also raises the domestic demand for the foreign bond, and therefore the demand for foreign currency, so that the domestic currency depreciates, raising the home and foreign demands for the domestic good. There is thus a trade balance effect that swamps the direct absorption effect.)

Returning to the process of insulation against goods-market disturbances, let us see why it is not instantaneous. Consider the effects of a goods-market disturbance that raises domestic output and income, and therefore the demand for money. As the supply of money cannot respond endogenously under a floating rate, the home currency must appreciate to reduce the demand for money, and there are two ways in which it does so. First, the trade balance worsens, reducing income. Second, households suffer capital losses on their holdings of foreign bonds, reducing wealth. If households held no such bonds, the trade balance effect would have to do the whole job of clearing the money market, and the exchange rate would have to appreciate sufficiently to offset completely the income raising effect of the initial disturbance. When they do hold foreign currency bonds, however, the capital loss effect is called into play and reinforces the decline in the demand for money. The trade balance does not have to offset the entire income raising effect of the disturbance.

IV

What does this model have to say about the powers of fiscal and monetary policies under a floating exchange rate and about the influence of capital mobility? Answers are supplied by Table 2. Let us begin with fiscal policy, represented in the short run by an increase in the budget deficit $\bar{D}$, and in the long run by an increase in the stock of debt $\bar{B}$. In the short run it raises output and income, even in the case of "perfect" capital mobility—when foreign and domestic bonds are perfect substitutes. It can be shown, however, that the short-run effect of a budget deficit is *smaller* with a floating exchange rate than with a pegged rate, regardless of the degree of capital mobility.

TABLE 2—THE INFLUENCE OF CAPITAL MOBILITY ON THE EFFECTIVENESS OF
MONETARY AND FISCAL POLICIES UNDER FLOATING
AND PEGGED EXCHANGE RATES

Outcome	Floating Rate		Pegged Rate	
	Impact Effect	Steady State	Impact Effect	Steady State
Sign of Income Change				
With Imperfect Substitutability Between Bonds				
Budget deficit	+	+[a]	+	0
Open-market purchase	+	+	+	0
With Perfect Substitutability Between Bonds				
Budget deficit	+	0	+	0
Open-market purchase	+	+	0	0
Effect of Increase in Substitutability on Size of Income Change				
Budget deficit	Decreases	Decreases[a]	Increases	None
Open-market purchase	Increases[b]	Increases	Decreases	None
Effect of Increase in Domain of Foreign Bond on Size of Income Change				
Budget deficit	Increases	None	None	None
Open-market purchase	Ambiguous[c]	None	None	None

[a] On the assumption that crowding out does not dominate.
[b] The assumption that crowding out does not dominate is sufficient, but not necessary for this result.
[c] Will decrease the size of the increase in income in the case in which an open-market purchase causes the exchange rate to depreciate.

These results are new. Robert Mundell argued that with no capital mobility fiscal policy is more effective under a floating rate. In his model, however, capital mobility diminishes its influence under a floating rate while increasing its influence under a pegged rate. In the limiting case of perfect mobility, fiscal policy is utterly ineffective under a floating rate. While the signs of the effects of an increase in capital mobility are the same in my model as in Mundell's, the presence of foreign-currency bonds prevents an increase in capital mobility from depriving fiscal policy of all its influence under a floating rate. The capital loss effect limits the change in the exchange rate, and the size of the increase in income due to a budget deficit goes to a lower but positive limit as we approach perfect mobility.

There is no need to dwell on the long-run effects of fiscal policy summarized in Table 2. They resemble those obtained from many other models, including the one used by Ronald McKinnon and Wallace Oates when they introduced the vital distinction between the short-run and long-run effects of macro policies. Thus a budget deficit has no permanent effect on income under a pegged exchange rate, and the size of its effect under a floating rate varies inversely with the degree of capital mobility (falling to zero in the long run with perfect mobility).

Turning next to the effects of monetary policy, we encounter new results that do not depend directly on the presence in this model of a foreign currency bond. It can be shown, for example, that monetary policy is not always more effective under a floating rate than under a pegged rate. An open-market purchase is more effective in the short run only when it causes the exchange rate to depreciate—which does not always happen in this model. Furthermore, the degree of capital mobility does not necessarily raise the short-run effectiveness of monetary policy under a floating rate; we can be sure that it will do so only when we are willing to assume that crowding out does not dominate.

Finally, on the last two lines of Table 2, I explore a neglected dimension of capital mobility—the influence of the domestic *domain* of the foreign currency bond. It has, of course, no relevance for the functioning of policies under a pegged rate, as there are then no capital gains or losses on holdings of foreign bonds. Under a floating rate, however, an increase in the size of the domain of the foreign bond has important implications for the sizes of the short-run effects of domestic policies.

V

What does my econometric model say about the degree of insulation provided by a floating rate and about the influence of the exchange-rate regime on the operations of domestic policies? The model has much in common with the abstract model I have been describing. Foreign currency assets do not appear explicitly in any of the equations, and there are thus no capital gains or losses due to exchange rate changes. Nevertheless, exchange rate changes prove to be influential not only on trade and service flows, but also on capital flows, and there are proxies in the model for expectations of exchange rate changes. Furthermore, capital flows are treated as once and for all adjustments of actual to desired stocks, and significant stock adjustment terms appear in most of the capital flow equations. Finally, trade and other current account flows react with long lags to exchange-rate changes, and these lags have large implications for the ability of a floating rate to insulate the economy from the effects of external disturbances.

The balance-of-payments sector of the model contains more than thirty-five behavioral equations; it is similar in size to the model developed by S. Y. Kwack, although different in specification. The domestic sector contains more than forty behavioral equations; it is a conventional Keynesian model of the U.S. economy, but it deals in some detail with the determination of the price level and with financial relationships.

Three pairs of simulations are summarized in Table 3. The first pair is addressed to the question of insulation. It describes the effect of a permanent increase in the level of real economic activity in the outside world (a disturbance resembling an increase in $\bar{C}^f$ in my theoretical model). When the exchange rate is pegged, as in the first simulation, there is an increase of real gross national product in the United States, an improvement in the current account balance, and an increase in the overall balance-of-payments surplus. When the exchange rate floats without official intervention, insulation is incomplete, but it is not inconsequential. The dollar begins to appreciate immediately, limiting the increase in the current account surplus and, therefore, the increase in real *GNP*.

In the second pair of simulations, we ask what happens when income taxes are reduced in the United States (a policy change resembling an increase of $\bar{D}$ in my theoretical model, although tax collections are not adjusted continuously to hold the budget deficit at some desired level). Under a pegged exchange rate, there is an increase in real GNP and a modest deterioration in the current account balance. The overall balance of payments improves initially owing to a reduction in capital outflows. Analogously, the dollar appreciates at first under a floating rate, just as it did in my theoretical model, and the changes in real *GNP* are very slightly smaller in the first three quarters of the simulation. Later, moreover, the dollar depreciates as in my model and the depreciation strengthens the current account balance. As a result, the medium-term effect of a tax cut is larger with a floating rate.

In the third pair of simulations, we ask what happens when the supply of high powered money is made to grow faster in the United States (a policy change resembling an increase of $\bar{B}^c$ in my theoretical model). A large capital outflow reduces the balance-of-payments surplus under a pegged rate and causes the dollar to de-

TABLE 3—Effects of Disturbances and Policy Changes under Pegged and Floating Exchange Rates in Simulations using a Quarterly Econometric Model of the *U.S.* Balance of Payments and Domestic Economy

Simulation and Variable	Differences Between Simulations and Control Solutions							
	1Q	2Q	3Q	4Q	8Q	12Q	16Q	20Q
Increase in Foreign Activity								
With pegged exchange rate								
Real *GNP*	0.46	0.72	0.82	0.88	1.05	1.04	0.97	0.89
Current account surplus	0.33	0.31	0.31	0.31	0.32	0.30	0.31	0.32
Balance-of-payments surplus	0.04	0.15	0.18	0.97[a]	0.19	0.21	0.21	0.23
With floating exchange rate								
Real *GNP*	0.42	0.53	0.50	0.49	0.44	0.37	0.43	0.41
Current account surplus	0.29	0.21	0.17	0.14	0.09	0.10	0.15	0.14
Composite exchange rate	−0.21	−1.06	−1.60	−1.98	−1.78	−1.88	−2.74	−3.57
Reduction in Income Taxes								
With pegged exchange rate								
Real *GNP*	0.24	0.44	0.63	0.81	1.26	1.44	1.51	1.50
Current account surplus	−0.02	−0.04	−0.05	−0.06	−0.12	−0.19	−0.28	−0.37
Balance-of-payments surplus	0.01	0.01	0.01	−0.02	−0.10	−0.17	−0.24	−0.33
With floating exchange rate								
Real *GNP*	0.24	0.43	0.62	0.82	1.46	1.91	2.20	2.35
Current account surplus	−0.03	−0.04	−0.04	−0.05	−0.09	−0.03	−0.05	−0.08
Composite exchange rate	−0.01	−0.06	−0.03	0.08	1.01	1.60	2.17	3.58
Increase in Growth Rate of Supply of High Powered Money								
With pegged exchange rate								
Real *GNP*	0.01	0.09	0.37	0.78	1.85	3.25	3.24	3.82
Current account surplus	0.00	0.03	0.02	−0.02	−0.07	−0.24	−0.36	−0.56
Balance-of-payments surplus[b]	−0.04	−0.52	−0.57	−0.14[a]	−0.65	−0.22	−0.78	−1.69
With floating exchange rate								
Real *GNP*	0.05	0.64	1.38	1.62	3.32	4.25	4.70	5.40
Current account surplus[c]	0.02	0.38	0.49	0.25	0.49	−0.01	0.19	0.14
Composite exchange rate[c]	0.27	3.16	5.24	3.97	4.91	2.49	8.07	11.87

Note: Data used and actual simulations may be obtained from the author. Exchange rates and foreign activity refer to trade weighted indices.

[a] Reflects a reduction in capital outflows resulting from an endogenous abatement of speculation against the dollar.

[b] Outcomes in certain quarters affected by capital flows resulting from changes in the discount rate.

[c] Outcomes in certain quarters affected by capital flows mentioned in fn. b above; under a floating rate, these affect the current account balance by way of the exchange rate.

preciate under a floating rate. There is an increase in real *GNP* in both instances, but it is much larger, as expected under a floating rate, because the depreciation of the dollar improves the current account balance.

There is thus a remarkable degree of consistency between the signs and relative sizes of the outcomes in these simulations and the predictions summarized in earlier tables. It would be nice to know that this is not an accident—that the econometric model behaves as it does because it cap-

tures the chief features of the abstract model. I could point to several fortuitous consistencies, as well as citing many analytical consistencies in the spirit if not the particulars of specification. I therefore draw the usual conclusion that much work remains to be done.

REFERENCES

A. S. Blinder and R. M. Solow, "Does Fiscal Policy Matter?," *J. Publ. Econ.*, Nov.

1973, *2*, 319–37.

R. S. Boyer, "Devaluation and Portfolio Balance," *Amer. Econ. Rev.*, Mar. 1977, *67*, 54–63.

W. H. Branson, "Portfolio Equilibrium and Monetary Policy with Foreign and Non-Traded Assets," in Emil-Maria Claassen and P. Salin, eds., *Recent Issues in International Monetary Economics*, Amsterdam 1976.

R. Dornbusch, "Expectations and Exchange Rate Dynamics," *J. Polit. Econ.*, Dec. 1976, *84*, 1161–76.

———, "Capital Mobility and Portfolio Balance," in Robert Z. Aliber, ed., *The Political Economy of Monetary Reform*, Montclair 1977.

L. Girton and D. Henderson, "Central Bank Operations in Foreign and Domestic Assets under Fixed and Flexible Exchange Rates," in Peter Clark et al., eds., *The Effects of Exchange Rate Adjustments*, Washington 1977.

Peter B. Kenen, *A Model of the U.S. Balance of Payments*, forthcoming.

———, "The Balance of Payments and Policy Mix: Simulations Based on a U.S. Model," *J. Finance*, May 1974, *29*, 631–54.

——— and Polly R. Allen, *Asset Markets, Exchange Rates, and Economic Integration*, forthcoming.

P. J. K. Kouri, "The Exchange Rate and the Balance of Payments in the Short Run and in the Long Run," *Scand. J. Econ.*, No. 2, 1976, *78*, 280–304.

S. Y. Kwack, "Simulations with a Model of the U.S. Balance of Payments: The Impact of the Smithsonian Exchange-Rate Agreement," in Peter Clark et al., eds., *The Effects of Exchange Rate Adjustments*, Washington 1977.

Ronald I. McKinnon and Wallace E. Oates, *The Implications of International Economic Integration for Monetary, Fiscal, and Exchange-Rate Policies*, Princeton 1966.

Robert A. Mundell, *International Economics*, New York 1968.

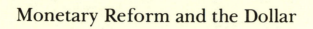

Monetary Reform and the Dollar

INTERNATIONAL LIQUIDITY: THE NEXT STEPS

By Peter B. Kenen

The international monetary system is in better health today than for many years. The stock of reserve assets is adequate for now and for the next decade. The central banks have shown great skill and vigor in their efforts to defend the monetary system. The recent growth in European reserves has been achieved at the expense of the United States, but this country can still purchase all the time it needs to solve its payments problem if only it is willing to pay out reserves and to use the time it buys for a good adjustment. The less developed countries have inadequate reserves, but their payments problems cannot be resolved by a simple increase in liquidity, for they will spend any cash they can earn or borrow.

Yet there is a lingering concern about the future. Few critics still take aim at the margin, arguing the need for more reserves. But many still complain that the structure of reserves is unsatisfactory, arguing the need for consolidation to protect the quality of the reserve media. And too few people have examined the implications of the new arrangements connecting central banks.

The problems of the margin and of asset structure cannot, of course, be segregated. Concern about prospective growth first drew our attention to the structure of reserves. Critics argued that such growth could impair the quality of the dollar as a reserve currency.[1] Then the critics' own proposals met with similar objections. Triffin's plan for reform of the IMF, for example, could expose the Fund to a dangerous gold drain as it went about incurring liabilities.[2]

But recent history calls direct attention to the structure of reserves. There has been a quiet drift toward gold, with several central banks increasing their gold holdings or running down their dollar assets as they lost reserves. And though gold production has grown steadily since 1957, the annual accretion to official holdings has been falling off. Recent changes in the monetary system likewise stress consolidation rather than expansion. They seek to discourage or offset massive flows of private money that could drain reserves from New York and Lon-

---

[1] Robert Triffin, *Gold and the Dollar Crisis* (New Haven, 1960), pp. 64-69, and my own "International Liquidity and the Balance of Payments of a Reserve-currency Country," *Q.J.E.*, Aug., 1960, pp. 572-86.

[2] U.S. Congress, Joint Economic Committee, *Hearings: International Payments Imbalances and Need for Strengthening International Financial Arrangements* (Washington, 1960), pp. 193-96.

don, impairing the confidence of other central banks. They also seek to supplement national reserves and the lending powers of the IMF. These changes are described with great candor in two recent articles,[3] but a brief summary may be helpful here.

To forestall speculation and related cash flows, the U.S. Treasury and Federal Reserve System have begun to intervene in the foreign exchange markets. In adroit maneuvers against speculation, they have forced the forward mark and Swiss franc toward their interest parities. The United States, United Kingdom, and European governments have also forged a common policy toward the London gold market, which apparently includes a set of ground rules governing central bank transactions and provision for joint intervention to contain the price of gold.

This new activity has been financed by intricate credit arrangements. In some cases, the United States has made outright purchases of foreign currency or borrowed by issuing special obligations denominated in a foreign currency. More often, it has drawn on new stand-by credits set up in its favor by foreign central banks. Under these arrangements, each central bank agrees to swap its currency for dollars. The two countries then agree to liquidate their balances at a fixed exchange rate and a fixed date three to six months later. Some of the foreign currencies drawn under these arrangements have apparently been used in spot operations; some were set aside to meet the deferred obligations incurred by the United States in its intervention on the forward markets.

The details of these "swap" transactions vary from instance to instance. So do the operations in each foreign currency. The American authorities have tried to mesh their interventions with the money-market tactics of the other central banks. Because there is a shortage of money-market assets in most European countries, commercial banks hold foreign currencies, especially dollars, as secondary cash reserves, and central banks must operate in the foreign exchange markets to carry out domestic monetary policies.[4] They cannot control bank reserves using the familiar tools; they have instead to influence Eurodollar flows. Paradoxically, the development of the Eurodollar market may delay the formal monetary integration of Western Europe—the creation of a common currency for the European Economic Community. The many kinds of Eurodollar credit substitute for more familiar money-market instruments, and the Eurodollar market gives the EEC and adjacent countries a unified money market. We may have to wait

[3] Charles A. Coombs, "Treasury and Federal Reserve Foreign Exchange Operations," *Fed. Res. Bul.*, Sept., 1962; Robert V. Roosa, "Assuring the Free World's Liquidity," Federal Reserve Bank of Philadelphia, *Bus. Rev.*, Sept., 1962. See, also, Bank for International Settlements, *Thirty-Second Annual Report* (Basle, 1962), pp. 125-27.

[4] Oscar L. Altman, "Foreign Markets for Dollars, Sterling, and Other Currencies," IMF *Staff Papers* (Dec., 1961), pp. 339-42.

some years for a European reserve currency to join the dollar and the pound.

The United Kingdom has also used central bank credits to strengthen its reserve position. After the revaluation of the deutsche mark and guilder in the spring of 1961, there was a massive run on sterling. But other central banks supplied the equivalent of $900 million in short-term credit to supplement Britain's own reserves. A few months later, the United Kingdom turned to the IMF and purchased $1.5 billion worth of foreign currencies. It used part of this record drawing to repay its debts under the so-called "Basle arrangements." In effect, Britain used the IMF to consolidate its short-term obligations and supply an indirect but uniform exchange guarantee.

In order that the IMF may continue serving this important function, ten major countries have agreed to place $6 billion worth of convertible currencies at the disposal of the Fund should it need this money to finance a major drawing. (These commitments are listed in the second column of Table 1.) This agreement is embodied in a protocol, the General Arrangements to Borrow, which provides that the Managing Director of the IMF shall propose a call on these currencies if a participating country applies for a drawing on the Fund to "forestall or cope with an impairment of the international monetary system" and if IMF resources are inadequate to finance the drawing. A call must then be approved by a complex qualified majority of the ten participants, and any member may opt out of its obligations by giving notice that its "present and prospective balance of payments and reserve position" cannot honor further calls.[5] Money borrowed by the Fund under the General Arrangements will be repaid within three to five years, when the drawing on the Fund is itself repaid, but may be paid back earlier if any of the lending countries encounters a payments problem of its own.

These credit arrangements are an intriguing mixture of reserve transfer and reserve creation. All of them involve the creation of new reserve media. A swap transaction between the United States and Germany adds dollars to German reserves and deutsche mark to U.S. reserves. It is not a transfer of outstanding reserve assets from one country to another. Nor is it reserve growth in the ordinary sense. The reserves created by the swaps will be extinguished as soon as they are used. When the United States uses its deutsche mark in the foreign ex-

[5] International Monetary Fund, *International Financial News Survey* (Jan. 12, 1962). The Baumgartner letter attached to the protocol provides that the prospective drawer shall not vote and that a call shall not be issued without (1) a two-thirds majority of the number of participants voting and (2) a three-fifths majority of weighted votes, with weights based on the size of the participants' commitments. These provisions mean that any four countries listed in Table 1 could block a U.S. drawing, but that the United Kingdom and Germany could also do so, likewise the United Kingdom or Germany, plus France or Italy, plus any third country.

change market, its balance at the Bundesbank is eradicated rather than transferred to a third country.[6] Furthermore, the cash assets created by the swaps and by special loans to the IMF are matched by liabilities and slated for repayment within a brief time; they do not bring a lasting increase in owned reserves.

But the architects of these new arrangements envisage further innovations that could enlarge owned reserves. When the United States moves over into payments surplus, it can accumulate European currencies instead of forcing other countries to run off dollar assets or to sell us gold. New reserves may also be created by more swap transactions, but larger and without express provision for repayment. Presumably, these balances could be used in any way—transferred to another country or converted into a third currency.

Underlying all these innovations is the fact and expectation of close co-operation among the key central banks. Such co-operation is essential to orderly official intervention in the foreign exchange markets and to an alignment of fundamental policies affecting trade and payments within the industrial community. But it may not be the proper basis for an international monetary standard. Reserve-asset structure can only pose a problem if some central bank decides to hold less of one reserve asset and more of another, or because a central bank does not want to hold its new reserves in the form they take when they are created. A monetary standard based on "close co-operation" rather than binding commitments and arrangements is built on a bad premise: It relies on acquiescence to cope with a crisis that can only be brought on if one central bank has declined to co-operate. Despite the talk and evidence of close co-operation, moreover, the reservoir of good will could easily run dry. During the last year or so, the London gold price has been kept a shade below $35.20 an ounce—a limit that may not allow sufficient variation to penalize potential speculators. Why this very narrow spread? Is it because central bank gold arbitrage becomes profitable when the gold price rises above $35.20 and some central banks might engage in arbitrage despite the new ground rules? Why, too, the current obsession with fixed exchange rates? Is it because some central banks would be compelled to sell off certain reserve assets if they foresaw changes in the key exchange rates?

Finally, *ad hoc* acquiescence in collective measures may have a high price. The Under Secretary of the Treasury, Robert Roosa, has opposed exchange rate guarantees because, he says, "one country after another will interpose conditions on its readiness to accept a guarantee—conditions that will at the least interpose their judgments more

[6] The same thing will happen to dollar balances held by a foreign government, but in only one of several likely cases—if the balances are used to buy up foreign currency from Americans.

specifically into the determination of our military, aid, or investment activities abroad." "And where would we find ourselves," he goes on to ask, "when the demands of one of our guaranteed creditors conflicted with those of another?"[7] If Mr. Roosa is convinced that we would have to pay for the privilege of giving a guarantee, how much more costly might it be to purchase close co-operation without giving any guarantee? And what would be our price for co-operation once the United States had begun to hold large amounts of foreign currency? One might reply that every country would then have a club with which to beat the other into close co-operation. But this apparent parity would soon vanish if one country ran a payments deficit and lost reserves—and that would surely be the time when other countries would be nervous about holding the first country's currency.

All of this is not to say that the central banks are fair weather friends. I merely argue that we should obtain binding assurances and more automaticity when the weather is its fairest so that every country can count on help when the sky begins to cloud. I shall not succumb to temptation and present another "plan" for reform of the monetary system. It would be quite wrong to backtrack now, searching for perfection, when the recent innovations offer a foundation on which to build a very strong monetary system.

In my view, these recent innovations start a major change in financial practice. They begin to substitute governmental credits for a further growth in national reserves. Carried further, these arrangements can provide liquidity without doing damage to the reserve position of any center country of the IMF. They point to a system of overdraft financing rather than the more familiar methods of deposit growth. I shall therefore urge some minor changes that will make the credit network a more perfect substitute for growth in owned reserves—changes aimed at automatic access to existing credits and at steady growth in overdraft facilities.[8]

As a first step toward a stronger system, I would favor the rapid completion of the stand-by network. Every major central bank should undertake to lend $150 million or $200 million to the United States and a like amount to the United Kingdom, obtaining a reciprocal commitment from each of those two countries. One might even want asymmetry in each overdraft agreement, with the United States committed to lend more than it is allowed to borrow. Many countries use the dollar when they intervene in the foreign exchange markets. Granted larger dollar credits, they would not need to draw on one another. In

[7] Roosa, *op. cit.*, p. 6.
[8] I do not claim any originality for these proposals or for the way in which I have combined them. Readers who have followed the burgeoning literature will recognize bits of Triffin, Angell, Bernstein, Zolotas, and others. All remaining faults are, of course, those of the gold exchange standard.

brief, bilateral asymmetry would give rise to over-all symmetry; each other country could draw dollars to defend its currency, and the United States could draw every other money.

These stand-by arrangements should be permanent, with provision for immediate drawings and for repayment in six months at the exchange rate that prevailed when the drawing first took place. A country should be able to use its stand-by credits whenever its currency falls beneath its parity with that of its partner. It should not be allowed to use borrowed funds for purchasing a third currency. With these restrictions and, perhaps, an end to cross-crediting, no country could do damage to its partners, nor influence its partners' economic policies.

There is, of course, one danger in a credit network connecting the United States with every other country. The United States might find itself financing a French deficit with some other country, say Germany or Britain. At present, by contrast, such a deficit is financed by a transfer of existing dollar balances, not with newly drawn dollars. But if American financing went on very long, the dollar would tend to a discount on the foreign exchange market and the United States could draw marks or pounds to correct the situation.

Next, I would favor two important changes in the General Arrangements to Borrow, making those arrangements fully automatic and allowing them to grow. Under the existing agreement, two or three potential lenders can prevent Fund borrowing merely by casting negative votes. Furthermore, each country is the final judge of its own ability to lend. I would consequently urge that the IMF be empowered to invoke the General Arrangements at its own discretion—power that Per Jacobssen tried hard to obtain—and that every country be compelled to participate unless the Fund's holdings of that country's currency are above the usual three-fourths of quota.

The General Arrangements also fix each participant's commitment. As time goes on and trade and payments grow, these commitments may prove far too small. They may even be too small to cope with the next crisis. The IMF cannot draw the whole $6 billion because that sum includes the currency of the deficit country. Each country's obligation should therefore be tied to its own reserves. Its commitment should be equal to, say, half its gross reserves less an exemption fixed in advance. Table 1 shows how this arrangement would work out. I have inverted my formula and calculated the fixed exemptions implied by each country's commitment under the existing General Arrangements and by its gross reserves at June, 1962. The exemptions total $29.1 billion; they are listed in the fourth column of the table. I have also listed alternative exemptions for the ten participants, cutting those of Germany and

TABLE 1

RESERVES AND CONTINGENT COMMITMENTS TO THE IMF, ACTUAL AND PROPOSED
(Billions of Dollars)

COUNTRY	GROSS RESERVES, 6/30/62	CONTINGENT IMF COMMITMENT		PROPOSED EXEMPTION	
		Actual	Calculated*	Implied†	Adjusted
Belgium.................	1.60	.15	.15	1.30	1.30
Canada.................	1.81	.20	.16	1.40	1.50
France.................	3.48	.55	.44	2.40	2.50
Germany................	6.23	1.00	1.36	4.25	3.50
Italy..................	3.24	.55	.62	2.15	2.00
Japan..................	1.62	.25	.06	1.10	1.50
Netherlands............	1.79	.20	.25	1.40	1.30
Sweden.................	.73	.10	.11	.55	.50
United Kingdom.........	3.44	1.00	.22	1.45	3.00
United States.........	17.08	2.00	2.54	13.10	12.00
Total‡.................	41.02	6.00	6.00	29.10	29.10

* Equal to 0.5(gross reserves less adjusted exemptions).
† Equal to gross reserves less 2×actual commitments, so that 0.5(gross reserves less implied commitments) = actual commitments.
‡ Detail may not add to total because of rounding.
SOURCES: Basic data from International Monetary Fund, *Annual Report* (Washington, 1962), and *International Financial Statistics* (October, 1962).

the United States and raising those for Britain and Japan. These revised exemptions make allowance for Britain's large monetary liabilities and do not reward Germany for its reserve appetite of 1956-61. But the structure of exemptions is of secondary interest. The more important feature of this formula is its flexibility. A 1 per cent annual increase in gross reserves would give the IMF power to borrow an extra $200 million. And if this were insufficient, a $200 million cut in the exemptions, spread across all countries, would give the Fund another $100 million. The IMF might even be allowed to cut exemptions by $200 million in every year that saw gross reserves rise by less than 1 per cent. Otherwise, there might be insufficient credit to replace renewed growth in national reserves. Exemptions might someday turn negative, but this would simply say that each country has a fixed commitment in addition to the one depending on reserves.

These amendments to the General Arrangements would have one other virtue. They would help to curb the reserve appetite of a surplus country. An increase in one country's gross reserves would enlarge its contingent obligation to the IMF and permit the Fund to supply its currency to deficit countries. They could then slow down their own reserve losses, though not offset more than half the surplus country's gains.

I come now to the vexed question of exchange rate guarantees.

Many people look upon a guarantee as the painless way to run a payments deficit—to lodge extra dollars with nervous foreigners. Viewed this way, guarantees hold a dangerous contradiction. "In giving a guarantee," Roosa writes, "the United States would expect to release its domestic economic performance . . . from the constraints imposed by the need for balance of payments equilibrium; in accepting a guarantee, other countries would expect the United States to maintain their confidence in its internal and external economic performance. . . ."[9] Put differently, the very growth of guaranteed claims might sap this country's will to honor its commitment (or, at least, cause other countries to distrust this nation's pledge). But this is to misconstrue the function of a guarantee. It should help the foreigner retain the dollars he already holds, not seek to seduce him into holding more. Furthermore, a guarantee would free the United States from the chief constraint imposed by its role as a reserve center. It could change its exchange rate without wrecking the international monetary system. Guarantees are often urged to forestall devaluation as they might stave off runs on major currencies. They should actually be urged because they would allow a devaluation when it is required. Without guarantees, moreover, we may confront a general exchange rate paralysis; when the United States has come to hold European currencies, the European countries may also feel a compulsion to keep their exchange rates still.

There are grave problems of practice and principle lurking in this simple case for a guarantee. But I must not spike the discussants' guns by a pre-emptive strike. Let me merely raise two common questions and sketch out the briefest answers:

1. Could the United States afford to honor a firm guarantee on some $13 billion of official dollar claims? Here, I think, the critics confuse the burden of a guarantee with the burden of devaluation. If foreign governments were told that the United States planned to devalue the dollar, they would doubtless take our gold before the devaluation. In that case, the dollar value of their gross reserves would rise by just as much as with a guarantee—and they could exercise the same extra claims on American resources. A guarantee would impose a net resource-cost only if the foreigner had imperfect foresight, or the United States gave no notice of its plans. The United States, moreover, could control the resource-cost by attaching its exchange rate guarantee to a special instrument rather than covering all dollar assets held by foreigners. The Treasury could issue nonmarketable bills carrying a guarantee (and a lower rate of interest than its other obligations). It

---

[9] Roosa, *op. cit.*, p. 6. His objections would apply with special force to the recent suggestions of the United Kingdom for an indirect IMF guarantee on new foreign exchange holdings. He has, in fact, anticipated this proposal in a trenchant passage (*ibid.*, pp. 7-8).

might then decline to issue more such bills, save at stated intervals and in such amounts as it thought appropriate to secure desired growth in total dollar claims.[10] It might even limit the amount it would sell to a single country. But this would create two kinds of dollar balances and might give rise to new gold losses; the giving of a guarantee on some dollar assets could itself stir rumors of devaluation and cause foreigners to convert their other dollar assets into gold.

2. Could the United States give a firm guarantee when, in fact, it broke its word back in the thirties? Here, I think, there is misunderstanding of the old gold clause case. In my inexpert reading of the jurists' jargon, the Supreme Court did not sanction abrogation of the gold clause. On the contrary, it held that the government could not break a contract. But it then declined to grant redress because U.S. citizens were not injured by the abrogation; their other obligations were denominated in paper dollars, not in gold. This argument on damages could not be applied to foreign central banks that have obligations outside the United States. In any case, we could assuage foreign doubts about the sanctity of a U.S. guarantee by accepting the compulsory jurisdiction of the World Court in all matters that pertain to the guarantee.

Some critics of the present monetary system would like to give the IMF a much larger role. They would dispense with stand-by credits and rely directly on drawings from the Fund. They would give guarantees through the IMF by having it take dollars in exchange for new deposits. But bilateral arrangements have a place in any system; they can be invoked quickly and quietly, giving faster aid than a drawing on the Fund. They can then be paid off by a drawing on the Fund when calm is again restored. As I see it, moreover, expansion of the IMF comes at a later stage. When it comes time to enlarge national reserves, the necessary growth should be secured by a further change in the General Arrangements to Borrow. The Fund's obligations should be made transferrable (or exchanged for deposits at the IMF). The IFM could then create reserves when countries came to it for aid, and the attendant growth in total reserve assets would be a response to manifest needs. At that point, too, the IMF would become quite Triffinesque. But most of the sensible proposals lead in this direction. They differ more in rates of change than in their objectives. And while all roads may lead through Yale, after some meandering, we do not have to travel them at a breakneck speed.

[10] One might link this arrangement to the Posthuma proposals under which, it is reported, central banks would keep the gold content of their gross reserves below a specified percentage.

Financing and Adjustment:
The Carrot and the Stick

PETER B. KENEN

NEAR the start of any treatise on international monetary problems, the author is sure to declare that the problem of international liquidity cannot be divorced from the problem of balance-of-payments adjustment. On this point, indeed, professors and practitioners fully agree, although they are at odds on most other issues. The creation of reserves or liquidity, the author will point out, serves to "finance" the deficit countries, enabling them to defer the adoption of policies required to end their deficits. Reserve creation or "financing" is thereby portrayed as a pernicious alternative to the correction of imbalances, otherwise described as "adjustment."

There is, to be sure, a small band of heretics who advocate the generous financing of deficits. They stress the possibility of transitory imbalances and the capacity of households and firms to make adaptations by themselves, offsetting payments deficits without changes in policy. They would therefore provide a deficit country with ample access to reserves so that it can take time to diagnose its payments problem, and should that problem be temporary, abstain from any change in its economic policies.

The more orthodox view, however, contends that most major imbalances are not accidents, but result from imprudent financial policies—excessive credit creation or government spending—and believe that extended financing is far inferior to a prompt attempt at decisive adjustment. A deficit country ought not to have easy access to reserves; it must be barred from procrastination. On this more common view, adjustment is virtually inevitable, however painful, and should not be delayed. Otherwise, inflationary pressures will be transformed into obdurate cost-price disparities that are not easy to eradicate.

This brief note proposes that financing and adjustment should be considered as complements rather than rivals—that there is another way to look at the connection between them. It is too often argued that reserve creation should regulate the speed with which a deficit country begins to adjust, when, in fact, reserve creation ought also to govern the rate at which a country corrects its imbalance once it has decided to do so. When a deficit country does decide to act upon its payments problem, it formulates a program of policy changes. Even then, however, the effects of that program on its economy and balance of payments may take hold rather slowly. This is true even of devaluation, the most abrupt of all policy changes, for consumers and producers do not at once readjust long-established habits (and even if they did, their new patterns of consumption and production might not be reflected in the foreign-exchange market and in official reserves until goods and cash started to move in response to newly placed orders). In brief, a deficit country always requires financing, and the rate of reserve creation must be aligned with the desired pace of adjustment. The promptness and pace of adjustment, moreover, are separate desiderata, and the former ought not to preempt all of our attention.

We do not know very much about the "optimum" pace of payments adjustment, but are not wholly ignorant on this score. Consider, for example, the case of a country facing that most painful affliction—domestic unemployment combined with a payments deficit. The textbook prescription for this affliction is, of course, devaluation.[1] But let us be stubborn—like most finance ministers—and stick to fixed exchange rates. Let us also be puritanical and insist that the deficit country refrain from imposing new trade barriers or restrictions on capital movements. Hemmed-in this way, the deficit country has now to take a nasty dose of medicine—to reduce domestic prices relative to those abroad. It may not have to cut money-wage rates; if man-hour output is rising, labor costs and prices may perhaps be made to fall merely by holding the

[1] See any textbook.

rate of increase of money wages below the rate of growth of productivity. To do so, though, the deficit country may have to endure an increase in unemployment, and if it faces a particularly belligerent "Phillips curve," the requisite increase in unemployment may be rather large. In this case, the deficit country may prefer to stretch out the process of adjustment, choosing a little unemployment for a long time, rather than a lot of unemployment for a short time. Its choice, however, must be "validated" by the international monetary system which, with slow adjustment, must provide financing for the entire interim period.

There are, assuredly, other aspects to the choice of an "optimal" time path—for deficit and surplus countries alike. They might try to manipulate domestic policies, à la Mundell, so as to restore full employment through fiscal policy while using monetary policy to regulate capital movements. The preceding example, however, should suffice to illustrate the basic point that "financing" and "adjustment" are not entirely competitive, but are partial complements, and has the further implication that any attempt to regulate reserve creation solely to prevent procrastination by the deficit countries will strip away what little freedom of choice a country enjoys under fixed exchange rates. It will foreshorten the process of adjustment, once begun, and may thereby raise the welfare costs of external balance.

There is, however, one more point to be made about the relationship between financing and adjustment, and this point is also overlooked by many authors. The rate of reserve creation is apt to affect the quality of the restoration of balance, not just its timing and pace. Countries that are forced to correct imbalances rapidly because they do not have sufficient reserves (or access to reserves), may do so in destructive ways—by resort to controls on trade and investment. Any reader familiar with recent policies in the developed countries, let alone the less-developed countries, can readily provide his own example.[2] The attempt to enforce "discipline" on national policies by limiting the creation of reserves has,

[2] See any country.

as its unfortunate byproduct, the effect of relaxing "discipline" in the choice of policy instruments.

Just as a country with two distinct economic objectives has usually to use two policy instruments in the pursuit of its objectives, the international monetary system, with several objectives regarding the correction of imbalances, has also to employ a series of instruments. It cannot use the rate of reserve creation to control simultaneously the timing of national policy decisions, the pace of their application, and the quality of the techniques employed. But it is an unfortunate fact of life that the international community is not yet endowed with a sufficient range of instruments to pursue these separate objectives efficiently. It must rely on the cooperation of sovereign governments and, as the ultimate penalty for failure to cooperate, on the denial of credit facilities to a deficit country. It is likewise obvious, and most unfortunate, that this ultimate penalty applies chiefly to the deficit countries; there is no comparable way to control the behavior of surplus countries. Under these circumstances, it must be decided whether reserve creation shall be used as a carrot or a stick—whether the provision of reserves should serve to "validate" an appropriate pace and quality of measures to restore balance or be strictly limited to compel an early adoption of rapidly acting policy measures.

My own answer should be clear by now, if only because I have raised the question and challenged the conventional view. If a choice must be made, reserve creation should be used as a carrot, to purchase slow but sure progress in the correction of imbalances, not brandished like a stick to punish misbehavior. One must nonetheless remember that both carrot and stick are used to keep the donkey moving, and that the stick can be applied continuously without being consumed, while the carrot has always to be dangled a safe distance from the donkey; once it has eaten the carrot, the donkey will stop.[3] I therefore suggest that reserves-as-a-carrot ought to be provided conditionally, not as an all-around distribution of CRU (collective reserve units) or an increase

[3] See any donkey.

in automatic drawing rights on the IMF. Otherwise, countries may use up their reserves before taking action, confirming the expectations of those who call for "discipline." If countries are granted conditional access to reserves, they may be led to comply with accepted norms regarding all three attributes of the process of restoring balance—timing, pace, and quality. If the donkey is allowed to eat the carrot bite by bite, and made to jog along between the bites, the process of adjustment may improve substantially.

The International Position of the Dollar in a Changing World

PETER B. KENEN

INTERDEPENDENCE IN FINANCIAL POLICY

PEACEABLE relations between states require that each nation affected by another's acts be induced to acquiesce in all those acts, but this acquiescence may take many forms. It may be quite positive, involving affirmation and, at times, concerted action, or it may be negative, involving mere silence or *pro forma* protest and, most importantly, total abstinence from countervailing acts. Economic and financial relations between states display all forms of acquiescence and too often demonstrate the sad results of failure to obtain consent. Their history, however, manifests gradual progress from an erratic reliance on tacit consent to a wide-ranging reliance on positive, explicit undertakings frequently accompanied by concerted action. Increasingly, moreover, that concerted action has been multilateral, not just bilateral. The tariff warfare of the twenties and earlier decades has now given way to the formal regulation of tariff policies, and the bilateral trade agreements of the 1930's, covering exclusively tariff reductions, have been replaced by a single comprehensive multilateral arrangement, the General Agreement on Tariffs and Trade (GATT) dealing with all aspects of commercial policy. The competitive exchange-rate depreciations of the thirties have likewise given way to formal regulation, beginning with the Tripartite Declaration of 1936 involving the United Kingdom, France, and the United States and culminating in the Articles of Agreement adopted by the Bretton Woods Conference of 1944 establishing the International Monetary Fund (IMF).

The domain of acquiescence is as yet incomplete, and the evolution of

PETER KENEN is Professor of Economics at Columbia University, New York. The author is indebted to the Editors of *International Organization* and to the members of his graduate seminar for comments on an earlier draft of this article. He is also indebted to several former students, especially Richard Meyer and Christopher Beauman, for some of the thoughts developed here.

foreign trade and investment has thrust contentious new issues to the fore more rapidly than nations have devised the instruments required to resolve them. The recent appearance and startling growth of multinational corporations has generated controversy over jurisdiction in matters of exchange control, taxation, and trade policy. More importantly, the practice of accommodation is as yet imperfect. A nation claiming to be injured when another raises tariffs will ordinarily come to GATT, but failing an agreed solution, GATT has no recourse but to authorize limited retaliation. In international monetary matters, moreover, frequent acquiescence in other countries' policies and less frequent but important acts of active cooperation have been punctuated by disruptive challenges to concerted action, and that action, when taken, has too often been limited to the provision of large-scale credits to deficit countries. Despite very frank discussions of policies in the Organization for Economic Cooperation and Development (OECD) and the Bank for International Settlements (BIS) active cooperation has rarely extended to the most important realm—mutually agreed alterations in national monetary and fiscal policies or in the exchange rates.

One can, indeed, contend that monetary cooperation between the major countries has not advanced much beyond the better moments of the twenties. Then, as now, central banks readily gave large amounts of credit to one another or organized consortia of private lenders. Now, as then, however, those credits are too often the visible confessions of failure to agree on changes in exchange rates or on other measures to end the imbalances that credits can merely finance. It is widely argued, for example, that United States leadership in organizing aid to sterling early in the sixties was born of Washington's belief that the alternative—devaluation of the pound—would weaken the American balance of payments. Sterling was regarded as the first line of defense for the United States dollar. Eventually, of course, the pound was devalued without disastrous consequences for the United States dollar, and the long delay before devaluation served merely to prolong the painful austerity which must go with devaluation without also allowing Britain to enjoy the gains from devaluation. The United Kingdom, moreover, incurred large external debts to protect the pound (and dollar) so that its present payments target cannot be mere balance but has instead to be a surplus large enough to pay those debts. Most recently, in 1968, the major central banks advanced some $2 billion in credits to France but did so to stave off the crisis created by the refusal of the Federal Republic of Germany to revalue the mark and France's refusal to devalue the franc (alternating with the French threat to devalue hugely). International monetary history from the Tripartite Declaration of 1936 through Bretton Woods and on to the crisis of the sixties can be described as acquiescence purchased by commitments to defend the status quo—to maintain virtually rigid exchange rates.

One could live with this regime if acquiescence were achieved in another realm. If nations could agree that some would run surpluses and others would run deficits and each would lend or borrow—gain or lose reserves—accordingly, no country would be forced to seek acquiescence in policies to alter its balance of payments. Any such agreement, however, has also to include consensus on components, not just on totals, and on the whole array of national policies required to evoke the proper patterns. All countries might agree, for instance, that continental Europe should reduce its surplus and that the United States should reduce its deficit, but any such agreement must come unstuck if the United States tries to bolster exports by, say, tax incentives while Europe seeks a decrease of American direct investment. Despite a decade of continuous consultation in OECD, BIS, and other institutions no such detailed consensus on targets or instruments has as yet emerged.

It is not hard to understand why full acquiescence has been so elusive in monetary matters. Many acts by governments affect other countries, but trade and payments policies are perceived to have a peculiar, symmetrical gain-loss effect, and international monetary policy has the further feature that explicit collaboration, not simple consent, is required to implement the most important measures.

One normally encounters this sense of gain-loss symmetry because decisions on international economic policies affect transactions between individuals in two or more countries altering the balance of advantage between them. Even here, however, explicit collaboration is not always needed to implement a policy. Tacit consent— failure to retaliate—may sometimes suffice. The United States can raise its tariffs unilaterally. Doing so, it aids its import-competing producers and injures foreign suppliers; this is perceived as gain-loss symmetry.[1] It can do so, however, without the assistance of other governments; its policy will be effective as long as other countries refrain from explicit countervailing acts. The United States can also declare a reduction in the gold value of the dollar, seeking thereby to devalue the dollar in terms of foreign currencies. If successful, it would make American goods more attractive than foreign goods, aiding its import-competing producers and export industries and injuring competitors throughout the world; devaluation would be gain-loss symmetrical. Under present institutional arrangements, however, the United States cannot devalue the dollar in terms of foreign currencies without the collaboration of all other governments. The foreign-currency price of the dollar is determined by foreign central banks which buy and sell dollars against their own currencies in the foreign-exchange markets. If they refuse to change the

---

[1] An increase of United States tariffs could, of course, injure American consumers and might also injure foreign consumers. Unfortunately, this more important effect is rarely perceived; it is the direct gain-loss effect on home and foreign output that too often dominates tariff policy (and exchange-rate policy, discussed below).

currency prices at which they intervene to stabilize exchange rates, they will completely frustrate American policy.[2]

The financing of long-lasting payments imbalances—deficits and surpluses resulting from the failure to adjust exchange rates or change other policies—is likewise symmetrical and calls for collaboration. No deficit country can maintain a fixed exchange rate unless it possesses a stock of foreign currencies to use for market intervention; it must buy up its own currency with foreign currency to prevent the excess supply of its currency from depressing its market exchange rate. A change in its holdings or borrowings, however, involves a symmetrical change in the asset position of a foreign country, and one country's operations in the foreign-exchange markets may also call for active help from a foreign central bank.

Even the majestic neutrality of gold does not solve the problem. No country can count upon financing a deficit by selling gold unless some other country is committed to buy gold, performing a positive act. Gold transfers, moreover, involve symmetrical changes in national balance sheets. Active collaboration and gain-loss symmetry were a vital part of the old gold standard.

Unfortunately, the full, mutual interdependence of financial policies was not clearly recognized in the days of the gold standard. Prior to 1914 each central bank pegged its own currency to gold and regarded the maintenance of that gold parity as its chief obligation. Taken together, the system of gold parities implied a network of national exchange rates—a full set of foreign-currency prices for each nation's money. But because the central banks maintained those exchange rates by dealing in gold bullion, not by intervening in the foreign-exchange markets, they looked upon a change in the gold value of a nation's currency as that nation's sovereign right despite its effect on exchange rates. Such a change was deemed damaging to national prestige and to financial stability but was nonetheless regarded as a unilateral, practicable act.

This view carried over into the twenties. In 1925, for instance, the United Kingdom hitched the pound to gold at its prewar parity. Economists, including John Maynard Keynes, criticized the move, warning that the old gold parity would put sterling out of line with other currencies—that the exchange rates would be all wrong. The critics, however, spoke to ears deafened by repeated assertions that the gold parity mattered most, not the exchange rates implied by that parity. Full understanding of gain-loss symmetry and the need for active collaboration did not dawn until the thirties, following the forced de-

[2] There has been much confusion on this point generated by a loose use of words. The United States defines the international value of the dollar in terms of gold (at $35 an ounce) and can change that valuation unilaterally. A change in the declared gold price of the dollar, however, is not devaluation in the strict sense of the term. The United States cannot alter the foreign-currency price of the dollar if foreign central banks continue to stabilize their own currencies in terms of the dollar (tacitly altering their currencies' gold values). More on this matter later.

valuation of the pound in 1931 and the not-so-forced devaluation of the United States dollar in 1933. Having cut the ties to gold, London and Washington each faced two options—to let exchange rates fluctuate freely in the markets or to intervene directly in those markets to stabilize exchange rates by dealing in currencies. Drifting toward the second course, they came soon to understand that their intervention had to be coordinated; the dollar price of sterling could easily be fixed by the British Exchange Equalization Account or by the American Exchange Stabilization Fund, but both could not be in the market at the same time unless they were agreed on aims and tactics.

The Final Act of Bretton Woods gave formal recognition to these facts, establishing a basis for consistent market operations in a new, ingenious way. Under that agreement, as put into practice, all major central banks undertook to stabilize their currencies by purchasing and selling United States dollars. Doing so, of course, they also undertook to stabilize the price of the dollar in terms of their own currencies. There was to be no need for market intervention by the United States. To carry out their operations, however, foreign central banks must hold or have access to the necessary dollars, and it was to be the special function of the United States to satisfy their needs. Some central banks have long held some of their reserves in dollars, but others, mainly European, prefer to hold gold, for a mixture of motives that need not be recited here. This second group of countries, however, was promised access to the dollars they would need for intervention; the United States Treasury promised to buy gold for dollars and also to sell gold to countries that had taken dollars from the foreign-exchange markets. A working division of labor was established between the United States and all other countries. The others undertook to stabilize exchange rates; the United States, in turn, undertook to accommodate the others' asset preferences by dealing in gold and dollars. A strict reading of the Final Act of Bretton Woods would make it seem that governments are still much concerned with gold; they may, in fact, declare their parities in terms of gold. In practice, however, these declared parities serve only to define the dollar prices of foreign currencies, thereby providing the benchmarks needed to govern market intervention.

The Passivity of Power

Whether in full knowledge of their implications or under a misapprehension, the United States agreed to these arrangements at Bretton Woods, surrendering direct control over the foreign-currency price of the dollar. Other countries can devalue or revalue their currencies vis-à-vis the dollar and can implement those acts by market intervention. The United States can therefore experience change in its exchange rate but only at the initiative of other countries. It has, in fact, experienced a substantial revaluation of the dollar since the Second World War in consequence of other countries' devaluations, a revaluation that has surely exacerbated its current payments problem.[3]

The importance of the problem, viewed prospectively, can best be illustrated by reciting the favorite scenario of those who argue for decisive unilateral action to end the United States payments deficit. The United States, it is suggested, should suspend the conversion of dollars into gold in order to produce two results. First, foreign central banks and governments could not buy gold with dollars they already hold and with those they might acquire in future exchange-market operations. Second, there would be no official gold price for the dollar—the convention that has helped other countries to stabilize their currencies in relation to the dollar. One cannot deny that this single step would solve the United States payments problem. The method by which it would be solved, however, would depend entirely upon the acts of other governments, not upon the American initiative. Other countries could follow one of two routes. They might continue to stabilize the prices of their currencies in terms of the dollar, buying additional dollars in the foreign-exchange markets as United States deficits fed dollars into the markets; they might solve the American payments problem by accumulating dollars that could not be converted into gold. They might instead abstain from intervention and allow the flow of dollars to raise the dollar prices of their own currencies rather than adding dollars to their reserves; they might permit the depreciation of the dollar required to increase American exports, decrease American imports, and improve the United States balance of payments.

It is hard to know how many countries would follow each of these two routes as decisions in these matters are not independent. If many countries go one way initially, others are quite apt to follow. It should be clear, however, that the United States cannot control the final outcome, save by exerting political pressures or throwing extraneous issues into a bargaining process, and that either solution would leave much to be desired. The need to accumulate inconvertible dollars rather than allow exchange rates to change would surely cause some governments to criticize and combat those United States policies they deemed to be the basic cause of the American deficit. Gaullist complaints about United States direct investments and overseas bases would echo in other quarters. But the alternative to open-ended involuntary lending,

[3] That revaluation amounts to some 375 percent since 1948, if measured by the weighted-average change in fourteen countries' exchange rates (Canada, Japan, Australia, India, the United Kingdom, France, West Germany, the Netherlands, Belgium, Italy, Spain, Brazil, Mexico, and Venezuela) but Brazil accounts for all but 39 percent. It amounts to some 485 percent if measured by the weighted average change in the exchange rates of all countries (except the Republic of Korea) accounting for more than 0.5 percent of United States exports. Notice, however, that most countries have suffered more rapid inflation than the United States so that a "purchasing-power-parity" computation based on changes in exchange rates and consumer prices would show a modest *devaluation* of the United States dollar: 59 percent for fourteen countries (and 17 percent without Brazil), or 113 percent for all major trading countries. Data from International Monetary Fund, *International Financial Statistics;* indexes weighted by United States exports in 1967. I am indebted to Miss Carol Gerstl for these computations.

a depreciation of the dollar, would shift the balance of competitive advantage toward the United States, leading to new demands for import restrictions and export subsidies, and these demands are already too loud in too many countries. Resort to these protective measures, it should be added, could not prevent solution of the United States payments problem. A free market in foreign exchange would respond to trade restrictions by forcing an additional compensatory depreciation of the United States dollar; if foreigners handicap American exports, the price of the dollar would fall further to make them more attractive. Those who impose restrictions, however, would succeed in shifting the burden of adjustment onto other countries, generating similar demands for more protection in those other countries and, generally, restricting world trade.

One should not preclude the better possibility of orderly adjustment in the key exchange rates. General agreement on a modest devaluation of the dollar, or, more to the point, a modest revaluation of the Deutschmark and certain other currencies, may not be out of sight. But experience in 1968, when France and West Germany declined to change their parities, suggests that agreement is still out of mind, and the universal acquiescence required to change the price of the dollar would be even more difficult to achieve. Whatever the practical prospects, moreover, one basic fact remains. Acquiescence is required and, in this particular case, the initiative lies abroad, not with the United States.

American initiative is constrained a second way, likewise a consequence of Bretton Woods. During the wartime consultations between Washington and London the British, led by Lord Keynes, proposed the creation of an institution quite different from the IMF. It would have been a global clearing union *cum* central bank operating on an overdraft principle. A country requiring dollars to stabilize its currency in the foreign-exchange market could have drawn on its credit line at the clearing union, transferring its drawing rights to the United States in exchange for dollars. The global supply of reserve assets could have been increased at will under this arrangement, merely by enlarging all countries' drawing rights. The very different IMF that emerged at Bretton Woods lacks this flexibility. It is, instead, a fixed pool of gold, dollars, and other currencies which countries can purchase against their own currencies. Those purchases, moreover, cannot be made freely; once a nation has purchased foreign currencies equal in value to its own gold subscription (one quarter of its total quota in the IMF) it must satisfy increasingly restrictive conditions to make additional purchases. In consequence, drawing rights beyond the so-called gold tranche are not perfect substitutes for national reserves (or for the automatic drawing rights envisaged in the Keynes plan). The Articles of Agreement do provide for a quinquennial review of quotas, and quotas have been enlarged on two occasions. An increase of quotas, however, does not provide an increase of reserves, nor does it substitute for larger reserves; automatic access to the IMF is enlarged by just one-fourth of any quota increase, and that same automatic access to the IMF is purchased by a further gold subscription—an exchange of one reserve asset for another.[4]

The Bretton Woods system then, did not provide ways to augment reserves in a regular, systematic way. It did not generate a new reserve asset under IMF control, as Keynes' clearing union would have done, but left the process of reserve creation to the vagaries of gold production and the willingness of individual central banks to hold foreign currencies as part of their reserves. Most importantly, central banks as a group could not increase their *net* reserves beyond the limits set by new gold supplies as the currency claims of one central bank are the liabilities of some other central bank. In effect, all countries but one could increase their reserves provided the remaining country willingly ran deficits in its balance of payments (and that its currency was regarded as a satisfactory reserve asset by other central banks).

The United States assumed this special role. From 1949 through 1957 United States payments deficits totaled $5.8 billion, of which a mere $0.5 billion was financed by gold and other reserve losses while $5.3 billion was financed by dollars transferred to foreign central banks and added to their reserves. From 1958 through 1968 United States deficits totaled $15.6 billion, of which $9.1 billion was transferred in gold and other reserve assets while $6.5 billion took the form of newly created dollar reserves.[5] At the end of 1968 United States reserves totaled $15.7 billion, of which $10.9 billion was gold, but dollar liabilities to foreign central banks totaled $15.2 billion.[6]

Some observers have suggested that the United States sought this special role,[7] which view would explain its opposition at Bretton Woods to the creation of a global central bank strong enough to do the job. My own reading of the record is quite different. The United States willingly ran deficits until the mid-fifties, seeking to establish a more balanced distribution of gold and other reserve assets, especially to restore the reserve positions of European countries. But it would have been quite willing to lose gold rather than accumulate dollar liabilities. The United States did not seek reserve-currency status for the dollar but allowed other countries to attach that status to the

[4] It should be pointed out that certain IMF transactions do increase reserves (automatic drawing rights) but only in an indirect, imperfect way. When one country buys another's currency, beyond its automatic (gold tranche) drawing rights, the other obtains additional automatic drawing rights known in the jargon as super-gold-tranche drawing rights. But the size and distribution of these extra drawing rights depends haphazardly on the size and currency distribution of conditional drawings at any point in time.

[5] Deficit computed on the "official settlements" basis.

[6] Data from Board of Governors, Federal Reserve System, *Federal Reserve Bulletin,* and International Monetary Fund, *International Financial Statistics.* Figures for early years approximate.

[7] See, e.g., John R. Karlik, "The Costs and Benefits of Being a Reserve-Currency Country" (unpublished Ph.D. dissertation, Columbia University, 1966), Chapter III.

dollar as they took on dollar assets through the middle fifties.[8] Forswearing regulation of its own reserve position by agreeing to trade gold for dollars, the United States foreclosed the choice between holding reserve assets (gold and foreign currencies) and incurring reserve debts (dollar liabilities to foreign central banks). It left the composition of its reserve balance sheet to other countries' asset choices and, more importantly, assumed a special obligation for the stability of the entire system. Decisions concerning its own balance of payments became, perforce, decisions to regulate the growth rate of global reserves, and as its liabilities grew through time, its policies affected the quality of those reserves. Growth in foreign dollar holdings relative to United States gold, necessary to enlarge total reserves by more than global gold accretions, impaired foreign confidence in the convertibility of existing dollar balances. To make matters worse the United States could not enforce decisions regarding the growth of reserves. Conscious American decisions to increase reserves by running deficits—if such decisions were ever made—could be vetoed by conversions of dollars into gold.

Why did the United States accept these constraints on its initiative in exchange-rate policy and its independence in managing its own reserves? One need not extract explicit answers from the record. One has merely to recall the unique economic and political position of the United States in the mid-forties—a position of enormous strength but also of special vulnerability. The then-accepted reading of interwar experience blamed the United States for most of the disasters of the thirties. Its enormous net creditor position, representing interallied debts and United States lending in the twenties, gave the United States a decisive role in interwar negotiations on financial matters. More importantly, the sensitivity of American imports to the domestic business cycle and their very large share in total world trade caused all other nations to share the fortunes of the American economy. Conversely, United States exports, while very large absolutely, were not a large share of domestic output so that the American economy was thoroughly insulated from disturbances arising abroad. Looking back upon the thirties, economists could justly say: "Whenever the United States sneezes, the rest of the world catches pneumonia." Finally, most observers feared that the postwar world would not be too different and that, in particular, the overwhelming economic problem after reconstruction would be another enormous American depression.

Hints of this consensus can be found in Keynes' proposal for a clearing union. It was explicitly designed to give other countries a blank check on the United States in case the American economy should take ill again, reducing

[8] The United States decision to buy and sell gold, reaffirmed at Bretton Woods, is sometimes cited as contrary evidence—that the United States sought to make the dollar a more attractive reserve asset. This is to miss the point. The decision was designed to make gold more attractive. Nations needing dollars for intervention would not have dared to hold gold as a reserve asset without the American pledge to buy gold for dollars.

American imports and driving other countries into payments deficit. The IMF's Articles of Agreement rejected this device but proffered an alternative to serve the same aim. If the United States slid into another depression, causing other countries to use up their reserves (and their dollar drawing rights at the IMF) the dollar could be declared a "scarce currency," and other countries could discriminate against American exports, thereby balancing their external accounts without resorting to deflation or devaluation.

The United States forswore the initiative in monetary matters because the postwar world looked to have a single economic center—one to which all other countries had to forge their separate links. It was not to be bipolar, let alone polycentral. The overwhelming size and apparent instability of the United States made it seem as though other countries would need the initiative in monetary matters. That same size, moreover, seemed to preclude unilateral acts by the United States, for anything it did would so much affect all other countries that they would have usually and collectively to neutralize its acts.

By now, of course, this country is not the sole center of economic strength. The other industrial countries, taken together or in subgroups, come near to matching its production and surpass its trade. Indeed, one can discern several emerging centers, including the European Economic Community (EEC) and, by itself, Japan. Significantly, the slowdown of European economic expansion after 1965 affected third-world trade no less severely than the United States recession of 1960-1961. What may be more important, the overseas activities of major American firms, including their trade and overseas production, account for a large share of their total output and their total profits. Compared to most other industrial countries, the United States remains relatively insulated from external disturbances, but that isolation is much less complete than it was in the interwar period. Changes in other countries' economic policies can have profound effects on vital American interests.

The United States retains enormous power, and changes in the international economy, underway or undetected, are quite apt to give it more. The overseas activities of United States firms, mentioned several times, cause decisions made in Washington, Detroit, and Pittsburgh greatly to influence the economic life of other countries. The emergence of the Eurodollar market has given the United States dollar new uses and prestige and created new channels to transmit the impact of domestic policy. Even as American monetary policies and, to less extent, fiscal policies have now to be attuned to the balance of payments, so too those same policies have come to affect credit conditions in other countries and cannot be conducted without this fact in mind. In 1968-1969, for instance, United States banks sought to escape the stricter policies of the Federal Reserve by borrowing billions of Eurodollars, thereby driving interest rates to new highs in the Eurodollar market and putting upward pressure on the home interest rates of other countries. Finally, the enormous political influence of the United States gives Washington considerable leverage in international financial affairs. It is not surprising that West Germany, the country most concerned to preserve the American military presence in Western Europe, has been the most willing to finance the United States payments deficit by buying American Treasury securities rather than acquiring ordinary short-term dollar claims or buying additional gold.

But the continued influence of United States policies, specific and general, is at once a source of strength and a constraint. Other countries cannot be entirely passive in the face of credit-market trends that undermine their aims. Further, United States efforts to combat inflation or to attract capital may have long-term consequences adverse to basic American aims, slowing economic growth throughout the world and curtailing world trade. More importantly, the use of political influence to accomplish short-term financial objectives can be counterproductive. Having played on German fears to finance its deficit, Washington is now constrained by its own success. It cannot think of pulling troops out of Western Europe without also asking whether West Germany would not turn its dollars in for gold.

As at Bretton Woods, though in different ways, the massive impact of the United States economy and of American policy continues to limit American autonomy. Though largest in size and power, even now, the United States must continue to behave as though it were but slightly more than one among equals.

Toward a Better System

The special role of the United States, defined at Bretton Woods, has to be perpetuated. The United States must still forswear full freedom in financial policy if only because autonomous acts may be self-defeating. Nevertheless, self-imposed parity with other countries, accomplished by accepting certain policy constraints, should earn full equality for the United States in certain critical domains. The United States must require the right to demand the acquiescence presently accorded acts of other major countries and, *a fortiori*, of weaker countries. It must press for three important changes in the international monetary system.

Acknowledging, at once, that there is just one exchange rate connecting any pair of national currencies, one has also to acknowledge that this same exchange rate cannot be decided by one of two governments. The Bretton Woods regime must give way to one of two new systems. On the one hand, governments may concur in total abstention from stabilization, leaving private markets to determine the exchange rates. This is the option favored by many economists, if only for want of workable alternatives. Abstention, however, would not be enough. Nations would have still to concert many vital policies in order to prevent wide movements in exchange rates adverse to their common interests and to the working of free-market rates, and they would have to abstain from using trade taxes and controls to offset any change in the free exchange rates. On the other hand, governments could agree on a set of rules to govern intervention and, in particular, to introduce needed changes in otherwise fixed rates when movements in reserves or other indexes argue for such changes. History suggests that it will be difficult to work out those rules, but it may not be impossible if governments will work to write *general* rules governing all future changes in rates rather than, as now, *ad hoc* agreements concerning a specific rate. A system of general rules would probably call for early changes as imbalances appeared and, therefore, modest changes, whereas *ad hoc* consultation (and, too often, deadlock) over specific changes tends now to take place too late, when large changes may be needed and, correspondingly, are more bitterly resisted.[9]

Noneconomists concerned with the development of general rules to govern relations between states may properly prefer this second option—regulated rates with rules for change. But if that is their choice, they must bring their influence and argument to bear against those of the economists, as we too often tend to favor the rule of markets over that of men.

Next, prompt action must be taken to remedy the major defect of the Articles of Agreement of the IMF. Adequate reserve-creating machinery must be started up in order to supply reserves at a regular rate and to reconcile national policy objectives. It will always be impossible to obtain consistent, comprehensive agreements on financial policies if nations are competing for a fixed or slow-growing stock of reserves. If global reserves do not increase to match the global total of desired surpluses, one country or another will fail to achieve its aims and may then adopt economic policies inconsistent with others' aims. Steady growth of reserves is not itself a sufficient condition for harmonizing policies, thereby to maintain stable exchange rates, but it is surely necessary. Here, of course, the basic reform has been accomplished; new machinery has been designed and is ready for use. Under an agreement reached a year ago the IMF is authorized to credit each member country with special drawing rights (SDR's) to be used in much the same way as Keynes' overdrafts. At the start of every five-year period the Managing Director of the IMF is authorized to propose the creation of SDR's in fixed annual amounts. If his proposal is adopted by the member governments, SDR's will be distributed among the countries in amounts proportionate to their IMF quotas. Each

---

[9] For a brief survey of current proposals for reform of the exchange-rate system, including formulas to regulate changes, see the *Economic Report of the President* (Washington: U.S. Government Printing Office, January 1969), pp. 145ff. See also J. R. Williamson, *The Crawling Peg* (Princeton Essays in International Finance, No. 50) (Princeton, N.J: International Finance Section, Department of Economics, Princeton University, 1965); and F. Modigliani and P. B. Kenen, "A Suggestion for Solving the International Liquidity Problem," *Quarterly Review* (Banca Nazionale del Lavoro), March 1966, pp. 3–17.

member, in turn, can transfer SDR's to another country in order to acquire that country's currency (or buy back its own currency held by the other country). Strict rules are proposed to prevent abuse of the new drawing rights. Any country can draw its account down to zero but may not remain there continuously. It need not reconstitute its total holdings (as with ordinary drawings on the IMF) but over any five-year period its holdings must equal at least 30 percent of its cumulative annual allotment. A country can use all its SDR's some of the time and some of its SDR's all of the time but cannot use all of them all of the time. Further, no member need accept SDR's from any other country if it has already accepted (from all sources) an amount twice as large as its own allotment. This last rule is designed to remedy one defect of the Keynes plan; SDR's cannot become a blank check on one member country. The new plan has been cast as a series of amendments to the IMF's Articles of Agreement and these have been ratified by a large number of countries. The machinery is ready for use as soon as governments are ready to begin.

Finally, there is urgent need for a consolidation of existing reserve holdings as these now comprise an untidy and unstable mixture of dollars, pounds, French francs, claims on the IMF, and national gold holdings. There is, in particular, a need to protect the monetary system against any massive switch from currencies to gold. Modest steps have been taken in this direction. The major central banks have now agreed to help the United Kingdom convert sterling into dollars by extending medium-term credits. No similar device, however, can be applied to the large number of dollars held by foreign governments. Central banks are willing to lend dollars to the United Kingdom but would not be as willing to lend gold to the United States. It would, indeed, be difficult to work out gold loans, if only because the countries holding the gold needed to meet a run on the United States gold stock are quite apt to join the run (if not, indeed, to start it). An increase in the price of gold could solve the problem by revaluing United States gold reserves sufficiently to repay foreign dollar holdings. But a higher gold price has several drawbacks. It would be inequitable in impact because it would reward the countries that have held gold relative to those that have held dollars. It would be uncertain in effect because we do not know how gold production would respond, and it is not at all clear that the increase in price needed to revalue existing gold holdings would thereafter evoke the "right" rate of increase through new gold production. Finally, it would be inefficient as it would draw additional real resources into the production of a commodity for purely monetary use; if central banks persist in the primitive belief that settlements between them must involve transfers of physical assets, one can surely find a cheaper poker chip than gold. There are, in short, better ways to forestall instability resulting from shifts between gold and dollars. Consider, for example, a simple plan proposed by several experts. Let all central banks deposit all their gold, dollars, and other reserve assets with the IMF, obtaining in exchange a new composite reserve asset backed by all the gold and other assets that had been held separately. Each nation would then have a *pro rata* claim on all the gold and dollars—and the dollars would no longer be a claim on United States gold. Some observers have objected that this consolidation would forever deny gold to those that had held dollars. These critics, however, ignore the fact that the American gold stock is by now too small to honor all the claims upon it—that no one has an undisputed claim to gold. Other critics argue that central banks already understand this simple fact and would not perpetrate a run on gold. This objection makes more sense but counts on rationality at moments of crisis. Rules that obtain in normal times tend often to break down amid uncertainty, political or economic. Consolidation is possible only when workable arrangements can be devised by reasoned argument. It will be impossible when it is most needed—when one can no longer appeal to reason and common interest.

Convertibility and Consolidation: A Survey of Options for Reform

By Peter B. Kenen*

Previous discussions of our general subject have focused narrowly upon the costs and benefits to the United States of its special role in the monetary system. They have sought to measure the principal effects on the conduct of American domestic policy—on the ability of the United States to achieve internal economic aims.[1] This approach is not appropriate to the time or place at which we meet. It was, indeed, defective from the start. It involved comparisons with the effects of alternative policies, requiring subjective political judgments concerning those policies. It neglected effects on other countries, including the effects of policies they would have adopted had the dollar not been available or acceptable as a reserve asset. It ignored costs and benefits to the international economic system, even the U.S. share in the global totals, of the several financial services furnished by the dollar.

Appraisals of that systematic role are now found abundantly in the debate on reform. A few are made explicitly; more are made implicitly, especially by those who urge an early resumption of convertibility and strict limitations on the role of

dollar reserves.[2] These judgments, moreover, are bound to loom large in the negotiations that have just begun. Governments obliged to choose among proposals for reform must look to their effects on the incentives to correct or finance imbalances, to their implications for the choice and timing of corrective measures, and to the ways the system will distribute praise and blame for taking or failing to take initiatives. These are the dimensions that impinge most importantly on national autonomy in the pursuit of domestic objectives.

I plan to paraphrase some of the calculus that seems to be implicit in governments' attitudes, then to look at ways of reducing the role of the dollar, in order to accommodate an emerging consensus concerning the net cost of its continued use.

First, however, a few words about the past. The defects we now see in the postwar system (and in our perceptions of it) must not obscure a vital fact. The system put together at and after Bretton Woods served its founders' aims quite well. It permitted and probably fostered directly the dismantling of burdensome restrictions, an enormous expansion in the volume of international trade and investment,

---

* Professor of economics and international finance and Director, International Finance Section, Princeton University.
[1] See, e.g., Karlik and the works by Aliber, Aubrey, Grubel, and Salant cited there.

[2] For explicit cost-benefit analyses, see C. F. Bergsten and R. N. Cooper; for conflicting implicit analyses, see the presentations by G. Shultz and V. Giscard d'Estaing at the 1972 International Monetary Fund meetings.

and the successful pursuit simultaneously of domestic prosperity and growth. The economic annals of the last two decades compare impressively with those of any others in the past century. It would be wrong, however, to give most of the credit to the monetary system, especially to single out the role of the dollar. Foundations for the liberalization and growth of the world economy were laid very early after the war, at a time when the United States was prepared to run deficits in its international accounts, but before it was fully possessed or conscious of its role as a reserve center. The United States was willing to countenance continuing deficits so that other countries could rebuild their reserves, but looked to gold losses, not the growth of dollar holdings, as the likely outcome.

There is, in addition, a point to be made about terminology and another to be made about ends and means. When, hereafter, I talk about convertibility, understand me to address the rights and duties of governments and central banks, not of individuals and firms. The convertibility of currencies, one into another, by private parties is impaired only by barriers to dealings in foreign exchange—when access to markets is limited by class of transaction or transactor, or when currencies cannot be transferred freely between residents and foreigners. It is not even impaired, on my definition, by the possibility of changes in exchange rates. (It is, perhaps, impaired *de facto* by large uncertainties concerning exchange rates and by inadequate forward facilities, and may therefore be limited more seriously when pegged rates are not fully fixed than when there are no pegs at all. It is also impaired by nonprice controls over foreign trade and investment, but these can best be analyzed on their own demerits.) The dollar, then, remains as fully convertible for private parties as most other currencies. If, indeed, its convertibility in the first sense was impaired in 1971, it was not by the United States, but by other governments, especially France, that restricted systematically access to their currencies.

Convertibility, in strict and proper use, denotes only the commitment by a government to make official settlements in a particular subset of assets designated by law or custom. It is the substance of the obligation contained in Article VIII (4) of the Bretton Woods Agreement to repurchase one's currency when it is presented by a foreign official institution. Furthermore, it is a one-sided commitment; it does not convey the corresponding obligation to demand "asset settlements" at all times—to refrain from accumulating other countries' currencies. This is a different, important matter to which we must turn before long. (Notice, in addition, that another term often used for this obligation, "interconvertibility among reserve assets," is misleading. Used with particular reference to the United States, it may be taken to imply that the dollar should continue to be a reserve asset, and that the obligation to pay out gold or Special Drawing Rights (*SDR*'s) in exchange for dollars is meant only to accommodate the asset preferences of foreign central banks. The term may also be construed incorrectly to suggest that the obligation in question is unique to the United States, when other countries have assumed it for many years.)

Convertibility in this second, governmental sense is not a moral attribute. Countries that honor the obligation do not thereby attain a state of grace, and those that default on it may not sin grievously. Some countries have maintained official convertibility only by restricting private convertibility—by limiting trade and investment. Others, including Canada, have not maintained official convertibility, allowing exchange rates to fluctuate instead, but will not have to answer for too many sins when called to final judgment. W. Fellner reminds us emphatically that convertibility is a means to an end. It is a crude device to force the harmonization of national policy targets and useful only if it improves the selection and timing of policy responses.[3] A monetary system with or without convertibility works well only when it provides incentives and penalties to foster the rectification of deep-seated imbalances, but it must also provide financing, official or private, sufficient to ride out imbalances that do not call for therapy.

To be more concrete, the United States should resist the temptation to do penance for refusing to resume convertibility if, in its judgment, convertibility would interfere with the efficient choice and timing of payments policies. This would leave the world on a dollar standard, but that standard may be no worse than others from the standpoint of harmonization and policy selection. A dollar standard might be more efficient than some others in forcing frequent changes in exchange rates, including the resort to floating rates. Surely it would be more efficient than a gold or *SDR* standard established prematurely, without first securing sufficient reserves for the United States (and the means to defend its reserves by changing its exchange rate). In language used before, the premature restoration of official convertibility could invite or compel the United States to interfere with private convertibility, hampering the conduct of trade and investment.

[3] The word "crude" needs special emphasis here. As movements of reserves do not have symmetrical implications for surplus and deficit countries, unless central banks obey the "rules of the game," they do not always force the right country to act. More important, they cannot harmonize national aims regarding the current and capital accounts. M. V. Posner stresses this shortcoming, suggesting that the harmonization of these aims might substitute for institutional reform, and that reform can be no substitute for harmonization.

I.

The current debate on costs and benefits takes place in semantic disguise, cloaked in the dialogue concerning asymmetries in the monetary system. To compound confusion, several asymmetries enter the debate, and the participants rarely define them precisely.

There is, first, asymmetry in the signals the system gives to deficit and surplus countries. As movements in reserves are bounded in but one direction, deficit countries have more reason to act. The same point is sometimes made differently. The Bretton Woods agreement, it is said, contains a strong bias toward devaluation, which works out as a bias against the dollar. (Earlier formulations of this assertion, that the system contains a deflationary bias, have been drowned by more recent complaints that the chief deficit country is exporting inflation to the outside world.)

There is, next, a pervasive asymmetry arising from differences in country size, especially the difference in size between the U.S. economy and its major partners. The external transactions of the United States are smaller in relation to its economy than those of most other countries but bulk large absolutely in the global totals. For this reason, we are told, the United States is preoccupied with its domestic objectives; it tends to neglect external commitments. More to the point, its domestic policies have large effects on other countries by way of trade and capital flows. Changes in monetary policy lead to flows of short-term capital that are small in relation to the New York money market and the U.S. credit base but large enough to alter substantially credit conditions abroad.[4] Fi-

[4] This particular asymmetry could be reduced by the successful integration of European capital markets, and this may be sufficient cause for the United States to support present plans for integration.

nally, this same difference in country size is said to cause the U.S. preference for payments policies that have the smallest impact on its economy, especially for changes in exchange rates, rather than for policies that discipline domestic activity.

A third asymmetry arises from the widespread use of dollars by other countries' traders and investors, which sensitizes foreign economies to U.S. policies. Changes in expectations concerning the dollar affect the conduct of world trade, producing huge financial flows between international credit markets based on the dollar and the smaller national markets.

The fourth asymmetry derives from the third. Because the dollar is the most important "vehicle" currency, it has become the "intervention" currency—the one used by central banks in the foreign exchange markets—and is also used to state the par values of many currencies. These two features of the system restrict the United States's freedom to change its own exchange rate simply and effectively; it cannot change its parity unilaterally vis-à-vis currencies denominated in dollars or make a new parity effective unless all other countries agree to intervene appropriately in the foreign exchange markets. Parities relate to market rates only by way of the limits they set for changes in market rates —the limits at which central banks undertake to intervene. The United States could perhaps impose new exchange rates for the dollar by intervening directly in spot markets. To do so at cross-purposes with others, however, is to invite a breakdown of day-to-day cooperation vital to the functioning of a pegged-rate system. This same fourth source of asymmetry has another implication—one that has achieved great prominence recently. Because the dollar is the intervention currency, market exchange rates involving the dollar can move by only half as much as exchange rates involving other currencies. This phe-

nomenon was not very important when exchange rates were confined within a narrow band. The wider bands installed by the Smithsonian Agreement and the recent U.S. suggestion that bands be widened further have caused it to attract much more interest and innovative energy.[5]

Note that U.S. exchange-rate policy is circumscribed by a number of asymmetries —including some I have not yet mentioned. The United States cannot declare a new parity simply or uniformly, as other countries use the dollar to declare their own. This particular problem can be solved only by altering the Bretton Woods Agreement, to replace the present options, gold and the dollar, with gold or SDR's. The United States cannot make a new rate effective unless other governments alter consistently the rates at which they intervene in foreign exchange markets. This problem cannot be solved by changing the *numéraire* for par values, not even by moving to multiple-currency intervention of the type implied by U.S. proposals designed to achieve symmetrical bands. The United States cannot alter its par value without inducing some other countries to do so too. Its trade is vital to many economies. Finally, any change in exchange rates for the dollar has meant heretofore a change in the relative values of reserve assets. The devaluation of 1971 reduced the gold and SDR values of dollar reserves to the particular detriment of countries that have held their reserves in dollars.

There is a fifth asymmetry in the monetary system. Because the dollar has been the chief reserve currency, U.S. deficits have been financed differently from those of other countries. The United States has not always lost reserves; it has instead accumulated debts to foreign governments

[5] To complicate matters, the European Community has been working to narrow the bands within which its currencies fluctuate against one another. On these dimensions of asymmetry see Cooper and J. Williamson.

and central banks. This unique privilege is the main target of the many new proposals for ending the reserve role of the dollar. The objections are not new; they were one reason for French gold purchases in the mid-1960's. They are endorsed more widely today, however, partly because the U.S. decision to close the gold window has forced financing in dollars, but partly because the advent of the *SDR* has made possible growth in world reserves without a corresponding growth in dollar balances. The world does not need the dollar as a reserve asset, and the benefit-cost calculation is seen to come out much closer to zero. As in most other zero-sum situations, moreover, this perception has produced new tensions; the players have less cause to play the game together—to maximize their joint gain.

Furthermore, the players tend to stress in their dialogue costs to themselves and benefits to others. The United States contends that it has been burdened unfairly by two features of the system. The special constraints imposed by the use of the dollar for intervention and reserve accumulation have made it difficult for the United States to change its exchange rate. On this view, the United States has been forced by other countries' policies to choose continuing deficits rather than impose harsh domestic discipline.[6] Other countries, by contrast, deem themselves burdened because they are affected profoundly by U.S.

[6] No one says that this was so in the late 1960's when the domestic situation called for the same discipline. It is said, however, about earlier years and, again, about the last few years. One hears, in addition, that the United States was obliged to maintain interest rates higher than those desired domestically in order to make the dollar attractive as a reserve asset. It is hard to find evidence supporting this assertion (save perhaps in the days of "operation twist"). Notice, in any case, that the need to offer an attractive yield on reserve-currency balances is not different from the need to maintain high interest rates for domestic deflation and payments adjustment—a need that would have been quite strong if other countries had not financed U.S. deficits by holding dollar reserves. The two obligations are not additive.

policies but cannot much influence its choice of policies. They cannot compel the United States to take corrective measures by converting dollars bought in support of exchange rates or by altering the composition of existing reserves. In the 1960's, moreover, they could not make *any* change in composition, even one that was not meant to prod U.S. policy, without threatening the U.S. reserve position, global confidence in the dollar, and the stability of the system as a whole. No one country was large enough to blackmail Washington by demanding gold for dollars, but each was large enough to fear that its actions could undermine the monetary system.

The current debate on asymmetries and burdens reflects more fundamental disagreement concerning the mix and timing of corrective measures. Some say, indeed, that no country would care about the asymmetries if all could agree on the ways in which imbalances should be removed. The U.S. interest in using exchange rates (or forcing others to do so) contrasts quite sharply with European views.

This contrast derives in part from ideology. Changes in exchange rates are still treated far too widely as confessions of failure in economic policy. Deficits are due to the mismanagement of money. By implication, they are the responsibility of deficit countries and amenable to monetary therapy. Even as economists are overly inclined to start discussions of payments adjustment by introducing a spontaneous change in tastes or technology (which leads always to a "dilemma" case), so men of affairs are too much prone to start their discussions by speeding up the printing press at the central bank. These intellectual prejudices are reinforced by political preferences. The desire, widespread abroad, to curb U.S. direct investment leads to the recommendation that the United States eliminate its deficit by restricting sharply capital outflows, and this recommendation is opposed in Washington. The United States has imposed controls on capital outflows, but these are not especially effective—which may be no accident. The United States prefers to improve its current account, to accommodate capital outflows rather than restrict them. Finally, there are sound pragmatic reasons for the difference in outlook. Changes in exchange rates could correct the U.S. balance of payments without depressing the American economy, but they would do so by depressing other countries' production and employment.

The U.S. proposals for reform of the system, set forth in September 1972, reflect directly the American assessment but seek also to accommodate other countries' views. The United States would be willing to resume some form of convertibility, leaving others to decide whether or not to accumulate more dollars, if the rest of the world would agree to more flexible exchange rates and new rules to limit the use of trade policies and capital controls as substitutes for changes in exchange rates. It would be willing to give up the benefit of being a reserve-currency country if it could also shed what it deems to be the cost. The U.S. proposals, however, may not go far enough. Many countries now prefer to prohibit formally additions to dollar reserves, and some want to remove all dollars from official reserves.[7]

II.

It would be wrong to look upon proposals to remove these holdings, the so-called dollar overhang, as merely symbolic of the quest for symmetry. They are re-lated intimately and functionally to other important dimensions of most plans for reform. A consolidation of existing balances is prerequisite to any prohibition on additional holdings. In its absence, imbalances between countries other than the United States could lead to serious drains on U.S. reserves. A deficit country holding dollars would begin to sell them in the exchange market. The surplus country gaining them from the market would have to present them to the United States for conversion into an acceptable reserve asset. More important, consolidation may be required if the United States is to resume convertibility in the near future, even if there is to be no prohibition on new accumulations. It is, indeed, essential to the United States's own plan for reform. The United States cannot return to convertibility without first enlarging its reserves. It needs more reserves to finance the short-term imbalances no country can hope to avoid. And it cannot enlarge its reserves by running a surplus if the countries with the corresponding deficits are able to run down their present dollar holdings. Consolidation is needed merely to prevent a simple unwinding of recent history—the financing of U.S. surpluses by dollar decumulation—not only to forestall future demands for the conversion of dollar reserves already in the system.

One wonders, in fact, whether the United States can earn enough reserves to achieve convertibility in the next few years. It is not prepared to curb severely long-term capital outflows, and other countries are reluctant to let it improve its current account. There is some danger, then, that its promise to resume convertibility may be delayed disadvantageously for the new U.S. plan taken as a whole. Other governments may reject other parts of the plan because the net benefits—as they perceive and weigh them—are too long deferred. This possibility affects my

[7] The United States is willing to "study" proposals for transforming dollar holdings and other reserve-currency balances into *SDR*'s but opposes any outright prohibition on new accumulations. In Secretary Shultz's words, "official foreign currency holdings need be neither generally banned nor encouraged." His reasons are parallel to those given by Cooper.

own recommendation concerning the character of consolidation.

Proposals for consolidation of the dollar overhang take many forms. They range from the compulsory conversion of all dollar balances into *SDR*'s issued for that purpose—without the eventual amortization of the corresponding U.S. debts to the International Monetary Fund—to suggestions for a series of partial, voluntary, bilateral fundings into medium-term U.S. debt.[8]

The several proposals for consolidation may be classified analytically according to three attributes: (1) whether they would require eventual amortization by the United States, (2) how they would alter the level of international reserves, and (3) how completely they would deal with the overhang itself.

The first of these features has produced much rhetoric. Some have said that the United States has a moral obligation to repay what it has borrowed while financing its deficits. Others, including Bergsten, suggest that total forgiveness would do no more than compensate for past U.S. aid, including the Marshall Plan. I dislike these arguments. They threaten always to regress indefinitely, for there is no original sin or virtue in international relations. The question of amortization, moreover, should be viewed pragmatically. The burden upon the United States is itself a function of two negotiable elements—the rate at which it will receive newly created *SDR*'s and the interest rate on its consolidated debt. If the United States can expect to receive large *SDR* allocations, it will not have to generate a large current-account surplus in order to repay its debts. If the interest rate it would have to pay on irredeemable debt is much higher than the rate on redeemable debt, the total burden of redemption would not be large.[9]

The effect on world reserves may be a more important characteristic. Plans that would replace all dollar balances with *SDR*'s would not affect the present stock of reserves. Those that would fund the dollars into long-term U.S. debt would reduce reserves immediately. But funding into *SDR*'s might depress the growth rate of reserves. The creation at one time of enough *SDR*'s to replace all dollar reserves would increase hugely the stock of *SDR*'s.[10] Governments might then be reluctant to

---

[8] For consolidation into *SDR*'s, see Bergsten; for voluntary bilateral arrangements, see O. Emminger; for plans involving the creation of new instruments and institutions, see R. Triffin and the report of the Atlantic Council. One must also mention a recent proposal by J. Rueff to return in stepwise fashion to a pure gold standard. Earlier, Rueff proposed an increase in the price of gold to raise the dollar value of U.S. gold reserves and permit the repurchase with gold of foreign dollar balances. As U.S. gold reserves are quite small now, this would require a huge increase in the gold price. Hence, Rueff suggests instead that other countries lend to the United States some of what they would garner from a more modest increase in the price of gold and that the United States use the borrowed gold to redeem dollar balances. This proposal, however, has the same defect as his earlier plan. It would redistribute world assets arbitrarily—in favor of countries that have held reserves in gold. Those who favor a gold standard would not object to this redistribution; it would merely reward those who have abstained virtuously from accumulating dollars. But the United States and its present creditors would oppose it as unfair.

[9] Notice, moreover, that the interest costs of consolidation should be calculated net of the interest paid now on foreign official dollar holdings; these costs should be measured by the difference between the rate that would have to be paid on long-term or irredeemable debt and the rate now paid on Treasury bills and similar instruments.

[10] On September 30, 1972, the stock of *SDR*'s totaled $10.1 billion, while U.S. liabilities to foreign official institutions (liquid and nonliquid) totaled $60 billion. The second figure, however, does not include official holdings in the Eurodollar market, nor does it include holdings of sterling and other reserve-currency balances. At June 30, 1972, central-bank currency holdings totaled $91.5 billion. Bergsten has suggested that consolidation must also encompass privately held dollars, as these could someday migrate into official hands. But foreign private holdings are unusually low; they are more likely to rise than fall. If, further, consolidation includes official holdings in Eurodollars, it will cover a significant fraction of the liabilities to foreign banks appearing on the books of the United States.

vote new allocations for some years to come. If this reluctance reflected a belief that total reserves are adequate, even excessive, and the belief were universal, a moratorium on *SDR* creation would not be harmful. But if it reflected distrust of the *SDR* as a reserve asset, or were not unanimous, such a moratorium could be harmful. Unhappily, I cannot shed much light on this issue. It is hard to disentangle governments' discomfort about their dollar holdings from possible concerns about the sizes of their own or others' total reserves.

Compulsory funding into *SDR*'s or long-term dollar debt would, by definition, impound the whole overhang, removing the entire threat to U.S. reserves. Partial or voluntary funding would not do so. But some observers argue that it should not be removed. They argue that the recent growth in foreign official dollar holdings is an aberration, reflecting private speculation against the dollar. On this view official holdings will decline when confidence returns, as central banks will use their dollars to meet the reflux of private demand. There is disagreement, however, on the size of the prospective reflux. R. V. Roosa dismisses proposals for funding because he believes that most of the dollars will flow back into private hands. Others suggest that the events of 1971–72 amount to a permanent shift out of dollars into other currencies, especially those of the European Community. Prudence, then, requires that any plan to deal with the dollar balances be sufficiently flexible to deal with all outcomes. Funding into *SDR*'s would furnish this flexibility; if the reflux were large, central banks could transfer *SDR*'s to the United States in exchange for dollars needed to meet the private demand. Compulsory consolidation into long-term debt would be less suitable from this standpoint; central banks might have to give up a large fraction of their remaining non-dollar reserves. Partial, bilateral funding

has the appearance of flexibility. Central banks could hang onto some of their dollars. But the amounts retained might not match the reflux when and if it came.

None of the plans considered thus far deals explicitly with one remaining problem—the need to rebuild rapidly total U.S. reserves. Compulsory funding into *SDR*'s might do so indirectly if it was followed by a reflux of private demand for dollars. But the size of the resulting increase of U.S. reserves cannot be forecast or guaranteed; it would depend on the size of the reflux. And we need more certainty to risk convertibility. This leads me, then, to argue for a hybrid plan—one that combines bilateral consolidation with a special issue of *SDR*'s, the two together to provide for the total displacement of dollar balances *and* a once-for-all increase in U.S. reserves.[11] I suggest that the U.S. Treasury issue special nonmarketable bonds, denominated in *SDR*'s and equal in total value to foreign official dollar holdings plus, say, $10 billion to borrow *SDR*'s immediately for the United States. This special issue should be offered first for dollars that central banks are willing to relinquish directly in exchange for long-term claims on the United States. The remainder of the issue should then be lodged with the International Monetary Fund in exchange for new *SDR*'s. These *SDR*'s would be used to repurchase the dollars still held by central banks and to augment U.S. reserves.

I recommend this plan for its simplicity in dealing with the problem of stability, the composition of reserves, and the U.S. reserve position. I recommend it also for its flexibility. It allows for the reduction of total reserves (and limits correspondingly immediate, large *SDR* creation) insofar as

[11] The proposal outlined here is similar to one set out by T. de Vries and bears a functional resemblance to the plan for a "substitution account" contained in the recent report of the Executive Directors of the International Monetary Fund.

central banks demonstrate by their own choices that this is desired. It allows them also to hold *SDR*'s against a resurgent private demand for U.S. dollars. Finally, it can be amended to deal with other aspects of the dollar problem.

What does one do about central banks that *want* to hold some dollars as working balances to earn interest, or to secure their own and their citizens' relations with American financial institutions? These countries could be made to go through two steps—to give up their dollars for *SDR*'s, then to repurchase the dollars they desire by shifting *SDR*'s to the United States. These *SDR*'s would be held in a special escrow account, apart from other U.S. reserves. They would not be available to finance U.S. deficits. The United States might even be allowed to charge a custody fee, thereby to discourage other countries from swapping *SDR*'s that earn little interest for dollars that earn more.

What would happen if other countries were too willing to accept U.S. debt and found themselves unable later to finance a reflux of private demand for dollars? One might allow them to present the long-term U.S. bonds for early or special amortization by the United States, but only in the smaller of two amounts—a fraction (to be specified) of the corresponding increase in U.S. reserves, or a fraction of the drop in the countries' own reserves.

The problem of consolidation raises other issues, and I have not dealt with several separate aspects of the reserve system, notably the role of gold. I have sought instead to emphasize the case for dealing promptly with the dollar overhang and with the reserve position of the United States. Both call for quick attention if convertibility is to be restored in the near future—if there is to be an acceptable balance of benefits and costs in comprehensive reform. The United States cannot agree to resume convertibility without adequate reserves. Even if it can obtain agreement to more frequent changes in exchange rates and, therefore, is able to correct its own position more rapidly than in the past, it will need reserves to finance those imbalances that should not be corrected.

I close with one more formulation of this same warning: Failure to reconstitute U.S. reserves will handicap the system as a whole for a long time to come. The United States will be tempted to rig the rules for exchange-rate changes in order to protect or rebuild gradually its own inadequate reserves. If it succeeds, the new system will be asymmetrical and, therefore, the cause of new recriminations. If it fails, but agrees to resume convertibility, it will have to break the rules as it did in August 1971 or to use controls and domestic policies that damage or offend its trading partners.

REFERENCES

Atlantic Council, *To Modernize the International Monetary System,* Interim Report of the Monetary Committee of the Atlantic Council of the United States, Washington 1972.

C. F. Bergsten, *Reforming the Dollar: An International Monetary Policy for the United States,* Council on Foreign Relations, New York 1972.

R. N. Cooper, "Eurodollars, Reserve Dollars, and Asymmetries in the International Monetary System," *J. Int. Econ.,* Sept. 1972.

T. de Vries, *An Agenda for Monetary Reform,* Essays in International Finance, International Finance Section, Princeton 1972.

O. Emminger, "The Changing Pattern of the International Monetary System," in *The Smithsonian Agreement and Its Aftermath,* Council on Foreign Relations, New York 1972.

Executive Directors of the International Monetary Fund, *Reform of the International Monetary System,* International Monetary Fund, Washington 1972.

W. Fellner, "The Dollar's Place in the International System: Suggested Criteria for the

Appraisal of Emerging Views," *J. Econ. Lit.*, Sept. 1972.

V. **Giscard d'Estaing**, "Statement to the Annual Meeting of the International Bank for Reconstruction and Development and the International Monetary Fund," *Summary Proceedings of the Twenty-Seventh Annual Meeting*, International Monetary Fund, Washington 1972.

J. R. **Karlik**, "The Costs and Benefits of Being a Reserve-Currency Country," in P. B. Kenen and R. Lawrence, eds., *The Open Economy*, New York 1968.

M. V. **Posner**, *The World Monetary System: A Minimal Reform Program*, Essays in International Finance, International Finance Section, Princeton 1972.

R. V. **Roosa**, "Approaching International Reform," in *The Smithsonian Agreement and its Aftermath*, Council on Foreign Relations, New York 1972.

J. **Rueff**, "They Used to Call Me Cassandra," in W. Schmitz, ed., *Convertibility, Multilateralism and Freedom*, Vienna 1972.

G. **Schultz**, "Statement to the Annual Meeting of the International Bank for Reconstruction and Development and the International Monetary Fund," *Summary Proceedings of the Twenty-Seventh Annual Meeting*, International Monetary Fund, Washington 1972.

R. **Triffin**, "International Monetary Collapse and Reconstruction in April 1972," *J. Int. Econ.*, Sept. 1972.

J. **Williamson**, *The Choice of a Pivot for Parities*, Essays in International Finance, International Finance Section, Princeton 1971.

After Nairobi—beware the rhinopotamus

PETER B. KENEN

The rhinopotamus could be dangerous, as some of the delegates at this year's IMF conference may discover.

Corridor Cassandras at the IMF meetings spent most of their time predicting failure to agree on reform of the international monetary system. Terrible things will happen, they warned, if there is no agreement by 31 July 1974, the deadline announced at the Nairobi meeting and proclaimed as its major accomplishment.

They may be right about the prospects for an early compromise. None of the parties is sufficiently disturbed about the state of the foreign exchange markets to contemplate large concessions. Each blames others for the delay, but no government appears to value progress toward reform more than it cherishes its own position. The trade talks begun at Tokyo will not be stalled by deadlock on reform—you cannot stall something that is not moving. And agreement on the monetary system would not even revive Washington's dream of a new design for transatlantic relations.

A stronger dollar?

Yet there may be no great danger in failure to agree: 31 July is only two weeks away from 15 August, but deadlock on plans for reforming the system need not be cause for anyone to go into another tantrum. If, indeed, the current consensus is correct, the monetary system may reform itself to some significant extent on its own. The US dollar is, in any case, undervalued and oversold. Price trends are ominous everywhere, but they are no worse for the United States than for its chief competitors. Energy needs will add to US imports, but this problem in its full gravity is still some years away. The fuel shortage forecast for this winter testifies to domestic mismanagement—an incredible failure to use and enlarge refining, transport and storage facilities—not to sudden growth in the consumption of fossil fuels or an imminent upsurge of oil imports. In brief, the dollar should strengthen in the months ahead.

A stronger dollar will pose problems. European central banks will have to decide whether—and by how much—to allow changes in the pattern of exchange rates. Should the dollar be permitted to appreciate until market rates converge upon the parities or central rates established last February? How fast should the exchange rates move? Some officials have started to ponder these questions and trial balloons were floated over the Kenyatta Conference Centre. But the problems posed by a stronger dollar are tactical, not strategic. There are no important obstacles to their solution.

Were the dollar to strengthen more rapidly than now seems likely—allowing for the prospect of slower growth in US exports, changes in interest rates, Watergate and other headaches—the scale of official intervention required to prevent too much appreciation would simplify the bargaining over reform. Central banks would have to feed their dollar balances into the foreign exchange markets, as the Japanese did earlier this year, and would thereby help to solve two problems facing the reformers. They would reduce the size of the dollar overhang requiring consolidation—bilateral funding or conversion into Special Drawing Rights—and they would reduce the excess of international liquidity so often cited as a reason for halting the creation of new SDRs. A stronger dollar would change the climate for reform, resolving some of the issues cluttering the conference table and dissolving some of the preconceptions bedevilling communication. It is, indeed, the hope of new strength for the dollar which causes some negotiators to welcome delay. The US Secretary of the Treasury said so bluntly at Nairobi, but in a context which led his listeners to infer that the United States will not budge from its present position until the dollar shows its strength, not as a bystander's innocent prognosis.

The more important risk is not deadlock in July, but agreement on an unworkable compromise. A new monetary system must be built to last for several turbulent decades. There is grave danger, however, that political processes and pressures—including the negotiators' own desire to succeed—will lead to agreement on a system that cannot survive its first test in the market. The central banks that will have to defend it against massive money flows—the markets' manifestation of disbelief—will be forced to back away, confirming the suspicion now approaching dogma that free markets alone can regulate exchange rates properly.

The creation at Nairobi of four working parties to study the technical characteristics of plans for reform is, perhaps, implicit recognition of the danger. But a reading of the 'Outline of Reform' published at Nairobi suggests that the danger of bargaining is grave indeed. The reformers may be bringing back from Africa a rhinopotamus—a beast that sometimes glides or jumps, but is more apt to float in a puddle of liquidity.

The logical and plausible dimensions of compromise are apparent even now. The United States presses for a system in which there will be strong inducements to alter exchange rates or domestic policies when imbalances appear in international payments. Movements in reserves would warn of the need for adjustment and failure to heed the signal given by the indicator would expose a delinquent government to financial sanctions of increasing severity. American officials argue forcefully that a par-value system lacking such signals and sanctions would be asymmetrical. Deficit countries would always experience pressures to act. Their reserves would fall. But surplus countries would experience no comparable pressures.

At first glance, of course, the European view seems quite different and the appearance of deep cleavage is magnified by the Europeans' vigorous objections to the quasi-automatic or presumptive use of a reserve indicator. Europeans stress another aspect of asymmetry—the capacity of countries like the United States, whose currencies are held as reserves, to finance payments deficits indefinitely, avoiding losses of reserves and the familiar financial pressures to modify policies. They would correct this serious flaw by restoring convertibility, but changing it from right into obligation. Surplus countries would be obliged to present for conversion currencies acquired in the foreign-exchange markets, not merely guaranteed the opportunity to do so. Mandatory transfers of reserves—asset settlements—through the IMF or bilaterally would be the cutting edge of monetary discipline.

As usual, the parties are arguing from history as each reads it. Americans believe that the US deficits of the 1950s and 1960s were prolonged and led finally to the collapse of the par-value system because surplus countries—the Europeans and Japan—could not be compelled to alter their policies, and the United States could not easily initiate a change in exchange rates. Europeans read this same post-war history to argue that the blame and obligation to change policies rested with the United States, yet it was not compelled to act because it was not losing reserves.

Reserve indicators

Differences in views about the past and extrapolations into the future animate other aspects of the debate. Europeans dislike the US proposal for a reserve indicator because, in their opinion, it might betray them into acting when no action is warranted by underlying circumstances. Under a system of mandatory asset settlements of the type they advocate reserve movements might be misleadingly symmetrical. Deficit countries would lose reserves, surplus countries would gain them, and both would have to change their policies or the pattern of exchange rates. There would be no way of assigning blame for the imbalances reflected in movements of reserves—even to assess size or probable duration—and no way of fixing responsibility for taking corrective measures. Americans, by contrast, distrust the plan for mandatory settlements. These, they say, would be too rigid; the stock of reserves and reserve credit would not be sufficiently elastic. They fear that massive capital flows could drain off completely a country's reserves before it could respond to the first signs of imbalance or before its policies would take full effect. They worry, quite properly, about the reserve position of the United States and argue that convertibility should be a right, not obligation, of surplus countries, which would then be free to accumulate reserve currencies. They suggest, moreover, that a surplus country should lose its right to ask for the conversion of currencies when its reserves reach a predetermined level, thereby to protect deficit countries and the system as a whole from a single country's appetite for surpluses. (This device recalls the Scarce Currency Clause written into the Bretton Woods Agreement when it was feared that the United States would be the villain of the piece, draining other countries of reserves.) Unfortunately, Europeans view these concerns and their incarnation in the US proposals as reflecting a desire to preserve the special reserve-currency role of the dollar.

Fundamentally, however, the parties are not far apart. Both sides seem to be saying that the new system must foster prompt adjustment, something which many Americans used to oppose. Both sides, moreover, understand quite clearly the logic of their shared commitment to convertibility and par values. A system which contains powerful incentives to alter exchange rates and national policies is the only one in which governments can exercise the right of convertibility. If, then, the Europeans continue to insist upon mandatory settlements, they will find it difficult to oppose the use of a reserve indicator backed by effective graduated sanctions. If, instead, the United States continues to insist upon presumptive use of a reserve indicator, it will find it difficult to oppose mandatory asset settlement. Putting the same trade-offs positively, those who would circumscribe the role of the reserve indicator may have to mute their objections to an elastic reserve system, while those determined to resist mandatory settlements may have also to mute their demand for the presumptive use of an indicator. (It should be noted, however, that the European need not also agree to the continued use of the dollar as a reserve asset; there are suggestions in the 'Outline of Reform' for reserve credit facilities administered by the IMF and for implicit short-term lending by deferring settlements or making them infrequently. Furthermore, discretionary use of a reserve indicator need not interfere with the automatic application of financial sanctions against delinquent countries. Indeed, one of the governments that has opposed vehemently the presumptive use of an indicator has itself proposed that pressures be applied automatically to surplus countries, by way of a tax or negative interest rate on accumulations of reserves.

In brief, the countries know where to find common ground—when they decide it is time to agree. In all likelihood the US reserve indicator will be used to signal the need for adjustment, but the decision to alter national policies or exchange rates will be taken only on the basis of supplementary information and, no doubt, extensive consultation. Countries will be expected to convert all currencies acquired in the course of intervention to defend par values, but reserve settlements may be scheduled from time to time to impart substantial elasticity to the monetary system.

Unhappily a compromise along these lines may be worse than no agreement at all as the recipes blended in the 'Outline of Reform' are not compatible. The chief defect of the scheme which seems to be emerging derives from an agreement reached early on, symbolized by the commitment to 'stable but adjustable' exchange rates.

This phrase mixes ends and means. Stability is a characteristic of markets. It has no intrinsic connection with the choice between exchange regimes—their formal fixity, adjustability or free market flexibility. The US dollar price of the Canadian dollar was very stable for most of the years in which it was free to float. The dollar price of the mark was far from stable even when it was pegged formally; it rose by some 70% in just one decade. The declaration of par values can sometimes enhance the stability of markets, but only if traders who live in the markets believe that central banks are willing to defend the par values they declare. Central banks, however, have laboured prodigiously to undermine the traders' respect for their tenacity. Repeatedly, and with increasing speed, they have backed away from the defence of parities, allowing exchange rates to float under speculative pressures. There is, of course, a good case for the temporary float. It may be the least fallible way to locate a new parity—until the econometricians learn more about their craft. But floating under pressure from the market itself is hardly the way to establish credibility and enhance market stability. It is instead a good way to breed contempt for official pronouncements and commitments.

Yet the fault in the phrase 'stable but adjustable' cannot be cured by clarification, nor even by persuading the foreign exchange markets that the authorities mean what they say. For what they may now mean is wrong fundamentally.

Somewhere in transit between the Smithsonian and the Kenyatta Conference Centre the consensus in favour of greater flexibility was transformed perversely. At the start it seemed to imply that reformers and professors were talking the same language, favouring more play for market forces by widening the bands or the use of 'gliding parities' that might change from week to week by very small amounts. Now it appears to imply that parities should change no more than once or twice a year and, correspondingly, by a larger amount on each occasion than would be required or desired if they were to glide. The 'Outline of Reform' contemplates changes in exchange rates much like those endorsed in the Bretton Woods Agreement.

Changes of this type would not have to exceed a few percentage points if they were to take place promptly—to correct emerging disequilibria rather than to offset disparities which had been neglected for several years. Nevertheless, the changes required by discrete, stepwise procedures would be large enough to confer large profits on those with the wisdom to anticipate them well.

This is why the rhinopotamus is likely to float. The combination of a reserve indicator—available for all to read—with infrequent discrete changes in parities guarantees the advent of huge speculative flows whenever the indicator signals an imbalance. The central banks are bound to be overwhelmed.

There are, in fact, two defects in this combination, one of which would also afflict the better combination of a reserve indicator and a gliding parity. This first defect arises directly from the mechanical characteristics of a par value system. Changes in reserves take place when central banks intervene to stabilize exchange rates. Intervention, however, is apt to occur when market rates have reached the limits of their bands, not when they are still moving. Thus, reserve movements and changes in parities are most likely to happen when market rates are close to their limits, and changes in parities, shifting those limits, will make the next change in market rates easy to predict. A reserve indicator, unlike others one might use, minimizes the risks attendant on speculation.

The second, more serious, defect of the scheme now in prospect arises from the marriage in the 'Outline of Reform' of a reserve indicator and parities which jump, not glide. Infrequent sizeable changes in parities will enlarge the profitability of riskless speculation. (There is a third defect in the 'Outline of Reform'—in the three-part combination of a reserve indicator, large changes in parities, and plans for multi-currency intervention. The last will not work without rules to prevent central banks from intervening at cross-purposes, and the only simple enforceable rule is an outright prohibition on intervention before rates reach the limits of their bands—the prohibition that was tried with imperfect success to manage the Europeans' 'snake'-in-the-tunnel. Such a rule, however, increases the likelihood that movements in reserves, guiding changes in parities, will cause corresponding movements in market rates, reducing even further the risks of speculation.)

The question of gold sales

The reformers' migration to middle ground poses other risks. Consider briefly the new view on getting rid of gold. The 'Outline of Reform' reports widespread agreement on this aim—and a measure of agreement on the way to achieve it. It suggests that central banks be free to sell gold in private markets. This plan pleases those who want to phase out gold. It seems also to appease those who would prefer to raise the official price of gold—to value 'realistically' their total gold holdings. But think for a moment about the implications, especially the interaction of this plan for gold with provisions for mandatory settlements.

Suppose that the Bank of France decides to sell gold. If the buyers are Frenchmen who pay in francs, the transaction will have no important effects on the international monetary system, apart from reducing the stock of reserves. It will resemble an open market operation of the type which central banks employ to regulate domestic credit. If the buyers are foreigners, however, or pay in foreign currency, the sale has important international effects. If, for example, the bank of France acquires dollars for its gold, it will be obliged to present them for conversion into an acceptable reserve asset, and the United States will lose reserves.

Far from serving to demonetize gold reserves, the plan proposed in the 'Outline of Reform' would make gold convertible *de facto* into SDRs and, more to the point, a potential claim on the reserves of countries that would be unable to honour the claim. Clearly, gold sales to private markets must be restricted and subject to surveillance. Sales for foreign currencies cannot be countenanced unless the seller needs the currency for intervention in the foreign exchange markets.

Observers at Nairobi were fond of remarking that agreement on reform awaits only the political will to compromise—that the problems cannot be resolved by technicians. This view can only produce a rhinopotamus. Political will is required to move off dead centre, but it is not enough for successful reform. The technical issues are difficult, and those which are not rooted out for study and solution before reforms are put in place are capable of wrecking the new system completely. Reforms must be designed, not traded at the conference table.

Reforming the monetary system—
you can't get there from here

PETER B. KENEN

The author introduces this article: 'These words are written three full years after the collapse of practically everything, on 15 August 1971. They are written as we near the first anniversary of the agreement at Nairobi to put everything together again by 31 July 1974. They are written to answer some of the questions evoked by reciting these two dates.'

If the decisions of 15 August 1971 and those that followed them—the termination of gold-dollar convertibility and suspension of the par-value system—destroyed the international monetary system set up at Bretton Woods, why do international trade and investment continue to flourish? Or were the obituaries we read at the time a bit premature? And if the major governments were determined, as they said, to draft a plan for a new system by 31 July 1974, why did they fail? Could they have succeeded if there were no increase in the price of oil and no worldwide inflation? Could they have succeeded if there had not been political upheavals in the United States, France, Germany and elsewhere? Finally, and most important, where do we go from here?

The manner in which I pose these questions hints at the way I will answer them. The events of 15 August 1971 did not destroy the monetary system. The obituaries were premature. They served only to accelerate and ratify changes that had started several years before—changes in the way that governments perceive the system and in the way they react to it. They signalled the need to recognize the obsolescence of certain rules written at Bretton Woods, or, more precisely, of interpretations and departures from the rules that had been sanctioned by practice during two decades.

Efforts to reform the monetary system began long before the crisis of 1971 dramatized the need, and the most significant change in the system—the definition and creation of Special Drawing Rights—took place before the crisis. The negotiations that began after the crisis were attempts to write a new code of conduct that would reflect more faithfully attitudes and conduct already in being, thereby to render that conduct more regular and predictable and to forestall new confrontations which might cause disagreements about monetary matters to poison other relationships, economic and political. That effort has not succeeded yet and may not succeed for some time, but we must not exaggerate its importance. The work of the Committee of Twenty and of its successors is not to build a monetary system but to describe in accurate, enduring terms the system that exists and to accommodate additional change.

Abrogation of the rules, formal and informal, did not interfere importantly with the institutions, arrangements and practices that serve international trade and investment. It did not impair the convertibility of one currency into another for purposes of buying goods, services, or assets—the right to buy or sell in the foreign exchange market. It even allowed some major governments to relax or remove restrictions on the freedom of action of traders and investors. The suspension of the par-value system altered only the manner in which central banks react to events in the market-place and, vitally for monetary policy, changed the way in which international events impinge on domestic autonomy. Central banks need no longer do battle against events and opinions in the foreign exchange market, at enormous cost to their domestic aims and at greater cost to their credibility when they decide to retreat. They are no longer obliged to behave as though foreign trade and investment should involve no risk of changes in exchange rates, then to introduce uninsurable risks by retaining the right to alter exchange rates.

Experience under the new non-rules has not been painless. Dealers in currencies and, to some lesser extent, dealers in goods, services and assets have had to learn anew the ways to recognize risk and opportunity, and some, we have discovered, did not learn fast enough. The authorities, moreover, have yet to identify and to enunciate their residual responsibilities as managers and guarantors of the system, especially to recognize their responsibility for protecting foreigners against imprudent behaviour by their own nationals. It is not enough to act as lender of last resort to domestic banks or to insure the deposits of one's own citizens. The safety of the system and health of the international economy requires that central banks declare their joint concern for the solvency and efficiency of the private institutions that make markets work.

The failure of a few institutions is not disastrous. It may indeed be salutary. It would be far worse to subsidize recklessness. Herstatt is not the Credit Anstalt. But it is the job of central banks to protect the innocent victims of others' recklessness. Otherwise the innocents are sure to panic.

The failure to agree on a new system by 31 July 1974 is often blamed on the increase in the price of oil and the need to stabilize national economies before they are locked together again by a new monetary constitution. But the promise to achieve comprehensive agreement on long-run reform was unrealistic even when it was announced on the eve of the Nairobi meetings. The differences among official positions was very large, and the differences in premises was larger still. Most fundamentally, no major government saw reason to sacrifice national advantage in the interests of agreement. No government identified national destiny with the rehabilitation of the international system. None was able to say or believe that its own strength and security would be enhanced significantly by accepting limits on its freedom of action.

Those who thought that an agreement was possible were perhaps deceived by their own apprehensions and by the example of Bretton Woods. Exaggerated fears of disintegration led to the conviction that an agreement *had* to be reached. And imperfect memories of events and circumstances three decades earlier led to the belief that agreement *could* come easily.

The American dimension

Armed with almost perfect hindsight, we are able now to see that the events and decisions that followed Richard Nixon's speech on 15 August 1971 did not provoke disintegration. American conduct invited it. There was no consultation before the event. There was no promise of co-operation after the event. There was bombast, recrimination and the threat of worse to come if the offender did not get his way. But bad manners did not overwhelm good judgment, not even in Washington. Some would say, indeed, that bad manners helped to underscore the need for decisions more drastic than those that usually emerge from more civilized modes of consultation and to stress the fact, sometimes forgotten, that the United States was not in full control of its economy or its policy. Congressional initiatives in trade and payments policy, especially passage of the Burke-Hartke Bill, would have done more damage than the rhetoric of the Administration.

American habits of mind, moreover, led to misinterpretation of American behaviour and its implications for the monetary system. Many observers—I was one—mistook specific violations of the law for the collapse of the rule of law and identified the rule of law with the preservation of orderly economic relations.

Americans since Woodrow Wilson, even before, have longed to codify the conduct of nations, even though there is as yet no policeman to catch those who break the law, no court that has jurisdiction to try them, and no jail in which to put them. The League of Nations was an American notion. The United Nations was another—and began its career with strong support from the United States, born of American faith in the rule of law and of guilt arising from earlier isolation. Furthermore, the Bretton Woods Agreement establishing the IMF and IBRD was an offspring of the effort to organize world peace. The Fund and the Bank are specialized agencies of the United States. The Bretton Woods Agreement proclaims the conviction that international economic conduct must be governed and constrained by an explicit code and by decisions taken collectively. It articulates its members' belief that adherence to the rules is advantageous on balance, even if it seems disagreeable at times to an individual government.

I do not belittle the faith that brought forth this first formal constitution for the international monetary system. The need for it was the unmistakable lesson of history. The reconstruction and collapse of the monetary system after the First World War is replete with episodes that testify to the need for the multilateral determination of exchange rate relationships and the joint management of reserve creation.

The separate, sequential decisions of Great Britain, France and others to return to fixed parities in the 1920s, decisions that focused on the prices of currencies in terms of gold rather than their prices in terms of each other, established exchange rates that could not be sustained. The use of sterling as a reserve currency, sanctioned by practice and ratified after the fact by the Genoa Resolution of 1922, placed responsibility for maintaining confidence on a nation that had lost economic preeminence before the First World War, was weakened further by the war, and was rent by internal economic strife. And the unravelling of the system after 1931 proved again the costs of failing to acknowledge the implications of economic interdependence. Parities came unstuck sequentially, just as they had been declared sequentially. Central banks intervened in the foreign exchange markets without consultation and, from time to time, at cross-purposes. There were no rules for reconciling and confirming collectively policies to achieve internal and external aims. Some countries, like the United States, felt free to place their domestic objectives ahead of external commitments, compounding their neighbours' problems. Others, like the gold bloc countries, punished their economies.

My aim is to recall the attitudes and very special circumstances that allowed the writing of a monetary constitution in 1944. There was the vivid recollection of recent history—of failures to consult and cooperate in making decisions about exchange rates, decisions that cannot be unilateral because an exchange rate is bilateral. There was the determination of the United States, overly optimistic but perfectly sincere, to establish the rule of law in international relations. And there was the unique, dominant position of the United States, political and economic, which gave it the power to shape decisions concerning the new system and to make concessions for the sake of the system without placing its own interests in serious jeopardy.

This last fact needs emphasis. It is the one that distinguishes the first from the third decade following the Second World War, explaining the change in perceptions and in realities that caused the crisis of 1971 and the suspension of efforts at reform in 1974.

The Bretton Woods Agreement embodied an implicit commitment on the part of the United States—the commitment to forgo certain rights and opportunities that other governments would enjoy. The roles that the dollar would come to play—as *numeraire* and reserve asset for the system—are written into the agreement and must have been foreseen, even if imperfectly, by those who drafted the agreement.

Some, of course, would say that the United States was not being altruistic. Having the political influence to marshall majorities in the International Monetary Fund and an overwhelming economic pre-eminence at the close of the Second World War, the United States could agree to asymmetries in the new system without undertaking to make major sacrifices. But this is not the whole truth. Those who deplore the 'arrogance' of the United States in the years before *detente* forget that this was not its mood before the outbreak of the Cold War.

The United States was more insecure than arrogant at the end of the Second World War. It was uncomfortable with nuclear monopoly. It was fearful of its economic future. Remember the concerns of American leaders with the needs and problems of domestic reconversion and their reluctance to give a 'blank cheque' to other countries with which to draw on American resources. Remember the predictions of post-war depression and long-term stagnation in the United States. Remember, finally, the importance attached at the time to the scarce-currency clause in the Bretton Woods Agreement, the clause that was designed to quarantine an American depression and prevent a repetition of the 1930s.

The United States, moreover, was willing to make some real sacrifice of autonomy—not essential sovereignty to be sure—because it identified its interest and image with the rule of law. Many observers have compared the United States to Gulliver among the Lilliputians. The metaphor may be more apt than they themselves intended. It describes vividly the difference in size that has had so much effect on relations between the United States and other countries. It also describes the manner in which the United States began to conduct its foreign relations after the Second World War. Gulliver could have extracted by force or threat of force the food and other things he needed from the Lilliputians. But Gulliver was an amiable man, unlike Jonathan Swift. He was the personification of civilized conduct and chose to write a treaty with the Emperor of the Lilliputians. They were to supply what he needed, and he was to respect their rights. He would give warning when coming to town, would confine his walks to the principal high-roads, and would take the utmost care not to trample on the bodies of the Lilliputians, their horses or carriages. Gulliver preferred to earn goodwill if he could have what he needed that way.

But times change and so do the sizes of nations. The United States is still quite powerful and its mistakes can have serious consequences for the rest of the world economy. Its fiscal and monetary errors in the 1960s, compounded by blunders in the early 1970s, are one major cause of worldwide inflation. The United States, however, is not preeminent and, what is more important, believes itself to be very much less powerful than it did before. Acutely conscious of the limitations of political influence, it is not prepared to rely on persuasion or power to limit the cost of conferring initiatives on other countries or on international institutions. And acutely conscious of declining domestic support for its traditional image—the civilized Gulliver—it is unwilling to forgo the right to use any instrument of economic policy that might protect its own economy from the shocks and injuries it is apt to import from the outside world. The United States continues to enunciate belief in the rule of law—its own proposals for reform of the monetary system were perhaps too formal and legalistic—but seems determined to achieve the appearance and substance of symmetry in new rules for the system.

Thus, economic and political conditions, combined with current styles in American diplomacy, deprive the international rule-making process of the ingredient that made it work in 1944. No government is willing or able to declare that agreement on a new monetary constitution is a major aim of national policy. No government is moved to take a self-denying stance in the interests of the system. This is the reason for my choice of title. There is no easy way to get from where we are to where we used to think we would like to be.

The impasse, however, is not calamitous. We can stay where we are for some time to come while we try to clarify aims and attitudes. We can do so if we recognize two vital facts.

Where do we want to go . . . ?

First, the changes in conditions and attitudes I have been describing require a reordering of objectives. Ever since the Second World War western governments have proclaimed as a major objective the closer integration of national economies, including not only the integration of Western Europe. Integration, however, has three dimensions, and the connections between them have not received sufficient attention. Integration calls for the unification of markets—the elimination of barriers to trade, payments and migration. It calls for the coordination of policies—the consistent use of national instruments and, in some important cases, the joint use or merging of national instruments. It calls for the harmonization of targets—the articulation of joint aims.

We have, of course, been prone to stress the first of these three processes and sometimes to assume that the second would happen quite naturally. But recent experience in Europe and elsewhere has taught us that the second is very difficult. And this is because we have not made much progress with the third—the harmonization of aims. In fact, the thesis I have been developing has as one chief implication the pessimistic inference that governments find it increasingly hard to declare joint aims. They are subject to intense domestic pressures and can achieve internal consensus only by making domestic commitments that cannot then be modified by external bargaining. Progress in the unification of markets has therefore exposed national economies to deep interpenetration without also fostering agreements and arrangements to manage economies collectively, and governments have responded to external disturbances, including other governments' policy errors, by re-erecting barriers to market integration. They have done so, moreover, unilaterally and have sometimes struck out at the most important links between economies, movements of goods and persons.

It would, of course, be pleasant to forecast a change in mood—to say that we will see a resumption of policy coordination, reflecting new movement toward harmonization of policy aims. But this is not likely. Indeed, we are more likely to see a gradual unravelling of agreements and arrangements already in place, at a time when they are needed urgently to consolidate the economic gains from the unification of markets and to confront unprecedented changes in the structure and terms of trade.

Governments must not abandon the attempt to harmonize national aims, especially to deal jointly with emergencies like the increase in the price of oil and impending shortages of certain foodstuffs, which no consuming country can resolve alone. At this juncture, however, efforts to rebuild the monetary system and make lasting changes in modes of conduct are unlikely to succeed, and failure may exacerbate the climate for cooperation. The immediate objective must be modest. It is time to ask how best to *separate* national economies, to grant governments the leeway they will need to deal with domestic pressures and problems without severing the most important links between economies. It is time to formulate what I have called elsewhere a *theory of optimum disintegration* that would take account of obstacles to the synchronized unification of markets, coordination of policies and harmonization of targets. Speaking less abstractly, it is time to recognize that flexible exchange rates are less damaging to trade and payments than the direct controls which governments impose when they seek to fend off foreign threats to their domestic commitments and aims. The drift to flexibility should not be viewed as a retreat from an attainable first-best world but, more realistically, as the least damaging way to face the inescapable political facts of a second-best world.

... and how do we get there?

Second, monetary policies and institutions cannot handle real problems. Monetary policies cannot cope efficiently with the domestic counterparts of higher prices for oil, wheat and fertilizer. Financial intermediation cannot make good the governments' failures to articulate a strong and joint response to the cartelization of the market for petroleum. Monetary policies must be tuned properly to real trends; higher prices for vital commodities like oil and wheat will be passed on easily, causing other prices to rise rapidly, if central banks are made to conceal the sins of governments by spewing out vast quantities of money. Financial intermediation can buy time for governments to make decisions and for their decisions to take effect. But changes in the structure and terms of trade require adaptations of a type that cannot even start unless and until someone begins to hurt.

The proper response to the cartelization of world trade in petroleum is, surely, to deploy countervailing power. It would make more sense to tax harshly the use of gasoline—on top of the increase in cost—than to prevent consumers from feeling any pain. It would make more sense for consuming countries to withhold technology and arms than to compete with each other in an effort to pay for high-priced oil.

There are, of course, two reasons for our errors. No two countries face the same situation—now or prospectively—and governments decline to acknowledge that, though they are not in the same boat, none can expect smooth sailing ahead. Governments, moreover, earn no rewards at home for helping foreigners, even when the costs to their citizens are small. To make matters worse, the burden of retrenchment and adaptation are distributed unevenly within and between countries. An energy policy that taxed gasoline heavily enough to reduce imports sharply, raising the cost of continued cartelization, would redistribute incomes and wealth in the consuming countries.

There are ways to compensate those who would be hurt by concerted efforts of this kind—partly by taxing those who might benefit. But the problem of compensation between nations is very difficult, and will get worse in the next few years. There are apt to be grave shortages of grain during the rest of the decade—the gods cannot seem to manage food production any better than the ministers of agriculture—and the nations that will suffer most acutely are those that have had the unhappiest histories during the last few years. The problems and solutions, however, are not monetary. Financial institutions cannot solve the problems facing India—they cannot even offer significant relief without damaging themselves. Here, above all, there is need to reaffirm the commitment to international cooperation. The major producers of grain, for example, must be asked to guarantee minimum supplies to the rest of the world, even if their own citizens must eat less. At the very least they must forswear the hoarding of their own production—the use of export quotas or prohibitions. And countries that will have to spend more than they earn, merely to feed themselves, will have to be able to tap anew wellsprings of goodwill which have been left to run dry in recent years.

International Monetary Relations after Jamaica:

An Overall View

by Peter Kenen

I have been asked to give an overall view of the international monetary situation. I cannot hope to rise to the Olympian objectivity implied by that assignment. All of us are closest to the problems of our own countries, and you are bound to detect an American perspective in my comments as well as my accent. In my intervention, however, I shall try to do three things.

First, I shall make some suggestions concerning the perspective from which we should judge recent events and decisions affecting the international monetary system. Second, I shall offer my own assessment of those events and decisions, having in mind not only the Jamaica Agreement to amend the Articles of Agreement of the International Monetary Fund, but also the several agreements which went before, including the agreement to change the valuation of the SDR, the agreement among the Group of Ten concerning transactions in gold, and the Rambouillet agreement or communiqué. Third, I shall list some of the problems which seem to me to call for further work at the political level and, even more importantly, further thought at the analytical level. I, for one, do not believe that the reform of the monetary system is complete or that its completion can be postponed for long.

When we look back upon what academics and officials, but especially academics, have written about international monetary problems in the last twenty-five years, one fact stands out. Without always knowing it, most of us have judged events, decisions, and proposals by an idealistic, cosmopolitan criterion. We have asked how far each step has taken us toward the creation of a world money to which national monies would be subordinated and by which they might some day be supplanted. This perspective is the one from which Robert Triffin has proceeded when arguing for the gradual transformation of the International Monetary Fund into a world central bank. It is also the perspective adopted by those like Jacques Rueff who have called for the reinstatement of gold as the only acceptable international money. And it is the perspective of those like Robert Mundell who dismiss the Jamaica agreement as being wholly irrelevant to the important work of international monetary reform.

There are, of course, important differences between Triffin and Rueff, in their readings of history and their aspirations for the future. Triffin, for example, has always called for orderly growth, collectively decided, in the stock of international money. Rueff, less sanguine perhaps about the sagacity of governments, has emphasized the need for firm, impersonal control of growth in supplies of national monies to safeguard against inflation. But common to their views and those of many others is the optimistic supposition that governments are willing and able to sacrifice or compromise national aims—to accept international rules or to establish international institutions that would limit severely and permanently national autonomy in monetary matters.

This optimistic consensus, which has only recently broken down, was the intellectual by-product of international economic trends in the 1950s and 1960s. Those trends led us to accept the desirability, even the inevitability, of closer international economic integration. It was the consensus that Richard Cooper celebrated intellectually in his brilliant book on international economic interdependence. It was the consensus that Europeans celebrated politically in their ambitious plans for full-fledged economic integration. And there went together with this optimistic consensus an agreement, more or less explicit, on the virtues of stable exchange rates—an agreement enshrined in the commitment to par values that we identify with the Bretton Woods system.

Economists have commonly interpreted the rigidity of par values as a reflection of politicians' reluctance to admit mistakes. Governments, we said, cling too long to par values because they are loath to admit that they cannot continue to defend them. The consensus and conventions of that period, however, invite another interpretation. Under the Bretton Woods system, as it evolved, any change in an exchange rate was also a failure to honour obligations central to the vision of progressive integration.

Throughout the period to which I refer, some academic economists advocated flexible exchange rates. Remember, however, from what quarters this advocacy came in the 1950s and 1960s. It came from economists like Milton Friedman, for whom freely flexible exchange rates are the international monetary counterpart of a general prescription that governments should not intervene in economic affairs but should instead acknowledge and enhance the efficiency of free markets: *laissez faire partout*. It came also from British and Canadian economists for whom flexibility promised to confer the largest measure of national autonomy—scope for the pursuit of domestic objectives. For the Canadians, in particular, exchange-rate flexibility appeared to be the best defense against monetary annexation by their large next-door neighbour.

Academic sentiment did not coalesce in favour of flexible exchange rates until it was altogether obvious that par values had become extremely rigid, that decisions to change them could consume vast quantities of political capital, and that the measures governments were taking to defend par values were coming to threaten the achievements of the 1950s and 1960s—the liberalization of trade and capital flows that confer the chief benefits of international economic integration. Even after this shift in sentiment, moreover, economists continued to judge international monetary events, decisions, and proposals from the cosmopolitan world-money viewpoint, and many of us go on doing so today.

It is not my purpose here to praise the early advocates of flexibility. Some of them were right for very wrong reasons. Market flexibility has not brought about smooth, painless changes in exchange rates to offset differences in national inflation rates. It has not been visibly successful in fostering the reallocations of resources required to deal with real disturbances. And it has not replaced the jerky adjustment of par values with small, smooth movements in market exchange rates, as forecast by some of its advocates. There have instead been large, unproductive oscillations in the mark-dollar and other exchange rates.

Nor is it my purpose to criticize those who apply the world-money view in their assessments of events and agreements. I would be the wrong one to do so, for I was one of them. It is my purpose merely to suggest that another, more modest criterion has also to be used when we attempt to weigh the implications of events, agreements, and new plans to modify the international monetary system.

In the unhappy circumstances of the 1970s, it is the proper and pre-eminent task of international monetary institutions to preside over a world of national monies, not to supplant them with a world money. It is their task to conserve and reward the habits of consultation and co-operation that have been acquired since the Second World War. They should seek to articulate rules to forestall conflicts in strategies or tactics, as when governments intervene in the foreign-exchange markets, and rules to proscribe national conduct inimical to global welfare, as in matters of trade policy. It is too much to ask today, however, that they devise or administer rules whose application in particular circumstances would require a country, large or small, to sacrifice announced national aims. When, then, we must judge events and agreements in the international monetary realm, it is most realistic and sensible to ask what they can contribute to orderly relations among existing national monies.

I have adopted this more modest criterion as events have led me to be more pessimistic about the willingness of governments everywhere to subordinate their national goals to their international obligations. Ours is an era of defensive nationalism—a nationalism born of anxiety, not assertiveness, and marked by domestic dissension, not imperial ambition. It is therefore an era in which international institutions must accommodate their members' yearnings for autonomy without also abdicating their own obligations to conserve for the future the achievements of the past, looking to the day when we have mastered our current anxieties and are again prepared to honour onerous commitments.

Time does not permit me to explore the many implications of this shift in perspective. I must be content with one illustration. I turn, then, to the Jamaica Agreement and the agreements that went before it, to ask what those agreements can contribute to the peaceful coexistence of autonomous national currencies and autonomous national policies.

Were we to use a cosmopolitan standard when judging these agreements, we would have to say that they are retrogressive. This is, indeed, Mundell's conclusion, because he refuses to abandon a world-money view. And it would be foolish to deny that we are further now from the installation of a world money than we were ten years ago. Par values will not be re-established for many years, not perhaps for many decades. And this I say with more regret: the SDR will not move to the centre of the monetary system as its foremost reserve asset for many years to come, although this would be feasible technically and desirable politically even in the near term.

Adopting instead the modest standard I have proposed assessing our progress in the regulation of relations among national currencies, there is, I believe, some cause for cautious gratification. The Jamaica Agreement would be welcome if it did nothing more than to bring international monetary law into congruence with international monetary practice. Laws that bear no resemblance to practice are bound to incur contempt and to corrode respect for those who are charged with enforcing them. There were, however, other achievements at Jamaica, and it would be wrong to belittle them.

There was, first, an important procedural agreement on rules for making any major change in existing exchange-rate arrangements or, to be exact, for restricting the choice of exchange-rate regimes available to individual countries. What I have been saying about current attitudes leads me also to believe that it is foolish to write universal rules for exchange-rate management and, *a fortiori,* foolish to suppose that a mere majority of governments can command obedience by every government in matters that epitomize economic sovereignty.

There was, in addition, the tacit agreement, long overdue, that a regional currency bloc does not at all resemble a regional trading bloc. A currency bloc does not imply discrimination against outsiders, nor does it necessarily imply the internal exploitation that arose in some blocs during the 1930s. Monetary integration, whether by the unilateral decision of one country to peg its currency to that of a neighbour, or by the multilateral decision of several countries to keep their exchange rates closely aligned, should not be viewed suspiciously, in the way we look at preferential trade policies.

There was, next, a series of decisions that serve together to enlarge the resources of the IMF and to make those resources more freely available. I, for one, had hoped for a larger increase in Fund quotas in order to compensate fully for the demise of the oil facility and, in the longer run, to enhance the authority of the Fund. I am glad, nonetheless, that Jamaica did not ratify either of the two absurd contentions advanced in opposition to an increase of quotas —that international liquidity is super-abundant, or that the private recycling of OPEC surpluses has been successful, doing away with the need for any official financing of current-account deficits.

Finally, I cite as a major accomplishment the earlier agreement to prohibit any increase in the gold holdings of the IMF and the major industrial countries, taken together. If that agreement is honoured and, more importantly, if it is renewed when it expires in 1977, it may prove to be the most effective single step taken with respect to gold in the last few years. It is, I believe, the principal cause of the decline in the gold price, being much more influential than the lukewarm response of my country's citizens to the United States' legislation that allowed them to buy gold. It announced that the largest central banks would not support the price of gold. It implied that they would continue to regard the level and composition of international reserves as matters for collective decision and action, even if they are unable to agree for the time being on a single, comprehensive reform of the reserve system. And taken in conjunction with the earlier decision to redefine the SDR in terms of a "basket" of currencies, it gives practical significance to the decision reached at Jamaica expunging all references to gold from the rules governing exchange-rate practices and the day-to-day operations of the Fund. These steps, by themselves, do not bring the SDR to the centre of the system, least of all as its principal reserve asset, but they do increase the likelihood of movement in that direction over the longer run, and that is the direction in which we should move to achieve eventually the cosmopolitan objective of a world money.

There is room for disagreement and dissatisfaction concerning some other things that have been done with gold. I venture to suggest, indeed, that no one can be very happy with the outcome at Jamaica. The demonetization of gold *de jure* is not a demonetization *de facto*. Law and practice are less thoroughly congruent in this regard than they were before. Today, moreover, gold has no regulatory role; since no national currency is freely convertible into gold, the continuing presence of gold in the system does nothing to discipline national policies. And because there are no rules governing gold holdings, apart from the loose two-year agreement I have already mentioned, no one has the obligation to regulate gold holdings. Finally, it was a major mistake to reduce the gold holdings of the IMF. Official disclaimers notwithstanding, this decision precludes the creation of a gold substitution account, to swap national gold holdings for new SDRs and thereby consolidate all gold holdings in the vaults of the Fund, and that was the right way to go. To sum up, the present status of gold is at best ambiguous and could become the cause of acrimonious debate not too many years from now.

I have in these last comments started my third task—to talk about the work that has still to be done. But let me draw back momentarily to say something more about the cosmopolitan and national criteria I have been juxtaposing throughout my remarks, especially to comment on the shift in perspectives that took place in official thinking, not just academic work, in the years that preceded the Jamaica Agreement.

Those who have tried to explain the sequence of events that led to this agreement, especially the failure to adopt the *Outline of Reform* produced by The Committee of Twenty, have emphasized the outbreak of inflation in 1972-73 and the increase of the oil price in 1974. These, it is said, made it all too clear that we could not return to pegged exchange rates, even to the "stable but adjustable parities" proposed by the Committee of Twenty.

This explanation is superficial. It is transparently clear—with hindsight—that a fundamental shift in official thinking was under way before 1973, when we backed our way into floating exchange rates. The anxious, defensive nationalism that is so prominent today had already begun to undermine the principles of universality and supranationality in international monetary matters. Looking back at the debates in the Committee of Twenty, one can detect a mixture of the old and new perspectives, and they are also mingled in the *Outline of Reform*. The proposals for asset settlement (and the American amendment calling for the use of an "objective" indicator to trigger changes in national policies) echo the old view: the international monetary system should be designed to discipline national policies. The endorsement of adjustable parities—the notion that exchange rates should be changed not in the last resort but as an optimal mode of adjustment —was the harbinger of the newer view that the chief task of the exchange-rate system is to accommodate monetary sovereignty and national economic vulnerability.

But I have begun to wonder whether we have gone too far. The triumph of the new view at Jamaica—the explicit endorsement of floating exchange rates and the tacit agreement to postpone further work on the structure and governance of the reserve system—is dangerous in two ways. On the one hand, it threatens to denigrate the contribution of international economic integration to national prosperity. On the other hand, it promises too much. It is wrong, I submit, to believe for a moment that flexible exchange rates can accommodate or reconcile very large differences in national policies or shifts in policies, that they can insulate any economy from what is happening in the outside world, or that they can do away with the need for consultation in international monetary matters.

We have learned from theory and from experience that floating exchange rates do not confer complete national autonomy. They do not reconcile policy differences automatically. A flexible exchange rate will always clear the foreign-exchange market, yet recent developments in exchange-rate theory convey these three warnings:

(1) When the disturbances afflicting trade and payments are those that emanate from financial markets or financial policies, including monetary policies, the exchange-rate changes produced by floating rates can destabilize national price levels. With much international capital mobility, and this is what we have today, flexible exchange rates do not confer insulation or autonomy to the degree that was once thought possible.

(2) When the disturbances in question emanate from the goods markets, and these include differences in national inflation rates, flexible exchange rates can confer insulation but not instantaneously. In most current versions of the theory of exchange-rate determination, including the one on which I am working, insulation occurs only in the long run—in the so-called steady state.

(3) When flexibility is managed as it is today, we are bound to encounter once again the age-old problem of reconciling interventions in the foreign-exchange markets.

I am not much concerned with the possibility of day-to-day conflicts between central banks—intervention at cross purposes. Central banks communicate with one another; each of them knows what the others are doing. I have in mind a different and more serious problem. Most governments appear to hold fairly strong views about exchange rates. They believe that they know where rates should be or should be moving over the long run. They seem to have in mind well-defined targets or target zones for exchange rates. They do not always publicize their views, but one can find references to targets or zones in recent pronouncements from London and Rome, and one can detect them too in recent patterns of central-bank intervention.

Under managed floating, moreover, targets and target zones must be consistent—no less so than under a par-value regime. The sterling-dollar rate is also the dollar-sterling rate; views about the one must be consistent with views about the other, and the governments concerned will come into conflict if they act on different views.

There are many ways to achieve consistency, even as there were many ways to do so under the Bretton Woods system. I am concerned, however, lest we adopt the one that we used for the twenty-five years before the crisis of 1971. Consistent exchange-rate policies were possible then only because the United States abstained from having or imposing a view about its own exchange rate; it allowed other countries to decide what their rates should be *vis-à-vis* the dollar. Today, two countries are playing strategically passive roles—the United States and the Federal Republic of Germany. If either one ceases to do so, if they begin to hold strong views about their exchange rates, we will face serious problems of reconciliation.

The crisis that wrecked the Bretton Woods system was precipitated when the United States decided that it could no longer be indifferent to the level or trend of dollar exchange rates—that it had to achieve a change in exchange rates, even at considerable political cost to itself and the rest of the world. This is what happened in August, 1971. We will face another such crisis some day, even under managed floating, if the targets that countries come to adopt for their exchange rates are not mutually consistent and if no country is prepared to give way passively.

Much has been written recently about rules for managed floating, and some of the proposed rules make use of a reference rate for each currency. Under one such rule, for example, a central bank could buy its currency, supporting the exchange rate, only when the market rate for its currency was below the reference rate. Much ingenuity has been expended on the articulation of these rules. Little attention has been paid to the most important problem—how to reconcile and adjust over time the reference or target rates for the various currencies. Those who recommend these rules appear to have forgotten the history of the last few years. It is the adjustment of the reference or target rates that provokes international political controversy and raises the question of exchange-rate policy to the highest political levels, where it does not belong. This is the problem that must be resolved if managed floating is to be the viable successor to the Bretton Woods regime. It is the most urgent unfinished business left over from Jamaica.

Techniques to Control
International Reserves

PETER B. KENEN

IN THIS, the bicentennial year of Adam Smith's *Wealth of Nations*, it would be unkind to quarrel with the principle of specialization. A division of labor enhances efficiency in the production of goods. It may also enhance efficiency in the production of ideas. The sponsors of our conference would seem to think so, for they have given each of us a specialized task. But the case for specialization in the production of goods assumes that producers have perfect knowledge, including knowledge of the future, and similar assumptions would seem to be needed to prove the case for specialization in the production of ideas. I am convinced of it, being at a disadvantage as the last specialist on the program.

When I present this paper at the conference table, I will have perfect knowledge. Professors Cooper and Giersch will have explained why and how the IMF should exercise surveillance over exchange rates. Professors Haberler and Grubel will have explained why we should want to control international reserves. My task, to discuss techniques for controlling reserves, will be well defined. The exchange of ideas around the conference table will take place under conditions of diminishing uncertainty. But the act of production—the preparation of my paper—is encumbered by a great deal of uncertainty. I do not know why I am supposed to tell you how we should control international reserves.

When we must make decisions under uncertainty concerning the behavior of others, we can try to guess what they will do by looking at what they have done in the past. But this is an expensive option, especially when trying to forecast the opinions of four distinguished, prolific economists. Furthermore, it does not promise to be helpful at this juncture, when all of us are trying to assimilate new facts, including the law and philosophy of the Second Amendment to the IMF Articles of Agreement, and to understand new problems, including those of managing economic policies at a time when recovery is far from exuberant, inflation far from dormant, and the distributions of trade balances, capital flows, and stocks of debt very sharply skewed.

When we cannot guess what others will do or say, we fall back to a second way of dealing with uncertainty. We ask what we would do or say were we in their places. I use this introspective method here to sort out my own thinking on some of the questions that have to be answered before I can specialize efficiently, as I was asked to do, in the production of ideas concerning techniques to control international reserves. My paper, then, deals with three sets of questions, not just one, and takes them up more or less sequentially:

1. What are the implications of the Second Amendment, especially the portions dealing with exchange rates, for the manner in which reserves are created, the location of the power to create reserves, and the virtues of various techniques to guard against abuse of that power?

2. What role, if any, should be given to reserves, national or global, in IMF surveillance of exchange-rate practices and, more mechanically, in any set of guidelines promulgated to control central-bank intervention in the foreign-exchange markets?

3. What are the implications of answers to these questions for efforts to control the creation or destruction of individual reserve assets, to control relationships among reserve assets, including the terms on which they are exchangeable and the proportions in which they are held, and to control the totality of reserves?

I am not especially happy with my answers to these questions. They lead me to wonder whether the reform of the monetary system embodied in the Second Amendment is sufficiently coherent internally and sufficiently consistent externally with the aspirations of major governments. I wonder, too, whether the reform portends a satisfactory role for the IMF, the custodian of global influence over national monetary policies.

To launch an exploration of the issues raised by my three questions, it is useful to identify the chief features of the present reserve system. Risking excessive simplification, let me suggest that there are today three types of reserve assets: those whose supplies are determined collectively, by governments acting through the IMF and other international institutions; those whose supplies are determined unilaterally, by governments acting individually; and those whose supplies are determined by a mixture of these principles—by way of transactions between international and national institutions or by the actions of national agencies pursuant to rules or limitations on which they have agreed collectively.

The supply of SDRs is, of course, the one that is most clearly and decisively determined collectively. Special drawing rights are created and distributed by the IMF under rules that require the consent of countries accounting for an 85 percent majority of the votes in the IMF. The rules are so strict that we may see no substantial growth in the supply of SDRs for some years to come, a prospect that causes me to wonder how IMF members plan to achieve the objective to which they subscribe in Article VII, Section 7, of the amended articles—to make the SDR the principal reserve asset in the international monetary system. These familiar words have now migrated from the pious, inconsequential context of a ministerial communiqué to the formal, binding context of a treaty having the force of law. To make them meaningful in this century, it will not suffice to use the SDR as a unit of account in IMF transactions and statistics. It is necessary also to plan now for a gradual but sizeable growth in the supply of SDRs—a matter to which I return below.

At the opposite pole, the supply of any reserve currency is determined unilaterally, not collectively. Dollars, pounds, francs, and marks become reserve assets when and only when they are acquired and held by governments and central banks. The supply of a reserve currency is not, I emphasize, determined by the issuer. It is determined by the sum of the decisions of holders. I will return to this point too, because it epitomizes the spirit of the Second Amendment and has far-reaching implications for the feasibility and necessity of controlling international reserves.

Reserve positions in the IMF and national gold holdings belong, for different reasons, to the third, mixed category of reserve assets. Reserve positions in the IMF are determined initially by discrete decisions taken collectively concerning the sizes of IMF quotas and the manner in which IMF members must "pay" for their quotas. But the sizes of reserve positions are not fixed thereafter; they vary with the volume and composition of drawings on the IMF, and these are initiated by individual governments, subject to IMF rules and policies.

Changes in reserve positions are not always or exclusively the results of decisions taken by the countries whose positions are affected. The size of any country's reserve position in the IMF depends on IMF holdings of its currency, and these depend in part on transactions undertaken by other countries. Thus reserve positions are jointly determined by collective decisions, holders' decisions, and decisions by other countries.

I say that gold holdings belong today to this third category because of the agreement reached last year among the members of the Group of Ten. In August 1975 they decided that they would refrain from any action to peg the price of gold and that "the total stock of gold in the hands of the Fund and the monetary authorities of the Group of Ten will not be increased" during the two-year life span of the agreement.[1] By virtue of this self-denying ordinance and the decision taken soon afterward to distribute to the IMF members one-sixth of IMF gold holdings and to auction off a second sixth on the free market, the supply of monetary gold to the members of the Group of Ten is subject temporarily to collective control. Decisions of the IMF concerning its gold holdings place an upper limit on the holdings of the Group of Ten. Their gold holdings can, of course, fall below this limit; members of the Group of Ten can decide individually to sell gold. Furthermore, collective control is incomplete, in that other countries are free to buy gold (or will be when the Second Amendment comes into force). Nevertheless, it is accurate to say that gold holdings are jointly determined by the decisions of the IMF, the Group of Ten, and individual governments.

There is reason to believe, however, that this situation will not last. The ten-country agreement may not be renewed in its present form. And

[1] The passage quoted is from the communiqué issued by the Interim Committee of the IMF Board of Governors, reproduced as Appendix III to the 1976 *Annual Report* of the IMF.

there have been suggestions, by Italy and other countries, that the IMF suspend or limit its gold auctions in order to prevent the price of gold from falling. We may thus be approaching a worrisome situation in which gold holdings, like currency holdings, will be determined entirely by the decisions of individual countries, by way of their transactions with gold producers and gold hoarders.

This is perhaps the point to pause for lamenting. I am, like many others, deeply disappointed by the manner in which the Second Amendment deals with gold. The aim, we have been told, is to reduce the role of gold in international monetary affairs. But this is to be done by sedulous neglect, not by restricting governments' rights to buy or sell gold at free-market prices or to value as they wish gold that they already hold. It is one achievement of the Amendment to the IMF articles that it brings international monetary law into conformity with monetary practice in matters pertaining to exchange rates. Laws that are not consonant with practice breed contempt for the rule of law and for those who must enforce it. But the Amendment marches in a different direction when it faces the gold problem. It achieves demonetization *de jure* by removing gold entirely from IMF cognizance and depriving the IMF of any right or power to regulate national gold holdings or policies.

As gold will continue to be a reserve asset for some time to come and gold holdings will be governed in growing degree by the decisions of gold holders, demonetization *de jure* will not accomplish demonetization *de factor*. Law and practice may become totally orthogonal. Governments, moreover, are not now and will not soon become indifferent to the price of gold, and their views about gold holdings and the prospects for gold prices will continue to affect their judgments regarding the need to adjust collectively the supplies of other reserve assests, including SDRs.

Those who have participated in the running debate on reform of the reserve system are apt to balk at my assertion that decisions affecting supplies of currency reserves have today to be regarded as resting with the governments that *hold* those reserves. The supply of any national currency is, after all, determined to a first approximation by the decisions of the government issuing that currency.

A currency becomes a reserve asset, however, only when another country chooses to acquire it, and the decision to acquire any currency is today discretionary, not an obligation of participation in the international monetary system. This is what I meant by my suggestion that the present classification of currency reserves epitomizes the dramatic change in philosophy that is reflected in the Second Amendment.

When countries were obligated to declare and defend par values for their currencies, as they were in practice before the advent of floating and in law before the Second Amendment, responsibility for the control of reserve-currency supplies was said to rest with the countries issuing the currencies. It was indeed that very view that led to a decade of transatlantic recrimininations concerning the responsibilities of the United States. The supply of dollars to the stock of reserves was the joint result of U.S. policies affecting the size of the U.S. payments deficit, the obligation of other countries to take up the dollars supplied by the deficit so as to defend par values, and the obligation assumed by large countries—not all of them to be sure, nor with equal formality—to refrain from converting the dollars they acquired.

It is not my intention to rehearse that transatlantic argument, and still less to apportion moral responsibility for the huge growth of dollar holdings that took place in the final years of the par value system. There are some who still believe that the U.S. deficit, the underlying source of dollar supplies, was fundamentally demand-determined. Other countries, it is argued, had an appetite for dollars that was reflected in their policies, and those policies ordained the U.S. deficit. I recall the argument only to stress its irrelevance under present circumstances.

What was an obligation of each government to declare and defend a par value is today an option, but only one of many. Under the new Article IV, "each member [of the IMF] undertakes to collaborate with the Fund [IMF] and other members to assure orderly exchange arrangements and to promote a stable system of exchange rates." To this end, it must notify the IMF "of the exchange arrangements it intends to apply in fulfillment of its obligations," and these may include "(i) the maintenance by a member of a value for its currency in terms of the special drawing right or another denominator, other than gold, selected by the member, or (ii) cooperative arrangements by which members maintain the value of their currencies in relation to the value of the currency or currencies of other members, or (iii) other exchange arrangements of a member's choice." No member, moreover, is bound by its choice; it is free to change its exchange arrangements.

This text might be described as codified anarchy, and it conceals a number of difficulties. Not so long ago, for example, economists had to explain why it was nonsense to say that floating exchange rates were good for all countries except the United States; if all currencies were floating against the dollar, and that was a good thing, then the dollar would be floating against all other currencies, and that would have to be a good thing, too. Now, it would appear, we are required to warn that no country can choose an exchange arrangement for its currency without impinging on the freedom of others to choose arrangements for themselves. If all countries other than the United States undertake to manage their exchange rates by intervening in foreign-exchange markets, the dollar will be managed too, whatever the wishes of the United States.[2]

---

[2] The U.S. Government seems to be worried about this problem, and not without justification. The managed float toward which we are drifting contains the seeds of grave international disorder. Large numbers of countries would appear to hold strong views about exchange rates. Many have chosen to peg their currencies; others are intervening actively to prevent or attenuate movements in floating rates. It is not too wrong to say that we have devised a system of gliding parities in which the parities and rates of glide do not have to be announced and are thus hidden from the scrutiny required to guarantee overall consistency. There is, then, the danger that the dollar will become again the nth currency in the system—that practice, if not law, will come to resemble in this respect the par value system we have just supplanted. Should this occur, the United States may seek someday to free itself from the constraints imposed by others, by acting as it did in 1971, with convulsive consequences for international financial, economic, and political relationships. Were I to advise the U.S. Treasury, however, I would counsel a response different from the one it appears to have adopted. I would urge the rapid, complete articulation of explicit rules to regulate intervention, rules proscribing any intervention designed to drive exchange rates away from target rates or zones that the IMF, acting on its own initiative, would promulgate from time to time. I leave open a number of complicated questions—whether the IMF should publish the targets and how it should obtain them, to what extent it should rely on its own research, including its own econometric models, and to what extent it should proceed by consultation with the governments concerned. I do believe, however, that we need to move in this direction. Proposals to impose rules for floating that do not include well-defined procedures for setting and altering target rates or zones miss the basic point at issue. The nth country problem will not go away. It is sure to arise from the verbiage of Article IV, to plague us when we are most vulnerable to its implications.

But this is not my chief point. My main aim is to insist that the change in the language of Article IV has, as I have stated, shifted completely the locus of responsibility for determining the volume of currency reserves. No country has any constitutional obligation, other than one it may assume freely for itself or in concert and reciprocity with like-minded countries, to acquire or hold another country's currency. The creation of currency reserves results from the manner in which each IMF member resolves the question posed by Article IV. Is it to acquire currency reserves by intervening to influence the exchange rate, or is it to allow the exchange rate to vary?

From this interpretation there follows a second. It is the logical implication of what I have been saying, and quite directly of Article IV, that no country should be required to redeem in any "primary" reserve asset the holdings of its currency acquired by another in the course of intervention. There may be a case, based on prior law and practice, for redeeming or converting in some gradual fashion reserve currencies acquired under the par value system. This is the old problem of consolidation. It is not unneighborly or obstinate, however, for the United States to persist in its opinion that it should not be compelled to redeem dollar balances acquired since the termination of the par value system. That obligation was reciprocal to the one accepted by other countries—the obligation to defend par values—and it has lapsed in principle, not only in practice, with the expiration of its counterpart.

The same conclusion follows just as forcefully from a different view of Article IV. The case for the new text is basically the case for national autonomy in monetary policy. In some significant respects, of course, autonomy is unattainable. With tight international integration of financial markets, no country can assert complete control over its own national markets. In one important respect, however, resort to floating under Article IV does confer autonomy. It allows each government or central bank to decide whether, to what extent, and at what times it will assert control over the supply of money. We all know by now that intervention in the foreign-exchange market does not differ in its impact on bank reserves from intervention in the money market. The right to undertake or abstain from purchases and sales of foreign exchange, the right rehabilitated by

Article IV, is the right of each country to determine its domestic money stock.

To impose on the United States or any other country the obligation to pay out reserves on demand, because of the policies pursued by other countries in respect of their exchange rates, would be to replace the famous asymmetries of the par value system with new asymmetries. It would withhold from countries with intervention currencies the degree of domestic autonomy that the Second Amendment purports to confer on all IMF members.

In answer, then, to part of my first question, I conclude that the Second Amendment precludes, as a matter of principle and logical consistency, resort to any form of asset convertibility, mandatory or at the option of the holder, as a way to regulate currency reserves or the evolution of total reserves. It does so because no country has any remaining obligation to defend a par value, and no other country has the corresponding obligation to conduct its affairs with a view to sparing its neighbors the domestic monetary consequences of reserve-currency accumulations. The choice between reserve accumulation and a change in the exchange rate is open to every country.

These are strong words, with large implications for the management of world reserves. They are not, however, altogether nihilistic. I propose to argue in the balance of this paper that the close control of global reserves is not the important objective it was (or should have been) under the par value system, that it is not in any case an efficient way to discipline the domestic policies of a large country such as the United States, and that it is not a promising technique for governing the management of floating exchange rates—the volume or character of intervention under the new monetary system.

The United States and other large countries have an obligation to pursue domestic policies, especially domestic monetary policies, that foster global economic stability. By virtue of its size alone, the United States should seek always to avoid insofar as possible policies that force other countries to choose between painful alternatives. And currency appreciation, the chief option open to a country when its neighbors err in an inflationary manner, is far from being painless, economically or politically.

What we have been learning and preaching recently—the asset-market theory of exchange-rate determination—says, among other things, that fluctuations in exchange rates occur in the first instance as responses to disturbances in financial markets and that changes in national monetary policies are among the most influential disturbances. It is a corollary to this proposition that day-to-day changes in exchange rates bear no clear-cut relationship to changes needed for insulation from swings in foreign prices or, by extension, from the expenditure and price effects of other countries' policies. On the contrary, any change in one country's monetary policy can, by its short-term effects on floating exchange rates, destabilize domestic prices and production in neighboring economies. Moving to the real world, a classic case in point is furnished by recent experience in Europe. Market forces, driven by monetary policies in Europe and the United States, have caused certain European currencies to appreciate. The domestic price effects of the appreciations have not been unwelcome, but the cyclical and secular effects on important traded-goods industries have been quite painful.

Yet these considerations do not argue for limiting reserve supplies, even if it were possible to do so without undermining the philosophy of the Second Amendment. If reserve-currency accumulations had been limited in the years before 1971, it might have been possible to avoid that debacle. Acting under a reserve constraint, the American authorities would have been compelled to end the U.S. payments deficit. I venture to suggest, however, that they would have started to consider changes in exchange rates—an earlier realignment—not to contemplate any major change in domestic monetary and fiscal policies. It was in part because they were concerned to maximize the world's appetite for dollars, thereby to finance U.S. deficits without losses of reserves, that they refused to entertain, let alone discuss, thoughts about a realignment, including a concomitant change in the gold price. Had it been known in, say, 1965 that the U.S. deficit would not disappear in two or three years, as forecast by an influential study, and that U.S. reserves had been falling steadily for five years or so under an asset-settlement rule, the U.S. authorities would have had cause to talk about changing exchange rates, rather than suppressing any secret thoughts they or their aides may have harbored. But asset convertibility would not have caused them to deflate the U.S. economy as rapidly or sharply as might have been required to terminate the deficit before U.S. reserves were exhausted.

It is, I believe, a fair generalization that no large country can agree to subordinate the imperatives of domestic policy to the requirements of convertibility. It will instead jettison its external obligations, if not by obtaining agreement to a change in the exchange rate through the ordinary methods of consultation, then by throwing a tantrum to extort the concurrence it requires. I will go further. It may be possible someday to foster in all countries a decent respect for the needs of neighbors. Today, however, it is sometimes difficult for democratic governments to generate adequate support for measures to achieve domestic stability. The disciplines of democracy do not always work to foster sound policies. Under these circumstances, it is utterly unrealistic to suppose that limitations on reserve supplies can prevent or rectify damaging policies. If governments are not rewarded by their own citizens for taking the steps necessary to maintain domestic economic health, they cannot expect to be rewarded for submitting to the arcane constraint of reserve scarcity.

My suggestion that restrictions on reserve creation might have induced an earlier devaluation of the dollar, forestalling the crisis of 1971, has its counterpart in the proposal made by the United States during the deliberations of the Committee of Twenty. Confronting demands for restrictions on the creation of currency reserves, demands for mandatory asset settlement, the United States suggested that movements in reserves be treated as "presumptive" indicators of the need for changes in par values and in domestic financial policies aimed at the correction of payments imbalances. The insistence of Europeans on more symmetry in access to official financing was met by American insistence on more symmetry in the initiation of adjustment.

As described in the Report of the Committee of Twenty (Annex 1 to the Outline of Reform), the plan for a reserve indicator could have been implemented in the absence of mandatory asset settlement. It was not even necessary to have close control over the global supply of reserves. The only requirement—and this pertained to symmetry—was that the reserves of participating countries be defined in net rather than in gross terms. Had that not been done, the signals transmitted to surplus and deficit countries might not have been equally strong.

The use of reserves—levels, trends, or changes—to regulate the management of floating exchange rates is subject only to this same minimal requirement. It would not be essential to control total reserves. It would be important to define reserve levels, trends, or changes in net terms. Otherwise, a rule that prohibited France from selling francs for dollars, because it had acquired large dollar reserves, would not necessarily prevent the United States from doing the same thing; U.S. liabilities to France would not count against U.S. reserve assets, and the latter might be large. The aim of such a rule, after all, is to bar any intervention that would block a change in the franc–dollar rate, and it must therefore operate to prohibit intervention by either country having an interest in that rate.

Furthermore, the use of reserve levels in rules to manage floating rates would be free of one objection made against their use to regulate par values. A mechanical use of reserve levels to mandate changes in par values, combined with the requirement of intervention to defend those par values, could have caused large oscillations in exchange rates. A country with low reserves would have had to devalue until it began to run a surplus, and this would have caused the country's reserves to rise until the reserve-level rule signaled the need for revaluation. Par values would have moved up and down, dragging exchange rates with them.[3] A reserve-level rule to govern a managed float would not necessarily destabilize exchange rates, because it would not be combined with mandatory intervention. A country with low reserves would be required to abstain from further support of its currency, and the currency might then depreciate. But the country would not be required to ratify the depreciation by selling its currency and building up reserves, the source of cyclical instability under a par value system.

These observations, however, fall short of making a good case for using reserves in rules to govern intervention under floating rates. There are, on the contrary, two arguments against reserve-based rules.

[3] For simulations illustrating this possibility, see my previous paper, Peter B. Kenen, "Floats, Glides, and Indicators: A Comparison of Methods for Changing Exchange Rates," *Journal of International Economics* (May 1975), 5:107–51.

First, reserve movements are, at best, historical testimony. They do not necessarily tell us much about the present, let alone the future of exchange-rate relationships. An accumulation or high level of reserves is *prime facie* evidence that a government or central bank has been acting to depress the price of its national currency (or at least, to limit the increase that would have occurred in the absence of intervention). Yet this information does not always indicate that the currency should be allowed to appreciate now or in the near future, and this is the question to which an intervention rule should be addressed. The history of policies told by reserves may not be altogether irrelevant to judgments concerning the future. Data relating to recent changes in net reserves, if current and comprehensive, may shed some light on the propriety of further intervention.[4] But I would want to use that information only as an input to the process of deciding where to set and how to change target rates or target zones, and then to use those rates or zones as the norms in rules to regulate intervention.

Second, it is difficult to interpret changes in reserves, especially in net reserves, under floating rates. I have in mind a feature of the present situation neglected in my brief description of the reserve system. With floating rates, the prices of reserve assets are not fixed in terms of any single asset or in terms of any index. (There is, in addition, no fixed official price for gold under the Second Amendment, but this merely complicates the situation, and I defer discussion of the gold price to another context.) The level of reserves is, of course, more stable in terms of the SDR than in terms of any national currency. But the dollar bulks larger in total reserves than in the "basket" of currencies defining the SDR, so that changes in dollar exchange rates can cause variations in the value of reserves, even when measured in terms of the SDR.

To illustrate, consider the changes in global reserves recorded in 1975.[5] Total reserves rose by SDR 14.4 billion during that year. Omit-

---

[4] Movements of reserves can also be employed to check on compliance with an intervention rule, but they are not perfect indicators even for this purpose. A country that has violated an intervention rule, thereby acquiring currency reserves, would not have great difficulty hiding the reserves. It might indeed be easier to conceal changes in reserves from the statistical scrutiny of the IMF than to conceal the fact of intervention from the market and financial press.

[5] The data come from Table 14 in the IMF 1976 *Annual Report*.

ting the reserves of oil-exporting countries, they rose by SDR 4.0 billion. But three quarters of that total, SDR 3.0 billion, reflected changes in exchange rates, chiefly the appreciation of the U.S. dollar. The increase in the volume of reserves was only SDR 1.0 billion. These statistics warn that data on reserves may tell us very little, even retrospectively, about the rights and wrongs of intervention. They also raise questions about the functioning of intervention rules based on the evolution of reserves. Does an appreciation of a country's currency, increasing its net reserves by reducing the foreign-currency value of its liabilities, affect in any significant way the justification for intervention to prevent a further appreciation? If we were concerned with the country's ability to meet demands for the conversion of its liabilities into "primary" reserve assets —demands that do not and should not arise under the Second Amendment—we might answer affirmatively. If we are concerned (as we should be) with the implications of the appreciation for the pattern of trade and payments, we must answer negatively. The story told by such a change in net reserves can signify little.

It is, in brief, my answer to the second question posed at the start of this paper that the need to regulate intervention is no reason for concern with the control of total reserves.

This may be the best juncture to look at a proposal that has been advanced in many forms and contexts, to harmonize the composition of reserves and limit their volume by imposing holding limits. Each country's holdings of other countries' currencies could be no larger than some fixed multiple of its holdings of "primary" assets.

In its most recent incarnation, an address by the managing director of the IMF delivered a year ago in Frankfurt, the proposal would employ the SDR as the "primary" reserve asset and would thereby confer on the IMF the power to limit the volume of reserves by limiting the volume of SDRs—the one component of the total reserve supply over which the IMF has adequate control. Some of the implications of this proposal were explored by J. Marcus Fleming in an internal memorandum drafted in his last weeks at the IMF, and my own views have been influenced by that memorandum. He should not be held responsible, however, for what I have to say.

I have already given one reason to doubt the need for a holding limit. With the legalization of floating exchange rates, it is no longer necessary to exercise close control over the volume of currency reserves. Even if there were need to do so, however, a holding limit might not be a good way to achieve control. Consider the plight of a country that has reached its holding limit. If it is unable to obtain additional SDRs, its holding limit is transformed into an absolute injunction against intervention to prevent appreciation of the country's currency. As such, it is exposed to all of my complaints about reserve-based rules to regulate intervention— and to the additional complaint that an injunction against intervention could be imposed by the composition as well as the level of a country's reserves, an accident of history that can have little bearing on the desirability of intervention.

There are, of course, two ways in which a country can acquire additional SDRs: it can buy them or can borrow them. No country, however, is entitled automatically to buy SDRs from another; France is not empowered to demand that the United States sell them in exchange for U.S. dollars. To confer this right on any country would be to impose on other countries the obsolete obligation of asset convertibility. The Second Amendment does allow countries to deal more freely in SDRs than they could before; voluntary transfers, presumably including loans or sales subject to repurchase, can be agreed between two countries without specific IMF approval. But the removal of restrictions on transfers not mandated by "designation" is no guarantee that a country will find a voluntary seller or lender, and the likelihood of finding a supplier is itself inversely related to the effectiveness of a holding limit.

Thanks to the Second Amendment, it is now possible to foresee the development of an SDR loan market akin to the Federal Funds market in the United States. But that possibility may not be realized until the IMF becomes a lender of last resort, and it is not now authorized to perform that function. The Second Amendment makes no major change in the rigid rules relating to new distributions and cancellations of SDRs. And in the absence of an SDR loan market, holding limits could function unevenly across countries and time, affecting arbitrarily the allowable amounts of intervention in various currency markets.

The point I made earlier about reserve statistics—how difficult it is to interpret them under floating rates—raises another general issue. When there were par values and a fixed official price for gold, the global total of reserves was easy to define. It was the sum of its parts. There were, to be sure, difficulties in deciding how to measure net reserves. Was it right, for example, to regard Eurodollars held by governments and central banks as reserve liabilities of the United States? But these and other problems, both conceptual and statistical, were simple by comparison with those we face today. The SDR prices of reserve currencies can change from day to day. The gold price is SDR 35 per ounce in IMF reserve statistics, is different in certain national statistics, and is on its way into legal limbo. It is difficult to ascertain whether the total of reserves, gross or net, is larger or smaller than the sum of its parts, valued at any set of prices one might choose to use.

Furthermore, the *liquidity* of certain reserve assets—their transferability at stable prices—has been much impaired. Do the French authorities, who value their gold holdings at market-related prices but cannot be sure of selling gold at those prices, regard themselves to be three or four times richer than they would be if they valued their gold holdings at SDR 35 but knew that they could sell freely at that price?

A few years ago there was a rash of academic papers showing that the national demand for reserves could be derived from models in which the need to use reserves is described by stochastic disturbances affecting external payments and in which the cost of foregoing their use is described by the reductions of real income associated with devaluations or deflations required to stabilize external payments. Under present circumstances, one would have to add another stochastic dimension. The expected value of a country's reserves is itself uncertain. The problem of determining, even in theory, the optimal quantity of reserves has become, *inter alia*, an exercise in portfolio theory.[6]

[6] To use this term is to raise another problem. Because the prices of individual reserve assets can vary in terms of any *numeraire*, holders have incentives to diversify. To diversify reserves, however, a country must swap one reserve asset for another in the foreign-exchange markets, and in so doing, it can contribute to the variability of exchange rates, with the incidental effect of reducing further the liquidity of all reserve assets by increasing uncertainty about the prices at which one asset can be converted into others.

One thing is reasonably clear. The growth of international reserves, measured at prices used by the IMF, has slowed down dramatically. In 1970–72, the years of large U.S. deficits, gross reserves rose by SDR 67.8 billion (by 86 percent of reserves outstanding at the end of 1969). In 1973–75 they grew by another SDR 48.2 billion (by 33 percent of reserves outstanding at the end of 1972), but most of the increase accrued to oil-exporting countries. The reserves of all other countries rose by only SDR 8.9 billion (6.5 percent). It can be argued that these numbers are misleading because the appropriate gold price is higher than SDR 35 per ounce, the one used by the IMF, but this argument cuts two ways. Were gold valued at market-related prices after 1968 (the year in which the two-tiered gold market was abandoned), total reserves would be much larger; using SDR 100 per ounce, for example, global reserves would have been SDR 274 billion at June 30, 1976, rather than SDR 208 billion. The same procedure, however, would underscore the fact that reserves are rising slowly at present. The market price of gold has been falling, reducing the market-related value of gold reserves.

There is, of course, another answer to my numbers. The increase of reserves in 1970–72 was much too large; slower growth is needed to offset it. But the inflation caused by the policies that gave rise to the earlier increase of reserves has by now revenged itself upon the real value of reserves. Using the familiar ratio of reserves to imports, the crudest but simplest available yardstick, the story of slow growth in nominal reserves turns into a tale of rapid decline, to levels below those prevailing before the "explosion" of reserves. Citing once again figures published by the IMF, the ratio of reserves to imports was 30 percent for all countries together in 1969 (and for industrial countries as well). It rose to 33 percent in 1972 (and to 37 percent for industrial countries). But by 1975, it had fallen to 28 percent (and to 22 percent for industrial countries).

In its own judicious assessment of trends in reserves, the IMF in its 1976 *Annual Report* gives reasons for distrusting these familiar calculations. It points out, for instance, that the balance between financing and adjustment has shifted, "so that aggregate payments imbalances are likely to be smaller relative to the volume of international transactions than they would have been if, with the magnitude of balance of payments disturbances given, the world economy were still functioning under the Bretton Woods par value system." Nevertheless, it proceeds to remind us that the majority of countries continue to peg their currencies. The pegs are altered more frequently than in the days when devaluation was regarded as a confession of failure, and some countries have adopted gliding parities or methods of pegging exchange rates (as to the SDR) that allow for gradual changes in exchange rates. At the same time, countries with floating rates intervene extensively in currency markets to smooth out day-to-day fluctuations and to attenuate longer-term trends. There is by now evidence that countries with floating rates make less use of reserves than other countries, but the difference in usage is a matter of degree, not a textbook difference in kind.[7]

When this point is made, another emerges. The reserves of countries with pegged rates are not on average higher than those of countries with floating rates. I summarize some evidence in Table 8.1 (albeit diffidently, because it is so hard to classify the exchange arrangements of various countries). In 1975 the unweighted average ratios of reserves to imports was just under 24 percent for the thirty-six large countries represented in that table. But the ratios for the countries with floating rates were slightly higher than those for the countries with pegged rates. The ratios for the former, excluding the United States, the United Kingdom, and Italy, averaged about 26 percent.[8] Those for the members of the European "snake" averaged only 21 percent, and only 17 percent without Germany.[9] And those for the countries that peg to the dollar, to other currencies, and to the SDR averaged under 25 percent, a shade below the average for the floating-rate countries. There is, in brief, no reason to believe that the countries which have chosen to peg their exchange rates are the ones well endowed with reserves to do so.

[7] See Esther Suss. "A Note on Reserve Use Under Alternative Exchange Rate Regimes," *IMF Staff Papers* (July 1976), 23:387-94.

[8] I remove these three countries because the United States has never used reserves in the same way as other countries, the dollar being the intervention currency, while the United Kingdom and Italy were obliged to float separately from their partners in the EEC *because* they were short of reserves.

[9] If Germany is transferred to the floating-rate group, because for practical purposes the "snake" is a group of countries that peg to the mark while the mark floats freely *vis-à-vis* the dollar, the unweighted average for the floating-rate group rises to 26.5 percent.

Table 8.1

Ratios of Reserves to Imports, Large Trading Countries, 1975

(percent)

Country Group	Weighted [a]	Unweighted [b]
All Large Trading Countries [c]	21.9	23.6
Except United States	23.0	23.8
Floating Exchange Rates [d]	19.1	23.7
Except United States	20.3	24.1
Except US, UK, Italy	23.8	25.7
European Snake [e]	27.9	21.4
Except Germany	18.3	17.5
Other Pegged Exchange Rates [f]	23.7	24.6

SOURCES: Data from International Monetary Fund, *International Financial Statistics*, September 1976. Reserves are year-end figures; imports are annual figures (cf.). Country classification from International Monetary Fund, *Annual Report 1976*, Table I.1.

[a] Reserves for country group divided by imports for country group.

[b] Average of ratios of members of group.

[c] All countries reporting exchange arrangements to the IMF and having imports larger than $3 billion in 1975. For individual countries, see notes below.

[d] Australia, Austria, Canada, Finland, France, Greece, India, Italy, Japan, Malaysia, Morocco, New Zealand, Philippines, Portugal, Singapore, Spain, Turkey, United Kingdom, United States, Yugoslavia.

[e] Belgium, Denmark, Germany, Netherlands, Norway, Sweden.

[f] Argentina, Brazil, China (Taiwan), Egypt, Ireland, Israel, Korea, Mexico, South Africa, Thailand.

Much of this paper has been concerned with the problem of limiting reserve creation. It has in this sense echoed preoccupations generated by the "explosion" of currency holdings in 1970–72. The figures I have cited, however, together with the variability of exchange rates and the gold price, lead me to believe that there may now be the serious danger of a shortage in usable reserves and to ask what should be done about it.

It is no answer to say that IMF quotas have just been enlarged. The Sixth General Review of quotas was an exercise in bloc politics, in its intent and in its effect. Its chief results were to increase the quotas of the oil-exporting countries, to preserve in the face of that increase the voting hegemony of other countries, and to compensate for the termination of the Oil Facility (an aim that was not achieved in full, since the once-and-for-all increase in the quotas of the oil-importing developing countries was much smaller than their two-year use of the Oil Facility).

Where there is a will to increase reserves there is, of course, a way. It is necessary only to resume the distribution of SDRs. This process should begin quite soon, if only to honor the pledge enshrined in the IMF Articles to move the SDR to the front and center of the international monetary system. It would be wrong, however, to create new reserves in an effort to offset declines in the liquidity of other reserve assets, especially to offset declines in the liquidity of gold holdings.

Perceptions concerning the usability of gold holdings can change abruptly, and attempts to compensate for shifts in perceptions by increasing or decreasing the stock of SDRs would be cumbersome, to say the least, and grossly unfair in their consequences for the distribution of reserves. It would be more sensible to shore up the liquidity of gold reserves, even at the expense of acknowledging what the Second Amendment denies—the continuing role of gold in the monetary system.

I had hoped that the Second Amendment would move to centralize gold holdings in the IMF, and not to disperse the IMF's own holdings. I wish, even now, that it were possible to revive the proposal for a gold-substitution account. It is, I fear, too late for that. There nevertheless remain several ways to underwrite the liquidity of gold holdings or, less ambitiously, to prevent large variations in their usability that could influence the policies of major governments—policies concerning their exchange rates and domestic economies and policies concerning IMF activities, including the creation of SDRs. These would no doubt require a third amendment, but let us not pretend that the second is the last.

The IMF, for example, could shift to the other side of the gold market, becoming a buyer rather than a seller. It could hold periodic auctions to sell new SDRs to the highest bidders, with the bids expressed and payable in gold. The gold acquired in this fashion could be held by the IMF indefinitely or sold at subsequent auctions for the benefit of the trust fund that is the recipient of profits from the current auctions. (I would prefer that the IMF retain the gold, consonant with my view that gold should be demonetized by centralization, not decentralization, but this is not essential to the purpose at hand.)

This first proposal, however, has disadvantages. It might work in the long run to gather gold into the IMF, but would lead to lumpy substitutions of SDRs for gold, could increase the volatility of the gold price, and would do nothing between auctions to maintain the liquidity of national gold holdings. A second plan makes more sense. The IMF might be authorized to lend new SDRs against gold, at an SDR gold price based on (but well below) a moving average of free-market prices. Decisions concerning a country's right to borrow against its gold holdings could be vested in the IMF or based on the sizes of countries' gold holdings at some base date, their quotas in the IMF, or a combination of the two.

It would be neater to remove completely the risk of instability in reserves and, more importantly, in national policies resulting from the complicated composition of reserves. But my proposal may be a partial solution. I offer it here to provoke discussion—to emphasize my concern about the disparity between the roles of gold *de jure* and *de facto*—and to be told what may be wrong with it.

Debt Relief as Development Assistance
Peter B. Kenen

It was agreed that I would survey here old and new sources of development assistance. It soon became clear to me, however, that the rescheduling of international indebtedness deserves the most urgent attention. There are two reasons. First, the debt-service problems of developing countries and proposals to relieve them are drifting to the top of the international agenda, and we must confront such problems analytically before seeking to resolve them politically. Second, debt relief may be the most promising way to increase the flow of resources to developing countries.

This work, then, concentrates on the debts of developing countries and ways to reduce debt-service burdens. It begins by describing the problem in general terms that will be familiar to many readers, but it offers new data that may alarm even those who have been watching the problem. It goes on to survey proposals for debt relief and to assess their short-run impact on debt-service flows. It concludes with some thoughts on financing debt relief.

The Sources of Development Assistance

Transfers of resources by gross lending have been taking place on a scale unforeseen a few years ago. In 1969, the Pearson Commission projected gross borrowing and debt-service payments for developing countries. Hypothesizing terms slightly more liberal than those prevailing in the late 1960s, the commission predicted that debt-service flows on official development assistance would reach $6 billion in 1981. (Pearson, et al., 1969, Chart 7, assumption 1.) They have already reached that rate. To make matters worse, borrowing from private lenders has grown very rapidly, raising total debt-service flows above $10 billion in 1974, and, I fear, above $17 billion in 1976. Let us look more closely at some of these trends, using the data on debts and debt-service flows in Tables 2.1 through 2.3.

By the end of 1973, the sixty-seven countries included in the World Bank's reporting network (and in the statistics summarized in Table 2.1) had accumulated long-term debts larger than $70 billion, and short-term debts to U.S. banks and other U.S. lenders larger than $8 billion.[1] Two years later, after the increase in oil prices and the commodity-price cycle, their long-term debts exceeded $105 billion, and their short-term debts to U.S. lenders totaled $18 billion.[2] Borrowing from private sources increased rapidly from

Table 2.1 The Debts of Developing Countries, 1973 and 1975 (All Developing Countries Except Oil Exporters) ($ billion)

Type	1973	1975
Disbursed Long-Term Debt		
To Private Creditors		
Suppliers' Credits	7.1	7.9
Bank Credits	10.9	22.4
Other Credits	6.8	7.5
To Public Creditors		
International Organizations	11.9	20.9
DAC Governments	29.3	35.6
East Bloc Governments	3.6	5.1
Other Governments	1.2	6.2
Total	70.8	105.6
Short-Term Debt to U.S. Creditors		
To U.S. Banks	6.0	14.5
To U.S. Nonbanking Concerns	2.1	3.4[a]
Total	8.1	17.9

Source: Long-term debt in 1973 from World Bank, *World Debt Tables*, October 1975 (EC-167/75), Table 7; long-term debt in 1975 estimated in accordance with methods detailed in the Appendix. Short-term debt from Treasury Department, *Treasury Bulletin*, February 1976, Tables CM-II-2 and CM-IV-2. Short-term debts to banks exclude U.S. claims on the Bahamas, Panama, and Other Latin America, as well as on oil-exporting countries (1973 claims on Middle Eastern and African oil exporters estimated at $300 million and $75 million, respectively); debts to nonbanking concerns exclude claims on the Bahamas and Other Latin America, Indonesia, and Venezuela. Short-term debts include those of countries and private entities not covered by the World Bank data on long-term debt.
[a]September 1975.

1967 to 1973 (World Bank, 1975a, Table A), and this faster rate of increase has compounded the borrowers' problems. Private credits are available only on market-related terms, and the growth of borrowing from banks, private capital markets, and suppliers has hardened average terms. Interest rates are higher and maturities shorter than those forecast a few years ago.[3]

The figures in Tables 2.2 and 2.3 dramatize the size and urgency of the debt-service problem. In 1976, interest and amortization payments on long-term debts will probably exceed $14 billion, an increase of almost $5 billion in two years. They will be larger than gross loan disbursements were just two or three years ago.[4] If, in addition, some of the short-term debt incurred in 1974/1975 has to be repaid, as assumed in Table 2.3, total debt-service payments will climb to $17 billion, a figure far higher than anything projected five years ago.

There is no need to belabor the obvious. To exchange current for future

Table 2.2 Projected Debt-Service Flows, 1976

Type of Debt	Implicit Service Rates Interest (percent)	Amorti-zation (years)	Projected Service Flow in 1976 ($ million) Interest	Amorti-zation	Total
Suppliers' Credits	5.42	4.67	428	1,692	2,120
Bank Credits	7.72	7.30	1,729	3,068	4,797
Other Private Credits	5.52	9.17	414	818	1,232
International Organizations	4.86	23.25	1,016	899	1,915
DAC Governments	2.90	17.24	1,032	2,065	3,097
East Bloc Governments	1.66	9.43	85	541	626
Other Governments[a]	2.90	17.24	181	360	541
Total, Long-term Debt	–	–	4,885	9,443	14,328
Estimate, 1974[b]	–	–	3,126	6,459	9,585
Increase, 1974 to 1976	–	–	1,759	2,984	4,743

Source: Implicit rates from same source as those in Table 2.10 of the appendix; debt-service flows calculated using implicit service rates and debt projections in Table 2.1.

[a]Actual implicit service rates were 2.89 percent and 10.42 years in 1973; it is assumed here, however, that the relevant rates for this category, dominated now by debts to oil-exporting countries, resemble rates on debts to DAC governments.

[b]Sum of projected flows from Table 2.10 of the appendix.

resources at recent rates and on current terms is not a prudent way to foster larger flows of resources to developing countries. To do so would only exacerbate a problem that may now be acute.

There is, then, only one way to transfer more resources. Developed countries must give them away by larger grants and grant-equivalent transfers. It is, of course, fashionable to be pessimistic about their willingness to do so, and nothing in the numbers can allay that pessimism. The growth of bilateral development assistance has barely kept pace with world inflation, and no large donor has achieved the target accepted by the majority of OECD countries—an annual transfer of official development assistance equal to 7/10 of 1 percent of GNP.[5]

The international political atmosphere is hardly conducive to enlarging grant and grant-equivalent transfers. Nations, like individuals, can be persuaded to part with resources only by appealing to their self-esteem or self-interest, and much has happened recently to weaken the donors' belief that development assistance serves their self-interest.

Denunciations, declarations, and diplomatic opposition to policies of the United States have led many Americans to reappraise the commitment to global values that has been a mainspring of public support for U.S. bilateral

Table 2.3 An Estimate of Debt-Service Flows on Short-Term Debt 1974 and 1976

Item	Rate	Amount ($ million)	
		1974	1976
Interest on Short-Term Debt			
To U.S. Banks	7.72 percent[a]	463	1,119
To U.S. Nonbanking Concerns	5.42 percent[b]	114	184
Total Interest		577	1,303
Amortization of Increase in Short-Term Debt			
To U.S. Banks	7.30 years[a]	—	1,164
To U.S. Nonbanking Concerns	4.67 years[b]	—	278
Total Amortization		—	1,442
Total Interest and Amortization		577	2,745
Debt-Service Flow, All Debt[c]		10,166	17,073

Source: Debt data from Table 2.1; implicit service rates from Table 2.2.
[a] Average rate for long-term bank credits.
[b] Average rate for long-term suppliers' credits.
[c] Sum of short-term debt, above, and long-term debt from Table 2.2.

aid and for U.S. contributions to multilateral aid agencies. It would be wrong to suppose that the blunt words of U.S. representatives at United Nations' meetings reflect only momentary anger with particular resolutions. They convey a deeper disenchantment that may be hard to dispel.

Current Third World rhetoric, moreover, can hardly revive support for development assistance. Demands for reform of the international economic system that are prefaced by catalogs of past wrongs convey the distressing suggestion that international economic relations are a zero-sum game. An increase in the power or wealth of Third World countries is to be accomplished by diminishing the power or wealth of First World countries. Whether this inference is right or wrong, it is influential, and its implications are discouraging to those who would advocate an enlargement of development assistance.

Finally, the new demands for equity seem sometimes to border on hypocrisy. Governments that have done little indeed to rectify internal inequality are not embarrassed to demand an international rectification. Governments that invoke the liberal values of the West to justify their aims and programs are themselves sinners against those values, and their sins also tarnish what is left of the belief that development promotes democracy. We have long known that poverty breeds tyranny. We are beginning to realize that this proposition has no neat obverse. And we have seen too many instances in which growth has been ultrabiased toward guns, not butter.

I do not say these things to excuse the faults of the rich, at home or abroad. I recite them only to warn that extravagant rhetoric and conduct inconsistent with what one asks of others are here, as in all things, counterproductive. Now I turn to debt relief as one of the few devices that may evoke perceptions of self-interest and solicitude and may thereby generate a larger flow of development assistance.

The Case for Debt Relief

During the last two decades, several developing countries have sought and received debt relief in varying amounts.[6] Others will do so in the next few years. Judging from the growth of total debt-service flows and other indexes, debt burdens are higher now than ever before for many developing countries. Bankers and financial journalists are predicting large-scale defaults, and some developing countries are themselves hinting that they will default if relief is not forthcoming.

Defaults by developing countries, even if widespread, would not seriously threaten the stability of the international financial system, loose talk to that effect notwithstanding. Some banks and other private lenders would be hurt. A few might be wounded mortally. But there is little justification for the fear that defaults would wreck the Eurocurrency market or would do grave damage to national financial systems.

There are good reasons, however, for seeking to head them off. First, unilateral defaults would injure relations between developed and developing countries at a time when those relations are already strained by the policies and attitudes of many developing countries toward foreign investors and creditors. Private lenders who believe that they have been mistreated turn to their own government for support. The governments are forced to interpose themselves—to represent the interests of their citizens abroad—in a manner that often invites and sometimes earns the accusation of interference. Second, the prospect of default can have inequitable effects on the level and distribution of resource transfers. Lenders who worry about their debtors' ability to pay sometimes throw good credits after bad to keep them afloat, and borrowers whose own policies have impaired their ability to pay are rewarded, not punished, for their imprudence. Third, piecemeal default, when it takes place, is also apt to reward improvidence. Those who have borrowed too heavily or pursued policies inconsistent with their debt-service obligations escape those obligations. More importantly their conduct tarnishes the creditworthiness of others. Defaults by a handful of developing countries with relatively small debts would make it difficult for many others with good records and prospects to borrow anew.

Some of these objections to defaults are also objections to case-by-case debt relief. It, too, can favor the improvident and damage the creditworthiness of others. There is, at the very least, the need for agreed upon international rules to govern debt relief. There may be need for new multilateral institutions.

Above all, in my judgment, there is need to regard debt relief as a form of development assistance, not as a device for protecting the integrity of the lenders' balance sheets.

This last point is emphasized frequently by those who direct our attention to the problem. Summarizing debt-relief operations in the last two decades, Islam (1975, p. 34) has written:

Debt relief in the past was mainly related to service payments due in the immediate future. In some cases, it related only to a part of the total debt burden. Most of the creditor countries preferred a "short leash" approach, and kept their options open to review debt service problems after a few years. In some cases, the debt rescheduling exercises were undertaken more than once. A very long-term rescheduling, it was feared, might not ensure sufficiently strict economic discipline and sound debt management policies. In many cases, the interest rate applied to the rescheduled debt was the commercial rate; only in a few cases was it a concessional rate.

If there is any principle which may be said to guide debt relief operations, it is that relief afforded should be the minimum needed to ensure the early resumption of debt service payments and that the cost to the creditors of any postponement of amortization and interest payments, whether by means of rescheduling or refinancing, should be matched by additional interest charged at commercial rates. . . .

The debt relief I have in mind would be more comprehensive in scope and larger in grant content than has been typical heretofore. It would be a way of easing ex post the terms of official and private lending over the last twenty years.

Proposals along these lines were made by the Pearson Commission (1969, pp. 156-160) and have received official sanction. At its Seventh Special Session, the United Nations General Assembly called for comprehensive debt relief (Res. 3362, II, para. 8):

The burden of debt on developing countries is increasing to a point where the import capacity as well as reserves have come under serious strain. At its fourth session the United Nations Conference on Trade and Development shall consider the need for, and the possibility of, convening as soon as possible a conference of major donor, creditor and debtor countries to devise ways and means to mitigate this burden, taking into account the development needs of developing countries, with special attention to the plight of the most seriously affected countries. . . .

Anticipating the discussion at UNCTAD IV, the Group of 77 made a formal proposal at their Manila meeting in February 1976. I quote the operative paragraphs in their entirety:

3. Debt relief should be provided by bilateral creditors and donors in the form of waivers or postponement of interest payments and/or amortization, cancellation of principal, etc., of official debt to developing countries seeking such relief. In that framework, the least developed, the developing landlocked and the developing island countries should have their official debts cancelled. . . .

4. Multilateral development finance institutions should provide programme

assistance to each developing country in an amount no less than its debt service payments to these institutions.

5. Agreement should be reached to consolidate commercial debts of interested developing countries and to reschedule payments over a period of *at least* 25 years. The consolidation of commercial debts and the rescheduling of payments would require the establishment of suitable financial arrangements or machinery which might include, *inter alia*, a multilateral financial institution, such as a fund or a bank, designed to fund the short-term debts of interested developing countries.

This resolution addresses itself to a number of economic and political questions: Who should receive debt relief? Who should grant it? What form should it take? It is silent on certain other questions, including the one most often raised by those who are asked to grant relief: Can conditions be attached to debt relief to discourage developing countries from borrowing themselves back into difficulty very soon again?

No single set of answers to these and other questions will satisfy debtors and creditors. It may be difficult to satisfy even the debtors. Notice how often the ministerial resolution qualifies its own proposal with references to "interested" countries and to special claimants like landlocked and island countries. There are large differences, too, in the interests of lenders and in the characteristics of their claims. Loans by East Bloc countries, for example, bear lower interest rates but shorter maturities than those of Western governments (see Table 2.2).[7]

All of these differences lead some observers to despair of reaching any comprehensive agreement. They propose instead ad hoc arrangements subject only to loose principles and guidelines. This is the position taken by Bitterman (1973, pp. 228-229):

The practical problems of refinancing à la Pearson, or generally refunding for all willing debtors, are formidable. It has taken long and difficult negotiation to get international agreement in the acute refunding cases. More general agreements would be practically impossible without the establishment of an international debt refunding agency financed pro rata by the creditors. Otherwise the refunding countries or those giving equivalent grants or soft loans would pay off the harder creditors. . . .
In sum, a general refunding for all the aid recipients is not feasible either by consolidation or the Pearson method. From the standpoint of both creditors and debtors refunding should not be carried beyond necessity. Economic development will have to muddle through with a combination of credits, soft loans and grants punctuated by refundings as needed. . . .

I am not much more optimistic. But the problem itself has grown graver, and support for a comprehensive approach seems also to be growing. In my view, moreover, debt relief is one of the few policy domains in which developed countries can be forthcoming rather than reluctant in responding to demands from developing countries. Debt relief is not a zero-sum game. It can confer economic and political benefits on grantors and grantees and on the international system. It will at least remove a major irritant from the international body politic.

I do not minimize the difficulties or depth of differences in view that continue to separate developed and developing countries. The answers one gives to the questions I raised—to whom, from whom, and how—depend importantly on one's views about the role of debt relief.

If relief were granted, as in the past, primarily to preserve the integrity of the lenders' balance sheets, the following might be the answers: Relief should be granted only to countries that are now or will soon be unable to honor their obligations at an acceptable internal political cost. It should be granted directly by the creditors whose claims are in jeopardy. It should defer current debt-service payments but should not reduce substantially the present value of creditors' claims—it should not have a large grant element. On this view, moreover, countries that qualify for debt relief should agree to abstain from new borrowing, or, at the very least, to subordinate new obligations to those of their existing creditors. These answers are less generous than those implied by some of the arrangements made in recent years, but are not gross caricatures of those arrangements.

If relief is viewed instead as a form of development assistance, whether as a substitute or complement to others, the answers are different indeed. All developing countries should be eligible, although they need not be equally eligible. Relief should be granted by the chief suppliers of concessional assistance, even those that are not large creditors, and it should reduce significantly the present value of future debt-service flows, not just postpone current flows. Finally, the conditions imposed on the recipients should not be especially onerous, nor should they subordinate new borrowing to the claims of creditors that grant debt relief.

The questions I have raised and answered are not truly independent. The form in which debt relief is granted, for example, will determine in large measure the incidence of benefits. Turning the same point on end, distributional desiderata must figure prominently in the design of a debt-relief proposal. This point is recognized explicitly by the ministerial resolution quoted earlier, when it proposes canceling the debts of the least developed countries. The same point can be made quite plainly by asking what countries would benefit most from various forms of debt relief.

Using statistics furnished in the appendix, working with three country classes (based on the countries' incomes per capita), and expressing the reductions in first-year debt-service flows as percentages of debt disbursements, consider the effects of two proposals:[8]

1. A one-year forgiveness of interest on all long-term debt covered by the World Bank's debt tabulations would have reduced the debt-service payments of the higher-income countries by $2,155 million in 1974, that is, by 37 percent of concurrent debt disbursements. It would have reduced the payments of the lower-income countries by $519 million, in other words, by only 24 percent of debt disbursements. The higher-income countries have the largest debts at the highest interest rates and would have been the largest beneficiaries.

2. A one-year forgiveness of all interest on long-term bilateral debts to governments would have reduced the debt-service payments of the higher-income countries by $877 million, or 15 percent of disbursements. It would have reduced the payments of the lower-income countries by $392 million, or 18 percent of disbursements. The lower-income countries would have captured a larger share of the reduction in debt-service payments because they are the larger debtors to governments. The size of the reduction, however, is much smaller for all countries, absolutely and in relation to disbursements.

Clearly, any comprehensive plan that seeks to decrease substantially the probability of default by large debtor countries, but also to afford meaningful assistance to the lower-income countries, must include several types of concessions, tailored to the needs of the various countries.

The ministerial resolution calls attention to another set of issues impinging on one's answer to my question about sources of debt relief. It is not difficult to say who should grant relief in respect of debts to governments. The creditors themselves are the ones to do so. The answer is not as obvious, however, when one comes to the claims of multilateral lenders, especially the World Bank and regional development banks. These are financial intermediaries, obtaining most of their loanable funds from private financial markets. They cannot grant relief to their debtors without impairing their ability to service their own debts. Recognizing this particular difficulty, the ministerial resolution distinguishes clearly between bilateral creditors (para. 3) and multilateral institutions (para. 4), although the solution it proposes in respect of the latter seems to me unsatisfactory, because it could freeze new lending into a pattern that would discriminate against the newest, poorest countries.

Turning to credits from private institutions, it is easily argued that suppliers' credits should be refinanced by the creditors' national governments. Suppliers' credits finance exports and are not different in purpose or form from official export credits. As a matter of fact, many of these credits (and some bank loans) are insured or guaranteed by governmental entities. The fiscal, legal, and administrative arrangements required for something resembling refinancing are already in place. Most bank loans, however, pose difficult problems. Even those that financed exports to developing countries may bear no geographic congruence to the corresponding flows of goods. Loans by U.S. banks, for example, finance exports from many developed countries (and from one developing country to another). Furthermore, the largest long-term bank loans have been made recently by non-national (Eurocurrency) banks.

In debates about the regulation of these institutions, it is argued that responsibility for their integrity should rest with the governments of the countries from which they come. On this principle, the burden of refinancing credits extended by the foreign branches of U.S. banks would rest with the United States. This line of argument makes some sense when the aim is to defend the solvency or liquidity of the banks concerned; the U.S. government or one of its instrumentalities should be the lender of last resort to U.S. banks, wherever located. (Even in this somewhat different context, however, there are problems at the fringes. Who should be lender of last resort to banks that are truly non-national, like the so-called consortium banks?) Applied to the problem of debt relief, moreover, the principle itself is less cogent. The burden of concessional debt relief, a form of development assistance, should be allocated in accordance with some agreed upon notion of equity, not borne by those countries whose banks and their branches happen to have been large lenders to the developing countries. The refinancing of bank credits, to the extent that it occurs, should be handled multilaterally, as suggested by the ministerial resolution (para. 5).

Finally, what should be done about other forms of debt, including the bonds issued by developing countries in national and international capital markets? Were these to be refinanced, they might be treated like bank credits. There are reasons, however, for excluding them entirely from any comprehensive plan. First, an attempt to refinance or otherwise to modify the terms of bond issues would undo the progress made so slowly and painfully to open international capital markets to developing countries. I would prefer to proceed in a different direction—to adopt some of the measures proposed recently for easing access to private capital markets, including interest subsidies and guarantees.[9] Second, the bond issues of developing countries are marvelously heterogeneous. It would be very difficult to grant significant debt relief on terms that would be comparable across securities, let alone countries or groups of countries.

There is no way to guarantee that countries relieved of their debts will not immediately borrow again so heavily and on such terms that they will soon confront debt-service obligations as large as those they bear today. Once relief is granted, after all, the creditors' leverage is greatly diminished. It should not be impossible, however, to devise rules for new borrowing that would keep debt-service flows from growing more rapidly than current-account receipts (to keep so-called debt-service ratios from rising much above the levels to which they would be pared in consequence of debt relief). A country might still experience an unanticipated increase in its debt burden on account of a shortfall of export earnings. Such a country, however, would qualify for compensatory financing from the International Monetary Fund. In fact, the same moving average of export receipts that is used to measure shortfalls in current-account receipts and qualify a country for such financing might also be used to define the permissible rate of growth in debt-service payments and, therefore, the permissible level of new borrowing.[10]

A solemn undertaking to obey this rule would probably be honored by most governments, but sanctions might help. These could include denial of access to compensatory financing and to new official development assistance when a country borrows excessively or fails to meet its debt-service obligations once these are scaled down. The international community has by now acknowledged explicitly and liberally that developing countries should receive preferential treatment and should be exempted from certain obligations. But they cannot be allowed to renege on obligations assumed freely or to claim that all commitments made in the past were undertaken out of weakness and dire need. There can be no international order, old or new, if the doctrine of "changed circumstances" is allowed to prevail over fundamental principles of law. Countries that repudiate obligations cannot be permitted to claim rights and privileges.

Finally, one cannot guarantee that debt relief will increase the net flow of resources to any or all developing countries. Some of the funds required may well be diverted from other aid programs—including those that may be judged to be superior developmentally or distributionally. Debt relief is "high quality" aid in that it is untied. If administered in the fashion suggested here, moreover, it would have a large grant content. Yet it would also be unencumbered by conditions on its use, apart perhaps from limitations on new borrowing of the type proposed above, and the manner in which some developing countries have spent their freely available funds—on guns, not butter—has led many advocates of aid to retreat from their earlier belief that aid should be entirely unconditional.

Critics of debt relief have emphasized these points, and I do not minimize their importance. Nor do I know of any way to obviate the possibility of substitution. It is naive to suppose that governments or legislatures can be deceived. It is morally wrong and stupidly arrogant to propose deception.[11] I do suggest an unconventional method of financing relief toward the end of this paper, but even this may not prevent substantial substitution. In my judgment, however, the threat of substitution is not a decisive objection. My own reasons for urging that debt relief receive consideration—reasons set out above—have to do with the political and economic consequences of widespread default. A general debt crisis would prolong and intensify North-South confrontation and most certainly would cause a sharp reduction in resource flows of all types, public and private, to all developing countries. On this view, debt relief is a defensive measure, not a device to enlarge the flow of resources.

The Size and Distribution of Benefits from Debt Relief

Several attempts have been made recently to gauge the effects of debt relief on debt-service burdens and on the net flow of resources to developing countries (UNCTAD, 1976). The one examined here is designed to show who would gain and by how much if there were a comprehensive international agreement reflecting the considerations I have already mentioned, if all developing countries took advantage of it, and if there were no substitution for other forms of aid. The proposal deals subsequently with four classes of long-term debt. The analysis asks what such an agreement would do to first-year debt-service flows, absolutely and in relation to gross flows of credit (measured as before by disbursements of long-term loans projected for 1974). I look at two base years, 1974 and 1976. Using 1974, the last year for which we have data broken down by groups of countries, I am able to ask *who* would benefit. Using 1976, I am able to ask how large the benefits would be, given current levels of debt and debt-service flows.[12]

The specific proposal analyzed here is not necessarily best. It is not a recommendation, merely an example on which to base an estimate of changes in debt-service burdens. It embodies the following features:

1. The governments of all developed countries would forgive absolutely fractions of their own long-term claims on developing countries. The fractions would be 25 percent for higher-income debtors, 50 percent for middle-income debtors, and 75 percent for lower-income debtors. In addition, the creditors would reduce the interest rates and lengthen the maturities on their remaining claims. The interest rates and maturities used here are based on averages attaching to bilateral DAC government loans at the end of 1973, listed on line 1 of Table 2.4. Interest rates would be reduced by one-half of one percent and maturities lengthened by about 50 percent for all debtors taken together, as shown on line 3 of Table 2.4.

2. Multilateral institutions would not forgive any of their claims but would agree to a similar reduction of interest rates and lengthening of maturities. In some instances, this would require new lending by a soft-loan agency such as the International Development Association (IDA) to pay off quasi-commer-

Table 2.4 Rates Used to Estimate Effects of Alternative Debt-Relief Proposals, 1974

	Interest (percent)			Amortization (years)		
Rate Structure	Higher Income	Middle Income	Lower Income	Higher Income	Middle Income	Lower Income
1. Actual Official Bilateral[a]	3.50	3.00	2.25	13	16	27
2. Actual Official Multilateral[b]	6.25	5.50	2.25	19	22	37
3. Reduced Official Bilateral	3.00	2.50	1.75	20	30	40
4. Reduced Official Multilateral	5.75	5.00	1.75	25	35	50
5. Hypothetical Supplier	5.00	4.50	3.75	10	15	20
6. Hypothetical Bank	6.25	5.50	2.25	10	15	20

[a]Based on rates for DAC governments in Table 2.10 of the appendix.
[b]Based on rates for international organizations in Table 2.10 of the appendix.

cial loans by, say, the World Bank; relief would be accomplished by substituting one form of indebtedness for another. Actual interest rates and years to maturity are shown on line 2 of Table 2.4; proposed rates and maturities are shown on line 4.

3. Governments would agree to take over or refinance long-term suppliers' credits granted by their nationals. They are not likely to do so, however, on terms as generous as those proposed to consolidate governmental loans. Here, then, I examine the consequences of two proposals. The first and more generous assumes governments that would offer terms resembling those actually attaching to governmental loans at the end of 1973 (line 1 of Table 2.4). The second and less generous proposal assumes that they would offer terms more liberal than those offered by suppliers but less generous than those offered on their own loans (line 5 of Table 2.4).

4. A new multilateral institution would be established to furnish debt relief in respect of long-term debts to banks. Here, as with suppliers' credits, two sets of terms are studied. The first and more generous are those actually offered by multilateral institutions at the end of 1973 (line 2 of Table 2.4). The second and less generous set of terms contains the same interest rates but requires more rapid repayment (line 6 of Table 2.4).

Table 2.5 shows what would have happened if the most generous option had been offered in each instance above, and all developing countries had taken advantage of it. It assumes the progressive forgiveness of official bilateral debt, and the consolidation of suppliers' and bank credits at the relatively low interest rates and long maturities shown on lines 1 and 2, respectively, of Table 2.4 The table also shows what would have happened had less generous terms been offered (consolidation of official bilateral debt without progressive forgiveness, and consolidation of suppliers' and bank credits on the terms shown by lines 5 and 6, respectively, of Table 2.4).[13]

Table 2.6 calibrates the calculations detailed in Table 2.5. It expresses the reductions in first-year debt-service flows as percentages of total debt-service flows and of loan disbursements in 1974. Three points emerge at once.

First, unless consolidation is accompanied by the progressive forgiveness of governmental loans, there will not be substantial relief for lower-income countries. Compare the first-year reductions with and without forgiveness. Second, relief in respect of suppliers' and bank credits on the terms described here would be most helpful absolutely to the higher-income countries, but the gains to the middle- and lower-income countries would not be inconsiderable as fractions of total debt-service flows or loan disbursements. Third, debt relief may be well worth the effort. A comprehensive consolidation of long-term indebtedness on the best terms described above, taken together with the progressive forgiveness of governmental loans, could have increased the flow of resources to developing countries by $4.5 billion in 1974 and by $6.7 billion in 1976. Each of these numbers was slightly larger than 45 percent of total debt-service flows in the corresponding year.

Table 2.5 Estimated First-Year Effects of Alternative Debt-Relief Proposals, Long-Term Debt, 1974 and 1976 ($ million)

Proposal	Estimated Debt-Service Flows, 1974				Im- plicit Rates[a]	Projected All Countries, 1976
	Higher Income	Middle Income	Lower Income	All Coun- tries		
Consolidation of official bilateral debt with forgiveness:						
Interest	314	78	61	453	2.65[b]	621[c]
Amortization	524	104	87	715	23.87[b]	982[c]
Reduction in debt service	741	459	764	1,964	–	2,660
Consolidation of official bilateral debt without forgiveness:						
Interest	419	156	243	818	2.40	1,126
Amortization	699	208	346	1,253	27.20	1,725
Reduction in debt service	461	277	322	1,060	–	1,412
Consolidation of official multilateral debt:						
Interest	360	74	72	506	4.26	890
Amortization	251	42	83	376	31.57	662
Reduction in debt service	117	33	53	203	–	363
Consolidation of suppliers' credits at actual official bilateral rates:						
Interest	155	50	23	228	3.19	252
Amortization	340	104	39	483	14.78	534
Reduction in debt service	673	289	182	1,144	–	1,332
Consolidation of suppliers' credits at hypothetical suppliers' rates:						
Interest	221	75	39	335	4.69	370
Amortization	442	111	52	605	11.80	669
Reduction in debt service	505	257	153	915	–	1,081
Consolidation of bank credits at actual official multilateral rates:						
Interest	578	46	18	642	5.88	1,317

Table 2.5 (continued)

Proposal	Estimated Debt-Service Flows, 1974				Implicit Rates[a]	Projected All Countries, 1976
	Higher Income	Middle Income	Lower Income	All Countries		
Consolidation of bank credits at actual official multilateral rates: *(continued)*						
Amortization	487	38	22	547	19.95	1,123
Reduction in debt service	908	131	109	1,148	–	2,357
Consolidation of bank credits at hypothetical bank rates:						
Interest	578	46	18	642	5.88	1,317
Amortization	925	56	41	1,022	10.68	2,097
Reduction in debt service	470	113	90	673	–	1,383
Summary for Selected Categories						
Bilateral and multilateral debt						
Reduction with forgiveness	858	492	817	2,167	–	3,023
Reduction without forgiveness	578	310	375	1,263	–	1,775
Suppliers' and bank credits						
Reduction on actual official terms	1,581	420	291	2,292	–	3,689
Reduction on hypothetical terms	975	370	243	1,588	–	2,464
Total reduction on best terms[d]						
With forgiveness	2,439	912	1,108	4,459	–	6,712
Without forgiveness	2,159	730	666	3,555	–	5,464

Source: Based on debt and debt-service data in Tables 2.1 through 2.3 and Table 2.10 of the appendix and terms proposed in Table 2.4.

[a]Calculated service payment as a percentage of multiple of all-country debt in 1973.

[b]After deducting forgiveness from all-country debt.

[c]After deducting debt forgiveness (at all-country average of 50 percent).

[d]Best terms are actual official terms applied to suppliers' and bank credits.

Table 2.6 Perspectives on Debt-Relief Proposals, 1974 and 1976

Proposal	Estimated Debt-Service Flows, 1974				Projected All Countries, 1976
	Higher Income	Middle Income	Lower Income	All Countries	
Reductions as Percentages of Total Debt-Service Flows					
Bilateral and multilateral debt					
With forgiveness	13.6	29.5	51.2	22.6	21.1
Without forgiveness	9.1	18.5	23.5	13.2	12.4
Suppliers' and bank credits					
Official terms	25.0	25.2	18.2	23.9	25.7
Hypothetical terms	15.4	22.2	15.2	16.6	17.2
Total reduction on best terms[a]					
With forgiveness	38.6	54.7	69.4	46.5	46.8
Without forgiveness	34.2	43.8	41.7	37.1	38.1
Reductions as Percentages of Loan Disbursements					
Total reduction on best terms[a]					
With forgiveness	41.5	50.5	50.4	45.1	–
Without forgiveness	36.7	40.4	30.3	35.5	–

Source: Debt-service reductions from Table 2.5; debt-service flows and loan disbursements from same source as Table 2.10 of the appendix.

[a] Best terms are actual official terms applied to suppliers' and bank credits.

The distribution of benefits from debt relief, even with progressive forgiveness, would not be strongly skewed in favor of the poorest countries. When first-year reductions are compared to total debt-service flows, the outcomes appear to be skewed in their favor. Using my 1974 figures, the lower-income countries would have garnered a 69 percent reduction in debt-service flows, compared with only 39 percent for the higher-income countries. But when the same reductions are compared to loan disbursements—the current gross flow of resources are a better measure for this purpose—the benefits appear to be distributed quite uniformly. The same figures for 1974 imply (in the absence of substitution) a 50 percent increase in gross flows to middle- and lower-income countries and a 41 percent increase in gross flows to higher-income countries. Without progressive forgiveness, moreover, debt relief would have been regressive. The absolute and relative benefits would have been largest for the higher-income countries.

Table 2.7 shows calculations for three countries, Argentina, Korea, and India, one from each country class in Table 2.6. The summary statistics

Table 2.7 First-Year Reductions in Debt-Service Flows, Selected Countries, 1973 ($ million)

Item	Argentina	Korea	India
Consolidation of official bilateral loans			
With forgiveness	30	41	375
Without forgiveness	22	6	141
Consolidation of official multilateral loans	23	6	22
Consolidation of suppliers' credits			
Official terms	166	134	45
Hypothetical terms	141	116	38
Consolidation of bank credits			
Official terms	68	32	22
Hypothetical terms	49	29	20
Total reduction on best terms[a]			
With forgiveness	287	213	464
Without forgiveness	279	178	230
Total as percentage of 1973 debt service			
With forgiveness	41	58	73
Without forgiveness	40	48	36
Total as percentage of 1973 loan disbursements			
With forgiveness	34	29	55
Without forgiveness	33	24	27

Source: Debt and debt-service data from World Bank, *World Debt Tables*, October 1975 (EC-167/75), Table 9; debt-relief proposals from Table 2.4.
[a]Best terms are actual official terms applied to suppliers' and bank credits.

shown there suggest that the conclusions drawn above for broad country classes are valid also for important members of those classes. Once again, progressive forgiveness is required if India, the lowest-income country, is to obtain substantial relief and if the distribution of benefits is not to be skewed in favor of the wealthier countries.

The Costs of Debt Relief

I conclude with some numbers and thoughts on the costs of the analyzed proposal. The costs, like the benefits, are expressed on a first-year basis, not as present values. They are, then, readily comparable to figures on annual aid flows, but not to figures on grant equivalents.

Table 2.8 shows how much it would cost developed countries to forgive

Table 2.8 First-Year Costs of Debt-Relief Proposals ($ million)

Item	Cost 1974	1976
Consolidation of official bilateral loans with forgiveness		
Interest forgiven	430	649
Amortization forgiven	972	1,483
Cost of forgiveness[a]	1,402	2,132
Interest foregone	61	27
Interest cost of deferred amortization[b]	37	38
Total costs	1,500	2,197
Consolidation of official bilateral loans without forgiveness		
Interest foregone	126	171
Interest cost of deferred amortization[b]	70	93
Total costs	196	264
Total costs of other proposals		
Consolidation of official multilateral loans	81	144
Consolidation of suppliers' credits		
Official terms	233	263
Hypothetical terms	117	135
Consolidation of bank credits		
Official terms	272	558
Hypothetical terms	236	485
Total costs of best terms[c]		
To governments		
With forgiveness	1,733	2,460
Without forgiveness	429	527
To multilateral institutions	353	702

Source: Based on debt-relief proposals outlined in Table 2.4.

[a]If computed as the interest cost of borrowing the principal of total debt forgiven, using a 7.5 percent interest rate, the figures would be $1,276 million for 1974 and $1,759 million for 1976.

[b]Cost of borrowing at a 7.5 percent interest rate to cover the reduction in first-year amortization payments.

[c]Best terms are actual official terms applied to suppliers' and bank credits.

progressive fractions of their claims on developing countries and to consolidate the remaining claims on more generous terms. The costs are (1) interest forgiven, (2) amortization forgiven, (3) interest foregone in consequence of lower interest rates, and (4) interest incurred by lengthening maturities (that is, the cost of borrowing at 7.5 percent to cover the first-year difference between old and new amortization payments). The total first-year cost of this package would have been $1.5 billion if implemented in 1974 and about $2.2 billion if implemented in 1976. The largest part of the cost is interest and amortization forgiven. Without progressive forgiveness, the package would have cost about $200 million in 1974 and some $256 million in 1976.

Table 2.8 also shows the total costs of the other components (each of which consists of interest foregone on account of reduced rates and interest incurred on account of longer maturities). The totals at the bottom of the table assume that governments take responsibility for consolidating official bilateral loans and suppliers' credits and that multilateral institutions (including a new one to deal with bank credits) take responsibility for the other two components.

Costs to governments have to be borne in the usual way—by budgetary appropriations or public borrowing. Costs to multilateral institutions, which have no power to levy taxes and cannot borrow on terms as favorable as those on which they would be lending, have to be financed some other way. In the short run, the financing might be made available from the Trust Fund established with profits from gold sales by the International Monetary Fund. In the long run, however, there is need to tap new sources of revenue.

I close with one suggestion along these lines. It borrows from one frequently made for the use of royalties generated by the exploitation of seabed resources.[14] Producers of all nonrenewable resources, wherever they may be, should be taxed on their output, and the proceeds should be used in aid of development. It is by now generally acknowledged that the world's nonrenewable resources are or should be subject to global regulation for purposes of conservation. It is a simple, logical extension of this principle to assert that rents arising from ownership and exploitation are or should be placed at the disposal of the international community. If the accident of ownership does not justify reckless exploitation, neither can it justify unilateral appropriation.

I do not propose that all of these rents be devoted to international use. I would not even know how to calculate them. Instead, I suggest that a tax be levied at one percent of the value of output and that some of the revenue raised be used to finance the multilateral institutions' share of the costs of debt relief.

Table 2.9 attempts to show how much revenue could be raised by a tax on twelve commodities and the countries that would pay it. It derives from calculations based on output in 1971 and prices in 1971 and 1974. A one percent tax would have raised $1.3 billion at 1971 prices and $3.5 billion at

Table 2.9 Revenues from a One Percent Tax on Outputs of Nonrenewable Resources ($ million)

Commodity or Producer	1971 Prices	1974 Prices
Total, Twelve Commodities[a]	1,276.2	3,551.4
Coal[b]	798.5	1,519.6
Petroleum[c]	333.3	1,778.7
Metals[d]	117.9	212.4
Chemicals[e]	26.9	40.7
United States	271.9	811.9
European Community	134.6	253.6
Other Developed Countries	95.0	225.2
Eastern Europe	97.5	184.6
Oil-Exporting Countries[f]	199.6	1,065.4
Other Developing Countries	89.5	169.8
Unallocated[g]	388.5	840.9

Source: Output and price data from published sources; details available on request.

[a] Excludes production in the U.S.S.R., the People's Republic of China, East Germany, North Korea, and North Vietnam.

[b] Valued at the German export price.

[c] Valued at the price for light Iranian crude.

[d] Aluminum, copper, iron, lead, tin, and zinc. Outputs of nonferrous metals were valued arbitrarily at 75 percent of the price for final (refined) output quoted on the London Metals Exchange; iron ore is valued at the Lake Superior price.

[e] Nitrates, phosphates, potash, and sulphur, valued at U.S. domestic prices.

[f] Includes revenue from products other than petroleum.

[g] Revenue from countries producing less than one percent of world output; country composition varies across commodities.

1974 prices (because most commodity prices were higher). The United States would have paid one-fifth of the tax. The oil-exporting countries would have paid about 15 percent at 1971 prices and about 30 percent at 1974 prices. This distribution reflects the fact that oil and coal, the two nonrenewable fuels included in the calculation, account for most of the revenue. The large contributions of the United States and OPEC are neither unreasonable nor punitive. These countries sit on precious resources whose worth is in no way due to the genius, industry, or abstinence of their citizens. Resources are the gift of God, no matter what language we use to address Him.

The one percent tax proposed here would have covered twice over the costs to the multilateral institutions of the debt-relief plan outlined above, even if the tax were based on 1971 prices. No one, however, would have trouble devising ways to use the rest of the revenue. A tax of this type, indeed, may be the most promising way to finance interest subsidies on future borrowing by the developing countries, including their borrowing through multilateral institutions. Subsidies may be required over the long term to prevent an early reemergence of debt-service problems, even with guidelines and sanctions to limit extravagant borrowing.

Notes

I am indebted to several colleagues for comments on the first version of this paper, especially to C. Fred Bergsten, Hollis Chenery, Richard Cooper, Charles Frank, Lawrence Krause, John Lewis, W. Arthur Lewis, and Paul Streeten. Some gave me their comments personally; others raked me over the coals at the MIT Workshop. They may notice some change in the tone of this revised version, but it will be too large to satisfy some of them and not large enough to satisfy others. I am grateful to Nancy Marion of Princeton University for gathering and processing the data used to illustrate the tax proposal made at the end of the paper.

1 There are no comprehensive data on the short-term debts of developing countries. The U.S. data used in this paper, however, account for a large slice of total short-term bank credit and may also serve to gauge the trend in total short-term suppliers' credit.

2 The 1975 projections in Table 2.1 use data and methods described in the appendix. The increase of long-term debt in 1974/1975, $35 billion, may understate net borrowing during those years, but does not fall far short of the figure produced independently by Holsen and Waelbroeck (1976) reproduced in the Appendix.

3 Several readers have urged me to recognize that worldwide inflation has reduced real interest rates, offsetting in whole or part the tendency described in the text. The point is well taken but needs qualification. It is the improvement in a debtor's terms of trade, not the rate of inflation *per se*, that reduces real *external* indebtedness, and the terms of trade of developing countries were not much better at the beginning of 1976, after the recent price cycle, than in 1971, before it started.

4 World Bank (1975a), Table 1D. Gross disbursements to developing countries (other than oil-exporting countries) totaled $11.8 billion in 1972 and rose to $15.6 billion in 1973, averaging $13.7 billion in the two years together.

5 Recent trends are summarized in World Bank (1975b), p. 8. There is one cause for guarded optimism—a gradual increase in the grant component of official development assistance—but it was not sustained in 1974.

6 The major cases are surveyed by Bitterman (1973).

7 Some of them, moreover, are repayable in the debtors' own currencies, which is to say that they are in effect repayable in the debtors' exports.

8 Here and hereafter, I use disbursements to calibrate debt relief, because they can be deemed to measure to a first approximation the level of gross flows of development assistance. The debt-service flows and debt disbursements used in this particular calculation are those projected by the World Bank, using debt data through 1973. Actual disbursements may have been quite different in 1974, since new borrowing was large (and some of it was utilized quickly to finance the current-account deficits resulting from the increase in oil prices and the decline of other raw-material prices). For present purposes, however, projected disbursements may be the better yardstick, as they were not so heavily influenced by the need for balance-of-payments financing, reflecting instead the distribution of undisbursed credits and, therefore, the distribution, ex ante of development assistance. The country classification used here and later is the one in World Bank (1975a); the countries labeled lower-income include most of those classified as Most Seriously Affected in UN usage.

9 See, for example, Michalopoulos (1975) and the proposals made in the resolution of the Ministerial Meeting of the Group of 77 (para. 12). One reader suggests that this option be pursued to its logical limit: the poorest developing countries should be granted debt relief (approaching debt cancellation); the more affluent should not be granted any debt relief but should be afforded easier access to credit and export markets in the developed world.

10 I admit to slighting one major difficulty. Some governments do not know how much their countries owe, and many do not have comprehensive controls to keep total borrowing, including private borrowing, in line with permissible levels.

11 I would still urge that development assistance be funded on a long-term basis, not annually through complex legislative processes. The aim, however, is not to bypass the legislature, but rather to reduce the costs and uncertainties involved in guiding an appropriation through the legislature each and every year (and exposing aid programs to volatile swings in public opinion concerning the policies of individual foreign governments).

12 The analysis for 1974 uses the statistics on debt and debt-service payments shown in Table 2.10 of the appendix; the totals for all countries are sums of the subtotals for the three country groups that are analyzed separately. The analysis for 1976 is based on global figures; I had neither the resources nor data to project separately the debts and debt-service payments of the three country groups. To obtain the results for 1976, I have had to assume that the reductions in interest rates and extensions of maturities that were applied to the three country groups individually in respect of 1974 would give the same global changes in interest rates and maturities in 1976 as they did in 1974. This assumption is inaccurate, as the pattern or borrowing has changed, but I had no other way to estimate effects of debt relief on current debt-service burdens. The calculations for 1974 and 1976 are independent, not consecutive. If the proposals analyzed here had been applied in 1974, debts and debt-service flows would have been different in 1976, invalidating my calculations for 1976. In other words, each set of calculations assumes that the year to which it refers is the first year of debt relief. Another methodological qualification: I have not tried to calculate the *total* relief afforded by each component of the proposal (to calculate the change in the present value of future debt-service flows, thereby to measure the concessional element in each component). But because each component involves a reduction of interest rates as well as an extension of maturities, each one probably contains a significant concessional element.

13 One cannot estimate the effects of consolidating short-term debt, since there are no comprehensive data with which to work. A partial calculation, however, shows that the effects are large. If short-term debts to U.S. banks and suppliers were refinanced at 6 percent and if all of the increase in 1974/1975 were amortized across ten years, not on the terms shown in Table 2.3, these would be the first-year effects in 1976:

Interest	1,074
Amortization	890
Reduction in debt service	781

14 See Oda, *et al.* (1976). Proposals similar to my own have been made before, as by Ul Haq (1975, p. 161).

References

Bitterman, H. J., 1973, *The Refunding of International Debt* (Duke University Press, Durham).

Holsen, J., and J. Waelbroeck, 1976, LDC Balance of Payments Policies and the International Monetary System (World Bank Staff Working Paper No. 226).

Islam, N., 1975, *New Mechanisms for the Transfer of Resources to Developing Countries* (United Nations Economic and Social Council, Doc. E/AC.54/L.83).

Kenen, P. B., and C. S. Voivodas, 1972, Export Instability and Economic Growth, *Kyklos*, 25, 791-804.

Michalopoulos, C., 1975, *Financing Needs of Developing Countries: Prospects for International Action* (International Finance Section, Princeton University, Princeton).

Oda, S., et al., 1976, *A New Regime for the Oceans* (Trilateral Commission, New York).

Pearson, L. B., et al., 1969, *Partners in Development: Report of the Commission on International Development* (Praeger, New York).

Ul Haq, M., 1975, Negotiating a New Bargain with the Rich Countries, in G. Erg and V. Kallab, eds., *Beyond Dependency* (Overseas Development Council, Washington).

UNCTAD, 1976, *International Financial Co-operation for Development: Debt and Debt Service* (United Nations Conference on Trade and Development, Doc. TD/188/Supp.1, Ch. III).

World Bank, 1975a, *World Debt Tables* (EC-167/75).

World Bank, 1975b, *Annual Report.*

Appendix
Projecting Long-Term Debts to 1975

Under normal circumstances, two years are not long to wait for a definitive statistical compilation like the one provided by the World Bank in *World Debt Tables.* But the events of 1974/1975 caused large changes in the volume, and, no doubt, the composition of international indebtedness. Thus, the effort to project long-term indebtedness summarized in Table 2.1 of the text and described in more detail by this appendix.

The appendix discusses line-by-line the entries in Table 2.1, and uses the following abbreviations to denote data sources:

BIC *Borrowing in International Capital Markets*, World Bank, November 1975 and January 1976 (EC-181/753 and 754).
IFS *International Financial Statistics*, International Monetary Fund, February 1976.
TB *Treasury Bulletin*, U.S. Treasury Department, February 1976.
USW *The U.S. and World Development*, Overseas Development Council, 1975.
WB *World Bank Annual Report*, World Bank, 1974, 1975.
WDT *World Debt Tables*, World Bank, October 1975 (EC-167/75, I & II).

The benchmark figures mentioned below are those that appear in Table 7 of WDT; unless otherwise indicated, they refer to total *disbursed* debt at the end of 1973 and exclude the debts of oil-exporting countries.

Suppliers' credits were projected directly from the 1973 bench mark figures by assuming an invariant relationship between the number in WDT and the corresponding country total for the long-term claims of U.S. *nonbanking concerns* in TB. (There has in fact been some slight decrease in the WDT-TB ratio since 1970, but no allowance was made for a further decline in 1974 or 1975.) In September 1975, the latest date for which TB data were available, the long-term claims of U.S. nonbanking concerns were $1,880 million. Multiplying by the WDT-TB ratio, we obtain as the 1975 projection the $7.9 billion in Table 2.1.

Private bank credits were projected separately for U.S. and other banks. Credits owed to U.S. banks are represented by the long-term claims of U.S. banks in TB. In December 1973, the total for developing countries was $3,358 million; in December 1975, it was $5,529 million. The difference between the 1973 bench mark in WDT and the TB figure was taken to represent total credits owed to other banks, including Eurocurrency banks, and was projected on the following assumptions: (1) that undisbursed credits at the end of 1973 were distributed between U.S. and other banks in the same proportion as total disbursed credits; (2) that published Eurocurrency credits in BIC were the only new credits extended by banks outside the United States in 1974 and 1975; (3) that new debt disbursements in each quarter of 1974 and 1975 were 25 percent of the sum of undisbursed credits at the start of the quarter and new Eurocurrency credits extended during the quarter; and (4) that annual repayments to banks outside the United States bore the same relationship to total disbursed debt that repayments projected for 1974 in WDT bore to total disbursed debt in December 1973 (that they were 15.3 percent of disbursed debt at the start of each year).

To illustrate the application of these assumptions, consider the annual estimates for 1974 (in millions of U.S. dollars):

Undisbursed credits, December 1973 (69.2 percent of
   total undisbursed credits in WDT) $1,941
New Eurocurrency credits, 1974 (from BIC) 8,222
Disbursements in 1974 (sum of quarterly estimates) 5,589
Repayments in 1974 (15.3 percent of disbursed debts
   in December 1973, WDT less TB) 1,156
Net increase in disbursed credits owed, 1974 4,433
Estimate of undisbursed credits, December 1974 4,574

The 25 percent disbursement rate is somewhat larger than the one implied by the annual projections of disbursements in WDT. It is nevertheless reasonable to assume some acceleration of disbursements in the special circumstances of 1974/1975. Performing the corresponding calculation for 1975 and adding the two-year increase in disbursed credits owed to the 1973 total in WDT, disbursed credits from all banks outside the United States were projected at $16,905 million in December 1975.

Other private credits were projected on the assumption that new international and foreign bond issues were the only source of other private credit in 1974 and 1975, that these were fully disbursed, and that there was no amortization of the new bonds in whole or in part during 1974 or 1975. Thus, the projection in Table 2.1 is the sum of the projection in WDT (which allows for the disbursement and repayment of credits extended before 1974) and of new bond issues listed in BIC.

Loans from international organizations were projected by amending the projection in WDT. That projection allows for the disbursement and repayment of loans approved before 1974. Four amendments allow for disbursements of loans approved in 1974 and 1975:

1. Disbursements of new loans by the World Bank and its affiliates were projected by assuming that half of the loan commitments made in fiscal 1974 came before December 31, 1973, and are included in the WDT projection (the rest being made in the first half of 1974), and that half of the commitments made in fiscal 1975 were made before December 31, 1974 (the rest being made in the first half of 1975). The World Bank and its affiliates committed approximately $3,650 million in fiscal 1974, apart from new commitments to oil producers, and another $5,300 million in 1975. Thus, an additional $1,830 million was deemed to be available for disbursement by June 30, 1974, and 10 percent was assumed to be disbursed in the second half of 1974. Similarly, $4,400 million of newly committed funds was deemed to be available by December 31, 1974 ($2,650 million of commitments in the first half of fiscal 1975 and 90 percent of the balance from 1974), and 10 percent was assumed to be disbursed in the first half of 1975. Carrying this procedure forward, disbursements of new credits were projected at $1,250 million for the two years ending in December 1975.

2. Disbursements of new loans by other development banks were projected crudely by assuming that they were one-fourth the size of new-loan disbursements by the World Bank and its affiliates. This ratio was derived from data on commitments in WDT, Table B. (Commitments by regional development banks and other multilateral institutions averaged 27.8 percent of commitments by the World Bank and IDA from 1970 to 1973 but the percentage was falling with the rapid growth of World Bank lending.)

3. Disbursements by the multilateral aid agencies established by the OPEC countries were projected arbitrarily at $250 million per year for two years.

4. Obligations to the IMF oil facility, excluding those of developed countries, are given in IFS at SDR 3,015 million for December 31, 1975, and this was equivalent to $3,530 million. (As this facility did not exist before 1974, all of its lending must be added to this debt category.)

The sum of these amendments is $5,590 million, bringing the total for the whole category to the $20.9 billion in Table 2.1.

Loans from DAC governments were projected on the basis of net lending reported or forecast in OECD data on the flow of Official Development Assistance (ODA) from DAC countries. This rubric does not include official export credit or lending for arms purchases. Some ODA, moreover, is destined for countries omitted from the totals in Table 2.1. In fact, the growth of ODA bears only a crude statistical relationship to the growth of total debt reported in WDT. From 1971 to 1973, for example, net bilateral lending reported as ODA amounted to $4.9 billion, while the increase of debt to DAC governments in WDT was $7.8 billion (including the increase of undisbursed debt but excluding oil-exporting countries). At the same time, lending reported as ODA was larger in 1974 than what is implied by the projection in Table 7 of WDT (a projection that makes no allowance for disbursements of new credits).

Development lending by DAC governments will be known with certainty by 1977, but the data for 1975 were not at hand when the projections were made. The figure in Table 2.1 is the sum of the actual number for 1974 (the $2,970 million in WB, 1975) and a forecast for 1975. The latter was obtained by assuming that actual ODA will exceed the forecast for 1975 in USW, Table D-4, by the same percentage that actual ODA exceeded the forecast for 1974, and that the bilateral loan component will be 26.3 percent of total ODA, its actual share in 1974. These assumptions give a loan forecast of $3,306 million for 1975 and, therefore, a two-year total of $6,276 million, the figure used in Table 2.1.

Loans from East Bloc governments were projected to grow slightly faster than in 1972/1973, when total debt, including undisbursed debt, rose by only $900 million. Table 2.1 shows an increase of $1.5 billion for 1974 and 1975 taken together. This is in the same neighborhood as the one implied by the extrapolation in WDT, Table 7. There, the projections from known commitments yield an increase of $660 million for 1974. Making only small allowance for disbursements of new loans—small because the data in WDT suggest that there are long lags between commitments and disbursements of East Bloc credits—one comes to the $750 million rate implied by the projection in Table 2.1.

Loans from other governments were projected by assuming that the only "other" governments making new loans in 1974/1975 were those of the OPEC countries and by amending the projection in WDT for disbursements of new credits by those governments. There is, however, much uncertainty concerning these disbursements. OECD figures in USW, Table D-9, put disbursements at $2.0 billion in 1974, and this number is not much different from the one implied by more recent data in WB, 1975. (Gross disbursements are given there at $5.0 billion, including $2,680 million to the World Bank and IMF. Subtracting this last sum and the $250 million mentioned above as the annual rate of disbursement through other multilateral aid agencies, one comes out with $2.1 billion for 1974.) But we know very little about disbursements in 1975. Bilateral commitments were very large in 1974 (they are put at $7.2 billion in USW, Table D-9), and there were additional commitments in 1975, some of which may have been disbursed. Here, then, it is assumed that disbursements in 1975 were half again as large as in 1974, so that total debts to "other" governments are listed as being $5.0 billion larger than the projection in WDT.

The two-year increase of debt shown in Table 2.1 is $34.8 billion, and, though it was estimated from fragmentary data, it is not vastly different from an estimate compiled by Holsen and Waelbroeck (1976) from more comprehensive and up-to-date sources:

Consolidated Balance of Payments for Non-Oil Developing Countries,
1974/75 ($ billion)
Goods and Services Deficit $69.7
Official Grants 8.2
Direct Investment 9.8
Long-Term Public Borrowing (including oil facility) 40.3
Other Borrowing (including errors and omissions) 9.9
Reserve Use (including other IMF drawings) 1.5

The figures shown here for long-term borrowing are similar to those shown in Table 2.1. Reclassifying the net changes shown there to match the components used by Holsen and Waelbroeck, we find:

	Holsen and Waelbroeck	Table 2.1
Loans from Banks	13.9	11.5
Loans from OPEC Sources	6.8	5.5
Other (including oil facility)	19.6	17.8

It would appear, then, that the estimates developed here are deficient chiefly in underestimating bank loans (because they rely entirely on U.S. and Eurocurrency data) and are too low also in respect of OPEC disbursements.

Note, finally, that the "other borrowing" estimated by Holsen and Waelbroeck comes close to the estimate of short-term borrowing from U.S. banks and nonbanking concerns that appears at the bottom of Table 2.1.

Table 2.10 Disbursed Long-Term Debt and Debt-Service Data by Country Class and Type of Debt, 1973

Type of Debt	Amount (in $ million)			Implicit Service Rates	
	Princi-pal in 1973	Projected Service Flow		Inter-est (percent)	Amorti-zation (years)
		Inter-est	Amorti-zation		
Higher-Income Countries					
Total disbursed debt[a]	39,624	2,155	4,165	5.44	9.5
Suppliers' credits	4,417	237	931	5.37	4.7
Bank credits	9,249	715	1,258	7.73	7.3
Other private credits	5,716	326	546	5.71	10.5
International organizations	6,265	400	328	6.39	19.1
DAC governments	12,875	445	961	3.46	13.4
East Bloc governments	771	19	94	2.47	8.2
Middle-Income Countries					
Total disbursed debt[a]	10,817	452	1,216	4.18	8.9
Suppliers' credits	1,673	104	399	6.21	4.2
Bank credits	844	66	149	7.77	5.7
Other private credits	589	30	130	5.12	4.5
International organizations	1,476	82	67	5.53	21.9
DAC governments	4,638	139	288	3.00	16.1
East Bloc governments	1,066	18	151	1.66	7.0
Lower-Income Countries					
Total disbursed debt[a]	20,352	519	1,078	2.55	18.9
Suppliers' credits	1,047	46	198	4.38	5.3
Bank credits	820	62	87	7.54	9.4
Other private credits	491	19	65	3.85	7.6
International organizations	4,128	95	113	2.30	36.7
DAC governments	11,800	266	445	2.25	26.5
East Bloc governments	1,783	23	138	1.31	12.9

Source: World Bank, *World Debt Tables*, October 1975 (EC-167/75), Table 7.

aIncludes debts to other governments not shown separately.

Index

Library of Congress Cataloging in Publication Data

Kenen, Peter B   1932-
   Essays in international economics.

   (Princeton series of collected essays)
   Includes bibliographical references.
   1.   International economic relations—Addresses,
essays, lectures.   I.   Title.
HF1411.K399   337   80-7540
ISBN 0-691-04225-X
ISBN 0-691-00364-5 (pbk.)